Meet the *Southern Living* Foods Staff

On these pages we show the Foods Staff (left to right in each photograph) at work as they compile, test, taste, and photograph the recipes that appear each month in *Southern Living*.

Catherine Garrison, Editorial Assistant; Nancy Nevins, Test Kitchens Director

Jean Wickstrom Liles, Foods Editor

Above: *Peggy Smith and Carole King, Test Kitchens Staff*

Right: *Susan Payne (seated) and Margaret Chason Agnew, Associate Foods Editors*

Nola McKey (seated) and B. Ellen Templeton, Assistant Foods Editors

Karen Brechin (seated) and Jodi Jackson, Editorial Assistants

Above: *Deborah Lowery, Assistant Foods Editor; Charles Walton, Senior Foods Photographer; Beverly Morrow, Photo Stylist*

Left: *Diane Hogan, Test Kitchens Staff; Kaye Adams, Assistant Test Kitchens Director*

Southern Living.

1985 ANNUAL RECIPES

Oxmoor
House.

Copyright 1985 by Oxmoor House, Inc.
Book Division of Southern Progress Corporation
P.O. Box 2463, Birmingham, Alabama 35201

Southern Living®, Breakfasts & Brunches®, Summer Suppers®, Holiday Dinners®, Holiday Desserts®, and *Cooking Light®* are federally registered trademarks of Southern Living, Inc.

Library of Congress Catalog Number: 79-88364
ISBN: 0-8487-0679-X
ISSN: 0272-2003

Manufactured in the United States of America
First Printing 1985

Southern Living® 1985 Annual Recipes

Southern Living®
Foods Editor: Jean Wickstrom Liles
Associate Foods Editors: Margaret Chason Agnew,
Susan Payne
Assistant Foods Editors: Deborah G. Lowery, Nola McKey,
B. Ellen Templeton
Editorial Assistants: Catherine Garrison, Karen Brechin,
Jodi Jackson
Test Kitchens Director: Nancy Nevins
Assistant Test Kitchens Director: Kaye Adams
Test Kitchens Staff: Diane Hogan, Carole King, Peggy Smith
Photo Stylist: Beverly Morrow
Senior Foods Photographer: Charles Walton. Additional
photography by *Southern Living* photographers: John
O'Hagan, pages 27, 140, 141, 162, 170 top, 173, 204; Jim
Bathie, ii bottom left and right, iii top left, 11, 62, 63 top,
128, 129, 174, 175, 220, 246; Van Chaplin, 283; Mary-Gray
Hunter, 166
Production: Clay Nordan, Wanda Butler

Oxmoor House, Inc.
Executive Editor: Ann H. Harvey
Senior Editor: Joan Denman
Editor: Olivia Kindig Wells
Editorial Assistant: Mary Ann Laurens
Production Manager: Jerry Higdon
Art Director: Bob Nance
Designer: Carol Middleton
Illustrator: Janie Farley
Production: Rick Litton, Jane Bonds, Diane Ridley

Cover: Christmas means lots of pretty cookies in all sizes, shapes, flavors, and colors. For identification of cookies, see page 322.

Page i: Our cozy fireside meal for two features Cream of Mushroom Soup, Stuffed Cornish Hens, Green Salad with Italian Dressing, and Aloha Carrots. (Recipes begin on page 261.)

Page iv: Bake one of these surprising layer cakes for your next party: (front to back) Chocolate Triangle Cake, with crystallized violets; Jellyroll Layer Cake, with unusual vertical layers; and stately Six-Layer Black Forest Cake. (Recipes begin on page 124.)

Back cover: Warm Praline Fruit Compote (page 260) uses canned fruit as a starter, but there's nothing plain about this elegant dish.

Table of Contents

Honolulu Chicken (page 52)

Stir-Fried Green Beans (page 148)

Grape Pie (page 212)

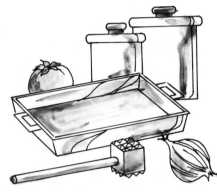

May   101

June   123

July   149

August   183

September   199

Our Year at Southern Living®

The question our foods staff hears most often is, "Where do you get all your ideas?" We're proud to say that many of these ideas come from *you*, our readers, who for years have shared your favorite recipes with us. Most of you consider it an honor to have a recipe published in *Southern Living*. You've often told us how you've become a celebrity in your hometown and have even been invited for radio or newspaper interviews.

Just as you enjoy sharing your recipes with us, receiving response from you is one of the greatest joys of our foods staff. From corresponding with you and from visiting in your home or on the phone, we learn what you cook and how you entertain. This communication with you serves as a barometer in helping us stay on target in planning the food features that our readers need.

Because we stay closely attuned to your food needs and preferences, we know that changes are taking place in Southern kitchens. Let's briefly explore some of the trends that are affecting the cooking and eating habits in the South, as well as how these trends are reflected in our food pages.

We find that most of you enjoy cooking and are excited about food. And if you have an active lifestyle, time and convenience are big concerns. Quick-and-easy recipes to cook during the week are a must. To help trim cooking time, we often emphasize these recipes and quick-cooking methods, such as stir-frying, sautéeing, and microwaving.

Speaking of microwaving, interest in this form of cooking continues to climb, with over 67% of our subscribers now owning a microwave oven. And to help you better utilize your microwave oven for daily meals, we offer recipes in our monthly "Microwave Cookery" feature.

Another trend we're noticing is that Southern meals are becoming simpler, with fewer side dishes. Many of the frills and fancy trimmings are saved for special occasions. We offer one-dish meals, quantity cooking, and make-ahead dishes to help you save time.

In contrast to the emphasis on quick-and-easy recipes for daily meals, most of you like to be creative and splurge on time and ingredients when you entertain. Through our entertainment stories, you can duplicate some of the South's best parties. And for the creative cook, each month we spotlight a specialty food involving intricate preparation. We include technique photos so that you can achieve the same results in your kitchen.

We're finding, too, that it's not just the women who are being creative with food. More men are finding their way into the kitchen, and for them cooking has become a hobby and family activity.

Concern about nutrition is high as Southerners are becoming more interested in developing good eating habits and cutting calories. Not only are we decreasing our sugar and salt consumption, but we're cooking with less fat, and we're seasoning with more herbs and lemon juice. Our monthly *Cooking*

Light® feature, prepared by a registered dietitian, proves that you don't have to give up all the favorite foods you love when on a diet.

With the health and fitness factors, we're seeing increased use of fresh fruits and vegetables. It's amazing what fresh products are available today in Southern supermarkets.

Although it appears that Southerners are interested in nutrition and calories, we're seeing an increased desire for rich chocolates, pastries, ice cream, and cheesecakes. Desserts still seem to be a favorite with us!

There is a fascination for "more flavor" in food, and this is reflected in increased use of herbs, spices, and spirits in cooking. While Southern regional foods are being spotlighted throughout the country, the South is showing a great interest in ethnic favorites, particularly Italian, Mexican, and Oriental dishes.

Even though Southern foods, generally speaking, are becoming lighter and fresher, they still offer down-home appeal with typically Southern ingredients. We are grateful to *you*, our readers, for sharing with us your treasured recipes that are unequaled in any other region of the country.

Now, for the seventh time, we offer a whole year of *Southern Living* recipes in a single volume. *1985 Annual Recipes* brings together all the recipes published in *Southern Living* during the past year. This book offers recipes for every occasion and for every type of cook.

Enjoy your *1985 Annual Recipes*. It represents a busy year of testing and tasting the best recipes of 1985. We believe you'll find this cookbook a welcome addition to your kitchen library.

Jean Wickstrom Liles

Seasoned Dishes Spice Up The Menu

The rich legacy of Southern cooking includes a variety of highly seasoned, hot dishes. Blessed with several major seaports and many inland waterways, the South has had access to spices and flavorings from all over the world. And Southern cooks have reaped the bounty, creating or adapting pungent, flavorful specialties that have become an important part of our heritage.

Southern cooks today still enjoy using generous amounts of seasonings. If anything, they're even more adventurous, often experimenting with spicy, exotic dishes from many different cuisines.

Mongolian Beef is a good example. This Chinese classic is stir-fried and served over fried rice noodles for a dramatic effect. Spaghetti is another foreign favorite. Pasta lovers can choose between Italian Zucchini Spaghetti and Spicy Spaghetti With Mushrooms.

And hot-flavored Cheddar-Jalapeño Cornbread has become a standby with cooks all across the South because it goes so well with favorites such as black-eyed peas and pinto beans.

While we may not want a steady diet of hot, spicy foods, most of us appreciate an occasional dish that has some bite to it. The spiciness stimulates our senses and helps bring out the flavor in other foods as well.

SEAFOOD GUMBO WITH WHOLE CRABS

3 tablespoons bacon drippings
¾ cup all-purpose flour
1 teaspoon salt
1 teaspoon pepper
1½ cups diced onion
1½ cups diced celery
1 (16-ounce) can tomatoes, undrained
2 (7½-ounce) cans tomatoes and jalapeño peppers, undrained
1 (10-ounce) package frozen sliced okra or 10 pods fresh okra, sliced
½ cup diced shallots
8 bay leaves, finely crushed
⅛ teaspoon garlic salt
½ teaspoon hot sauce
2 quarts water
8 to 10 whole crabs, cooked and cleaned
1 pound fresh crabmeat
1 pound fresh shrimp, peeled
1 teaspoon gumbo filé
Hot cooked rice

Heat bacon drippings in a heavy skillet over high heat; stir in flour, salt, and pepper. (Mixture will have the consistency of paste.) Cook, stirring constantly, about 5 minutes or until mixture is the color of a copper penny. Reduce heat; add onion and celery, and cook 10 to 15 minutes or until tender, stirring occasionally. Remove from heat.

Combine next 8 ingredients in a 4-quart Dutch oven. Stir in onion mixture. Add whole crabs. Bring to a boil; cover, reduce heat, and simmer 2 hours, stirring occasionally. Stir in crabmeat and shrimp; cover and cook an additional 30 minutes. Add gumbo filé. Serve over rice. Yield: about 2 quarts.
Lynn E. Young,
Mobile, Alabama.

MONGOLIAN BEEF

1 (2-pound) boneless sirloin tip roast
½ cup soy sauce
2 tablespoons dry sherry
2 teaspoons sesame oil
3 tablespoons cornstarch
2 tablespoons brown sugar
2 teaspoons crushed red pepper
4 to 6 dried whole red peppers
¼ cup plus 2 tablespoons vegetable oil, divided
4 bunches green onions, cut into 2-inch pieces
Fried rice noodles or hot cooked rice
3 strips fresh red chile (optional)

Partially freeze roast; slice diagonally across grain into 3- x ½-inch strips, and set aside. Combine next 7 ingredients, mixing well; add beef. Cover and refrigerate at least 20 minutes.

Pour 2 tablespoons vegetable oil around top of preheated wok, coating sides; heat at medium high (325°) for 1 minute. Add green onions; cover, reduce heat to low (200°), and cook 6 minutes or until tender. Remove green onions.

Add remaining ¼ cup vegetable oil; allow to heat at medium high (325°) for 1 minute. Add beef mixture, and stir-fry 5 minutes or until done. Return onions to beef mixture; stir-fry 30 seconds or until thoroughly heated. Remove whole red peppers, if desired. Serve over fried rice noodles. Garnish with fresh red chile, if desired. Yield: 6 to 8 servings.

Note: Use packaged rice sticks (sometimes called rice vermicelli) to make fried rice noodles.
Kaye Adams,
Birmingham, Alabama.

SPICY SPAGHETTI WITH MUSHROOMS

1 pound ground beef
¼ cup chopped onion
3 (8-ounce) cans tomato sauce
1 (6-ounce) can tomato juice
1 (3-ounce) can sliced mushrooms, drained
½ teaspoon garlic salt
½ teaspoon chili powder
½ teaspoon dried whole oregano
½ teaspoon crushed red pepper
½ teaspoon dried whole basil
½ teaspoon paprika
½ teaspoon salt
½ teaspoon pepper
½ teaspoon parsley flakes
½ teaspoon chopped chives
1 bay leaf
1½ cups water
Hot cooked spaghetti

Combine ground beef and onion in a large Dutch oven. Cook until browned; drain. Stir in remaining ingredients except spaghetti. Cover, reduce heat, and simmer 2 hours. Remove bay leaf. Spoon sauce over spaghetti. Yield: 4 servings.
Trisha Mullan,
Trenton, South Carolina.

ITALIAN ZUCCHINI SPAGHETTI

1½ pounds hot Italian sausage links, cut into bite-size pieces
2 medium green peppers, chopped
1 cup chopped onion
2 cloves garlic, minced
3 medium zucchini, coarsely shredded
2 cups chopped peeled tomato
1 (7½-ounce) can tomatoes and jalapeño peppers, undrained
1 teaspoon dried Italian seasoning
1 teaspoon chili powder
½ teaspoon salt
1 teaspoon lemon juice
½ teaspoon hot sauce
½ cup grated Parmesan cheese
Hot cooked spaghetti

Cook sausage, green pepper, onion, and garlic in a Dutch oven until meat is browned; drain well. Add next 8 ingredients; cook over medium heat 10 to 15 minutes or until zucchini is tender, stirring occasionally. Remove from heat; stir in cheese. Serve sauce over spaghetti. Yield: 8 servings.

Sarah J. Phelps,
Baltimore, Maryland.

CHEDDAR-JALAPEÑO CORNBREAD

5 slices bacon
2 eggs
1¼ cups milk
2 cups self-rising cornmeal
1 tablespoon sugar
¼ teaspoon garlic powder
1 (8½-ounce) can cream-style corn
1 cup chopped onion
¾ cup (3 ounces) shredded mild Cheddar cheese
2 tablespoons canned chopped jalapeño peppers
2 tablespoons chopped pimiento

Cook bacon in a 9-inch cast-iron skillet until crisp; remove bacon, crumble, and set aside. Drain skillet, reserving 5 tablespoons drippings. Coat bottom and sides of skillet with 1 tablespoon of reserved drippings. Heat skillet in 400° oven while mixing ingredients.

Beat eggs in a medium mixing bowl; stir in milk and 4 tablespoons reserved bacon drippings. Add bacon and remaining ingredients, and mix well. Remove skillet from oven; pour batter into skillet. Bake at 400° for 35 minutes or until cornbread is golden brown. Yield: 8 to 10 servings.

Mrs. E. M. Whitesides,
Brighton, Tennessee.

Pour On The Seasoning

It's time to pull bottles of hot sauce, steak sauce, soy sauce, and others from your pantry shelves and put them to use in some unusual ways. With these recipes see how soy sauce adds zest to more than a stir-fry, and hot sauce turns toasted pecans into a spicy appetizer.

MARINATED ROAST

1 (5-ounce) bottle soy sauce
½ cup red wine vinegar
1 tablespoon brown sugar
2 tablespoons lemon juice
1 tablespoon Worcestershire sauce
Dash of garlic powder
Dash of onion powder
1 (3-pound) boneless rump or chuck roast

Combine all ingredients, except roast; mix well. Place roast in a shallow dish; pour marinade over roast. Cover; marinate 24 hours in refrigerator, turning roast once.

Bake roast in marinade at 350° for 2 hours. Remove roast to serving platter; serve with pan drippings. Yield: 6 to 8 servings.

Ann Burris,
Hennessey, Oklahoma.

TENDER GRILLED ROUND STEAK

3 pounds (½-inch-thick) boneless round steak
1 teaspoon coarsely ground pepper
⅔ cup teriyaki sauce
⅓ cup soy sauce
1½ teaspoons instant meat tenderizer
⅛ teaspoon garlic powder

Sprinkle round steak with pepper; pierce at 1-inch intervals with a meat fork. Place in a large shallow container. Combine remaining ingredients; mix well, and pour over steak. Cover dish; marinate 8 to 10 hours or overnight in refrigerator.

Cook over hot coals 3 to 5 minutes on each side or until desired degree of doneness. Yield: 6 servings.

Skip Weeks,
Columbus, Georgia.

PINEAPPLE CHICKEN

4 chicken breast halves, skinned
Salt and pepper
1 tablespoon lemon juice
1 tablespoon soy sauce
1 tablespoon butter or margarine
¼ cup water
1 medium-size green pepper, sliced into rings
1 medium onion, sliced and separated into rings
1 (15¼-ounce) can pineapple chunks, undrained
3 tablespoons all-purpose flour
1 tablespoon water
2 teaspoons browning and seasoning sauce

Sprinkle chicken with salt and pepper; place in a lightly greased 12- x 8- x 2-inch baking dish. Drizzle lemon juice and soy sauce over chicken; dot with butter. Add ¼ cup water to chicken; top with green pepper and onion rings. Cover and bake at 350° for 40 minutes.

Drain pineapple, reserving 2 tablespoons juice. Combine flour, 1 tablespoon water, browning and seasoning sauce, and pineapple juice; mix well. Stir into drippings in baking dish; add pineapple. Return to oven and bake, uncovered, an additional 20 minutes, basting chicken with sauce occasionally. Yield: 4 servings.

Jo Novotny,
Robertsdale, Alabama.

CHICKEN À LA DIXIE MANOR

6 chicken breast halves
2 bay leaves
½ teaspoon salt
¼ teaspoon pepper
¼ cup olive oil
2 medium onions, chopped
1 large red pepper, chopped
2 stalks celery, chopped
1 (4.5-ounce) can sliced mushrooms, drained
¼ cup chopped fresh parsley
1 (16-ounce) can whole tomatoes, undrained and chopped
½ cup catsup
1 teaspoon garlic salt
1 tablespoon seafood seasoning
2 tablespoons steak sauce
Dash of red pepper
Hot cooked yellow rice
1 large avocado, peeled and sliced (optional)

Place chicken in a Dutch oven; cover with water. Add bay leaves, salt, and pepper. Bring to a boil; cover, reduce heat, and simmer 45 minutes or until tender. Remove bay leaves. Remove chicken from broth and cool. Reserve 1 cup chicken broth. Bone chicken and chop meat; set aside.

Heat olive oil in a Dutch oven; sauté onion, red pepper, and celery 3 minutes. Combine 1 cup reserved chicken broth and remaining ingredients except rice and avocado; add to sautéed vegetables. Simmer, uncovered, 15 to 20 minutes or until liquid is reduced and mixture is thickened. Add chicken, and cook until well heated.

Serve over rice. Garnish with avocado slices, if desired. Yield: 8 servings.

Irene R. Smith,
Covington, Georgia.

CRAB SOUFFLÉ SPREAD

1 (6-ounce) can crabmeat, drained and flaked
1 cup mayonnaise
1 egg, beaten
1½ tablespoons drained capers
1 tablespoon prepared horseradish
½ teaspoon prepared mustard
¼ teaspoon hot sauce
⅛ teaspoon pepper
¼ cup (1 ounce) shredded Cheddar cheese

Combine all ingredients except cheese; mix well. Spoon into a greased 1-quart casserole; bake at 350° for 15 minutes. Sprinkle cheese over top; bake 5 minutes. Serve hot with assorted crackers. Yield: 2 cups.

Mrs. E. W. Hanley,
Palm Harbor, Florida.

HOT PEPPER PECANS

2 cups pecan halves
¼ cup butter or margarine, melted
1 tablespoon plus 1 teaspoon soy sauce
1 teaspoon hot sauce

Spread pecans evenly in a 13- x 9- x 2-inch baking dish; bake at 300° for 25 to 30 minutes or until lightly browned.

Combine remaining ingredients; mix well. Pour over pecans; stir gently. Let stand 30 minutes; drain on paper towels. Yield: 2 cups. *Mrs. Jim Mack, Midland, Texas.*

ZIPPY CHEESE SPREAD

2 cups (8 ounces) shredded Fontina cheese
2 cups (8 ounces) process cheese spread
2 tablespoons mayonnaise
¼ cup chopped pimiento-stuffed olives
2 tablespoons finely chopped onion
2 to 3 teaspoons hot sauce

Combine all ingredients; mix well. Chill at least 1 hour. Serve with crackers. Yield: about 3½ cups.

Linda E. Whitt,
Missouri City, Texas.

Tip: Shop alone and after you have eaten. Studies show that people tend to buy more when hungry or when accompanied by others.

From Our Kitchen To Yours

With hot, spicy dishes gaining in popularity throughout the South, peppers are becoming a widely used ingredient. Here are a few commonly asked questions about peppers and some answers.

Which mild and hot types of peppers are most available at the market? Of the mild peppers, you'll often find the Anaheim or California chile and the banana pepper available. The **Anaheim** is usually about 4 to 5 inches long, about 1½ inches around, and has a medium to yellow-green color with some orange tinting. It's used in the popular main dish called chiles rellenos, other egg-and-cheese dishes, and for stuffing. The **banana** pepper is usually smaller than the Anaheim and is about 2 to 3 inches long and 1 inch in diameter. It most often has a distinct yellow-green color.

Popular hot peppers include the jalapeño, serrano, and cayenne. The **jalapeño** is usually 2 to 3 inches long and plump but not round. Its skin can be bright to dark green. A **serrano** pepper is smaller and thinner than a jalapeño, but has the same skin color. Its outer skin is thinner than a jalapeño too, yet it's just as hot. If the serrano is not readily available, you can use the jalapeño. Fresh **cayenne** peppers are long and skinny with a very thin outer skin that's a deep, dark-red color. It's so hot that it's usually added to dishes during cooking and removed before serving.

If fresh peppers are not available when preparing a recipe, are there any substitutes? Canned peppers can be substituted for fresh in most recipes. It's best to drain canned peppers when you're preparing a quiche, casserole, or other dishes that don't require any extra liquid. You can also use crushed dried chiles, ground red pepper (cayenne), or hot pepper sauce in place of fresh hot peppers. Of course, the amount depends on the desired degree of hotness.

What's the best way to work with hot peppers? Be careful; wear rubber gloves to keep from burning your skin. It's best to run cold water over chiles when removing the seeds and ribs.

How do I remove skins from peppers? To peel peppers, begin by either broiling, grilling, or deep-fat frying them until they look blistered all over. After the skin has blistered, put peppers in a plastic or paper bag to steam 10 to 15 minutes. Let them cool before you handle them. Start with the stem end, and the skins should peel off easily.

Can I freeze homegrown peppers? They are one of the few vegetables that can be frozen without being blanched first. Freeze green peppers by cutting them in half and removing the seeds and ribs. Dry them well, and wrap tightly in plastic wrap. Cover completely to keep the pepper aroma from spreading to other foods in freezer.

Any peppers can be frozen either peeled or unpeeled. If you freeze them unpeeled, the peeling will come right off after thawing. Mild peppers frozen too long may lose some flavor; hot ones will lose some hotness.

The Bread Is Homemade, With Flavor Extras

Nothing tastes as good as homemade bread, unless it's homemade bread filled with chunks of apple, almonds, and cinnamon, flavored with shredded Cheddar cheese, spiced with dillweed and onion, or topped with a sweet chocolate glaze.

Use your imagination to come up with your own favorite flavored breads. You can use other bread recipes and substitute spices, herbs, or ingredients that suit your own tastes. If you substitute vegetables and fruit in bread recipes, make sure you use another one similar in texture and sweetness for the best end product.

APPLE SWIRL BREAD

1 package dry yeast
1 cup warm water (105° to 115°)
3 tablespoons sugar
2 tablespoons shortening
1 egg
¾ teaspoon salt
3 to 3½ cups all-purpose flour, divided
Apple filling (recipe follows)

Dissolve yeast in warm water in a large bowl. Add sugar, shortening, egg, salt, and half the flour; beat at low speed of an electric mixer until smooth. Stir in enough of the remaining flour to make a soft dough.

Place dough in a greased bowl, turning to grease top. Cover and let rise in a warm place (85°), free from drafts, 1 hour or until doubled in bulk.

Punch dough down; turn out onto a lightly floured surface, and knead 4 or 5 times. Roll dough into a 15- x 7-inch rectangle on a lightly floured surface; sprinkle apple filling evenly over dough. Roll up jellyroll fashion, starting at short side. Pinch seams and ends together. Place roll, seam side down, in a greased 9- x 5- x 3-inch loafpan.

Cover and let rise in a warm place (85°), free from drafts, about 40 minutes or until doubled in bulk. Bake at 350° for 50 to 55 minutes or until loaf sounds hollow when tapped. Remove from pan; cool completely on a wire rack. Yield: 1 loaf.

Apple Filling:

2 cups finely chopped, peeled apple
¼ cup plus 2 tablespoons firmly packed brown sugar
1 tablespoon water
½ teaspoon ground cinnamon
¼ cup chopped almonds, toasted
¼ teaspoon vanilla extract

Combine first 4 ingredients in a saucepan; cover and cook over medium heat 5 minutes. Remove cover, and continue to cook 10 minutes or until all liquid evaporates. Stir in almonds and vanilla. Yield: about 1 cup.

WHOLE WHEAT ORANGE BREAD

1½ cups whole wheat flour
1½ cups all-purpose flour
¾ cup sugar
2 teaspoons baking powder
½ teaspoon salt
½ teaspoon grated orange rind
1 egg, beaten
¾ cup orange juice
½ cup milk
½ cup vegetable oil
½ cup chopped pecans
1 tablespoon sugar
½ teaspoon ground cinnamon

Combine first 6 ingredients in a large bowl; mix well. Combine egg, orange juice, milk, and oil; add to dry ingredients, stirring just until moistened. Fold in pecans. Pour into a greased 9- x 5- x 3-inch loafpan. Combine 1 tablespoon sugar and cinnamon; sprinkle mixture over batter. Bake at 350° for 55 to 60 minutes or until a wooden pick inserted in center comes out clean. Cool loaf in pan 10 minutes; remove from pan, and cool completely on a wire rack. Yield: 1 loaf. *Katie Harville, Grenada, Mississippi.*

EASY ONION-DILL BREAD

½ cup milk
1½ tablespoons sugar
1 teaspoon salt
2¼ teaspoons butter or margarine
1 package dry yeast
½ cup warm water (105° to 115°)
2¼ cups all-purpose flour
1 tablespoon instant minced onion
½ teaspoon dried whole dillweed
1 tablespoon butter or margarine, melted
⅛ teaspoon salt (optional)

Scald milk; remove from heat. Add sugar, salt, and 2¼ teaspoons butter; stir until sugar dissolves and butter melts. Cool to 105° to 115°. Dissolve yeast in warm water in a large bowl. Add cooled milk mixture, flour, onion, and dillweed; beat at medium speed of an electric mixer until smooth. Cover and let rise in a warm place (85°), free from drafts, 45 minutes or until tripled in bulk.

Punch dough down. Beat with a wooden spoon for 30 seconds. Place in a greased 9-inch piepan. Bake at 350° for 1 hour. Brush top with melted butter; sprinkle with salt, if desired. Yield: 1 loaf. *Annette Crane, Dallas, Texas.*

CHEESY ONION BUNS

1 package dry yeast
¼ cup warm water (105° to 115°)
2 cups milk, scalded
¼ cup butter or margarine
½ cup sugar
1 teaspoon salt
1 egg, beaten
6 to 7 cups all-purpose flour
2 cups (8 ounces) shredded sharp Cheddar cheese
2 tablespoons instant minced onion
1 tablespoon butter or margarine, melted

Dissolve yeast in warm water; set aside. Combine milk, ¼ cup butter, sugar, and salt in a mixing bowl; stir until butter melts. Cool to 105° to 115°. Add egg, yeast mixture, and 2 cups flour; mix well. Stir in cheese, onion, and enough remaining flour to make a soft dough.

Turn dough out onto a well-floured surface; knead 8 to 10 minutes or until smooth and elastic. Shape into a ball. Place dough in a well-greased bowl; brush top with melted butter. Cover and let rise in a warm place (85°), free from drafts, 1½ hours or until doubled in bulk.

Punch dough down; cover and let rest 10 minutes. Divide dough in half; divide each half into 10 equal pieces. Roll each piece into a ball, and place on greased baking sheets about 2 inches apart. Press each ball down lightly with fingertips to resemble a bun.

Cover and let rise in a warm place (85°), free from drafts, 1½ hours or until doubled in bulk. Bake at 375° for 15 minutes or until golden brown. Yield: 20 buns. *Jean Pashby, Memphis, Tennessee.*

CHOCOLATE-CINNAMON BUNS

1 package dry yeast
¾ cup warm water (105° to 115°)
¼ cup shortening
½ teaspoon salt
¼ cup sugar
1 egg
⅓ cup cocoa
2¼ cups all-purpose flour, divided
1 tablespoon butter or margarine, softened
3 tablespoons sugar
1½ teaspoons ground cinnamon
¾ cup sifted powdered sugar
1 tablespoon plus 1½ teaspoons milk
¼ cup chopped pecans

Dissolve yeast in warm water. Add shortening, salt, ¼ cup sugar, egg, cocoa, and 1 cup flour. Beat at medium speed of electric mixer until smooth. Stir in enough of remaining flour to make a stiff dough. Place in a well-greased bowl, turning to grease top. Cover and let rise in a warm place (85°), free from drafts, 1 hour or until doubled in bulk.

Punch dough down. Turn dough out onto a lightly floured surface; roll into a 12- x 8-inch rectangle, and spread with butter. Combine 3 tablespoons sugar and cinnamon; sprinkle mixture over rectangle. Roll up jellyroll fashion, beginning at long side; moisten edges with water to seal. Cut rolls into 1-inch slices; place slices cut side down in a lightly greased 9-inch square baking pan. Cover; let rise in a warm place (85°), free from drafts, 1 hour or until doubled in bulk.

Bake at 375° for 20 to 25 minutes. Combine powdered sugar and milk, mixing well. Drizzle glaze over warm rolls. Sprinkle tops with pecans. Yield: 1 dozen. *Debbie C. Fadeley, Toms Brook, Virginia.*

SWEET POTATO MUFFINS

½ cup butter or margarine, softened
1¼ cups sugar
2 eggs
1¼ cups canned mashed sweet potatoes
1 cup milk
1½ cups all-purpose flour
2 teaspoons baking powder
¼ teaspoon salt
1 teaspoon ground cinnamon
¼ teaspoon ground nutmeg
½ cup raisins, chopped
¼ cup chopped pecans

Cream butter; gradually beat in sugar. Add eggs, one at a time, beating well after each. Stir in sweet potatoes and milk. Combine flour, baking powder, salt, cinnamon, and nutmeg; add to creamed mixture, stirring just until moistened. Stir in raisins and pecans. Spoon into greased muffin pans, filling two-thirds full. Bake at 400° for 25 minutes. Yield: 1½ dozen.

Clonelle G. Jones,
Nashville, Tennessee.

CHOCOLATE-GLAZED POTATO DOUGHNUTS

1 package dry yeast
¼ cup warm water (105° to 115°)
1 egg, slightly beaten
½ to ¾ cup warm water (105° to 115°)
3 cups bread flour
½ cup instant mashed potato flakes
⅓ cup sugar
¼ cup instant nonfat dry milk powder
6 tablespoons butter or margarine, softened and cut into 6 pieces
¾ teaspoon salt
Vegetable oil
Chocolate glaze (recipe follows)

Dissolve yeast in ¼ cup warm water; set aside. Combine egg and ½ cup water; set aside.
Position knife blade in food processor bowl. Add next 6 ingredients, and top with cover. Process 10 seconds or until well mixed. With processor running, pour yeast mixture and egg mixture through food chute in a slow, steady stream; process 5 seconds or until dough pulls away from the sides of bowl and forms a ball. If dough does not form a ball, add 1 to 2 tablespoons water and pulse several times.

Turn dough out onto a lightly floured surface; knead 3 to 4 minutes or until smooth and elastic. Place dough in a greased bowl, turning to grease top. Cover and let rise in a warm place (85°), free from drafts, 1 hour and 30 minutes or until doubled in bulk. Punch dough down, and turn out onto a lightly floured board; let rest 15 minutes. Roll dough out to ¾-inch thickness; cut with a 2½-inch doughnut cutter. Place doughnuts on a lightly floured surface. Cover and let rise in a warm place (85°), free from drafts, 30 minutes or until doubled in bulk.
Heat 2 to 3 inches of oil to 375°; drop in 2 to 3 doughnuts at a time. Fry 30 seconds or until golden brown on one side; turn and cook other side 30 seconds. Drain well. Dip each doughnut in chocolate glaze while warm; cool on wire racks. Yield: 16 doughnuts.

Chocolate Glaze:

2 cups sifted powdered sugar
2 to 3 tablespoons cocoa
¼ cup boiling water

Combine powdered sugar and cocoa; mixing well. Gradually stir in water until mixture is smooth. Yield: 1 cup.
Susie Lavenue,
Ridgely, Tennessee.

CHEESE POPOVER PUFFS

1 cup all-purpose flour
½ teaspoon salt
1 cup milk
2 eggs
1 tablespoon butter or margarine, melted
¼ cup (1 ounce) shredded Cheddar cheese

Combine all ingredients except cheese. Beat at medium speed of an electric mixer until smooth. Stir in cheese.
Heat a well-greased muffin pan at 425° for 3 minutes or until very hot. Spoon in batter, filling two-thirds full. Bake at 425° for 15 minutes; reduce heat, bake at 350° for 25 minutes or until golden brown. Serve immediately. Yield: 8 popovers. –*Linda Lawson,*
Salem, Virginia.

Tip: Measure ingredients accurately. For liquids, use a glass measuring cup; this allows you to see that you are measuring correctly. Use a metal or plastic measuring cup for solids or dry ingredients; fill cup to overflowing, and level off with a knife or spatula.

Start The Year With Lucky Peas

In many households, New Year's Day just isn't complete without serving black-eyed peas. If you follow this tradition, you'll enjoy these recipes offering new ways to prepare your lucky dish.

BEEFY BLACK-EYED SOUP

2 pounds ground beef
½ cup chopped green pepper
½ cup butter or margarine
½ cup all-purpose flour
2 quarts water
1 (28-ounce) can whole tomatoes, undrained
1 (16-ounce) package frozen black-eyed peas
1 cup chopped onion
1 cup diced carrots
1 cup chopped celery
2 tablespoons beef-flavored bouillon granules
1 tablespoon pepper
½ teaspoon salt
⅛ teaspoon garlic powder
⅛ teaspoon onion powder

Cook beef and green pepper until beef is browned; stir to crumble. Drain.
Melt butter in a Dutch oven; add flour, stirring until smooth. Cook 1 minute, stirring constantly. Gradually add water; cook, stirring constantly, until bubbly. Stir in beef mixture and remaining ingredients. Bring to a boil; cover and simmer 45 minutes to 1 hour. Yield: 4½ quarts.

CREOLE BLACK-EYES AND RICE

1 (16-ounce) package dried black-eyed peas
½ pound salt pork
3 cups chopped onion
1 bunch green onions, chopped
1 cup chopped fresh parsley
1 cup chopped green pepper
2 cloves garlic, pressed
1 to 1½ teaspoons salt
1 teaspoon red pepper
1 teaspoon pepper
3 dashes of hot sauce
1 tablespoon Worcestershire sauce
1 (8-ounce) can tomato sauce
¼ teaspoon dried whole oregano
¼ teaspoon dried whole thyme
2 pounds smoked sausage, cut into 1-inch pieces
Hot cooked rice
Green onion fan (optional)

Sort and wash peas; place in a Dutch oven. Cover with water, and soak overnight. Drain peas. Add pork to peas; cover with water. Cover and cook over low heat 45 minutes. Add next 13 ingredients; cover and cook over low heat 45 minutes to 1 hour, stirring occasionally. Add sausage; cook, uncovered, over low heat 45 minutes. Serve over rice, and garnish with a green onion fan, if desired. Yield: 10 servings.

HEARTY BLACK-EYED PEAS

1 (16-ounce) package dried black-eyed peas
3 cups water
1 (1 pound) ham steak, cut into ½-inch cubes
6 pearl onions
3 bay leaves
1 teaspoon pepper
½ teaspoon salt

Sort and wash peas; place in a large Dutch oven. Cover with water, and bring to a boil; cook 2 minutes. Remove from heat. Cover and let soak 1 hour; drain.
Combine peas, 3 cups water, and remaining ingredients; bring to a boil. Cover, reduce heat, and simmer 1 hour or until peas are tender. Remove bay leaves. Yield: 8 servings.
Gary McCalla,
Birmingham, Alabama.

HOT BACON AND BLACK-EYED SALAD

1 (10-ounce) package frozen black-eyed peas
¼ cup sugar
¼ cup vinegar
¼ cup water
8 slices bacon
1 small head cauliflower
½ cup diced celery
4 green onions with tops, chopped
1 (2-ounce) jar diced pimiento, drained
1 tablespoon brown sugar
2 tablespoons vinegar
½ teaspoon salt

Cook peas according to package directions, omitting bacon and salt; drain well. Combine peas and next 3 ingredients; stir well. Cover; chill 3 hours.
Cook bacon until crisp; drain well, reserving 2 tablespoons drippings in pan. Crumble bacon, and set aside.
Break cauliflower into flowerets; place in steaming rack. Cover; steam 10 to 15 minutes or until crisp-tender.

Drain peas; add cauliflower, celery, onions, pimiento, and bacon. Combine 2 tablespoons bacon drippings, brown sugar, 2 tablespoons vinegar, and salt in a saucepan. Cook over low heat until thoroughly heated; pour over vegetables, tossing gently. Yield: 6 servings.

COOKING LIGHT®

Lose Weight The Light Way

Another New Year is here—and you've resolved to get serious about losing those extra pounds. Keep in mind that it's necessary to cut back on the food eaten so that fewer calories are taken in than the body can burn.
Exercise increases the metabolism, or burning of calories. That's why most reasonable diet plans recommend an increase in physical activity along with a decreased intake of calories.
As you start your diet, remember that it probably took several months of overeating to put on the extra pounds, and it will take time to get them off. Set your goal to lose only 1 to 2 pounds a week. Women can accomplish this by keeping to a diet of about 1,200 calories a day, while men should restrict themselves to 1,600 calories daily. If you eat less than these recommended amounts, you will probably not obtain the nutrients your body needs. In addition, you'll be eating so little that you'll be more likely to stay hungry and eventually stray from your diet plan.
The safest and surest way to lose weight and keep it off is to eat three meals a day of regular food: meat, vegetables, fruit, bread, cereal, and milk. You can avoid unnecessary calories by limiting the fat and sugar added during food preparation. Be conscious of serving sizes in order to keep total calories at about 1,200 or 1,600 daily.
A guide to the amount and type of food you should eat on a 1,200-calorie diet is shown in our menu plans for breakfast, lunch, and dinner. Recommended guidelines suggest about two servings of protein foods (meat, fish, poultry, and dried beans and peas), four servings of fruit and vegetables, four servings of breads and cereal, and two servings of milk or other dairy products.

(Milk needs for children, teenagers, and pregnant and lactating women are greater than two servings a day.) If you're on a 1,600-calorie diet, just increase the servings of these nutritious foods, and avoid high-calorie foods such as candy, chips, and nuts.
For our breakfast menu, you can prepare 1 egg in a number of ways. It can be poached or scrambled in a non-stick utensil. Or you may want to prepare your favorite omelet recipe, using water or skim milk.

BREAKFAST
One-egg omelet
Bran-Buttermilk Muffin
Broiled Grapefruit
½ cup skim milk

BRAN-BUTTERMILK MUFFINS

1½ cups buttermilk
1½ cups whole bran cereal
2 tablespoons sugar
2 tablespoons vegetable oil
1 egg, beaten
1¼ cups all-purpose flour
2 teaspoons baking powder
½ teaspoon baking soda
½ teaspoon salt
Vegetable cooking spray

Combine buttermilk and cereal; let stand 5 minutes or until liquid is absorbed. Mix in sugar, oil, and egg.
Combine remaining ingredients except cooking spray; make a well in center of mixture. Add bran mixture to dry ingredients, stirring just until moistened. Spoon into muffin pans coated with cooking spray, filling two-thirds full. Bake at 400° for 20 to 25 minutes. Yield: 12 muffins (about 115 calories each). *Susan Buckmaster,*
Charlotte, North Carolina.

BROILED GRAPEFRUIT

2 medium grapefruit
2 teaspoons sugar
½ teaspoon ground cinnamon
½ teaspoon ground nutmeg

Cut grapefruit in half crosswise; remove seeds, and loosen sections. Place cut side up in a broiler pan. Combine sugar and spices; sprinkle ¾ teaspoon mixture on each grapefruit half. Broil 6 inches from heat 2 to 3 minutes or until sugar is bubbly. Yield: 4 servings (48 calories per serving).
Harriet O. St. Amant,
Newport, Rhode Island.

LUNCH
Open-Face Ham Sandwich
Mushroom-Zucchini Salad
10 fresh grapes
1 cup skim milk

DINNER
Chicken Cutlets With Lemon
½ cup unbuttered cooked rice
Sesame Broccoli
Green salad
Peaches With Strawberry Sauce
Water

PEACHES WITH STRAWBERRY SAUCE

1½ cups frozen unsweetened strawberries, partially thawed and drained
1 tablespoon Grand Marnier or other orange-flavored liqueur
2 tablespoons unsweetened white grape juice or apple juice
2 (16-ounce) cans unsweetened sliced peaches, chilled and drained

Combine strawberries, liqueur, and grape juice in container of an electric blender; process until smooth. Spoon sauce into 4 individual serving dishes. Arrange 6 peach slices over sauce in each dish; reserve remaining peach slices for other uses. Yield: 4 servings (about 74 calories per serving).

OPEN-FACE HAM SANDWICHES

1 (10-ounce) package frozen asparagus spears
Lettuce leaves
6 slices whole wheat bread, toasted
12 (4/5-ounce) slices lean, cooked ham
6 (¾-ounce) slices Swiss cheese
¼ cup plus 2 tablespoons plain low-fat yogurt
¼ cup plus 2 tablespoons reduced-calorie mayonnaise
1½ teaspoons lemon juice
¼ teaspoon dry mustard
Pimiento strips

Cook asparagus according to package directions, omitting salt; drain.

Place lettuce leaves on each toast slice; top each with 2 ham slices, 1 cheese slice, and 3 asparagus spears.

Combine next 4 ingredients in a small saucepan; cook over medium heat, stirring constantly, until heated (do not boil). Spoon sauce over sandwiches; garnish with pimiento. Yield: 6 servings (about 259 calories per serving).

CHICKEN CUTLETS WITH LEMON

4 chicken breast halves (about 2 pounds), skinned and boned
1 egg
Pinch of red pepper
½ cup wheat germ
Vegetable cooking spray
1 tablespoon margarine
3 tablespoons lemon juice
Lemon slices or chopped fresh parsley

Place each piece of chicken between 2 sheets of waxed paper, and flatten to ½-inch thickness using a meat mallet or rolling pin.

Combine egg and red pepper. Dip each chicken breast in egg mixture, and coat with wheat germ. Coat a large skillet with cooking spray; add margarine, and place over medium heat until margarine melts. Add chicken, and cook 3 to 4 minutes on each side; remove to a serving platter, and keep warm.

Pour lemon juice in pan; cook over high heat 1 minute, stirring constantly. Pour juice over chicken; garnish with lemon slices or parsley. Yield: 4 servings (about 238 calories per serving).

Burnell Huff,
Dallas, Texas.

MUSHROOM-ZUCCHINI SALAD

½ pound fresh mushrooms, sliced
1 medium zucchini, thinly sliced
1 medium tomato, diced
¼ cup sliced scallions or green onions
2 to 3 tablespoons white vinegar
1 tablespoon olive or vegetable oil
½ teaspoon coarsely ground pepper
½ teaspoon dried whole marjoram, crumbled
Lettuce leaves (optional)

Combine mushrooms, zucchini, tomato, and scallions. Combine next 4 ingredients, mixing well. Pour over vegetables; toss gently. Serve on lettuce, if desired. Yield: 6 servings (about 47 calories per serving).

Lynn F. Wootan,
Broussard, Louisiana.

SESAME BROCCOLI

1 (1-pound) bunch fresh broccoli
1 tablespoon vinegar
1 tablespoon soy sauce
1 teaspoon sugar
1½ teaspoons vegetable oil
1½ teaspoons water
1 tablespoon sesame seeds, toasted

Trim off large leaves of broccoli, and remove tough ends of lower stalks. Wash broccoli thoroughly, and separate into spears. Cook broccoli in a small amount of boiling water 8 to 10 minutes or until crisp-tender; drain.

Combine remaining ingredients in a small saucepan; bring to a boil. Pour sauce over broccoli; toss. Yield: 4 servings (about 57 calories per serving).

Pam Burleson,
Birmingham, Alabama.

Tip: After purchasing fresh mushrooms, refrigerate immediately in their original container. If mushrooms are in a plastic bag, make a few holes in the bag for ventilation.

Give Winter Squash A Try

With its colorful shell, distinct shape, and excellent storage life, winter squash may be more familiar as a decorative, seasonal centerpiece than as the nutritious vegetable it actually is. But beneath the attractive shell is a firm, dry flesh that is an excellent source of vitamin A and suitable for recipes ranging from soup to dessert.

For a filling entrée, try Acorn Squash With Sausage; pork sausage and a hint of brown sugar complement this mellow-flavored squash. Enjoy our Sherried Acorn Squash served as a spirited side dish. Or for dessert, bake Spicy Squash Pie. The sweet and nutty taste of butternut squash is enhanced with spices for a taste that will remind you of pumpkin pie.

Select winter squash that is fully mature as indicated by a hard, tough shell. A tender shell indicates immaturity, a sign of poor eating quality in winter squash. Generally speaking, the deeper the color of the flesh, the higher the vitamin A content. Figure 1 pound of fresh winter squash to yield about 1 cup of mashed, cooked squash.

ACORN SQUASH WITH SAUSAGE

3 medium acorn squash
½ teaspoon salt
1½ pounds bulk pork sausage
¼ cup plus 2 tablespoons firmly packed
    brown sugar
3 tablespoons butter or margarine

Cut squash in half lengthwise, and remove seeds; sprinkle with salt. Place cut side down in a shallow baking dish, and add ½ inch boiling water. Bake, uncovered, at 375° for 35 minutes; drain.

Cook sausage in skillet over medium heat until browned, stirring to crumble meat. Remove from heat; drain.

Place 1 tablespoon brown sugar and 1½ teaspoons butter in each squash cavity. Spoon sausage into squash halves. Bake, uncovered, at 350° for 25 minutes or until tender. Yield: 6 servings. *Helen Rainwater,*
Weslaco, Texas.

SKILLET BUTTERNUT AND BACON

2 (2-pound) butternut squash
6 slices bacon, cut into ½-inch pieces
1 medium onion, finely chopped
2 tablespoons butter or margarine, melted
⅛ teaspoon salt
⅛ teaspoon pepper

Peel squash; slice in half lengthwise, and remove seeds. Cut into slices; place in saucepan, and cover with water. Cover and cook 15 minutes or until tender; drain. Mash pulp thoroughly. Set aside 3¾ cups mashed squash; store remainder in refrigerator for other uses.

Sauté bacon and onion in a medium skillet, stirring constantly until bacon is crisp; do not drain. Add squash and remaining ingredients. Cook until thoroughly heated. Yield: 6 to 8 servings.
Mrs. Grant A. Begley,
Dumfries, Virginia.

SHERRIED ACORN SQUASH

2 medium acorn squash
Salt
2 tablespoons brown sugar
2 teaspoons grated orange peel
2 tablespoons dry sherry
1 tablespoon plus 1 teaspoon butter or
    margarine

Cut squash in half lengthwise, and remove seeds; sprinkle with salt. Place cut side down in a shallow baking dish, and add ½ inch boiling water. Bake, uncovered, at 375° for 35 minutes; do not drain. Turn cut side up; prick squash cavities with fork. Sprinkle each cavity with 1½ teaspoons brown sugar, ½ teaspoon orange peel, and 1½ teaspoons sherry; dot each cavity with 1 teaspoon butter. Bake, uncovered, at 350° for 30 minutes or until squash is tender. Yield: 4 servings. *Mrs. Donald D. Sisson,*
Wimberley, Texas.

SPICY SQUASH PIE

1 (2-pound) butternut squash
1 cup evaporated milk
2 eggs, beaten
¾ cup firmly packed brown sugar
¾ teaspoon salt
1 teaspoon ground cinnamon
½ teaspoon ground nutmeg
½ teaspoon ground ginger
1 unbaked 9-inch pastry shell
Whipped cream (optional)

Peel squash; slice in half lengthwise, and remove seeds. Cut into slices; place in saucepan, and cover with water. Cover and cook 15 minutes or until tender; drain. Mash pulp thoroughly. Set aside 1¾ cups mashed squash; store remainder in refrigerator for other uses.

Combine squash, milk, eggs, brown sugar, salt, cinnamon, nutmeg, and ginger in a medium bowl; mix well. Pour squash mixture into pastry shell. Bake at 450° for 15 minutes. Reduce heat to 300°; continue baking an additional 45 minutes. Let cool; garnish with whipped cream, if desired. Yield: one 9-inch pie. *Davi Uher,*
Ocean Springs, Mississippi.

Southern Chowders Are Robust Fare

Chowder may have originated in New England, but through the years Southerners have come to claim this thick, hearty dish as one of their own. Not surprising when you consider that the main ingredient in the original chowders was fish or clams and that much of the South has easy access to the sea. Of course, chowders today may have meat, vegetables, or cheese in them, as well as seafood. Note the variety in these tantalizing chowder recipes.

SEAFOOD CHOWDER

4 medium onions, chopped
1 large green pepper, chopped
¼ cup vegetable oil
2 tablespoons all-purpose flour
3 (14½-ounce) cans stewed tomatoes,
    undrained
1 tablespoon celery salt
1 teaspoon garlic powder
1 teaspoon sugar
1 teaspoon hot sauce
½ teaspoon pepper
2 pounds fresh medium shrimp, peeled
    and deveined
½ pound crabmeat
½ pint oysters, drained
1 large fish fillet, cut into bite-size pieces

Sauté onion and green pepper in oil in a large saucepan until tender; add flour, stirring until smooth. Cook 1 minute, stirring constantly. Stir in tomatoes and seasonings; bring to a boil. Cover, reduce heat, and simmer 15 minutes. Add remaining ingredients; cover and allow to simmer an additional 15 minutes. Yield: 12 cups. *Lora Blocker,*
Dade City, Florida.

CLAM CHOWDER

4 slices bacon, chopped
3 (6½-ounce) cans whole shelled clams
3 tablespoons butter or margarine
½ cup chopped celery
½ cup chopped onion
2 green onions with tops, chopped
2 cups chopped potatoes
3 tablespoons all-purpose flour
2 cups milk
2 cups half-and-half
¼ teaspoon hot sauce
½ teaspoon salt
¼ teaspoon white pepper
Paprika
Fresh parsley sprigs (optional)

Sauté bacon in a Dutch oven until crisp; pour off pan drippings. Set aside.

Drain clams, reserving 1 cup juice; set clams aside. Add clam juice, butter, and vegetables to bacon. Bring to a boil; cover, reduce heat, and simmer 15 minutes or until potatoes are tender.

Chop clams coarsely; set aside.

Combine flour and milk; stir until flour is dissolved. Add milk mixture, clams, half-and-half, hot sauce, salt, and pepper to soup mixture. Cook over medium heat, stirring constantly, until thoroughly heated. Sprinkle each serving with paprika, and garnish with parsley, if desired. Yield: 8 cups.
Frances Rigsby,
Daphne, Alabama.

TURKEY CHOWDER

2 tablespoons butter or margarine
2 tablespoons all-purpose flour
2 cups milk
2 cups cubed process cheese
2 cups chopped cooked turkey
1½ cups sliced cooked potatoes
1 (10-ounce) package frozen mixed
    vegetables
1 teaspoon chicken-flavored bouillon
    granules
½ teaspoon instant minced onion
¼ teaspoon dry mustard
⅛ teaspoon pepper

Melt butter in a large saucepan over low heat; add flour, stirring until smooth. Cook 1 minute, stirring constantly. Gradually add milk and cheese; cook over medium heat, stirring constantly, until mixture thickens and cheese melts. Add remaining ingredients, and mix well. Cook over low heat, stirring occasionally, until the vegetables are tender. Yield: 5 cups.

Kathy Russell,
Austin, Texas.

CORN CHOWDER

1 cup chopped onion
½ cup chopped celery
2 tablespoons butter or margarine, melted
3 cups fresh corn, cut from cob
1½ cups peeled, cubed potatoes
1½ cups water
2 chicken-flavored bouillon cubes
1 teaspoon salt
¼ teaspoon pepper
¼ teaspoon dried whole thyme
2 cups milk
1 cup half-and-half

Sauté onion and celery in butter in a large saucepan until tender. Stir in next 7 ingredients; cover and simmer 15 minutes. Add milk and half-and-half; cook, stirring constantly, until thoroughly heated. Yield: 8 cups.

Note: 3 cups of frozen corn may be substituted for fresh. *Larra Andress, Birmingham, Alabama.*

Enjoy Dates In Any Season

If you have dates left over from holiday baking, take a look at the variety of delicious possibilities for using them. We've included desserts, a bread, and even a snappy appetizer.

Dates are a natural source of sweetness—the sugar content of the dried fruit we usually see on the market runs about 65%. They're also a good source of fiber and potassium as well as many other minerals and vitamins.

APPLE-DATE DREAM CAKE SQUARES

2 cups all-purpose flour
1 cup sugar
1½ teaspoons baking soda
1 teaspoon salt
1 teaspoon ground cinnamon
½ teaspoon ground allspice
2 eggs, slightly beaten
1 (21-ounce) can apple pie filling
½ cup vegetable oil
1 teaspoon vanilla extract
1 cup chopped dates
¼ cup chopped walnuts
Sweetened whipped cream (optional)
Walnut halves (optional)

Combine flour, sugar, soda, salt, cinnamon, and allspice; stir gently. Combine eggs, pie filling, oil, and vanilla; stir into dry ingredients. Stir in chopped dates and chopped walnuts; pour mixture into a greased and floured 13- x 9- x 2-inch baking pan. Bake at 350° for 35 to 40 minutes; cool.

Cut cake into squares. Garnish each serving with sweetened whipped cream and a walnut half, if desired. Yield: 15 servings. *Marie A. Davis, Morganton, North Carolina.*

DATE-NUT LOAF

1 teaspoon baking soda
1 cup boiling water
1 (8-ounce) package chopped dates
¼ cup butter or margarine, softened
¾ cup sugar
1 egg
1¼ cups all-purpose flour
¼ teaspoon baking powder
¼ teaspoon salt
1 cup chopped pecans

Dissolve baking soda in boiling water; stir in dates, and set aside.

Cream butter with an electric mixer; gradually add sugar, beating well. Add egg, and mix well.

Combine flour, baking powder, and salt; add to creamed mixture. Add date mixture, and mix well. Stir in pecans.

Pour batter into a greased and floured 8½- x 4½- x 3-inch loafpan. Bake at 350° for 55 to 60 minutes or until a wooden pick inserted in center comes out clean. Yield: 1 loaf.

Alice K. Liles,
Sylacauga, Alabama.

LAYERED OATMEAL-DATE BARS

⅔ cup chopped dates
3 tablespoons all-purpose flour
⅓ cup firmly packed brown sugar
½ cup butter or margarine, softened
⅔ cup firmly packed brown sugar
1 cup whole wheat flour
½ teaspoon baking powder
¼ teaspoon salt
1 cup quick-cooking oats, uncooked
½ cup sesame seeds

Combine dates, flour, and ⅓ cup brown sugar in a medium bowl; toss to coat dates. Set aside.

Cream butter; gradually add ⅔ cup brown sugar, beating well. Combine remaining ingredients; add to creamed mixture, and mix well.

Press half of oats mixture into a greased 9-inch square pan. Top with date mixture. Press remaining half of oats mixture over dates. Bake at 350° for 35 to 40 minutes. Let cool, and cut into bars. Yield: 2 dozen.

Sharon Bramlett,
Clyde, North Carolina.

DATE-NUT BALLS

1 cup butter, softened
¼ cup sugar
2 teaspoons vanilla extract
2 cups all-purpose flour
2 cups finely ground pecans
1 cup diced dates
About 1½ cups sifted powdered sugar

Cream butter; gradually add sugar, beating until light and fluffy. Add vanilla and flour, stirring well. Stir in pecans and dates. Chill 2 hours.

Shape dough into 1-inch balls; place on a lightly greased baking sheet. Bake at 350° for 20 to 25 minutes or until lightly browned. Roll in powdered sugar; cool. Roll in powdered sugar again. Yield: about 4 dozen.

Kathy C. Tucker,
Raphine, Virginia.

JUNE BUGS

½ cup butter or margarine, softened
1 cup (4 ounces) shredded Cheddar cheese
1½ cups all-purpose flour
⅛ teaspoon red pepper
Dash of paprika
25 pitted dates (about 6 ounces)

Combine butter and cheese; beat until smooth. Combine flour, red pepper, and paprika. Add to cheese mixture, mixing well.

Cut dates in half crosswise; wrap each half with dough. Place on ungreased baking sheets; bake at 400° for 15 to 18 minutes. Cool on wire racks. Yield: 50 appetizers.
*Jean Head,
Boaz, Alabama.*

MICROWAVE COOKERY

Plan An Oriental Menu For Six

Our complete Oriental menu may look like a feast, but it's easy to prepare when you use your microwave oven. The dishes are microwaved one at a time and reheated briefly, if needed. The end result is a menu filled with a variety of flavors and contrasting colors.

Plan ahead by making Mandarin-Almond Pudding a day in advance. That way it will be firm enough to unmold and cut into squares when the rest of the menu is ready.

With that out of the way, microwave the rice next. Keep in mind that you won't be saving much time over conventional cooking. In fact, you may prefer to cook the rice conventionally while microwaving other items. Another option is to microwave the rice ahead and reheat it just before serving.

Stir-fry Ginger Chicken and Cashews in the browning skillet rather than a wok. The browning dish absorbs microwaves as it preheats. When the chicken is added to the skillet, it browns at the contact point as in a wok.

You can save time by making Egg-Drop Soup while preparing the chicken. For this simple soup, just slowly stir beaten eggs into the boiling broth mixture; fine, lacy egg strands should appear right away.

Save the broccoli until last. It takes only a few minutes to cook and can be served straight from the microwave.

A preheated browning dish makes it a snap to stir-fry Ginger Chicken and Cashews.

GINGER CHICKEN AND CASHEWS

1 egg white
1 tablespoon soy sauce
1 teaspoon cornstarch
1 teaspoon sugar
⅛ teaspoon salt
⅛ teaspoon pepper
1½ pounds boneless chicken breast halves, skinned and cut into 1-inch pieces
2 tablespoons vegetable oil
½ cup cashews
1 (8-ounce) can sliced bamboo shoots, drained
3 medium green onions with tops, cut into 1-inch pieces
1 tablespoon vegetable oil
2 teaspoons grated fresh gingerroot
1 tablespoon soy sauce
2 teaspoons dry sherry
2 green onions (optional)

Combine first 6 ingredients in a medium bowl, stirring well. Add chicken; toss well, and refrigerate 15 minutes. Place a 10-inch browning skillet in microwave oven; preheat, uncovered, at HIGH for 6 minutes. Add 2 tablespoons oil to hot skillet, tilting to coat surface. Drain chicken; add to preheated skillet, stirring well. Microwave at HIGH for 3 to 3½ minutes or until no longer pink, stirring well after 2 minutes. Set aside.

Combine cashews, bamboo shoots, green onions, oil, and gingerroot in a 1-quart casserole. Cover and microwave at HIGH for 2 to 3 minutes or until onion is crisp-tender. Stir well.

Add cashew mixture and 1 tablespoon soy sauce to chicken mixture; stir well. Cover and microwave at HIGH for 1 minute. Stir in sherry; garnish with 2 green onions, if desired.

Note: Recipe can be made ahead; let stand, covered, until remainder of menu is ready. Reheat at HIGH for 1 minute before serving. Yield: 6 servings.

Tip: Store spices in a cool place and away from any direct source of heat as the heat will destroy their flavor. Red spices will maintain flavor and retain color longer if refrigerated.

EGG-DROP SOUP

4 cups hot water
1 (10¾-ounce) can chicken broth,
  undiluted
1 (3-ounce) can sliced mushrooms, drained
2 cloves garlic
1 teaspoon soy sauce
1 teaspoon chicken-flavored bouillon
  granules
⅛ teaspoon white pepper
2 eggs, well beaten
⅓ cup sliced green onions with tops

Combine hot water, chicken broth, mushrooms, garlic, soy sauce, and bouillon granules in a 3-quart casserole. Cover and microwave at HIGH for 10 to 12 minutes or until boiling. Add pepper, stirring well. Pour eggs in a thin stream into soup, stirring constantly. Cover and let stand 3 minutes. Remove garlic; sprinkle soup with green onions. Yield: 6 cups.

CHINESE BROCCOLI

1 (1½-pound) bunch broccoli
3 tablespoons water
1 tablespoon soy sauce
1½ teaspoons sesame seeds
2 teaspoons lemon juice

Trim off large leaves of broccoli, and remove tough ends of lower stalks. Wash broccoli thoroughly; cut into bite-size pieces. Place in a 1½-quart casserole; add water. Cover with heavy-duty plastic wrap, and microwave at HIGH for 4 to 4½ minutes or until broccoli is crisp-tender. Drain. Combine remaining ingredients, and pour over broccoli; toss well. Yield: 6 servings.

ORIENTAL RICE

2¾ cups hot water
1½ cups uncooked regular rice
1 large carrot, scraped and diced
½ teaspoon salt
⅛ to ¼ teaspoon garlic powder

Combine all ingredients in a 2½-quart casserole. Cover and microwave at HIGH for 5 minutes. Reduce to MEDIUM (50% power), and microwave 18 to 20 minutes or until liquid is absorbed. Allow to stand 5 minutes; fluff with a fork.
Note: Rice can be made in advance; to reheat, microwave at MEDIUM HIGH (70% power) for 4 minutes. Yield: 6 servings.

MANDARIN-ALMOND PUDDING

1 (11-ounce) can mandarin oranges,
  drained
1 envelope unflavored gelatin
2 cups milk, divided
¼ cup plus 2 tablespoons sugar
2 teaspoons almond extract
Additional mandarin oranges (optional)

Reserve 12 mandarin orange sections to be used for garnish. Coarsely chop ⅔ cup remaining sections; drain again, and set aside.
Combine gelatin and ¾ cup milk in a small bowl; set aside. Combine remaining 1¼ cups milk and sugar in a 1½-quart casserole. Microwave at HIGH for 4 to 5 minutes or until heated but not boiling. Add gelatin mixture, stirring until dissolved. Stir in almond extract and chopped oranges; pour into a lightly oiled 9- x 5- x 3-inch loafpan.
Chill overnight or until set. Unmold gelatin; cut into 6 squares. Carefully transfer each square to a serving plate; garnish tops with the 12 reserved mandarin orange sections. Arrange additional mandarin orange sections around sides, if desired. Yield: 6 servings.

Serve It With Mustard

If you think of mustard as just something to put on a hot dog, think again. In recent years, a variety of mustards and mustard sauces have become popular with a wide range of foods, including chicken, turkey, pork, fruit, and vegetables. We've rounded up some spicy mustard concoctions for you.

HOT SWEET MUSTARD

½ cup dry mustard
⅔ cup white vinegar
⅔ cup sugar
1 egg

Combine all ingredients in container of an electric blender, and process until smooth. Pour mixture into top of a double boiler; bring water to a boil. Reduce heat to low; cook, stirring constantly, about 7 minutes or until smooth and thickened. Store in an airtight container; refrigerate. Yield: 1⅓ cups.
Judy Hutchings,
Birmingham, Alabama.

SWEET MUSTARD SAUCE

1 tablespoon sugar
1 tablespoon all-purpose flour
2 teaspoons salt
⅛ teaspoon white pepper
2 teaspoons dry mustard
⅓ cup water
2 egg yolks, slightly beaten
⅓ cup vinegar
⅓ cup light corn syrup
2 tablespoons honey
½ teaspoon dried whole tarragon
½ cup corn oil

Combine sugar, flour, salt, pepper, and mustard in a medium-size heavy saucepan; mix well. Gradually add water, stirring until smooth. Add remaining ingredients except oil and cook over low heat 5 minutes or until thick, stirring constantly. (Do not boil.) Remove from heat; slowly add oil in a thin, steady stream, stirring constantly with a wire whisk. Cover and chill 2 to 3 hours. Stir before serving. Yield: about 2 cups.
Maybelle Pinkston,
Corryton, Tennessee.

SWEET-AND-SOUR SAUCE

2 teaspoons wine vinegar
1½ to 2 tablespoons sugar
2 tablespoons prepared mustard
¼ cup plus 2 tablespoons crushed
  pineapple, undrained
2 teaspoons cornstarch
¼ cup plus 2 tablespoons water

Combine vinegar and sugar in a small saucepan; cook over medium heat, stirring constantly, until sugar dissolves. Remove from heat; stir in the mustard and pineapple.
Dissolve cornstarch in water. Gradually stir about one-fourth of hot mixture into cornstarch mixture; add to remaining hot mixture, stirring constantly. Cook over medium heat, stirring constantly, until smooth and thickened. Yield: about 1 cup.
Denise Smith,
Oneonta, Alabama.

CHINESE HOT MUSTARD

¼ cup dry mustard
1 teaspoon sugar
¼ cup boiling water
1 tablespoon vegetable oil

Combine mustard and sugar; mix well. Stir in water and oil. Let stand overnight. Yield: ⅓ cup.
Lane A. Harris,
Jacksonville, North Carolina.

HONEY-MUSTARD SAUCE

¾ cup mayonnaise
3 tablespoons honey
3 tablespoons prepared mustard
1 tablespoon lemon juice

Combine all ingredients; stir well. Cover and chill for 2 to 3 hours. Yield: 1¼ cups.
Chris Tortorici,
Pelham, Alabama.

Sample These Recipes For Spaghetti And Sauces

Have you ever thought of stirring ground turkey into spaghetti sauce? Or adding bacon pieces and a can of beer to an otherwise basic ground beef spaghetti sauce? Try these spaghetti sauces as well as other variations.

BEER SPAGHETTI SAUCE

4 slices bacon
2 pounds ground beef
1 large onion, chopped
1 large green pepper, chopped
1 (12-ounce) can beer
1 (10¾-ounce) can tomato soup
1⅓ cups water
1 (6-ounce) can tomato paste
2 tablespoons grated Parmesan cheese
2 bay leaves
1 teaspoon garlic powder
1 tablespoon parsley flakes
1 teaspoon dried whole basil
1 teaspoon dried whole oregano
1 teaspoon celery flakes
½ teaspoon salt
½ teaspoon pepper
Hot cooked spaghetti

Cook bacon in a Dutch oven until crisp; remove bacon, reserving drippings in the Dutch oven. Crumble bacon and set aside.

Add ground beef, onion, and green pepper to Dutch oven; cook until beef is browned, stirring to crumble meat. Drain off drippings; stir in beer. Reduce heat and simmer, uncovered, 10 minutes. Add next 12 ingredients; simmer, uncovered, 30 minutes. Remove bay leaves, and stir in bacon. Spoon sauce over spaghetti. Yield: 8 cups.
Barbara Dobbs,
Lampasas, Texas.

HERBED SPAGHETTI SAUCE

1 pound ground beef
1 pound hot bulk pork sausage
1 cup chopped onion
2 cloves garlic, minced
2 (15-ounce) cans tomato sauce
2 (6-ounce) cans tomato paste
2 cups water
1 (6-ounce) can sliced mushrooms, drained
¼ cup chopped fresh parsley
1 tablespoon brown sugar
1½ teaspoons dried whole oregano
¼ teaspoon ground thyme
1 bay leaf
Salt to taste
Hot cooked spaghetti

Combine ground beef, sausage, onion, and garlic in a Dutch oven; cook until meat is browned, stirring to crumble meat. Drain off drippings. Add remaining ingredients except spaghetti; bring to a boil. Cover, reduce heat, and simmer 2 hours, stirring occasionally. Uncover and simmer an additional hour, stirring occasionally. Remove bay leaf, and spoon sauce over spaghetti. Yield: 10 cups.
Joyce Petrochko,
St. Albans, West Virginia.

SHRIMP SPAGHETTI WITH BLACK OLIVES

8 ounces uncooked vermicelli
⅓ cup olive oil
1 to 1½ pounds fresh medium shrimp, peeled and deveined
1 cup chopped onion
3 cloves garlic, crushed
2 (16-ounce) cans tomatoes, undrained and chopped
2 teaspoons dried whole basil
½ teaspoon salt
¼ teaspoon pepper
½ cup chopped fresh parsley
¾ cup sliced ripe olives
3 tablespoons grated Parmesan cheese

Cook vermicelli according to package directions; drain and set aside.

Heat oil in a large Dutch oven over medium-high heat. Add shrimp, onion, and garlic; cook, stirring constantly, 5 minutes or until shrimp are pink. Remove shrimp, and set aside.

Add tomatoes, basil, salt, and pepper; bring to a boil. Cook, uncovered, 5 to 7 minutes. Add vermicelli, shrimp, and parsley; toss until mixture is well coated. Transfer to serving dish. Sprinkle with ripe olives and Parmesan cheese. Yield: 6 servings.
Jeanette Shedd,
Roswell, Georgia.

TURKEY SPAGHETTI SAUCE

¾ cup chopped onion
1 clove garlic, minced
3 tablespoons olive or vegetable oil
1½ pounds ground uncooked turkey
1 (28-ounce) can whole tomatoes, undrained and chopped
2 (6-ounce) cans tomato paste
1 cup water
1 bay leaf
1½ teaspoons dried whole oregano
1½ teaspoons sugar
¾ teaspoon salt
¼ teaspoon pepper
Pinch of dried whole basil
½ pound mushrooms, sliced
2 tablespoons grated Parmesan cheese
Hot cooked spaghetti

Sauté onion and garlic in oil in a large Dutch oven until onion is tender. Add turkey; cook until done, stirring to crumble meat. Stir in next 9 ingredients; simmer, uncovered, 1 hour. Add mushrooms and cheese; simmer, uncovered, 20 minutes. Remove bay leaf. Spoon sauce over spaghetti. Yield: 6¼ cups.
Becky Foster,
Dallas, Texas.

Kids Enjoy Cooking, Too!

Here are some recipes kids can make themselves with a minimum of help. We purposely chose recipes with their tastes in mind.

BLACK FOREST DUMP CAKE

1 (8-ounce) can crushed pineapple
1 (21-ounce) can cherry pie filling
1 (18.5-ounce) package devil's food cake mix
1 cup chopped pecans
½ cup butter or margarine, melted
Whipped topping

Drain pineapple, reserving liquid.

Spread pineapple in a lightly greased 13- x 9- x 2-inch pan; add pie filling, spreading gently. Sprinkle dry cake mix on pie filling; top with pecans. Combine butter and reserved pineapple liquid; drizzle on mixture in pan. Bake at 350° for 35 to 40 minutes. Cut into squares; top with whipped topping. Yield: 15 servings.
Elaine Winters,
College Park, Maryland.

CHOCOLATE-PEANUT BUTTER CUPS

1 (15-ounce) roll refrigerated ready-to-slice
   peanut butter cookie dough
48 miniature peanut butter cup candies

Slice cookie dough into ¾-inch slices. Cut each slice into quarters. Place each quarter into ungreased 1¾-inch muffin pans. Bake at 350° for 8 to 10 minutes. (Dough will rise during baking.) Remove from oven, and immediately press a miniature peanut butter cup gently and evenly into each cookie. Cool before removing from pan. Refrigerate until firm. Yield: 4 dozen.

Dorothy Martin,
Frost, Texas.

CHOCOLATE-PEANUT BUTTER CONES

40 cone-shaped corn snacks
¼ cup peanut butter
3 (1-ounce) squares semisweet chocolate

Stuff each corn snack with peanut butter; set aside.

Melt chocolate in top of double boiler; dip open end of each corn snack in chocolate. Place on waxed paper. Yield: 40 cones. *Doris T. Ramsey,*
Martinsville, Virginia.

EASY PINEAPPLE BUNS

1 (8-ounce) can crushed pineapple,
   drained
½ cup firmly packed brown sugar
¼ cup butter or margarine, softened
1 teaspoon ground cinnamon
1 (10-ounce) package refrigerated biscuits

Combine first 4 ingredients in a bowl; mix well. Spoon mixture evenly into 10 greased cups of a 12-cup muffin pan. Place 1 biscuit in each cup. Bake at 425° about 10 minutes. Cool 5 minutes. Invert pan on plate; serve warm. Yield: 10 servings. *Mrs. Troy Rainwater,*
Weslaco, Texas.

NO-COOK CANDY BALLS

1 cup creamy peanut butter
1 cup sifted powdered sugar
½ cup chopped walnuts
2 tablespoons butter or margarine,
   softened
1 cup flaked coconut

Combine first 4 ingredients in a medium mixing bowl; mix well. Shape into ½-inch balls; roll each ball in coconut. Chill. Yield: about 3 dozen.

Carolyn T. Camden,
Chesterfield, Virginia.

Fry Some Fritters And Hush Puppies

Stir fruit, vegetables, or meat into a flour-based bread batter; drop small amounts in hot oil to fry, and you'll have a platterful of fritters. Substitute a cornmeal batter and the crisp bread pieces are known as hush puppies.

Be sure the oil is hot enough (at least 350°) before adding the uncooked batter. Hot oil fries the outside quickly for a crisp crust and leaves the inside moist and tender. If the oil is too cool, it will be absorbed by the batter, and the crust will not be crisp.

EASY HUSH PUPPIES

2 (7½-ounce) packages corn muffin mix
2 eggs, beaten
¼ cup minced onion
Vegetable oil

Measure 2¼ cups corn muffin mix. (Save remainder of mix for other uses.) Combine mix, eggs, and minced onion, stirring well.

Carefully drop batter by tablespoonfuls into deep, hot oil (370°); cook only a few at a time, turning once. Fry 1½ minutes or until hush puppies are golden brown. Drain on paper towels. Yield: 2 dozen. *Patsy Gowen,*
Amherst, Virginia.

ONION HUSH PUPPIES

1 cup yellow cornmeal
½ cup all-purpose flour
1½ teaspoons baking powder
1 teaspoon salt
1 teaspoon sugar
¼ teaspoon garlic powder
¼ teaspoon pepper
Dash of ground red pepper
1 egg, beaten
¼ cup milk
¾ cup minced onion
2 tablespoons finely chopped green onions
Vegetable oil

Combine all ingredients except oil; stir until smooth. Drop batter by heaping teaspoonfuls into deep, hot oil (350°); cook only a few at a time, turning once. Fry 1 to 2 minutes or until golden brown. Drain on paper towels. Yield: about 2 dozen. *Rose Alleman,*
Prairieville, Louisiana.

APPLE FRITTERS

1½ cups all-purpose flour
1 tablespoon sugar
2 teaspoons baking powder
½ teaspoon salt
3 cups peeled, finely chopped apples
⅔ cup milk
2 eggs, beaten
1 tablespoon vegetable oil
Vegetable oil
Powdered sugar

Combine flour, sugar, baking powder, and salt in a large bowl, stirring well. Add apples, milk, eggs, and 1 tablespoon oil; stir mixture just until moist.

Carefully drop batter by rounded tablespoonfuls into deep, hot oil (370°); cook only a few at a time, turning once. Fry 2 to 3 minutes or until fritters are golden brown. Drain well on paper towels. Sift powdered sugar over fritters. Yield: 3 dozen. *Regina Evers,*
Florence, Alabama.

SKILLET-FRIED CORN FRITTERS

1 (17-ounce) can whole kernel corn,
   undrained
⅓ cup evaporated milk
2 eggs, beaten
1½ cups all-purpose flour
2 teaspoons baking powder
¾ teaspoon salt
Vegetable oil

Drain corn, reserving liquid; set corn aside. Add enough corn liquid to milk to equal ½ cup. Combine milk mixture and eggs; mix well.

Combine remaining ingredients except oil; gradually add milk mixture, stirring until smooth. Stir in corn.

Heat ¼-inch deep oil (350°) in a large skillet. Drop in corn mixture by heaping teaspoonfuls; cook only a few at a time, turning once. Fry 3 to 5 minutes or until fritters are golden brown. Drain on paper towels, and serve immediately. Yield: about 3½ dozen. *Janis Moyer,*
Farmersville, Texas.

Mold A Chocolate Garnish

Present someone with a piece of pie garnished with a chocolate cutout, and he's likely to nibble on the chocolate before the pie.

For eye-catching garnishes, start with semisweet chocolate in the square or chip form. Either form can be melted down and shaped; then it hardens back up and holds its fancy new form.

Handle With Care

Since chocolate scorches easily, melt it in a double boiler over hot, not boiling, water. To do this, place the chocolate in the top of a double boiler, and bring the water to a boil. Then immediately reduce the heat, and cook until the chocolate melts. Do not let any steam or water droplets get into the chocolate, or the mixture will thicken and be hard to work with. All cooking utensils should be absolutely dry.

You can also melt chocolate in your microwave oven. Place chocolate morsels or coarsely chopped chocolate squares in a small glass bowl. Microwave at HIGH until melted, stirring once or twice. About ½ cup of chocolate morsels (3 ounces) will take 1 to 1½ minutes. Larger or smaller amounts will take slight time adjustments. Always watch chocolate carefully; do not overcook.

Store unmelted chocolate in a cool, dry place, but not in the refrigerator. When chocolate is exposed to extremes in temperature, the cocoa butter rises to the surface and gives the chocolate a grayish color. But, even then, only the appearance is affected, not the flavor. The chocolate will still be suitable for melting and for cooking.

Chocolate melts, and then it firms back up into pretty garnishes for all kinds of desserts: (from front) dipped chocolate on strawberries and rosettes, rolled chocolate shaped into leaves on a cheesecake, webbed chocolate and drizzled chocolate border on a cake, and chocolate cutouts on a pie.

Dip Foods Into Chocolate

Chocolate coats all kinds of food with a pretty shine as well as flavor—a variety of fruits will work, as well as cookies, candies, pastries, and pretzels. Dip the edges of rosettes for a delicate touch, or completely cover cherries for bursts of flavor. Strawberries, orange sections, even clusters of grapes can be partially dipped in chocolate to make attractive garnishes or delicious additions to a fruit-and-cheese platter.

Just make sure the fruit is perfectly dry before dipping. You may want to rinse the fruit earlier in the day, and drain on paper towels; allow to dry in the air for several hours, or gently pat dry with paper towels.

For dipping, melt chocolate and let it cool slightly. Dip food items into the chocolate; set aside for chocolate to harden.

To dip one pint of strawberries, melt 4 ounces of semisweet chocolate; transfer to a small bowl, and let cool slightly. Grasp a strawberry by the cap, dip it in the chocolate, and turn it to coat the bottom two-thirds of the fruit. Allow any excess to drip back into the bowl. Lay the strawberry on its side on a baking sheet lined with waxed paper.

Allow coated strawberries to stand at room temperature until the chocolate hardens, or place in the refrigerator about 10 minutes if the chocolate takes too long to harden. Don't store coated fruit in the refrigerator, however; the chocolate coating will sweat when returned to room temperature and will lose its satiny sheen.

Keep in mind that you must use chocolate-dipped fruit within six hours, because moisture in the fruit will break down the coating. However, chocolate-dipped cookies, rosettes, candies, or pretzels may be layered between waxed paper in airtight containers and stored for several days in a cool, dry place.

Pipe; Then Pull Chocolate

Perk up frosted cakes, cookies, pies, or cheesecakes with either a linear or round webbed design. To make either pattern across the top of a cake, melt 2 ounces of semisweet chocolate, and let it stand until cooled and thickened, but not set. Next, spoon the melted chocolate into a decorating bag fitted with No. 2 round tip.

For a linear pattern, pipe chocolate in parallel lines ½ inch apart across the top of cake. Pull the point of a wooden pick back and forth perpendicular to the lines to create the webbed pattern. Let stand until chocolate hardens; you may want to chill briefly to set the chocolate, if necessary.

For a round webbed design, pipe chocolate in concentric circles ½ inch apart on the top of the cake. Pull the point of a wooden pick across the chocolate circles from the center to the outer edge.

Drizzle a Chocolate Border

Make any cake or cheesecake more tempting by drizzling its edge with chocolate. Simply melt 3 ounces semisweet chocolate, and let it cool slightly. Drizzle the chocolate from a spoon around the edge of the cake, a small amount at a time, letting some of the chocolate drip down the side. Let stand until the chocolate hardens; if necessary, chill briefly to set the chocolate.

Melt chocolate with corn syrup, and roll the cooled mixture through a pasta machine to make thin sheets of rolled chocolate for creating garnishes.

Roll Chocolate Like Pasta

If you own a pasta machine, you can roll chocolate for garnishes. Cut the rolled chocolate sheets into strips to wrap around a cake, or cut and mold shapes to garnish a cheesecake.

To make rolled chocolate, combine 6 ounces semisweet chocolate and 3 tablespoons light corn syrup in the top of a double boiler over hot water; cook over low heat, stirring occasionally, until the chocolate melts. Transfer chocolate to a bowl; let stand 20 minutes or until it becomes a "paste," stirring gently every 5 minutes. Do not beat the chocolate, or air bubbles will form.

Place the chocolate paste on a marble or laminated plastic surface, and knead until it begins to firm up. Cut into 4 pieces, and keep covered with plastic wrap when not in use. Working with 1 piece at a time, pat the chocolate into a rectangle the width of the pasta machine roller. Run the chocolate rectangle through the thickest setting of the

Cut rolled chocolate sheets into leaves or other shapes. As the chocolate begins to dry, curl the edges for a three-dimensional effect with the leaves or other shapes.

pasta machine (about ⅛ inch). Knead the chocolate again for 10 seconds; pat it into a rectangle, and run it through a thinner setting (about 1/16 inch). Continue kneading and running it through this setting as many times as it takes to form a smooth, glossy sheet.

Cut chocolate sheets into desired shapes by freehand, using cookie cutters, or by tracing around patterns using a sharp knife; transfer shapes to waxed paper to dry. Allow the chocolate to harden slightly; then curve the pieces into three-dimensional shapes, if desired. (If curved too early, the chocolate will not hold its shape.) Repeat kneading, rolling, and shaping procedure with remaining chocolate pieces.

Melted cocoa butter present in the chocolate will collect on your hands and the marble surface as you work with it. This moisture will help keep the chocolate from sticking to the surface and the pasta machine. The shapes will lose this oily appearance as they dry and harden.

To make a webbed chocolate design, first pipe melted chocolate in parallel lines across the top of a cake.

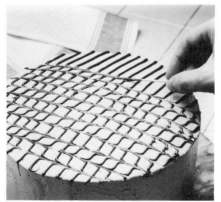

To complete the webbed pattern, pull the point of a wooden pick back and forth perpendicular to the piped lines.

For a drizzled border, spoon melted chocolate all around the edges of a cake, letting some drip down the sides.

Melt Chocolate for Cutouts

Melting and cooling chocolate is almost all it takes to make chocolate cutouts that add a finished touch to cakes, pies, pastries, and ice cream. Let your favorite cookie or canapé cutters "draw" the shapes for you.

To make a dozen 1½-inch cutouts, melt 6 ounces semisweet chocolate, and cool slightly. Line a baking sheet with aluminum foil; pour the chocolate onto the baking sheet, and gently shake it until the chocolate is smooth and level and is about ⅛ inch thick. Let stand until partially set.

Press a cookie or canapé cutter halfway through the chocolate to outline shapes. Remove the cutter, and let stand until the chocolate is firm. When chocolate hardens, reposition the cutter over the outlines, and press down to cut the chocolate smoothly. Lift the cutter up, and remove the cutout by gently pressing through the cutter with a small wooden utensil. (Don't use your fingers, or you'll leave prints on the chocolate.)

To make chocolate cutouts, pour melted chocolate on a foil-lined baking sheet. When partially set, press cutter into the chocolate to define shapes; then let stand until firm.

When the chocolate is firm, reposition cutter on outlines, and press firmly to cut through chocolate. Remove cutout from cutter by gently pressing it with a small wooden utensil.

Try This Garnish, Too

You can grate unsweetened, semisweet, or milk chocolate to sprinkle on top of pies, puddings, or ice cream. It's easiest done in a food processor, but you can hand-grate it. When hand-grating, hold chocolate with a paper towel or waxed paper so heat from your hand will not soften or melt the chocolate.

Sweeten With Honey—Nature's Own Nectar

There's no prettier sight than a jar of honey glistening in the sunlight. This golden nectar is available in several different forms, the most common being liquid and chunk. Chunk honey contains a piece of the honeycomb. Creamed honey, similar to a buttery spread and sold in refrigerated cases, is not as widely available as liquid or chunk.

Honey should be stored in a dry place because it tends to absorb moisture, causing it to become granulated. If this occurs, place the honey container in a bowl of warm water to liquefy.

For cooking, measure the butter, oil, or shortening first, and then the honey. This way, the honey will slide right out of the measuring cup.

Recipes created especially for honey, such as Honey-Orange Butter and Honey Wheat Bread, usually yield the best results. But if you want to substitute honey for sugar in other recipes, try replacing one cup of granulated sugar with two-thirds or three-fourths cup of honey, depending on desired sweetness. For every cup of sugar replaced by honey, reduce the total liquid by one-fourth cup. Also reduce the baking temperature 25 degrees.

OVEN-FRIED CHICKEN WITH HONEY-BUTTER SAUCE

1 cup all-purpose flour
2 teaspoons paprika
½ teaspoon salt
¼ teaspoon pepper
1 (2½- to 3-pound) broiler-fryer, cut up and skinned
½ cup butter or margarine, melted
Honey-Butter Sauce

Combine flour, paprika, salt, and pepper, stirring well; dredge chicken in flour mixture. Set aside.

Pour butter into a 13- x 9- x 2-inch baking pan. Place chicken in pan, turning to coat with butter. Cover and bake, meaty side down, at 400° for 30 minutes. Turn chicken pieces, and pour Honey-Butter Sauce over each piece. Bake, uncovered, an additional 25 to 30 minutes or until tender, basting occasionally with sauce. Yield: 4 servings.

Honey-Butter Sauce:

¼ cup butter or margarine, melted
½ cup honey
¼ cup lemon juice

Combine all ingredients; beat well. Yield: about ¾ cup.

Jennifer B. Lewis,
Columbia, South Carolina.

HONEY-GLAZED CARROTS

8 medium carrots, scraped
¾ cup water
2 teaspoons sugar
¼ cup honey
2 tablespoons orange juice
2 tablespoons butter or margarine
½ teaspoon salt

Cut carrots in half crosswise; slice halves lengthwise into quarters. Combine carrots, water, and sugar in a saucepan. Cover and cook 5 to 8 minutes or until crisp-tender; drain carrots, reserving ¼ cup of the cooking liquid. Set aside.

Combine ¼ cup carrot liquid and remaining ingredients in a saucepan; bring to a boil, and cook 5 minutes. Add carrots; reduce heat, and simmer 2 to 3 minutes. Yield: 4 to 6 servings.

Jeanette Guess,
Edinburg, Virginia.

HONEY WHEAT BREAD

¼ cup vegetable oil
¼ cup honey
2 packages dry yeast
1 tablespoon salt
2½ cups hot water (120° to 130°)
1 cup instant nonfat dry milk powder
3 eggs, slightly beaten
7 to 8 cups whole wheat flour, divided

Combine oil, honey, yeast, and salt in large mixing bowl; stir in hot water. Add dry milk powder and eggs; mix well. Stir in 2 cups flour. Gradually add enough remaining flour to make a soft dough.

Turn dough out on a floured surface,

and knead until smooth and elastic (about 8 to 10 minutes). Place in a well-greased bowl, turning to grease top. Cover and let rise in a warm place (85°), free from drafts, 1 hour or until doubled in bulk.

Punch dough down, and divide into 3 portions; shape each into a loaf. Place in 3 well-greased 8½- x 4½- x 3-inch loafpans. Cover and let rise in a warm place (85°), free from drafts, 30 to 40 minutes or until doubled in bulk. Bake at 375° for 35 minutes or until loaves sound hollow when tapped. Transfer to wire racks to cool. Yield: 3 loaves.

La Juan Coward,
Brookeland, Texas.

MAPLE-HONEY-CINNAMON SYRUP

1 cup sugar
2 tablespoons brown sugar
½ cup water
½ cup honey
½ teaspoon ground cinnamon
⅛ teaspoon maple flavoring

Combine sugar and water in a heavy saucepan; bring to a rapid boil. Remove from heat; stir in remaining ingredients. Yield: 1⅓ cups.   *Louise Holmes,*
Winchester, Tennessee.

HONEY-ORANGE BUTTER

½ cup butter, softened
¾ cup honey
½ teaspoon grated orange rind

Cream butter until light and fluffy; slowly add honey, and beat well. Beat in orange rind. Refrigerate several hours or overnight. Serve with biscuits, waffles, or pancakes. Yield: about 1⅓ cups.   *Norma Sorenson,*
Birmingham, Alabama.

PEANUT BUTTER-HONEY DIP

1 cup crunchy peanut butter
⅓ cup honey
⅔ cup milk
1 cup golden raisins
½ teaspoon ground cinnamon
2 tablespoons slivered almonds, toasted

Combine peanut butter, honey, and milk in a medium mixing bowl; stir until smooth. Stir in raisins and cinnamon; sprinkle with almonds. Serve with apple and banana slices. Yield: 3 cups.

Nancy A. Yates,
Decatur, Alabama.

From Our Kitchen To Yours

The South is known for tasty desserts and breads sweetened with sugar, honey, molasses, and syrup. Since each of these sweeteners varies in makeup and consistency, there are often many questions about substitutions, accurate measuring, and storing. We would like to answer some of the questions.

What's the difference in granulated and powdered or confectioners' sugar? Powdered sugar comes from granulated sugar that has been crushed and screened. You can tell the degree of fineness of powdered sugar by the number of x's indicated on the package—the fine powdered is 4x, the very fine powdered is 6x, and the ultra-fine powdered is 10x. The 10x type is what we use in our test kitchens when a recipe calls for powdered sugar.

Granulated sugar is also available in different forms. There is regular sugar, which is uniform in granulation, as well as extra-fine sugar that has smaller crystals resulting from additional processing. In making a Swiss meringue or a fine-textured cake in which quick mixing or dissolving is important, you often need to use an extra-fine sugar. If you can't find extra-fine sugar, you can make your own by processing regular granulated sugar in the blender until you have finer crystals.

What am I actually getting when I buy cane, sorghum, or maple syrup? Cane syrup comes from sugar cane that has been boiled down to the consistency of syrup. Sorghum comes from a coarse grass by the same name. Sorghum grass is processed until you have juice, which is concentrated by boiling until it becomes syrup. Maple syrup comes from the sap of the sugar maple tree. Like sugar cane, it's boiled down to the consistency of syrup.

Can I substitute honey, molasses, or maple syrup for sugar in a recipe? If you decide to make a substitution, remember that honey, molasses, and syrup are about 20% to 30% water. These sweeteners have a very distinct flavor and vary in their sweetening power. In "Sweeten With Honey—Nature's Own Nectar" on facing page, read how to measure and substitute honey for sugar. If you're using molasses for granulated sugar, use the same amount of molasses as sugar, and reduce the liquid by ¼ cup for each cup of sugar used in the recipe.

To replace sugar with maple syrup when baking, use the amount of maple syrup equal to the sugar called for in the recipe. Then reduce the liquid ingredient by half, and add ¼ teaspoon baking soda for each cup of maple syrup used. If you're cooking on the cook surface, it's best to use ¾ cup of maple syrup in place of each cup of sugar, since maple syrup is a little sweeter than sugar.

How do I accurately measure powdered and brown sugar? Regular sugar measures easily because, unlike powdered and brown sugar, it's free flowing. Measure powdered sugar as you would flour. Always sift powdered sugar to get rid of all lumps. Then when measuring, spoon it into a measuring cup, being careful not to pack it when filling; then level it off with a metal spatula or knife. Press brown sugar into a measuring cup or spoon to get an accurate measurement. It should be packed so that it keeps its shape when it's unmolded. That's why we always call for firmly packed brown sugar.

How can I keep brown sugar from drying out? Brown sugar will dry out easily after opening because it's more moist than granulated sugar. After we open a package, we transfer the unused part to an airtight container. This keeps it soft and moist. To soften hardened brown sugar, put it in an airtight container and add an apple or bread slice.

Can I use liquid or granulated brown sugar in place of regular brown sugar? Since liquid brown sugar is more concentrated than regular brown sugar, substituting one type for the other is not recommended.

Granulated brown sugar can be substituted for regular brown sugar cup for cup, but you may have a slight loss in flavor intensity.

Garlic Gives It Flavor

Mince it, crush it, simmer it, sauté it, or leave it whole, and a clove of garlic will take on a new taste. This sensational seasoning offers a flavor that ranges from subtle to pungent, depending on the method of preparation.

For example, you'll release the strongest flavor of garlic by crushing the cloves with a garlic press or knife handle. But once you sauté the garlic or heat it, the sharp flavor diminishes. In our recipe for Perky Squash Soup, the garlic clove is crushed, then sautéed with the onion and added to the remaining ingredients right away. For a stronger garlic flavor, you may prefer to skip the sautéing step and add the garlic during the last few minutes of cooking. The longer it simmers, the milder the flavor becomes. In fact, tossing whole, peeled garlic cloves into soup or stew that simmers for a few hours will render an almost sweet, nutty flavor.

Garlic is minced and left uncooked for a zesty twist to Creamy Wine Dressing and Garlic Cheese Log. Remember that the finer you chop the garlic, the sharper the flavor.

When buying garlic, you'll find bulbs ranging from white to deep wine. Choose bulbs with a dry, paper-like covering that completely encases each clove. Store in a cool, dry place (not in the refrigerator), and use as needed.

ORIENTAL BEEF

1½ pounds boneless sirloin steak
2 tablespoons soy sauce
2 cloves garlic, crushed
1 teaspoon sugar
½ teaspoon ground ginger
3 tablespoons vegetable oil
1 (6-ounce) package frozen Chinese pea pods, thawed and drained
2 cups sliced Chinese cabbage
1 cup sliced fresh mushrooms
3 green onions with tops, cut in 1-inch pieces
1 (8-ounce) can sliced water chestnuts, drained
1 teaspoon beef-flavored bouillon granules
2 tablespoons cornstarch
½ teaspoon salt
1 cup warm water
Hot cooked rice

Trim excess fat from steak. Partially freeze steak; slice diagonally across grain into 2- x ¼-inch strips. Set aside.

Combine soy sauce, garlic, sugar, and ginger; add steak, tossing to coat. Cover and refrigerate 1 hour.

Coat wok or skillet with oil; allow to heat at medium high (325°) for 2 minutes. Add steak; stir-fry 1 minute. Add pea pods; stir-fry 1 minute. Add cabbage, mushrooms, green onions, and water chestnuts; stir-fry 2 minutes.

Dissolve bouillon granules, cornstarch, and salt in water; stir into steak mixture. Cook until thickened. Serve over rice. Yield: 6 servings.

Julia Garmon,
Alexandria, Virginia.

POTATO PANCAKE

3 ounces Parmesan cheese, cubed
2 pounds baking potatoes, peeled
1 clove garlic
1 small onion, cubed
2 eggs
¼ cup all-purpose flour
½ teaspoon seasoned salt
⅛ to ¼ teaspoon red pepper
¼ cup butter or margarine, divided
1 tablespoon vegetable oil

Position knife blade in food processor bowl; add cheese. Process until finely grated (about 1 minute); remove cheese, and set aside.

Position shredding disc in processor bowl. Place potatoes in food chute, cutting to fit, if necessary. Shred, applying moderate pressure with food pusher. Roll potatoes in a towel to squeeze out excess moisture; place in a bowl, and set aside.

Reposition knife blade in processor bowl. With processor running, drop garlic through food chute; process 3 to 5 seconds until minced. Add onion; process until chopped. Add eggs, flour, seasoned salt, and red pepper; process until blended, pulsing 4 or 5 times. Pour mixture over potatoes; add cheese, and toss well.

Melt 2 tablespoons butter with oil in a 10-inch nonstick skillet; add potato mixture, and press down evenly with a spatula to form pancake. Cover and cook over medium heat 12 to 15 minutes or until browned and crisp on bottom. Place a flat skillet lid or a large plate over skillet; invert potato pancake onto lid. Melt remaining 2 tablespoons butter in skillet, and slide potato pancake back into skillet, cooked side up. Cook, uncovered, over medium heat an additional 10 minutes or until browned and crisp on other side. Slide potato pancake onto a serving plate; cut into wedges to serve. Yield: 6 to 8 servings.

RICOTTA-STUFFED MUSHROOMS

18 medium-size fresh mushrooms
1 slice bread, torn into small pieces
2 eggs, slightly beaten
½ cup ricotta cheese
2 cloves garlic, minced
1½ teaspoons chopped fresh parsley
Pinch of salt
Pinch of pepper
Grated Parmesan cheese
Olive oil

Clean mushrooms with damp paper towels. Remove mushroom stems, and chop. Combine stems and next 7 ingredients; mix well.

Spoon mixture into mushroom caps; sprinkle each with Parmesan cheese. Grease a 12- x 8- x 2-inch baking dish with olive oil. Place mushrooms in dish, and bake at 350° for 20 minutes. Yield: 1½ dozen.

Lynn Young,
Knoxville, Tennessee.

PERKY SQUASH SOUP

1 medium onion, coarsely chopped
1 clove garlic, crushed
2 tablespoons butter or margarine, melted
4 medium-size yellow squash, sliced ¼ inch thick
1 cup chicken broth
1 (8-ounce) can tomato sauce
1½ cups water
½ teaspoon salt
½ teaspoon freshly ground pepper
½ teaspoon parsley flakes
¼ teaspoon dried whole thyme
⅛ teaspoon dried whole oregano
Grated Parmesan cheese

Sauté onion and garlic in butter in a Dutch oven until tender. Add remaining ingredients except the cheese. Cover and simmer 20 minutes or until squash is tender. Top with cheese. Yield: about 6 cups.

Mrs. John J. O'Neill,
Welaka, Florida.

CREAMY WINE DRESSING

3 tablespoons red wine vinegar
1 tablespoon Dijon mustard
2 cloves garlic, minced
1 tablespoon capers
¾ cup vegetable oil

Combine first 4 ingredients, stirring well. Combine vinegar mixture and oil in a jar. Cover tightly, and shake vigorously. Chill. Shake well before serving. Yield: 1 cup.

Susan Houston,
Tucker, Georgia.

GARLIC CHEESE LOG

1 (8-ounce) package cream cheese, softened
1 (6-ounce) roll bacon-cheese spread, softened
1½ cups (6 ounces) shredded Cheddar cheese
1 clove garlic, minced
1 teaspoon Worcestershire sauce
½ cup chopped pecans
1 tablespoon parsley flakes
Pimiento

Combine first 5 ingredients; mix well. Shape into a log. Combine pecans and parsley; roll log in mixture. Chill. Garnish with pimiento. Yield: one 6-inch cheese log.   *Rebecca Sharpton, Jasper, Alabama.*

meat on a rack in a roasting or broiler pan so that the melted fat drips away.

Our recipe for Open-Face Pizza Sandwiches illustrates yet another way to remove fat. After browning the ground chuck, transfer the meat to a colander, and drain away any excess fat.

These less tender cuts of meat become more tender and flavorful if marinated for several hours in a mixture containing an acidic ingredient, such as wine, lemon juice, vinegar, orange juice, or tomato juice.

You can seal in natural juices by quickly browning the outside of a piece of meat as with Apricot-Sauced Pork Chops. Cook the chops slowly in liquid to prevent drying of the meat. Just be sure to trim away excess fat before cooking. Also, drain off fatty pan drippings after browning and before adding the cooking liquid.

Trim excess fat from steak; score steak in a diagonal design ⅛ inch deep on both sides. Coat a large skillet with cooking spray; add steak. Cook steak over medium heat until lightly browned on both sides. Sprinkle each side of steak with 1 teaspoon flour; cook until browned. Add wine, green onions, parsley flakes, lemon juice, and poultry seasoning. Cook steak 8 to 10 minutes on each side or to desired degree of doneness. Remove steak to warm serving platter; sprinkle with salt and pepper.

Simmer sauce in skillet until thickened. Slice steak across the grain into thin slices; serve with sauce. Yield: 8 servings (about 159 calories per serving).   *Ruth Jacobsen, Madison, Wisconsin.*

COOKING LIGHT®

Trim Calories From Meat

Confused when you go to the meat counter of your grocery store? A general rule to remember when shopping for meat is that the tenderest cuts usually contain the most fat. The marbling (streaks of fat) in a choice rib-eye steak melts into the meat during cooking, leaving the cooked meat juicy and tender. That extra fat is what makes the calorie count per ounce of rib-eye steak, T-bone steak, rib roast, and ground beef higher than that of leaner cuts such as round steak, flank steak, tip roast, and ground chuck.

For many years pork was considered fatty and high in calories. However, the reputation of today's pork has changed. Some of the leaner cuts include trimmed chops, loin roast, tenderloin, and Canadian bacon.

Since lamb and veal are meats from very young animals, excessive marbling has not built up in the muscle. So when you want to add variety to your low-calorie meals, choose lean cuts of lamb and veal. Lamb loin chops, leg of lamb, veal cutlets, and veal round are all lean.

A layer of fat usually surrounds even the leanest cuts of meat, such as beef top round steak. Before cooking the meat, use a sharp knife to remove as much of this excess fat as possible. Another way to get rid of extra fat (and calories) is to broil, bake, or roast the

MARINATED POT ROAST

1 (3-pound) boneless eye-of-round roast
1 cup unsweetened pineapple juice
½ cup red wine vinegar
½ cup water
2 teaspoons Worcestershire sauce
1 medium onion, thinly sliced
1 clove garlic, minced
1 bay leaf
¼ teaspoon freshly ground pepper

Trim excess fat from roast; set aside. Combine remaining ingredients in a large shallow dish. Add meat; cover and marinate overnight in the refrigerator, turning meat occasionally.

Place meat and marinade in a Dutch oven. Cover and simmer 1½ to 2 hours or until desired degree of doneness.

To serve, thinly slice roast. Yield: 9 servings (about 188 calories per 3-ounce slice).   *Mrs. Delbert R. Snyder, Williamsburg, Virginia.*

SKILLET STEAK IN RED WINE SAUCE

1 (2-pound) flank steak
Vegetable cooking spray
2 teaspoons all-purpose flour
1 cup dry red wine
½ cup chopped green onions
1 tablespoon dried parsley flakes
1 tablespoon lemon juice
½ teaspoon poultry seasoning
¼ teaspoon salt
⅛ teaspoon pepper

PEPPER-BEEF STEAK

1 pound boneless round steak
Vegetable cooking spray
1 (16-ounce) can tomatoes, undrained and chopped
½ cup chopped onion
1 clove garlic, minced
1 teaspoon beef-flavored bouillon granules
1 large green pepper, cut into ¾-inch pieces
2 tablespoons cornstarch
1 tablespoon soy sauce
1 tablespoon water
3 quarts water
½ teaspoon beef-flavored bouillon granules
3 ounces uncooked vermicelli
1 cup fresh bean sprouts

Trim excess fat from steak; cut into 1-inch pieces, and set aside.

Coat a large skillet with cooking spray; place over high heat until hot. Add meat, and cook until browned. Add tomatoes, onion, garlic, and bouillon granules; bring to a boil. Cover, reduce heat, and simmer 1 hour. Add green pepper; cover and simmer an additional 10 minutes.

Combine cornstarch, soy sauce, and 1 tablespoon water, stirring until blended; stir into beef mixture. Cook 1 to 2 minutes or until slightly thickened.

Combine 3 quarts water and ½ teaspoon bouillon granules in a Dutch oven; bring to a boil. Add vermicelli, and return to a boil. Cook, uncovered, 6 to 9 minutes or until tender, stirring occasionally; drain. Combine vermicelli with bean sprouts. Serve steak over vermicelli mixture. Yield: 4 servings (about 271 calories per serving).

Betty Quillen, Rogers, Arkansas.

OPEN-FACE PIZZA SANDWICHES

½ pound ground chuck
¼ cup chopped onion
2 tablespoons chopped green pepper
1 (6-ounce) can tomato paste
1 tablespoon water
½ teaspoon dried whole oregano
¼ teaspoon pepper
⅛ teaspoon garlic powder
2 whole wheat English muffins, split
½ cup (2 ounces) shredded mozzarella
  cheese
2 tablespoons grated Parmesan cheese
4 pimiento-stuffed olives, sliced

Combine beef, onion, and green pepper in a skillet. Cook over medium heat, stirring to crumble, until beef is browned and vegetables are tender. Drain in a colander, and pat dry with a paper towel.

Combine beef mixture and next 5 ingredients. Spread over cut sides of muffin halves; top with cheese. Bake at 400° for 5 to 6 minutes or until sandwich is heated and cheese is bubbly. Garnish with sliced olives. Yield: 4 servings (about 229 calories per serving).

COMPANY VEAL AND CARROTS

1 pound veal cutlets
3 tablespoons all-purpose flour
⅜ teaspoon salt
⅜ teaspoon garlic powder
¾ teaspoon freshly ground pepper
⅜ teaspoon dried whole marjoram
Vegetable cooking spray
1 tablespoon vegetable oil
12 baby carrots, scraped and cut in half
  lengthwise
¾ cup dry white wine

Trim excess fat from veal. Flatten veal to ⅛-inch thickness, using a meat mallet or rolling pin. Cut veal into 2-inch pieces.

Combine next 5 ingredients; dredge veal in flour mixture. Coat a large skillet with cooking spray; add oil, and place over medium-high heat until hot. Add veal, and cook 1 minute on each side or until lightly browned. Add carrots and wine; cover, reduce heat, and simmer 10 minutes or until veal is tender. Yield: 4 servings (about 278 calories per serving).

BROILED LAMB CHOPS

4 (1-inch-thick) lamb chops
2 bay leaves
½ cup Italian reduced-calorie salad
  dressing
¼ cup reduced-calorie catsup
2 teaspoons water
1 teaspoon Worcestershire sauce

Trim excess fat from lamb chops; place chops in a shallow dish. Add bay leaves; pour dressing over chops, and cover. Marinate overnight in refrigerator, turning occasionally. Combine catsup, water, and Worcestershire sauce; set aside.

Remove lamb chops from marinade. Discard marinade. Broil 5 inches from heat 5 minutes, brushing with catsup mixture after 3 minutes. Turn chops, and broil an additional 5 to 7 minutes, brushing with remaining catsup mixture after 3 minutes. Yield: 4 servings (about 250 calories per serving).

APRICOT-SAUCED PORK CHOPS

4 (1-inch-thick) lean center-cut pork chops
¼ teaspoon salt
¼ teaspoon freshly ground pepper
Vegetable cooking spray
¾ cup unsweetened orange juice
1 (16-ounce) can unsweetened apricot
  halves, undrained
1 tablespoon cornstarch
½ teaspoon grated orange rind
⅛ teaspoon ground cinnamon

Trim excess fat from pork chops; sprinkle with salt and pepper. Brown chops in a large skillet coated with cooking spray. Add orange juice, and bring to a boil; cover, reduce heat, and simmer 55 to 60 minutes or until the pork chops are tender. Remove chops from skillet, and keep warm.

Drain apricots, reserving liquid; set aside. Combine cornstarch, 2 tablespoons apricot liquid, orange rind, and cinnamon; stir well. Gradually stir cornstarch mixture into liquid in skillet. Cook, stirring constantly, 1 minute or until thickened and bubbly. Add apricots and remaining apricot liquid; cook until thoroughly heated.

Spoon sauce over pork chops to serve. Yield: 4 servings (about 330 calories per serving).

Tip: Freeze small portions of leftover meat or fowl until you have enough for a pot pie, curry, or casserole.

Winter Is Salad Time Too

It doesn't have to be summertime to enjoy a good salad. With winter's fresh produce and canned or frozen vegetables, you can put together a salad that's every bit as appealing as one made from summer's bounty.

APPLE-CARROT SALAD

2 cups shredded carrots
1½ cups diced, unpeeled apples
½ cup raisins
¼ cup chopped walnuts
½ cup mayonnaise or salad dressing
1 tablespoon lemon juice
1 tablespoon honey
Lettuce leaves (optional)

Combine first 4 ingredients; set aside. Combine mayonnaise, lemon juice, and honey, stirring well. Pour dressing over carrot mixture, and toss until coated. Cover and chill 2 to 3 hours. Serve on lettuce leaves, if desired. Yield: about 6 servings.
                              Terry Mitchum,
                        Germantown, Tennessee.

RICE-AND-BEAN SALAD

1 (16-ounce) can red kidney beans,
  drained
3 hard-cooked eggs, chopped
1 cup cooked regular rice
½ cup chopped sweet pickles
¼ cup chopped green pepper
¼ cup chopped onion
¼ cup chopped celery
½ cup mayonnaise or salad dressing

Combine all ingredients; toss gently to mix. Cover and chill 1 to 2 hours. Yield: 4 to 6 servings. *Shana Wartes,*
                              Lipan, Texas.

LEMON-VEGETABLE CONGEALED SALAD

1 (6-ounce) package lemon-flavored gelatin
¾ cup boiling water
¼ teaspoon salt
½ cup evaporated milk
¼ cup vinegar
1 (12-ounce) carton small curd cottage
  cheese
1 cup finely chopped celery
3 tablespoons shredded carrot
1 tablespoon chopped green pepper
1 tablespoon chopped green onion
½ cup mayonnaise

Dissolve gelatin in boiling water. Add salt, milk, and vinegar; mix well. Stir in remaining ingredients; pour into a lightly oiled 5-cup mold. Chill until firm. Yield: 8 to 10 servings.

Mrs. Quentin Bierman,
Dunwoody, Georgia.

HOT BROCCOLI-POTATO SALAD

6 medium-size new potatoes, peeled and cubed
1 (1-pound) bunch broccoli
¼ cup vegetable oil
3 tablespoons white wine vinegar
3 tablespoons orange juice
2 tablespoons minced fresh parsley
2 tablespoons olive oil
1 clove garlic, minced
1 teaspoon salt
1 teaspoon dried whole basil
2 green onions with tops, thinly sliced
3 drops of hot sauce
Cherry tomatoes, halved (optional)
Additional chopped fresh parsley (optional)

Cook potatoes in a small amount of boiling water 10 minutes or until tender; drain. Set aside, and keep warm.

Trim off large leaves of broccoli. Remove tough ends of lower stalks, and wash broccoli thoroughly; cut flowerets and stems into bite-size pieces. Cook broccoli in a small amount of boiling water 7 minutes or until tender; drain. Set aside, and keep warm.

Combine vegetable oil, vinegar, orange, parsley, olive oil, garlic, salt, and basil in a small saucepan; bring to a boil. Remove from heat; stir in green onions and hot sauce. Arrange potatoes and broccoli on serving platter; pour hot oil mixture over top. Garnish with cherry tomatoes and parsley, if desired. Yield: 8 servings.　*Jeanette Guess,*
Edinburg, Virginia.

Sip A Hot Beverage

Steaming cups of Johnny Appleseed Tea, sweetly flavored with apple juice concentrate and brown sugar, offer a warm welcome to neighbors when they stop by on a chilly afternoon. So will mugs of Old-Fashioned Hot Chocolate, topped with marshmallows or dollops of whipped cream. And Cranberry Wine Cup will be a favorite, especially on cold nights in front of a fire.

OLD-FASHIONED HOT CHOCOLATE

2 (1-ounce) squares unsweetened chocolate
1⅓ cups boiling water
1 quart milk, scalded
⅓ cup sugar
Pinch of salt
½ teaspoon vanilla extract
Marshmallows or whipped cream (optional)

Place chocolate in top of a double boiler; bring water to a boil. Reduce heat to low; cook until chocolate melts. Gradually add 1⅓ cups boiling water, stirring constantly. Remove from heat; set aside.

Combine scalded milk, sugar, and salt in a saucepan; add chocolate mixture, stirring well. Cook over low heat, stirring occasionally. Remove from heat; stir in vanilla. If desired, top with marshmallows or whipped cream. Yield: 6 cups.　*Sarah Watson,*
Knoxville, Tennessee.

JOHNNY APPLESEED TEA

2 quarts water, divided
6 tea bags
1 (6-ounce) can frozen apple juice concentrate, thawed and undiluted
¼ cup plus 2 tablespoons firmly packed brown sugar

Bring 1 quart water to a boil; add tea bags. Remove from heat; cover and let steep 5 minutes. Remove tea bags.

Add remaining 1 quart water and remaining ingredients. Cook over low heat until thoroughly heated. Serve hot. Yield: 9 cups.　*Evelyn Milam,*
Knoxville, Tennessee.

CRANBERRY WINE CUP

2 cups cranberry juice cocktail
1 cup water
½ cup sugar
1 (2-inch) stick cinnamon
6 whole cloves
1 (25.4-ounce) bottle Lambrusco or other sparkling red wine
2 tablespoons lemon juice

Combine first 5 ingredients in a large Dutch oven; mix well. Cook over low heat, stirring constantly, until sugar dissolves. Reduce heat, and simmer, uncovered, 15 minutes. Remove cloves and cinnamon stick; stir in wine and lemon juice. Simmer until thoroughly heated. Serve hot. Yield: 6 cups.

Judi Grigoraci,
Charleston, West Virginia.

Shortcuts To Quick Soup

If you want a bowl of hot, steaming soup but don't have time to wait while it simmers for hours, try one of these fast ideas.

CLAM FLORENTINE SOUP

1 (10¾-ounce) can creamy chicken mushroom soup, undiluted
1 (9-ounce) package frozen creamed spinach, thawed
2 (5-ounce) cans minced clams, undrained
1 cup milk
¼ cup dry white wine
¼ teaspoon pepper
Croutons (optional)

Combine all ingredients except croutons in a large saucepan; cook over low heat, stirring constantly, until mixture is heated. (Do not boil.) Ladle into serving bowls; garnish with croutons, if desired. Yield: 5 cups.　*Patti Leonard,*
Manassas, Virginia.

ASPARAGUS-POTATO SOUP

1 (14½-ounce) can chicken broth, undiluted
3 medium-size red potatoes, peeled and diced
⅓ cup chopped onion
⅛ teaspoon ground nutmeg
1¼ cups half-and-half
1 (10½-ounce) can cut asparagus, drained
1 (5-ounce) jar process pimiento cheese spread

Combine first 4 ingredients in a Dutch oven; bring to a boil. Cover, reduce heat, and simmer 5 minutes or until potatoes are tender. Stir in remaining ingredients; simmer, uncovered, stirring frequently, until thoroughly heated. (Do not boil.) Yield: 6 cups.　*Aileen Halcomb,*
Huntsville, Alabama.

CREAMED BROCCOLI SOUP

3 cups water
1 (10-ounce) package frozen chopped
    broccoli
2 tablespoons butter or margarine
1 (10¾-ounce) can Cheddar cheese soup,
    undiluted
1 cup instant nonfat dry milk powder
⅛ teaspoon pepper
⅛ teaspoon hot sauce
Dash of garlic powder

Combine water, broccoli, and butter in a large saucepan. Bring to a boil; cover, reduce heat, and simmer 5 to 7 minutes or until broccoli is tender. Add remaining ingredients; cook over low heat, stirring frequently, just until thoroughly heated. Yield: 5 cups.

Tawanda Gordon,
Douglas, Georgia.

QUICK VEGETABLE SOUP

3 (14½-ounce) cans chicken broth,
    undiluted
1 (10¾-ounce) can tomato soup, undiluted
1 (16-ounce) package frozen mixed
    vegetables
1 (8½-ounce) can whole kernel corn,
    drained
2 cloves garlic, minced
2 tablespoons instant minced onion
¼ teaspoon pepper

Combine all ingredients in a Dutch oven; bring to a boil. Reduce heat, and simmer 15 to 20 minutes. Yield: about 8 cups.

Mrs. N. L. Coppedge,
Shreveport, Louisiana.

TOMATO-AND-RICE SOUP

1 large onion, finely chopped
¼ cup butter or margarine, melted
2 (14½-ounce) cans stewed tomatoes
2½ cups water
⅓ cup uncooked regular rice
1 teaspoon dried whole thyme

Sauté chopped onion in butter in a large saucepan until tender.

Puree tomatoes in container of electric blender. Add tomato puree, water, rice, and thyme to onion mixture; mix well. Bring to a boil; cover, reduce heat, and cook 25 to 30 minutes until rice is tender. Yield: about 7 cups.

Linda Keith,
Dallas, Texas.

Cook These Meals In A Pressure Saucepan

If you're like many other busy homemakers, your pressure saucepan may be sitting, unused, in the back of the kitchen cabinet. But this handy piece of equipment cooks three times faster than conventional methods, it saves you time and energy, and it helps retain food nutrients and flavor. Our menus and recipes show you how to cook complete meals for two—from main dish to dessert—all at the same time in the pressure saucepan.

The secret to cooking entire meals in the pressure saucepan is to choose foods that cook in the same amount of time. Our recipes may direct you to cut a food a certain way or to leave it whole so that all items get done at the same time. Follow directions carefully for best results.

We tested our menus in a 6-quart stainless steel pressure saucepan. This size is needed to accommodate an entire meal for two. If you're cooking just for one, you can half the recipes and use a 4-quart pressure saucepan, but cook the food for the same amount of time.

Liquid is needed to generate steam to cook the food. Use 1½ cups water in a 6-quart pressure saucepan or 1 cup water in a 4-quart pressure saucepan.

Once the food is cooked, additional liquid will accumulate in some of the food packets. This is normal. It may be removed or served with the food for extra nutrients and flavor.

Miniature Meat Loaves
Yellow Rice With Water Chestnuts
Dilled Carrots
Apricot Bread Pudding

MINIATURE MEAT LOAVES

½ pound ground beef
¼ cup fine, dry breadcrumbs
¼ cup chopped fresh mushrooms
1 tablespoon finely chopped onion
2 teaspoons prepared horseradish
½ teaspoon Worcestershire sauce
¼ teaspoon salt
⅛ teaspoon pepper
1 egg, slightly beaten
1 tablespoon catsup
2 fresh mushrooms, sliced

Combine all ingredients except catsup and mushrooms in a medium bowl; mix well. Divide mixture evenly; shape into two loaves of equal size. Brush tops with catsup. Garnish with sliced mushrooms.

Place meat loaves on a 15-inch piece of foil. Pinch corners of foil to make a packet with high sides; leave top open. Set aside, and prepare Yellow Rice With Water Chestnuts.

YELLOW RICE WITH WATER CHESTNUTS

¾ cup water
⅓ cup uncooked regular rice
1 tablespoon sliced water chestnuts
½ teaspoon dried parsley flakes
¼ teaspoon salt
⅛ teaspoon ground turmeric
2 teaspoons butter or margarine

Combine first 6 ingredients in a small bowl, mixing well. Divide mixture evenly between two 4-ounce custard cups; dot with butter. Cover loosely with foil.

Place custard cups on rack in bottom of a 6-quart pressure saucepan containing 1½ cups water. Place meat loaf packet on the top.

DILLED CARROTS

2 large carrots, scraped
⅛ teaspoon salt
⅛ teaspoon dried whole dillweed
2 teaspoons butter or margarine

Place whole carrots on a 15-inch piece of foil. Pinch corners to make a packet with high sides; leave top open. Sprinkle with salt and dillweed, and dot with butter. Set aside, and prepare Apricot Bread Pudding.

APRICOT BREAD PUDDING

½ cup cubed whole wheat bread
⅓ cup milk
¼ cup canned apricot halves, drained and
    chopped
2½ tablespoons brown sugar
¼ teaspoon ground cinnamon
¼ teaspoon vanilla extract
1 egg, beaten
2 tablespoons apricot preserves
2 pecan halves

Combine all ingredients except preserves and pecans in a small bowl; mix well. Divide evenly between two 4-ounce custard cups; cover loosely with foil. Set aside remaining ingredients.

Place custard cups on rack in bottom of a 6-quart pressure saucepan next to Yellow Rice With Water Chestnuts, stacking cups, if necessary. Place the carrot packet on top.

To Cook:

Once meal is assembled in pressure saucepan, secure lid; set weighted control at 15 pounds pressure, and cook on high heat until control jiggles or rocks steadily; reduce heat, and cook 15 minutes. Remove from heat; run cold water over saucepan to reduce pressure instantly. Remove lid so that steam escapes away from you.

Remove foil from Apricot Bread Pudding. Spread tops with apricot preserves; garnish with pecan halves. Yield: 2 servings.

Seasoned Browned Chicken
Mashed Sweet Potatoes
Lemony Brussels Sprouts With Celery
Peanutty Stuffed Apples

SEASONED BROWNED CHICKEN

⅓ cup all-purpose flour
½ teaspoon paprika
¼ teaspoon garlic salt
⅛ teaspoon pepper
2 (3-ounce) chicken breast halves
2 (2-ounce) chicken thighs
3 tablespoons vegetable oil

Combine first 4 ingredients in a plastic bag; mix well. Add chicken, and shake to coat on both sides. Sauté chicken in pressure saucepan in hot oil about 5 minutes or until browned.

Transfer chicken to a 15-inch piece of foil. Pinch corners of foil to make a packet with high sides; leave top open. Remove remaining oil from saucepan with a paper towel. Place chicken on rack in bottom of a 6-quart pressure saucepan containing 1½ cups water.

MASHED SWEET POTATOES

1½ cups uncooked sweet potatoes, peeled and diced
2 teaspoons butter or margarine
¼ to ⅓ cup milk
1½ teaspoons sugar
⅛ teaspoon ground cinnamon

Place potatoes on a 15-inch piece of foil; dot with butter. Set aside remaining ingredients. Pinch corners of foil to make a packet with high sides; leave top open. Place in a pressure saucepan next to Seasoned Browned Chicken.

LEMONY BRUSSELS SPROUTS WITH CELERY

18 small to medium brussels sprouts
1 stalk celery, cut into ½-inch pieces
¼ to ½ teaspoon grated lemon rind
⅛ teaspoon salt
2 teaspoons butter or margarine

Score bottoms of brussels sprouts; place brussels sprouts and celery on a 15-inch piece of foil. Pinch corners of foil to make a packet with high sides; leave top open. Sprinkle with lemon rind and salt; dot with butter. Place vegetables in a pressure saucepan on top of Mashed Sweet Potatoes.

PEANUTTY STUFFED APPLES

¼ cup finely crushed peanut brittle
1 tablespoon raisins
1 medium baking apple, unpeeled
1 teaspoon butter or margarine

Combine peanut brittle and raisins; mix well. Wash and core apple; cut in half crosswise. Fill apple cavities with peanut mixture, heaping remaining mixture on top. Dot with butter.

Place apples on a 15-inch piece of foil. Pinch corners of foil to make a packet with high sides; leave top open. Place in a pressure saucepan on top of Seasoned Browned Chicken.

To Cook:

Once meal is assembled in pressure saucepan, secure lid; set weighted control at 15 pounds pressure, and cook over high heat until control jiggles or rocks steadily. Reduce heat, and cook 10 minutes. Remove from heat; run cold water over saucepan to reduce pressure instantly. Remove lid so that steam escapes away from you.

Place sweet potatoes in a small bowl; mash. Add milk, sugar, and cinnamon, mixing well. Yield: 2 servings.

Enjoy Eating Avocados

When you think of avocados, do warm, balmy days come to mind? If so, then you may not realize the fruit is available year-round. This once hard-to-find fruit is now a common item in salads, soups, and dips.

Creamy Avocado-Mushroom Soup can be served hot or cold, but when making it, add the avocado during the last minutes of preparation and only heat through. A bitter taste results when the fruit is exposed to high or prolonged heat.

CREAMY AVOCADO-MUSHROOM SOUP

1 medium onion, chopped
1 cup sliced fresh mushrooms
2 tablespoons chopped celery
2 tablespoons butter or margarine, melted
2 tablespoons all-purpose flour
4 cups chicken broth
2 cups milk
2 medium avocados, mashed
½ teaspoon white pepper
Croutons (optional)

Sauté onion, mushrooms, and celery in butter in a large saucepan until vegetables are tender. Add flour; cook 1 minute, stirring constantly. Gradually add chicken broth and milk, stirring constantly. Bring to a boil; reduce heat, and simmer 5 to 10 minutes. Add avocado and pepper; cook until thoroughly heated. Garnish with croutons, if desired. (Soup may be served cold, if desired.) Yield: 8 cups. *Hazel Sellers, Albany, Georgia.*

BACON-GUACAMOLE DIP

2 medium avocados, mashed
⅓ cup mayonnaise
¼ cup diced pimiento-stuffed olives
2 tablespoons lemon juice
1 tablespoon grated onion
¼ teaspoon chili powder
Dash of red pepper
4 slices bacon, cooked and crumbled
Sliced pimiento-stuffed olives (optional)

Combine all ingredients except bacon and olives; mix well. Cover and chill. Stir half of bacon into dip; sprinkle remaining bacon on top. Garnish with olive slices, if desired. Serve with corn chips. Yield: 2½ cups.

Vertie Vandervort, Austin, Texas.

CONGEALED AVOCADO CRUNCH SALAD

1 (6-ounce) package lime-flavored gelatin
2 cups boiling water
1½ cups mashed avocado
1 cup mayonnaise
1 cup diced green pepper
1 cup chopped pecans
⅓ cup chopped pimiento
2 teaspoons minced onion
Lettuce leaves
Additional pimiento (optional)

Dissolve lime gelatin in boiling water; stir until dissolved. Add avocado and mayonnaise; mix well. Chill until the consistency of unbeaten egg white. Stir in next 4 ingredients. Pour into a lightly oiled 5½-cup mold. Chill until set. Unmold on lettuce leaves. Garnish salad with additional pimiento, if desired. Yield: 10 servings. *Hattie McNeely, Archer City, Texas.*

AVOCADO-GRAPEFRUIT SALAD

3 grapefruit, peeled, seeded, sectioned, and drained
1 (11-ounce) can mandarin oranges, drained
3 medium avocados, halved and seeded
Lemon juice
Creamy Dressing
Paprika (optional)

Combine grapefruit sections and mandarin oranges; set aside. Brush avocado halves with lemon juice. Spoon fruit mixture into avocado cavities. Top with Creamy Dressing; sprinkle with paprika, if desired. Yield: 6 servings.

Creamy Dressing:
½ cup mayonnaise
½ cup commercial sour cream
¼ cup chopped green pepper
¼ cup chopped celery
¾ teaspoon onion salt

Combine all ingredients; mix well. Chill 1 to 2 hours. Yield: 6 servings.
Mary Gervais, Matthews, North Carolina.

Add A Rare Touch Of Saffron

Of all spices, saffron is the most treasured. This is because each saffron thread must be painstakingly collected by hand from crocus blossoms—a process that takes months to complete.

Fortunately, when used in cooking, a little saffron goes a long way. You can usually find it ground or in threads at supermarkets. To sample the exotic flavor this spice adds, try these recipes.

SPANISH PAELLA

⅓ cup olive oil
2 cloves garlic, minced
3 pounds chicken breasts, thighs, and legs, skinned
1 (28-ounce) can whole tomatoes, undrained and chopped
½ teaspoon salt
¾ cup uncooked regular rice
¼ to ½ teaspoon ground saffron
¼ cup boiling water
1 cup cut fresh green beans
¾ to 1 cup frozen English peas, thawed
1 pound medium fresh shrimp, peeled and deveined

Heat oil in a large skillet or paella pan; add garlic, and cook 1 minute. Add chicken, and brown on both sides. Add tomatoes and salt; cover and cook over low heat 20 to 30 minutes. Remove chicken, and stir in rice. Dissolve saffron in boiling water; stir into rice mixture. Return chicken to skillet; cover and simmer 20 to 30 minutes. Do not stir. Arrange the beans, peas, and shrimp over rice; cover and cook 10 to 12 minutes or just until the shrimp are pink. Yield: 6 to 8 servings.

SAFFRON TEA BREAD

1 cup sugar
½ cup shortening
⅛ teaspoon ground saffron
2 eggs
1½ cups all-purpose flour
1½ teaspoons baking powder
¼ teaspoon salt
½ cup milk
2 teaspoons grated lemon rind
2 teaspoons lemon juice

Combine sugar, shortening, and saffron, beating well. Add eggs, one at a time, beating well after each addition. Combine flour, baking powder, and salt; add to creamed mixture alternately with milk, beginning and ending with flour mixture. Mix well after each addition. Stir in lemon rind and lemon juice. Pour into a greased 9- x 5- x 3-inch loafpan. Bake at 350° for 55 to 60 minutes. Cool in pan 10 minutes. Remove from pan, and cool completely on a wire rack. Yield: 1 loaf.

A Cheesecake With Chocolate

For a rich, eye-catching dessert to serve company, choose Chocolate Swirl Cheesecake. It's sure to be a hit.

CHOCOLATE SWIRL CHEESECAKE

2 cups graham cracker crumbs
1½ teaspoons ground cinnamon
½ cup butter or margarine, melted
2 (1-ounce) squares semisweet chocolate
2 (8-ounce) packages cream cheese, softened
1 cup sugar
6 eggs
¼ cup plus 1 tablespoon all-purpose flour
1½ teaspoons grated lemon rind
3 tablespoons lemon juice
1 teaspoon vanilla extract
1 cup whipping cream, whipped
Grated chocolate (optional)

Combine graham cracker crumbs, cinnamon, and butter, mixing well; firmly press into bottom and up sides of a 9-inch springform pan. Then refrigerate.

Place chocolate in top of a double boiler; bring water to a boil. Reduce heat to low; cook until chocolate melts. Set aside to cool slightly.

Beat cream cheese with electric mixer until light and fluffy; gradually add sugar, mixing well. Add eggs, one at a time, beating after each addition; stir in flour, lemon rind, lemon juice, and vanilla. Fold in whipped cream.

Combine 1 cup cheesecake mixture and melted chocolate. Pour remaining cheesecake mixture into prepared crust. Pour chocolate mixture over cheesecake mixture; gently swirl with a knife.

Bake at 300° for 1 hour. Turn off oven, and let cheesecake stand in closed oven 1 hour. Open oven door, and allow cheesecake to stand in oven 2 to 3 hours or until completely cooled. Chill several hours. Garnish with grated chocolate, if desired. Yield: one 9-inch cheesecake. *Lynn Koenig, Charleston, South Carolina.*

Right: *Add warm and nourishing excitement to winter meals with (front to back) Creole Black-Eyes and Rice, Hot Bacon and Black-Eyed Salad, or Beefy Black-Eyed Soup (recipes on pages 6 and 7).*

Page 28: *Mongolian Beef is served over fried rice noodles and garnished with strips of fresh red chile (recipe on page 2).*

Speed Up Ground Beef Entrées

Ground beef is the star in these recipes, and with the microwave oven, you'll put the entrées on the table quicker than with a conventional oven.

Don't forget the microwave when it comes to defrosting, too. Use the guide of 5 to 7 minutes per pound at LOW (30% power) or 3¾ to 4¾ minutes per pound when defrosting at MEDIUM.

Place frozen ground beef packaged in paper or plastic in the microwave, and defrost for one-third of the recommended time. Turn the package over, and repeat. At this time you can remove the packaging, scrape away soft pieces of beef, and set aside. Place the still-frozen beef in a casserole dish, and break it up as much as possible with a fork. Defrost for the remaining one-third of the time. (If you're defrosting over 1 pound of ground beef, you'll need to check periodically to remove soft pieces.) After defrosting, allow the beef to stand 5 to 10 minutes. The meat will still be icy, but soft and pliable.

SHERRIED BEEF CRÊPES

¾ pound ground beef
1 cup minced fresh mushrooms
1 medium onion, finely chopped
1 clove garlic, minced
2 cups (8 ounces) shredded sharp Cheddar cheese, divided
¾ cup grated Parmesan cheese, divided
⅓ cup catsup
3 tablespoons dry sherry
1 tablespoon steak sauce
1 teaspoon dry mustard
1 teaspoon chopped fresh parsley
¼ teaspoon dried whole oregano
¼ teaspoon dried whole rosemary, crushed
1 bay leaf
¼ teaspoon salt
Dash of pepper
Crêpes (recipe follows)
Paprika

Combine beef, mushrooms, onion, and garlic in a large glass mixing bowl or baking dish; stir to crumble beef. Cover tightly, and microwave at HIGH 5 to 6 minutes or until beef is browned, stirring at 2-minute intervals. Drain.

Set aside ¾ cup Cheddar cheese and ¼ cup Parmesan cheese for topping.

Stir remaining cheese and next 10 ingredients into beef mixture; cover and microwave at MEDIUM HIGH (70% power) for 1½ to 2 minutes, stirring at 1-minute intervals, until mixture is hot. Remove the bay leaf.

Spoon about ½ cup beef mixture in the center of each of 8 crêpes. Roll up, and place seam side down in a lightly greased 12- x 8- x 2-inch baking dish. Sprinkle with reserved cheese and paprika. Cover and microwave at MEDIUM HIGH for 3 to 4 minutes or until the cheese melts, rotating dish after 1½ minutes. Yield: 8 servings.

Crêpes:

1 cup all-purpose flour
½ teaspoon salt
1¼ cups milk
2 eggs, beaten
2 tablespoons butter or margarine, melted
Vegetable oil

Combine flour, salt, and milk, beating until smooth. Add eggs, and beat well; stir in butter. Refrigerate batter 1 hour. (This allows the flour particles to swell and soften so that the crêpes will be light in texture.)

Brush the bottom of a 7-inch crêpe pan or heavy skillet with vegetable oil; place the pan over medium heat until just hot, not smoking.

Pour 2 tablespoons batter into pan; quickly tilt pan in all directions so that batter covers the pan with a thin film. Cook about 1 minute.

Lift edge of crêpe to test for doneness. Crêpe is ready for flipping when it can be shaken loose from pan. Flip crêpe, and cook about 30 seconds on other side. (This side is rarely more than spotty brown and is the side on which the filling is placed.)

Place crêpes on a towel to cool. Stack them between layers of waxed paper to prevent sticking. Yield: 12 crêpes.

Note: Freeze extra crêpes not used for later use.

TACO SALAD CUPS

¾ pound ground beef
¼ cup plus 2 tablespoons barbecue sauce
2½ teaspoons minced onion
1 to 2 teaspoons brown sugar
4 medium tomatoes
3 cups shredded lettuce
1 cup (4 ounces) shredded Cheddar cheese
⅓ cup coarsely crushed taco chips
Commercial sour cream
Sliced ripe olives
Commercial taco sauce

Crumble ground beef into a glass mixing bowl or casserole dish. Cover tightly, and microwave at HIGH for 3 to 5 minutes, stirring once; drain. Stir in barbecue sauce, onion, and brown sugar; set aside.

Remove stems from tomatoes, and place stem side down. Cut almost through each tomato, making six wedges. Place lettuce on serving plate; top with tomatoes; separate wedges slightly to form a cup. Microwave beef mixture at HIGH 1 minute or until thoroughly heated. Spoon mixture evenly into tomato cups. Sprinkle with cheese and taco chips. Top with sour cream and olives. Serve with taco sauce. Yield: 4 servings.

VEGETABLE MEAT LOAF

¾ cup chopped onion
½ cup chopped green pepper
2 tablespoons water
1½ pounds ground beef
1 (8-ounce) can mushroom stems and pieces, drained and chopped
1 (2-ounce) jar diced pimiento, drained
2 eggs, slightly beaten
¼ cup fine, dry breadcrumbs
1 tablespoon Worcestershire sauce
½ teaspoon salt
⅛ teaspoon garlic powder

Combine chopped onion, chopped green pepper, and water in a 1-quart casserole. Cover and microwave at HIGH for 2 to 2½ minutes or until softened; drain and set aside.

Combine remaining ingredients in a large bowl. Add onion mixture, mixing well. Shape meat mixture into a loaf; place in a lightly greased 9- x 5- x 3-inch microwave-safe loaf dish. Place waxed paper loosely over meat loaf; microwave at HIGH for 5 minutes. Microwave at MEDIUM (50% power) for 18 to 22 minutes or until meat loses pink color. Give dish a half-turn after 10 minutes. Pour off excess juices. Let meat loaf stand 5 minutes before serving. Yield: 6 servings.

Use Frozen Fruit In Dessert

When fresh fruit isn't in season, take advantage of the packaged frozen kind. Frozen raspberries, strawberries, and blueberries turn into great desserts.

STRAWBERRY DELIGHT CAKE

48 large marshmallows
Juice of 1 lemon
1 (10-ounce) package frozen sliced strawberries, thawed and undrained
2 cups whipping cream, whipped
1 (8-inch) commercial pound cake

Place marshmallows in top of a double boiler; bring water to a boil. Reduce heat to low; cook until marshmallows melt. Stir in lemon juice. Remove from heat. Add strawberries, mixing well. Fold whipped cream into strawberry mixture.

Split pound cake horizontally into 4 layers. Spread each layer with two-thirds cup strawberry mixture. Frost top and sides of cake with remaining mixture. Cover and refrigerate overnight. Yield: one 8-inch cake.

Gail Thompson,
Brundidge, Alabama.

BLUEBERRY BUCKLE

½ cup shortening
¼ cup sugar
1 egg
1 cup all-purpose flour
2 teaspoons baking powder
¼ teaspoon salt
½ cup milk
1 (16-ounce) package frozen blueberries, thawed and drained
2 teaspoons lemon juice
½ cup all-purpose flour
¼ cup sugar
¼ cup butter or margarine, softened
½ teaspoon ground cinnamon

Cream the shortening with an electric mixer; gradually add ¼ cup sugar, beating the mixture until light and fluffy. Add egg, and beat well.

Combine 1 cup flour, baking powder, and salt; add to creamed mixture alternately with milk, beginning and ending with flour mixture. Mix well after each addition. Spread batter into a greased 9-inch square pan.

Combine blueberries and lemon juice; sprinkle over batter.

Combine ½ cup flour, ¼ cup sugar, butter, and cinnamon; mix well. Crumble over blueberries. Bake at 350° for 45 to 55 minutes or until a wooden pick inserted in center comes out clean. Serve warm. Yield: 9 servings.

Mrs. John Shoemaker,
Louisville, Kentucky.

SNOWFLAKE PUDDING

2 envelopes unflavored gelatin
1 cup sugar
½ teaspoon salt
1¼ cups milk
1 teaspoon vanilla extract
1 (3½-ounce) can flaked coconut
2 cups whipping cream, whipped
Crimson Raspberry Sauce

Combine first 3 ingredients; gradually stir in milk. Cook over medium heat until sugar and gelatin dissolve. Chill until the consistency of unbeaten egg white. Stir in vanilla. Fold in coconut and whipped cream. Pour into a lightly oiled 1½-quart mold. Chill 4 hours or until firm. Unmold onto serving platter, and top with Crimson Raspberry Sauce. Yield: 12 servings.

Crimson Raspberry Sauce:

1 (10-ounce) package frozen red raspberries, thawed and drained
1½ teaspoons cornstarch
½ cup red currant jelly

Combine raspberries and cornstarch; stir in jelly. Bring mixture to a boil. Reduce heat to medium and cook, stirring constantly, until mixture is clear and thick. Press through a sieve or food mill, and chill. Yield: 1 cup.

Nancy L. Holstad,
Knoxville, Tennessee.

SO EASY INDIVIDUAL CHEESECAKES

14 vanilla wafers
4 (3-ounce) packages cream cheese, softened
⅔ cup sugar
2 eggs
1 teaspoon vanilla extract
¾ cup commercial sour cream
¼ cup sugar
1 (10-ounce) package frozen sliced strawberries, thawed and drained

Line muffin pans with paper liners. Place a vanilla wafer in each cup. Set pans aside.

Beat cream cheese with electric mixer until light and fluffy; gradually add ⅔ cup sugar and mix well. Add eggs and vanilla, beating well. Spoon mixture into liners filling two-thirds full. Bake at 350° for 10 minutes. Cool.

Combine sour cream and ¼ cup sugar; mix well. Spread over each cheesecake. Top each with a heaping teaspoonful of strawberries. Freeze until firm. Remove from freezer 5 minutes before serving. Yield: 14 servings.

Cheryl Daniel,
Austin, Texas.

Serve A Saucy Stroganoff

Stroganoff—this Russian word creates visions of a rich, creamy dish with thin strips of sliced beef. That's the classic version, but as you can see from the recipes below, stroganoff can take many other forms as well.

EUROPEAN VEAL MEATBALLS

1 pound ground veal
½ cup fine dry breadcrumbs
¼ cup milk
1 egg, beaten
2 tablespoons chopped fresh parsley
1 clove garlic, minced
1 teaspoon pepper
¾ teaspoon salt
2 tablespoons vegetable oil
2 tablespoons all-purpose flour
1 (4-ounce) can sliced mushrooms, undrained
1½ cups commercial sour cream
1 teaspoon browning and seasoning sauce
¼ teaspoon salt
⅛ teaspon pepper
½ to ¾ cup milk
6 ounces egg noodles
1 tablespoon poppy seeds

Combine first 8 ingredients in a large mixing bowl, and mix well. Shape mixture into 1½-inch balls; brown in 2 tablespoons hot oil 5 to 6 minutes in a large skillet. Remove meatballs, reserving pan drippings in skillet. Add flour to pan drippings; stir until blended. Reduce heat; add mushrooms, sour cream, browning and seasoning sauce, salt, and

Tender and savory European Veal Meatballs top a base of poppy seed-sprinkled egg noodles. Choose salad ingredients that will add color to the menu.

BEEF BURGUNDY STROGANOFF

½ pound fresh mushrooms, sliced
¼ cup chopped onion
1 clove garlic, minced
¼ cup butter or margarine, melted
1 pound boneless sirloin, cut into 3- x ½-
   x ¼-inch strips
2 tablespoons all-purpose flour
1 (10½-ounce) can consommé, undiluted
3 tablespoons lemon juice
3 tablespoons Burgundy
¼ teaspoon pepper
1 cup commercial sour cream
Hot cooked noodles

Sauté mushrooms, onion, and garlic in butter until onion is tender. Add beef; cook, stirring constantly, until browned. Stir in flour, consommé, lemon juice, Burgundy, and pepper; bring to a boil. Reduce heat, and simmer 15 minutes, stirring occasionally. Stir in sour cream; cook until thoroughly heated. (Do not boil.) Serve over noodles. Yield: 4 servings.

MEATBALLS PAPRIKASH WITH RICE

1 pound lean ground beef
¾ cup commercial breadcrumbs
1 teaspoon salt
½ teaspoon pepper
1 egg, beaten
¼ cup milk
Vegetable oil
3 tablespoons all-purpose flour
1 tablespoon paprika
¼ teaspoon pepper
1½ cups warm beef broth
¾ cup commercial sour cream
Hot cooked rice

Combine first 6 ingredients, mixing well. Chill 2 hours. Shape mixture into 1½-inch meatballs; brown in hot oil in a large skillet over medium heat. Remove meatballs, and drain on paper towels, reserving pan drippings in skillet.

Add flour, paprika, and ¼ teaspoon pepper to pan drippings; mix well. Gradually add broth, stirring until smooth. Remove from heat; cool slightly. Add sour cream and the meatballs; cook over medium heat, stirring constantly, until thoroughly heated. Serve over rice. Yield: 6 servings.

Barbara L. Boyle,
Germantown, Maryland.

Tip: Lightly mix and shape ground meat or meat loaf mixtures. Excessive handling results in a compact mixture.

pepper, stirring constantly. Gradually stir in milk. Return meatballs to skillet, and cook over low heat 10 minutes.

Cook noodles according to package directions; drain. Sprinkle with poppy seeds. Serve meatballs and sauce over noodles. Yield: 6 servings.

Elsie Finley,
Houston, Texas.

STEAK STROGANOFF WITH PARSLIED NOODLES

1 medium onion, thinly sliced and
   separated into rings
1 tablespoon vegetable oil
¼ cup all-purpose flour
1 teaspoon salt
4 (4-ounce) cubed steaks
¼ cup vegetable oil
1 (4-ounce) can mushroom stems and
   pieces, undrained
½ cup commercial sour cream
Parslied Noodles

Sauté sliced onion in 1 tablespoon oil in a large skillet. Remove onion, and set aside.

Combine flour and salt; dredge steaks in flour mixture. Heat remaining oil in skillet; add steaks. Cover and cook over medium heat 4 minutes on each side or until done. Remove steaks, and keep warm. Add onion, mushrooms, and sour cream to pan drippings; cook until thoroughly heated. (Do not boil.)

Arrange steaks on Parslied Noodles, and spoon on sauce. Yield: 4 servings.

Parslied Noodles:

4 cups water
2 teaspoons salt
4 ounces wide egg noodles
1 tablespoon butter or margarine
1 teaspoon dried parsley flakes

Combine water and salt; bring to a rapid boil. Add noodles, and boil 7 to 9 minutes, stirring occasionally; drain. Combine noodles, butter, and parsley. Yield: 4 servings. *Patricia Andrews,*
McAlester, Oklahoma.

Enjoy Cabbage At Its Best

Whether there's snow on the ground or flowers in bloom, cabbage is always available at the grocery store. The economical vegetable is particularly welcome when supplies of other fresh produce are less abundant.

When buying cabbage, rest assured that you're getting your money's worth. It's a good source of vitamins C and A, is high in fiber, and has a high yield. One medium head, about 2½ pounds, makes about 16 one-inch slices, 9 cups shredded raw cabbage, or 7 cups of cooked cabbage. And don't throw away the dark-green outer leaves. They're perfect for stuffing and have a higher vitamin A content than the lighter colored leaves on the inside.

Proper storage will help protect raw cabbage against loss of nutrients and texture. It will keep for one to two weeks if you wrap the head in a moist paper towel, seal it in a plastic bag, and refrigerate. Some vitamin C will be lost during preparation, but this can be minimized if you use a sharp knife to shred the cabbage and cook it in as little liquid as possible.

CRUNCHY CABBAGE-RICE ROLLS

8 large cabbage leaves
4 cups cooked brown rice
1 (8-ounce) can sliced water chestnuts, drained
1 (4-ounce) can mushroom stems and pieces, drained
3 tablespoons butter or margarine, melted
½ cup chicken broth
1 tablespoon butter or margarine, melted

Cook cabbage leaves in a small amount of boiling water 8 minutes or until just tender; drain and set aside.

Combine next 4 ingredients; mix well. Spoon ½ cup of rice mixture onto each cabbage leaf; roll up and place seam side down in a 12- x 8- x 2-inch baking dish. Pour chicken broth on and around cabbage rolls; brush rolls with remaining butter. Cover and bake at 350° for 1 hour. Yield: 8 servings.
Mrs. E. F. Whitt,
Attalla, Alabama.

CARAWAY CABBAGE

8 cups (about 1 to 1½ pounds) shredded cabbage
2 eggs, beaten
1 cup milk
2 tablespoons butter or margarine, melted
1 teaspoon salt
1 teaspoon caraway seed
¼ teaspoon pepper
Paprika (optional)

Cook cabbage in a small amount of boiling water 7 minutes or until just tender; remove from heat. Drain.

Combine remaining ingredients except paprika; mix well. Stir into cabbage. Place mixture in a greased 2-quart shallow casserole; cover and bake at 375° for 30 minutes. Garnish with paprika, if desired. Yield: 6 servings.
Louise Sanders,
Union, South Carolina.

RED CABBAGE AND APPLES

1 onion, chopped
2 tablespoons butter or margarine, melted
2 pounds red cabbage, shredded
½ cup raisins
1 large apple, peeled and chopped
½ teaspoon salt
⅛ teaspoon pepper
½ teaspoon mixed pickling spices
1½ tablespoons sugar
2 tablespoons cider vinegar

Sauté onion in butter in a Dutch oven until tender; stir in next 5 ingredients. Tie spices in a wet piece of cheesecloth; add to cabbage mixture. Cover, reduce heat, and simmer 30 minutes. Combine sugar and vinegar; stir into cabbage, and simmer 5 minutes. Remove spice bag. Yield: 6 to 8 servings.
Lynn R. Koenig,
Charleston, South Carolina.

QUICK VEGETABLE SOUP

1 cup chopped onion
1 cup diced celery
¼ cup butter or margarine, melted
6 cups beef broth
1 cup peeled, diced potato
1 cup peeled, diced turnip
⅔ cup scraped, diced carrots
2 tablespoons chopped fresh celery leaves
2 tablespoons chopped fresh parsley
¼ teaspoon dried whole thyme
½ to 1 teaspoon pepper
2 cups shredded cabbage

Sauté onion and celery in butter in a large Dutch oven 5 minutes. Add next 8 ingredients; bring to a boil. Cover, reduce heat, and simmer 30 minutes. Add cabbage; simmer an additional 5 minutes. Yield: about 2 quarts.
Mildred Sherrer,
Bay City, Texas.

Cheese Flavors These Breads

Cheese is a natural for adding flavor to bread. Stir it into biscuits for a quick bread, or add it to yeast rolls or a loaf.

CHEESE BISCUITS

2 cups all-purpose flour
1 tablespoon plus 1 teaspoon baking powder
1 teaspoon salt
½ cup shortening
½ cup (2 ounces) shredded sharp Cheddar cheese
¾ cup milk

Combine flour, baking powder, and salt in a mixing bowl; cut in shortening with a pastry blender until the mixture resembles coarse meal.

Add cheese and milk, stirring until dry ingredients are moistened. Turn dough out onto a lightly floured surface; knead 8 to 10 times.

Roll dough to ½-inch thickness; cut with a 2-inch biscuit cutter. Place biscuits on an ungreased baking sheet. Bake at 450° for 12 to 14 minutes or until golden brown. Yield: 1 dozen biscuits.
Wendy Smith,
Peterman, Alabama.

ITALIANO DINNER ROLLS

3¼ to 4 cups all-purpose flour, divided
2 packages dry yeast
2 tablespoons sugar
2 teaspoons garlic salt
1 teaspoon Italian seasoning
1 teaspoon parsley flakes
1 cup milk, scalded
½ cup warm water (105° to 115°)
2 tablespoons butter or margarine
1 egg
¾ cup grated Parmesan cheese, divided
2 tablespoons butter or margarine, melted

Combine 1½ cups flour and next 5 ingredients in a large bowl; mix well. Combine milk, water, and 2 tablespoons butter in a small bowl; stir until butter melts. Cool to lukewarm (105° to 115°).

Add milk mixture to flour mixture; beat at medium speed of an electric mixer 3 to 4 minutes or until smooth. Add egg, and beat until well blended. Stir in ½ cup cheese and enough of remaining flour to make a stiff dough. Turn dough out onto a floured surface, and knead until smooth and elastic (about 6 to 8 minutes).

Place in a greased bowl, turning to grease top. Cover and let rise in a warm place, free from drafts, 15 minutes or until doubled in bulk.

Punch dough down, and divide into 16 pieces; shape each into a ball. Dip tops in 2 tablespoons melted butter and ¼ cup Parmesan cheese. Place in a well-greased 13- x 9- x 2-inch baking pan. Cover and let rise in a warm place, free from drafts, for 10 minutes. Bake at 375° for 20 to 25 minutes or until brown. Yield: 16 rolls.

La Juan Coward,
Brookeland, Texas.

CHEESE-CARAWAY BATTER BREAD

1 package dry yeast
¾ cup warm water (105° to 115°)
2 eggs, beaten
1 cup (4 ounces) shredded sharp Cheddar cheese
¼ cup shortening
2 tablespoons sugar
1 teaspoon salt
1 teaspoon caraway seeds
2⅔ cups all-purpose flour, divided
1 tablespoon butter or margarine, melted

Dissolve yeast in warm water in a large bowl. Stir in next 6 ingredients. Gradually add 2 cups flour, beating at medium speed of an electric mixer until smooth. Stir in enough of remaining flour to make a stiff dough. Cover and let rise in a warm place, free from drafts, 30 minutes or until doubled in bulk. Stir dough down. Pour into a greased 9- x 5- x 3-inch loafpan. Smooth out top of dough with floured hands. Cover and let rise in a warm place, free from drafts, 40 minutes or until doubled in bulk. Bake at 375° for 40 to 45 minutes or until loaf sounds hollow when tapped. Brush top with melted butter. Remove loaf from pan, and cool on a wire rack. Yield: 1 loaf.

Susan Key,
Houston, Texas.

SOUR CREAM-CHEESE BREAD

1 package dry yeast
¼ cup warm water (105° to 115°)
2⅓ cups all-purpose flour, divided
2 tablespoons sugar
1 teaspoon salt
¼ teaspoon baking soda
½ teaspoon pepper
1 (8-ounce) carton commercial sour cream
1 egg, beaten
1 cup (4 ounces) shredded Cheddar cheese

Dissolve yeast in warm water in a large bowl; let stand 5 minutes. Add 1½ cups flour, sugar, salt, baking soda, pepper, sour cream, and egg; beat at low speed of an electric mixer 30 seconds. Beat at high speed 2 minutes; stir in remaining flour and cheese.

Divide dough in half; place in two well-greased 1-pound coffee cans. Cover and let rise in a warm place, free from drafts, 1 hour. (Dough will not double in bulk.) Bake at 350° for 40 minutes or until loaves sound hollow when tapped. Yield: 2 loaves.

Linda Davidson,
Midland, Texas.

Easy Entrées For The Family

If your family seems to think that everyday meals could use a lift, then take a look at these entrées. You'll find each one to be enticing and easy. In fact, they are so simple you may want to get everyone involved in preparing the night's main course.

CHEESE-BEEF PIE

1½ pounds ground beef
½ cup chopped onion
1 (8-ounce) can tomato sauce
1 (4-ounce) can chopped green chiles, drained
2 teaspoons chili powder
½ teaspoon garlic salt
1 egg, beaten
1½ cups (6 ounces) shredded Cheddar cheese, divided
½ cup commercial sour cream
1 (10-ounce) can refrigerated buttermilk biscuits

Cook beef and onion in a large skillet until meat is browned, stirring to crumble. Drain off pan drippings; stir in tomato sauce, chiles, chili powder, and

garlic salt. Reduce heat, and cook, uncovered, over low heat 10 minutes, stirring occasionally; remove from heat. Combine egg, ½ cup Cheddar cheese, and sour cream; mix well. Add to meat mixture, stirring well; set aside.

Separate each biscuit into two halves, making 20 biscuit rounds. Press 10 rounds into a greased 8-inch baking dish. Top with meat mixture. Cover with remaining biscuit rounds. Bake, uncovered, at 350° for 25 minutes. Sprinkle with remaining 1 cup cheese; bake an additional 5 minutes. Yield: 6 to 8 servings.

Mary Rudolph,
Fort Worth, Texas.

LINK-SAUSAGE PIZZA PIE

1 cup all-purpose flour
1½ teaspoons baking powder
¼ teaspoon salt
¼ teaspoon dried Italian seasoning
⅛ teaspoon garlic powder
2 tablespoons shortening
⅓ cup milk
6 brown-and-serve sausage links
⅓ cup commercial pizza sauce
1 tablespoon vegetable oil
Dash of ground oregano
¼ cup ripe olives, sliced
½ cup (2 ounces) shredded sharp process American cheese

Combine flour, baking powder, salt, Italian seasoning, and garlic powder in a bowl; cut in shortening with a pastry blender until mixture resembles coarse meal. Sprinkle milk evenly over surface; stir mixture with a fork until all dry ingredients are moistened.

Turn dough out on a floured surface; knead lightly about 5 times. Roll dough into a 10-inch circle. Fit dough into a 9-inch pieplate; crimp edges.

Cook sausage until brown; drain and cut into ½-inch slices. Set aside.

Combine pizza sauce, oil, and oregano; spread evenly over crust. Top with sausage and olives; sprinkle with cheese. Bake at 450° for 12 to 15 minutes. Yield: one 9-inch pizza.

Alice McNamara,
Eucha, Oklahoma.

SPAGHETTI CARBONARA

1 large onion, chopped
3 cloves garlic, minced
2 tablespoons butter or margarine, melted
1½ cups cubed cooked ham
10 slices bacon, cooked and crumbled
1 cup Chablis or other dry white wine
5 eggs, beaten
1 cup whipping cream
1½ to 2 cups grated Parmesan cheese
½ teaspoon pepper
¼ teaspoon dried whole thyme
¼ teaspoon dried whole oregano
1 (16-ounce) package spaghetti

Sauté onion and garlic in butter in a skillet until onion is tender. Stir in ham, bacon, and wine; cook, uncovered, over low heat 30 minutes or until liquid is absorbed. Set aside.

Combine eggs, whipping cream, grated Parmesan cheese, pepper, thyme, and oregano; mix well.

Cook spaghetti according to package directions; drain. Add ham mixture and egg mixture to warm spaghetti, tossing gently. Serve immediately. Yield: approximately 8 servings.

Mary I. Newsom,
Etowah, North Carolina.

SWEET-AND-SOUR PORK

1 pound boneless pork, cut into ¾-inch cubes
2 teaspoons soy sauce
1 teaspoon salt
About 1 cup all-purpose flour
2 eggs, beaten
⅔ cup vegetable oil
2 small onions, quartered
1 small green pepper, cut into ¾-inch pieces
2 medium tomatoes, cut into 8 wedges
2 (15¼-ounce) cans pineapple chunks, drained
Sweet-and-sour sauce (recipe follows)
Hot cooked rice

Combine pork, soy sauce, and salt; stir well. Dredge pork in flour; dip in beaten egg. Dredge again in flour. Pour oil around top of preheated wok, coating sides; allow to heat at medium high (325°) for 1 minute. Add pork; stir-fry 4 to 5 minutes or until browned. Remove from wok; set aside. Drain off oil, reserving 1 tablespoon drippings in wok.

Add onion and green pepper; stir-fry 30 seconds. Add pork, tomatoes, and pineapple; stir-fry 4 to 5 minutes. Stir in sweet-and-sour sauce; cook until bubbly. Serve over rice. Yield: 4 servings.

Sweet-and-Sour Sauce:

½ cup malt vinegar
½ cup sugar
¼ cup orange juice
¼ cup pineapple juice
¼ cup tomato paste
½ teaspoon salt
1½ tablespoons cornstarch

Combine all ingredients except cornstarch in a small saucepan; mix well. Remove ¼ cup mixture; stir in cornstarch, and set aside.

Cook juice mixture over medium heat until bubbly. Stir in cornstarch mixture, and cook over medium heat until smooth and thickened. Yield: 1 cup.

Sue-Sue Hartstern,
Louisville, Kentucky.

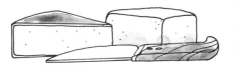

CHEESY CHICKEN CASSEROLE

3½ cups chopped cooked chicken
1½ cups cooked medium egg noodles
1 cup (4 ounces) shredded sharp Cheddar cheese
¼ cup grated Parmesan cheese
½ cup chicken broth
¼ cup dry white wine
½ cup mayonnaise
1 (2-ounce) jar diced pimiento, drained
1 tablespoon minced onion
1 tablespoon parsley flakes
1 tablespoon celery flakes
½ teaspoon salt
½ teaspoon coarsely ground black pepper

Combine all ingredients; spoon into a greased 8-inch square baking dish. Cover and bake at 350° for 30 minutes or until casserole is thoroughly heated. Yield: 4 to 6 servings. *Sandra R. Utt,*
Bassett, Virginia.

Try Peanut Butter And Jelly In A Cake

With over a dozen Southern states growing peanuts commercially, it's no wonder that peanut butter is the South's favorite spread. Those who like the combination of peanut butter and jelly don't stop with sandwiches, either. Here, for instance, is a recipe for Peanut Butter-and-Jelly Cake.

PEANUT BUTTER-AND-JELLY CAKE

½ cup butter or margarine, softened
¼ cup creamy peanut butter
1⅓ cups sugar
2 eggs
2 cups all-purpose flour
1 tablespoon baking powder
1 teaspoon salt
1 cup milk
1 teaspoon vanilla extract
¾ cup grape jelly
Peanut Butter Frosting
Chopped unsalted peanuts (optional)

Cream butter and peanut butter; gradually add sugar, beating at medium speed of an electric mixer until light and fluffy. Add eggs, one at a time, beating well after each addition. Combine flour, baking powder, and salt; add to creamed mixture alternately with milk, beginning and ending with flour mixture. Mix well after each addition. Stir in vanilla.

Pour batter into 2 greased and floured 9-inch round cakepans. Bake at 350° for 30 to 35 minutes or until a wooden pick inserted in center comes out clean. Cool in pan 10 minutes; remove layers from pans, and let cool completely on wire racks.

Spread jelly between layers; spread top and sides with Peanut Butter Frosting. Garnish top with chopped peanuts, if desired. Yield: one 2-layer cake.

Peanut Butter Frosting:

2½ tablespoons butter or margarine, softened
¼ cup plus 2 tablespoons creamy peanut butter
1¼ teaspoons vanilla extract
2 cups sifted powdered sugar
3 to 4 tablespoons milk

Cream butter and peanut butter until light and fluffy. Add vanilla; mix well. Add sugar to creamed mixture alternately with milk, beating until spreading consistency. Yield: enough for one 2-layer cake. *Mrs. Bob Renfro,*
Louisville, Kentucky.

Tip: To keep cake layers from sticking in the pan, grease the bottom and sides of the pan and line bottom with waxed paper. (Trace outline of pan on waxed paper and cut out.) Pour batter in pan and bake. Invert cake layer on rack to cool; gently peel off waxed paper while the cake is still warm.

March

Five Meals From A Leg Of Lamb

Start with a whole leg of lamb. Have your butcher make the first few cuts; then finish carving it at home into meal-size portions according to these directions. You'll have enough tender meat for five varied meals, from a white tablecloth affair to a backyard barbecue.

Talk to the Butcher

To make these recipes, you'll need a leg of lamb that weighs about 10 pounds. Have the butcher slice off four 1-inch-thick **sirloins** from the loin end. Most butchers are happy to cut special orders and usually do so without charge. Wrap up the sirloins to make Lamb Steaks With Béarnaise Sauce, a succulent grilled version of the meat.

Ask the butcher to remove the bone from the remaining lamb. Have him do the rest of the cutting, or do it yourself with these directions and the sketch. The task will be easy, since there's no more bone to cut through.

Next, slice off the **top round.** Cut into four 1-inch-thick boneless fillets to make Fillets of Lamb With Vegetables, an elegant offering of lamb served with julienned vegetables and a wine sauce.

Cut away the **bottom round,** weighing about 1 pound, from which to slice stir-fry strips for Curried Lamb With Rice Mold. For an attractive presentation, spoon the lamb into the center of the rice mold, and then arrange assorted condiments around it.

Next, slice off the **sirloin tip.** It will yield about 1 pound of tender meat to cube and grill into Shish Kabobs Teriyaki. For extra flavor, baste kabobs with leftover marinade as they cook.

The meat left on the **shank** should yield about 1 pound of meat for Lamb Stew-in-a-Loaf.

If additional meat remains, grind it for making lamb loaves or burgers. And don't throw away the bones; boil them in water to make a tasty soup stock.

Before You Cook

Store fresh lamb no more than two days in the refrigerator before cooking it. If you don't plan to use the lamb immediately, wrap it in freezer paper in serving-size portions. It can be frozen for up to nine months.

Fat left on lamb during cooking can give the meat an undesirable flavor. So trim all visible fat away before cooking.

Leg of lamb is covered with a parchment-like skin called fell. The fell is sometimes left on whole roasts to hold in natural juices during cooking, but if left on individual steaks, the skin will shrink and cause the steaks to curl. If your butcher hasn't trimmed the fell, be sure to remove it before cooking.

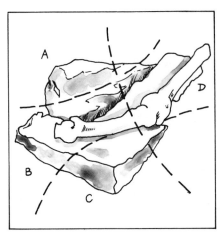

Leg of Lamb, Sirloins Removed

Have butcher remove the bone; then cut lamb into these portions:
A. Top round for boneless fillets
B. Bottom round for stir-fry strips
C. Sirloin tip for kabob cubes
D. Shank portion for stew meat

FILLETS OF LAMB WITH VEGETABLES

2 large carrots, cut into julienne strips
2 stalks celery, cut into julienne strips
1 tablespoon butter or margarine
¼ teaspoon salt
⅛ teaspoon white pepper
¼ cup chopped green onions with tops
2 tablespoons sesame or vegetable oil
4 (1-inch-thick) boneless lamb fillets
3 tablespoons dry white wine
2 tablespoons soy sauce

Cook carrots and celery in a small amount of boiling water until crisp-tender; drain and return to saucepan. Stir in butter, salt, and pepper; set aside.

Sauté green onions in hot oil in a large skillet 1 minute. Add lamb fillets, and cook over medium-high heat 10 minutes, turning once. Remove fillets; keep warm. Add wine and soy sauce to skillet; cook over medium-high heat 5 minutes or until sauce is reduced to about ¼ cup.

Arrange three-fourths of vegetables in 4 stacks on serving platter; top with lamb fillets. Spoon green onions and glaze over lamb, and top lamb with remaining vegetables. Yield: 4 servings.

CURRIED LAMB WITH RICE MOLD

1 pound boneless lean lamb
¾ cup sliced fresh mushrooms
¼ cup chopped onion
1 tablespoon butter or margarine, melted
1 tablespoon all-purpose flour
1 cup beef or lamb broth
1½ tablespoons bacon drippings
½ teaspoon curry powder
½ teaspoon salt
⅛ teaspoon pepper
Curried Rice Mold
Assorted condiments

Partially freeze lamb; slice diagonally across grain into 2- x ¼-inch strips. Set lamb aside.

Sauté mushrooms and onion in butter; add flour, stirring until smooth. Cook 1 minute, stirring constantly. Gradually add broth; cook over medium heat until gravy is thickened and bubbly. Set aside.

Stir-fry lamb in bacon drippings in a heavy skillet; drain. Add gravy mixture, curry powder, salt, and pepper; cover and simmer 10 minutes or until lamb is tender.

Spoon lamb and gravy into Curried Rice Mold, and surround mold with several of the following condiments: chopped tomato, chopped green pepper, shredded carrot, toasted slivered almonds, bean sprouts, raisins, and flaked coconut. Yield: 4 servings.

Curried Rice Mold:

2 cups water
2 teaspoons chicken-flavored bouillon granules
1 cup uncooked medium-grain regular rice
2 tablespoons toasted slivered almonds
2 tablespoons butter or margarine, melted
½ teaspoon curry powder
¼ teaspoon ground turmeric
¼ cup raisins

Combine water and bouillon granules in a large heavy saucepan; bring water to a boil. Gradually add rice, stirring constantly. Cover, reduce heat, and simmer 15 to 20 minutes or until rice is tender and water is absorbed.

Sauté almonds in butter until golden. Stir almonds, curry powder, turmeric, and raisins into cooked rice. Pack hot rice mixture into a well-oiled 4-cup ring mold, pressing firmly with back of spoon; let stand 5 minutes. Invert onto serving platter. Yield: 4 servings.

Tip: Store food in coolest area of kitchen, away from oven and range.

SHISH KABOBS TERIYAKI

¼ cup soy sauce
¼ cup vinegar
¼ cup vegetable oil
1 clove garlic, minced
¼ teaspoon ground ginger
1 pound boneless lamb, cut into 1-inch
   cubes
4 cherry tomatoes
1 green pepper, cut into 1-inch pieces
1 (8-ounce) can pineapple chunks, drained
1 (8-ounce) can whole water chestnuts,
   drained
Hot cooked rice
Fresh parsley sprigs

Combine soy sauce, vinegar, vegetable oil, garlic, and ginger in a large shallow container. Add lamb; cover and marinate in refrigerator several hours or overnight.

Remove lamb from marinade. Alternate lamb and next 4 ingredients on skewers. Grill kabobs over medium coals 5 minutes on each side or to desired degree of doneness, basting frequently with marinade. Serve over hot cooked rice; garnish with parsley. Yield: 4 servings.

LAMB STEAKS WITH BÉARNAISE SAUCE

2 tablespoons soy sauce
1 tablespoon catsup
1 tablespoon vegetable oil
½ teaspoon coarsely ground pepper
1 clove garlic, minced
4 (1-inch-thick) lamb sirloins
Béarnaise sauce (recipe follows)
Carved tomato shell
Fresh watercress

Combine first 5 ingredients, mixing well. Brush the garlic mixture over both sides of each lamb steak. Place the steaks in a large shallow dish. Cover and refrigerate meat overnight.

Grill steaks over medium coals 5 to 8 minutes on each side or to desired degree of doneness. Serve steaks with béarnaise sauce in tomato shell; garnish with watercress. Yield: 4 servings.

Béarnaise Sauce:

3 egg yolks
3 tablespoons tarragon vinegar
¼ teaspoon salt
¼ teaspoon coarsely ground pepper
⅔ cup butter or margarine, melted
2 tablespoons dry white wine
1 teaspoon dried whole tarragon
2 teaspoons minced green onions

Combine first 4 ingredients in container of an electric blender; process 3 seconds at high speed.

Turn blender to low speed; with blender running, add hot butter to yolk mixture in a very slow, steady stream. Turn blender to high speed, and process until thick.

Combine wine, tarragon, and green onions in a small saucepan; cook over high heat until almost all liquid evaporates. Add to mixture in blender, and process 4 seconds at high speed. Yield: 1⅓ cups.

Note: To make tomato shell, cut off top of tomato; scallop cut edge of tomato, using a sharp knife. Scoop out pulp, leaving shell intact. (Reserve pulp for other uses.) Invert tomato shell on paper towel to drain.

LAMB STEW-IN-A-LOAF

1 pound lean lamb, cut into 1-inch cubes
2 tablespoons all-purpose flour
2 tablespoons vegetable oil
1 large tomato, peeled and coarsely
   chopped
¾ cup water
1 teaspoon beef-flavored bouillon granules
1 small bay leaf, crumbled
½ teaspoon chili powder
⅛ teaspoon pepper
⅛ teaspoon dried whole thyme
3 small new potatoes, peeled and cut into
   eighths
3 small carrots, pared and cut into 1-inch
   pieces
1 small onion, coarsely chopped
1 stalk celery, sliced
½ cup frozen English peas
Crusty French Loaves
Lettuce leaves (optional)

Coat lamb with flour, and brown in hot oil in a Dutch oven. Add tomato, water, bouillon granules, and seasonings; cover and simmer over low heat 1 hour or until lamb is almost tender, stirring occasionally. Stir in vegetables except peas; cover and cook 30 minutes. Add peas; cover and cook an additional 15 minutes, stirring occasionally.

Slice tops from Crusty French Loaves. Hollow out center of loaves, leaving a ¾-inch-thick shell. (Reserve center of loaves for breadcrumbs or other uses.) Spoon stew into bread shells, and replace tops of loaves, slightly off center. Serve on a bed of lettuce, if desired. Yield: 4 servings.

Crusty French Loaves:

¼ cup warm water (105° to 115°)
1 teaspoon sugar
1 package dry yeast
¾ cup plus 2 tablespoons warm water
   (105° to 115°)
1 tablespoon sugar
1 tablespoon butter or margarine, melted
1 teaspoon salt
3 to 3½ cups all-purpose flour, divided

Combine first 3 ingredients; let stand 5 minutes.

Combine ¾ cup plus 2 tablespoons warm water, 1 tablespoon sugar, butter, salt, and 1 cup flour in a large bowl; mix well. Stir in yeast mixture and enough of remaining flour to make a soft dough.

Turn dough out onto a floured surface, and knead until smooth and elastic (about 5 minutes). Place in a well-greased bowl, turning to grease top. Cover; let rise in warm place, free from drafts, 1 hour or until doubled in bulk.

Punch dough down, and divide into fourths. Shape each fourth into a ball, and place on well-greased baking sheets.

Make intersecting slits about ¼ inch deep across top of loaves with a sharp knife. Cover and let rise in a warm place, free from drafts, until doubled in bulk (about 40 minutes).

Place a pan of boiling water on lower rack of oven to obtain steam. Bake loaves at 400° for 15 to 20 minutes or until golden brown. Yield: 4 loaves.

Note: Commercial rounds of bread may be substituted for homemade bread, if desired.

Tip: Use finely chopped fresh herbs whenever possible. Dried whole herbs are usually the next best choice since they maintain their strength longer than the commercially ground form. Remember to use 3 times more fresh herbs in a recipe if it calls for the more potent dried form.

Irresistible Cheesecakes!

You don't have to wait until you're at a restaurant to enjoy fabulous cheesecake. With our easy-to-follow recipes, you can make these pretty cheesecakes anytime you get a craving.

Keep in mind that because of their delicate crusts, cheesecakes are traditionally baked in springform pans, which have breakaway sides for easy removal. Remove pan just before you are ready to garnish and serve cheesecake.

If your cake cracks or sinks on top, remember that it's not your fault—just the nature of cheesecake. We have found that gradual cooling reduces this problem. Lighter, more moist versions of cheesecake do not crack very often.

Denser, drier cheesecakes will almost always crack as they cool. To help prevent this, turn the oven off when the cheesecake is done, allowing it to remain there until cooled. Some recipes suggest opening the oven door during this cooling process.

ORANGE CHEESECAKE

1½ cups graham cracker crumbs
3 tablespoons sugar
¼ cup plus 2 tablespoons butter, melted
1 teaspoon Grand Marnier or other orange-flavored liqueur
3 (8-ounce) packages cream cheese, softened
1 cup sugar
1 tablespoon all-purpose flour
3 eggs
2 tablespoons butter, melted
1 tablespoon Grand Marnier or other orange-flavored liqueur
1 (11-ounce) can mandarin oranges, drained

Combine first 4 ingredients, mixing well. Press into bottom and up sides of a 9-inch springform pan; set aside.

Beat cream cheese with electric mixer until light and fluffy. Gradually add 1 cup sugar and flour, mixing well. Add eggs, one at a time, beating well after each addition. Stir in 2 tablespoons butter and 1 tablespoon Grand Marnier. Spoon into prepared pan; bake at 375° for 30 minutes. Let cool to room temperature on a wire rack; refrigerate 12 hours. Remove sides of pan; garnish with mandarin oranges. Yield: 10 to 12 servings.

Bill Shealy,
Columbia, South Carolina.

ULTIMATE PINEAPPLE CHEESECAKE

1 cup graham cracker crumbs
2 tablespoons sugar
¼ cup butter, melted
3 (8-ounce) packages cream cheese, softened
1 cup sugar
4 eggs
1 tablespoon vanilla extract
¼ teaspoon salt
Pineapple Glaze

Combine graham cracker crumbs, 2 tablespoons sugar, and butter, mixing well. Press into bottom of a 9-inch springform pan. Beat cream cheese with electric mixer until light and fluffy; gradually add 1 cup sugar, mixing well. Add eggs, one at a time, beating well after each addition. Stir in vanilla and salt. Spoon into prepared pan. Bake at 350° for 50 minutes. Let cool to room temperature on a wire rack; refrigerate several hours.

Spread Pineapple Glaze over chilled cheesecake; refrigerate overnight. Remove sides of pan before slicing. Yield: 10 to 12 servings.

Pineapple Glaze:

1 (8¾-ounce) can crushed pineapple, undrained
½ cup sugar
3 tablespoons cornstarch
1 egg, beaten
1 tablespoon butter or margarine

Drain pineapple, reserving juice. Add water to juice to equal ½ cup.

Combine pineapple, juice mixture, sugar, and cornstarch in a saucepan. Cook over medium heat, stirring constantly, just until thickened. Add egg and butter; cook an additional 2 minutes, stirring constantly. Cool before spreading. Yield: about 1½ cups.

Alice Slaton Grant,
Concord, North Carolina.

PECAN CHEESECAKE

1½ cups graham cracker crumbs
2 tablespoons sugar
¼ cup plus 2 tablespoons butter, melted
5 (8-ounce) packages cream cheese, softened
1⅔ cups firmly packed light brown sugar
5 eggs
1 teaspoon vanilla extract
1 cup chopped pecans
Whipped cream (optional)
Additional chopped pecans (optional)
Pecan halves (optional)

Combine first 3 ingredients, mixing well. Press mixture into bottom of a 10-inch springform pan; chill.

Beat cream cheese with electric mixer until light and fluffy; gradually add brown sugar, mixing well. Add eggs, one at a time, beating well after each addition. Stir in vanilla and 1 cup chopped pecans. Spoon into prepared pan. Bake at 325° for 1 hour. Turn oven off; allow cheesecake to cool in oven 30 minutes. Let cool to room temperature; refrigerate 8 hours.

Remove sides of springform pan. If desired, garnish cheesecake with whipped cream, top with additional chopped pecans and pecan halves, and gently press additional chopped pecans onto sides of cake. Yield: 12 servings.

Cynthia Ward,
Winston-Salem, North Carolina.

RICH CHOCOLATE CHEESECAKE

1½ cups chocolate wafer crumbs
¼ teaspoon ground nutmeg
½ cup butter, melted
2 (8-ounce) packages cream cheese, softened
¾ cup sugar
3 eggs
1 (8-ounce) carton commercial sour cream
6 (1-ounce) squares semisweet chocolate, melted
1 tablespoon plus ¾ teaspoon cocoa
1½ teaspoons vanilla extract
½ cup whipping cream, whipped
Additional whipped cream (optional)
Chocolate curls (optional)
Almonds (optional)
Maraschino cherries (optional)

Combine first 3 ingredients, mixing well. Press mixture into bottom of a 9-inch springform pan; chill.

Beat cream cheese with electric mixer until light and fluffy; gradually add sugar, mixing well. Add eggs, one at a time, beating well after each addition. Stir in sour cream, melted chocolate, cocoa, and vanilla; mix well. Gently fold in whipped cream; spoon into prepared pan.

Bake at 300° for 1 hour. Turn oven off; allow cheesecake to cool in oven 30 minutes. Open door, and allow cheesecake to cool in oven an additional 30 minutes. Refrigerate 8 hours. Remove sides of springform pan, and garnish with additional whipped cream, chocolate curls, almonds, and cherries, if desired. Yield: 10 to 12 servings.

Lynn R. Koenig,
Charleston, South Carolina.

BREAKFASTS&BRUNCHES®

Start The Day–Deliciously

In the South, the sun rises on some fabulous food. While fluffy biscuits, sausage patties, grits, and scrambled eggs have been standard fare to start the day, take a look through our *Breakfasts & Brunches* section, and see how you can embellish the old favorites for fresh new ideas.

A brunch menu is already planned for you, thanks to Mary and Sandy Pike, a couple in Marietta, Georgia, who make parties something special in their 18th-century home.

Brunch in Georgia

The Pikes agree that a brunch is ideal for entertaining their friends. You'll find their favorite morning menu and recipes on the pages to follow.

The party begins with appetizers on the back patio. A platter of sliced melon, Shrimp Pâté With Dill Sauce, and Curried Chicken Bites whet appetites for the meal to come. Of course, Sandy makes sure that everyone is greeted with a refreshing taste of his mint juleps that are served from antique silver julep cups.

In the sunroom, a buffet brunch of cheese grits, hot biscuits, chilled fruit salad, and asparagus with basil butter awaits. And in the kitchen, Sandy serves omelets fresh from the oven.

For a finale, the Pikes serve Tipsy Squire, a chilled custard and sherry-soaked cake dessert typical of colonial days. It was the early English colonists version of English trifle, Sandy explains.

You can enjoy the Pikes' brunch menu at your own party with the recipes you'll find here. (Notice that although this menu serves twelve, not all of the recipes make twelve servings. With so many dishes, the Pikes offer half-servings of omelets and small servings of cheese grits.) Prepare the appetizers, Orange Salad Cups, and basil butter the day before to save time the day of the party.

> Melon Platter
> **Shrimp Pâté With Dill Sauce**
> **Curried Chicken Bites**
> **Mint Juleps**
> **Puffy Omelets With Mushroom Sauce**
> **Bacon, Ham, and Sausage**
> **Orange Salad Cups**
> **Asparagus With Basil Butter**
> **Baked Cheese Grits**
> **Mile-High Biscuits**
> **Tipsy Squire**
> **Champagne**

SHRIMP PÂTÉ WITH DILL SAUCE

2 quarts water
1 quart dry white wine
3 shallots, chopped
3 cloves garlic, crushed
½ cup chopped celery leaves
1 large carrot, scraped and coarsely chopped
1 leek top, coarsely chopped
1 bay leaf
1 teaspoon salt
½ teaspoon crushed peppercorns
¼ teaspoon dried whole thyme
2 pounds unpeeled medium shrimp
1 teaspoon unflavored gelatin
2 tablespoons butter, softened
2 teaspoons finely chopped fresh chives
¼ teaspoon salt
Crème Fraîche (recipe follows)
Fresh dill sprigs
Additional cooked shrimp
Dill Sauce

Combine first 11 ingredients in a large Dutch oven; bring to a boil. Reduce heat; simmer 30 minutes. Strain to remove vegetables and seasonings. Bring stock to a boil; add shrimp, and cook 3 to 5 minutes. Drain shrimp; reserve 1 cup stock. Cool shrimp; peel, devein, and chill. (Set aside 4 shrimp.)

Strain reserved stock through 2 layers of damp cheesecloth into saucepan. Sprinkle gelatin over stock; let stand several minutes. Cook over medium heat, stirring constantly, until gelatin dissolves. Cool slightly.

Position knife blade in food processor bowl. Combine shrimp, gelatin mixture, butter, chives, and salt in processor bowl. Cover and process 30 seconds or until shrimp is finely chopped. Stir in ½ cup Crème Fraîche. (Reserve remaining Crème Fraîche for use in Dill Sauce.)

Slice reserved whole shrimp in half lengthwise. Arrange shrimp and dill sprigs on bottom and sides of a 4-cup mold; spoon in shrimp mixture. Cover and chill overnight. Garnish pâté with dill sprigs and additional shrimp. Serve with crackers and Dill Sauce. Yield: 10 to 12 servings.

Crème Fraîche:

1 cup whipping cream
1 tablespoon buttermilk

Combine whipping cream and buttermilk; stir well. Cover and let stand at slightly warm room temperature 10 to 12 hours or until thickened. Chill. Yield: about 1 cup.

Dill Sauce:

⅓ cup Crème Fraîche
⅓ cup mayonnaise
⅓ cup commercial sour cream
1 tablespoon lemon juice
1½ tablespoons chopped fresh dill
Fresh dill sprig

Combine all ingredients except dill sprig; mix well. Cover and chill. Transfer to serving container, and garnish with dill. Yield: 1 cup.

CURRIED CHICKEN BITES

1 (8-ounce) package cream cheese,
    softened
3 tablespoons mayonnaise
2 cups finely chopped, cooked chicken
1½ cups finely chopped almonds, toasted
3 tablespoons chutney, chopped
2 teaspoons curry powder
1 teaspoon salt
2 cups flaked coconut

Beat cream cheese and mayonnaise until light and fluffy. Stir in next 5 ingredients, mixing well. Shape mixture into 1-inch balls; roll in coconut. Chill several hours. Yield: 4½ dozen.

MINT JULEPS

4 cups water
2 cups sugar
4 cups loosely packed fresh mint sprigs,
    chopped
4 cups bourbon
Crushed ice
Fresh mint sprigs

Combine water and sugar in a medium saucepan; bring to a boil. Reduce heat to medium, and cook 10 minutes. Reduce heat to low, add chopped mint sprigs, and simmer 30 minutes. Let syrup stand at room temperature overnight. Strain.

Fill julep cups with crushed ice. Combine bourbon and mint syrup; pour over ice. Garnish with mint. Yield: 7½ cups.

PUFFY OMELETS WITH
MUSHROOM SAUCE

12 eggs
¾ cup half-and-half
¾ teaspoon salt
⅛ teaspoon pepper
2 tablespoons butter or margarine
Mushroom Sauce
Fresh parsley sprigs

Separate 2 eggs, and beat whites (at room temperature) until stiff but not dry; set aside. Beat yolks in a medium bowl until thick and lemon colored. Stir in 2 tablespoons half-and-half, ⅛ teaspoon salt, and a dash of pepper into yolks; fold whites into yolks.

Heat an ovenproof 7-inch omelet pan or heavy skillet over medium heat until hot enough to sizzle a drop of water. Add 1 teaspoon butter; rotate pan to coat bottom. Pour in egg mixture all at once, and gently smooth surface. Reduce heat, and cook omelet about 5 minutes or until puffy and lightly browned on bottom, gently lifting omelet at edge to judge color. Bake at 350° for 10 minutes or until lightly browned on top. Loosen omelet with spatula, and fold in half. Transfer to serving plate, and top with about 3 tablespoons Mushroom Sauce. Make 5 additional omelets with remaining ingredients. Spoon remaining sauce over omelets, and garnish with parsley sprigs. Yield: 6 omelets.

Mushroom Sauce:

1 cup sliced fresh mushrooms
1 teaspoon grated onion
2 tablespoons butter or margarine, melted
2 tablespoons all-purpose flour
1 cup milk
½ teaspoon salt
⅛ teaspoon pepper

Sauté mushrooms and onion in butter in a heavy saucepan about 5 minutes. Add flour, stirring until mushrooms are coated. Cook 1 minute, stirring constantly. Gradually add milk; cook over medium heat, stirring constantly, until thickened and bubbly. Stir in salt and pepper. Yield: about 1¼ cups.

ORANGE SALAD CUPS

6 medium oranges
1 banana, halved and sliced
1 apple, peeled and shredded
1 cup miniature marshmallows
⅓ cup seedless green grapes, halved
⅓ cup seedless red grapes, halved
1 (8-ounce) carton commercial sour cream,
    divided
2 tablespoons honey
¼ teaspoon salt
Additional red grape halves
Boston lettuce leaves

Cut oranges in half crosswise. Clip membranes, and carefully remove pulp. (Do not puncture bottom.) Using kitchen shears, cut edges of orange cups into scallops. Set orange cups aside.

Dice orange pulp; drain. Combine orange pulp, banana, apple, marshmallows, and grapes in a medium bowl.

Combine ¼ cup sour cream and honey; mix well. Stir in remaining sour cream and salt. Combine fruit mixture and ¾ cup sour cream mixture; toss gently. Stuff each orange cup with fruit; garnish tops with remaining sour cream mixture and red grape halves. Place orange cups on a platter lined with Boston lettuce leaves. Yield: 12 servings.

ASPARAGUS
WITH BASIL BUTTER

¼ cup plus 2 tablespoons unsalted butter,
    cut into pieces
⅓ cup firmly packed fresh basil leaves
2 tablespoons fresh parsley
1 teaspoon salt
⅛ teaspoon ground nutmeg
Freshly ground pepper to taste
Additional fresh basil leaves
3 pounds fresh asparagus spears
Cherry tomato halves

Position knife blade in food processor bowl; add first 6 ingredients. Cover and process about 1 minute or until thoroughly mixed. Spoon mixture into a ½-cup mold or small bowl. Cover and store in refrigerator until hard. Turn butter out onto serving plate; set out about 30 minutes before serving to soften. Garnish with basil.

Snap off tough ends of asparagus. Remove the scales from stalks with a knife or vegetable peeler, if desired. Cook asparagus, covered, in boiling water 6 to 8 minutes or until crisp-tender. Drain. Arrange on serving platter, alternating tips. Garnish with basil leaves and cherry tomato halves. Serve with basil butter. Yield: 12 servings.

Tip: Cooking vegetables with the least amount of water possible will preserve vitamins and maintain flavor.

BAKED CHEESE GRITS

4 cups water
1 teaspoon salt
1 cup uncooked regular grits
1 cup (4 ounces) shredded sharp Cheddar
  cheese
½ cup butter or margarine
1 teaspoon Worcestershire sauce
3 eggs, slightly beaten
Fresh mushroom slices
Fresh parsley sprigs

Bring water and salt to a boil; stir in grits. Cook grits about 30 minutes or until done. Remove from heat, and add next 3 ingredients; stir until Cheddar cheese and butter melt.

Gradually stir about one-fourth of hot grits into eggs; add to remaining grits, stirring well. Pour grits into a lightly greased 9-inch quiche dish. Bake at 350° for 1 hour. Garnish with mushrooms and parsley. Yield: 6 to 8 servings.

MILE-HIGH BISCUITS

3 cups all-purpose flour
2 tablespoons sugar
1 tablespoon plus 1½ teaspoons baking
  powder
¾ teaspoon cream of tartar
¾ teaspoon salt
¾ cup shortening
1 egg, beaten
¾ cup milk

Combine first 5 ingredients, mixing well; cut in shortening with a pastry blender until mixture resembles coarse meal. Combine egg and milk; add to flour mixture, stirring until dry ingredients are moistened. Turn dough out onto a lightly floured surface; knead 8 or 10 times.

Roll dough to 1-inch thickness; cut with a 2½-inch biscuit cutter. Place biscuits on an ungreased baking sheet. Bake at 450° for 15 minutes or until golden brown. Yield: 15 biscuits.

TIPSY SQUIRE

Custard Sauce (recipe follows)
2 (10¾-ounce) frozen commercial pound
  cakes, thawed
½ cup dry sherry
1¼ cups slivered almonds, toasted
1 cup whipping cream
¼ teaspoon almond extract
Candied cherries

Prepare two recipes of Custard Sauce two days before serving Tipsy Squire. (Do not double recipe.)

Slice each pound cake into 12 slices. Arrange 12 slices in the bottom of a 13- x 9- x 2-inch baking dish. Place remaining cake slices in another dish. Sprinkle sherry evenly over all cake slices. Cover and refrigerate 3 hours.

Pour about 1½ cups Custard Sauce over cake slices in baking dish; top with remaining cake slices. Sprinkle with half of almonds. Pour remaining Custard Sauce over cake slices. Cover cake mixture, and refrigerate overnight.

Whip cream until soft peaks form; fold in almond extract. Dollop whipped cream over cake mixture; sprinkle with remaining almonds. Garnish with cherries. Yield: 12 to 15 servings.

Custard Sauce:

3 eggs
¼ cup sugar
⅛ teaspoon salt
2 cups milk
1 teaspoon vanilla extract

Beat eggs until frothy; add sugar and salt, beating until thick.

Scald milk in top of a double boiler. Gradually stir about one-fourth of hot milk into egg mixture; add to remaining milk, stirring constantly.

Bring water in bottom of double boiler to a boil. Reduce heat to low; cook custard over hot water, stirring occasionally, about 20 minutes or until mixture thickens and coats a metal spoon. Stir in vanilla. Cover and chill 48 hours. Yield: 2 cups.

Bake The Best Breads

They're so good they melt in your mouth. That's the best way to describe these delicious breads.

CHEDDAR-NUT BREAD

3¾ cups biscuit mix
1½ cups (6 ounces) shredded sharp
  Cheddar cheese
¼ teaspoon salt
1 egg, slightly beaten
1 cup evaporated milk
½ cup water
½ cup chopped pecans

Combine first 3 ingredients in a large bowl; set aside. Combine egg, milk, and water; add to dry ingredients, stirring just until moistened. Stir in pecans.

Spoon batter into a lightly greased 9- x 5- x 3-inch loafpan. Bake at 350° for 55 to 60 minutes or until a wooden pick inserted in center comes out clean. Let cool in pan 10 minutes. Yield: 1 loaf.

Carol Harris,
Raleigh, North Carolina.

CHEDDAR CHEESE POPOVERS

3 eggs, beaten
1 cup whole wheat flour
1 cup milk
3 tablespoons butter or margarine, melted
¼ teaspoon salt
¼ cup (1 ounce) shredded Cheddar
  cheese, divided

Combine first 5 ingredients; beat with an electric mixer just until smooth.

Place a well-greased muffin pan in oven at 450° for 3 minutes or until a drop of water sizzles when dropped in pan. Remove pan from oven; pour 1 tablespoon of batter into each cup. Sprinkle each with 1 teaspoon cheese; fill cups three-fourths full with remaining batter. Bake at 450° for 25 minutes. Serve immediately. Yield: 1 dozen.

Helen Maurer,
Christmas, Florida.

ENGLISH MUFFIN LOAVES

6 cups all-purpose flour, divided
2 packages dry yeast
1 tablespoon sugar
1½ teaspoons salt
¼ teaspoon baking soda
2 cups milk
½ cup water
Cornmeal

Combine 3 cups flour, yeast, sugar, salt, and soda in a large mixing bowl; set aside.

Combine milk and water in a small saucepan; heat until very warm (120° to 130°). Gradually add milk mixture to dry ingredients, mixing on low speed of electric mixer 2 to 3 minutes. Stir in enough remaining flour to make a soft dough. Divide dough in half; shape each half into a loaf. Grease two 8½- x 4½- x 3-inch loafpans; sprinkle bottom and sides with cornmeal. Place dough into prepared pans, and sprinkle tops with cornmeal.

Cover and let rise in a warm place (85°), free from drafts, 45 minutes or until doubled in bulk. Bake at 400° for 25 minutes. Yield: 2 loaves.

Julie L. York,
Asheboro, North Carolina.

FLAKY BUTTER CROISSANTS

1 package dry yeast
¼ cup warm water (105° to 115°)
¾ cup milk, scalded
2 tablespoons sugar
1 tablespoon shortening
1 teaspoon salt
1 egg, beaten
About 3 cups all-purpose flour
¾ cup butter, softened and divided

Dissolve yeast in warm water; let stand 5 minutes. Combine milk, sugar, shortening, and salt in a large bowl; mix well. Cool to 105° to 115°. Add egg and yeast mixture, mixing well. Gradually stir in enough flour to make a soft dough. Place in a well-greased bowl; turn to grease top. Cover; chill 1 hour.

Place dough on a lightly floured surface; roll into a 12-inch square. Spread ¼ cup butter evenly over dough. Fold corners to center; then fold dough in

half. Wrap in waxed paper, and chill 30 minutes. Repeat rolling, buttering, and folding procedure twice; cover and chill dough at least 1 hour after last time.

Divide dough in half; roll each portion into a 14-inch circle on a lightly floured surface; cut into 8 wedges. Roll up each wedge tightly, beginning at wide end. Seal points, and place point side down on greased baking sheets; curve into crescent shapes. Cover and let rise in a warm place (85°), free from drafts, 45 minutes or until doubled in bulk. Bake at 400° for 10 to 12 minutes or until lightly browned. Yield: 16 croissants.
Mrs. J. H. Nichols,
Franklin, North Carolina.

QUICK APPLE PINWHEEL

1 (8-ounce) package refrigerated crescent dinner rolls
1 medium apple, peeled and finely chopped
¼ cup raisins
2 tablespoons sugar
½ teaspoon grated lemon rind
Dash of ground nutmeg
Milk
1 tablespoon brown sugar

Separate crescent rolls into triangles. Arrange the triangles so that they overlap on a greased baking sheet with points outward and the bases forming a circle. Press overlapping part of triangle slightly to mesh bases and form a 2-inch circle in the center.

Combine next 5 ingredients; mix well. Spoon mixture onto crescent pinwheel, forming a ring. Bring points of triangles over apple mixture and secure tips under the edges of the circle, stretching triangles slightly as necessary. Brush with milk; sprinkle with brown sugar. Bake at 350° for 25 minutes or until golden brown. Yield: 6 servings.
June Bostick,
Greenwood, Delaware.

CAROLINA MARMALADE BISCUITS

2 cups all-purpose flour
1 tablespoon plus 1 teaspoon baking powder
½ teaspoon salt
¼ cup plus 1 tablespoon shortening
1 egg, slightly beaten
⅓ cup milk
⅓ cup orange marmalade

Combine first 3 ingredients; mix well. Cut in shortening with pastry blender until mixture resembles coarse meal.

Combine egg, milk, and marmalade; mix well. Add to flour mixture, stirring until moistened. Turn dough out onto a lightly floured surface; knead lightly 8 or 10 times.

Roll dough to ½-inch thickness; cut with a 2-inch biscuit cutter. Place biscuits on an ungreased baking sheet. Bake at 450° for 8 to 10 minutes or until golden brown. Yield: 1½ dozen.
Mary M. Hoppe,
Kitty Hawk, North Carolina.

Sunny Side-Dish Ideas

You've settled on a favorite entrée and a refreshing beverage. But if the brunch is to be a success, you'll need a side dish that complements your menu.

HAWAIIAN SAUSAGE CASSEROLE

1 (20-ounce) can pineapple chunks, undrained
1 (16-ounce) can whole sweet potatoes, drained and cut into ½-inch slices
¾ pound smoked sausage, sliced
3 tablespoons brown sugar
2 tablespoons cornstarch
¼ teaspoon salt
1 tablespoon butter or margarine

Drain the pineapple chunks, reserving the juice. Add enough water to the pineapple juice to measure 1¼ cups. Set aside.

Place pineapple chunks, sweet potatoes, and sausage in a 10- x 6- x 2-inch baking dish. Set aside.

Combine sugar, cornstarch, and salt in a saucepan. Gradually add pineapple juice mixture, stirring until blended. Cook, stirring constantly, until mixture thickens and comes to a boil; boil 1 minute, stirring constantly. Remove from heat, and add butter, stirring to melt. Pour over sausage mixture. Cover and bake at 350° for 35 to 40 minutes. Yield: 6 to 8 servings.   *Judy Irwin,*
Mabank, Texas.

ASPARAGUS WITH ORANGE BUTTER SAUCE

⅓ cup butter
2 tablespoons grated orange rind
¼ cup orange juice
1½ pounds fresh asparagus
Peeled orange slices

Combine butter, orange rind, and juice in a saucepan; bring to a boil. Reduce heat, and simmer until mixture is reduced by half and slightly thickened, stirring occasionally. Set aside, and keep warm.

Snap off tough ends of asparagus, and remove scales from stalks with a knife or vegetable peeler.

Cook asparagus, covered, in a small amount of boiling water 6 to 8 minutes or until crisp-tender; drain. Arrange asparagus in a serving dish. Pour orange sauce over asparagus. Garnish with orange slices. Yield: 6 servings.
Mina De Kraker,
Holland, Michigan.

BAKED CHEDDAR TOMATOES

5 medium tomatoes, cut in half crosswise
Olive oil
¾ teaspoon salt
1 cup soft breadcrumbs
1 cup (4 ounces) shredded Cheddar cheese
¼ cup butter or margarine, melted
1 teaspoon dried whole basil
½ teaspoon red pepper

Brush cut surface of tomato halves with olive oil; sprinkle with salt. Place tomato halves in a 13- x 9- x 2-inch baking dish.

Combine remaining ingredients; mix well. Spoon over cut surface of tomatoes. Bake at 350° for 12 to 15 minutes or until tomatoes are thoroughly heated and cheese melts. Yield: 10 servings.
Mrs. John M. Burner,
McGaheysville, Virginia.

JALAPEÑO CHEESE GRITS

4½ cups water
1 teaspoon salt
1½ cups quick-cooking grits
4 cups (1 pound) shredded sharp Cheddar cheese
¼ cup butter or margarine
2 canned jalapeño peppers, seeded and chopped
2 tablespoons chopped pimiento
1 teaspoon salt
3 eggs, beaten

Combine water and 1 teaspoon salt in a large saucepan; bring to a boil. Gradually stir grits into water; cover, reduce heat to low, and cook 5 minutes, stirring occasionally. Add cheese and butter; stir until melted. Stir in peppers, pimiento, and 1 teaspoon salt.

Add a small amount of hot grits to eggs, stirring well; stir egg mixture into the remaining grits. Pour grits into a lightly greased 12- x 8- x 2-inch baking dish. Bake, uncovered, at 350° for 30 minutes. Yield: 8 to 10 servings.
Dorothy Burgess,
Huntsville, Texas.

Choose From These Breakfast Beverages

Weekends usually allow more time to enjoy a morning beverage as you entertain guests, relax with the newspaper, or pamper yourself with breakfast in bed. At times like these, the meal calls for a special beverage that adds sparkle to your day.

QUILTER'S BREW

9 cups water
9 small tea bags with paper tags removed
12 to 14 whole allspice
8 whole cloves
Peel from ½ orange, cut into small strips
2 cups water
1 (12-ounce) can frozen orange juice concentrate, thawed and undiluted
½ cup lemon juice
½ cup sugar
¼ cup honey

Pour 9 cups water into a 12-cup percolator. Combine next 4 ingredients in percolator basket. Perk through complete cycle of electric percolator. When percolating is completed, remove the basket. Add the remaining ingredients to tea mixture; stir. Heat thoroughly. Yield: 13 cups.   *Nora Hendrix,*
Augusta, Georgia.

TROPICAL FRUIT DRINK

1 (46-ounce) can pineapple juice
1 (15.5-ounce) can cream of coconut
1 (12-ounce) can frozen orange juice concentrate, thawed and undiluted
7½ cups water

Combine all ingredients in a large container; stir well. Serve chilled. Yield: 1 gallon.   *Mary Morgan,*
Plantersville, Mississippi.

ALMOND TEA

2 tablespoons lemon-flavored iced tea mix
2 cups hot water
1½ cups sugar
10 cups water, divided
1 (12-ounce) can frozen lemonade concentrate, thawed and undiluted
1 tablespoon almond extract
2 teaspoons vanilla extract

Dissolve iced tea mix in 2 cups hot water; set aside.

Combine sugar and 2 cups water in a Dutch oven; bring to a boil, and boil 5 minutes. Add tea mixture, and remaining water and ingredients to sugar syrup; heat thoroughly. Yield: 3 quarts.   *Dorothy Burgess,*
Huntsville, Texas.

BRANDY MILK PUNCH

3 cups vanilla ice cream
1 cup milk
¼ cup light rum
3 tablespoons bourbon
2 tablespoons brandy
Ground nutmeg

Combine ice cream, milk, rum, bourbon, and brandy in container of an electric blender; process until smooth. Pour into glasses; sprinkle each serving with nutmeg. Serve milk punch immediately. Yield: about 1 quart.

Nancy Rounsefell,
Baton Rouge, Louisiana.

MIMOSA HAWAIIAN

1 (12-ounce) can apricot nectar
1 (12-ounce) can pineapple juice
1 (6-ounce) can frozen orange juice
   concentrate, thawed and undiluted
¾ cup water
1 (25.4-ounce) bottle dry white
   champagne, chilled

Combine first 4 ingredients in a large pitcher; stir well. Chill. Stir in champagne immediately before serving. Yield: about 7½ cups. *Judi Grigoraci, Charleston, West Virginia.*

Enjoy Eggs In A Main Dish

Eggs—most of the time we eat them fried, poached, or scrambled without complaint. But for a special occasion, we look for a little more variety. Something we can be proud to serve to guests. And, let's face it, something that eliminates asking the question, "How do you want your eggs?" and getting six different orders.

We've helped solve the problem for you with the entrées below. These selections are substantial enough to make them hearty breakfast fare, yet special enough to serve to company.

BRUNCH EGGS

12 slices Canadian bacon
12 (1-ounce) slices Swiss cheese
12 eggs
1 cup whipping cream
⅓ cup grated Parmesan cheese
Pepper to taste
Paprika
Chopped parsley

Place Canadian bacon in a lightly greased 13- x 9- x 2-inch baking dish; top with Swiss cheese. Break eggs into baking dish, spacing evenly; carefully pour whipping cream over eggs. Bake at 450° for 10 minutes; sprinkle with Parmesan cheese, pepper, and paprika. Bake an additional 8 to 10 minutes or until set. Sprinkle with parsley. Let stand 10 minutes before serving. Yield: 6 to 8 servings. *Pat Campbell, Temple, Texas.*

APPLE-EGG CASSEROLE

4 cooking apples, peeled and thinly sliced
2 tablespoons sugar
2 cups (8 ounces) shredded sharp Cheddar
   cheese
1 pound bacon, cooked and crumbled
1½ cups biscuit mix
1½ cups milk
4 eggs, beaten

Combine apples and sugar; mix well. Spread evenly in a lightly greased 13- x 9- x 2-inch baking dish. Sprinkle cheese and bacon on top.
Combine remaining ingredients; beat at medium speed of an electric mixer 30 seconds or until smooth. Pour over cheese and bacon; bake at 375° for 30 to 35 minutes or until golden brown. Serve warm. Yield: 10 servings.

Carin Usry,
Oklahoma City, Oklahoma.

COTTAGE EGGS

4 eggs, beaten
¼ cup cream-style cottage cheese
Dash of pepper
1½ teaspoons butter or margarine
3 slices bacon, cooked and crumbled

Combine eggs, cottage cheese, and pepper; set aside.
Melt butter in a skillet over medium heat; add egg mixture. Cook, stirring often, until eggs are almost firm. Add bacon; cook until eggs are firm but still moist. Yield: 2 servings.

Beverly Van Stee,
Chapel Hill, North Carolina.

BREAKFAST PIZZA

1 pound bulk pork sausage
1 (8-ounce) package refrigerated crescent
   rolls
1 cup frozen loose-pack hash brown
   potatoes, thawed
1 cup (4 ounces) shredded sharp Cheddar
   cheese
5 eggs, beaten
¼ cup milk
½ teaspoon salt
⅛ teaspoon pepper
2 tablespoons grated Parmesan cheese
Whole pimientos (optional)
Fresh oregano (optional)

Cook sausage in a medium skillet until browned; drain. Set aside.
Separate crescent dough into 8 triangles; place triangles with elongated points toward center in a greased 12-inch pizza pan. Press bottom and sides to form a crust; seal perforations. Spoon sausage over dough; sprinkle with hash brown potatoes and Cheddar cheese.
Combine eggs, milk, salt, and pepper; pour over sausage mixture. Bake at 375° for 25 minutes. Sprinkle with Parmesan cheese, and bake an additional 5 minutes. Garnish with pimiento and fresh oregano, if desired. Yield: 6 to 8 servings. *Linda Tarleton, Mabank, Texas.*

Tip: Unless otherwise specified, always preheat the oven at least 20 minutes before baking.

BREAKFAST BAKE

1¼ cups uncooked regular rice
2 cups (8 ounces) shredded Cheddar
 cheese, divided
12 slices bacon, cooked, crumbled, and
 divided
1 (15-ounce) can tomato sauce
½ cup chili sauce
12 eggs
12 thinly sliced green pepper rings

Cook rice according to package directions, omitting salt.

Combine rice, 1¼ cups cheese, ½ cup crumbled bacon, tomato sauce, and chili sauce. Spoon into a lightly greased 13- x 9- x 2-inch baking dish; pat firmly. Make twelve 2-inch wells in rice mixture using back of a spoon. Cover and bake at 350° for 25 minutes. Remove from oven; break an egg into each well; press a green pepper ring around each egg. Cover and bake at 350° for 30 minutes or until eggs are set. Top eggs with remaining cheese and bacon; cover and let stand 5 to 10 minutes or until cheese melts. Yield: 12 servings.
Mary Ann Shewbridge,
Virginia Beach, Virginia.

ITALIAN BROCCOLI QUICHE

1 (10-ounce) package frozen chopped
 broccoli
½ cup chopped onion
1 tablespoon vegetable oil
1 cup milk
½ teaspoon salt
¼ teaspoon Italian seasoning
4 eggs
½ cup grated Parmesan cheese, divided
4 slices bacon, cooked and crumbled

Thaw broccoli; drain on paper towels.

Sauté chopped onion in oil in a saucepan; add milk, salt, and Italian seasoning. Heat thoroughly.

Beat eggs well. Gradually stir about one-fourth of milk mixture into eggs; add to remaining milk mixture, stirring constantly. Add broccoli and ⅓ cup cheese; pour into a lightly greased 9-inch quiche dish. Sprinkle with bacon and remaining cheese. Bake at 350° for 25 to 30 minutes or until set. Yield: 6 servings.
Edna Earle Moore,
Hueytown, Alabama.

BROCCOLI-MUSHROOM OMELET

1 (10-ounce) package frozen chopped
 broccoli
½ cup sliced fresh mushrooms
1½ teaspoons butter or margarine, melted
5 eggs
⅓ cup water
Pinch of salt
Dash of pepper
2 tablespoons butter or margarine
1 cup (4 ounces) shredded sharp Cheddar
 cheese
Sautéed sliced mushrooms (optional)
Fluted mushroom (optional)

Cook broccoli according to package directions; drain. Set aside.

Sauté mushrooms in 1½ teaspoons butter until tender; set aside.

Combine eggs, water, salt, and pepper; beat well. Heat a 10-inch omelet pan or heavy skillet over medium heat until hot enough to sizzle a drop of water. Add 2 tablespoons butter or margarine; rotate pan to coat bottom.

Pour egg mixture into skillet. As mixture starts to cook, gently lift edges of omelet with a spatula and tilt pan so uncooked portion flows underneath.

When egg mixture is almost set, spoon broccoli over half of omelet; top with mushrooms and cheese. Place skillet under broiler just until the cheese melts. Loosen the omelet with a spatula, and fold in half.

Slide omelet onto a warm serving platter. Garnish with sautéed sliced mushrooms and fluted mushroom, if desired. Yield: 2 servings.   *Ken Magee,*
Elgin, South Carolina.

EGG-AND-CHEESE PUFF

2 tablespoons butter or margarine,
 softened
6 slices white bread
2 cups (8 ounces) shredded Cheddar
 cheese
2½ cups milk
4 eggs
½ teaspoon salt
½ teaspoon dry mustard
½ teaspoon Worcestershire sauce

Spread butter on one side of 3 bread slices. Top with remaining bread. Cut each sandwich into quarters. Place 6 of the quarters in a buttered 8-inch square baking dish. Sprinkle with half of cheese. Repeat procedure with remaining quarters and Cheddar cheese.

Combine remaining ingredients, and beat with a wire whisk until blended; pour over casserole. Cover dish and chill overnight.

Remove dish from refrigerator, and allow casserole to reach room temperature. Uncover and bake at 300° for 1 hour and 15 minutes or until set. Serve immediately. Yield: 6 servings.

Sweeten Your Morning

Coffee cakes and fruit dishes are often a part of morning meals in the Southland. You will find that these recipes, such as Orange-Pecan Baked Apples, offer just the right sweet taste.

Regal Bananas, a recipe from Cathy Allen of Staunton, Virginia, will impress your guests and satisfy their appetites for something sweet. Just sauté bananas with coconut, rum, and orange rind; then add more rum to the pan and ignite. You'll keep the fruit from becoming mushy if you use bananas that aren't too ripe and avoid overcooking.

ORANGE-PECAN BAKED APPLES

6 medium baking apples, cored
¼ cup orange marmalade
2 tablespoons finely chopped pecans
Ground cinnamon
Ground nutmeg

Place apples in a shallow baking dish; add water to cover bottom of dish.

Combine marmalade and pecans; mix well. Fill center of apples with marmalade mixture; sprinkle with cinnamon and nutmeg. Bake, uncovered, at 350° for 1 hour or until tender. Yield: 6 servings.   *Charlotte Watkins,*
Lakeland, Florida.

REGAL BANANAS

⅓ cup flaked coconut
¼ cup firmly packed brown sugar
½ teaspoon grated orange rind
¼ cup butter or margarine
4 bananas, cut in half crosswise
¼ cup rum, divided

Combine coconut, brown sugar, and orange rind, mixing well; set aside.

Melt butter in a large skillet; add bananas. Sprinkle with coconut mixture and 2 tablespoons rum. Cook over low heat about 3 minutes or until lightly browned on all sides.

Add remaining 2 tablespoons rum to skillet. (Do not stir.) Ignite with a long match, basting bananas with sauce until flames die down. Serve immediately. Yield: 4 servings. *Cathy Allen, Staunton, Virginia.*

BANANA CREAM COFFEE CAKE

2 (3-ounce) packages cream cheese, softened
⅓ cup sugar
1 tablespoon all-purpose flour
½ teaspoon ground nutmeg
1 egg
½ cup butter or margarine, softened
1½ cups sugar
2 eggs
1 teaspoon baking soda
3 tablespoons hot water
3 cups all-purpose flour
1 teaspoon baking powder
½ teaspoon salt
½ teaspoon ground nutmeg
½ teaspoon ground cinnamon
⅓ cup orange juice
1 teaspoon vanilla extract
3 medium bananas, mashed
1 cup chopped pecans
1 tablespoon butter or margarine, melted
1 tablespoon sugar
¼ teaspoon ground cinnamon

Combine first 4 ingredients, beating until smooth. Add 1 egg, mixing well. Set mixture aside.

Cream ½ cup butter; gradually add 1½ cups sugar, beating well. Add 2 eggs, one at a time, beating after each addition. Combine soda and water; add to creamed mixture, mixing well.

Combine flour, baking powder, salt, nutmeg, and cinnamon; add to creamed mixture alternately with juice, beginning and ending with flour mixture. Stir in vanilla, bananas, and pecans.

Spoon 1½ cups banana mixture into a greased and floured 10-inch Bundt pan. Spread cream cheese mixture over batter. Spoon remaining batter over cream cheese mixture. Bake at 350° for 50 to 55 minutes. Cool in pan 10 minutes; remove from pan, and cool completely on a wire rack. Brush with melted butter. Combine 1 tablespoon sugar and ¼ teaspoon cinnamon; sprinkle over cake. Yield: one 10-inch cake.

Ferrilyn Welsh, Warner Robins, Georgia.

STRAWBERRY COFFEE CAKE

1 (8-ounce) package cream cheese, softened
½ cup butter or margarine, softened
¾ cup sugar
¼ cup milk
2 eggs
1 teaspoon vanilla extract
2 cups all-purpose flour
1 teaspoon baking powder
½ teaspoon baking soda
¼ teaspoon salt
1 (18-ounce) jar strawberry preserves
1 tablespoon lemon juice
½ cup chopped pecans
¼ cup firmly packed light brown sugar

Cream first 2 ingredients; gradually add ¾ cup sugar, beating until fluffy. Add milk, eggs, and vanilla; beat well.

Combine flour, baking powder, soda, and salt; add to creamed mixture, and beat until blended. (Batter will be stiff.)

Spread half of batter in a greased and floured 13- x 9- x 2-inch baking pan. Combine preserves and lemon juice; spread over batter in pan. Dot remaining batter evenly over preserves.

Combine pecans and brown sugar; sprinkle over top. Bake at 350° for 40 minutes or until a wooden pick inserted in the center comes out clean. Yield: about 15 servings. *Brenda Blalock, Lawrenceville, Georgia.*

PINEAPPLE-APPLE BETTY

3 cups peeled apple slices
1 (8-ounce) can crushed pineapple, drained
½ cup all-purpose flour
½ cup firmly packed brown sugar
½ teaspoon ground cinnamon
¼ teaspoon salt
¼ cup butter or margarine, softened

Alternate layers of apples and pineapple in a greased 1-quart baking dish.

Combine flour, sugar, cinnamon, and salt; add butter, and stir with a fork until crumbly. Sprinkle the flour mixture over fruit. Bake, uncovered, at 375° for 30 minutes. Serve warm. Yield: about 4 to 6 servings.

Mrs. Gary Taylor, Afton, Virginia.

Fruit Rounds Out The Menu

Fruit starts the day out right. And simple fruit side dishes become a morning eye-opener when prepared or served in an unexpected way.

FRISKY FRUIT SALAD

2 cups cubed fresh pineapple
1 cup halved strawberries
1 pear, cubed
1 orange, sectioned
2 tablespoons sugar
2 tablespoons brandy
1 tablespoon orange juice
1 tablespoon lime juice
1 tablespoon Cointreau or other orange-flavored liqueur

Combine fruit; set aside. Combine remaining ingredients, mixing well; pour over fruit. Cover and chill 1 hour. Yield: 6 servings.

Note: This salad is best when made and served the same day.

Cyndee Kannenberg,
Brown Deer, Wisconsin.

FRUIT CUP MEDLEY

½ cup commercial sour cream
½ cup orange juice
3 tablespoons honey
2 cups unpeeled, chopped apple
1 large banana, sliced
1 tablespoon lemon juice
1 (15¼-ounce) can pineapple chunks, drained
¼ cup chopped peanuts

Combine first 3 ingredients; chill mixture 1 hour.

Coat apple and banana with lemon juice; add pineapple, tossing gently. Spoon fruit into individual serving dishes; top with sour cream mixture and peanuts. Yield: 6 servings.

Susan S. Watkins,
Raleigh, North Carolina.

BAKED MUSTARD FRUIT COMPOTE

1 (8-ounce) can pineapple chunks, undrained
2 bananas, sliced
1 (16-ounce) can peach slices, drained
1 (16-ounce) can pear slices, drained
1 (10-ounce) jar maraschino cherries, drained
½ cup firmly packed brown sugar
¼ cup butter or margarine
1½ tablespoons prepared mustard

Drain pineapple, reserving juice. Toss bananas in pineapple juice; drain. Combine pineapple, bananas, and next 3 ingredients in a 1½-quart baking dish.

Combine remaining ingredients in a small saucepan. Cook over medium heat, stirring constantly, until smooth and bubbly; pour over fruit. Bake, uncovered, at 325° for 20 to 25 minutes or until thoroughly heated. Yield: 8 servings.

Jane Ellis,
Due West, South Carolina.

STUFFED PRUNES

12 to 15 large pitted prunes
⅓ cup small curd cottage cheese
2 tablespoons finely chopped peanuts
1 teaspoon grated orange rind
Peanut halves (optional)

Place prunes in a saucepan; cover with water. Bring to a boil; cover, reduce heat, and simmer 5 minutes. Drain; set aside.

Combine next 3 ingredients, mixing well. Spoon mixture into a pastry bag fitted with a large tip; pipe mixture into cavity of each cooled prune. Garnish with peanut halves, if desired. Yield: 12 to 15 prunes.

Irene Murry,
Herculaneum, Missouri.

CITRUS SALAD IN ORANGE CUPS

⅓ cup honey
1 tablespoon plus 1 teaspoon lime juice
2 teaspoons lemon juice
1 egg, beaten
6 large oranges
1½ cups grapefruit sections
1½ cups halved fresh strawberries
¼ cup whipping cream

Combine first 4 ingredients in a small saucepan; cook over medium heat, stirring constantly, until thickened. Remove from heat; cover and chill 1 hour.

Cut a ½-inch slice from the stem end of each orange; clip membrane, and carefully remove pulp. (Do not puncture rind.) Drain orange cups on paper towels. Remove membrane from orange pulp; cut pulp into bite-size pieces. Combine orange pieces, grapefruit sections, and strawberries; drain. Spoon fruit mixture evenly into orange cups; set aside.

Beat whipping cream until stiff peaks form; fold into chilled honey mixture. Spoon mixture over orange cups. Yield: 6 servings.

Tip: Remember that deep green, yellow, and orange fruit and vegetables are good sources of vitamin A.
Sources of vitamin C are citrus fruit, deep green vegetables, and potatoes.

Favorites From The Processor

Save time and energy by letting a food processor do the work for you. Take note of our breakfast bread and Banana Milkshake recipes, and see how you can eliminate steps by using a food processor. Then apply the same principles to your favorite recipes.

For our Crunchy Walnut Waffles, chop the walnuts at the same time you combine the dry ingredients. Just add flour, baking soda, baking powder, salt, and nuts to the processor bowl and pulse until the walnuts are chopped. Any time a bread recipe calls for chopped nuts, you can use this same procedure. However, if the mixture will be processed several times with the addition of ingredients, you may want to add the nuts at a later step to keep them from being too finely chopped.

The food processor takes the messiness out of mixing soft bread doughs, as you'll see when you make Processor Cream Cheese Loaves. Place the flour in the processor bowl, and add the remaining dough ingredients through the food chute with the motor running.

Then to save time, don't wash the processor bowl after removing the dough. Just scrape the bowl as much as possible with a rubber spatula; it's ready for mixing the filling ingredients.

As with any food processor recipe, you'll get best results if you avoid overprocessing. Get in the habit of using the pulse button, and watch the mixture carefully as you process.

BANANA MILKSHAKE

2 small ripe bananas
1½ cups milk
2 cups vanilla ice cream

Position knife blade in food processor bowl. Cut each banana into 4 pieces. Place bananas and milk in processor bowl, and top with cover; process about 30 seconds. Add ice cream, and pulse until well mixed but not pureed. Serve immediately. Yield: about 4 cups.

Dorothy Gilbert,
Victoria, Texas.

PROCESSOR CREAM CHEESE LOAVES

1 package dry yeast
¼ cup warm water (105° to 115°)
3¼ cups all-purpose flour
¾ cup commercial sour cream, scalded
¼ cup plus 2 tablespoons butter or margarine, melted
⅓ cup sugar
¾ teaspoon salt
1 egg, beaten
Filling (recipe follows)
Glaze (recipe follows)

Dissolve the yeast in warm water, and set aside.

Position knife blade in food processor bowl; add flour. Combine sour cream, butter, sugar, salt, and yeast mixture in a small bowl; stir in egg. With processor running, pour mixture through the food chute in a slow, steady stream. Process until well blended. (Dough will be soft.) Place dough in a well-greased bowl, turning to grease top. Cover and let rise in a warm place, free from drafts, 1½ hours or until doubled in bulk.

Divide dough into 2 equal portions. Turn each portion out onto a heavily floured surface, and knead 4 or 5 times. Roll each into a 14- x 10-inch rectangle. Spread half of filling over each rectangle, leaving a ½-inch margin around edges. Carefully roll up jellyroll fashion, beginning at long side. Firmly pinch edge and ends to seal. Carefully place rolls, seam side down, on greased baking sheets.

Make 6 equally spaced X-shaped cuts across top of each loaf. Cover and let rise in a warm place, free from drafts, 1½ hours or until doubled in bulk. Bake at 375° for 15 to 20 minutes. Spread loaves with glaze while warm. Yield: 2 loaves.

Filling:

1 (8-ounce) package cream cheese, softened
½ cup sugar
1 egg yolk, beaten
Dash of salt
1 teaspoon vanilla extract

Position knife blade in processor bowl; add all ingredients. Top with cover; process until well blended. Chill 20 to 30 minutes. Yield: about 1 cup.

Glaze:

1¼ cups sifted powdered sugar
2½ tablespoons milk
1 teaspoon vanilla extract

Combine all ingredients, mixing well. Yield: about 1 cup.   *Susie Lavenue, Ridgely, Tennessee.*

CRUNCHY WALNUT WAFFLES

2 cups all-purpose flour
1½ teaspoons baking powder
½ teaspoon baking soda
¼ teaspoon salt
½ cup walnut halves
2 eggs
1½ cups buttermilk
½ cup maple-flavored syrup
⅓ cup shortening
Fresh strawberries (optional)

Position knife blade in food processor bowl. Combine first 5 ingredients in processor bowl; top with cover, and process 3 seconds or until walnuts are coarsely chopped. Add remaining ingredients except strawberries, and process 5 seconds or until batter is smooth. Bake in a preheated, lightly oiled waffle iron about 5 minutes. Top with strawberries, if desired. Yield: 16 (4-inch) waffles.   *Erma Jackson, Huntsville, Alabama.*

REFRIGERATOR YEAST BISCUITS

1 package dry yeast
¼ cup warm water (105° to 115°)
5 cups all-purpose flour
¼ cup sugar
1 tablespoon baking powder
1 teaspoon baking soda
1 teaspoon salt
1 cup shortening
2 cups buttermilk

Dissolve the yeast in warm water, and set aside.

Position knife blade in food processor bowl. Add flour, sugar, baking powder, baking soda, and salt; top with cover, and pulse 1 time to mix. Add shortening, and process until mixture resembles coarse meal. Add yeast mixture and buttermilk; process until dry ingredients are moistened. Pour into a lightly greased bowl; cover and refrigerate until needed.

Turn dough out onto a floured surface, and knead lightly 4 or 5 times. Roll dough to ½-inch thickness; cut with a 2-inch biscuit cutter. Place on lightly greased baking sheets. Bake at 450° for 12 to 15 minutes. Yield: about 2 dozen.

Note: Biscuits may be frozen. To freeze, place unbaked biscuits on an ungreased baking sheet; cover and freeze until firm. Transfer frozen biscuits to plastic bags. To bake, place frozen biscuits on a lightly greased baking sheet, and allow to stand 30 minutes. Bake biscuits at 450° for 12 to 15 minutes.

Vera H. Clary, Gasburg, Virginia.

COOKING LIGHT®

Wake Up To A Light Menu

A breakfast of poached eggs and dry toast may be low in calories, but it's certainly not very exciting. Imagine instead Eggs Benedict, Spinach Quiche, or Mexican-Style Scrambled Eggs. These are just a few of the enticing entrées our readers have submitted for this special feature of *Cooking Light*.

Today's dieter can choose from a variety of reduced-calorie or low-fat ingredients. You can find the lean Canadian-style bacon for Betty Quillen's Eggs Benedict among the luncheon meats in your grocery store. One slice is only 18 calories. Betty holds down calories in the Mock Hollandaise Sauce with plain low-fat yogurt. Keep the hollandaise sauce below a boil to prevent curdling of the yogurt.

Jean Sternberger uses low-fat cottage cheese in her Spinach Quiche. By not using a crust, she saves about 150 calories per serving. Another low-fat cheese, sliced low-fat process Cheddar, keeps calories to 147 for each serving of Cheesy Vegetable Omelet.

Almost all low-calorie diets recommend avoiding sausage because of its high fat content. However, Patra Sullivan's recipe called Dieters' Spicy Sausage is an exception. Made with lean ground pork and several spices, Patra's version has only 105 calories per patty.

EGGS BENEDICT

6 (½-ounce) slices lean Canadian-style
  bacon
Vegetable cooking spray
3 English muffins, split and toasted
6 poached eggs
Mock Hollandaise Sauce

Place bacon in a skillet coated with cooking spray; cook over medium heat until thoroughly heated, turning once. Remove bacon to paper towel to drain.

Place 1 bacon slice on each muffin half. Top each with a poached egg and 2 tablespoons Mock Hollandaise Sauce. Serve immediately. Yield: 6 servings (about 198 calories per serving).

Mock Hollandaise Sauce:

1 egg yolk, beaten
¾ cup plain low-fat yogurt, divided
1 tablespoon lemon juice
¼ teaspoon salt
⅛ teaspoon dry mustard

Combine egg yolk and ¼ cup yogurt in a small saucepan; cook over low heat, stirring constantly, until smooth and thickened. Stir in remaining yogurt and remaining ingredients; cook until thoroughly heated. (Do not boil.) Yield: ¾ cup. *Betty Quillen,*
Rogers, Arkansas.

DIETERS' SPICY SAUSAGE

1 pound lean ground pork
1 teaspoon rubbed sage
½ teaspoon freshly ground pepper
¼ to ½ teaspoon garlic powder
¼ teaspoon onion powder
¼ teaspoon ground mace
⅛ teaspoon ground allspice
⅛ teaspoon salt (optional)
Dash of ground cloves
Vegetable cooking spray

Combine all ingredients except cooking spray in a large mixing bowl; mix thoroughly. Shape into 6 patties. Cook patties in a large skillet coated with cooking spray over medium heat until browned on both sides. Yield: 6 servings (about 105 calories per serving).
Patra Collins Sullivan,
Columbia, South Carolina.

SPINACH QUICHE

3 eggs, beaten
1 (10-ounce) package frozen chopped
  spinach, thawed and well drained
2 cups low-fat cottage cheese
¼ cup grated Parmesan cheese
3 tablespoons shredded Swiss cheese
½ teaspoon Dijon mustard
¼ teaspoon instant minced onion
¼ teaspoon dry mustard
¼ teaspoon red pepper
⅛ teaspoon salt
Vegetable cooking spray

Combine all ingredients except cooking spray; mix well. Pour into a 9-inch pieplate coated with cooking spray. Bake at 350° for 35 to 40 minutes or until set. Yield: 6 servings (about 135 calories per serving). *Jean Sternberger,*
Annapolis, Maryland.

CHEESY VEGETABLE OMELET

Vegetable cooking spray
¼ cup chopped green pepper
¼ cup chopped onion
1 tablespoon chopped pimiento
2 eggs
2 egg whites
2 tablespoons water
⅛ teaspoon pepper
2 (¾-ounce) slices low-fat process sharp
  Cheddar cheese

Coat a 6-inch skillet with vegetable cooking spray; place over medium heat until hot. Add green pepper, onion, and pimiento; sauté until tender. Remove from skillet, and set aside.

Combine next 4 ingredients; beat well. Recoat the skillet with cooking spray; place over medium heat until hot enough to sizzle a drop of water. Pour in half of egg mixture. As mixture starts to cook, gently lift the edges of the omelet, and tilt the pan to allow any uncooked portion of egg mixture to flow underneath.

Spoon half of vegetable mixture over half of omelet when eggs are set and top is still moist and creamy; top with 1 slice of cheese. Fold unfilled side over filling; place on a warm platter. Repeat for second omelet. Yield: 2 servings (about 147 calories per serving).

COTTAGE-TOPPED
FRENCH TOAST

4 eggs, beaten
¼ cup skim milk
2 teaspoons sugar
1 teaspoon ground cinnamon
Pinch of salt
8 slices whole grain bread
Vegetable cooking spray
Topping (recipe follows)
1 kiwi, sliced or 1 cup fresh strawberries

Combine eggs, milk, sugar, cinnamon, and salt in a medium bowl; stir until blended. Dip bread slices, one at a time, into egg mixture, coating well; drain off excess.

Coat a large skillet with cooking spray; place over low heat until hot. Arrange bread in a single layer in skillet, and cook about 3 minutes on each side or until browned. Repeat with remaining bread slices, coating skillet with additional cooking spray as needed. Spoon 2 tablespoons topping over each hot bread slice. Garnish with kiwi slices or fresh strawberries. Yield: 8 servings (about 159 calories per serving).

Topping:

1 cup low-fat cottage cheese
2 tablespoons sugar
2 teaspoons vanilla extract
1 teaspoon lemon juice

Combine all ingredients in container of electric blender; process until smooth. Yield: 1 cup.
Marise Meier,
Kennesaw, Georgia.

MEXICAN-STYLE SCRAMBLED EGGS

6 flour tortillas
8 eggs
¼ cup water
2 tablespoons chopped canned green chiles
2 tablespoons taco sauce
¼ teaspoon salt
Dash of pepper
Vegetable cooking spray
¾ cup taco sauce, divided
½ cup plus 1 tablespoon shredded Cheddar cheese, divided

Wrap tortillas in foil, and bake at 350° for 7 minutes. Set tortillas aside, and keep warm.

Combine next 6 ingredients in a large bowl; mix well with a wire whisk. Pour egg mixture into a large skillet coated with cooking spray; cook over medium heat, stirring often, until eggs are firm but still moist.

Spoon one-sixth of egg mixture onto each tortilla. Top with 1 tablespoon taco sauce and 1 tablespoon cheese; fold opposite sides over. Garnish each tortilla with 1 tablespoon taco sauce and ½ tablespoon cheese. Yield: 6 servings (about 246 calories per serving).

Susan Buckmaster,
Charlotte, North Carolina.

Flowers For A Morning Fare

Whether you are decorating a simple breakfast tray or the buffet for a formal brunch, let potted annuals add freshness to your morning meal. Available across the South, flats and pots of geraniums, marigolds, petunias, pansies, and other annuals color nurseries and garden centers at this time of the year.

Pop two or three of these bright annuals from a flat, place them in small pots, and you have the perfect adornment for a breakfast tray. Or you may want to pot several small annuals in decorative containers and mix them with foliage plants for a fresh and colorful brunch centerpiece.

If the transplants from flats are too small for your decorating needs, then look for large pots of blooming annuals, such as geraniums, impatiens, or wax begonias, which are also available during the spring months. Slip several of these pots into jardinieres or cachepots to grace a formal buffet table or a sideboard in a striking way.

Once the transplants have adorned the meal, set them outdoors to add seasonal color to the garden.

Crisp, Cool Looks For Spring Tabletops

One way to add new life to traditional china patterns and table settings is to vary your color scheme. Colors can tie together a tabletop and create new looks for any china pattern. There are two basic ways to do this: by working with one solid color or by using two colors that complement each other.

A formal white china pattern becomes even more elegant with a white-on-white color scheme. This sophisticated monochromatic setting is created by using white accessories with fine crystal and silver. Using homespun fabric and handmade baskets and accessories would create a more casual look. For a variation on this monochromatic scheme, add accents of bright colors like red or orange or high-tech colors like black and silver.

A complementary color scheme of two colors, such as violet and yellow, gives a fresh look to a table setting. Other complementary schemes you might choose are blue with orange, red with green, or any shades of these.

Be confident when working with colors, but don't always aim for perfection. Mix your favorites, and follow your taste. Then your table setting will not only please family and guests but also become your own design.

In this stunning table setting, an elegant white china pattern becomes even more formal with the white-on-white color scheme.

Revive Menus With Sprouts

You may have noticed the pleasing colors and interesting shapes of fresh sprouts in the grocery store, but have you tried them? If so, you know that these nutritious, low-calorie tendrils add a new dimension to dishes.

At the market look for sprouts that are fresh and crisp; avoid those that are wilted or rotted and those with dry tips. Alfalfa sprouts should be green and white, and bean sprouts pale ivory. Shorter sprouts are younger and will be more tender.

Sprouts give a high yield. One pound of alfalfa sprouts will measure over 10 cups, and 1 pound of mung bean sprouts will yield over 6⅓ cups. All parts of sprouts are edible just as purchased. But for a more attractive appearance, briefly place sprouts in cold water before using to separate them from their seed cases.

SPROUT MEAT LOAF

1½ pounds ground beef
1½ cups chopped alfalfa sprouts, firmly
    packed
½ cup wheat germ
⅓ cup soft white breadcrumbs
1 medium onion, finely chopped
2 eggs, beaten
1 tablespoon lemon juice
1 teaspoon salt
Dash of pepper
½ cup catsup

Combine all ingredients except catsup in a large bowl; mix lightly. Spread mixture in a 7½- x 3- x 2-inch baking dish; top with catsup. Bake meat loaf at 350° for 1 hour. Yield: 6 servings.
Lenah Miller Elliott,
Destin, Florida.

POLYNESIAN SPROUT SANDWICHES

1 (8-ounce) can pineapple slices,
    undrained
¼ cup plus 1 tablespoon mayonnaise
½ teaspoon teriyaki sauce
¼ teaspon ground ginger
¼ cup teriyaki sauce
2 chicken breast halves, skinned and
    boned
4 (1-ounce) slices Swiss cheese
4 (¾-inch thick) diagonally cut slices
    French bread
1 cup alfalfa sprouts

Drain pineapple, reserving juice; set aside. Combine 2 teaspoons reserved pineapple juice with mayonnaise, ½ teaspoon teriyaki sauce, and ginger; mix well. Cover and chill.

Combine remaining pineapple juice and ¼ cup teriyaki sauce in a shallow dish; set aside. Place each chicken breast between 2 sheets of waxed paper, and flatten to ¼-inch thickness using a meat mallet or rolling pin. Cut each breast in half; add to teriyaki sauce mixture, turning once to coat. Cover; marinate 2 to 4 hours in refrigerator.

Remove chicken; reserve marinade. Broil chicken 5 inches from heat, 2 minutes on each side, basting once with reserved marinade. Top each chicken piece with a slice of cheese and pineapple; broil until cheese melts. Place chicken on bread; spread each sandwich with mayonnaise mixture, and top each with ¼ cup sprouts. Yield: 4 servings.

HAM-SPROUT PATTIES

1 cup mung bean sprouts
½ cup diced ham
½ cup diced green onions with tops
½ cup diced celery
1 large green pepper, chopped
5 eggs, well beaten
Vegetable oil
Commercial picante sauce (optional)

Combine first 6 ingredients, mixing well. Heat small amount of oil in a large skillet. Spoon ¼ cup vegetable-egg mixture into hot oil, shaping into a 3-inch circle with a spatula. Cook until browned on one side; turn and brown other side. Repeat with remaining mixture, adding oil to skillet as necessary. Serve with picante sauce, if desired. Yield: 10 patties.

VEGETABLE PUFF SANDWICH

1¼ cups biscuit mix
¾ cup mayonnaise
1 egg, beaten
2 cups (8 ounces) shredded Swiss cheese
1 cup alfalfa sprouts
1 medium tomato, chopped
½ medium cucumber, unpeeled and
    chopped
¼ teaspoon salt
6 slices bread

Combine biscuit mix, mayonnaise, and egg; stir until blended. Add remaining ingredients except bread to biscuit mixture; mix well. Spread mixture evenly on bread slices; place on an ungreased cookie sheet. Bake at 450° for 10 minutes or until golden brown. Yield: 6 servings.
Karen Rowell,
Berne, Indiana.

Custards At Their Best

A custard makes an incredibly delicious dessert. There are two basic types: baked and stirred. Baked custards are simple. Just place the custard cups or baking dish inside a larger dish filled with about 1 inch of hot water. After baking, remove the custard from the water and allow it to cool. Baked custards are typically topped with a sprinkling of nutmeg, or in the case of flan, with caramelized sugar syrup.

The secret to smooth, velvety stirred custard is to use a heavy saucepan or double boiler, and to stir often enough to keep the mixture evenly heated. Never allow a stirred custard to boil, as this will cause it to become lumpy.

SPANISH FLAN

½ cup sugar
1 (14-ounce) can sweetened condensed
    milk
1 cup milk
3 eggs
3 egg yolks
1 teaspoon vanilla extract
½ teaspoon almond extract

Sprinkle sugar evenly in a heavy saucepan; place over medium heat. Cook, stirring constantly, until sugar melts and syrup is a light golden brown. Pour hot caramel mixture into a 9-inch quiche dish, tilting to coat bottom; set dish aside.

Combine remaining ingredients in container of an electric blender; process at high speed for 10 seconds. Pour mixture into quiche dish. Place dish in a 14- x 11½- x 2¼-inch dish. Pour 1 inch of hot water into larger dish. Bake at 325° for 40 minutes or until a knife inserted in center comes out clean. Remove flan from water; cool. Refrigerate overnight.

Loosen edges with a spatula; quickly invert flan onto serving plate. Yield: 6 to 8 servings.
Connie George,
West Fork, Arkansas.

INDIVIDUAL FLANS

1 cup sugar
1 tablespoon hot water
8 eggs
1½ cups sugar
1 teaspoon vanilla extract
½ teaspoon salt
1 quart milk, scalded

Place 1 cup sugar in a heavy saucepan; place over medium heat. Cook, stirring constantly, until sugar melts and syrup is a light golden brown. Remove from heat; add water, stirring well. Pour hot caramel mixture into 12 custard cups; set aside.

Beat eggs until frothy. Add 1½ cups sugar, vanilla, and salt; beat well. Gradually stir about 1 cup milk into egg mixture; add to remaining milk, stirring constantly. Pour mixture into custard cups. Place cups in two 13- x 9- x 2-inch baking dishes. Pour 1 inch of hot water into larger dishes. Bake at 350° for 25 to 30 minutes or until a knife inserted in center comes out clean. Remove the cups from water, and cool. Refrigerate until chilled.

To serve, loosen edges of custard with a spatula; quickly invert onto dessert plates. Yield: 12 servings.
Karen Sue Woodall,
Mercedes, Texas.

EASY BAKED CUSTARD

3 eggs, slightly beaten
⅔ cup sweetened condensed milk
1 teaspoon vanilla extract
¼ teaspoon salt
1⅓ cups hot water
Dash of ground nutmeg

Combine eggs, milk, vanilla, and salt. Gradually stir in hot water. Pour mixture into a 1-quart lightly greased baking dish; sprinkle with nutmeg. Place dish in a 13- x 9- x 2-inch baking dish. Pour 1 inch of hot water into larger dish. Bake at 325° for 1 hour or until a knife inserted in center comes out clean. Remove custard from water; cool. Refrigerate until chilled, if desired. Yield: 4 servings.
Georgia Taylor,
Davisboro, Georgia.

OLD-FASHIONED STIRRED CUSTARD

2 eggs
½ cup plus 2 tablespoons sugar
1½ tablespoons all-purpose flour
3 cups milk, scalded
1 teaspoon vanilla extract

Beat eggs until frothy. Add sugar and flour, beating until thick. Gradually stir about 1 cup milk into yolk mixture; add to remaining milk, stirring constantly. Pour into top of a double boiler; bring water to a boil. Reduce heat to low; cook, stirring occasionally, for 30 minutes or until thickened. Stir in vanilla. Serve warm or cold. Yield: 3½ cups.
Mrs. Jimmy D. Pritchard,
Huntingdon, Tennessee.

Make The Most Of Homemade Jams And Jellies

The taste of homemade jams and jellies can't be beat, but don't limit yourself to putting the spreads on toast and biscuits. Jams and jellies can be used in many ways—from appetizer to main course to dessert.

TIPSY FRANKS

⅓ cup plum jelly
3 tablespoons prepared mustard
3 tablespoons bourbon
1 pound beef frankfurters, cut into 1-inch pieces

Combine jelly and mustard in a saucepan; cook over low heat, stirring until jelly dissolves. Add bourbon and frankfurters; cook until thoroughly heated. Spoon the mixture into a chafing dish; use wooden picks to serve. Yield: 4 dozen.
Sheree Garvin,
Wilkesboro, North Carolina.

HONOLULU CHICKEN

¼ cup all-purpose flour
½ teaspoon salt
Dash of pepper
4 chicken breast halves, skinned
2 tablespoons vegetable oil
1 cup peach preserves
½ cup commercial barbecue sauce
½ cup diced onion
2 tablespoons soy sauce
1 large green pepper, cut into strips
2 (8-ounce) cans sliced water chestnuts, drained
Hot cooked rice

Combine first 3 ingredients; dredge chicken in flour mixture. Heat oil in a large Dutch oven over medium-high heat; add chicken, and cook 2 to 3 minutes on each side or until browned. Remove chicken; drain off drippings, and return chicken to Dutch oven.

Combine preserves, barbecue sauce, onion, and soy sauce; mix well. Pour mixture over chicken. Bring to a boil; cover, reduce heat, and simmer 40 minutes, stirring occasionally. Stir in green pepper and water chestnuts; continue to cook an additional 15 minutes. Serve over hot cooked rice. Yield: 4 servings.
Lou Taylor,
Pine Bluff, Arkansas.

PEAR PRESERVE CAKE

1 cup butter or margarine, softened
2 cups sugar
4 eggs
2½ cups all-purpose flour, divided
1 teaspoon baking soda
1 teaspoon salt
1 teaspoon ground cinnamon
1 teaspoon ground cloves
1 teaspoon ground nutmeg
1 cup buttermilk
1 teaspoon vanilla extract
1 cup chopped pecans
1 cup raisins
1 cup pear preserves
Sifted powdered sugar (optional)

Cream butter; gradually add sugar, beating at medium speed of an electric mixer until fluffy. Add eggs, one at a time, beating after each addition.

Combine 2 cups flour, soda, salt, and spices; add to creamed mixture alternately with buttermilk, beginning and ending with flour mixture. Mix just until blended after making each addition; stir in vanilla.

Dredge pecans and raisins in remaining ½ cup flour. Stir pecan mixture and pear preserves into batter. Pour into a greased and floured 13- x 9- x 2-inch pan. Bake at 350° for 50 to 55 minutes or until a wooden pick inserted in center comes out clean; cool. Sprinkle with powdered sugar, if desired. Yield: 15 servings.
Brenda Heupel,
Florence, Alabama.

ORANGE MARMALADE CAKE

¾ cup shortening
1½ cups sugar
4 eggs
2¾ cups all-purpose flour
1 teaspoon salt
1 teaspoon ground cinnamon
½ teaspoon ground cloves
1¼ teaspoons baking soda
1¼ cups buttermilk
1 cup orange marmalade
1 cup finely chopped pecans
1 tablespoon grated orange rind
Frosting (recipe follows)

Cream shortening; gradually add sugar, beating at medium speed of an electric mixer until light and fluffy. Add eggs, one at a time, beating after each addition.

Combine flour, salt, and spices, and set aside.

Dissolve soda in buttermilk. Add dry ingredients to creamed mixture alternately with buttermilk, beginning and ending with flour mixture. Mix just until blended after each addition. Stir in marmalade, pecans, and orange rind.

Pour batter into 3 greased and floured 9-inch round cakepans. Bake at 350° for 20 to 25 minutes or until a wooden pick inserted in center comes out clean. Cool in pans 10 minutes; remove from pans, and cool completely.

Spread frosting between layers and on top and sides of cake. Yield: one 3-layer cake.

Frosting:

1 (8-ounce) package cream cheese, softened
1 (3-ounce) package cream cheese, softened
¾ cup butter or margarine, softened
5 cups sifted powdered sugar
1½ tablespoons grated orange rind
¾ teaspoon orange extract
½ teaspoon butter extract

Combine cream cheese and butter, beating until light and fluffy. Add remaining ingredients; beat until smooth. Yield: enough for one 3-layer cake.
*Robert L. King,
Columbus, Ohio.*

Tip: To keep the plate neat while frosting a cake, place three or four strips of waxed paper over the edges of the plate. Position the cake on the plate, and fill and frost it; then carefully pull out the waxed paper strips.

Catch The Fish Habit

For a light entrée, fish is a perfect choice. Its mild flavor is suited to a variety of cooking methods, and the addition of a sauce, topping, or stuffing adds an extra touch.

The key to preparing fish is to use good quality fresh or frozen fish that has been handled properly, and don't overcook it. Fish can usually be cooked directly from the frozen state, but if you're planning to stuff, bread, or cook it in a sauce, thawing is recommended. Since fish is delicate and spoils easily, be sure to handle it as little as possible and let it defrost in the refrigerator.

Cook fish only until the flesh becomes opaque and flakes easily with a fork. You can use the cook-by-the-inch method as an easy rule of thumb: measure fish at the thickest point, and cook 10 minutes for each inch of thickness. If cooking from the frozen state, double the cooking time; if cooking in foil or in a sauce, allow an extra 5 minutes per inch of thickness.

CATFISH PECAN

½ cup cornmeal
1 teaspoon salt
¼ teaspoon pepper
2 (10- to 12-ounce) pan-dressed catfish
3 tablespoons vegetable oil
½ cup pecans, finely chopped
Pecan Rice
Lemon slices (optional)

Combine cornmeal, salt, and pepper. Dredge the fish in cornmeal mixture.

Place coated fish in a lightly greased 13- x 9- x 2-inch pan; drizzle oil over fish. Bake at 500° for 10 minutes. Sprinkle with pecans; bake an additional 5 minutes or until fish flakes easily when tested with a fork. Transfer fish to a serving platter; serve over Pecan Rice. Garnish with lemon slices, if desired. Yield: 2 servings.

Pecan Rice:

¼ cup finely chopped onion
2 tablespoons butter or margarine, melted
2½ cups cooked brown rice
½ cup pecans, finely chopped
2 tablespoons minced fresh parsley
¼ teaspoon salt
¼ teaspoon pepper
¼ teaspoon ground ginger
¼ teaspoon dried whole basil

Sauté onion in butter until tender. Stir in remaining ingredients; reduce heat, and simmer until thoroughly heated. Yield: 2 servings.
*Martha Gayle Peeler,
Ocean Springs, Mississippi.*

FLOUNDER-GRAPEFRUIT BROIL

1 pound flounder fillets
3 tablespoons butter or margarine, melted
¼ teaspoon salt
⅛ teaspoon hot sauce
⅛ teaspoon poultry seasoning
Paprika
1 grapefruit, peeled and sectioned
1 tablespoon chopped fresh parsley

Place flounder in a 13- x 9- x 2-inch baking pan. Combine butter, salt, hot sauce, and poultry seasoning; mix well. Brush half of mixture over fish. Sprinkle with paprika. Broil 3 minutes 5 to 6 inches away from heat.

Top with grapefruit sections; brush with remaining butter mixture. Broil 2 minutes or until fish flakes easily when tested with a fork. Transfer to a serving dish; sprinkle with parsley. Yield: 4 servings.
*Cindy Murphy,
Cleveland, Tennessee.*

CHEESY TROUT FLORENTINE

2 (10-ounce) packages frozen chopped spinach, thawed and drained
2 pounds trout fillets
1 medium onion, chopped
2 tablespoons butter or margarine, melted
1 (10¼-ounce) can cream of shrimp soup, undiluted
½ cup milk
½ cup (2 ounces) shredded Swiss cheese
½ cup (2 ounces) shredded Cheddar cheese
⅛ to ¼ teaspoon curry powder
Dash of pepper
½ cup cracker crumbs
¼ cup grated Parmesan cheese

Spread spinach in a greased 13- x 9- x 2-inch baking dish. Place trout on top.

Sauté onion in butter in a saucepan until tender. Stir in next 6 ingredients; cook over low heat, stirring constantly, until cheese melts. Spoon cheese mixture on top of fish. Top with cracker crumbs and Parmesan cheese. Bake, uncovered, at 350° for 30 minutes or until fish flakes easily when tested with a fork. Yield: 4 servings. *Karla Stith,
Panama City, Florida.*

BAKED SALMON STEAKS

4 (8-ounce) salmon steaks, 1 inch thick
⅓ cup mayonnaise
2 lemons, cut into ¼-inch slices
4 slices bacon, cut in half crosswise
1 medium onion, cut into ¼-inch slices
1 (16-ounce) can whole tomatoes,
undrained and chopped

Place salmon steaks in a lightly greased 13- x 9- x 2-inch baking dish. Spread mayonnaise over top of steaks; top with lemon slices.

Place 2 pieces bacon over each steak; top with onion slices. Pour tomatoes over onion and around steaks. Cover and bake at 350° for 45 minutes or until fish flakes easily when tested with a fork. Yield: 4 servings.

FISH CAKES

2 cups (about 1¼ pounds) cooked, flaked
fish
1 cup cold mashed potatoes
¼ cup minced onion
2 teaspoons lemon juice
2 eggs, beaten
½ teaspoon salt
½ teaspoon pepper
½ cup all-purpose flour
½ cup vegetable oil
Cocktail sauce (optional)

Combine first 7 ingredients; mix well. Shape into 8 patties; dredge in flour. Fry fish cakes in hot oil (330°) about 10 minutes or until golden brown, turning once; drain well. Serve with cocktail sauce, if desired. Yield: 8 servings.

Note: Any canned or leftover fish may be used. *Norma Cowden,*
Shawnee, Oklahoma.

COOKING LIGHT®

Look What
Gelatin Can Do

Over the past few years we've tried hundreds of recipes in search of new ways to prepare low-calorie food. One ingredient we turn to repeatedly is unflavored gelatin. We've used it in expected ways, such as in congealed salads, and unexpected ways, such as in fruit spreads and salad dressings.

Try unflavored gelatin with fruits and fruit juices to come up with your own congealed salads at home. Just remember that it takes one envelope of gelatin to gel two cups of liquid.

When our home economists developed Pineapple-Poppy Seed Dressing, they cut calories by substituting pineapple juice for oil, an ingredient in most regular salad dressings. Without oil, however, the dressing was very thin. When a small amount of unflavored gelatin was added, the consistency of the dressing was just right.

If you've ever made jam or jelly, you know that both require several cups of sugar for a proper gel. But not a speck of sugar goes into Light Strawberry Spread. Once again, we depended on unflavored gelatin for thickening.

Reduced-calorie versions of whipped topping and frozen yogurt also benefit from unflavored gelatin. The gelatin aids in whipping evaporated skim milk to the stiff-peak stage. What a bonus this is to dieters! Calories per tablespoon of Reduced-Calorie Whipped Topping are only 5, compared to 25 calories for an equal amount of sweetened whipped cream.

APPLE CIDER SALAD MOLD

1 envelope unflavored gelatin
2 cups unsweetened apple cider
2 tablespoons sugar
1 tablespoon plus 1 teaspoon lemon juice
2 cups coarsely grated unpeeled apple
½ cup finely chopped celery
Vegetable cooking spray
Lettuce leaves

Sprinkle gelatin over apple cider in a saucepan; let stand 1 minute. Add sugar and lemon juice; cook over low heat, stirring constantly, until gelatin dissolves. Chill until consistency of unbeaten egg white; fold in apple and celery. Pour mixture into a 4-cup mold coated with cooking spray; chill until firm. Unmold on lettuce leaves. Yield: 8 servings (about 61 calories per serving). *Mrs. F. D. Heindel,*
Scott Depot, West Virginia.

PEACH MOUSSE

1 envelope unflavored gelatin
½ cup water
1 (16-ounce) can unsweetened sliced
peaches, undrained
½ cup frozen whipped topping, thawed
¼ teaspoon vanilla extract

Sprinkle unflavored gelatin over water in a small saucepan; let stand 1 minute. Cook over low heat, stirring constantly, until the gelatin dissolves; set aside.

Place undrained peaches in container of an electric blender; process 1 minute or until pureed. Combine peaches and gelatin mixture in a small bowl; mix well. Chill until consistency of unbeaten egg white. Add whipped topping and vanilla; stir with a wire whisk until smooth. Spoon into 4 individual serving dishes; chill until firm. Yield: 4 servings (about 82 calories per serving).
Kitty Sheehan,
Montgomery, Alabama.

MANDARIN SALAD MOLDS

1 envelope unflavored gelatin
2 cups unsweetened orange juice, divided
1 (11-ounce) can mandarin oranges in
light syrup, drained
Vegetable cooking spray
Lettuce leaves
Additional mandarin orange sections
(optional)
1 tablespoon plus 1 teaspoon Cointreau or
other orange-flavored liqueur

Sprinkle gelatin over ½ cup orange juice; let stand 1 minute. Bring remaining 1½ cups orange juice to a boil; add to gelatin mixture, and stir until gelatin dissolves. Chill until consistency of unbeaten egg white.

Stir drained mandarin oranges into gelatin mixture; pour into 4 (6-ounce) custard cups coated with cooking spray. Chill until firm. Unmold on lettuce leaves, and garnish with additional mandarin orange sections, if desired. Pour 1 teaspoon Cointreau over each mold. Yield: 4 servings (about 115 calories per serving without garnish).

Bettye Cortner,
Cerulean, Kentucky.

LEMON-CHIFFON
FROZEN YOGURT

½ cup sugar
1 envelope unflavored gelatin
Dash of salt
1 cup skim milk
2½ cups plain low-fat yogurt
3½ tablespoons lemon juice

Combine sugar, gelatin, and salt in a medium saucepan; add milk, and let stand 1 minute. Cook over low heat, stirring constantly, 5 minutes or until gelatin and sugar dissolve; let cool. Stir in yogurt and lemon juice; chill.

Pour mixture into freezer can of a 1-gallon hand-turned or electric freezer; freeze according to manufacturer's instructions. Serve immediately, or let ripen 1 hour. Yield: 5 cups (about 87 calories per ½-cup serving).

Patricia Ewer,
Cabot, Arkansas.

PINEAPPLE-POPPY SEED DRESSING

1 teaspoon unflavored gelatin
2 cups unsweetened pineapple juice
3 tablespoons honey
1½ tablespoons lemon juice
2 teaspoons poppy seeds

Combine gelatin and pineapple juice in a saucepan; let stand 1 minute. Cook over medium heat, stirring constantly, 2 to 3 minutes or until gelatin dissolves. Stir in remaining ingredients; chill overnight. Serve over fruit salads. Yield: 2¼ cups (about 13 calories per tablespoon).

REDUCED-CALORIE WHIPPED TOPPING

¼ cup evaporated skim milk
¾ teaspoon unflavored gelatin
¼ cup plus 1 teaspoon water
3 tablespoons sugar
1 teaspoon vanilla extract
½ teaspoon lemon juice

Pour evaporated milk into a metal mixing bowl; place in freezer until ice crystals form around edges.

Sprinkle gelatin over water in a small saucepan; let stand 1 minute. Cook over low heat, stirring constantly, until gelatin dissolves. Chill until the consistency of unbeaten egg white.

Beat milk until foamy; gradually add sugar, 1 tablespoon at a time, beating 5 minutes or until soft peaks form. Add gelatin, vanilla, and lemon juice; beat 3 to 4 minutes or until stiff peaks form. Yield: 3 cups (about 5 calories per tablespoon).

Emma Prillhart,
Kingsport, Tennessee.

LIGHT STRAWBERRY SPREAD

2 envelopes unflavored gelatin
1 cup unsweetened apple juice, divided
2 quarts fresh strawberries
1 tablespoon lemon juice

Sprinkle gelatin over ½ cup apple juice; set aside. Combine remaining ½ cup apple juice, strawberries, and lemon juice in a Dutch oven. Cook over medium-low heat 10 to 15 minutes, stirring constantly. Mash strawberry mixture with a fork. Add softened gelatin mixture; stir until gelatin dissolves.

Quickly spoon into hot sterilized jars, leaving ¼-inch headspace. Cover at once with metal lids, and screw bands tight. Cool. Store in refrigerator for up to 1 month. Yield: 6 half pints (about 6 calories per tablespoon).

Bake A Loaf Of Bread

If you love the taste of homemade bread, we have just the recipes for you. All of these breads bake into flavorful loaves to slice and serve anytime.

QUICK CHERRY-NUT BREAD

3 cups biscuit mix
½ cup sugar
⅓ cup all-purpose flour
1 teaspoon ground cardamom
1 egg
1 cup milk
1 cup chopped candied cherries
¾ cup chopped pecans

Combine first 6 ingredients; beat at medium speed of an electric mixer 30 seconds. Stir in cherries and pecans. Spoon into a greased and floured 9- x 5- x 3-inch loafpan; bake at 350° for 50 to 55 minutes or until a wooden pick inserted in center comes out clean. Cool in pan 10 minutes. Remove from pan; cool completely. Yield: 1 loaf.

Linda H. Sutton,
Winston-Salem, North Carolina.

CINNAMON LOAF

4 to 4½ cups all-purpose flour, divided
½ cup sugar
2 packages dry yeast
1½ teaspoons salt
1 cup milk
¼ cup butter or margarine
2 eggs, beaten
¾ cup sugar
1 teaspoon ground cinnamon
⅓ cup raisins
Powdered sugar glaze (recipe follows)

Combine 2 cups flour, ½ cup sugar, yeast, and salt in a large bowl; stir well. Heat milk in a small saucepan to 105° to 115°; add butter, stirring until melted. Gradually add to flour mixture; add eggs. Beat at medium speed of an electric mixer until smooth. Gradually stir in enough of the remaining flour to make a slightly stiff dough.

Turn dough out on a floured surface, and knead until smooth and elastic (8 to 10 minutes). Place in a greased bowl, turning to grease top. Cover and let rise in a warm place (85°), free from drafts, 1 hour or until doubled in bulk.

Punch dough down, and divide in half. Place dough on a lightly floured surface; roll each half into a 12- x 9-inch rectangle. Combine ¾ cup sugar, cinnamon, and raisins. Sprinkle half of cinnamon mixture over each rectangle, leaving a ½-inch margin on all sides. Roll up each rectangle jellyroll fashion, starting at long end. Pinch edges together to seal. Tuck ends under, and place seam side down in 2 greased 9- x 5- x 3-inch loafpans. Cover and let rise in a warm place (85°), free from drafts, for 50 to 60 minutes or until doubled in bulk. Bake at 350° for 40 minutes or until loaves sound hollow when tapped. Partially cool loaves on wire racks. Drizzle loaves with powdered sugar glaze while warm. Yield: 2 loaves.

Powdered Sugar Glaze:

1 cup sifted powdered sugar
½ teaspoon vanilla extract
1½ tablespoons milk

Combine all ingredients, mixing well. Yield: about ½ cup.

Katherine Wickstrom,
Pelham, Alabama.

Tip: To determine the capacity of a utensil, fill a liquid measure with water and pour into utensil. Repeat until utensil is full, noting amount of water used. To determine a utensil's dimensions, measure from the inside edges.

POTATO BREAD

2 medium potatoes, peeled and chopped
2 packages dry yeast
¼ cup warm water (105° to 115°)
2 eggs
About ¾ cup milk
½ cup shortening
¾ cup sugar
2 teaspoons salt
6½ to 7 cups all-purpose flour

Cook potatoes in boiling water to cover 10 minutes or until tender. Drain potatoes, reserving 1 cup liquid (add water to make 1 cup, if necessary). Mash potatoes; add reserved liquid to potatoes, and set aside.

Dissolve yeast in warm water; let stand 5 minutes, and set aside. Beat eggs; add enough milk to eggs to equal 1 cup liquid, and set aside.

Combine shortening, sugar, and salt in a saucepan; cook, stirring constantly, until shortening melts. Cool to 105° to 115°; stir in potatoes, egg mixture, and yeast mixture. Gradually stir in enough flour to make a soft dough.

Turn dough out on a floured surface, and knead until smooth and elastic (8 to 10 minutes). Place in a well-greased bowl, turning to grease top. Cover and let rise in a warm place (85°), free from drafts, 1 hour or until doubled in bulk.

Punch dough down, and divide in half; shape each into a loaf. Place in two well-greased 9- x 5- x 3-inch loaf-pans. Cover and let rise in a warm place (85°), free from drafts, 30 minutes or until doubled in bulk. Bake at 350° for 40 to 45 minutes or until loaves sound hollow when tapped. Yield: 2 loaves.
Sue Reeves,
Murfreesboro, Tennessee.

PIZZA BATTER BREAD

3 cups all-purpose flour, divided
1 package dry yeast
1 teaspoon dried whole oregano
¼ teaspoon garlic powder
1¼ cups water
2 tablespoons butter or margarine
1 tablespoon sugar
1 teaspoon salt
¼ cup finely chopped pepperoni
Grated Parmesan cheese (optional)

Combine 1½ cups flour, yeast, oregano, and garlic powder in a large mixing bowl. Combine water, butter, sugar, and salt in a small saucepan; place over low heat until very warm (120° to 130°), stirring to melt butter. Gradually add water mixture to dry ingredients, mixing at low speed of an electric mixer. Beat 3 minutes at high speed of mixer. Stir in the pepperoni and enough remaining flour to make a soft dough.

Cover and let rise in a warm place (85°), free from drafts, 45 minutes or until doubled in bulk.

Stir dough, and spread evenly in a well-greased 9- x 5- x 3-inch loafpan. Cover and let rise 30 minutes or until doubled in bulk. Sprinkle Parmesan cheese over top of bread, if desired.

Bake at 375° for 35 to 40 minutes or until loaf sounds hollow when tapped. Cool loaf in pan 10 minutes; then remove to wire rack, and cool completely. Yield: 1 loaf.
Deborah Alford,
Independence, Kentucky.

MICROWAVE COOKERY

Chicken Classics In Half The Time

Chicken is a Southern favorite whether it's stuffed and roasted; cooked, chopped, and served with a creamy sauce and dumplings; or wrapped in a crispy coating and oven fried. You'll find some classic recipes here adjusted for the microwave.

Can you imagine roasting a whole stuffed chicken in less than an hour? It's easy with the microwave. The key to a golden skin color is to remove any oily film by scrubbing the chicken with a vegetable brush and hot water before brushing on a browning sauce or glaze. By cooking the chicken uncovered in the microwave, you can achieve a comparable color to conventionally roasted chicken without a browning sauce. Just remember that the skin won't crisp in the microwave.

If you enjoy crispy oven-fried chicken, try our Crunchy Spiced Chicken. We use a mixture of herb-seasoned stuffing mix and spices for the coating, but you can substitute other ingredients. Try using crushed French-fried onions, cereal, or cracker crumbs. Then stir in your favorite spices, parsley, poppy seeds, or toasted sesame seeds for extra flavor. To cook, arrange the pieces on a roasting rack so the juices don't soak into the coating as the chicken cooks. Place the meatier pieces to the outside; then rearrange after half the cooking time, and place the least cooked pieces to the outside.

For another favorite, try our Chicken and Dumplings With Vegetables; it's ready to serve in just 45 minutes. Prepared the conventional way, it takes at least 1 hour to simmer the chicken before cooking the broth and dumplings. With this recipe, chicken pieces and vegetables cook together in a baking dish 22 to 30 minutes. The broth and dumplings take an additional 10 to 15 minutes. Even if you want to stay with your own recipe, cook the chicken in the microwave to save time.

CHICKEN AND DUMPLINGS WITH VEGETABLES

1 small onion, coarsely chopped
1 cup thinly sliced carrots
½ cup sliced celery
1 (2½- to 3-pound) broiler-fryer, cut up
1 (14½-ounce) can chicken broth, undiluted
¼ teaspoon salt
¼ teaspoon pepper
1 cup all-purpose flour
¼ teaspoon baking soda
¼ teaspoon salt
1½ tablespoons shortening
⅓ cup buttermilk
Chopped fresh parsley

Combine onion, carrots, and celery in a 12- x 8- x 2-inch baking dish. Arrange chicken, skin side up, over vegetables. Cover with waxed paper, and microwave at HIGH 22 to 30 minutes or until tender, giving dish a half-turn after 10 minutes. Remove chicken from dish and cool. Skin and bone chicken, and cut meat into bite-size pieces; set aside.

Drain juice from chicken and vegetables into a measuring cup; add water to equal 1 cup liquid. Combine liquid, cooked vegetables, chicken broth, ¼ teaspoon salt, and pepper in a 2½-quart shallow casserole. Cover and microwave at HIGH 5 to 9 minutes or until mixture boils, stirring once. Stir in chicken.

Combine flour, soda, and ¼ teaspoon salt; cut in shortening until mixture resembles coarse meal. Add buttermilk, stirring with a fork until the dry ingredients are moistened. Turn dough out onto a well-floured surface, and knead lightly 4 or 5 times.

Pat dough into ½-inch thickness. Pinch off dough in 1½-inch pieces, and drop into hot chicken mixture around outside edges of casserole. Cover and microwave at HIGH 5 to 6 minutes or until the dumplings are no longer doughy, turning dish once. Sprinkle with parsley. Yield: 4 to 6 servings.

CHICKEN WITH PECAN-RICE DRESSING

½ cup chopped celery
¼ cup chopped onion
1 tablespoon butter or margarine
1¾ cups cooked regular rice
⅓ cup chopped pecans
1 tablespoon commercial blue cheese salad dressing mix
1 tablespoon dried parsley flakes
1 (3½-pound) broiler-fryer
¼ teaspoon salt
1 tablespoon butter or margarine
1 tablespoon browning and seasoning sauce
¼ teaspoon paprika

Combine celery, onion, and butter in a 1-quart casserole. Cover and microwave at HIGH 3 to 4 minutes or until tender, stirring after 1½ minutes. Add rice, pecans, salad dressing mix, and dried parsley, stirring well.

Remove giblets from chicken; reserve for other uses. Scrub chicken lightly with a vegetable brush and hot water to remove any oily film from skin. Pat dry; sprinkle cavity with salt. Fold neck skin over back; secure with a wooden pick. Lift wing tips up and over back; tuck under chicken. Stuff cavity with rice mixture. Close cavity, and secure with wooden picks; truss chicken.

Place 1 tablespoon butter in a 1-cup glass measure, and microwave 45 seconds or until melted. Stir in browning and seasoning sauce and paprika. Place chicken, breast side down, on a microwave roasting rack; brush with browning sauce mixture. Microwave at HIGH 3 minutes. Microwave 20 minutes at MEDIUM (50% power). Turn chicken, breast side up, and brush with remaining butter mixture. Microwave at MEDIUM 25 to 30 minutes or until drumsticks are easy to move. Yield: 4 servings.

CRUNCHY SPICED CHICKEN

1¾ cups herb-seasoned stuffing mix, finely crushed
1½ teaspoons garlic salt
1½ teaspoons pepper
¾ teaspoon paprika
¼ to ½ teaspoon poultry seasoning
½ cup milk
1 egg, beaten
1 (2½- to 3-pound) broiler-fryer, cut up and skinned

Combine first 5 ingredients in a plastic bag; shake to mix, and set aside.
Combine milk and egg; mix well, and set aside.

Place 2 or 3 pieces of chicken in bag; shake well. Dip chicken in egg mixture; return to bag, and shake again. Repeat procedure with remaining chicken. Press coating into place, if necessary.

Place chicken, bone side down, on a microwave roasting rack, arranging meatier pieces to the outside. Cover with waxed paper; microwave chicken at HIGH for 10 minutes.

Rearrange chicken so less cooked pieces are to the outside. Microwave at HIGH 8 to 11 minutes or until juices run clear and meat near bone is no longer pink. Yield: 4 servings.

Stir Up A Skillet Entrée

Recipes don't come any simpler than those for skillet entrées. Since all the ingredients cook together in one utensil and require little attention during cooking, you can turn your efforts to the remainder of the meal.

PEPPER STEAK

2 pounds (½-inch-thick) boneless round steak
2 tablespoons vegetable oil
1 cup hot water
2 tablespoons soy sauce
1 teaspoon molasses
½ teaspoon ground ginger
1 clove garlic, crushed
1 medium onion, sliced
2 medium-size green peppers, cut into strips
1 (8-ounce) can sliced water chestnuts, drained
¼ cup water
1 tablespoon cornstarch
10 cherry tomatoes, halved

Partially freeze steak; slice diagonally across grain into 3- x ½-inch strips, and set aside. Heat vegetable oil in a large skillet; add steak. Cook, stirring often, until steak is browned.

Combine 1 cup water, soy sauce, molasses, ginger, and garlic; mix well, and pour over steak. Cover and simmer 30 minutes. Add onion; cover and simmer 15 minutes. Add green pepper and sliced water chestnuts; cover and simmer 10 minutes.

Combine ¼ cup water and cornstarch; mix well. Add to skillet; cook over medium heat, stirring until smooth and thickened. Stir in tomatoes. Yield: 6 servings. *Mrs. Hugh L. Mosher, Huntsville, Alabama.*

PICADILLO

1 pound ground beef
1 large onion, finely chopped
1 clove garlic, minced
2 tablespoons vegetable oil
1 large tomato, peeled and chopped
1 medium apple, peeled and chopped
1 to 2 jalapeño peppers, seeded and finely chopped
⅓ cup raisins
¾ teaspoon salt
¼ teaspoon pepper
¼ teaspoon ground cinnamon
¼ teaspoon ground cloves
Hot cooked rice

Brown ground beef, onion, and garlic in hot vegetable oil in a large skillet, stirring to crumble beef. Add the next 8 ingredients, mixing well; reduce heat, and simmer 25 minutes. Serve over rice. Yield: 6 servings. *Nora Henshaw, Castle, Oklahoma.*

APPLE CHICKEN

½ cup all-purpose flour
1 teaspoon salt
¼ teaspoon pepper
8 chicken breast halves, skinned and boned (about 2 pounds)
¼ cup butter or margarine
½ cup apple brandy or apple juice
2 tablespoons lemon juice
1 tablespoon honey
1 (20-ounce) can sliced apples, undrained

Combine flour, salt, and pepper in a plastic or paper bag; shake to mix. Place 2 or 3 pieces of chicken in bag; shake well. Repeat procedure with remaining chicken pieces.

Melt butter in a large skillet over medium heat; add chicken breast halves, and cook 5 to 8 minutes on each side or until golden brown.

Combine brandy, lemon juice, and honey; mix well, and pour over chicken. Turn chicken to coat; add sliced apples. Cover, reduce heat, and simmer for 20 minutes. Transfer chicken and apples to serving platter; drizzle pan drippings over top. Yield: 8 servings.

Marge Killmon, Annandale, Virginia.

WINE-POACHED CHICKEN BREASTS

4 chicken breast halves, skinned and
  boned
½ pound fresh mushrooms, sliced
2 tablespoons chopped fresh parsley
¾ teaspoon salt
½ teaspoon dried whole tarragon
¼ teaspoon pepper
¾ cup Chablis or other dry white wine

Place chicken and mushrooms in a large skillet; sprinkle with parsley, salt, tarragon, and pepper. Add wine; cover and cook over medium heat 20 to 25 minutes or until chicken is tender. Yield: 4 servings.

Martha Edington,
Knoxville, Tennessee.

From Our Kitchen To Yours

Herbs can make ordinary food extraordinarily good. Knowing how much of an herb to use, how to substitute dried for fresh, and which herbs to blend lets you enhance the flavors of foods without disguising them. You can capture the flavor of fresh herbs for later use by drying or freezing, as well. Here are some suggestions.

Gathering Fresh Herbs

If you're gathering herbs, use kitchen shears to trim leaves and stems. Do this on a sunny morning after the dew has evaporated but before the sun is very hot. Try to cut herbs when the leaves are still green and just before the plants start to bloom. Mint has the best flavor when it's harvested in full bloom. Some herbs, such as basil, summer savory, chives, and oregano, can be harvested only three or four times during the summer, while others, including rosemary, thyme, sage, and winter savory, can be gathered year-round.

Drying Herbs

This is the most common method of preservation. You can air-dry herbs or use a conventional oven, a microwave oven, or a dehydrator.

To air-dry, put herbs on a nylon screen in a room with low humidity, such as an air-conditioned room. Prop the screen or tray up to let air circulate above and below. To dry a small amount of herbs, just spread them in a thin layer on paper towels. You can also hang small bunches of herbs on a clothesline in a dry, well-ventilated place, such as an attic, screened porch, or air-conditioned room, until they are crispy dry. The drying time will vary from several days to more than a week, depending on the thickness of the herbs and stems.

Oven drying is faster, but be careful not to use too much heat. If you can smell the herbs, their natural oils are evaporating and the temperature is too high. Set the oven at the lowest temperature possible. It's difficult to keep the heat low enough in an electric oven, but the heat given off by the pilot light in a gas oven is perfect. Place a screen across the oven rack, and spread a single layer of herbs on it. Leave the door partially open to let moisture escape.

You can dry small amounts of herbs in a microwave oven. Put four or five leafy stems between paper towels; set the microwave on HIGH for two to three minutes. Check herbs, and microwave a little longer if necessary.

If you use the dehydrator, herbs take about two to three hours, depending on the thickness of the leaf. Arrange the herbs on the drying trays, and set the thermostat at 100 degrees.

Herbs are dry when they crumble easily. The stems should be brittle and break when bent. If they're not totally dry, they may mold. Herbs need to be stored as soon as they're dry, so flavor will not be lost. Store them in an airtight, opaque container or in an airtight jar in a dark place. Keep in the coolest place available, preferably below 60 degrees. This will keep the herbs from losing their color and flavor. It's best to keep only small quantities of herbs ready to use in your kitchen. Never store them over the cook surface.

Freezing Herbs

Parsley, dill, chives, and basil freeze well and keep their aroma and flavor. To freeze, don't blanch or steam them; just wash, and let dry. Then wrap small amounts in packets of foil, and freeze.

You can also pack chopped herbs into ice cube trays and add just enough water to cover; then freeze. When they're frozen, you can transfer the cubes to labeled plastic bags. If you're making a soup or spaghetti sauce, just drop in a cube.

Hints on Cooking With Herbs

—It's best to crush or grind herbs just before using. If this is done for storage purposes, the aroma as well as the flavor will be affected.

—Use herbs with a light hand. Their aromatic oils are strong. Remember that it's easy to add more herbs later.

—Blend herbs carefully. Choose a leading flavor, and combine one to four less-pronounced flavors with it. Never blend the strong herbs like rosemary, sage, or basil.

—Very finely cut or chop the leaves of fresh herbs. For some recipes, herbs should be ground in a mortar. The more cut surface exposed, the more completely the flavor can be absorbed.

—Always remember the flavor of dried herbs is much more concentrated than the fresh; therefore, use only about one-third of the amount of dried leaves to replace the fresh.

—Cooking too long can make herbs become bitter or lose their aroma and flavor, but a little heat makes them release flavor. So add herbs during the last few minutes of cooking, except for bay leaves, which should be added at the beginning. For cold foods, such as dips, cheese, vegetables, and salad dressings, herbs should be added at least several hours before serving.

Spruce Up Meals With Fresh Spinach

The arrival of spring signals warmer weather, budding trees, and garden-fresh spinach. To help you get the most from the early spinach harvest, we have tested some savory recipes.

Besides being tasty, spinach is very nutritious. The dark-green leaves have high levels of vitamin A, potassium, calcium, and iron. Although the body can't use iron from plants as easily as iron from meats, you can get more benefit from iron in spinach and other plants by serving them with a food that is high in vitamin C, such as orange juice.

SPINACH-LAMB SALAD

½ pound fresh spinach, torn into bite-size
  pieces
1 medium-size green pepper, cut into thin
  strips
½ cup sliced mushrooms
1 cup crumbled feta cheese
1½ cups cooked, thinly sliced lamb strips
1 medium tomato, cut into wedges
Yogurt Dressing

Combine spinach, green pepper, mushrooms, and cheese, tossing gently; arrange on a serving platter. Place lamb in center of platter, and garnish with tomato wedges. Serve with Yogurt Dressing. Yield: 4 servings.

Yogurt Dressing:
¾ cup plain yogurt
1 green onion with top, diced
1 clove garlic
1 tablespoon lemon juice
1 tablespoon olive oil
Pinch of salt
Pinch of white pepper

Combine all ingredients; stir well. Chill several hours. Remove garlic clove before serving. Yield: 1 cup.

*Ella C. Stivers,
Abilene, Texas.*

FRESH SPINACH SANDWICHES

1½ pounds fresh spinach
¾ cup mayonnaise
¾ teaspoon pepper
½ teaspoon garlic salt
12 slices whole wheat bread
½ pound bacon, cooked and crumbled

Remove stems from spinach; wash leaves thoroughly. Drain; finely chop, and set aside.

Combine mayonnaise, pepper, and garlic salt; stir well. Lightly toast bread, if desired. Spread mayonnaise mixture evenly over each slice of bread. Top half of slices with spinach and bacon; place remaining slices of bread, mayonnaise side down, over spinach mixture to make a sandwich. Cut into halves or wedges; secure with wooden picks. Yield: 6 servings.

*Barbara Beard,
Greenwell Springs, Louisiana.*

GREEK SPINACH PIE

2½ pounds fresh spinach
6 eggs, beaten
1 cup chopped green onions with tops
1 cup (4 ounces) shredded mozzarella cheese
½ cup grated Parmesan cheese
½ cup crumbled feta cheese
¼ cup vegetable oil
2 teaspoons dried whole dillweed
¼ teaspoon pepper
1 (16-ounce) package commercial frozen phyllo pastry, thawed
1 cup butter or margarine, melted

Remove stems from spinach; wash leaves thoroughly. Place fresh spinach in a large Dutch oven (do not add water), and cook, covered, 3 to 5 minutes or until tender. Drain spinach well, and coarsely chop.

Combine spinach and next 8 ingredients in a large bowl; mix well, and set spinach mixture aside.

Trim phyllo pastry to fit a 13- x 9- x 2-inch baking dish. Brush each of 7 sheets of phyllo with melted butter, and layer in a greased 13- x 9- x 2-inch baking dish.

Spoon half of spinach mixture evenly over pastry. Brush 7 more sheets of phyllo with butter, and layer over spinach mixture. Repeat procedure with remaining spinach mixture and phyllo sheets. Bake at 350° for 1 hour or until golden brown. Yield: 8 servings.

*Mary J. Ealey,
Smithfield, Virginia.*

Bacon—Not Just For Breakfast

Cooking with bacon comes naturally to Southerners, who enjoy its flavor and texture in salads, casseroles, quiches, and sandwiches.

Bacon is also used to help tenderize wild game and less tender cuts of meat as in Bacon-Wrapped Flank Steak. The bacon strips prevent the lean meat from drying out and becoming tough while it's cooking.

BACON-WRAPPED FLANK STEAK

1 (1½- to 2-pound) flank steak
1 teaspoon garlic salt
Salt and pepper to taste
4 slices bacon
1 medium-size green pepper, chopped
1 medium onion, chopped
1 (14½-ounce) can stewed tomatoes, undrained
2 (8-ounce) cans tomato sauce
2 teaspoons parsley flakes
2 tablespoons Worcestershire sauce
2 tablespoons soy sauce
5 to 6 drops of hot sauce

Score surface of steak with a knife; rub with garlic salt, salt, and pepper.

Cook bacon in large skillet until limp; remove bacon, reserving drippings in skillet. Arrange bacon crosswise over top of steak; secure on side with wooden picks. Brown steak in bacon drippings over medium heat; drain. Add remaining ingredients. Bring to a boil; cover, reduce heat, and simmer 1 hour. Yield: 6 servings.

*Barbara Carr,
North Little Rock, Arkansas.*

ITALIAN ZUCCHINI CASSEROLE

7 to 8 medium zucchini, cut into ¼-inch slices
8 slices bacon
1 large onion, chopped
1 large clove garlic, crushed
4 slices bread, torn
2 cups (8 ounces) shredded Cheddar cheese
1 (15-ounce) can tomato sauce
1 teaspoon Italian seasoning
⅛ teaspoon pepper
¼ cup grated Parmesan cheese

Cook zucchini in a small amount of boiling water 5 to 8 minutes; drain well.

Cook bacon in a medium skillet until crisp; remove bacon, reserving drippings in skillet. Crumble bacon, and set aside. Sauté onion and garlic in drippings until tender; drain. Combine onion mixture, zucchini, bacon, and remaining ingredients except Parmesan cheese; mix well. Pour into a lightly greased 13- x 9- x 2-inch baking dish. Bake at 350° for 20 minutes; sprinkle with Parmesan cheese, and bake 5 minutes. Yield: 10 to 12 servings.

*Daisy Cotton,
Edcouch, Texas.*

BACON-TOPPED POTATO SALAD

6 medium-size red potatoes
2 eggs, slightly beaten
¼ cup sugar
½ teaspoon salt
¼ cup vinegar
½ cup milk
6 slices bacon
½ cup chopped onion
2 tablespoons mayonnaise

Cook potatoes in boiling water until tender; peel and cut into large cubes.

Combine next 5 ingredients; beat until smooth. Set aside. Cook bacon in skillet until crisp; remove bacon, reserving ¼ cup drippings in skillet. Stir in egg mixture; cook over low heat, stirring constantly, until smooth and thickened. Crumble 4 slices bacon; stir crumbled bacon and egg mixture into potatoes. Cool. Stir in onion and mayonnaise. Crumble 2 slices bacon; sprinkle on top. Cover; chill 3 to 4 hours. Yield: 6 to 8 servings.

*Ruth Sherrer,
Fort Worth, Texas.*

BACON QUICHE

Pastry for 9-inch, deep-dish pie
8 slices bacon, cooked and crumbled
2½ tablespoons chopped pimiento-stuffed olives
2 tablespoons chopped green pepper
2 tablespoons chopped onion
1 (4-ounce) can sliced mushrooms, drained
2 cups (8 ounces) shredded Swiss cheese
5 eggs
2 cups half-and-half
¼ teaspoon dry mustard
Cooked bacon curls (optional)
Green pepper strips (optional)

Line a 9-inch, deep-dish pieplate with pastry. Trim excess pastry around edges; fold edges under, and flute. Prick bottom and sides of pastry with a fork. Bake at 400° for 3 minutes; remove from oven, and gently prick with a fork. Bake 5 minutes longer. Cool.

Sprinkle bacon, olives, green pepper, and onion evenly into pastry shell; top with mushrooms and cheese. Set aside.

Beat eggs; add half-and-half and mustard, mixing well. Pour mixture into pastry shell. Let stand 10 minutes. Bake at 350° for 45 to 50 minutes or until set. Let stand 10 minutes before serving. Garnish with bacon curls and pepper strips, if desired. Yield: one 9-inch quiche.
Cindy Black,
Gatlinburg, Tennessee.

A New Twist To Pasta

There's no better way to mix friendship with food than with pasta as the Italians do. But if you're tired of the usual lasagna or spaghetti with meat sauce, try stuffing the pasta.

CREAMY CHICKEN MANICOTTI

8 manicotti shells
1 (10¾-ounce) can creamy chicken mushroom soup, undiluted
½ cup commercial sour cream
2 cups chopped cooked chicken
¼ cup chopped onion
1 (4-ounce) can sliced mushrooms, drained
2 tablespoons butter or margarine, melted
¼ cup warm water
½ teaspoon chicken-flavored bouillon granules
1 cup (4 ounces) shredded Cheddar cheese

Cook manicotti shells according to package directions, omitting the salt; drain and set aside.

Combine soup and sour cream; mix well. Combine half of soup mixture and chicken; mix well. Reserve remaining soup mixture; set aside. Stuff manicotti shells with chicken mixture; place in a greased 12- x 8- x 2-inch baking dish.

Sauté onion and mushrooms in butter in a large skillet until tender; set aside. Combine water and bouillon granules, stirring until dissolved; add to reserved soup mixture, mixing well. Stir soup mixture into mushroom mixture; mix well. Spoon over manicotti; bake, uncovered at 350° for 15 minutes. Sprinkle with Cheddar cheese, and bake an additional 5 minutes. Yield: 4 to 6 servings.
Harriett Ransbottom,
Richmond, Texas.

CANNELLONI

12 cannelloni shells
3 cups tomato sauce
2 tablespoons grated Parmesan cheese
¼ cup diced onion
1 teaspoon minced garlic
2 tablespoons olive oil
1 (10-ounce) package frozen chopped spinach, thawed and drained
1 pound ground beef
¼ cup plus 1 tablespoon grated Parmesan cheese
2 tablespoons whipping cream
2 eggs, slightly beaten
½ teaspoon dried whole oregano
¼ cup plus 2 tablespoons butter or margarine
¼ cup plus 2 tablespoons all-purpose flour
1 cup milk
1 cup whipping cream
⅛ teaspoon white pepper
2 tablespoons butter or margarine

Cook cannelloni shells according to package directions; drain and set aside.

Combine tomato sauce and 2 tablespoons Parmesan cheese in a small saucepan; cook over medium heat, stirring constantly, until mixture is heated. Spread 1 cup tomato mixture in a lightly greased 13- x 9- x 2-inch baking dish; set aside remaining sauce.

Sauté onion and garlic in olive oil in a large skillet until tender. Add spinach; cook, stirring often, until the spinach is just tender. Remove spinach mixture, and set aside.

Add ground beef; cook over medium heat until brown, stirring to crumble; drain. Discard drippings from skillet. Add spinach, ¼ cup plus 1 tablespoon

Parmesan cheese, 2 tablespoons whipping cream, eggs, and oregano; mix well. Stuff cannelloni shells with ground beef mixture and place on tomato mixture in baking dish; set aside.

Melt ¼ cup plus 2 tablespoons butter in a heavy saucepan over low heat; add flour, stirring until smooth. Cook 1 minute, stirring constantly. Gradually add milk and 1 cup whipping cream; cook over medium heat, stirring constantly, until mixture is thickened and bubbly. Stir in pepper. Pour over cannelloni; spoon remaining tomato mixture over cream sauce. Dot with 2 tablespoons butter. Bake, uncovered, at 375° for 20 minutes. Yield: 6 servings.
Mark C. Carl,
Burke, Virginia.

SPINACH-STUFFED SHELLS

24 jumbo macaroni shells
1 (32-ounce) jar spaghetti sauce with mushrooms
1 (10-ounce) package frozen chopped spinach, thawed and drained
2 cups ricotta cheese
2 cups (8 ounces) shredded mozzarella cheese
1 small onion, diced
½ cup grated Parmesan cheese
2 tablespoons chopped fresh parsley
1 teaspoon dried whole oregano
Dash of hot sauce
Dash of ground nutmeg
¼ cup grated Parmesan cheese

Cook macaroni shells according to package directions; drain and set aside.

Spoon 1 cup spaghetti sauce into a lightly greased 13- x 9- x 2-inch baking dish; set aside remaining sauce.

Combine next 9 ingredients; mix well. Stuff each macaroni shell with 1½ tablespoons spinach mixture, and arrange in baking dish. Spoon remaining sauce over shells; sprinkle with ¼ cup Parmesan cheese. Cover and bake at 350° for 30 to 40 minutes. Yield: 6 to 8 servings.
Mrs. James A. Tuthill,
Virginia Beach, Virginia.

Right: *Try nature's sweetener on a slice of apple coated with Peanut Butter-Honey Dip, in crisp Honey-Glazed Carrots, or in thick slices of Honey Wheat Bread (recipes on pages 18 and 19).*

Page 64: *When it's time for dessert, no one will be able to resist these rich offerings: (clockwise from top) Rich Chocolate Cheesecake, Orange Cheesecake, or Pecan Cheesecake (recipes on page 38).*

Above: *For a change of pace, enjoy Broccoli-Mushroom Omelet (page 45) with morning coffee. Made in a 10-inch pan and packed with cheese and vegetables, this omelet is large enough to serve two.*

Left: *Each serving of Eggs Benedict (page 49) has only 198 calories, yet this dish is special enough for a fancy brunch. Fresh strawberries on the side give a bright splash of color.*

Far left: *Carolina Marmalade Biscuits (page 42) and sliced Cheddar-Nut Bread (page 41) are welcome ways to start the morning.*

Wild Rice Makes It Special

The grayish-brown grain we call wild rice remains relatively expensive, so most of us consider it a luxury item. But a little of this delicacy goes a long way when you want to make a menu extra special.

Although wild rice is technically not a true rice, it's prepared and served similarly. For plain wild rice, follow the package instructions or the basic procedure in the recipes below. Keep in mind that overcooking increases volume but makes the rice mushy. Sometimes undercooking is desirable for certain dishes, such as salads. The rice will have a chewier, nut-like texture. Undercooking is also best if the rice is going to be used in a casserole or in another dish with additional cooking.

For fun, try "popping" wild rice, and use it as a gourmet topping for soups and salads. You can also season it as you would popcorn and serve it that way. But don't expect the same volume as popcorn. The rice puffs only slightly; one tablespoon of wild rice yields only about two tablespoons when popped.

CHICKEN-WILD RICE CASSEROLE

1 (3-pound) broiler-fryer
⅔ cup uncooked wild rice
2 cups water
½ to 1 teaspoon salt
1 medium onion, chopped
1 medium-size green pepper, chopped
1 (10¾-ounce) can cream of mushroom soup, undiluted
1 (8-ounce) can water chestnuts, drained and sliced
1 (2-ounce) jar diced pimiento, drained
1 cup mayonnaise
1 cup (4 ounces) shredded Cheddar cheese

Place chicken in a Dutch oven, and add water to cover. Bring to a boil; cover, reduce heat, and simmer 1 hour or until tender. Remove chicken, and let cool. Bone chicken, and chop meat; set aside.

Wash wild rice in 3 changes of hot water; drain. Combine rice, 2 cups water, and salt in a medium saucepan; bring to a boil. Cover, reduce heat to low, and simmer 30 to 45 minutes or until the rice is tender.

Spoon cooked rice into a lightly greased 8-inch square baking dish.

Combine chicken and remaining ingredients except cheese; mix well. Spoon mixture over chicken. Bake, uncovered, at 350° for 25 minutes. Remove from oven, and sprinkle with cheese. Return to oven, and bake 5 minutes or until cheese melts. Yield: 6 to 8 servings.
Alice G. Pahl,
Raleigh, North Carolina.

SAUSAGE AND WILD RICE

⅔ cup uncooked wild rice
2 cups water
½ to 1 teaspoon salt
1 pound bulk pork sausage
1 medium-size red onion, chopped
1 pound fresh mushrooms, sliced
1 teaspoon Worcestershire sauce
1 (10¾-ounce) can cream of mushroom soup, undiluted
½ cup water

Wash wild rice in 3 changes of hot water; drain. Combine rice, 2 cups water, and salt in a medium saucepan; bring to a boil. Cover, reduce heat to low, and simmer 30 to 45 minutes or until rice is tender. Set aside.

Combine sausage, onion, and mushrooms in Dutch oven; cook over medium heat until meat is brown and vegetables are tender. Drain. Stir in cooked rice and remaining ingredients; mix well. Simmer 10 minutes or until heated. Yield: 6 servings.
Anna Lou Beckes,
Highlands, North Carolina.

WILD RICE SALAD

⅔ cup uncooked wild rice
2 cups water
½ to 1 teaspoon salt
3 green onions, cut into ½-inch pieces
1 (8-ounce) can sliced water chestnuts, drained
⅓ cup chopped walnuts
⅓ cup mayonnaise or salad dressing
Dash of pepper
Lettuce leaves

Wash wild rice in 3 changes of hot water; drain. Combine rice, 2 cups water, and salt in a medium saucepan; bring to a boil. Cover, reduce heat to low, and simmer 30 to 45 minutes or until the rice is tender.

Combine cooked rice, onions, water chestnuts, walnuts, mayonnaise, and pepper; stir well. Chill 3 to 4 hours. Serve on lettuce leaves. Yield: 8 servings.
Dorothy Burgess,
Huntsville, Texas.

POPPED WILD RICE

Vegetable oil
3 tablespoons uncooked wild rice

Heat 1 inch of oil in a small skillet to 390° or until very hot. Place 1 tablespoon wild rice in a small metal strainer; dip strainer into oil, and fry rice 20 to 25 seconds or until rice swells and rises to the surface of oil. Drain on paper towels.

Repeat frying process with remaining rice. Yield: approximately 6 tablespoons popped rice.

Note: If the oil is not hot enough, the rice will brown but not puff.

Perk Up Foods With Horseradish

Horseradish is one of the world's oldest and most popular condiments. The peppery root can add delicate flavor or a delightful punch to food, depending on the amount used. We were conservative when adding the potentially powerful ingredient, but you can add more if you desire.

Keep in mind that proper handling and storage of grated fresh or prepared horseradish is important since high heat and long exposure to air will destroy its pungent flavor. When using horseradish in dishes that are cooked, add it near the end of the cooking process, and do not boil. Be sure to refrigerate fresh and prepared horseradish.

CRANBERRY-HORSERADISH DIP

1 cup jellied whole-berry cranberry sauce
½ cup catsup
¼ cup lemon juice
2 green onions, chopped
2 tablespoons chopped celery leaves
2 tablespoons prepared horseradish
1 tablespoon prepared mustard
Cooked shrimp

Combine all ingredients except shrimp in container of an electric blender; process until smooth. Serve with chilled cooked shrimp. Yield: about 2 cups. *Myrtle P. Richardson,*
Grand Junction, Colorado.

CORNED BEEF ROLL

4 eggs, separated
2 tablespoons sugar
½ cup all-purpose flour
1 tablespoon chopped fresh parsley
1 (12-ounce) can corned beef
½ cup mayonnaise
½ cup diced celery
¼ cup sweet pickle relish
2 tablespoons prepared horseradish
1 tablespoon prepared mustard
16 to 18 pimiento-stuffed olives
1 (5-ounce) jar pimiento cheese spread
Chopped pecans (optional)
Chopped parsley (optional)

Grease an 18- x 12- x 1-inch jellyroll pan with vegetable oil; line with waxed paper. Grease waxed paper.

Beat egg yolks at high speed of an electric mixer until thick and lemon colored; set aside. Beat egg whites (at room temperature) until foamy. Gradually add sugar, beating until stiff peaks form. Fold egg yolks, flour, and 1 tablespoon parsley into egg whites. Spread batter evenly into prepared pan. Bake at 400° for 8 minutes.

Place waxed paper (longer than jellyroll pan) over bread. Holding both ends of waxed paper and pan, quickly invert pan. Remove pan, and carefully peel paper from bread. Starting at long side, carefully roll up bread jellyroll fashion. Place roll on a wire rack, seam side down, for 10 minutes.

Combine corned beef, mayonnaise, celery, pickle relish, horseradish, and mustard, mixing well. Unroll bread onto waxed paper; spread corned beef mixture evenly over surface. Arrange olives in a single row along edge of long side. Starting at the long side, carefully roll up bread jellyroll fashion.

Slide roll onto a serving plate, seam side down; chill 1 hour. Spread pimiento cheese on sides and top of roll. Garnish with chopped pecans and chopped parsley, if desired. Chill. Yield: 14 to 16 (1-inch) slices.

Bridget H. Bohince,
Leesburg, Virginia.

HORSERADISH SALAD

1 (3-ounce) package lemon-flavored gelatin
1 (3-ounce) package lime-flavored gelatin
2 cups boiling water
1 cup mayonnaise
3 tablespoons prepared horseradish
1 (15½-ounce) can crushed pineapple, undrained
1 (2-ounce) jar diced pimiento, undrained
Lettuce leaves (optional)

Dissolve gelatin in boiling water. Combine gelatin mixture, mayonnaise, and horseradish in container of an electric blender; process until smooth. Stir in pineapple and pimiento.

Pour mixture into an oiled 6-cup mold. Chill until firm. Unmold on lettuce leaves, if desired. Yield: 12 servings.

Virginia Salmon,
Natchez, Mississippi.

YOGURT-HORSERADISH SAUCE

1 cup plain low-fat yogurt
1½ tablespoons prepared horseradish
1 teaspoon lemon juice
¼ teaspoon red pepper
¼ teaspoon black pepper
⅛ teaspoon salt

Combine all ingredients, mixing well. Serve with fish or vegetables. Yield: about 1¼ cups.

Evelyn Milam,
Knoxville, Tennessee.

CARROTS WITH HORSERADISH GLAZE

2 pounds carrots, scraped and cut diagonally into ½-inch slices
¼ cup butter or margarine
⅓ cup honey
2 tablespoons prepared horseradish

Cook carrots, covered, in a small amount of salted water 18 to 20 minutes or until tender; drain.

Melt butter in a large saucepan over low heat; stir in honey and horseradish. Gently stir in carrots; cook until thoroughly heated. Yield: 6 to 8 servings.

Grace Bogema Setterholm,
Tulsa, Oklahoma.

Reach For Peanut Or Olive Oil

When a recipe calls for peanut or olive oil rather than vegetable oil, do you know the difference? While you can interchange types of cooking oil in many cases, it helps to know the special qualities of each to get the best result.

Peanut oil is ideal for frying. It's flavorless and doesn't transfer other flavors, so you can use it over and over. Oriental cooks often use it in recipes.

Green- to golden-colored olive oil offers a special fruity flavor to food. Since it does have a unique taste, use it in salad dressings or marinades where the flavor can be prominent. For the strongest olive oil flavor, select one with a green to green-gold color. The darker the color, the stronger the taste.

SCALLOPS PROVENÇAL

1 pound fresh scallops, cut in half
3 tablespoons lemon juice
½ pound fresh mushrooms, sliced
½ cup sliced green onions with tops
¼ cup plus 2 tablespoons olive oil, divided
2 large tomatoes, peeled and coarsely chopped
2 tablespoons chopped fresh parsley
½ teaspoon dried whole oregano

Combine scallops and lemon juice in a medium bowl; set aside. Sauté mushrooms and green onions in 2 tablespoons olive oil in a medium skillet until tender. Stir in tomato, parsley, and oregano; cook over low heat 5 minutes, and set aside.

Sauté scallops in ¼ cup olive oil in a medium skillet 3 to 5 minutes. Drain. Combine scallops and vegetable mixture. Yield: 4 servings.

Ashlyn Ritch,
Forsyth, Georgia.

CHICKEN TEMPURA DELIGHT

1 egg, beaten
2 tablespoons all-purpose flour
1 tablespoon water
½ teaspoon salt
2 pounds boneless chicken breasts, cut into 1-inch pieces
All-purpose flour
¾ cup peanut oil
Sweet-and-Sour Pineapple Sauce

Combine egg, flour, water, and salt; mix well, and chill 1 hour. Dip chicken pieces into batter; dredge in flour. Heat oil in a wok to 375°; cook chicken in hot oil until lightly browned. Drain. Serve with Sweet-and-Sour Pineapple Sauce. Yield: about 6 dozen appetizers.

Sweet-and-Sour Pineapple Sauce:

1 (8-ounce) can crushed pineapple
1 (6-ounce) can unsweetened pineapple juice
2 tablespoons sugar
1 tablespoon cornstarch
2 teaspoons prepared mustard
2 tablespoons cider vinegar

Drain pineapple, reserving liquid. Combine reserved liquid and pineapple juice, adding enough water if necessary to equal 1 cup liquid. Combine ¾ cup juice and sugar in a small saucepan; Cook over medium heat, stirring constantly until sugar dissolves. Combine cornstarch and remaining ¼ cup pineapple juice; stir into pineapple juice mixture in saucepan. Bring to a boil over medium heat, and boil 1 minute, stirring constantly. Add mustard, cider vinegar, and pineapple; mix well. Chill. Yield: 1¾ cups. *John N. Riggins, Nashville, Tennessee.*

SPAGHETTI WITH VEGETABLES

1 cup sliced fresh mushrooms
¾ cup chopped onion
3 cloves garlic, minced
6 large fresh basil leaves, chopped
¼ teaspoon finely ground fennel seeds
¼ cup plus 3 tablespoons olive oil, divided
1½ cups broccoli flowerets
1½ cups cauliflower flowerets
1 (15½-ounce) can red kidney beans, rinsed and drained
¼ to ½ teaspoon salt
2 quarts water
1 teaspoon salt
1 (7-ounce) package spaghetti
½ cup freshly grated Parmesan cheese
Freshly ground pepper

Sauté first 5 ingredients in 2 tablespoons olive oil 3 to 4 minutes or until onion is tender; remove from skillet. Add 3 tablespoons olive oil to skillet and sauté broccoli and cauliflower 5 minutes or until crisp-tender. Add onion mixture, beans, and ¼ to ½ teaspoon salt to vegetables; heat thoroughly. Set vegetable mixture aside, and keep warm.

Combine water, 1 tablespoon olive oil, and 1 teaspoon salt; bring to a boil, and add spaghetti. Cook spaghetti 10 to 13 minutes, stirring occasionally. Drain. Add 1 tablespoon olive oil to spaghetti, tossing to coat.

Combine spaghetti, vegetable mixture, and cheese in a large serving bowl, tossing well. Top with freshly ground pepper. Yield: 6 to 8 servings.
Marlene Rosenkoetter, Wilmington, North Carolina.

MARINATED VEGETABLES

2 cups cauliflower flowerets
2 cups sliced carrots
1½ cups broccoli flowerets
1½ cups sliced fresh mushrooms
3 stalks celery, diagonally sliced
1 medium zucchini, sliced
½ medium cucumber, cut in half lengthwise and sliced
⅔ cup diced green pepper
Dressing (recipe follows)

Combine all ingredients except dressing in a large bowl. Pour dressing over vegetables; toss gently. Cover; chill at least 12 hours. Yield: 10 servings.

Dressing:

¾ cup tarragon vinegar
¼ cup olive oil
2 tablespoons vegetable oil
2 tablespoons sugar
1 large clove garlic, crushed
½ teaspoon dried whole tarragon
¼ teaspoon prepared mustard
¼ teaspoon salt
¼ teaspoon pepper

Combine all ingredients, mixing well. Yield: about 1¼ cups.
Katie Kimbrough, Jackson, Mississippi.

GREEN SALAD WITH LEMONY FRENCH DRESSING

½ cup olive oil
2 cloves garlic, finely chopped
2 tablespoons white wine vinegar
2 tablespoons lemon juice
1¼ teaspoons salt
½ teaspoon pepper
10 cups torn mixed salad greens

Combine all ingredients except salad greens; mix well. Chill. Pour over salad greens; toss. Yield: 8 to 10 servings.
Virginia B. Stalder, Nokesville, Virginia.

Tip: Keep butter, margarine, and fat drippings tightly covered in the refrigerator. Vegetable shortening can be kept covered at room temperature. Homemade salad dressing should be kept in the refrigerator; mayonnaise and commercial salad dressings should be refrigerated after opening. Foods mixed with mayonnaise, such as potato salad or egg salad, should be refrigerated and used within a couple of days.

Enjoy Fresh Vegetables Year-Round

Broccoli, cauliflower, spinach, carrots, cabbage, and onions can generally be found in the produce section of your local grocery any time of the year. Take advantage of these hardy vegetables in their natural state; they'll add variety to your end-of-winter menus.

KIELBASA AND CABBAGE

6 slices bacon
1 medium head cabbage, cut into thin wedges
1 medium onion, chopped
¼ cup water
2 tablespoons brown sugar
1 clove garlic, minced
1 teaspoon seasoned salt
½ to 1 teaspoon dried crushed red pepper
1 pound kielbasa or Polish sausage, cut into 1-inch pieces

Cook bacon in a large skillet until crisp; remove bacon, reserving drippings in skillet. Crumble bacon, and set aside. Add next 7 ingredients to drippings; cover and cook 10 minutes over medium heat, turning cabbage once. Add sausage; cover and cook 5 minutes or until sausage is heated. Transfer to serving dish with a slotted spoon; sprinkle with bacon. Yield: 6 servings.
Judi Grigoraci, Charleston, West Virginia.

CREAMY CARROT BAKE

6 to 8 medium carrots, scraped and cut into ¼-inch slices
½ cup salad dressing or mayonnaise
¼ cup water
2 tablespoons dried onion flakes
2 tablespoons prepared horseradish
½ teaspoon salt
¼ teaspoon pepper
¼ cup dry breadcrumbs
2 teaspoons butter or margarine, melted

Cook carrots in boiling water 10 minutes or until tender; drain.

Combine next 6 ingredients; mix well. Add carrots; toss gently. Spoon into lightly greased 1½-quart casserole. Combine breadcrumbs and butter; mix well. Sprinkle over carrot mixture; bake at 375° for 20 to 25 minutes. Yield: 6 to 8 servings.
Marie H. Webb, Roanoke, Virginia.

BROCCOLI SUPREME

1½ pounds fresh broccoli
1 cup water
½ teaspoon salt
1 (10¾-ounce) can cream of chicken soup, undiluted
½ cup commercial sour cream
¼ cup grated carrot
1 tablespoon grated onion
1 tablespoon all-purpose flour
⅛ teaspoon pepper
¾ cup herb-seasoned stuffing mix
2 tablespoons butter or margarine, melted

Trim off large leaves of broccoli. Remove tough ends of lower stalks, and wash broccoli. Separate flowerets, and coarsely chop stalks. Bring water to a boil; add salt and broccoli. Cover, reduce heat, and simmer 5 minutes or until crisp-tender; drain and set aside.

Combine soup and next 5 ingredients, mixing well. Fold in broccoli; pour into a greased 2-quart casserole. Combine stuffing mix and butter; sprinkle around edge of casserole. Bake, uncovered, at 350° for 30 minutes. Yield: about 6 servings.   *Lynn Abbott,*
Southern Pines, North Carolina.

CHEESE-FROSTED CAULIFLOWER

1 medium head cauliflower
½ cup mayonnaise
2 teaspoons prepared mustard
¾ cup (3 ounces) shredded Cheddar cheese
Paprika
Tomato wedges (optional)
Parsley (optional)

Wash cauliflower; remove leaves, and cut out base. Cook, covered, in boiling, salted water 12 to 15 minutes or until tender; drain. Place in a shallow, ungreased baking pan. Combine mayonnaise and mustard; spread over cauliflower. Bake at 375° for 5 minutes. Top with cheese, and bake 5 minutes. Sprinkle with paprika, and garnish with tomato and parsley, if desired. Yield: 6 servings.   *Melissa Mathews,*
Orlando, Florida.

SAVORY PARMESAN SPINACH

½ to ¾ pound fresh spinach
2 tablespoons olive oil
1 small clove garlic, minced
¾ teaspoon minced fresh basil or ¼ teaspoon dried whole basil
¼ cup grated Parmesan cheese

Remove stems from the spinach. Wash leaves thoroughly; tear into bite-size pieces. Place spinach in a large saucepan (do not add water); cover and cook over high heat for about 3 minutes. Drain spinach well.

Heat oil in a medium skillet; add garlic, and sauté 3 to 5 minutes. Stir in basil and drained spinach.

Cook mixture until thoroughly heated. Then remove from heat, and stir in Parmesan cheese. Yield: 2 to 4 servings.   *Mrs. Donald MacMillan,*
Cartersville, Georgia.

These Squares Are The Best

Rich, dainty, and delicious is the best way to describe these Cream Cheese-Almond Squares—perfect food for stand-up get-togethers because they are easy to pick up and eat.

CREAM CHEESE-ALMOND SQUARES

½ cup butter or margarine, softened
2 teaspoons sugar
2 tablespoons milk
½ teaspoon grated lemon rind
1⅓ cups all-purpose flour
2 (8-ounce) packages cream cheese, softened
1 cup sugar
1 egg, slightly beaten
1 teaspoon grated lemon rind
1 cup chopped almonds, toasted
1 cup sifted powdered sugar
1 tablespoon water
1 teaspoon ground cinnamon
Toasted sliced almonds (optional)

Combine first 4 ingredients; beat until light and fluffy. Add flour; mix well. Press mixture into the bottom of a 9-inch square baking pan; set aside.

Combine cream cheese, sugar, egg, and lemon rind; beat until smooth. Stir in chopped almonds; pour mixture over layer in pan. Bake at 300° for 1 hour and 10 minutes or until set.

Combine powdered sugar, water, and cinnamon; mix well. Spread over hot mixture; let cool. Chill 3 to 4 hours; cut into squares. Garnish with toasted sliced almonds, if desired. Yield: 2½ dozen.
Phyllis Murell,
Birmingham, Alabama.

Beer Makes The Difference

Sparkling and tangy beer can transform a simple dip or spread into something worth noticing. Even vegetables are better when teamed with beer. And for the best fried fish, just stir some beer into the batter.

SAUCY MEATBALLS

2 slices white bread, crumbled
1 (12-ounce) can beer, divided
1 pound ground beef
½ cup (2 ounces) shredded process American cheese
½ teaspoon salt
Dash of pepper
2 tablespoons butter or margarine, melted
½ cup chopped onion
1 tablespoon brown sugar
1 tablespoon vinegar
1 teaspoon beef-flavored bouillon granules
1½ teaspoons cornstarch
1 tablespoon water
Hot cooked noodles

Soak crumbled bread in ½ cup beer; add ground beef, cheese, salt, and pepper, mixing well. Shape mixture into 1½-inch meatballs; cook in butter in a large skillet over medium heat until browned.

Drain meatballs on paper towels; pour off pan drippings, reserving 1 tablespoon in skillet. Add onion; sauté until tender. Add meatballs, remaining beer, sugar, vinegar, and bouillon; cover and simmer 20 minutes.

Combine cornstarch and water, mixing well; stir into meatball mixture. Bring to a boil; cook 1 minute, stirring constantly. Serve over noodles. Yield: 4 servings.   *Nell H. Amador,*
Guntersville, Alabama.

BEER-BATTER FISH

1 pound fish fillets
1¼ cups biscuit mix, divided
½ teaspoon salt
1 egg, beaten
½ cup beer
Vegetable oil

Coat fish fillets with ¼ cup biscuit mix; set aside.

Combine remaining 1 cup biscuit mix, salt, egg, and beer; stir until smooth.

Dip each fillet into beer mixture; fry in deep hot oil (350°) for 1 to 2 minutes on each side or until golden brown and fish flakes easily when tested with a fork. Yield: 4 servings.

Cheryl L. Blakney,
Sandersville, Georgia.

BRUSSELS SPROUTS IN BEER

1 pound fresh brussels sprouts or 2 (10-ounce) packages frozen brussels sprouts
1 (12-ounce) can beer
2 tablespoons butter or margarine, melted
½ teaspoon salt

Combine brussels sprouts and beer in a saucepan; bring to a boil. Cover, reduce heat, and simmer 10 to 12 minutes or until tender. Drain. Add butter and salt; toss. Yield: 4 to 6 servings.

Mary Jane Yost,
Huntsville, Alabama.

BEER-CHEESE SPREAD

2 cups (8 ounces) shredded sharp Cheddar cheese
2 cups (8 ounces) shredded process American cheese
1 (3-ounce) package cream cheese, softened
½ (4-ounce) package blue cheese, crumbled
¾ cup stale beer
2 tablespoons onion juice
1 large clove garlic, crushed
1 teaspoon hot sauce

Combine all ingredients; mix well. Cover and refrigerate. Serve with crackers. Yield: 1¾ cups. *David B. Hicks,*
St. Petersburg, Florida.

FRIED ONION RINGS

1½ cups all-purpose flour
1 (12-ounce) can beer
¼ teaspoon salt
2 large Bermuda or Spanish onions
Vegetable oil
Salt to taste

Combine flour, beer, and ¼ teaspoon salt, stirring well. Cover and let stand at room temperature 1½ to 2 hours.

Peel onions; cut into ¼-inch-thick slices, and separate into rings. Dip onion rings into beer mixture; fry in deep hot oil (375°) until golden brown. Drain on paper towels, and sprinkle with salt. Yield: 6 to 8 servings.

Mrs. Billie Taylor,
Fork Union, Virginia.

BRAUNSCHWEIGER-AND-BEER DIP

2 (8-ounce) rolls braunschweiger, softened
1 (8-ounce) package cream cheese, softened
½ cup commercial sour cream
1 tablespoon Worcestershire sauce
¼ teaspoon salt
¼ teaspoon garlic powder
½ cup beer

Combine the softened braunschweiger, cream cheese, and sour cream; beat until smooth. Add Worcestershire sauce, salt, and garlic powder. Gradually add beer, mixing well. Serve with crackers or rye bread. Yield: 4 cups.

Marge Brady,
Arlington, Texas.

Toss Salads With Hot Dressings

Most salads are supposed to be crisp, but these are topped with hot dressings, which leave them wilted and packed with flavor.

Lane Harris of Jacksonville, North Carolina, tells us that the secret to her Wilted Mixed Green Salad is in the vinegar. She always uses seasoned gourmet rice vinegar, most commonly found in Oriental food stores, to add the right sweet-and-sour taste.

WILTED MIXED GREEN SALAD

5 cups torn spinach
3 cups torn iceberg lettuce
¼ cup thinly sliced radishes
¼ cup thinly sliced celery
4 slices bacon
¼ cup seasoned gourmet rice vinegar
1 tablespoon sugar

Combine vegetables in a large bowl; set aside. Cook bacon in a skillet until crisp; remove bacon, reserving 3 tablespoons drippings in skillet. Crumble bacon, and add to vegetables.

Add vinegar and sugar to bacon drippings; bring to a boil, stirring constantly, until sugar dissolves. Pour over vegetables; toss gently. Serve immediately. Yield: 6 servings.

Lane A. Harris,
Jacksonville, North Carolina.

WILTED BACON-AND-LETTUCE SALAD

1 large head red leaf lettuce, torn into bite-size pieces
½ cup sliced fresh mushrooms
6 slices bacon
¼ cup plus 1 teaspoon vinegar
1½ teaspoons sugar
¼ teaspoon salt
¼ teaspoon pepper

Combine lettuce and mushrooms in a large salad bowl; set aside. Cook bacon in a skillet until crisp; remove bacon, reserving 3 tablespoons drippings in skillet. Crumble bacon, and add to the lettuce mixture.

Add vinegar, sugar, salt, and pepper to bacon drippings; bring to a boil, stirring constantly, until sugar dissolves. Pour over lettuce mixture; toss gently. Serve immediately. Yield: 6 servings.

Anna Joines,
Hickory, North Carolina.

TANGY WILTED SALAD

1 large head lettuce, torn into bite-size pieces
1 small onion, chopped
4 slices bacon
½ cup sugar
1 cup water
¼ cup vinegar
1 egg, beaten
1 tablespoon cornstarch
½ teaspoon salt

Combine lettuce and onion in a large bowl; set aside. Cook bacon in a large skillet until crisp; remove bacon, reserving drippings in skillet. Crumble bacon, and add to lettuce mixture.

Add sugar, water, and vinegar to bacon drippings. Stir in egg, cornstarch, and salt. Cook over medium heat, stirring constantly, until thickened. Pour over lettuce mixture; toss gently. Serve salad immediately. Yield: 6 servings.

Sharon Gwaltney,
Carrsville, Virginia.

Crusty Breads To Make At Home

Many of the dishes we feature call for a loaf of thick, crusty bread to round out the menu. If you're like most people, you probably buy a loaf of French or Italian bread. However, if you'd like to try your hand at making some crusty breads from scratch, we offer two possibilities.

Our baguettes are an easy version of the classic French bread; we made them in a food processor. This recipe makes two long loaves or eight small ones. Herb-Cheese Bread is a rich, savory bread that bakes in a round dish. It's great with soups as well as entrées.

HERB-CHEESE BREAD

½ cup milk
½ cup water
1 tablespoon butter or margarine
2½ to 2¾ cups all-purpose flour, divided
1 package dry yeast
1 tablespoon sugar
1½ teaspoons salt
½ cup (2 ounces) shredded Cheddar
    cheese
1 egg
1 tablespoon plus 1 teaspoon parsley
    flakes
¾ teaspoon caraway seeds
½ teaspoon dried whole tarragon

Combine milk, water, and butter in a small saucepan. Bring to a boil; remove from heat, and cool to lukewarm (105° to 115°).

Combine 1 cup flour, yeast, sugar, and salt in a large bowl. Add milk mixture; beat 2 minutes with an electric mixer. Add cheese, egg, parsley flakes, caraway seeds, and tarragon; beat 2 minutes. Gradually stir in enough remaining flour to make a stiff dough.

Cover and let rise in a warm place (85°), free from drafts, 1 hour or until doubled in bulk.

Stir dough down. Spoon into a greased 1½-quart round baking dish. Bake at 350° for 40 minutes or until the bread loaf sounds hollow when tapped. Yield: 1 loaf.

BAGUETTES

¼ cup warm water (105° to 115°)
1 package dry yeast
Pinch of sugar
3½ cups unbleached flour
1 tablespoon sugar
1 teaspoon salt
1 cup to 1 cup plus 2 tablespoons warm
    water (105° to 115°)
1 egg white
1 tablespoon water

Combine water, yeast, and sugar in a small bowl; let stand 5 minutes.

Position knife blade in food processor bowl. Add flour, 1 tablespoon sugar, and salt; top with cover, and process 10 seconds. With processor running, add yeast mixture and 1 cup warm water; process until dough forms a ball leaving sides of bowl. (Add additional water, if necessary.) Continue processing 15 to 20 seconds after dough forms a ball.

Place dough in a greased bowl, turning to grease top. Cover and let rise in a warm place (85°), free from drafts, 1 hour or until doubled in bulk.

Punch dough down, and turn out onto a floured surface. Run over dough with a rolling pin to remove air bubbles; divide dough in half. Roll up half of dough jellyroll fashion. Roll dough with hands back and forth across flat surface to form a thick rope about 15 inches long. Place in a greased baguette pan. Repeat procedure with remaining dough. (If mini-baguettes are desired, cut rope into 4 pieces. Place mini-baguettes in 2 greased baguette pans 3 inches apart.) Make deep diagonal slashes about 2 inches long in each loaf. Cover loaves, and let rise in a warm place (85°), free from drafts, 30 minutes or until doubled in bulk.

Combine egg white and 1 tablespoon water; mix well. Gently brush egg mixture on loaves.

Bake at 425° for 10 minutes; reduce heat to 375° and bake 8 minutes longer. (For mini-baguettes, bake at 425° for 10 minutes; reduce heat to 375°, and bake 6 minutes longer.) Remove to wire rack to cool. Yield: two 17-inch baguettes or eight 5-inch mini-baguettes.

Note: For a crustier bread, place a small pan of hot water on bottom rack of oven during baking. *Joan Purcell, Birmingham, Alabama.*

Tip: Bread will stay fresh in the freezer from two to three months; it's safe to eat after that time, but will lose flavor.

Tips For Good Cooks

Whether you're a novice or experienced cook, shortcuts in the kitchen are always welcome. The following tips will save time for you.

—Use an extra set of dry measuring cups as scoops in canisters of flour, sugar, and grains to save time and to cut down on dishwashing.

—Keep flour in a large shaker for quick flouring of a pan; just shake out the amount needed to cover the pan.

—Arrange spices in alphabetical order on a shelf. Always store all spices in tightly covered containers to help retain flavor.

—Measure dry ingredients before liquids; you won't have to wash spoons or cups in between measuring.

—To ensure even baking in heat-proof glass dishes, lower the oven temperature 25 degrees.

—Chill gelatin mixtures quickly for aspics or molds by pouring the mixtures into a metal pan and placing it in the freezer about 15 minutes.

—To prevent grease from spattering while frying, invert a metal colander over the skillet to catch grease and allow steam to escape.

—When recipes call for small amounts of canned tomato paste put the remainder in a container and freeze.

—If soups, stews, or other foods are too salty, add a teaspoon of vinegar and a teaspoon of sugar and reheat.

—Placing a jar of jam, jelly, syrup, or honey in a pan of simmering water dissolves the sugar crystals on top.

—Poach leftover egg yolks in an egg poacher; chop yolks for garnishes.

—Freeze very soft cheese 15 minutes to make shredding easier.

—Crumble extra pieces of cooked bacon and freeze. Use as a topping for casseroles or baked potatoes.

—To improve canned shrimp, soak shrimp 1 hour in ice water and drain.

—To speed up baking time for potatoes, parboil them 5 minutes; then bake at 400° about 40 minutes.

—To keep fresh beets from bleeding and fading when cooking, cook them whole with 2 inches of stem attached.

—Chopped onions have the best flavor if they are browned in shortening before being added to casserole dishes.

—For just a squirt of lemon juice, poke a hole in one end of a lemon and squeeze the lemon.

—To give the top crust of a pie a rich brown glaze, brush it lightly with milk before baking.

April

Cream Puff Pastry Filled With Variety

Whoever developed cream puffs deserves an award. When baked, the famous dough magically rises and creates a center cavity exactly the right size to hold sweetened whipped cream.

Just as cream puff dough can be shaped into dessert-size rounds, it can also be crafted into tiny balls for appetizers, fancy logs for luncheon sandwiches, and even a giant dessert puff so big you'll have to slice it like pie.

The dough used in making cream puffs and other pastry delicacies is called pâté à chou among the professionals—cream puff pastry in lay terms. It contains water, butter, and flour like regular pastry, but the addition of eggs makes it rise, and a larger amount of water makes piping possible and creates steam that evaporates to make the puff's center cavity.

To fill cream puffs for our Appetizer Chicken Puffs or Luncheon Shrimp Puffs, slice off the top of the puff, and pull out and discard the soft dough inside. Spoon in the filling, and replace the tops of the puffs. Don't cut the pastry at all when making Giant Fruit Puff. Just spoon the filling into the center of the ring. (See photograph of these pastries on page 133.)

Cream puffs look prettiest when piped from a decorating bag with a fluted tip. Use large fluted tips—No. 5 or 6B. They can be found at most stores that carry cake-decorating supplies.

You can also make cream puffs without special cake-decorating tips. Just spoon the dough directly onto the baking sheet, and the pastries will bake up smooth instead of fluted. Whether piping or spooning the dough, try to make all puffs the same size to ensure even

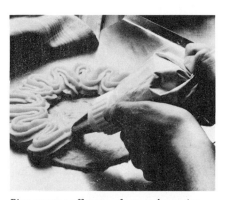

Pipe cream puff pastry from a decorating bag for its fanciest look; just spooning the dough onto the baking sheet will work, too.

baking. Space the puffs at least 2 inches apart on the baking sheet, because they "puff" a lot during baking.

Bake the cream puffs as soon as the dough is made; the longer you wait to bake them, the less they will rise. You can bake the puffs a day ahead, and store them in an airtight container, if desired. Don't fill them more than four hours before serving.

CREAM PUFF PASTRY

⅔ cup water
⅓ cup butter or margarine
⅔ cup all-purpose flour
⅛ teaspoon salt
3 eggs

Combine water and butter in a medium saucepan; bring to a boil. Add flour and salt, all at once, stirring vigorously over medium-high heat until mixture leaves sides of pan and forms a smooth ball. Remove from heat, and cool 4 to 5 minutes.

Add eggs, one at a time, beating thoroughly with a wooden spoon after each addition; then beat until dough is smooth. Shape and bake dough as recipe directs. Yield: enough to pipe one 7-inch, four 4-inch, or thirty 1-inch cream puffs.

LUNCHEON SHRIMP PUFFS

1 recipe Cream Puff Pastry
3 cups water
1 pound unpeeled shrimp
½ cup chopped celery
⅓ cup mayonnaise
1½ teaspoons lemon juice
½ to 1 teaspoon dried whole dillweed
½ teaspoon salt
¼ teaspoon coarsely ground pepper
Leaf lettuce

Spoon Cream Puff Pastry into decorating bag fitted with a No. 5 or 6B large fluted tip. Pipe dough into four 4-inch zigzag logs (2 inches apart) on a lightly greased baking sheet, using slightly more than half the dough. Pipe another zigzag log, slightly smaller, on top of each 4-inch log using remaining dough. Bake at 400° for 35 minutes or until puffed and golden brown. Cool away from drafts.

Bring water to a boil; add shrimp, and cook 3 to 5 minutes. Drain well; rinse with cold water. Chill. Peel and

devein shrimp; chop. Combine shrimp, celery, mayonnaise, lemon juice, dillweed, salt, and pepper; chill.

Just before serving, slice tops from cream puffs; pull out and discard soft dough inside. Line cream puff shells with lettuce, and spoon on shrimp salad. Replace tops. Yield: 4 servings.

APPETIZER CHICKEN PUFFS

3 tablespoons grated Parmesan cheese
1 recipe Cream Puff Pastry
1 cup chopped cooked chicken
⅓ cup finely chopped celery
¼ cup mayonnaise
2 tablespoons sweet pickle relish
¼ teaspoon salt
⅛ teaspoon pepper
2 tablespoons chopped almonds, toasted
Sliced pimiento-stuffed olives

Stir Parmesan cheese into Cream Puff Pastry; spoon mixture into decorating bag fitted with a No. 5 or 6B large fluted tip. Pipe mixture into 30 small balls on lightly greased baking sheets. Bake at 400° for 20 minutes or until puffed and golden brown. Cool away from drafts.

Combine chicken, celery, mayonnaise, relish, salt, pepper, and almonds, mixing well; chill.

Just before serving, cut top one-third off cream puffs; pull out and discard soft dough inside. Spoon chicken mixture into cream puffs; replace tops. Place an olive slice on top of each puff, and insert a decorative wooden pick lengthwise through center of each. Yield: 2½ dozen.

GIANT FRUIT PUFF

1 recipe Cream Puff Pastry
3 egg yolks
½ cup sugar
3½ tablespoons cornstarch
¼ teaspoon salt
1½ cups milk
1 tablespoon butter or margarine
1 teaspoon vanilla extract
½ cup whipping cream, whipped
6 fresh strawberries
1 kiwi, peeled and sliced

Spread ½ cup Cream Puff Pastry into a 7-inch circle on a lightly greased baking sheet. Spoon remaining dough into decorating bag fitted with a No. 5 or 6B large fluted tip. Pipe dough around outside edge of dough circle, leaving a 3½-inch circle in center. Bake at 425° for 15 minutes; reduce heat to 375°, and bake an additional 25 minutes or until puffed and golden. Cool on wire rack. Beat egg yolks on high speed of an electric mixer until thick and lemon colored. Set egg yolks aside.

Combine sugar, cornstarch, and salt in a medium saucepan; stir in milk, and bring to a boil, stirring constantly. Boil 1 minute, and remove from heat. Gradually stir about one-fourth of hot mixture into egg yolks; add to remaining hot mixture, stirring constantly. Cook, stirring constantly, over medium-low heat 3 to 4 minutes. Remove from heat, and gently stir in butter and vanilla. Cover with waxed paper, and cool completely. Fold in whipped cream. Spoon mixture in center of puff, and arrange fruit on top; chill. Serve within 4 hours. Yield: 6 servings.

Belgian endive lends a striking appearance to Shrimp-Endive Salad; black beans and alfalfa sprouts serve as flavorful accents.

Main-Dish Salads Take On New Sophistication

Here's a fresh approach to salads, one that focuses on them as a main course, opening up creative possibilities.

Foods can be combined to create salads with an interesting mix of flavors, colors, and textures. Presentation is an important part of the concept. Some salads, such as Spicy Italian Ham Salad and Marinated Chicken-Grape Salad, lend themselves to being tossed; others, such as Shrimp-Endive Salad, are striking in a more composed arrangement. The aim with both types of salads is to play up the unusual food combinations and present them in their most attractive form.

We offer a variety of main-dish salads as examples, but we also encourage you to experiment on your own. For starters, don't limit yourself to only one kind of salad green. Try combining one of the sweet-flavored types—leaf, Boston, or iceberg lettuce—with one of the more pungent—romaine, endive, watercress, chicory, roquette, or radicchio. (Roquette and radicchio may be available only at specialty food stores.)

Use the same principle when you choose the other ingredients, keeping in mind the importance of color and texture. For instance, in Marinated Chicken-Grape Salad, the purplish-red color in the lettuce is repeated in the red grapes on top, tying the different elements together. The crunchiness of the celery and cashews also contrasts effectively with the soft texture of the chicken and grapes.

SHRIMP-ENDIVE SALAD

7½ cups water
1 tablespoon plus 2 teaspoons salt
2½ pounds unpeeled fresh shrimp
½ head romaine
1 head curly endive
½ head Belgian endive
1 (8-ounce) can sliced water chestnuts, drained
1 medium-size green pepper, cut into thin strips
6 radishes, thinly sliced
2 medium tomatoes, cut into wedges
2 to 4 tablespoons alfalfa sprouts
¾ cup canned black beans, drained and rinsed
Herb-Mayonnaise Sauce

Bring water and salt to a boil; add shrimp, and cook 3 to 5 minutes. Drain well; rinse with cold water. Chill. Peel and devein shrimp.

Place romaine and curly endive on individual plates; arrange Belgian endive, shrimp, and remaining ingredients except Herb-Mayonnaise Sauce on top. Serve with Herb-Mayonnaise Sauce. Yield: 6 servings.

Herb-Mayonnaise Sauce:

½ cup mayonnaise
⅓ cup commercial sour cream
2 tablespoons chopped fresh parsley
2 tablespoons chopped fresh chives
2 tablespoons chopped fresh tarragon
2 hard-cooked eggs, finely chopped
2 teaspoons lemon juice
2 teaspoons white wine vinegar
1 teaspoon Dijon mustard
Salt to taste
Freshly ground black pepper to taste

Combine mayonnaise and sour cream, mixing well. Stir in remaining ingredients. Cover and chill at least 5 hours. Yield: 1¾ cups.

SPICY ITALIAN HAM SALAD

½ cup red wine vinegar
½ cup vegetable oil
¼ cup water
¼ to ½ pound thinly sliced
    black-peppered ham, cut into
    1- x 3-inch strips
¼ to ½ pound thinly sliced prosciutto, cut
    into 1- x 3-inch strips
3 stalks celery, diagonally sliced (1-inch
    slices)
1 medium-size green pepper, cut into thin
    strips
½ medium onion, sliced into thin rings
4 hot cherry peppers, finely chopped
1 head Boston lettuce
1 teaspoon chopped fresh oregano
Additional hot cherry peppers (optional)

Combine vinegar, oil, and water in a jar. Cover and shake vigorously. Set dressing aside.

Combine black-peppered ham, prosciutto, celery, green pepper, onion, and diced cherry peppers, tossing well. Tear lettuce into bite-size pieces; place on individual plates. Arrange ham mixture on lettuce. Shake dressing, and pour over salad; sprinkle with oregano. Garnish with whole cherry peppers, if desired. Yield: 4 to 6 servings.

Deborah L. Cooper,
Fayetteville, North Carolina.

TURKEY-ZUCCHINI SALAD

¼ cup lemon juice
3 tablespoons vegetable oil
2 tablespoons chopped fresh parsley
1¼ teaspoons sugar
1 clove garlic, crushed
3 cups chopped cooked turkey
1 (11-ounce) can mandarin oranges,
    drained
1 medium unpeeled apple, cut into thin
    wedges
1 medium zucchini, sliced
Red-leaf lettuce
2 tablespoons slivered almonds, toasted

Combine lemon juice, oil, parsley, sugar, and garlic in a jar. Cover jar tightly, and shake vigorously; set aside.

Combine turkey, mandarin oranges, apple, and zucchini in a shallow container. Pour half of dressing over mixture, tossing to coat. Cover and marinate in refrigerator 1 hour.

Place lettuce on salad platter. Arrange turkey mixture on lettuce in desired pattern; sprinkle with toasted almonds. Drizzle with remaining dressing. Yield: 4 to 6 servings.

Dixie Barger,
Enid, Oklahoma.

MARINATED CHICKEN-GRAPE SALAD

1 pound boneless chicken breasts
¼ teaspoon salt
Water
⅔ cup dry white wine
3 tablespoons lemon juice
1 cup mayonnaise
¼ teaspoon salt
⅛ teaspoon white pepper
Red-leaf lettuce
1 cup seedless green grapes, cut in half
1 cup seedless red grapes, cut in half
1½ cups diagonally sliced celery
½ cup cashews

Place chicken in a medium saucepan; add ¼ teaspoon salt and water to cover. Cook, covered, about 30 minutes or until done. Drain and cool. Slice chicken into strips.

Combine wine and lemon juice; pour over chicken, tossing gently. Cover and chill at least 2 hours. Drain, reserving marinade. Set chicken aside.

Strain marinade; set aside ¼ cup plus 2 tablespoons. Combine reserved marinade, mayonnaise, ¼ teaspoon salt, and white pepper.

Line individual plates with lettuce. Arrange chicken, grapes, celery, and cashews over lettuce. Serve with mayonnaise mixture. Yield: 4 servings.

Jeanne Hotaling,
Augusta, Georgia.

Cook Chinese By Regions

If you've eaten at any of the Chinese restaurants that have sprung up across the South, then you already know they serve a variety of interesting regional cuisines. To create these same tasty dishes in your own kitchen, just get out the wok and try our recipes. We'd like to acquaint you with the four main Chinese regional cuisines. We've tried to keep them authentic but also as practical as possible.

See "From Our Kitchen To Yours" on page 76 for additional information on utensils and techniques used in Chinese cooking.

Many Chinese dishes, such as Fish in Tomato Sauce or Shrimp With Snow Peas, may seem elaborate but are really quite simple to prepare. Chopping and slicing can be done ahead, and actual cooking time is brief.

Most ingredients for Pork-and-Onions With Bean Sauce and Shredded Beef Over Rice Noodles can be found in large supermarkets. Special ingredients, such as hoisin sauce or bean sauce, are available at Oriental food stores.

■ Szechuan cooking comes from the western part of China, where the climate is damp and humid. Spicy, hot foods are served here, for the Chinese believe they induce perspiration, causing a cooling effect. Dried peppers and gingerroot are often used. One word of caution, however—if you are a novice at eating spicy foods, proceed cautiously with Szechuan dishes.

SHREDDED BEEF OVER RICE NOODLES

1 pound sirloin steak
3 tablespoons soy sauce
1 teaspoon cornstarch
2 teaspoons grated fresh gingerroot
1 teaspoon rice wine
½ teaspoon sugar
¼ cup chicken broth
1 tablespoon water
1 tablespoon soy sauce
½ teaspoon cornstarch
¼ cup peanut or vegetable oil
1 clove garlic, crushed
4 dried whole red peppers
1 tablespoon hot bean sauce
1½ teaspoons hoisin sauce
1½ carrots, scraped and cut into julienne
    strips
1 stalk celery, cut into julienne strips
3 cups peanut or vegetable oil
2 (3-ounce) packages rice noodles

Partially freeze steak; slice diagonally across the grain into 3- x ¼-inch strips. Combine soy sauce, cornstarch, gingerroot, rice wine, and sugar in a bowl. Add the steak, and mix well; let stand 15 minutes.

Combine chicken broth, water, 1 tablespoon soy sauce, and ½ teaspoon cornstarch, mixing well; set aside. Pour ¼ cup oil around top of preheated wok. Allow to heat at medium high (325°) for 30 seconds. Add beef mixture and garlic; stir-fry 2 minutes or until beef is browned. Remove beef mixture, and drain on paper towels.

Reserve 2 tablespoons drippings in wok. Add red peppers and stir-fry 1 minute. Add bean sauce and hoisin sauce; stir-fry 15 to 20 seconds. Add vegetables; increase heat to high (350°), and stir-fry 1 minute. Add broth mixture, and cook until slightly thickened. Add beef, and mix well; remove from heat, and keep warm.

Pour 3 cups oil into wok; heat to 400°. Drop a few noodles at a time into oil; fry 2 to 3 minutes or until noodles expand. Remove from wok with a slotted metal spoon and drain on paper towels. Spoon beef over noodles. Serve immediately. Yield: 4 servings.

■ From the southeastern coast of China comes Cantonese-style cooking. Due to the mild climate, farmers produce vegetables like snow peas, and fishermen harvest an array of seafood. Cantonese cooking is basically casual; foods are quickly stir-fried or steamed, leaving ingredients crisp and colorful. Chicken broth, rice wine, and gingerroot are common seasonings, with rice usually accompanying each dish.

SHRIMP WITH SNOW PEAS

1 pound unpeeled medium-size fresh
   shrimp
½ teaspoon salt
1 teaspoon sesame oil
1½ teaspoons cornstarch
¼ cup chicken broth
3 tablespoons oyster sauce
½ teaspoon cornstarch
¼ cup peanut or vegetable oil
2 cloves garlic, crushed
2 teaspoons grated fresh gingerroot
½ pound fresh snow peas or 1 (6-ounce)
   package frozen snow peas, thawed
2 teaspoons rice wine

Peel and devein shrimp; rinse and pat dry. Sprinkle shrimp with salt and toss with sesame oil; dredge in 1½ teaspoons cornstarch. Set aside.

Combine chicken broth, oyster sauce, and ½ teaspoon cornstarch, and mix well; set the mixture aside.

Pour peanut oil around top of preheated wok, coating sides; allow to heat at medium high (325°) for 1 minute. Add garlic and gingerroot, and stir-fry 30 seconds. Add shrimp, and stir-fry 1½ minutes. Remove and drain on paper towels.

Add snow peas to wok, and stir-fry 30 seconds. Add broth mixture, stirring constantly until slightly thickened. Stir in shrimp and rice wine. Serve immediately. Yield: 4 servings.

■ About midway along the coast lies the home of Shanghai-style cooking. Western influence on this area's food is obvious by the use of various tomato and cream sauces. Rich with produce, meat, and seafood, Shanghai cooking offers a wide variety of tasty but relatively mild-flavored dishes served with steamed breads or dumplings.

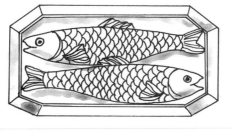

FISH IN TOMATO SAUCE

1 (1½- to 2-pound) whole dressed, fresh
   trout
¼ teaspoon salt
2 tablespoons cornstarch
¼ cup plus 2 tablespoons peanut or
   vegetable oil, divided
¼ cup diced green onion
1 small tomato, peeled and diced
¼ cup diced fresh mushrooms
¼ cup diced fresh carrot
¼ cup frozen English peas, thawed
2 tablespoons sugar
3 tablespoons chicken broth
2 tablespoons water
2 tablespoons rice vinegar
2 tablespoons tomato sauce
1 tablespoon soy sauce
2 teaspoons cornstarch
2 teaspoons water
Pinch of salt
Green onion fans (optional)

Clean fish, and pat dry. Score a crisscross design on each side. Sprinkle outside and cavity with salt, and let stand 10 minutes. Pat dry with a paper towel. Sprinkle each side with cornstarch. Heat ¼ cup oil in a large skillet at medium high (325°). Fry fish 3 to 5 minutes on each side or until lightly browned and fish flakes easily with a fork.

Remove fish from skillet, and keep warm on a serving platter. Drain off pan drippings. Add 2 tablespoons oil to skillet; stir-fry onions at medium heat (300°) for 1 minute. Add remaining vegetables; stir-fry 2 minutes.

Combine remaining ingredients except green onion fan, stirring well; add to vegetables. Cook at medium high (325°) 2 to 3 minutes or until slightly thickened. Spoon vegetable mixture over fish. Garnish with green onion fans, if desired. Serve immediately. Yield: 2 to 4 servings.

■ The Peking or Mandarin area, in the northernmost part of China, is much colder than the other regions. This means there are fewer fresh vegetables. Wheat, rather than rice, is more common and is used to make dumplings or pancakes. Soy sauce, bean curd, garlic, and green onions are often featured in this cuisine. Pork, beef, lamb, and duck are the most common meats.

MONGOLIAN BEEF

2 pounds boneless sirloin steak
⅓ cup soy sauce
3 tablespoons cornstarch
3 tablespoons rice wine
1 teaspoon sugar
1 teaspoon sesame oil
2 tablespoons peanut or vegetable oil
4 bunches green onions, cut into 3-inch
   pieces
2 tablespoons peanut or vegetable oil
¼ cup water
2 teaspoons sweet bean sauce
2 teaspoons hoisin sauce

Partially freeze steak; slice diagonally across grain into 3- x ¼-inch strips. Set aside. Combine soy sauce, cornstarch, wine, sugar, and sesame oil in a bowl; add beef and mix well.

Pour 2 tablespoons peanut oil around top of preheated wok; allow to heat at medium high (325°) for 1 minute. Add green onions; cover, reduce heat to low (200°), and cook 5 to 6 minutes, stirring occasionally. Remove onions, and drain on paper towels.

Pour 2 tablespoons peanut oil around top of wok; allow to heat at medium high (325°) for 1 minute. Add beef mixture; stir-fry 5 minutes or until lightly browned. (Add additional oil, if necessary.) Remove beef with slotted spoon, and drain on paper towels.

Reserve 2 tablespoons drippings in wok. Combine water, bean sauce, and hoisin sauce; stir well, and add to wok. Bring to a boil. Add green onions and beef; stir-fry 30 seconds or until thoroughly heated. Serve immediately. Yield: 6 servings.

Tip: Oriental stir-fry cooking is not only intriguing as a menu idea, it's also more energy efficient and nutritious than boiling or steaming. With this method, food is cut into small pieces so it can cook quickly.

PORK-AND-ONIONS WITH BEAN SAUCE

1 pound boneless pork loin
2 teaspoons cornstarch
2 tablespoons water
1 tablespoon plus 1 teaspoon soy sauce
1 teaspoon rice wine
2 teaspoons sugar
1 tablespoon plus 2 teaspoons sweet bean sauce
1 tablespoon soy sauce
1½ teaspoons rice wine
6 green onions with tops
¾ cup peanut or vegetable oil

Partially freeze pork; slice into 3- x ¼-inch strips. Combine cornstarch, water, 1 tablespoon plus 1 teaspoon soy sauce, and 1 teaspoon rice wine in a small bowl; add pork and mix well. Set aside. Combine sugar, bean sauce, 1 tablespoon soy sauce, and 1½ teaspoons rice wine; set aside.

Cut green onions into 3- to 4-inch pieces; finely slice each piece into lengthwise strips. Arrange green onions on a serving platter; set aside.

Pour oil into wok. Lower pork into hot oil (375°) with a slotted metal spoon. Fry pork 2 minutes or until no longer pink. Remove, and drain well on paper towels.

Reserve 3 tablespoons oil in wok. Add bean sauce mixture; stir-fry at medium high (325°) until slightly thickened. Add pork; mix well. Serve over green onions. Yield: 2 to 4 servings.

From Our Kitchen To Yours

You can enjoy Chinese foods in your own home. Although preparation may involve some new utensils, new ways of cutting, and new techniques for cooking, you'll have fun as you learn.

Getting Started

In "Cook Chinese by Regions" on page 74, you'll find that authentic Chinese recipes involve a lot of chopping and slicing. Since most Chinese eat with chopsticks rather than forks and knives, all the ingredients are bite-size. Also, because cooking time is short, foods need to be cut into similar shapes and sizes so that they will cook evenly and in the same length of time.

To do all this chopping and slicing, the Chinese chef uses a cleaver; it's a knife with a blade about 8 inches long and 3 inches wide. A thick, heavy cleaver is best for cutting through meats and chicken with bone. A lighter, thinner one works well when you're chopping vegetables and slicing boneless meat. A heavy, sharp knife can be used in place of the cleaver.

Most of our Chinese recipes using beef or poultry tell you to make thin slices diagonally across the grain. If you partially freeze the meat, slicing will be a lot easier. Once sliced, the meat can be marinated to make it more tender and tasty. When you're slicing fibrous vegetables, such as celery or broccoli, cut them diagonally to create more surface area and to reduce cooking time. You can just slice soft vegetables like mushrooms in the regular manner.

Whether you're slicing, shredding, chopping, or dicing, cut each piece uniformly; your care will show and definitely make the dish more attractive.

Cooking Equipment

If you're just learning about Chinese cookery, you can use standard kitchen utensils and equipment without making any new investments.

Most Chinese dishes are stir-fried. This is a cooking method in which food is cooked in a small amount of oil over high heat and stirred and turned almost constantly. It's a quick cooking method that retains the natural color, flavor, and nutritive value of the food.

To stir-fry, use a wok or heavy skillet with high sides. Woks all have the same classic bowl shape but are available in different styles. There are models that sit atop a cooking surface, as well as electric woks. They're available in aluminum, iron, or steel, and some are coated with a nonstick surface. If you've just bought a wok without a nonstick lining and plan to use it for the first time, it should be seasoned to keep food from sticking and the surface from rusting. You'll find instructions for seasoning included with your wok.

After using the wok, clean it with a mild detergent, and dry thoroughly to prevent rusting. After using it several times, you may need to rub a few drops of oil into the surface before storing.

Along with the wok, the Chinese chef uses a Chinese spatula and stirring spoon. The spatula is used to scoop and lift food from the sides and bottom of the wok, and a stirring spoon is useful for stir-frying. However, a ladle and long-handled spoon can be substituted for these utensils.

Chinese foods are also deep-fried. For this method, you'll need a Chinese strainer or a slotted spoon to lower food into the hot oil and lift it out when it's done. You also should have a thermometer to regulate oil temperature. If your oil gets too hot, the food will brown yet not be done inside. If it's too cool, the food will be soggy and greasy.

Cooking Tips

—Have all your ingredients prepared and at hand before heating the wok and oil to stir-fry.

—When stir-frying, be sure to heat the wok before adding the oil; then heat the oil before adding the food.

—Peanut oil is the best choice for use in the wok because it can be heated to a high temperature without causing smoke. Vegetable oil works well, too, but never use solid shortening, butter, or margarine.

—Add ingredients to the wok in the order according to the recipe so nothing will be undercooked or overcooked.

—When deep-frying, remember that the oil level shouldn't be over half the depth of the wok, or the oil might splash out.

—Dry food completely before lowering it into hot oil; water will cause the oil to splatter.

—Gently lower food into the hot oil with a spatula or strainer so that there's no splashing.

Adding the Finishing Touch

Although cooking takes only a little time, don't forget the final touch of garnishing before serving. Chinese dishes are attractive because of their colorfulness and variety of shapes, and garnishes enhance the dishes even more.

Onion or celery fans and carved vegetable roses are the most popular Chinese garnishes. For fresh and pretty garnishes, keep them in a bowl of ice water, and add just before serving. To learn how to make garnishes, turn to "Appendices" in this book.

Desserts Can Be Nutritious

Desserts are sometimes considered frivolous, non-nutritious endings to meals. But we've come up with some tasty ideas that satisfy the sweet tooth yet keep nutrition in mind. And although these desserts are not necessarily lower in calories, they emphasize ingredients that contribute to the day's total food needs.

Using fruits and vegetables in desserts is one easy way to increase nutritional value. Zucchini Bars are enhanced with raisins, which have a high level of iron. Whole wheat flour and wheat bran cereal make these bars a good source of dietary fiber.

Strawberries, high in vitamin C, and pineapple increase the vitamin and mineral content of Strawberry Yogurt Delight. You also get extra protein and calcium from the yogurt.

Brown Rice Pudding is a new twist on an old favorite. The substitution of brown rice for white rice increases the vitamin, mineral, and fiber content of our recipe. Top this pudding with a tangy lemon sauce.

ZUCCHINI BARS

1½ cups firmly packed brown sugar
½ cup butter or margarine, softened
¼ cup vegetable oil
2 eggs
2 tablespoons water
1 teaspoon vanilla extract
¼ teaspoon ground nutmeg
1½ cups shreds of wheat bran cereal
1½ cups all-purpose flour
½ cup whole wheat flour
1 teaspoon baking soda
½ teaspoon salt
2½ cups grated zucchini
1 cup raisins
1 cup flaked coconut

Combine brown sugar, butter, and oil in a large mixing bowl; beat at medium speed of an electric mixer until light and fluffy. Add eggs, water, vanilla, and nutmeg; mix just until blended.

Combine cereal, flour, soda, and salt; add to creamed mixture alternately with zucchini, beginning and ending with the flour mixture. Mix just until blended

after each addition. Stir in raisins and coconut.

Spoon batter into a greased 13- x 9- x 2-inch baking pan. Bake at 350° for 40 minutes. Cool, and cut into bars. Yield: 3 dozen.   *Ruth Cunliffe,*
Lake Placid, Florida.

STRAWBERRY YOGURT DELIGHT

1 (8-ounce) can unsweetened crushed pineapple, undrained
1 envelope unflavored gelatin
1 (10-ounce) package frozen strawberries, thawed and undrained
1 (8-ounce) carton strawberry low-fat yogurt
1 teaspoon grated lemon rind
Whipped topping (optional)
Lemon wedges (optional)

Drain pineapple, reserving juice; set aside. Sprinkle gelatin over pineapple juice in a small saucepan; let stand 1 minute. Stir mixture over low heat 2 to 3 minutes or until gelatin dissolves; remove from heat. Add strawberries, yogurt, and lemon rind; mix well.

Pour into 6 (4-ounce) dessert dishes. Chill thoroughly. Garnish each serving with whipped topping and lemon wedge, if desired. Yield: 6 servings.
Mary Pappas,
Richmond, Virginia.

BROWN RICE PUDDING

2 cups milk
1 cup half-and-half
2 tablespoons butter or margarine
3 eggs, beaten
2 cups cooked brown rice
⅔ cup sugar
½ cup raisins
¼ teaspoon ground cinnamon
¼ teaspoon ground nutmeg
Dash of salt
Lemon sauce (recipe follows)

Combine milk, half-and-half, and butter in a saucepan; cook until thoroughly heated. (Do not boil.) Remove mixture from heat.

Gradually stir about one-fourth of hot mixture into eggs; add to remaining hot mixture, stirring constantly. Stir in rice, sugar, raisins, spices, and salt. Pour mixture into a lightly greased 2-quart baking dish.

Place dish in a shallow pan; add 1 inch of water to pan. Bake at 350° for 45 minutes or until set. Remove dish

from pan; let cool. Serve with lemon sauce. Yield: 8 servings.

Lemon Sauce:
¼ cup sugar
1½ teaspoons cornstarch
½ cup plus 2 tablespoons hot water
1½ tablespoons lemon juice
1 tablespoon butter or margarine
½ teaspoon grated lemon rind

Combine sugar and cornstarch in a small saucepan; gradually stir in water. Cook over medium heat, stirring constantly, until mixture comes to a boil. Cook 1 additional minute, stirring constantly. Remove from heat; stir in remaining ingredients. Yield: ¾ cup.
Mrs. Harry Zimmer,
El Paso, Texas.

SNOW WHITE PUDDING

2 eggs, separated
¼ cup sugar
1½ tablespoons cornstarch
⅛ teaspoon salt
2 cups milk, scalded
½ teaspoon vanilla extract
3 medium-size oranges, peeled and sectioned
¼ cup sugar
2 tablespoons flaked coconut
⅛ teaspoon grated orange rind

Combine egg yolks, ¼ cup sugar, cornstarch, and salt in top of a double boiler; mix well. Slowly add scalded milk, stirring constantly. Bring water to a boil in bottom of double boiler. Reduce heat to medium; cook 10 minutes, stirring occasionally, until custard thickens and coats a metal spoon. Remove from heat, and stir in vanilla; cool mixture slightly.

Divide orange sections evenly into 6 (6-ounce) custard cups. Pour pudding over the oranges.

Beat egg whites (at room temperature) until foamy. Gradually add ¼ cup sugar, 1 tablespoon at a time, beating until stiff peaks form. Spoon or pipe meringue onto pudding, covering entire surface and sealing edges. Bake at 425° for 3 minutes or until golden brown. Combine coconut and orange rind, mixing well; sprinkle over meringue. Yield: 6 servings.   *Roberta E. McGrath,*
Hopkinsville, Kentucky.

Tip: To ensure even baking, lower oven temperature 25° when using heatproof glass dishes.

GRANOLA APPLE CRISP

1⅓ cups fruit-and-nut granola
¼ cup butter or margarine, melted
¼ cup firmly packed brown sugar
¼ cup chopped pecans
4 large baking apples, peeled and sliced
 ½-inch thick
1 cup (4 ounces) shredded Cheddar cheese
¾ teaspoon ground cinnamon

Combine granola, butter, brown sugar, and pecans; mix well, and set mixture aside.

Combine apples, cheese, and cinnamon; toss well. Place in a greased 12- x 8- x 2-inch baking dish; top with granola mixture. Cover and bake at 375° for 30 minutes; uncover, and bake an additional 15 minutes. Yield: 6 to 8 servings.
Cynthia Shipley,
Dallas, Texas.

Entrées For Two Of You

If you're planning dinner for just the two of you, choose your favorite of these entrée recipes, whether it's chicken, fish, beef, or pork. Add a crisp salad and some bread, and you'll have the meal ready.

Our Lemon-Butter Steak With Brandy Sauce is a real time-saver. The steak is sautéed for less than 5 minutes and then flamed with apricot-flavored brandy for a dramatic presentation.

LEMON-BUTTER STEAK WITH BRANDY SAUCE

1 (1½-pound) sirloin steak
½ teaspoon seasoned salt
¼ teaspoon pepper
1 teaspoon dried whole oregano
¼ cup butter or margarine
2 tablespoons lemon juice
½ teaspoon hot sauce
2 tablespoons Worcestershire sauce
½ cup apricot brandy, heated
Lemon slice
Fresh parsley

Sprinkle both sides of steak with seasoned salt, pepper, and oregano. Melt butter in a heavy skillet; stir in lemon juice and hot sauce. Add steak, and cook over high heat, quickly browning each side. Reduce heat to medium, and

cook steak 1 to 2 minutes on each side or until desired degree of doneness is almost reached. Remove from heat.

Pour Worcestershire sauce and heated brandy over steak; ignite. When flames die down, remove steak to a serving plate; spoon sauce over steak. Serve immediately. Garnish with a lemon slice and parsley. Yield: 2 servings.
T. O. Davis,
Waynesboro, Mississippi.

POLYNESIAN PORK

½ pound boneless pork, cut into ⅛-inch
 strips
2 tablespoons peanut oil
½ green pepper, cut into 1-inch pieces
½ cup drained pineapple chunks
½ cup diagonally sliced celery
¾ cup chicken broth, undiluted
¼ cup vinegar
¼ cup sugar
1 tablespoon catsup
¼ teaspoon salt
1 tablespoon cornstarch
3 tablespoons water
Hot cooked rice

Sauté pork in hot oil in a large skillet until browned. Add green pepper, pineapple, celery, chicken broth, vinegar, sugar, catsup, and salt, mixing well; cover and cook 6 minutes or until vegetables are crisp-tender.

Combine cornstarch and water, stirring well; stir into pork mixture. Cook, stirring constantly, until thickened. Serve over rice. Yield: 2 servings.
Carolyn S. Rosen,
Nashville, Tennessee.

FILLET OF SOLE PROVENÇAL

½ to ¾ pound sole fillets
1 tablespoon lemon juice
1 tablespoon olive oil
1 small tomato, thinly sliced
1 small onion, thinly sliced
¼ teaspoon dried whole basil
⅛ teaspoon salt
Freshly ground pepper to taste

Place fillets in a lightly greased 13- x 9- x 2-inch baking dish. Combine lemon juice and olive oil; sprinkle over fillets. Top fillets with tomato and onion slices; sprinkle with remaining ingredients. Bake, uncovered, at 350° for 10 to 14 minutes or until fish flakes when tested with a fork. Yield: 2 servings.
Patricia Llewellyn,
Silver Spring, Maryland.

CHICKEN SCALLOPINI WITH PEPPERS

2 chicken breast halves, skinned and
 boned
¼ cup all-purpose flour
½ teaspoon salt
¼ teaspoon pepper
2 tablespoons olive oil
1 small green pepper, cut into ½-inch
 wide strips
1 small red pepper, cut into ½-inch wide
 strips
1 small clove garlic, minced
¼ cup dry red wine
1 tablespoon red wine vinegar

Place each chicken breast half between 2 sheets of waxed paper; flatten to ¼-inch thickness, using a mallet or rolling pin.

Combine flour, salt, and pepper; stir well. Dredge chicken in flour mixture, shaking off excess; set aside.

Heat olive oil in a heavy skillet. Cook chicken in oil over medium heat 4 to 5 minutes on each side or until golden brown. Remove chicken to a warmed serving platter; keep warm.

Add pepper strips to remaining oil in skillet; sauté over medium heat 2 to 3 minutes. Add garlic, and sauté 1 minute. Stir in wine and vinegar; simmer 2 minutes. Spoon peppers and sauce over chicken. Yield: 2 servings.
Brenda Clark,
Phenix City, Alabama.

Make-Ahead Menu Makes Entertaining Easier

A busy life-style often means making choices about how we spend our time. Entertaining is sometimes the first thing to go. But that doesn't have to be the case if you plan carefully and prepare most of the food ahead of time.

Our make-ahead menu allows for easy entertaining, so there's time to relax and enjoy your company. It features Shrimp au Gratin, an elegant dish that's put together one day and baked the next. We chose to serve it over rice, but for a luncheon or lighter meal, you might want to serve it just plain.

Welcome your guests with a light appetizer, Parsley-Dill Dip With Fresh Vegetables. We suggest a tray arranged with carrot sticks, broccoli, cauliflower, and cherry tomatoes. Prepare the vegetables the same day as the meal, but the dip can be made the night before.

The salad and dessert can also be made ahead of time. Easy Amaretto Cake actually gets better if it's held a couple of days. Ruby-and-Emerald Salad gels the night before and needs only to be unmolded onto lettuce leaves to be ready for serving.

Brussels Sprouts Polonaise and commercial French bread round out the menu. The brussels sprouts have to be cooked just before serving, but this dish takes little time to make, especially if you have the egg-crumb topping already mixed up.

Parsley-Dill Dip With Fresh Vegetables
Shrimp au Gratin
Brussels Sprouts Polonaise
Ruby-and-Emerald Salad
Commercial French bread
Easy Amaretto Cake
Wine   Coffee

PARSLEY-DILL DIP
WITH FRESH VEGETABLES

⅔ cup mayonnaise
⅓ cup commercial sour cream
1 tablespoon chopped fresh parsley
1 to 2 teaspoons hot sauce
1 teaspoon minced onion
1 teaspoon dried whole dillweed
1 teaspoon seasoned salt
1 teaspoon Worcestershire sauce

Combine all ingredients; mix well. Chill 6 hours or overnight. Serve with fresh vegetables. Yield: 1 cup.
Evelyn Milam,
Knoxville, Tennessee.

SHRIMP AU GRATIN

2½ quarts water
2 tablespoons salt
3 pounds unpeeled fresh shrimp
1 chicken-flavored bouillon cube
1 cup boiling water
¼ cup plus 1 tablespoon butter or
    margarine
3 tablespoons all-purpose flour
1 cup milk
1 egg, beaten
2 tablespoons sherry
1 teaspoon Worcestershire sauce
4 drops of hot sauce
¼ teaspoon pepper
⅛ teaspoon salt
1 cup (4 ounces) shredded Cheddar cheese
Hot cooked rice

Bring water and salt to a boil; add shrimp, and cook 1 to 2 minutes. Drain well; rinse with cold water. Peel and devein shrimp. Set aside.

Dissolve bouillon cube in 1 cup boiling water; set aside.

Melt butter in a heavy saucepan over low heat; add flour, stirring until smooth. Cook 1 minute, stirring constantly. Gradually add bouillon and milk; cook over medium heat, stirring constantly, until mixture is thickened and bubbly. Remove from heat.

Gradually stir about one-fourth of hot mixture into egg; add to remaining hot mixture, stirring constantly. Cook over low heat 3 to 4 minutes, stirring constantly; remove from heat. Stir in sherry, Worcestershire, hot sauce, and seasonings; add shrimp. Pour into a shallow 1½-quart casserole. Top with cheese. Cover and refrigerate overnight.

Let stand at room temperature 30 minutes before baking; cover, and bake at 350° for 30 to 40 minutes or until thoroughly heated. Serve over rice. Yield: 6 servings.

Note: Dish can be prepared and baked immediately, if desired.
Chris Tortorici,
Pelham, Alabama.

BRUSSELS SPROUTS POLONAISE

1½ pounds fresh brussels sprouts
¼ cup butter or margarine, melted
¼ cup fine dry breadcrumbs
1 hard-cooked egg, sieved
2 tablespoons chopped fresh parsley

Cook brussels sprouts in a small amount of boiling water 12 to 15 minutes. Drain and place in a serving dish.

Combine remaining ingredients; sprinkle over brussels sprouts, and toss lightly. Yield: 6 servings.
Alberta Pinkston,
Corryton, Tennessee.

RUBY-AND-EMERALD SALAD

1½ cups tomato juice, divided
1 (3-ounce) package lemon-flavored gelatin
½ cup beer
1 tablespoon vinegar
2 green onions, chopped
½ cup finely chopped celery
¼ cup finely chopped green pepper
1 (2-ounce) jar diced pimiento, drained
Lettuce leaves
Green onion fan (optional)

Bring 1 cup tomato juice to a boil; pour over gelatin, stirring until dissolved. Stir in remaining tomato juice, beer, and vinegar. Chill until consistency of unbeaten egg white. Stir in green onions, celery, green pepper, and pimiento; pour into oiled individual molds or a 4-cup mold. Chill until firm. Unmold on lettuce leaves. Garnish with green onion fan, if desired. Yield: 6 to 8 servings.
Mrs. John W. Stevens,
Lexington, Kentucky.

EASY AMARETTO CAKE

1½ cups chopped almonds, toasted and
    divided
1 (18.5-ounce) package yellow cake mix
    without pudding
1 (3½-ounce) package vanilla instant
    pudding mix
4 eggs
½ cup vegetable oil
½ cup water
½ cup amaretto
1 teaspoon almond extract
½ cup sugar
¼ cup water
2 tablespoons butter or margarine
¼ cup amaretto
½ teaspoon almond extract

Sprinkle 1 cup almonds into bottom of a well-greased and floured 10-inch tube pan; set aside.

Combine cake mix, pudding mix, eggs, oil, water, amaretto, and almond extract in a mixing bowl; beat on low speed of an electric mixer until dry ingredients are moistened. Increase speed to medium, and beat 4 minutes. Stir in remaining ½ cup almonds.

Pour batter into prepared tube pan. Bake at 325° for 1 hour or until a wooden pick inserted in center comes out clean. Cool cake in pan 10 to 15 minutes; remove from pan, and cool completely.

Combine sugar, ¼ cup water, and butter in a small saucepan; bring to a boil. Reduce heat to medium, and gently boil 4 to 5 minutes, stirring occasionally, until sugar dissolves. Remove from heat, and cool 15 minutes. Stir in ¼ cup amaretto and ½ teaspoon almond extract. Punch holes in top of cake with a wooden pick; slowly spoon glaze on top of cake, allowing glaze to absorb into cake. Yield: one 10-inch cake.
Jan Weller,
Richmond, Virginia.

Simple, Pretty Fruit Appetizers

What better way to welcome guests than with some of the South's sweetest claims to fame—ruby-red strawberries, plump blueberries, or juicy oranges. Arrange the appetizers artistically on a plate or on party crackers—no artist could paint a prettier picture.

Most of these recipes are no-cook, so they are easy to assemble just before serving. In fact, you'll want to prepare our Fruit-Topped Canapés just a few hours before serving. If this dish is allowed to sit overnight, juices from the fresh fruit can make the crackers soggy. Toasting will keep the crackers crisp for several hours.

If your guests enjoy eating sweets, our Strawberries With Chocolate Cream will be a hit. Mix cocoa, powdered sugar, and whipped cream, and use fresh strawberries for dipping. Be sure to leave the berries capped to serve; once the caps are removed, the sweet flavor is released.

You'll find more recipes here, but it's easy to come up with your own ideas for fruit appetizers. Always keep color and shape of fruit in mind as you plan your party tray. Here are some ideas to get you started.

—Slice honeydew melons in half, scoop out the seeds, and fill with fresh raspberries, cherries, or strawberries.

—Arrange a mix of fresh fruit and cheese on trays and in containers for a help-yourself buffet.

—Use scooped-out fruit shell halves, such as pineapples, melons, grapefruit, or oranges, for salad or dip containers. Cut up the fruit pulp for dippers.

—Wrap a slice of prosciutto ham (thinly sliced Italian ham) around a fig or a slice of cantaloupe or honeydew melon for a tasty combination.

—Dip wedges of pear or nectarine, orange segments, or berries in white or dark chocolate. Cover only half the fruit to allow colors to show.

Tiny canapé cutters give the fruit in our Fruit-Topped Canapés their unusual shapes.

SHRIMP-PINEAPPLE APPETIZER

3 cups water
1 pound fresh unpeeled shrimp
1 cup mayonnaise
½ cup commercial sour cream
3 tablespoons red maraschino cherry juice
1 fresh pineapple, halved lengthwise
About 3 cups honeydew balls
About 3 cups cantaloupe balls

Bring water to a boil; add shrimp, and cook 3 to 5 minutes. Drain well; rinse with cold water. Chill. Peel and devein. Set shrimp aside.

Combine mayonnaise, sour cream, and cherry juice; mix until well blended; chill.

Scoop pulp from pineapple halves, leaving shells ½-inch thick; set pineapple shells aside. Cut pineapple pulp into bite-size pieces; discard core. Alternate pineapple, melon balls, and shrimp on plastic picks.

Pour mayonnaise mixture into pineapple shells. To serve, arrange pineapple shells on serving dish; surround with fruit and shrimp on plastic picks. Yield: about 5 dozen appetizers.

Tip: Fresh pineapple does not ripen further after it's picked. Choose one that is firm and fresh looking and use within 3 to 5 days.

FRUIT-TOPPED CANAPÉS

1 (8-ounce) package cream cheese, softened
1 teaspoon grated orange rind
2 tablespoons orange juice
½ teaspoon ground ginger
4 dozen multi-shaped crackers, lightly toasted
8 fresh strawberries
½ cup fresh blueberries
¼ medium honeydew
¾ cup red grapes
¾ cup green grapes
½ cup mandarin orange sections, drained
1½ cups fresh pineapple wedges, drained
1 or 2 kiwi
Small fresh mint leaves

Beat cream cheese until smooth; add orange rind, orange juice, and ginger, mixing well. Spoon into a pastry bag, and pipe mixture onto crackers; set aside. Cut fruit into various shapes and place on crackers, decorating tops as desired with fruit and mint leaves. Yield: 4 dozen canapés.

ORANGE-BERRY APPETIZER

6 small oranges, peeled and sectioned
1½ cups fresh blueberries
1 (10-ounce) package frozen raspberries, thawed and drained
Fresh mint sprigs

Arrange orange sections on 6 small salad plates. Place the sections in a row down the center of each plate. Place 2 tablespoons blueberries along each side of orange sections; set aside.

Put raspberries through a sieve or food mill. Drizzle puréed raspberries over oranges and blueberries. Garnish with mint sprigs. Yield: 6 servings.

STUFFED CHERRIES

1 (3-ounce) package cream cheese, softened
¼ cup finely chopped almonds, toasted
1 tablespoon half-and-half
1 tablespoon grated orange rind
1 pound fresh Bing cherries, pitted

Combine all ingredients except cherries; mix well. Spoon cream cheese mixture into a decorating bag fitted with No. 12 round tip. Pipe mixture into cherries, keeping index finger over bottom end of cherry so mixture does not come through. Fill the cherries completely, piping mixture out around the tops of cherries. Yield: about 55 appetizers.
Hazel Boschen,
Ashland, Virginia.

STRAWBERRIES WITH CHOCOLATE CREAM

1 cup whipping cream
3 tablespoons cocoa
¼ cup plus 1 tablespoon powdered sugar
2 quarts medium-size fresh strawberries

Beat whipping cream until foamy. Sift cocoa and powdered sugar together; add to cream, beating until soft peaks form. Serve with strawberries. Yield: about 6½ dozen appetizers.

Have A Heart—An Artichoke Heart

If you enjoy artichoke hearts but not the tedious process of cooking the fresh vegetable, then try these recipes from our readers. They call for canned or frozen artichoke hearts—a convenience item that can't be beat.

HOT ARTICHOKE-CRAB SPREAD

2 (9-ounce) packages frozen artichoke hearts
¼ teaspoon lemon-pepper seasoning
1 (6-ounce) can crabmeat, drained
1 cup grated Parmesan cheese
1 cup mayonnaise
½ to ¾ teaspoon garlic salt
Pimiento strips (optional)

Cook artichokes according to package directions, adding lemon-pepper seasoning. Drain well; chop.

Add remaining ingredients except pimiento to artichokes; mix well. Spoon into a lightly greased 10- x 6- x 2-inch baking dish; bake at 350° for 20 minutes. Remove from oven; garnish with pimiento strips, if desired. Serve spread hot with assorted crackers. Yield: about 3½ cups.
Carol Allen,
Dallas, Texas.

CREAMED DRIED BEEF WITH ARTICHOKES

2 tablespoons butter or margarine
1 (14-ounce) can artichoke hearts, drained and sliced
½ cup Chablis or other dry white wine
1½ tablespoons grated Parmesan cheese
2 (5-ounce) jars sliced dried beef, rinsed and coarsely chopped
1 (16-ounce) carton commercial sour cream
4 English muffins, halved and toasted
Paprika

Melt butter in a large skillet; add artichokes, Chablis, cheese, and dried beef, mixing well. Cook over medium heat, stirring often, until bubbly. Stir in sour cream; cook until thoroughly heated. (Do not boil.) Serve over English muffin halves. Sprinkle with paprika. Yield: 8 servings.
Mrs. Harland J. Stone,
Ocala, Florida.

ARTICHOKE-RICE SALAD

1 (6-ounce) package long grain and wild rice mix
1 (14-ounce) can artichoke hearts, drained and chopped
1 (2-ounce) jar chopped pimiento, drained
12 pimiento-stuffed olives, chopped
3 green onions with tops, chopped
1 cup chopped celery
½ cup mayonnaise
1 teaspoon curry powder
Tomato wedges (optional)

Cook rice according to package directions, omitting butter; cool.

Add remaining ingredients except tomato wedges; mix well. Cover and chill thoroughly. Garnish with tomato wedges, if desired. Yield: 8 servings.
Genell Vaughn,
Albertville, Alabama.

ITALIAN GREEN BEAN-AND-ARTICHOKE CASSEROLE

2 (16-ounce) cans cut green beans, drained
1 (14-ounce) can artichoke hearts, drained and quartered
½ cup commercial Italian salad dressing
¼ cup fine, dry breadcrumbs
¼ cup Parmesan cheese

Combine beans, artichokes, and salad dressing in shallow dish; cover and marinate overnight in refrigerator.

Drain vegetable mixture; spoon into a lightly greased 2-quart casserole. Combine breadcrumbs and cheese; sprinkle on top. Bake, uncovered, at 350° for 30 minutes or until heated. Yield: 6 to 8 servings.
Debbie Valenti,
Hammond, Louisiana.

TOMATO-AND-ARTICHOKE HEART BAKE

1 (14-ounce) can artichoke hearts, drained
1 (28-ounce) can whole tomatoes, drained
½ cup chopped green onions with tops
2 tablespoons butter or margarine, melted
1 tablespoon sugar
½ teaspoon dried whole basil
Salt and pepper to taste

Rinse artichokes with water; drain. Cut drained artichokes and tomatoes into quarters.

Sauté green onions in butter until tender. Stir in artichoke hearts, tomatoes, and remaining ingredients. Pour mixture into a lightly greased 1-quart baking dish. Bake at 325° for 10 to 15 minutes or until heated through. Yield: 4 to 6 servings.
Nancy J. Winslow,
Oak City, North Carolina.

Plan Lunch For The Ladies

Like many ladies' luncheons, our menus feature salads as the entrées. But main-dish salads often are not as light as they appear—the mayonnaise or oil they contain add 100 or more unwanted calories per tablespoon.

By using reduced-calorie mayonnaise in Special Chicken Salad, we removed about 60 calories per serving. Mandarin oranges and emerald-green kiwi enhance the salad's appearance and taste.

Serve the chicken salad with Company Asparagus and melba rounds. Calories are kept low in the asparagus dish by sautéing celery and green onions in vegetable cooking spray instead of butter. We're suggesting melba rounds because they're lower in salt and fat than most crackers.

Apple-Tea Punch
Special Chicken Salad
Company Asparagus
Melba rounds
Tart Lemon Soufflé

APPLE-TEA PUNCH

6 cups unsweetened apple juice
2 cups strong tea
1 cup club soda, chilled

Combine apple juice and tea, stirring well; chill.

To serve, combine chilled mixture and club soda. Serve punch over ice, if desired. Yield: 9 cups (about 40 calories per ½-cup serving).   *Leslie Haynes, Marion, Alabama.*

SPECIAL CHICKEN SALAD

3 cups water
¼ teaspoon dried whole rosemary
¼ teaspoon salt
2 pounds boneless chicken breasts, skinned
½ cup chopped green pepper
1 (11-ounce) can unsweetened mandarin oranges, drained
½ cup reduced-calorie mayonnaise
3 tablespoons slivered almonds, toasted
1 tablespoon lemon juice
2 kiwi
Lettuce leaves (optional)

Bring water, rosemary, and salt to a boil; add chicken. Return to a boil; cover, reduce heat, and simmer 20 minutes or until tender. Drain chicken; let cool. Coarsely chop chicken. Add green pepper, mandarin oranges, mayonnaise, almonds, and lemon juice; mix well. Cover and chill 2 to 3 hours.

Peel kiwi; cut into ¼-inch slices. Cut slices in half; stir into salad just before serving. Serve salad on lettuce leaves, if desired. Yield: 8 servings (about 217 calories per serving).

COMPANY ASPARAGUS

2 pounds fresh asparagus
Vegetable cooking spray
¾ cup sliced celery
½ cup sliced green onions
2 tablespoons lemon juice
1 (8-ounce) can sliced water chestnuts, drained
1 (2-ounce) jar diced pimiento, drained

Snap off tough ends of asparagus. Remove scales, if desired, with a knife or vegetable peeler. Cook asparagus, covered, in boiling water 6 to 8 minutes or until crisp-tender. Drain and place on a serving dish; keep warm.

Coat a large skillet with cooking spray; place over medium heat until hot. Add celery, onions, and lemon juice; sauté until vegetables are tender. Stir in water chestnuts and pimiento; cook until thoroughly heated. Spoon mixture over hot asparagus. Yield: 8 servings (about 33 calories per serving).

TART LEMON SOUFFLÉ

⅔ cup lemon juice
½ cup water
2 envelopes unflavored gelatin
4 eggs, separated
¼ cup plus 2 tablespoons sugar
2 cups skim milk
1 cup frozen whipped topping, thawed
2 whole fresh strawberries (optional)
Fresh mint leaves (optional)

Cut a piece of aluminum foil or waxed paper long enough to fit around a 6-cup soufflé dish, allowing a 1-inch overlap; fold lengthwise into thirds. Lightly oil one side of foil; wrap around outside of dish, oiled side against dish and extending 2 inches above rim. Secure with freezer tape.

Combine lemon juice, water, and gelatin in a small saucepan; let stand 1 minute. Combine egg yolks and sugar;

beat well, and add to gelatin mixture. Stir in milk. Bring to a boil over low heat, stirring constantly. Chill until the consistency of unbeaten egg white.

Beat egg whites (at room temperature) until stiff but not dry; fold into lemon mixture. Fold in whipped topping. Spoon mixture into soufflé dish; chill until firm. Remove collar. Garnish with strawberries and mint, if desired. Yield: 8 servings (about 147 calories per serving).   *Elaine Bell, Dexter, New Mexico.*

Marinated Shrimp Salad
Assorted fresh vegetables
Light Tomato Aspic
Glazed Fruit

MARINATED SHRIMP SALAD

2 quarts water
2½ pounds unpeeled medium-size fresh shrimp
1 large green pepper, coarsely chopped
4 green onions with tops, sliced
½ cup diagonally sliced celery
½ cup unpeeled, chopped cucumber
1 (2-ounce) jar diced pimiento, drained
1 cup unsweetened apple juice
⅔ cup cider vinegar
¼ teaspoon hot sauce
¼ teaspoon paprika
⅓ pound fresh snow peas

Bring water to a boil; add shrimp, and cook 3 to 5 minutes. Drain well; rinse with cold water. Peel and devein shrimp. Chill.

Combine shrimp and next 5 ingredients in a large shallow dish. Combine apple juice, vinegar, hot sauce, and paprika, mixing well; pour over shrimp mixture. Cover and refrigerate dish overnight.

Arrange snow peas on a steaming rack, and place over boiling water; cover and steam 3 to 5 minutes or until crisp-tender. Chill peas.

To serve, arrange peas on plate; top with shrimp mixture. Yield: 6 servings (about 154 calories per serving).

LIGHT TOMATO ASPIC

2 envelopes unflavored gelatin
½ cup water
3 cups tomato juice
2 teaspoons lemon juice
1 tablespoon plus 1 teaspoon minced fresh
    parsley
1 teaspoon onion powder
⅛ teaspoon white pepper
Vegetable cooking spray
Thin cucumber slices
Fresh parsley sprigs

Sprinkle gelatin over water; let stand
1 minute.

Combine tomato juice and lemon
juice in a saucepan; bring to a boil.
Remove from heat; add gelatin, stirring
until gelatin dissolves. Stir in parsley,
onion powder, and white pepper. Spoon
into 6 (¾-cup) molds coated with cooking spray. Chill until firm.

To serve, arrange cucumber slices and
parsley sprigs on salad plates; unmold
aspics on plates. Yield: 6 servings
(about 33 calories per serving).

Mary Peterson,
Houston, Texas.

GLAZED FRUIT

1 (16-ounce) can unsweetened sliced
    peaches, drained
1 (15¼-ounce) can unsweetened pineapple
    chunks, drained
1 (11-ounce) can unsweetened mandarin
    oranges, drained
1 cup seedless green grapes, halved
2 tablespoons cornstarch
1 (12-ounce) can peach nectar
2 tablespoons Cointreau or other
    orange-flavored liqueur
¼ to ½ teaspoon grated lemon rind
Fresh mint leaves (optional)

Combine peaches, pineapple, mandarin oranges, and grapes; spoon into 6
dessert dishes. Set aside.

Combine cornstarch and peach nectar
in a small saucepan, stirring constantly.
Add Cointreau and lemon rind; cook
over medium heat until thickened, stirring constantly. Spoon sauce over fruit;
chill thoroughly. Garnish with mint
leaves, if desired. Yield: 6 servings
(about 142 calories per serving).

*Tip: Mix liquid from canned fruit in a
jar as you acquire it; use it in a gelatin
dessert or as a punch drink.*

Rich Ideas For Rice

Rice doesn't have to be a plain side
dish. In these recipes, it becomes host
to a variety of ingredients.

Beef consommé and hot sauce add
new life to Cumin Rice. And chicken-
flavored bouillon combined with raisins
and curry powder gives Raisin Rice
With Curry a sweet, nutty flavor.

Our most unusual rice dish features a
combination of long grain and wild rice
mix and several different vegetables.
Scallions, Chinese pea pods, mushrooms, and water chestnuts turn Rice
With Vegetables into a colorful addition
to the menu.

CUMIN RICE

1 cup uncooked regular rice
¼ cup chopped onion
¼ cup chopped green pepper
1½ tablespoons vegetable oil
2 (10½-ounce) cans beef consommé,
    undiluted
¾ teaspoon cumin seeds
¼ teaspoon hot sauce

Sauté rice, onion, and green pepper
in oil in a saucepan until lightly brown.
Add remaining ingredients; mix well.
Bring to a boil; then cover, reduce heat,
and simmer 20 to 25 minutes. Yield: 4
servings.

Betty Rabe,
Plano, Texas.

RICE WITH VEGETABLES

2 scallions, chopped
1 tablespoon butter or margarine, melted
1 (6-ounce) package long grain and wild
    rice mix
2 cups chicken broth
1 (6-ounce) package Chinese pea pods,
    thawed and drained
4 large mushrooms, sliced
1 (4-ounce) can water chestnuts, drained
    and sliced
2 tablespoons vegetable oil

Sauté scallions in butter in a large
skillet. Add rice mix and chicken broth;
bring to a boil. Cover, reduce heat, and
simmer 20 to 25 minutes or until liquid
is absorbed.

Sauté pea pods, mushrooms, and
water chestnuts in hot oil 1 to 2 minutes. Toss vegetables with rice mixture
before serving. Yield: 6 servings.

Saralyn Bone Lundy,
Tallahassee, Florida.

RAISIN RICE WITH CURRY

¼ cup chopped onion
3 tablespoons butter or margarine, melted
1 cup water
1 chicken-flavored bouillon cube
1 cup uncooked instant rice
¼ cup raisins
½ teaspoon curry powder

Sauté onion in butter in a saucepan
until tender. Add water and bouillon
cube; bring to a boil. Stir in remaining
ingredients. Allow mixture to return to
a boil; cover and remove from heat. Let
stand 5 minutes. Yield: 4 servings.

Lura Edsall,
Asheville, North Carolina.

HONEY RICE

4 cups hot cooked rice
½ cup chopped roasted peanuts
¼ cup butter or margarine
¼ cup honey
1 teaspoon ground cinnamon
¾ teaspoon ground ginger
Chopped parsley (optional)

Combine rice and peanuts; set aside,
and keep warm.

Combine butter and honey in a saucepan; cook over low heat just until butter melts. Stir in cinnamon and ginger;
pour over rice mixture, stirring well.
Sprinkle with chopped parsley, if desired. Yield: 6 servings.

Lilly S. Bradley,
Salem, Virginia.

CALICO RICE

2½ cups water
3 chicken-flavored bouillon cubes
1 cup uncooked regular rice
1 (4-ounce) can sliced mushrooms, drained
½ cup chopped green pepper
2 tablespoons butter or margarine
2 tablespoons chopped pimiento, drained
⅛ teaspoon pepper

Combine water and bouillon cubes in
a medium saucepan; bring to a boil. Stir
in rice; cover, reduce heat, and simmer
20 to 25 minutes or until the liquid is
absorbed. Remove from heat; stir in remaining ingredients. Spoon into a
lightly greased 1½-quart casserole;
cover and bake at 300° for 20 minutes
or until heated through. Yield: 6
servings. *Mrs. Randall L. Wilson,*
Louisville, Kentucky.

Mexican Salad Spells Variety

With Mexico just across a narrow river from Texas, it's no wonder Mexican salads are popular. Southern cooks seem to agree that the basis for these hearty main-dish salads is lettuce, meat or poultry, cheese, and tomatoes. But how the rest of the ingredients differ is what makes these salads so well liked.

Take, for example, Mexican Chef Salad. Kidney beans, two types of lettuce, Italian dressing, and avocados make it unique. Evelyn Milam, of Knoxville, adds taco seasoning mix, corn, refried beans, and tortilla chips to her Taco Salad. She layers it in a glass bowl for appealing visual effect.

MEXICAN CHEF SALAD

1 pound ground beef
½ cup chopped onion
1 (15-ounce) can kidney beans, drained
1 tablespoon chili powder
2 (4-ounce) cans taco sauce
½ cup commercial Italian salad dressing
6 cups torn iceberg lettuce
3½ cups torn romaine lettuce
½ cup sliced green onions with tops
1 (7½-ounce) package tortilla chips
1 large tomato, chopped
1 cup (4 ounces) shredded sharp Cheddar cheese
1 small avocado, sliced and coated with lemon juice

Cook beef and onion in a large skillet until meat is browned, stirring to crumble meat. Drain. Stir in beans and chili powder; cook, uncovered, until thoroughly heated. Remove from heat; stir in taco sauce and salad dressing. Cool mixture slightly.

Combine lettuce and green onions; place in a large bowl. Crush chips, reserving several whole ones for garnish. Set aside a small amount of chopped tomatoes for garnish. Layer remaining tomato, meat mixture, crushed chips, cheese, and avocado on lettuce. Garnish with reserved whole chips and chopped tomato. Yield: 6 servings.
Marti Ledwidge,
Baton Rouge, Louisiana.

TACO SALAD

1 pound ground beef
1 (1¼-ounce) envelope taco seasoning mix
1 (16-ounce) can cream-style corn
1 (16-ounce) can refried beans
1 (7½-ounce) package tortilla chips, coarsely crushed
1 medium head lettuce, torn into pieces
2 cups (8 ounces) shredded Longhorn cheese
2 medium tomatoes, diced
Commercial taco sauce

Cook beef in a large skillet until browned, stirring to crumble meat. Drain. Stir in taco mix, corn, and beans, blending well. Cool slightly.

Layer half the chips, meat mixture, lettuce, cheese, and tomatoes in a serving bowl. Repeat layers. Serve with taco sauce. Yield: 6 to 8 servings.
Evelyn Milam,
Knoxville, Tennessee.

MEXICAN OLIVE SALAD

1 pound ground beef
2 cups (8 ounces) shredded Cheddar cheese
½ cup commercial spicy-sweet French salad dressing
1 (2.2-ounce) can sliced ripe olives, drained
⅓ cup sliced pimiento-stuffed olives
1 large head lettuce, shredded
3 medium tomatoes, coarsely chopped
3 cups corn chips

Cook beef in a large skillet until browned, stirring to crumble meat. Drain, and cool slightly. Combine beef, cheese, salad dressing, and olives; chill. Add remaining ingredients, tossing gently; serve immediately. Yield: 8 servings.
Irene Murry,
Herculaneum, Missouri.

MEXICAN CHICKEN SALAD

1 (10-ounce) can tomatoes and green chiles, drained and chopped
½ (10¾-ounce) can cream of chicken soup, undiluted
⅛ teaspoon garlic powder
⅛ teaspoon ground cumin
1 small onion, diced
1 tablespoon vegetable oil
3 cups chopped cooked chicken
1 small head lettuce, torn into pieces
½ (7½-ounce) package tortilla chips, coarsely crushed
¾ cup (3 ounces) shredded sharp Cheddar cheese
¼ cup sliced ripe olives
Commercial taco sauce (optional)

Combine tomatoes and green chiles, soup, garlic powder, and cumin, mixing well; set aside.

Sauté onion in oil in a large skillet until tender. Stir in soup mixture and chicken. Cook over medium heat, stirring until bubbly. Cool slightly. Place lettuce on a serving dish; top with chicken mixture. Sprinkle with tortilla chips, cheese, and olives. Serve with taco sauce, if desired. Yield: 6 servings.
Sue T. McMurry,
Tupelo, Mississippi.

Fresh Vegetables With A Light Touch

In spring, we want everything to be lighter and fresher, especially vegetables. Why not try Potato-Broccoli Vinaigrette? The distinctive flavor of new potatoes makes this dish delightful after a long winter. The vinaigrette mixture is poured on after the vegetables are cooked; it's flavored with green onions, garlic, basil, and hot sauce.

New potatoes also star in another simple vegetable dish, Caraway Potatoes. The potatoes are cooked in their jackets with only a narrow strip peeled around the middle; then they're tossed with butter, caraway seeds, and lemon-pepper seasoning. This makes an attractive dish that virtually shouts spring.

Remember that when some of the fresh vegetables we crave aren't in season, we can make the ones that are available more tasty by preparing them in a lighter way. For example, in Dilly Carrots, a winter standby like carrots takes on a springtime freshness when cooked with a little butter, vinegar, brown sugar, and dill.

POTATO-BROCCOLI VINAIGRETTE

1½ pounds fresh broccoli
3 cups cooked, cubed new potatoes
½ cup vegetable oil
¼ cup cider vinegar
2 green onions, sliced
1 clove garlic, minced
1 teaspoon salt
1 teaspoon dried whole basil
⅛ teaspoon hot sauce
Cherry tomatoes (optional)

Trim off large leaves of broccoli, and remove tough ends of lower stalks. Wash thoroughly, and cut into 1-inch pieces. Cook broccoli, covered, in a small amount of boiling water 8 to 10 minutes or until crisp-tender.

Combine broccoli and potatoes in a bowl; keep warm.

Combine remaining ingredients except tomatoes in a saucepan; bring to a boil, and pour over vegetables. Gently toss. Garnish with cherry tomatoes, if desired. Yield: 6 to 8 servings.

Georgia F. Chapman,
Bedford, Virginia.

CARAWAY POTATOES

8 medium-size new potatoes
¼ cup butter or margarine, melted
2 to 3 teaspoons caraway seeds
½ teaspoon lemon-pepper seasoning
Salt to taste
Freshly ground pepper to taste

Peel a ½-inch strip around middle of each potato. Cook, covered, in boiling water 20 minutes or until tender. Drain potatoes; add remaining ingredients, tossing to coat. Yield: 4 servings.

Sharon McClatchey,
Muskogee, Oklahoma.

DILLY CARROTS

3 tablespoons butter or margarine
3 tablespoons vinegar
2 tablespoons light brown sugar
1 pound carrots, scraped and cut into
   2-inch strips
⅛ teaspoon dried whole dillweed

Melt butter in a medium saucepan; add vinegar and sugar, and mix well. Add carrots and dillweed; bring to a boil. Cover, reduce heat, and simmer 10 to 12 minutes or until crisp-tender. Yield: 4 servings.

Mrs. John B. Wright,
Greenville, South Carolina.

SESAME CUCUMBERS

1 medium cucumber, unpeeled and thinly
   sliced
1 cup commercial bottled pearl onions
½ cup chopped celery
½ cup vinegar
2 tablespoons water
1 tablespoon sugar
¼ teaspoon salt
1 tablespoon sesame seeds, toasted

Combine cucumber, onions, and celery in a medium bowl; set aside. Combine vinegar, water, sugar, and salt in a small saucepan; bring to a boil. Cook 1 minute; remove from heat. Stir in sesame seeds. Pour over vegetables. Chill several hours. Yield: 4 servings.

Mrs. Robert L. Ralston,
Parkersburg, West Virginia.

Make The Meatballs Special

If ground beef is a staple at your house, look closely at these meatball recipes. You're sure to find some new ideas for a great family entrée. An appetizer rounds out the selection.

MUSHROOM-MEATBALL STROGANOFF

1 pound ground beef
1 egg, beaten
1 cup soft breadcrumbs
⅛ teaspoon seasoned salt
Dash of pepper
1 (1.25-ounce) envelope beef-flavored
   mushroom soup mix
1 (4½-ounce) jar whole mushrooms,
   drained
2 tablespoons all-purpose flour
1¼ cups water
½ cup commercial sour cream
Hot cooked rice or noodles

Combine ground beef, egg, breadcrumbs, seasoned salt, pepper, and 2 tablespoons soup mix, reserving remaining soup mix; mix well. Cover each mushroom with about 1 tablespoon meat mixture, carefully sealing all around. Place meatballs in a 15- x 10- x 1-inch jellyroll pan; bake, uncovered, at 375° for 20 to 25 minutes or until done. Drain on paper towels.

Combine remaining soup mix, flour, and water in a large saucepan; mix well. Cook over medium heat, stirring constantly, until smooth and thickened; stir in sour cream. Add meatballs; cook over medium heat, stirring constantly, until thoroughly heated. (Do not boil.) Serve meatballs over hot cooked rice or noodles. Yield: 6 servings.

Mrs. Martin Drobena,
Temple, Texas.

SAUERBRATEN MEATBALLS

1 pound ground beef
½ cup finely chopped onion
1 egg, slightly beaten
½ teaspoon salt
⅛ teaspoon pepper
1½ tablespoons butter or margarine,
   melted
½ cup wine vinegar
½ cup water
3 tablespoons brown sugar
8 gingersnaps, coarsely crumbled
8 whole cloves
6 peppercorns, crushed
1 bay leaf
½ cup commercial sour cream

Combine ground beef, onion, egg, salt, and pepper; mix well. Shape into 1½-inch meatballs. Brown meatballs in butter in a large skillet over medium heat; drain well.

Combine remaining ingredients except sour cream; mix well. Pour over meatballs; cover and cook over low heat for 30 minutes. Remove meatballs to a serving platter; keep warm.

Strain sauce; stir in sour cream, and pour over meatballs. Yield: 4 servings.

Allan Pollock,
Hendersonville, North Carolina.

RED DELICIOUS MEATBALLS

2½ pounds ground beef
¼ cup seasoned croutons
1 egg
2 tablespoons butter or margarine, melted
1 (1⅜-ounce) package onion soup mix
2 (14-ounce) bottles extra spicy catsup
1 (10-ounce) jar apple jelly
1 (8-ounce) can tomato sauce

Combine ground beef, croutons, egg, butter, and onion soup mix, mixing well; shape into 1¼-inch meatballs. Cook half the meatballs in a large skillet over medium-high heat 5 to 10 minutes or until browned. Repeat with remaining meatballs. Drain meatballs on paper towels; pour off pan drippings.

Combine remaining ingredients in skillet, mixing well; simmer 10 minutes. Place meatballs in a 14- x 12- x 2-inch baking dish; pour sauce over meatballs. Cover and bake at 325° for 30 minutes. Yield: about 6 dozen. *Connie Burgess,*
Knoxville, Tennessee.

Tip: Keep coupons organized according to product so that they'll be easy to locate when needed for shopping.

HAWAIIAN MEATBALLS

1 pound ground beef
1 egg, beaten
2 tablespoons finely chopped onion
1 tablespoon cornstarch
¾ teaspoon salt
Dash of pepper
1 tablespoon vegetable oil
1 (8-ounce) can pineapple chunks, undrained
About 1¼ cups pineapple juice
¾ cup sugar
½ cup plus 1 tablespoon water
¼ cup plus 2 tablespoons vinegar
1½ tablespoons soy sauce
2½ tablespoons cornstarch
2 green peppers, cut into strips
Hot cooked rice

Combine ground beef, egg, onion, cornstarch, salt, and pepper; shape into 1¼-inch meatballs. Heat oil in a large skillet, and add meatballs. Cook over medium heat, turning often, until done. Remove meatballs from skillet; drain off drippings, reserving 1½ tablespoons oil in skillet. Set meatballs aside.

Drain pineapple, reserving juice; set pineapple aside.

Add enough additional pineapple juice to reserved juice to make 1½ cups. Combine juice, sugar, water, vinegar, soy sauce, and 2½ tablespoons cornstarch; mix well. Stir into drippings in skillet. Cook over medium heat, stirring constantly, until smooth and thickened. Add meatballs, pineapple, and green pepper; stir gently. Cook over medium heat, stirring often, until thoroughly heated. Serve over hot cooked rice. Yield: 6 servings.
Mrs. Robert Bryce,
Fairport, New York.

PIZZA MEATBALLS

1 pound ground beef
1 cup Italian-style fine dry breadcrumbs
½ cup milk
2 tablespoons instant minced onion
1 teaspoon garlic salt
⅛ teaspoon pepper
4 ounces mozzarella cheese, cut into 24 (½-inch) cubes
1 (15-ounce) jar pizza sauce
Shredded lettuce (optional)
Sliced mushrooms (optional)

Combine ground beef, breadcrumbs, milk, onion, salt, and pepper; mix well. Cover each cheese cube with about 1 tablespoon meat mixture, carefully sealing all around. Place meatballs in a lightly greased 13- x 9- x 2-inch baking pan; bake uncovered at 350° for 20 to 25 minutes or until done.

Place pizza sauce in a large saucepan; cook over medium heat just until boiling. Add meatballs; stir gently, and cook until thoroughly heated. If desired, serve on shredded lettuce; garnish with sliced mushrooms. Yield: 6 servings.
Polly Hughes,
Tarpon Springs, Florida.

His Specialty Is Steak

If he isn't busy selling automobiles, you're likely to find Hoke Roberson, Jr., of Edenton, North Carolina, in the kitchen. He may be tossing together a cold pasta salad, unmolding a tasty appetizer, or slicing into his favorite steak.

Like many men, Hoke's specialty is steak, and over the years, he has perfected his technique for making sure almost any cut is tender and flavorful. According to Hoke, "Many people hesitate to cook flank steak because they think it's tough. But if marinated and sliced as thin as tissue paper, it will melt in your mouth."

Hoke's recipes are followed by favorite recipes from other men who also like to cook.

MARINATED FLANK STEAK

1 cup Chablis or other dry white wine
¼ cup soy sauce
1 (1-ounce) package meat marinade
1 tablespoon sugar
2 tablespoons olive oil
2 cloves garlic, crushed
½ teaspoon ground ginger
1 (2-pound) flank steak

Combine all ingredients except steak in a large shallow dish, mixing well. Place steak in dish. Cover and refrigerate 3 hours, turning steak occasionally.

Remove steak from marinade. Grill 5 inches from hot coals for 7 minutes on each side or until desired degree of doneness; baste frequently with marinade. To serve, thinly slice the steak diagonally across the grain. Yield: 6 to 8 servings.

PASTA PRIMAVERA

1 (8-ounce) package linguine, broken in half
1 tablespoon olive oil
3 green onions, cut into 1-inch pieces
2 cloves garlic, minced
2 tablespoons olive oil
¾ pound broccoli, broken into flowerets
½ pound asparagus, cut into 1-inch pieces
1 (10-ounce) package frozen English peas, thawed and drained
½ pound fresh mushrooms, sliced
1 small tomato, finely chopped
1 small green or red pepper, chopped
½ cup olive oil
¼ cup minced fresh parsley
¼ cup grated Parmesan cheese
¼ cup grated Romano cheese
2 tablespoons vinegar
½ teaspoon salt
½ teaspoon dried whole oregano
½ teaspoon dried whole basil
½ teaspoon dried whole thyme
¼ teaspoon pepper
⅛ teaspoon ground red pepper

Cook the linguine pieces according to package directions, and drain. Rinse with cold water; drain. Place the linguine in a large bowl. Sprinkle with 1 tablespoon olive oil, and set aside.

Sauté onions and garlic in 2 tablespoons olive oil until onion is crisp-tender; add to the linguine.

Arrange broccoli and asparagus in a steamer rack. Place over boiling water; cover and steam for 6 to 8 minutes or until crisp-tender.

Add vegetables and remaining ingredients to linguine; gently toss. Cover and chill 3 to 4 hours before serving. Yield: 8 servings.

CAVIAR MOUSSE

1 package unflavored gelatin
¼ cup lemon juice
1 teaspoon Worcestershire sauce
6 hard-cooked eggs, sieved
1 cup mayonnaise
2 (2-ounce) jars black caviar

Lightly oil a 4-cup mold; place in freezer for 30 minutes.

Combine gelatin, lemon juice, and Worcestershire sauce in top of double boiler. Bring water to a boil; reduce heat to low, and cook until gelatin dissolves. Remove from heat; add eggs and mayonnaise, mixing well. Spoon about three-fourths of egg mixture into prepared mold; spread to fill sides of mold, leaving a well in center of mixture. Freeze 10 minutes.

Combine remaining one-fourth of egg mixture and caviar; stir well. Remove mold from freezer; pour caviar mixture into center of mold. Refrigerate overnight. Serve with unsalted crackers. Yield: about 4 cups.

BEEF TIPS ON RICE

3 tablespoons all-purpose flour
1 teaspoon salt
½ teaspoon pepper
½ teaspoon paprika
2 pounds boneless sirloin top roast, cut into 1-inch cubes
2 tablespoons vegetable oil
2 large onions, chopped
1 beef-flavored bouillon cube
¾ cup boiling water
Hot cooked rice

Combine flour, salt, pepper, and paprika in a plastic bag; shake to mix. Place beef cubes in bag, and shake well. Heat oil in a Dutch oven; add beef, and cook until browned. Add onion; cook until tender.

Dissolve bouillon cube in boiling water; add to beef mixture. Cover, reduce heat, and simmer 2 hours, stirring occasionally. Serve over rice. Yield: 6 to 8 servings.
Bill Aston,
Birmingham, Alabama.

GOOD-AND-EASY CHICKEN KABOBS

1 (8-ounce) bottle Italian salad dressing
⅓ cup liquid smoke
1 tablespoon brown sugar
¼ teaspoon pepper
⅛ teaspoon garlic powder
4 chicken breast halves, skinned, boned, and cut into 1-inch cubes
2 medium onions, cut into 4 wedges
Cherry tomatoes
Hot cooked long-grain and wild rice

Combine first 5 ingredients in a shallow dish; stir well. Add chicken. Cover and marinate in refrigerator several hours, turning occasionally.

Remove chicken from marinade. Alternate chicken and vegetables on skewers. Broil 4 to 5 inches from heat for 8 to 10 minutes, turning after 4 minutes. Serve with rice. Yield: 4 servings.
Jerry Collums,
Brandon, Mississippi.

VEGETABLE-RICE SALAD

1 cup uncooked regular rice
2 cups sliced celery
2 cups mayonnaise
1 medium onion, finely chopped
1 tablespoon plus 1 teaspoon prepared mustard
8 radishes, sliced
1 medium cucumber, peeled and diced
2 hard-cooked eggs, chopped

Cook rice according to package directions. Chill. Combine rice, celery, mayonnaise, onion, and mustard in a large mixing bowl; stir well. Chill; stir in radishes and cucumber, and sprinkle with egg before serving. Yield: 8 to 10 servings.
O. W. Dollison,
Albany, Georgia.

QUICK CHOCOLATE MOUSSE

1 (6-ounce) package semisweet chocolate morsels
¾ cup milk, scalded
2 eggs
3 tablespoons brewed coffee
2 to 3 tablespoons bourbon, rum, or brandy
Whipped cream

Combine chocolate morsels and scalded milk in container of electric blender; process until smooth. Add eggs, coffee, and bourbon. Process at high speed for 2 minutes. Spoon into stemmed glasses or individual serving dishes; chill. Top mousse with whipped cream. Yield: about 4 to 6 servings.
James E. Boggess,
North Miami, Florida.

Plan A Meal Around These Soups Or Stews

If you're looking for a main course that's both nutritious and simple to prepare, these robust soups and stews have a lot to offer. They're packed with vegetables and a variety of meat and seafood. Most of them require only one pot for cooking, and most simmer on their own without much attention. Since each is practically a meal in itself, there's no need to do a lot of other preparation; just add bread to round out the menu.

SHRIMP-MUSHROOM SOUP

1½ cups water
½ pound unpeeled medium shrimp
¼ pound fresh mushrooms, sliced
¼ cup chopped green onions
1 clove garlic, minced
1½ tablespoons butter or margarine, melted
1 (10¾-ounce) can cream of mushroom soup, undiluted
1 (10¾-ounce) can New England clam chowder, undiluted
1 cup whipping cream
1 cup water
¼ teaspoon coarsely ground pepper

Bring 1½ cups water to a boil; add shrimp, and cook 3 to 5 minutes. Drain well; rinse with cold water. Chill. Peel and devein shrimp; set aside.

Sauté shrimp, mushrooms, onions, and garlic in butter in a Dutch oven about 2 minutes.

Combine soup, chowder, whipping cream, 1 cup water, and pepper; mix well. Add to shrimp mixture, stirring well. Cook just until thoroughly heated. Yield: 5 cups.
Julia L. Willard,
Wetumpka, Alabama.

SWEET-AND-SOUR BEEF AND VEGETABLE STEW

2 pounds boneless round steak, cut into 1-inch cubes
2 tablespoons vegetable oil
2 cups sliced carrots, ¼ inch thick
2 cups pearl onions
1 large green pepper, cut into 1-inch pieces
2 (8-ounce) cans tomato sauce
2 teaspoons paprika
½ cup vinegar
½ cup molasses
¼ cup sugar
2 teaspoons chili powder
1 teaspoon salt
Hot cooked rice

Brown steak in hot oil in a heavy skillet; remove steak and drippings to slow cooker. Add carrots, onions, and green pepper. Combine remaining ingredients except rice; mix well, and pour into slow cooker. Cover and cook on high setting 4 hours.

Spoon rice into serving bowls; serve stew over rice. Yield: about 2½ quarts.
Cheryl Richardson,
Fairfax Station, Virginia.

EGGPLANT CHILI

1 pound ground beef
1 medium onion, chopped
1 large eggplant, peeled and cubed
1 (16-ounce) can stewed tomatoes,
   undrained
1 (8-ounce) can tomato sauce
½ cup water
2 tablespoons chili powder
1 tablespoon all-purpose flour
2 teaspoons sugar
1 teaspoon salt
½ teaspoon garlic powder
1 (16-ounce) can kidney beans, undrained

Combine ground beef and onion in a Dutch oven; cook over medium heat until beef is browned, stirring to crumble meat. Drain off drippings. Add remaining ingredients except kidney beans, mixing well. Cover, reduce heat, and simmer 2 hours. Stir in kidney beans; cover and continue to cook 30 minutes. Yield: 2½ quarts.
Mrs. Harlan J. Stone,
Ocala, Florida.

CABBAGE SOUP

1 medium head cabbage, coarsely chopped
2 tablespoons butter or margarine, melted
4½ cups water
1 cup cubed cooked ham
¼ cup cream sherry
2 beef-flavored bouillon cubes
1 bay leaf
1 tablespoon sugar
1 teaspoon salt
¼ teaspoon pepper

Sauté cabbage in butter 5 minutes or until tender. Add remaining ingredients; bring to a boil. Reduce heat and simmer, uncovered, 30 minutes. Remove bay leaf. Yield: about 2 quarts.
Mrs. John J. O'Neill,
Welaka, Florida.

SAUSAGE-BEAN SOUP

1 (16-ounce) package dried red kidney
   beans
6 cups water
2 pounds beef soup bones
2 teaspoons salt
2 (8-ounce) cans tomato sauce
2 medium potatoes, cubed
2 medium carrots, thinly sliced
¾ pound Polish sausage, cut into ½-inch
   slices
2 stalks celery, chopped
2 medium onions, chopped
1 small head cabbage, coarsely chopped
Freshly ground pepper to taste

Sort and wash beans; place in a large Dutch oven. Cover with water 2 inches above beans; let soak overnight. Drain beans; add 6 cups water, soup bones, and salt. Bring to a boil. Cover, reduce heat to low, and cook 45 minutes or until beans are tender; discard bones. Add tomato sauce, potatoes, and carrots; cover and simmer 10 minutes. Add remaining ingredients; cover and simmer 10 to 15 minutes or until the vegetables are tender. Yield: 3½ quarts.
Mrs. A. J. Amador,
Decatur, Alabama.

MICROWAVE COOKERY

Quick Breads From The Microwave

Quick breads are really true to their name when you bake them in your microwave oven. Even starting from scratch, you'll have fresh, hot muffins or coffee cake in minutes.

Keep in mind that microwaved quick breads tend to cook unevenly and are often pale looking. However, if you are looking for convenience, we think you'll find these recipes very useful—especially when you consider how little time they take to prepare.

When microwaving quick breads, be sure to follow the cooking times. Overcooking will produce a dry, tough product. When done, the bread should spring back when lightly touched. As in conventional baking, if a wooden pick is inserted into the center of the bread, it should come out clean. It's important to remember this because microwaved breads don't brown, and it's difficult to tell if they are done.

Round or ring-shaped dishes are ideal for microwaving coffee cakes, since oblong or square shapes tend to cook faster at the ends and corners. To improvise a ring-shaped dish, place a glass or custard cup right side up in the center of a round baking dish. Be sure the dish has the same volume as the one called for in the recipe.

You can improvise a microwave muffin ring with paper hot-drink cups or custard cups filled with muffin liners and arranged in a circle on a plate.

Give color and flavor to quick breads by adding toppings, such as cinnamon, wheat germ, cracker crumbs, or nuts. A simple frosting or icing drizzled over a coffee cake makes it more appealing.

ORANGE COFFEE CAKE

1 cup sugar
½ cup vegetable oil
2 eggs
1 cup quick-cooking oats
1⅓ cups all-purpose flour
1½ teaspoons baking powder
½ teaspoon salt
¾ teaspoon ground cinnamon
1 cup milk
1 tablespoon grated orange rind
Glaze (recipe follows)

Cream sugar and oil; add eggs, one at a time, beating at medium speed of mixer until light and fluffy. Add oats, flour, baking powder, salt, cinnamon, and milk; mix just until smooth. Stir in orange rind.

Lightly grease a 2-quart microwave ring mold; line bottom with waxed paper, and lightly grease. Pour in batter; microwave at MEDIUM (50% power) for 10 minutes, rotating once. Microwave at HIGH 4 minutes, rotating dish once.

Invert onto a serving plate. Spoon glaze over hot cake. Serve immediately. Yield: 6 to 8 servings.

Glaze:

3 tablespoons butter or margarine
⅓ cup firmly packed brown sugar
½ cup chopped pecans
1½ tablespoons grated orange rind
3 tablespoons orange juice

Combine ingredients in a 2-cup glass measure, stirring well. Microwave at HIGH 3½ to 4 minutes or until slightly thickened, stirring once. Yield: 1 cup.

CINNAMON-NUT MUFFINS

2 cups all-purpose flour
1 tablespoon baking powder
½ teaspoon salt
½ cup sugar
½ cup chopped pecans
2 eggs, beaten
½ cup milk
½ cup vegetable oil
3 tablespoons sugar
1½ teaspoons ground cinnamon

Combine flour, baking powder, salt, ½ cup sugar, and pecans; stir well. Make a well in center of mixture. Combine eggs, milk, and oil. Add egg mixture to dry ingredients, and stir just until moistened.

Spoon batter into paper-lined microwave muffin cups, filling half full. Combine 3 tablespoons sugar and cinnamon; sprinkle about ½ teaspoon sugar mixture on each muffin.

Microwave at MEDIUM HIGH (70% power) for 2½ minutes, rotating once. Let cool in pan 1 minute; serve immediately. Repeat with remaining batter and sugar mixture. Yield: 1½ dozen.

APPLE-BRAN MUFFINS

⅔ cup milk
2 teaspoons vinegar
1 cup shreds of wheat bran cereal
1 egg, beaten
2 tablespoons vegetable oil
¼ cup sugar
½ cup all-purpose flour
¾ teaspoon ground cinnamon
½ teaspoon baking soda
½ cup peeled, finely chopped apple
2½ teaspoons wheat germ, toasted and
    divided

Combine milk and vinegar in a mixing bowl; let stand 1 minute. Add cereal; let stand 5 minutes. Beat in egg and oil; stir in sugar. Combine flour, cinnamon, and soda; add to cereal mixture, and stir just until moistened. Fold in apple.

Spoon batter into paper-lined microwave muffin cups, filling two-thirds full. Sprinkle with ¼ teaspoon wheat germ.

Microwave at HIGH 3 minutes, rotating once. Let muffins cool in pan 1 minute; serve immediately. Repeat procedure with remaining batter and wheat germ. Yield: 10 muffins.

COFFEE CAKE RING

¼ cup sugar
3 tablespoons graham cracker crumbs
1½ teaspoons ground cinnamon
3 tablespoons finely chopped pecans
2 cups all-purpose flour
1 tablespoon baking powder
¼ teaspoon salt
¼ cup butter or margarine
⅔ cup milk
¼ cup butter or margarine, melted
Vanilla glaze (recipe follows)

Combine sugar, graham cracker crumbs, cinnamon, and pecans, mixing well; set mixture aside.

Combine flour, baking powder, and salt in a mixing bowl; cut in ¼ cup butter with a pastry blender until mixture resembles coarse meal. Add milk; stir with a fork until all ingredients are moistened. Knead on a lightly floured surface 10 times.

Roll out dough to ½-inch thickness. Cut into 2¼-inch rounds. Dip each round into melted butter, then into sugar mixture. Stand rounds around edge of a 1-quart microwave ring mold, overlapping rounds. Sprinkle with remaining sugar mixture, and drizzle with any remaining butter.

Microwave at HIGH 4 to 4½ minutes or until top springs back when touched, rotating after 2 minutes. Cool 2 minutes; invert onto a serving plate. Drizzle with glaze while hot. Serve immediately. Yield: one 9-inch coffee cake.

Vanilla Glaze:

½ cup sifted powdered sugar
2 teaspoons milk
1½ teaspoons butter or margarine, melted
¼ teaspoon vanilla extract

Combine all ingredients in a small bowl; stir until smooth. Yield: ¼ cup.

EASY CARAMEL RING

¼ cup butter or margarine
½ cup firmly packed brown sugar
2 tablespoons light corn syrup
¾ cup pecan halves
1 (10-ounce) package refrigerated
    buttermilk biscuits

Place butter in a 9-inch round dish. Microwave at HIGH 55 seconds. Sprinkle sugar over butter, and add corn syrup; stir well. Place a drinking glass in center of dish. Arrange pecans, right side down, around circle.

Place biscuits over pecans, squeezing to fit, if necessary. Microwave at MEDIUM (50% power) for 6 to 8 minutes, rotating dish after 3 minutes.

Remove glass; invert onto serving plate. Let stand 1 to 2 minutes. Serve immediately. Yield: one 9-inch ring.

Bourbon Adds The Flavor

Years ago, Southerners discovered bourbon whiskey with its sharp, distinctive flavor that comes from aging in charred oak barrels. But besides enjoying it in a drink, have you ever thought of stirring it into sauces or cookie dough or using it to simmer an entrée?

The alcohol evaporates during cooking, and all that's left is the flavor. For example, you'll detect just a trace of bourbon in our recipe for Baby Carrots Bourbonnaise. And in Bourbon-Braised Pork Chops, the taste of bourbon seasoned with allspice clings to the meat for a delicately flavored entrée. Crunchy Bourbon Dunkers are waferlike cookies that are especially good served with wine—a real crowd pleaser.

BABY CARROTS BOURBONNAISE

¾ pound baby carrots, scraped
⅔ cup orange juice
2 tablespoons butter or margarine
2 tablespoons brown sugar
2 tablespoons bourbon
⅛ teaspoon salt
1 teaspoon chopped fresh dill

Place carrots in saucepan with orange juice. Cook, covered, for 12 to 15 minutes or until carrots are tender; drain, reserving juice.

Combine reserved juice, butter, sugar, bourbon, and salt; cook over low heat until butter melts, stirring occasionally. (Do not boil.) Pour over carrots, and sprinkle with chopped dill. Yield: 4 servings.

BOURBON-BRAISED PORK CHOPS

⅓ cup all-purpose flour
½ teaspoon salt
¼ teaspoon pepper
4 (1-inch-thick) pork chops
1 tablespoon vegetable oil
4 orange slices
2 tablespoons brown sugar
2 tablespoons cornstarch
⅛ teaspoon ground allspice
1 cup hot water
¼ cup orange juice
2 tablespoons bourbon
¼ cup currants or raisins

Combine flour, salt, and pepper; dredge pork chops in flour mixture.

Heat oil in a large skillet over medium heat; brown pork chops on both sides. Place an orange slice on top of each chop.

Combine brown sugar, cornstarch, and allspice in a small saucepan; gradually stir in water. Cook over medium heat, stirring constantly, until mixture thickens and comes to a boil. Cook 1 minute, stirring constantly. Remove from heat; stir in orange juice, bourbon, and currants. Spoon over pork chops. Cover, reduce heat, and simmer 1 hour or until pork chops are tender. Yield: 4 servings.   *T. O. Davis, Waynesboro, Mississippi.*

CRUNCHY BOURBON DUNKERS

5½ cups all-purpose flour
1 tablespoon baking powder
6 eggs, slightly beaten
2 cups sugar
1 cup butter or margarine, melted
¼ cup anisette
¼ cup anise seeds
3 tablespoons bourbon
2 cups chopped walnuts or almonds

Combine flour and baking powder, and set aside.

Combine remaining ingredients except walnuts in a large bowl; mix well on medium speed of an electric mixer. Reduce speed to low; add flour mixture gradually, mixing well. Stir in walnuts.

On greased baking sheets, shape dough into loaves 2 inches wide, ½ inch thick, and length of baking sheet. (Shape no more than 2 loaves on each sheet.) Bake at 375° for 20 minutes.

Remove from oven; loosen loaves from baking sheets with metal spatula. (Leave loaves on baking sheets.) Cut loaves into ¾-inch slices. Place slices cut side down; bake at 375° for 15 minutes or until lightly browned and crisp. Cool on wire racks, and store in moisture-proof containers. Yield: about 9 dozen.
Faye Creech,
Moore, Oklahoma.

BOURBON BARBECUE SAUCE

1 cup catsup
⅓ cup bourbon
¼ cup vinegar
¼ cup molasses
2 cloves garlic, crushed
1 tablespoon Worcestershire sauce
1 tablespoon lemon juice
2 teaspoons soy sauce
½ teaspoon dry mustard
¼ teaspoon pepper

Combine all ingredients, mixing well. Use to baste pork or beef when grilling. Yield: 2 cups.

CRANBERRY PUNCH

1 (32-ounce) bottle cranberry juice
2¼ cups pineapple juice
1½ to 2 cups bourbon
1 cup orange juice
½ cup lemon juice
7 cups ginger ale, chilled

Combine all ingredients except ginger ale; chill. Stir in ginger ale before serving. Serve over ice. Yield: 1 gallon.
D. J. Newton,
Kingsland, Georgia.

BOURBON-PECAN PIE

3 eggs, beaten
1 cup sugar
½ cup light corn syrup
½ cup dark corn syrup
⅓ cup butter or margarine, melted
2 tablespoons bourbon
⅛ teaspoon salt
1 cup chopped pecans
1 unbaked 9-inch pastry shell

Combine eggs, sugar, syrup, butter, bourbon, and salt; mix well. Place pecans in bottom of pastry shell; pour the sugar mixture over pecans. Bake at 375° for 35 to 40 minutes. Yield: one 9-inch pie.
Edna Lewis,
Fredericksburg, Virginia.

Decorate The Easter Ham

Welcome spring with a colorful and attractive entrée. Our Ham Véronique starts with a canned ham. But what happens afterward transforms it into an elegant creation.

We baste the ham with a combination of fruit juices, spices, and herbs. We then embellish it with red and green grapes and kiwi slices. And to give it a bright, polished look, we glaze it with aspic made from the juice mixture. You'll be proud to serve this decorative ham any time of the year.

HAM VÉRONIQUE

1 cup white grape juice
1 cup apple juice
2 (3-inch) sticks cinnamon
8 whole allspice
1 teaspoon dried whole rosemary
1 (3-pound) canned ham
1 envelope unflavored gelatin
Green grape halves
Red grape halves
Kiwi slices

Combine grape juice, apple juice, and spices in a small saucepan. Bring to a boil; reduce heat, and simmer, uncovered, 10 minutes. Remove from heat; strain mixture. Measure and reserve ⅔ cup juice mixture in refrigerator for aspic; reserve remaining juice mixture for basting.

Place ham on rack in a shallow roasting pan; bake at 325° for 1½ hours or until a meat thermometer registers 140°, basting frequently with reserved juice mixture. Transfer ham to a wire rack set in a larger pan; cover and allow to chill thoroughly.

Sprinkle gelatin over ⅔ cup reserved juice mixture in a small saucepan; let stand 1 minute. Cook over low heat, stirring until gelatin dissolves. Remove from heat; let stand until mixture is cooled and syrupy (just before mixture begins to set).

Arrange fruit garnishes on top of ham; brush a thin coating of aspic over top and sides of ham. Chill 10 to 15 minutes or until aspic sets; repeat brushing and chilling process until ham is coated with aspic. Chill until the aspic is firm. Yield: 8 to 10 servings.

Start With Chocolate And Peanut Butter

Two great tastes are better than one, especially when they're chocolate and peanut butter. It's no wonder that this is one of the South's favorite dessert duos. Our readers have some very tasty and tempting ideas for combining them.

CHOCOLATE-PEANUT BUTTER COOKIES

½ cup shortening
½ cup creamy peanut butter
½ cup sugar
½ cup firmly packed brown sugar
1 egg
¾ cup all-purpose flour
½ cup cocoa
2 teaspoons baking powder
½ teaspoon salt

Cream shortening and peanut butter; gradually add sugar, beating until light and fluffy. Add egg, beating well.

Combine dry ingredients; add to creamed mixture, beating well. Shape dough into 1-inch balls; place 2 inches apart on greased cookie sheets. Flatten cookies with a fork to ¼-inch thickness in a crisscross pattern. Bake at 350° for 10 minutes. Yield: about 4 dozen.
Mrs. James S. Stanton,
Richmond, Virginia.

FUDGY PEANUT BUTTER CAKE

2 cups all-purpose flour
2 cups sugar
1 teaspoon baking soda
1 cup water
1 cup butter or margarine
¼ cup cocoa
½ cup buttermilk
2 eggs, slightly beaten
1 teaspoon vanilla extract
1 cup creamy peanut butter
1 tablespoon vegetable oil
¼ cup plus 1 tablespoon butter or
    margarine
3 tablespoons cocoa
¾ teaspoon vanilla extract
3 to 5 tablespoons buttermilk
2½ cups sifted powdered sugar

Combine flour, sugar, and soda; mix well, and set aside.

Combine water, 1 cup butter, and ¼ cup cocoa in a heavy saucepan; bring to a boil, stirring constantly. Gradually stir into flour mixture. Stir in ½ cup buttermilk, eggs, and 1 teaspoon vanilla. Pour into a greased and floured 13- x 9- x 2-inch baking pan; bake at 350° for 30 minutes or until a wooden pick inserted in center comes out clean. Cool.

Combine peanut butter and oil; mix well. Spread on cooled cake.

Combine ¼ cup plus 1 tablespoon butter and 3 tablespoons cocoa in a small saucepan; cook over low heat, stirring constantly, until butter melts and mixture is smooth. Remove from heat; add remaining ingredients. Beat until spreading consistency; spread over peanut butter mixture. Yield: 15 servings.
Jacquelyn Christopher,
Asheville, North Carolina.

CHOCOLATE SURPRISE CUPCAKES

1 (3-ounce) package cream cheese,
    softened
¼ cup crunchy peanut butter
2 tablespoons honey
2 tablespoons powdered sugar
1 tablespoon milk
⅓ cup shortening
1 cup firmly packed brown sugar
2 eggs
1 cup all-purpose flour
⅓ cup cocoa
1 teaspoon baking soda
½ teaspoon salt
½ cup milk
1 teaspoon vanilla extract
Sifted powdered sugar

Combine first 5 ingredients in a small bowl, mixing well; set aside.

Cream shortening; gradually add brown sugar, beating well. Add eggs, one at a time, beating well after each addition. Combine flour, cocoa, soda, and salt; add to creamed mixture alternately with ½ cup milk, beginning and ending with flour mixture. Mix well after each addition. Stir in vanilla.

Spoon 1 heaping tablespoon batter into each paper-lined muffin pan. Drop 1 rounded teaspoonful cream cheese mixture into center of each cupcake. Gently press cream cheese filling into batter. Fill cups two-thirds full with remaining batter. Bake at 375° for 20 minutes. Remove from pan, and sprinkle tops with powdered sugar. Yield: 1½ dozen.
Margot Foster,
Hubbard, Texas.

CHOCOLATE-PEANUT BUTTER PIE

1⅓ cups chocolate wafer crumbs
¼ cup butter or margarine, softened
2 tablespoons sugar
¾ cup chunky peanut butter
1 (4-ounce) container frozen whipped
    topping, thawed
1 quart chocolate ice cream, softened

Combine chocolate wafer crumbs, butter, and sugar in small bowl; mix well. Press firmly on bottom and sides of a buttered 9-inch pieplate.

Fold peanut butter and whipped topping into ice cream; spread evenly over crust. Cover and freeze overnight or until firm. Yield: one 9-inch pie.
Connie Burgess,
Knoxville, Tennessee.

TIN ROOF PIE

⅓ cup creamy peanut butter
1 tablespoon light corn syrup
2 cups corn flakes
1 quart vanilla ice cream, softened
Chocolate syrup
Chopped salted peanuts

Combine first 3 ingredients; mix well. Press firmly on bottom and sides of a buttered 9-inch pieplate. Spread ice cream over crust; cover and freeze overnight or until firm.

To serve, drizzle with chocolate syrup and sprinkle with peanuts. Serve immediately. Yield: one 9-inch pie.
Darryl Taylor,
Louisville, Kentucky.

DOUBLE PEANUT FUDGE

2 cups sugar
⅔ cup milk
1 cup marshmallow cream
1 cup creamy peanut butter
1 (6-ounce) package semisweet chocolate
    morsels
1 teaspoon vanilla extract
½ cup coarsely chopped peanuts

Combine sugar and milk in a heavy saucepan. Cook over medium heat, stirring occasionally, until mixture reaches soft ball stage (234°). Remove from heat; add next 4 ingredients. Stir until mixture is well blended; fold in peanuts. Pour into a buttered 8-inch square pan. Cool and cut into squares. Yield: 3 dozen.
Lois Cavenaugh,
Tifton, Georgia.

Toss A Fresh-Tasting Salad

Since this is the time of year when most fresh fruit and vegetables are at their prime, why not toss them into a crisp salad while the flavor is best? Then add a simple dressing, herbs, or spices to make it extra special.

TROPICAL SALAD

½ cup mayonnaise
¼ cup vegetable oil
¼ cup chopped onion
2 tablespoons honey
1 tablespoon lemon juice
1 tablespoon chopped parsley
¼ teaspoon prepared mustard
1 large head iceberg lettuce
1 green pepper, thinly sliced
½ small cucumber, thinly sliced
1 (4½-ounce) can small shrimp, rinsed
    and drained
¼ cup chopped walnuts

Combine mayonnaise, oil, onion, honey, lemon juice, parsley, and mustard in container of an electric blender; process until smooth. Chill.

Tear lettuce into bite-size pieces in salad bowl. Add remaining ingredients; toss well. Serve with the reserved chilled dressing. Yield: 8 servings.
Michelle C. Weaver,
Birmingham, Alabama.

GREEN SALAD ORIENTAL

1 pound fresh spinach, torn into bite-size
    pieces
¼ pound fresh mushrooms, sliced
2 grapefruit, peeled, sectioned, and
    chopped
1 (8-ounce) can water chestnuts, chopped
Citrus Dressing

Combine spinach, mushrooms, grapefruit, and water chestnuts in a large bowl. Add Citrus Dressing to salad just before serving, tossing well to coat. Yield: 8 servings.

Citrus Dressing:

¼ cup vegetable oil
2 tablespoons vinegar
2 tablespoons grapefruit juice
1 tablespoon soy sauce
¼ teaspoon salt
¼ teaspoon dry mustard
¼ teaspoon hot sauce

Combine all ingredients in a jar. Cover tightly, and shake vigorously. Chill several hours. Yield: ½ cup.
Doris Garton,
Shenandoah, Virginia.

GARDEN SALAD

4 cups chopped cabbage
3½ cups torn lettuce
1 small green pepper, diced
1 carrot, grated
½ cup diced celery
3 tablespoons finely grated onion
½ cup mayonnaise
¼ cup vinegar
2 tablespoons sugar
¼ teaspoon salt
2 medium tomatoes, cut in wedges

Combine cabbage, lettuce, green pepper, carrot, celery, and onion. Combine mayonnaise, vinegar, sugar, and salt; mix well. Pour mayonnaise mixture over vegetables; toss gently to coat. Garnish with tomato wedges. Yield: 8 servings.
Joyce Dean Garrison,
Charlotte, North Carolina.

CRISP SUMMER SALAD

1 small head Bibb lettuce, torn
1 (11-ounce) can mandarin oranges,
    chilled and drained
½ small purple onion, sliced and
    separated into rings
¼ cup vegetable oil
2 tablespoons wine vinegar
1 teaspoon sugar
⅛ teaspoon salt
⅛ teaspoon pepper
Dash of dried whole basil

Combine lettuce, mandarin oranges, and onion in a large salad bowl; set salad combination aside.
Combine remaining ingredients in a jar; cover tightly and shake until mixed well. Quickly pour mixture over salad; toss gently to coat. Serve immediately. Yield: 4 servings.
Mrs. Otis James,
Bude, Mississippi.

REFRESHING FRUIT SALAD

1 (20-ounce) can crushed pineapple
½ cup sugar
1 egg, slightly beaten
2 tablespoons lemon juice
2 tablespoons butter or margarine
6 oranges, peeled and sectioned
3 apples, chopped
1 cup chopped pecans
3 bananas, sliced

Drain pineapple, reserving juice; set aside. Combine sugar and egg in a saucepan; gradually stir in reserved pineapple juice and lemon juice. Add butter; cook over medium heat, stirring constantly, until mixture is thickened and bubbly. Cool dressing.
Combine pineapple, oranges, apples, and pecans in a bowl; stir in dressing. Chill well. Add bananas just before serving. Yield: 10 servings.
Mrs. Donald C. Vanhoy,
Salisbury, North Carolina.

BLT's With A Sauce

For luncheons or Sunday night suppers, Martha Lou McGinty of Cape Girardeau, Missouri, often serves these open-face sandwiches. They're a quick and easy idea that everyone will like. Just add your favorite soup and beverage to make a complete meal.

CHEESY BLT'S

3 English muffins, split, buttered, and
    toasted
6 lettuce leaves
12 slices bacon, cooked and halved
6 slices tomato
Cheese Sauce
Paprika

Top each English muffin half with a lettuce leaf, 2 slices of bacon, 1 tomato slice, and Cheese Sauce. Sprinkle with paprika. Yield: 6 servings.

Cheese Sauce:

2 tablespoons butter or margarine
2 tablespoons all-purpose flour
1 cup milk
½ cup (2 ounces) shredded Cheddar
    cheese
4 pimiento-stuffed olives, sliced
¼ teaspoon prepared mustard
Pinch of salt
Dash of paprika

Melt butter in a heavy saucepan over low heat; add flour, and stir until smooth. Cook 1 minute, stirring constantly. Gradually add milk; cook over medium heat, stirring constantly, until thickened and bubbly. Add cheese, olives, mustard, salt, and paprika; stir until cheese melts. Yield: 1¼ cups.

You'll Want Seconds Of Ratatouille

Who needs meat when you can achieve the tasty blend of vegetables and spices you'll find in our hearty Ratatouille? Tomato, onion, eggplant, zucchini, and green pepper are seasoned and simmered in a tomato-wine mixture for a colorful main dish that's so good you'll go back for seconds.

RATATOUILLE

1 medium onion, chopped
2 cloves garlic, crushed
1 bay leaf
¼ cup olive oil
1 medium eggplant, peeled and cubed
¾ cup tomato juice
3 tablespoons Burgundy or other dry red
    wine
2 tablespoons tomato paste
½ teaspoon dried whole basil
½ teaspoon marjoram leaves
½ teaspoon dried whole oregano
½ teaspoon salt
⅛ teaspoon dried whole rosemary, crushed
⅛ teaspoon pepper
2 medium-size green peppers, cut into
    strips
1 medium zucchini, cubed
2 medium tomatoes, coarsely chopped
2 tablespoons chopped fresh parsley
Hot cooked rice
Grated Parmesan cheese
Sliced black olives

Sauté onion, garlic, and bay leaf in oil in a Dutch oven 3 to 5 minutes. Add eggplant, tomato juice, wine, tomato paste, and seasonings; cover and cook 10 minutes. Add green pepper and zucchini; cover and cook 10 minutes. Add tomatoes, and cook just until thoroughly heated; stir in parsley. Discard bay leaf.

Serve over rice. Top with cheese and olives. Yield: 6 servings.

Michele Poynton,
Huntington Woods, Michigan.

Combine 2 tablespoons sugar and cinnamon; sprinkle over apples and raisins. Combine sour cream, egg yolks, ⅓ cup sugar, and 1½ tablespoons brandy, stirring well, and pour over apple mixture. Bake at 350° for 55 minutes or until edges are browned. Cool slightly.

Refrigerate until completely cooled; remove from springform pan. Garnish with apple slices and whipped cream, if desired. Yield: 10 to 12 servings.

Ursula Bambrey,
Springfield, Virginia.

add flour, stirring well. Cook 1 minute, stirring constantly. Gradually add half-and-half and beef broth, stirring constantly; cook over medium heat until thickened and bubbly. Add remaining ingredients; simmer, uncovered, about 10 minutes. Yield: 4 cups.

Pankey Kite,
Macon, Georgia.

This Cake Features Apple Brandy

If you're looking for a special dessert to serve company, Apple Slice Cake fills the bill. Garnished with apple slices and whipped cream, it makes a perfect ending to a festive meal.

APPLE SLICE CAKE

1½ cups all-purpose flour
½ cup sugar
1½ teaspoons baking powder
½ cup butter or margarine
1 egg, beaten
1 teaspoon vanilla extract
3 medium-size cooking apples
½ cup raisins
⅓ cup apple brandy
2 tablespoons sugar
1 teaspoon ground cinnamon
1½ cups commercial sour cream
2 egg yolks
⅓ cup sugar
1½ tablespoons apple brandy
Apple slices dipped in lemon juice
    (optional)
Whipped cream (optional)

Combine flour, ½ cup sugar, and baking powder; cut in butter with pastry blender until mixture resembles coarse meal. Add egg and vanilla; stir until dry ingredients are moistened. Press mixture evenly into the bottom and one-third of the way up sides of a 9-inch springform pan; set aside.

Peel and core apples; cut into ⅛-inch-thick slices. Combine apples, raisins, and ⅓ cup brandy in a large saucepan; cover and cook over low heat 8 minutes or until apples are almost tender. Drain well; arrange in a pinwheel design over top of cake mixture.

Appease The Appetite With Soup

When that special meal calls for a first course, whet your appetite with soup. Hot or cold, soup can set the stage for a spectacular entrée.

Our Cream of Mushroom Soup is a well-balanced creation spiked with a touch of sherry. But it's the basil and angostura bitters that give it just the right amount of seasoning.

Speed mealtime preparation and make Blender Gazpacho ahead of time. The secret to this quick soup is contained in its title; you use an electric blender to process the ingredients. Chili powder and cumin seeds give it a spicy flair, and the buttermilk makes it a little different from other gazpacho recipes.

For a satisfying yet lighter taste, savor Lemon Soup. Its delicious flavor will make your guests wonder what ingredient makes it so good.

CREAM OF MUSHROOM SOUP

½ pound fresh mushrooms, sliced
¼ cup diced onion
2 tablespoons butter or margarine, melted
1 tablespoon butter or margarine
2 tablespoons all-purpose flour
1¾ cups half-and-half
1 (10½-ounce) can beef broth, undiluted
1 tablespoon dry sherry
¼ teaspoon dried whole basil
Dash angostura bitters
⅛ teaspoon white pepper

Sauté mushrooms and onion in 2 tablespoons butter in a saucepan until onion is tender. Remove vegetables with a slotted spoon, and set aside. Melt 1 tablespoon butter in saucepan;

CHILLED CUCUMBER-POTATO SOUP

1¾ cups peeled and diced cucumber
1 (10¾-ounce) can condensed cream of potato soup, undiluted
1¼ cups milk
½ teaspoon chicken-flavored bouillon granules
1 cup half-and-half

Combine cucumber, soup, milk, and bouillon granules in a heavy saucepan. Cook over low heat 10 minutes, stirring occasionally. Place half of mixture in container of an electric blender; process until smooth. Remove from blender container. Repeat procedure with remaining mixture. Combine mixtures; cover and chill.

Stir in half-and-half just before serving soup. Yield: 4½ cups.

Mrs. Herbert W. Rutherford,
Baltimore, Maryland.

BLENDER GAZPACHO

1 (28-ounce) can tomatoes, undrained
1 cup tomato juice
1 cup buttermilk
1 small onion, coarsely chopped
1 small cucumber, coarsely chopped
1 small green pepper, coarsely chopped
1 clove garlic
2 tablespoons olive oil
½ to 1 teaspoon chili powder
½ teaspoon salt
½ teaspoon cumin seeds
½ teaspoon pickapepper sauce

Combine all ingredients in a large mixing bowl. Place half of mixture in container of an electric blender; process until smooth. Remove from blender container. Repeat procedure with remaining mixture. Combine mixtures; cover and chill. Yield: about 7½ cups.

Gloria Different,
Harvey, Louisiana.

LEMON SOUP

4 (14½-ounce) cans chicken broth,
  undiluted
1 small onion, chopped
½ cup uncooked rice
2 egg yolks, beaten
¼ cup lemon juice
1 cup whipping cream
2 tablespoons grated lemon rind
1 tablespoon grated Parmesan cheese

Combine chicken broth and onion in
a Dutch oven; bring to a boil. Add rice;
reduce heat, and cook, covered, 15 minutes. Combine egg yolks and lemon
juice, mixing well. Gradually stir about
1 cup of hot mixture into yolk mixture;
add to remaining hot mixture, stirring
constantly. Stir in remaining ingredients. Cook just until thoroughly
heated. Yield: 7½ cups.

Ethel Jernegan,
Savannah, Georgia.

Slice Into A Pizza Sandwich

The original calzone, a yeast-raised
turnover filled with spicy ingredients,
was created in Italy. But Melissa Parks
of Maryville, Tennessee, has devised a
newer version of this pizza sandwich.
For serving, Melissa cuts the wide loaf
into slices.

Calzone is filled with a spicy mixture of sausage, mozzarella cheese, and tomato paste.

CALZONE

1 package dry yeast
1 cup warm water (105° to 115°)
1 teaspoon salt
¼ cup vegetable oil
2½ to 3 cups all-purpose flour, divided
½ pound bulk pork sausage, cooked and
  drained
2 cups (8 ounces) shredded mozzarella
  cheese
1 (6-ounce) can tomato paste
1 teaspoon dried whole basil
1 teaspoon dried whole oregano
1 egg white, slightly beaten
1 teaspoon sesame seeds

Dissolve yeast in warm water; let
stand 5 minutes. Combine yeast mixture, salt, oil, and 1 cup flour in a large
bowl; mix well. Gradually stir in enough
remaining flour to make a stiff dough.
Turn dough out on a floured surface,
and knead until smooth and elastic
(about 5 minutes). Place in a well-
greased bowl, turning to grease top.
Cover and let rise in a warm place
(85°), free from drafts, 1 hour or until
doubled in bulk.

Punch dough down; roll into a 14- x
10-inch rectangle. Place on a lightly
greased baking sheet.

Combine sausage, cheese, tomato
paste, basil, and oregano; mix well.
Spread mixture in a 5-inch strip down
center of dough. Fold long sides of
dough over filling, overlapping edges.
Pinch ends together to seal. Cover and
let rise in a warm place, free from
drafts, 30 minutes.

Score top of loaf to allow steam to
escape. Brush with egg white; sprinkle
with sesame seeds. Bake at 400° for 25
minutes or until golden brown. Slice.
Yield: 6 servings.

A Family Menu That's Quick And Easy

If you're in charge of preparing dinner for a family after coming home
from work, you know what a challenge
it can be. Everyone is hungry and wants
to be fed immediately, so time is a
major consideration. Here's a menu
that's designed to help you get dinner
on the table in less than 45 minutes.

The key is the main dish, Flounder
Dijon; it bakes in about 5 minutes.
Preparation is a snap—just brush flounder fillets with melted butter, spread on
a layer of mustard, and wait until the
rest of the meal is almost ready before
you pop the fish into the oven.

Mix up Pineapple-Celery Salad next
so it can be chilling. Then make Peanut
Butter Pudding, an easy dish that's sure

to be a favorite with any children in the house. Gingered Carrots and Parsley Rice round out the menu; make these two dishes last.

All that's left is to arrange the salad, make the tea, bake the fish, and call the family to dinner.

Flounder Dijon
Parsley Rice
Gingered Carrots
Pineapple-Celery Salad
Peanut Butter Pudding
Iced tea

FLOUNDER DIJON

6 flounder fillets
3 tablespoons butter or margarine, melted
2 tablespoons Dijon mustard
Paprika (optional)
Lemon and lime slices (optional)

Place fish fillets in a lightly greased 13- x 9- x 2-inch baking dish; brush with melted butter. Spread 1 teaspoon mustard over each fillet. Bake, uncovered, at 375° for 5 minutes or until flounder flakes easily. Garnish with paprika and lemon and lime slices, if desired. Yield: 6 servings. *Martha Heun,*
Louisville, Kentucky.

PARSLEY RICE

1½ cups uncooked regular rice
3 chicken-flavored bouillon cubes
3 cups water
¼ cup plus 2 tablespoons sliced green onions
3 tablespoons butter or margarine, melted
½ cup chopped fresh parsley

Combine rice, bouillon cubes, and water in a medium saucepan. Bring to a boil; cover, reduce heat, and simmer 20 minutes or until tender.

Sauté green onions in butter. Combine with rice and fresh parsley. Yield: 6 servings.

GINGERED CARROTS

10 medium carrots, scraped and cut into 1-inch diagonal slices
¾ cup water
3 tablespoons butter or margarine
2 tablespoons honey
½ teaspoon ground ginger
2 teaspoons sesame seeds, toasted

Combine carrots and water in a saucepan; bring to a boil. Cover, reduce heat, and simmer 10 to 15 minutes or until crisp-tender. Drain well. Stir in butter, honey, and ginger. Bring to a boil, stirring often. Cook about 3 minutes or until thickened. Sprinkle with sesame seeds. Yield: 6 servings.
Brenda Gilpatrick,
Albany, Georgia.

PINEAPPLE-CELERY SALAD

1 (15¼-ounce) can pineapple chunks, drained
⅔ cup chopped celery
½ cup chopped pecans
¼ cup mayonnaise
½ teaspoon salt
⅛ teaspoon paprika
1 small head lettuce, shredded
1 (11-ounce) can mandarin oranges, drained

Combine pineapple, celery, pecans, mayonnaise, salt, and paprika, mixing well. Chill.

Arrange lettuce on individual salad plates; top with pineapple mixture. Garnish with mandarin oranges. Yield: 6 servings. *Louise Denmon,*
Silsbee, Texas.

PEANUT BUTTER PUDDING

½ cup sugar
3 tablespoons cornstarch
½ teaspoon salt
3 egg yolks, slightly beaten
2½ cups milk
½ cup creamy peanut butter
1 teaspoon vanilla extract
Whipped topping
Chopped peanuts

Combine sugar, cornstarch, salt, egg yolks, and milk in a medium saucepan. Cook over medium heat, stirring constantly, until mixture boils; cook 1 additional minute, stirring constantly. Remove saucepan from heat; stir in creamy peanut butter and vanilla, and blend mixture well.

Pour into 6 individual serving dishes; top with whipped topping and peanuts. Yield: 6 servings. *Mrs. V. O. Walker,*
Pennington, Texas.

Tip: If peanut butter is stored in the refrigerator, it will keep its quality longer and taste fresher than stored at room temperature.

Start With A Commercial Cake

Next time you're at the grocery store, pick up a ready-made angel food cake, pound cake, or some jellyrolls. Then get ready to make some of the tastiest and easiest desserts ever.

Our Lime Layer Loaf is as pretty as a picture. Simply split an angel food loaf cake lengthwise, and layer it with cool, refreshing lime sherbet. Envelop the colorful creation in whipped cream frosting, and garnish it with piped whipped cream and fresh lime rind. Use a knife dipped in water to make cutting this cake easier.

If you like to keep ingredients for a quick family dessert on hand, Strawberry-Chocolate Combo is for you. Put frozen pound cake, instant chocolate pudding mix, canned strawberry pie filling, and whipped topping on your shopping list so that you'll have them on hand when needed.

You'll find preparation a breeze with Pineapple-Almond Delight, which you can make ahead of time. Raspberry-Jellyroll Dessert is another ideal dish to prepare and chill. We think you'll agree they're both delicious.

RASPBERRY-JELLYROLL DESSERT

4 (3-ounce) packages jellyrolls
½ cup cream sherry
1 (10-ounce) container frozen raspberries, thawed and undrained
1 (3-ounce) package raspberry-flavored gelatin
1 cup boiling water
½ cup cold water
1 (3-ounce) package egg custard mix
1 envelope whipped topping mix
Maraschino cherries with stems

Cut jellyrolls into ½-inch thick slices; place in the bottom of a 2-quart bowl or trifle dish. Pour sherry evenly over cake; top with raspberries. Set aside.

Dissolve gelatin in boiling water; add cold water. Pour over raspberries; chill 2 to 3 hours.

Prepare custard mix according to package directions; cool slightly, and pour over gelatin. Chill at least 1 hour.

Prepare topping mix according to package directions; spread over custard. Garnish with cherries. Yield: 8 servings. *Cathy Shoemaker,*
Boynton Beach, Florida.

LIME LAYER LOAF

1 (8-ounce) loaf commercial angel food
  cake
1 pint lime sherbet, softened
2 cups whipping cream
½ cup sifted powdered sugar
2 teaspoons vanilla extract
2 teaspoons grated lime rind
Lime twist (optional)

Slice cake lengthwise into 3 layers.
Place one layer on a serving plate.
Spread half of sherbet over first layer.
Top with second cake layer; spread with
remaining sherbet. Top with third cake
layer; freeze cake until firm.

Beat whipping cream until foamy;
gradually add sugar and vanilla, beating
until stiff peaks form. Remove cake
from freezer; spread half of whipped
cream on top and sides of cake. Spoon
remaining whipped cream into a decorating bag fitted with No. 5B fluted tip.
Pipe remaining whipped cream around
edges of cake. Sprinkle top with lime
rind; freeze, uncovered, until firm. Garnish with lime twist, if desired. Yield:
10 to 12 servings. *Mary Andrew,
Winston-Salem, North Carolina.*

PINEAPPLE-ALMOND DELIGHT

1 (15¼-ounce) can pineapple tidbits,
  undrained
½ cup sugar
½ cup ground blanched almonds
4 egg yolks, beaten
¼ teaspoon ground cinnamon
1 (8-ounce) loaf commercial angel food
  cake
½ cup orange marmalade
½ cup commercial sour cream
1 tablespoon sugar
¼ cup sliced almonds, toasted

Combine pineapple, ½ cup sugar, ½
cup ground almonds, egg yolks, and cinnamon in a saucepan; cook over low
heat, stirring constantly, until thickened. Remove from heat; cool.

Cut cake into ¾-inch cubes. Place
half of cake in a 1½-quart trifle dish or
bowl; spoon half the marmalade over
cake. Spoon half the pineapple mixture
over marmalade; repeat layers.

Combine sour cream and 1 tablespoon sugar; mix well. Spread over
pineapple mixture. Garnish with almonds. Yield: 8 to 10 servings.
*Gayle Wallace,
Porter, Texas.*

STRAWBERRY-CHOCOLATE
COMBO

1 (6-ounce) package instant chocolate
  pudding mix
1 (10¾-ounce) loaf frozen pound cake,
  thawed
1 (21-ounce) can strawberry pie filling,
  chilled
1 (8-ounce) carton frozen whipped
  topping, thawed

Prepare pudding mix according to
package directions; set aside.

Cut cake into ¾-inch cubes; place in
a 12- x 8- x 2-inch baking dish. Spread
pudding over cake; spoon pie filling
over pudding. Top with whipped topping. Chill 2 to 3 hours. Yield: 12 to 15
servings. *Martha Hardeman,
Gadsden, Alabama.*

Try A Curry-Spiced
Sandwich

If you're having friends over for a
sandwich, serve them a treat. This recipe for Curried Chicken Salad on Raisin
Bread turns an ordinary sandwich into
something special.

CURRIED CHICKEN SALAD ON
RAISIN BREAD

1 tablespoon sugar
1 package dry yeast
1 cup warm buttermilk (105° to 115°),
  divided
1 large ripe banana, mashed
½ cup raisins
2 tablespoons butter or margarine, melted
1 tablespoon grated orange rind
1 tablespoon ground cinnamon
1 teaspoon salt
3 to 4 cups all-purpose flour
1 egg, beaten
1 tablespoon milk
Curried Chicken Salad
Chopped peanuts
Lettuce leaves

Dissolve sugar and yeast in ¼ cup
warm buttermilk; let stand 10 minutes.
Add remaining ¾ cup warm buttermilk,
banana, raisins, melted butter, orange
rind, cinnamon, and salt; mix well.
Gradually stir in enough flour to make a
soft dough.

Turn dough out onto a floured surface, and knead about 10 minutes or
until smooth and elastic. Place in a well-
greased bowl, turning to grease top.
Cover and let rise in a warm place
(85°), free from drafts, about 1½ hours
or until dough is doubled in bulk.

Punch dough down; turn out onto a
floured surface, and knead 2 to 3 minutes. Shape into a loaf, and place in a
greased 9- x 5- x 3-inch loafpan. Cover
and let rise in a warm place (85°), free
from drafts, 45 minutes or until doubled
in bulk.

Combine egg and milk, and brush
over top of loaf. Bake at 375° for 50
minutes or until bread sounds hollow
when tapped. (Cover loaf with aluminum foil if it starts to get too brown
while baking.) Cool bread.

Cut loaf into 12 slices. Spread each of
6 slices with a heaping ⅓ cup Curried
Chicken Salad; top with peanuts, lettuce
leaves, and remaining bread slices. Cut
sandwiches in half to serve. Yield: 6
servings.

Curried Chicken Salad:

1½ cups chopped cooked chicken
¾ cup chopped red apple
2 tablespoons chopped fresh parsley
¼ cup plain yogurt
2½ tablespoons mayonnaise
2 tablespoons grated onion
1 tablespoon plus 1 teaspoon lemon juice
1½ teaspoons curry powder
Salt to taste
¼ teaspoon pepper

Combine chicken, apple, and parsley
in a medium bowl. Combine remaining
ingredients and add to chicken mixture,
tossing to coat. Cover and chill. Yield:
about 2½ cups. *Mrs. R. D. Walker,
Garland, Texas.*

Right: *Serve Galantine of Turkey (page
150) as an entrée for light summer meals.
Each slice reveals a pretty vegetable stuffing
studded with medallions of ham.*

Pages 98 and 99: *Southern waters produce a
bountiful supply of lobsters, blue crabs,
oysters, clams, crawfish, and shrimp. The
first step in preparation is selecting those
shellfish that look and smell fresh. (For
information and recipes, see page 103.)*

Page 100: *Heavenly Chocolate-Berry Pie
and Mocha Brownie Torte (page 102) are
two spectacular, delectable desserts that say
chocolate in each bite. Both recipes got high
ratings with the chocolate lovers on our
foods staff.*

May

Extravagantly Chocolate Desserts

Who can resist the tantalizing flavor of dark, rich chocolate? Judging by the number of recipes we receive, chocolate is a favorite with our readers. Some might even call it an addiction. For whatever reasons, chocolate seems to have almost universal appeal.

This information comes in handy when you're planning a dinner party or having someone over for dessert. Whether you serve a down-home chocolate cake or one of the special desserts we've featured here, you can't go wrong with chocolate.

Needless to say, if you're concerned about calories, desserts should be sampled judiciously. Remember that in the right setting, a small serving eaten very slowly can often be just as satisfying as a large serving. You may want to try this approach when you enjoy these luscious chocolate desserts.

CREAMY CHOCOLATE-ALMOND PIE

1 (7-ounce) chocolate-almond candy bar
18 marshmallows
½ cup milk
1 cup whipping cream, whipped
1 baked 9-inch pastry shell

Combine candy, marshmallows, and milk in a heavy saucepan. Cover and cook over low heat until melted, stirring occasionally. Remove from heat; cool. Fold in whipped cream. Pour mixture into pastry shell. Chill at least 8 hours. Yield: one 9-inch pie.

Betty Joyce Mills,
Birmingham, Alabama.

HEAVENLY CHOCOLATE-BERRY PIE

1¼ cups graham cracker crumbs
3 tablespoons sugar
⅓ cup butter or margarine, melted
½ cup plus 2 tablespoons semisweet chocolate morsels, divided
1 (8-ounce) package cream cheese, softened
¼ cup firmly packed brown sugar
½ teaspoon vanilla extract
1 cup whipping cream, whipped
1 pint fresh strawberries
1 teaspoon shortening

Combine first 3 ingredients, mixing well; firmly press onto bottom and sides of a lightly greased 9-inch pieplate. Bake at 325° for 10 minutes. Cool crust completely.

Place ½ cup chocolate morsels in top of a double boiler; bring water to a boil. Reduce heat to low; cook until chocolate melts. Set chocolate aside to cool slightly.

Beat cream cheese with an electric mixer until light and fluffy; add brown sugar and vanilla, mixing well. Add cooled chocolate; mix well. Fold the whipped cream into cream cheese mixture; spoon filling into prepared crust. Chill at least 8 hours.

Set aside 1 strawberry, and cut remaining strawberries into thick slices. Arrange slices over filling; place whole strawberry in center.

Combine remaining 2 tablespoons chocolate morsels and shortening in a small saucepan over low heat; cook until the chocolate morsels melt. Drizzle over strawberries. Yield: one 9-inch pie.

Sandy Hayes,
Morristown, Tennessee.

MOCHA BROWNIE TORTE

1 (15.5-ounce) package fudge brownie mix
2 eggs, beaten
2 tablespoons water
½ cup chopped pecans
1 cup whipping cream
3 tablespoons plus 1 teaspoon brown sugar
2 teaspoons instant coffee granules
Additional flavored whipped cream for piping (optional)
Shaved chocolate (optional)
Chocolate curls (optional)

Grease two 8-inch round baking pans, and line with waxed paper; grease waxed paper. Set aside.

Combine brownie mix, eggs, and water; mix well. Stir in pecans. Spread batter into pans. Bake at 350° for 15 to 18 minutes. Cool 5 minutes; remove cake from pans, and cool completely.

Beat whipping cream until foamy; gradually add sugar and coffee granules, beating until stiff peaks form.

Spread whipped cream mixture between layers and on top and sides of cake. Garnish with piped whipped cream mixture, shaved chocolate, and chocolate curls, if desired. Chill until serving time. Yield: one 8-inch torte.

Peggy Blackburn,
Winston-Salem, North Carolina.

BRANDY-CHOCOLATE MOUSSE

1 (6-ounce) package semisweet chocolate morsels
¼ cup plus 1 tablespoon butter
4 eggs, separated
2 tablespoons brandy
¼ cup sifted powdered sugar
Whipped cream (optional)

Place chocolate and butter in top of a double boiler; bring water to a boil. Reduce heat to low; cook until chocolate and butter melt. Remove from heat; stir in egg yolks, one at a time, beating well after each addition with a wooden spoon. Cool. Stir in brandy and sugar; beat well.

Beat egg whites (at room temperature) until stiff but not dry; gently fold egg whites into chocolate mixture. Spoon mousse into stemmed glasses, and refrigerate. Garnish with whipped cream, if desired. Yield: 6 servings.

Rick Reed,
Lubbock, Texas.

RUM-FLAVORED POTS DE CRÈME

8 (1-ounce) squares semisweet chocolate
2 cups half-and-half
1 tablespoon sugar
6 egg yolks, slightly beaten
2 tablespoons dark rum
Whipped cream
Slivered almonds, toasted

Combine chocolate, half-and-half, and sugar in top of a double boiler; bring water to a boil. Reduce heat; cook until chocolate melts. Gradually stir about one-fourth of chocolate mixture into yolks; add to remaining chocolate mixture, and stir. Add dark rum.

Pour mixture into six 4-ounce serving dishes. Chill at least 8 hours. To serve, garnish with whipped cream and almonds. Yield: 6 servings.

Susan Mitchell Davis,
Longwood, Florida.

Catch On To Shellfish

In Louisiana's Cajun country, the favorite catch is crawfish. Apalachicola Bay fishermen in Florida are known for the oysters they harvest. Chesapeake Bay residents boast of blue crabs. And shrimp, lobsters, scallops, and clams are all caught on the Southern coastline.

Shellfish are always popular to cook and serve, but because they are generally expensive, you'll want to get the best quality for your money. When purchasing shrimp, always select those that are firm textured, and cook them within one or two days. Otherwise, it's best to freeze the shrimp in their shells the day they're purchased.

Live oysters or clams should have tightly closed shells. If they have been shucked, select those that are plump and fresh smelling. Any liquid should be clear, not cloudy or pink.

When buying fresh uncooked crabs and lobsters, make sure they are still moving. A live lobster's tail is curled under the body rather than hanging down when picked up. You'll find cooked crabmeat available in several forms—solid white lump meat, flaked white meat, and brownish claw meat; frozen cooked lobster tail meat will be white with tinges of red.

As with lobsters, crawfish should still be alive at the time of purchase. If crawfish are kept cold and moist, they will keep for two or three days. They are also available parboiled, fully cooked, or fresh frozen.

Scallops are always shucked immediately upon harvesting. If you purchase them fresh, look for creamy white, light tan, or pinkish meat with a slightly sweet odor and almost no liquid.

For the most part, shellfish can be found either fresh or frozen year-round. There was a time, however, when everyone followed the old wives' tale from pre-refrigeration days that oysters must be eaten only in months containing an "r." Some still insist oysters just aren't as flavorful during summer months.

Shrimp are generally available any time of the year. Fresh blue crabs, clams, and scallops can be difficult to locate during winter months. On the other hand, spiny lobsters are plentiful when it's cold, and crawfish harvesting begins in January and continues through late spring.

Every Southern family seems to have at least one special recipe for shellfish. Here are some of the best.

LOBSTER THERMIDOR

2 quarts water
1 (1½-pound) fresh lobster tail
2 tablespoons butter or margarine
2 tablespoons all-purpose flour
1½ teaspoons dry mustard
½ teaspoon salt
Dash of red pepper
1½ cups half-and-half
1 (4-ounce) can mushroom stems and
   pieces, drained
2 tablespoons grated Parmesan cheese
Paprika

Bring water to a boil; add lobster tail. Cover, reduce heat, and simmer 12 to 15 minutes. Drain. Rinse with cold water. Split and clean tail. Cut lobster meat (about 1 pound) into ½-inch pieces; set aside.

Melt butter in a skillet over low heat; add flour and seasonings, stirring until smooth. Cook 1 minute, stirring constantly. Gradually add half-and-half; cook over medium heat, stirring constantly, until mixture is thickened and bubbly. Stir in lobster meat and mushrooms. Spoon mixture into six well-greased 6-ounce baking shells or dishes. Sprinkle with cheese and paprika. Bake at 400° for about 10 minutes or until lightly browned. Yield: 6 servings.

Vicky L. Murphy,
Atlanta, Georgia.

SHRIMP-AND-SCALLOP SAUTÉ

6 green onions with tops, cut into 1-inch
   pieces
2 teaspoons minced garlic
½ cup butter or margarine, melted
1 pound fresh shrimp, peeled and
   deveined
¾ pound fresh scallops
½ pound lump crabmeat
½ pound fresh mushrooms, sliced
1 (8-ounce) can sliced water chestnuts,
   drained
½ cup finely chopped green pepper
1 tablespoon plus ½ teaspoon salt-free
   herb-and-spice seasoning
1 tablespoon Worcestershire sauce
2 tablespoons chopped fresh parsley
Hot cooked rice (optional)

Sauté green onions and garlic in butter in a large, heavy skillet 1 minute. Add remaining ingredients except parsley and rice. Cook over medium heat 6 to 8 minutes, stirring occasionally. Stir in chopped parsley. Serve mixture over rice, if desired. Yield: 6 servings.

Emalyn Johnson,
Stapleton, Alabama.

GRILLED SHRIMP

4 cloves garlic, crushed
1 cup olive oil
½ cup finely chopped fresh basil
2 tablespoons vinegar
1 tablespoon Worcestershire sauce
½ teaspoon hot sauce
2 pounds large fresh shrimp, peeled and
   deveined

Combine all ingredients except shrimp in a shallow dish; mix well. Add shrimp, tossing gently to coat. Cover and marinate shrimp 2 to 3 hours in the refrigerator, stirring occasionally.

Remove shrimp from marinade, reserving marinade. Place shrimp on six 14-inch skewers. Grill over medium-hot coals 3 to 4 minutes on each side, basting frequently with marinade. Yield: 6 servings.

Ramona Kilgo,
Fort Worth, Texas.

PARMESAN-STUFFED SHRIMP

1 cup round buttery cracker crumbs
½ cup butter or margarine, melted
¼ cup grated Parmesan cheese
1½ tablespoons cooking sherry
1 teaspoon lemon juice
¼ teaspoon garlic powder
16 jumbo fresh shrimp
Paprika

Combine cracker crumbs, butter, cheese, sherry, lemon juice, and garlic powder; mix well. Set aside.

Peel shrimp; devein and butterfly. Place in a shallow baking dish. Fill each shrimp with cracker mixture. Bake at 250° for 25 minutes. Broil 1 minute or until shrimp is lightly browned. Sprinkle with paprika. Yield: 4 servings.

Cyndi Copenhaver,
Virginia Beach, Virginia.

FESTIVE BLUE CRABS

2 dozen small blue crabs, cleaned
3 to 4 tablespoons lemon juice
¼ cup Season-All
½ cup butter or margarine

Using a sharp knife, remove claws and legs from crabs. Discard legs, reserving claws. Clean crabs.

Place crabs and claws in two ungreased 13- x 9- x 2-inch baking dishes; sprinkle with lemon juice and Season-All. Let stand 45 minutes; dot with butter. Cover and bake at 300° for 30 minutes. Yield: 4 servings.

Donald R. Smith,
Panacea, Florida.

DEVILED CRAB

¼ cup butter or margarine
¼ cup all-purpose flour
2 cups milk
2 tablespoons Worcestershire sauce
2 teaspoons dry mustard
1 teaspoon celery seeds
¼ teaspoon salt
¼ teaspoon pepper
6 dashes of hot sauce
1 pound fresh crabmeat
½ cup cracker crumbs
1 tablespoon chopped fresh parsley
Mayonnaise
Paprika
Chopped fresh parsley (optional)
Lemon wedges (optional)

Melt butter in a heavy saucepan over low heat; add flour, stirring until smooth. Cook 1 minute, stirring constantly. Gradually add milk; cook over medium heat, stirring constantly, until thickened and bubbly.

Remove from heat; add Worcestershire sauce, dry mustard, celery seeds, salt, pepper, and hot sauce, mixing well. Stir in crabmeat, cracker crumbs, and chopped parsley. Spoon crabmeat mixture into eight 6-ounce lightly greased baking shells or dishes. Bake at 350° for 20 minutes.

Top each serving with a dollop of mayonnaise, and sprinkle with paprika. Bake an additional 5 minutes. Garnish with parsley and lemon wedges, if desired. Yield: 8 servings.

Mrs. William B. Bartling,
New Bern, North Carolina.

CLAMS OREGANATA

2 dozen cherrystone clams
½ cup fine, dry breadcrumbs
2 tablespoons olive oil
1 tablespoon lemon juice
1 tablespoon grated Parmesan cheese
1 tablespoon chopped fresh parsley
1 teaspoon anchovy paste or 2 mashed
  anchovies
1 large clove garlic, minced
¾ teaspoon dried whole oregano
⅛ teaspoon pepper
Fresh parsley sprigs

Wash clams thoroughly, discarding any open (dead) clams. Pry open shells, reserving 3 tablespoons clam juice. Discard top shells, and loosen meat from bottom shell. Drain bottom shells on paper towels. Mince clams, and set them aside.

Strain clam juice. Combine 2 tablespoons juice with remaining ingredients except parsley sprigs; stir until mixed and crumbly, adding remaining clam juice if mixture seems too dry.

Spoon about 1 tablespoon minced clams into each shell half; arrange shells on shallow baking pans. Top each of the shells with a heaping teaspoon of the breadcrumb mixture.

Bake at 350° for 6 to 7 minutes or until heated through. Before serving, garnish with fresh parsley sprigs. Yield: 12 appetizer servings. *Carol Alvine,*
Altamonte Springs, Florida.

CRAWFISH SPAGHETTI

2 medium onions, chopped
¼ cup chopped green pepper
3 tablespoons vegetable oil
1½ cups water
1 (16-ounce) can tomatoes, undrained and
  chopped
1 (8-ounce) can tomato sauce
½ cup chopped fresh parsley
4 cloves garlic, minced
1 teaspoon salt
¼ teaspoon pepper
2 pounds cleaned crawfish tails
Hot cooked spaghetti
Grated Parmesan cheese

Sauté onion and green pepper in oil in a Dutch oven until tender. Stir in water, tomatoes, tomato sauce, and seasonings. Bring mixture to a boil; reduce heat, and simmer 1½ hours. Add crawfish tails; cook over low heat 20 minutes. Serve over spaghetti; sprinkle with cheese. Yield: 6 servings.

Vanessa Courville,
Loreauville, Louisiana.

FRIED OYSTERS

1 cup cracker meal
½ cup cornmeal
¼ teaspoon salt
⅛ teaspoon pepper
1 (12-ounce) container fresh Select oysters,
  drained
2 eggs, beaten
Vegetable oil

Combine cracker meal, cornmeal, salt, and pepper in a medium bowl. Dip oysters in egg; then dredge in meal mixture. Fry oysters in deep, hot oil (375°) for 1½ minutes or until golden, turning once. Drain on paper towels; serve immediately. Yield: 4 servings.

Henry Minix,
Lynchburg, Virginia.

Capture The Garden In A Jar

Your neighbor has just brought over a bushel of corn, a sackful of green beans, and some of the prettiest tomatoes you've ever seen. While you certainly want to enjoy some of the fresh flavor for dinner tonight, preserve what you can't use right away by canning.

Whether you've been putting up food for years or are giving it your first try, you'll find the information here helpful. Processing and safety recommendations have changed even in the past few years. (Especially note those for preserving tomatoes.)

You can update your favorite recipes to ensure safe storage. And try some of our recipes for fruit, vegetable combos, and even soup.

Have the Right Equipment

Before you start canning, be sure you have the following items on hand: water-bath canner with rack, pressure canner with rack, jar filler or funnel, jar lifter, rubber spatula, and timer. Use only standard canning jars without any scratches, cracks, or chips. Don't try to save money by using commercial mayonnaise or peanut butter jars; they often hold more food than a regular canning jar, making the recommended processing times too short to be safe.

Jars should be as clean as possible. Wash them in warm, soapy water; rinse, and keep hot. A dishwasher works well for this. If the required processing time in a water-bath canner is under 15 minutes, the jars need to be sterilized by boiling in water 15 minutes.

You can reuse metal bands as long as they aren't rusted or dented, but be sure to buy new jar lids each time, since the sealing compound works only once.

Preparing the Fruit And Vegetables

Produce selected for canning should be perfect—firm, ripe, with no bruises or bad places. Gather only the amount you can process within a few hours. If you must wait until the next day to can, store the produce unwashed in the refrigerator, and use as soon as possible.

Wash produce well; prepare as directed in recipe. Meanwhile, heat water in canner. The water-bath canner needs enough water to come 1 to 2 inches above jar tops; a pressure canner needs 2 or 3 inches in the bottom.

Place fruit or vegetables in hot jars following recipe directions for cold- or hot-pack methods. Some types of produce are best preserved by one of the two methods, so check with your local Extension agent to learn the latest recommendations on selecting methods.

Fruit maintains better quality when packed in a sugar syrup rather than boiling water. See our chart for types and directions.

It's important to follow recipe directions for leaving headspace when filling jars with liquid. Too little headspace may cause the liquid to bubble up under the lid and prevent it from sealing. With too much headspace, processing time may not be long enough to push all the air out and form a vacuum seal.

Wipe jar rims clean before putting the metal lids in place. Then screw on metal bands.

How To Process Canned Food

Safety is the first word in canning, so it's essential that canned goods be processed in a boiling-water bath or a pressure canner. The open-kettle method (placing cooked food in jars and sealing them without processing) is no longer considered safe practice.

Use the boiling-water bath method for fruit and tomatoes. The water should be gently boiling when you add jars packed by the hot-pack method. For the cold-pack method, you'll need to heat the water just to warm to prevent jar breakage.

Place jars on the canner rack so that water flows evenly around them. Add or remove water so that it levels 1 to 2 inches above the lids. Cover and start to count processing time when water returns to a boil.

Vegetables, meat products, and vegetable-tomato combinations must be processed in a pressure canner to heat them above the boiling point of water. The 240° temperature obtained in this canner is sufficient to kill harmful bacteria that thrive in low-acid conditions.

Before using a dial-gauge pressure canner, be sure to allow steam to escape from the vent for at least 10 minutes after closing the lid. Check manufacturer's directions for weighted-gauge models. Close the vent; then regulate the heat source to maintain 10 pounds pressure. The weight on a weighted-gauge model should jiggle or rock gently about three or four times a minute. You should begin to count processing time after the canner reaches 10 pounds pressure.

After processing, remove the canner from the heat, and allow pressure to drop to 0. This will take 30 minutes to 1 hour. (Do not rush the cooling process by removing the weight or setting the canner in water.) Open the lid away from you; then remove the jars, and allow them to cool.

Once the jars, processed by either method, have cooled 12 to 24 hours, check to see that each is sealed properly. You may hear them pop as they seal and feel a downward curve to the lids. Another method of checking is to tap each lid with the back of a spoon. If the sound is a dull thud rather than a clear ring, turn the jar on its side for a few minutes to check for leakage. Leaky jars indicate there is no seal, so the jars should be stored in the refrigerator and used right away. Otherwise, mark the jar, and store with the others, but use the marked jar first.

If you're making several "runs" of the same product, it would be wise to mark each jar by lot number. Then if you find a problem with one jar later, you can easily trace others processed at the same time.

Serving Home-Canned Food

Provided you've followed all the recommended canning procedures and used clean equipment and surfaces, your canned goods should keep safely and maintain good quality for at least a year, if properly stored. However, spoiled home-canned products account for some deaths each year, so it pays to be extra careful when preparing them.

Some types of harmful bacteria, such as the one that causes botulism, show no typical signs of spoilage, such as a bulging lid or leaking jar, mold, off-odor, cloudy liquid, or spurting liquid upon opening. Because of this, it's important to boil all home-canned food in a covered saucepan for 10 minutes; canned corn and meat should be boiled for 20 minutes. Never taste the food before boiling.

If you notice signs of spoilage, throw the food away. It's a good idea to boil it before discarding or burn the food to keep from spreading food toxins in any way to other people and animals.

Following are some recipes and general directions for canning some of the most popular vegetables and fruit. Follow recommendations carefully to ensure safe storage.

GREEN, SNAP, OR WAX BEANS

Wash beans, trim ends, and string if necessary; cut into 1-inch lengths.

Hot pack: Cover beans with boiling water, and boil 5 minutes. Pack beans loosely in hot jars, leaving ½-inch headspace. Add ½ teaspoon salt to pints and 1 teaspoon to quarts, if desired. Cover with boiling liquid, leaving ½-inch headspace. Cover at once with metal lids, and screw bands tight. Process in pressure canner at 10 pounds pressure (240°). Process pints for 20 minutes and quarts for 25 minutes.

Cold pack: Pack beans tightly into hot jars, leaving ½-inch headspace. Add ½ teaspoon salt to pints and 1 teaspoon to quarts, if desired. Cover with boiling water, leaving ½-inch headspace. Cover at once with metal lids, and screw on bands. Process in pressure canner at 10 pounds pressure (240°). Process pints for 20 minutes and quarts 25 minutes.

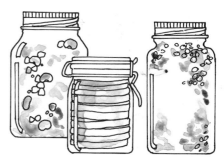

SUMMER SQUASH

Wash and trim ends from squash; do not peel. Cut squash into ½-inch slices; then cut slices into uniform pieces.

Hot pack: Add just enough water to cover squash; bring to a boil. Pack hot squash loosely into hot jars, leaving ½-inch headspace. Add ½ teaspoon salt to pints and 1 teaspoon to quarts, if desired. Cover with boiling liquid, leaving ½-inch headspace.

Cover at once with metal lids, and screw on bands. Process in pressure canner at 10 pounds pressure (240°). Process pints for 30 minutes and quarts for 40 minutes.

Cold pack: Pack squash tightly into hot jars leaving 1-inch headspace. Add ½ teaspoon salt to pints and 1 teaspoon to quarts, if desired. Cover with boiling water, leaving ½-inch headspace.

Cover at once with metal lids, and screw on bands. Process in pressure canner at 10 pounds pressure (240°). Process pints for 30 minutes and quarts for 40 minutes.

WHOLE KERNEL CORN

Husk corn, and remove silks; wash. Cut corn from cob at about two-thirds the depth of kernel; do not scrape.

Hot pack: Add 2 cups boiling water to 4 cups cut corn; boil 3 minutes. Pack corn into hot jars, leaving 1-inch headspace. Cover at once with metal lids, and screw on bands. Process in pressure canner at 10 pounds pressure (240°). Process pints for 55 minutes and quarts for 1 hour and 25 minutes.

Cold pack: Pack corn in hot jars; leaving 1-inch headspace. Do not shake or press down. Add ½ teaspoon salt to pints and 1 teaspoon to quarts. Cover with boiling water, leaving ½-inch headspace. Cover at once with metal lids, and screw on bands. Process in pressure canner at 10 pounds pressure (240°). Process pints for 55 minutes and quarts for 1 hour and 25 minutes.

CREAM-STYLE CORN

Husk corn and remove silks; wash. Cut corn from cob at about center of kernel; scrape cob.

Hot pack: Add 2½ cups water to 4 cups cut corn; boil 3 minutes. Pack loosely into hot pint jars, leaving 1-inch headspace. Add ½ teaspoon salt to each pint, if desired. Cover with boiling liquid, leaving 1-inch headspace. Cover at once with metal lids, and screw on bands. Process in pressure canner at 10 pounds pressure (240°). Process pints for 1 hour and 25 minutes.

Cold pack: Pack corn loosely into hot pint jars, leaving 1½-inch headspace. Add ½ teaspoon salt to each pint, if desired. Cover with boiling water, leaving ½-headspace. Cover at once with metal lids, and screw on bands. Process in pressure canner at 10 pounds pressure (240°). Process pints for 1 hour and 35 minutes.

Note: Do not can cream-style corn in quart jars.

TOMATOES

Peel tomatoes; remove stem and blossom ends. Leave whole, or cut as desired. Use hot-pack method only.

Hot pack: Bring tomatoes to a boil, stirring to keep from sticking; boil 5 minutes. Pack hot tomatoes into hot jars, leaving 1-inch headspace. Add ½ teaspoon salt to pints and 1 teaspoon to quarts, if desired. Cover tomatoes with boiling juice, leaving ½-inch headspace. Cover jars at once with metal lids, and screw on bands. Process in boiling-water bath 35 minutes for pints; process 45 minutes for quarts.

VEGETABLE SOUP

2 quarts (about 12 large) peeled, chopped tomatoes
1½ quarts (about 6 medium) peeled, cubed potatoes
1 quart shelled fresh lima beans
1 quart (about 10 ears) fresh corn, cut from cob
1½ quarts (about 15 medium) ¾-inch-thick carrot slices
2 cups 1-inch-thick celery slices
2 cups chopped onion
1½ quarts water
1¾ teaspoons salt, divided

Combine vegetables and water in a large kettle; bring to a boil, and cook 5 minutes, stirring often.

Ladle hot vegetable mixture into hot jars, leaving 1-inch headspace; remove air bubbles. Add ¼ teaspoon salt to each pint, ½ teaspoon salt to each quart. Cover jars at once with metal lids, and screw on bands. Process in a pressure canner at 10 pounds pressure (240°). Process pints for 55 minutes and quarts for 1 hour and 25 minutes. Yield: 15 pints or 7½ quarts.

SUCCOTASH

10 ears fresh corn
1½ quarts shelled fresh lima beans
1 tablespoon plus ½ teaspoon salt, divided
Boiling water

Place corn in a large Dutch oven, and cover with water. Bring to a boil; cook 5 minutes. Remove from heat; cool.

Cook beans, uncovered, in boiling water for 5 minutes. Drain beans, and reserve liquid.

Cut corn from cob; combine with beans. Pack into hot jars, leaving 1½-inch headspace. Pour in hot bean liquid, leaving 1½-inch headspace. Add ½-inch boiling water. Add ½ teaspoon salt to each pint, 1 teaspoon salt to each quart. Cover at once with metal lids, and screw on bands. Process in pressure canner at 10 pounds pressure (240°). Process pints for 1 hour and quarts for 1 hour and 25 minutes. Yield: 7 pints or 3½ quarts.

TOMATOES WITH OKRA

2 quarts peeled and coarsely chopped ripe tomatoes (about 4½ pounds)
6 cups sliced fresh okra (about 2 pounds)
1¼ teaspoons salt, divided

Cook tomatoes, uncovered, in a large Dutch oven 20 minutes. Add okra; bring to a boil and cook, uncovered, 5 minutes. Pour into hot jars, leaving 1-inch headspace; remove air bubbles. Add ¼ teaspoon salt to each pint, ½ teaspoon salt to each quart. Cover at once with metal lids, and screw on bands. Process in pressure canner at 10 pounds pressure (240°). Process pints for 30 minutes and quarts for 35 minutes. Yield: about 5 pints or 2½ quarts.

PEACHES AND PEARS

Peel fruit; cut in halves or quarters, and remove cores or pits. Cut in slices, if desired. To prevent fruit from darkening during preparation, use commercial ascorbic-citric powder according to manufacturer's directions, or immerse the fruit after peeling in a sugar-syrup or lemon-juice solution (¾ cup lemon juice to 1 gallon water).

Prepare a medium syrup. (See chart.)

Canning Syrups for Fruit

Type of Syrup	Sugar (Cups)	Liquid (Cups)	Yield (Cups)
Thin	2	4	5
Medium	3	4	5½
Heavy	4¾	4	6½

Directions: Combine sugar and water or fruit juice. Heat, stirring constantly, until sugar dissolves. Keep syrup hot.

Hot pack: Simmer peaches or pears in hot syrup 3 to 5 minutes. Pack fruit into hot jars, leaving ½-inch headspace. Cover fruit with boiling syrup, leaving ½-inch headspace; wipe rims clean. Cover jars at once with metal lids, and screw on bands. Process in boiling-water bath 20 minutes for pints; process 25 minutes for quarts.

Cold pack: Pack raw peaches or pears into hot jars, leaving ½-inch headspace. Cover fruit with boiling syrup, leaving ½-inch headspace; wipe rims clean. Cover jars at once with metal lids, and screw on bands. Process in boiling-water bath 25 minutes for pints; process 30 minutes for quarts.

FRUIT JUICES

Hot pack: Wash fruit, remove pits or seeds, if desired, and crush fruit. Heat to simmering, stirring constantly. Strain through cheesecloth or jelly bag. Add ½ to 1 cup sugar per gallon juice, if desired. Return to heat and simmer, stirring until sugar dissolves. Pour hot juice into hot, sterilized jars, leaving ½-inch headspace. Cover at once with metal lids, and screw on bands. Process in boiling-water bath 10 minutes for pints and quarts.

HONEY-SWEET PEACHES

2 quarts cold water
1 tablespoon salt
1 tablespoon white vinegar
15 firm, ripe medium Cling peaches (5¾ pounds)
1 quart water
1 cup sugar
1 cup honey

Combine water, salt, and vinegar in a large container; set aside. Peel peaches; cut in half, and pit. Scrape pit cavities to remove pink or red fibers. Place peach halves in salt-vinegar mixture to prevent darkening. (Do not allow to stand in mixture more than 20 minutes.) Drain peaches, and rinse well.

Combine 1 quart water, sugar, and honey in a saucepan; cook over medium heat until the sugar dissolves and mixture is hot.

Pack peaches in hot jars, cavity side down, overlapping layers and leaving ½-inch headspace. Pour hot syrup over peaches; leaving ½-inch headspace; remove air bubbles. Cover at once with metal lids, and screw on bands. Process in boiling-water bath 25 minutes for pints and 30 minutes for quarts. Yield: 6 pints or 3 quarts.

CINNAMON-APPLE RINGS

Ascorbic citric powder
14 medium cooking apples (about 6 pounds), unpeeled
4 cups sugar
1 quart water
1½ teaspoons ground cinnamon
10 to 12 drops red food color

Prepare ascorbic-citric solution according to the manufacturer's directions; set aside.

Core apples, and slice into ¼-inch rings. Drop apple rings into ascorbic-citric solution, and set aside. (Do not allow apples to stand in solution more than 20 minutes.)

Combine remaining ingredients in a large Dutch oven, and bring to a boil; boil 5 minutes. Remove syrup from heat. Drain apple rings, and add to syrup; let stand 10 minutes. Return apple mixture to heat, and bring to a rolling boil; reduce heat, and simmer 20 minutes, stirring occasionally. Remove from heat, and let cool.

Drain apples, reserving syrup. Bring syrup to a boil. Pack apple rings into hot jars, leaving ½-inch headspace. Cover apple rings with boiling syrup, leaving ½-inch headspace; remove air bubbles. Cover jars at once with metal lids, and screw on bands. Process in boiling-water bath 15 minutes for pints and 20 minutes for quarts. Yield: 6 pints or 3 quarts.

Canning is the first in a four-part series on food preservation. See the June, July, and August sections for information on making jams and jellies, pickling, and freezing fruits and vegetables.

COOKING LIGHT®

Liven Up Your Diet With Fruit

When you're dieting, it's important that the low-calorie food you eat is high in vitamins and minerals. After all, the most important reason for eating is to take in necessary nutrients for tissue building and maintenance and for daily physical activity.

That's why it makes good sense for a dieter to enjoy fruit often. Not only is fruit high in vitamins, minerals, and fiber, but it contains little, if any, fat or sodium—and no cholesterol. (An exception is the avocado, which is high in fat and calories.)

Fresh fruit is especially easy to enjoy—plain, in its natural state, or dressed up in a variety of fancy ways. In appetizers, soups, salads, and desserts, fruit will give new life to any diet.

CURRIED FRUIT SALAD

½ cup unsweetened orange juice
1 teaspoon curry powder
2 teaspoons lemon juice
½ cup cubed fresh pineapple
1 fresh peach, peeled and cubed
1 medium apple, unpeeled and cubed
20 seedless green grapes
4 (1-inch) slices honeydew
Lettuce leaves
2 cups low-fat cottage cheese

Combine orange juice, curry powder, and lemon juice in a medium bowl. Add pineapple, peach, apple, and grapes, stirring to coat. Cover and chill.

Place honeydew slices onto 4 individual lettuce-lined serving dishes; top each with ½ cup cottage cheese. Drain fruit mixture; spoon fruit around cottage cheese. Yield: 4 servings (about 167 calories per serving).

Harriet O. St. Amant,
Newport, Rhode Island.

PLUM SOUP

3½ cups peeled, diced ripe plums
1¾ cups unsweetened apple juice
1 cup water
1 (3-inch) stick cinnamon
½ teaspoon vanilla extract
¼ teaspoon ground allspice

Combine all ingredients except vanilla and allspice in a medium saucepan. Bring to a boil; cover, reduce heat, and simmer 30 minutes. Remove from heat, and stir in vanilla and allspice. Discard cinnamon. Pour half of mixture into container of an electric blender; process until smooth. Repeat with remaining mixture. Serve cold. Yield: 4½ cups (about 110 calories per 1-cup serving).

NECTARINE COCKTAIL

1 cup cubed cantaloupe
1 cup fresh raspberries
1 tablespoon lime juice
2 teaspoons grated orange rind
½ cup unsweetened orange juice
3 fresh nectarines, unpeeled and sliced
2 tablespoons slivered almonds, toasted

Combine cantaloupe, raspberries, lime juice, orange rind, and orange juice; chill 2 hours, stirring occasionally. Arrange nectarines vertically in 6 stemmed dishes. Spoon chilled fruit into center of nectarines; sprinkle with almonds. Yield: 6 servings (about 81 calories per serving).

STRAWBERRY ICE

2 cups fresh strawberries
¼ cup sugar
½ cup water
2 tablespoons unsweetened orange juice
2 egg whites
¼ teaspoon cream of tartar
Pinch of salt

Combine strawberries, sugar, water, and orange juice in container of an electric blender; process until smooth. Pour mixture into a medium saucepan, and cook over low heat 5 minutes, stirring occasionally. Let cool, and pour into a medium mixing bowl; freeze 45 minutes or until slushy.

Combine egg whites (at room temperature), cream of tartar, and salt in mixing bowl; beat until soft peaks form.

Beat strawberry mixture until fluffy and smooth. Fold in egg whites. Freeze until firm. Yield: 6 servings (about 57 calories per serving).   *Jan Hughes,*
Batesville, Arkansas.

RAINBOW FRUIT DESSERT

1 large mango (about 1 pound), peeled
  and diced
2 cups fresh blueberries
2 bananas, sliced
2 cups fresh strawberries, halved
2 cups seedless green grapes
2 nectarines, unpeeled and sliced
1 kiwi, peeled and sliced
Honey-Orange Sauce

Layer fruit in order listed in a serving bowl. Just before serving, pour on Honey-Orange Sauce. Yield: 12 servings (about 102 calories per 1-cup serving).

Honey-Orange Sauce:

⅓ cup unsweetened orange juice
2 tablespoons lemon juice
1½ tablespoons honey
¼ teaspoon ground ginger
Dash of ground nutmeg

Combine all ingredients in a bowl; mix well. Yield: ½ cup. *Audrey Joffre,*
Memphis, Tennessee.

PEACHES
WITH HONEY-LIME WHIP

2 tablespoons honey
1 teaspoon grated lime rind
2 tablespoons lime juice
⅛ teaspoon ground mace
6 medium peaches, peeled and sliced

Combine honey, lime rind, lime juice, and mace in a small bowl; mix well with

a wire whisk. Pour honey mixture over peaches, and toss gently. Yield: 6 servings (about 61 calories per serving).
Mrs. James E. Krachey,
Guymon, Oklahoma.

Vegetables:
Stir-Fried And Fresh

If you want to cook fresh vegetables with a light touch, do it quickly by stir-frying. That's one of the best ways to preserve their natural flavor, color, and nutrient value.

When stir-frying, start by heating a small amount of oil in either a wok or large skillet. As the vegetables are added, stir them continuously to ensure even cooking.

Always assemble the ingredients for Oriental Vegetables, or any of these recipes, before you heat the wok. The vegetables, of course, must be sliced and ready to cook. Once the stir-frying process begins, it proceeds rapidly.

Try to slice less tender vegetables, such as carrots, in a diagonal pattern to expose the largest possible area to the heat. Delicate vegetables, like mushrooms or tomatoes, should be cut into thicker pieces.

ORIENTAL VEGETABLES

2 tablespoons soy sauce
1 tablespoon vinegar
3 tablespoons light corn syrup
2 teaspoons cornstarch
2 tablespoons vegetable oil
2 medium zucchini, cut into thin
  2-inch-long strips
2 carrots, cut diagonally into thin slices
1 small onion, cut into thin wedges
½ teaspoon salt

Combine soy sauce, vinegar, syrup, and cornstarch, stirring well; set aside.

Pour oil around top of a preheated wok or large skillet; allow to heat at medium high (325°) for 2 minutes. Add vegetables and salt, and stir-fry 4 minutes or until crisp-tender. Add corn syrup mixture, stirring constantly. Bring to a boil; cook 1 minute. Serve immediately. Yield: 4 servings.
Mildred Sheppard,
Crawfordville, Florida.

ASPARAGUS AND MUSHROOMS

1 pound fresh asparagus
1 tablespoon butter or margarine, melted
½ pound fresh mushrooms, sliced
½ teaspoon beef-flavored bouillon granules
¼ cup boiling water
¼ teaspoon pepper

Snap off tough ends of asparagus. Remove scales from stalks with a knife or vegetable peeler, if desired. Cut asparagus into 1-inch pieces.

Melt butter in a wok or large skillet. Add asparagus and mushrooms; stir-fry over medium high heat (325°) for 2 to 3 minutes. Dissolve bouillon in water; add to vegetables. Bring to a boil; cover, reduce heat, and simmer 1 to 2 minutes or until asparagus is crisp-tender. Sprinkle with pepper, and serve immediately. Yield: 4 servings.   *Charlotte Watkins,*
Lakeland, Florida.

GREEN BEAN MEDLEY

½ pound fresh green beans
3 tablespoons vegetable oil
2 cups broccoli flowerets
3 firm medium tomatoes, cut into wedges
2 scallions or green onions, cut into
  2-inch pieces
¼ pound fresh mushrooms, sliced
1 (8-ounce) can sliced water chestnuts,
  drained
1 tablespoon soy sauce
¼ teaspoon salt

Wash green beans; trim ends, and remove strings. Cut beans diagonally into 2-inch pieces.

Pour oil around top of a preheated wok or large skillet; allow to heat at medium high (325°) for 2 minutes. Add beans and broccoli; stir-fry 2 minutes. Add tomatoes, scallions, mushrooms, and sliced water chestnuts; stir-fry 2 minutes. Stir in soy sauce and salt. Serve immediately. Yield: 6 servings.
Sue Smith,
Morristown, Tennessee.

ZUCCHINI-AND-TOMATO
STIR-FRY

2 tablespoons vegetable oil
2 medium onions, sliced
4 medium zucchini, sliced
2 large tomatoes, cut into wedges
1 (4-ounce) can sliced mushrooms, drained
½ teaspoon salt
¼ teaspoon pepper

Pour oil around top of a preheated wok or large skillet; allow to heat at medium high (325°) for 2 minutes. Add onion, and stir-fry 2 minutes. Add zucchini; stir-fry 6 to 8 minutes. Add remaining ingredients, and stir-fry 2 minutes. Yield: 8 servings.

Nancy Drechsler,
Hendersonville, North Carolina.

STIR-FRIED CABBAGE

3 slices bacon, chopped
1 small head cabbage, shredded
1 large green pepper, sliced
1 large onion, sliced
1 large tomato, peeled and chopped
3 stalks celery, cut diagonally into thin
   slices

Fry bacon in a wok or large skillet until crisp; remove bacon, reserving drippings in wok. Set bacon aside. Add vegetables to wok; stir-fry over high heat (350°) for 8 to 10 minutes. Cover, reduce heat, and simmer 5 minutes. Sprinkle with bacon. Yield: 6 servings.

Jan Aaron,
Fort Walton Beach, Florida.

VEGETABLE MEDLEY STIR-FRY

3 tablespoons vegetable oil
1 small head cabbage, coarsely shredded
1 medium red onion, sliced
1 large carrot, cut diagonally into thin
   slices
2 medium tomatoes, cut into wedges
1 tablespoon minced fresh dillweed
¼ teaspoon salt
¼ teaspoon cracked black pepper

Pour oil around top of a preheated wok or large skillet; allow to heat at medium high (325°) for 2 minutes. Add cabbage, onion, and carrot; stir-fry 4 minutes. Add remaining ingredients, and stir-fry 1 to 2 minutes. Yield: 6 to 8 servings.

Mrs. Bernard W. Reiben,
Bothell, Washington.

Easy But Elegant Entrées

You had a long, busy day; the guests are on their way, and you have little time and energy left to prepare that spectacular entrée you planned for dinner. If you've found yourself in this situation before, chances are you'll welcome these alternatives.

Beef Tenderloin Deluxe or Company Pork Chops are sure to please your guests. Let Veal Supreme be the dish you choose when you want to serve veal. Tender scallops combine with mushrooms, green pepper, purple onion, and vermouth. Ask for veal scaloppines or very thin sliced veal cutlets at the butcher shop.

BEEF TENDERLOIN DELUXE

1 (3- to 4-pound) beef tenderloin
½ cup chopped onion
1½ tablespoons butter or margarine,
   melted
1 cup dry sherry
3 tablespoons soy sauce
2 teaspoons dry mustard
⅛ teaspoon salt
⅛ teaspoon pepper

Trim excess fat from beef tenderloin. Place beef tenderloin in a large shallow baking pan; bake, uncovered, at 400° for 10 minutes.

Sauté onion in butter until tender; add remaining ingredients. Bring to a boil; pour over tenderloin. Reduce heat to 325°; bake 35 minutes or until a meat thermometer reaches 140° to 170°. Baste often with drippings. Slice tenderloin; serve with remaining drippings. Yield: 10 to 12 servings.

Judi Grigoraci,
Charleston, West Virginia.

VEAL SUPREME

1 cup all-purpose flour
¼ teaspoon salt
⅛ teaspoon pepper
1½ pounds veal scallops
10 fresh mushrooms, sliced
1 medium-size green pepper, cut into
   strips
1 medium-size purple onion, sliced and
   separated into rings
¼ cup butter or margarine, melted and
   divided
Additional melted butter or margarine
   (optional)
¾ cup dry vermouth
⅓ cup cream of chicken soup, undiluted

Combine flour, salt, and pepper. Dredge veal scallops with flour mixture, and set aside.

Sauté vegetables in 2 tablespoons butter until crisp-tender. Remove vegetables from skillet; set aside. Place remaining 2 tablespoons butter in skillet; add veal. Cook over medium heat

until browned on both sides, adding more butter, if necessary; remove veal to serving platter.

Add vermouth to skillet; cook over low heat, stirring constantly, 3 to 5 minutes. Stir in soup and sautéed vegetables; cover and simmer until heated. Serve with veal. Yield: 6 servings.

Mrs. R. D. Walker,
Garland, Texas.

COMPANY PORK CHOPS

2 tablespoons vegetable oil
4 (¾-inch-thick) center cut loin pork
   chops
1 small onion, sliced and separated into
   rings
1 clove garlic, minced
½ cup orange juice
1½ tablespoons cider vinegar
1 teaspoon paprika
1 teaspoon honey
⅛ teaspoon salt
⅛ teaspoon pepper
1 cup chicken broth, divided
2 tablespoons all-purpose flour
Chopped parsley (optional)
Orange wedges (optional)

Heat oil in a large heavy skillet; brown pork chops on both sides. Add onion, garlic, orange juice, vinegar, paprika, honey, salt, pepper, and ½ cup chicken broth; bring to a boil. Cover, reduce heat, and simmer 1 hour. Remove chops to platter, and keep warm.

Gradually stir remaining ½ cup broth into flour. Stir mixture into drippings in skillet; cook, stirring constantly, until thickened. Serve with chops. Garnish with parsley and orange wedges, if desired. Yield: 4 servings. *Cathy Darling,*
Grafton, West Virginia.

LAMB CHOPS TERIYAKI

⅓ cup firmly packed brown sugar
¼ cup soy sauce
2 tablespoons catsup
1 tablespoon lemon juice
½ teaspoon salt
½ teaspoon ground ginger
¼ teaspoon pepper
⅛ teaspoon garlic powder
4 (1-inch-thick) lamb chops

Combine all ingredients except lamb in a small bowl; stir until smooth.

Broil chops 11 inches from heat about 25 minutes, brushing often with sauce. Yield: 4 servings. *Barbara Davis,*
Lilburn, Georgia.

Casual Party Dishes For Teens

If your teenager is planning an end-of-school party, you'll want to take a close look at these casual entrées. (They're also good for an informal adult gathering or family meal, as well.)

Spicy food is usually a favorite with this age group, so consider serving Fiesta Dinner as the main course. Actually, guests serve themselves and make their own creations. This way they can choose what they like. Deciding which ingredients to use and layering the dish is part of the fun.

Steak fingers are always a hit, and our foods staff thought Golden Steak Fingers seasoned with a hint of lemon were especially good. We thought you might also want to use them as a family entrée, so we kept the number of servings small; just be sure to increase the recipe if you plan to serve this dish to hungry teenagers.

Spicy Beef Rolls are hot sandwiches special enough to serve company. The Italian-flavored ground beef filling is served on a Kaiser roll seasoned with garlic and paprika. The rich pizza flavor makes these unusual sandwiches a good bet for the teenage set and pizza lovers of all ages.

GOLDEN STEAK FINGERS

1 pound boneless round steak
1 teaspoon lemon-pepper seasoning
½ teaspoon salt
½ cup buttermilk
1 cup all-purpose flour
¾ cup vegetable oil

Pound steak to ¼-inch thickness. Sprinkle with lemon-pepper seasoning and salt; cut into 4- x ½-inch strips. Dip steak in buttermilk, and dredge in flour. Brown steak on both sides in hot oil in a large skillet. Drain well. Yield: 4 servings.
Carolyn Webb,
Jackson, Mississippi.

Tip: When cooking for a crowd, plan your menu so you can utilize several cooking appliances rather than just your oven. Don't forget to use the stove top, microwave, electric skillet, and toaster oven.

BEEF KABOBS

1 pound lean, boneless sirloin steak
½ cup olive oil
¼ cup dry red wine
2 cloves garlic, minced
2 bay leaves, crumbled
½ teaspoon salt
2 (8-ounce) cans pineapple chunks, drained
18 cherry tomatoes
1 large green pepper, cut into 18 pieces

Trim all visible fat from meat; cut meat into 1¼-inch cubes. Place meat in a shallow dish; set aside.

Combine oil, wine, garlic, bay leaves, and salt, mixing well; pour over meat. Cover and marinate in the refrigerator 3 hours. Drain, reserving marinade.

Alternate meat, pineapple, tomatoes, and green pepper on six 14-inch skewers. Coat grill with cooking spray. Grill kabobs over medium-hot coals for 12 minutes or until the desired degree of doneness is reached, turning and basting frequently with marinade. Yield: 6 servings.
Jane G. Kreer,
Arlington, Virginia.

STEAK STROGANOFF SANDWICHES

⅔ cup beer
⅓ cup vegetable oil
1 teaspoon salt
¼ teaspoon garlic powder
Dash of pepper
2 pounds flank steak
4 medium onions, thinly sliced
2 tablespoons butter or margarine, melted
½ teaspoon paprika
Dash of salt
1 (8-ounce) carton commercial sour cream
½ teaspoon prepared horseradish
8 slices French bread, lightly toasted
Additional paprika

Combine beer, oil, salt, garlic powder, and pepper in a shallow dish, stirring well. Place steak in marinade, spooning marinade on top. Cover and refrigerate at least 8 hours.

Remove steak from marinade; broil 5 inches from heat about 5 minutes on each side or until the desired degree of doneness is reached. Cut steak diagonally across the grain into thin slices, and set aside.

Sauté onion in butter until tender; add paprika and salt. Set aside. Combine sour cream and horseradish in a small saucepan; cook over low heat just until thoroughly heated.

To serve, place one-fourth each of steak, onion mixture, and sour cream mixture on tops of 2 slices of bread; sprinkle with paprika. Repeat procedure 3 times with remaining ingredients. Yield: 4 open-face sandwiches.
Karen Davage,
Woodland Hills, California.

FIESTA DINNER

2 pounds ground beef
1 (16-ounce) can chili hot beans, undrained
1½ cups water
1 (1¾-ounce) package chili seasoning mix
1½ cups uncooked regular rice
1 (8-ounce) package corn chips, crushed
2 cups (8 ounces) shredded Cheddar cheese
1 medium onion, chopped
1 medium head iceberg lettuce, shredded
2 large tomatoes, chopped
1 (4-ounce) can chopped black olives, drained
1 cup flaked coconut
1 cup chopped pecans
Whole black olives (optional)
Picante sauce

Cook ground beef in a large skillet until browned, stirring to crumble. Drain well.

Combine ground beef, beans, water, and seasoning mix. Bring mixture to a boil over medium heat; reduce heat to low, and simmer 20 minutes.

Cook rice according to package directions. Set aside.

Spread a layer of corn chips on 10 individual serving plates. Top each serving with rice and meat mixture, and serve with cheese, onion, lettuce, tomatoes, chopped black olives, coconut, and pecans as condiments. Garnish with whole black olives, if desired. Serve with picante sauce. Yield: 10 servings.
Kathy Russell,
Austin, Texas.

SPICY BEEF ROLLS

1 pound ground beef
1 tablespoon finely chopped onion
½ cup tomato sauce
½ cup catsup
2 tablespoons grated Parmesan cheese
½ teaspoon garlic powder
¼ teaspooon fennel seeds
⅛ teaspoon ground oregano
Garlic Spread
6 Kaiser rolls, split
6 (3-inch square) slices mozzarella cheese

Combine ground beef and onion in a heavy skillet; cook over medium heat until beef is browned, stirring to crumble meat. Drain. Add tomato sauce, catsup, Parmesan cheese, and seasonings; mix well. Simmer 20 minutes.

Spread ½ teaspoon Garlic Spread on cut edges of each roll. Spoon beef mixture evenly on bottom halves; place a cheese slice over beef. Replace top halves. Wrap sandwiches in aluminum foil; bake at 350° for 15 minutes or until thoroughly heated. Yield: 6 sandwiches.

Garlic Spread:

2 tablespoons butter or margarine, softened
¼ teaspoon garlic powder
½ teaspoon paprika

Combine all ingredients; mix well. Yield: 2 tablespoons.

Nancy Eisele,
Valrico, Florida.

Bake The Bread In A Can

Remember when coffee-can breads were so popular a few years ago? Well, baking bread in a can is still fun, and we've rounded up some new recipes you may want to try. Some of them are yeast breads rather than the quick breads you probably baked the first time around. For variety, we've also included instructions in a couple of recipes for baking mini-loaves in 12-ounce tomato juice cans.

Be sure to wash and dry all cans thoroughly; you may want to let new cans air for a day or so before you use them for baking. Save the cans for reuse after baking, but discard any cans that have rust spots.

Swedish Orange-Rye Bread has the dense texture characteristic of many rye breads, but the subtle flavoring of orange rind gives it an unusual taste. It rises first in a bowl and then again in the coffee cans in which it's baked. Use the plastic lids that come with the cans for handy covers while it's rising.

Zucchini Bread was a favorite in our test kitchens. It's a sweet bread with shredded zucchini in the batter, which gives it a rich texture and unusual flavor. You can bake it in either coffee or tomato juice cans, depending on the size loaves you may want to serve.

ZUCCHINI BREAD

3 cups all-purpose flour
1 teaspoon baking powder
1 teaspoon baking soda
1 teaspoon salt
1 tablespoon ground cinnamon
3 eggs
2 cups sugar
1 cup vegetable oil
2 teaspoons vanilla extract
2 cups shredded zucchini
1 cup chopped pecans
Whipped cream cheese (optional)
Chopped pecans (optional)

Combine flour, baking powder, soda, salt, and cinnamon; set aside. Combine eggs, sugar, oil, and vanilla in a large bowl; beat at medium speed of an electric mixer until well blended. Stir in zucchini and pecans. Add dry ingredients, stirring just until moistened.

Spoon batter into 3 greased and floured 1-pound coffee cans. Bake at 350° for 55 to 60 minutes or until a wooden pick inserted in center comes out clean. Cool in cans 10 minutes; remove to wire rack, and cool completely. Top with whipped cream cheese and pecans, if desired. Yield: 3 loaves.

Note: For mini-loaves, spoon batter into 7 greased and floured 12-ounce tomato juice cans. Bake at 350° for 35 to 40 minutes or until a wooden pick inserted in center comes out clean. Yield: 7 loaves. *Mrs. Adolph Marek, Jr.,*
Victoria, Texas.

SWEDISH ORANGE-RYE BREAD

1 package dry yeast
1¾ cups warm water (105° to 115°)
⅓ cup sugar
¼ cup light molasses
2 tablespoons vegetable oil
2½ to 3 cups all-purpose flour
2½ cups rye flour
2 tablespoons grated orange rind
2 teaspoons salt

Dissolve yeast in 1¾ cups warm water in a large mixing bowl; let stand 5 minutes. Add sugar, molasses, and oil; stir until mixture is well blended.

Combine 2½ cups all-purpose flour and remaining ingredients, mixing well; add to yeast mixture, stirring until a soft dough forms.

Turn dough out on a well-floured surface, and knead until smooth and elastic (5 to 8 minutes). (Add extra flour as necessary while kneading to prevent dough from sticking to hands.)

Place dough in a well-greased bowl, turning to grease top. Cover; let rise in warm place (85°), free from drafts, 1 hour or until dough is doubled in bulk.

Punch dough down; divide into thirds. Place each third into a well-greased 1-pound coffee can. Cover with plastic coffee can lids, and let rise in a warm place (85°), free from drafts, 45 minutes or until the dough is doubled in bulk. Remove lids.

Bake at 375° for 30 minutes or until loaves sound hollow when tapped. Cool in cans 10 minutes. Remove loaves from cans; cool completely on wire racks. Yield: 3 loaves. *Ruby Berger,*
Cushing, Oklahoma.

MOLASSES-WHOLE WHEAT COFFEE CAN BREAD

½ cup milk
½ cup water
½ cup vegetable oil
¼ cup dark molasses
1 teaspoon salt
2 cups all-purpose flour, divided
2 packages dry yeast
2 eggs
1½ cups whole wheat flour
¼ cup wheat germ
¼ cup unprocessed bran

Combine milk, water, oil, molasses, and salt in a saucepan, and mix well. Cook mixture over medium heat (105° to 115°) until warm.

Combine 1½ cups all-purpose flour and yeast. Add milk mixture; beat with an electric mixer until smooth. Add eggs, mixing well. Gradually add remaining ½ cup all-purpose flour, whole wheat flour, wheat germ, and bran; beat until smooth and elastic. (Dough will be very stiff.)

Spoon dough into 3 well-greased 1-pound coffee cans. Cover with plastic coffee can lids; let rise in a warm place (85°), free from drafts, 45 minutes or until doubled in bulk. Remove lids. Bake at 375° for 30 to 35 minutes or until bread sounds hollow when tapped. Cool in cans 10 minutes; remove from cans, and cool on wire racks. Yield: 3 loaves. *Martha Edington,*
Oak Ridge, Tennessee.

BANANA-NUT ROLL

½ cup butter or margarine, softened
2 cups sugar
2 eggs
2 cups all-purpose flour
1½ teaspoons baking soda
¼ teaspoon salt
¼ cup plus 2 tablespoons buttermilk
1½ cups mashed ripe banana (about 3 medium)
1 cup chopped pecans
1 teaspoon vanilla extract

Cream butter and sugar, beating well at medium speed of an electric mixer. Add eggs, one at a time, beating well.

Combine flour, soda, and salt; add to creamed mixture alternately with buttermilk, beginning and ending with flour mixture. Stir in remaining ingredients.

Spoon batter into 3 greased and floured 1-pound coffee cans. Bake at 350° for 55 minutes or until a wooden pick inserted in center comes out clean. Cool in cans 10 minutes; remove loaves to wire rack, and cool completely. Yield: 3 loaves.

Note: For mini-loaves, spoon batter into 9 greased and floured 12-ounce tomato juice cans. Bake at 350° for 35 minutes or until a wooden pick inserted in center comes out clean. Yield: 9 loaves. *Mrs. C. W. Carden, Ooltewah, Tennessee.*

MICROWAVE COOKERY

Here's An Easy Menu To Make Ahead

Having company for dinner takes planning, even if you use a microwave oven. With these recipes, you can prepare most of the meal the day before. Then you can finish the dinner in about 30 minutes the day of the event.

The day before your dinner, marinate the lamb; prepare the dressing for Sweet-Sour Spinach Salad, and chill; make Almond Rice, and refrigerate; and bake the shell for Lemon Meringue Pie. Then check to be certain you have all the remaining ingredients on hand.

The day of the party, start by completing the lemon pie. It takes under 15 minutes to cook the filling and the meringue. And since the filling sets quickly, you won't have to worry about cutting pretty slices when it's time for serving dessert.

Next, assemble the Shish Kabobs, and microwave them about 12 minutes. As the kabobs cook, you can toss the vegetables for the spinach salad and prepare the rice for reheating.

The microwave is excellent for reheating rice to the original freshly cooked fluffiness. Simply add 2 tablespoons of water for every 2 cups of cooked rice, cover and microwave at MEDIUM HIGH (70% power) for 3 to 4 minutes or until hot.

Shish Kabobs
Almond Rice
Sweet-Sour Spinach Salad
Lemon Meringue Pie
Red wine or water

SHISH KABOBS

1 small onion, finely chopped
¼ cup vegetable oil
¼ cup sherry
1½ to 2 teaspoons cumin seed
1 teaspoon salt
¾ teaspoon dried whole rosemary, crushed
½ teaspoon coarsely ground black pepper
½ teaspoon garlic salt
1½ pounds boneless lamb, cut into bite-size pieces
12 cherry tomatoes
2 small green peppers, cut into 24 pieces
1/2 (16-ounce) jar boiling onions, drained

Combine onion, oil, sherry, and seasonings. Place lamb pieces in a shallow container, and pour marinade over meat. Cover and marinate meat 24 hours in refrigerator.

Remove meat from marinade. Alternate lamb and vegetables on 12 wooden skewers, packing loosely. Place kabobs on a microwave roasting rack or a shallow microwave-safe baking dish. Cover with waxed paper, and microwave at MEDIUM (50% power) 6 minutes. Rearrange kabobs; microwave additional 5 to 7 minutes or until desired degree of doneness. Yield: 6 servings.

ALMOND RICE

2 cups uncooked instant rice
1 teaspoon butter or margarine
½ teaspoon salt
1⅔ cups hot water
¾ cup slivered almonds
¾ cup golden raisins

Combine rice, butter, and salt in a deep 2-quart casserole; stir in hot water. Cover with heavy-duty plastic wrap, and microwave at HIGH for 8 minutes. Let stand 3 minutes.

Spread almonds in a pieplate; microwave at HIGH 4 to 5 minutes. Stir almonds and raisins into rice; fluff rice with a fork. Yield: 6 servings.

SWEET-SOUR SPINACH SALAD

¼ cup sugar
2 tablespoons vinegar
¼ cup vegetable oil
¼ teaspoon celery seeds
¼ teaspoon paprika
⅛ teaspoon salt
1 pound fresh spinach, torn into bite-size pieces
6 medium-size fresh mushrooms, sliced
1 small purple onion, thinly sliced and separated into rings

Combine sugar and vinegar in a small microwave-safe bowl. Microwave at HIGH 2 to 3 minutes, stirring once, until sugar dissolves. Pour vinegar mixture into a jar; add oil, celery seeds, paprika, and salt. Cover tightly, and shake vigorously. Chill dressing.

Combine spinach, mushrooms, and onion in a serving bowl. Pour chilled dressing over salad, tossing lightly. Yield: 6 servings.

LEMON MERINGUE PIE

1 cup sugar
⅓ cup cornstarch
Dash of salt
1½ cups water, divided
3 eggs, separated
1 teaspoon grated lemon rind
¼ cup plus 2 tablespoons lemon juice
Basic microwave pastry (recipe follows)
1 teaspoon lemon juice
¼ cup plus 2 tablespoons sugar
Fresh mint leaves (optional)
Lemon rind curls (optional)

Combine 1 cup sugar, cornstarch, salt, and ¼ cup water in a 1½-quart microwave-safe mixing bowl; mix well. Stir in remaining water. Microwave at HIGH for 6 minutes or until thickened and clear, stirring at 2-minute intervals.

Beat egg yolks until thick and lemon colored. Gradually stir about one-fourth of hot mixture into yolks; add to remaining hot mixture. Microwave at HIGH for 1 minute. Stir in lemon rind and ¼ cup plus 2 tablespoons lemon juice. Cool slightly, and pour mixture into the microwaved pastry shell.

Beat egg whites (at room temperature) and 1 teaspoon lemon juice at high speed of an electric mixer 1 minute. Gradually add ¼ cup plus 2 tablespoons sugar, 1 tablespoon at a time, beating until stiff peaks form and sugar dissolves (about 2 to 4 minutes).

Spread meringue over hot filling, sealing to edge of pastry. Microwave at MEDIUM (50% power) for 2 minutes or until meringue is set. Garnish with mint leaves and lemon rind curls, if desired. Yield: one 9-inch pie.

Note: If a browned meringue is desired, microwave at MEDIUM for 1 minute; then place pie under broiler 8 inches away from heat for 30 seconds or until lightly browned.

Basic Microwave Pastry:

1 cup all-purpose flour
½ teaspoon salt
⅓ cup plus 1 tablespoon shortening
2 to 3 tablespoons cold water

Combine flour and salt; cut in shortening with pastry blender until mixture resembles coarse meal. Sprinkle 2 to 3 tablespoons water evenly over flour mixture, and stir with a fork until all ingredients are moistened.

Shape dough into a ball, and place on a lightly floured surface; roll dough into a circle 2 inches larger than inverted 9-inch pieplate. Fit pastry loosely into pieplate. Trim edges, and fold under to form standing rim; then flute.

Place a piece of heavy-duty plastic wrap over pastry, and cover with dried peas or beans. Gently prick rim of pastry. (This will help maintain fluted shape.) Microwave at HIGH for 6½ to 7 minutes or until pastry is opaque and the bottom is dry. Yield: one 9-inch pastry shell.

Reach For The Olives

You might know green olives best as an easy appetizer—just pop one in your mouth, and enjoy. But we're discovering olives in more and more recipes that we think you'll like.

Because olives are pickled, they're frequently included in appetizer recipes. In our recipe for Cheesy Olive Appetizers, the pungent green rounds are stirred into a cheese mixture, which is spread on party rye bread. They are then broiled for tasty and attractive canapés. Olives are wrapped jellyroll fashion with thin slices of ham and cheese in our Ham-and-Swiss Rollups, which are sliced into party appetizers.

You'll also find olives in salads, side dishes, and entrées. Teamed with chicken and Spanish rice, olives are a major ingredient in Chicken-and-Rice Valencia.

Refrigerate olives in their original brine once they're opened. And to prevent color loss during storage, place a lemon slice on top of olives in the jar.

HAM-AND-SWISS ROLLUPS

1 (8-ounce) carton French onion dip
1 (3-ounce) package cream cheese, softened
¼ cup finely chopped pimiento-stuffed olives
6 (6- x 4-inch) slices cooked ham
6 (6- x 4-inch) slices Swiss cheese
About 30 whole pimiento-stuffed olives

Combine dip, cream cheese, and olives; mix well. Chill 1 hour.

Spread half of cream cheese mixture evenly on ham slices; top with cheese slices. Spread remaining mixture evenly on cheese. Line up whole olives along one long side of each piece of cheese; roll up jellyroll fashion, starting at end lined with olives. Wrap in plastic wrap, and chill at least 2 hours. Just before serving, cut each roll into ½-inch slices. Yield: about 4½ dozen. *Bonnie Taylor, Jackson, Tennessee.*

VEGETABLE-PORK COMBO

1 cup chopped onion
1 clove garlic, minced
¼ cup vegetable oil, divided
2 pounds boneless pork, cut into ½-inch pieces
2½ cups beef broth
1½ cups uncooked regular rice
1 (16-ounce) can tomatoes, undrained and chopped
¾ cup finely chopped green pepper
¾ teaspoon salt
½ cup chopped pimiento-stuffed olives

Sauté onion and garlic in 2 tablespoons oil in a large skillet until tender; remove from skillet, and set aside. Add remaining oil to skillet; add pork, and cook until browned. Drain.

Add sautéed onion and garlic, broth, rice, tomatoes, green pepper, and salt to pork; spoon into a lightly greased, shallow, 2-quart casserole. Cover and bake at 325° for 40 minutes; sprinkle with olives, and bake 5 minutes more. Yield: 8 servings. *Sharon M. Crider, Evansville, Wisconsin.*

CHICKEN-AND-RICE VALENCIA

1 (3-pound) chicken, cut up
¼ cup olive oil
¾ cup pimiento-stuffed olives
1 onion, diced
1 green pepper, cut into thin strips
1 (8-ounce) can tomatoes, undrained
Pinch of ground saffron
1 bay leaf
½ cup chopped celery
¼ cup sliced celery leaves (optional)
Hot cooked commercial Spanish rice

Sauté chicken in hot olive oil in a large Dutch oven. Add olives, onion, green pepper, tomatoes, saffron, and bay leaf; cover and cook over low heat 45 minutes or until chicken is tender. Stir in celery and celery leaves, if desired; remove from heat. Remove bay leaf from mixture.

To serve, spoon Spanish rice onto serving platter, and arrange chicken pieces over rice. Spoon olive mixture over chicken. Yield: 4 servings.

Betty Beske, Arlington, Virginia.

CHEESY OLIVE APPETIZERS

1 cup (4 ounces) shredded Swiss cheese
6 slices bacon, cooked and crumbled
¼ cup chopped pimiento-stuffed olives
¼ cup mayonnaise
2 tablespoons chopped onion
20 slices party rye bread
Sliced pimiento-stuffed olives

Combine cheese, bacon, chopped olives, mayonnaise, and onion; mix well. Spread about 1 tablespoon cheese mixture on each slice of bread. Top each with an olive slice. Broil 2 minutes or until the cheese melts; serve hot. Yield: 20 appetizer servings.

Pat Boschen, Ashland, Virginia.

OLIVE-POTATO SALAD

6 cups cubed new potatoes
½ cup chopped green pepper
½ cup chopped pimiento-stuffed olives
¼ cup chopped onion
¾ cup mayonaise
3 hard-cooked eggs, chopped
1 tablespoon vinegar
1 tablespoon olive juice
1 tablespoon sweet pickle juice
1 teaspoon celery seeds
1 teaspoon prepared mustard
½ teaspoon salt
⅛ teaspoon pepper
Dash of garlic salt

Cook potatoes in boiling water 15 minutes or until tender; drain.

Combine potatoes and remaining ingredients, stirring well. Chill thoroughly. Yield: 8 servings.

Mrs. Stuart Rominger,
Greeneville, Tennessee.

TOMATOES WITH OLIVE SPREAD

1 (3-ounce) package cream cheese, softened
3 tablespoons mayonnaise
2 tablespoons chopped pimiento-stuffed olives
1½ tablespoons chopped walnuts
⅛ teaspoon salt
8 slices tomato
Mayonnaise
Whole pimiento-stuffed olives
Lettuce leaves

Combine cream cheese and mayonnaise; mix well. Add chopped olives, walnuts, and salt. Spread cream cheese mixture on 4 tomato slices; top with remaining tomato slices. Garnish each with a dollop of mayonnaise and an olive; chill. Serve on lettuce leaves. Yield: 4 servings. *Amelia M. Brown,*
Pittsburgh, Pennsylvania.

EASY ANTIPASTO

1 large head iceberg lettuce
1 small bunch parsley, coarsely chopped
2 (6½-ounce) jars marinated artichoke hearts, drained
1 (11½-ounce) jar pickled cauliflower, drained
1 (9-ounce) jar pickled peppers
1 (3-ounce) jar almond-stuffed olives
1 bunch green onions, cut into 3-inch pieces
1½ cups cherry tomatoes
1 cup radishes
¾ cup pimiento-stuffed olives
¾ cup ripe olives
¾ cup commercial Italian salad dressing

Line a platter with outer leaves of lettuce. Tear remaining lettuce into bite-size pieces. Combine lettuce pieces and parsley, and arrange over lettuce leaves. Arrange remaining ingredients, except dressing, over lettuce mixture. Cover and chill. Pour dressing over salad just before serving. Yield: 10 to 12 servings. *Grace Owens,*
Pride, Louisiana.

Make It A Favorite With Chocolate Chips

Dark and sweet, chocolate chips are impossible to resist, especially in these delectable treats. Each is a rich combination of ingredients that your whole family will love.

Perhaps the richest of all is Chocolate Chip Cheesecake. It's thick with cream cheese, sour cream, and chocolate chips. For an extra measure of goodness, sprinkle some additional chips around the top before serving.

Chocolate Chip Pie is a first cousin to pecan pie. Like pecan pie, it contains eggs, sugar, butter, and pecans, but it also has chocolate chips and coconut. If the pie is served hot, you might want to top each delicious slice with a scoop of vanilla ice cream.

CHOCOLATE CHIP CHEESECAKE

1 cup vanilla wafer crumbs
¼ cup butter, melted
2 (8-ounce) packages cream cheese, softened
¾ cup sugar
1 (8-ounce) carton commercial sour cream, divided
4 eggs
1 teaspoon vanilla extract
1 (6-ounce) package semisweet chocolate morsels
½ cup sugar
1½ teaspoons lemon juice
1½ teaspoons vanilla extract
Additional semisweet chocolate morsels (optional)

Combine wafer crumbs and butter, mixing well. Press mixture into bottom of a 9-inch springform pan; set aside.

Beat cream cheese with an electric mixer until light and fluffy; gradually

add ¾ cup sugar and ½ cup sour cream, mixing well. Add eggs, one at a time, beating well after each addition. Stir in 1 teaspoon vanilla and 1 package chocolate morsels. Spoon mixture into prepared pan. Bake at 325° for 1 hour. Let cool at room temperature on a wire rack 20 minutes.

Combine remaining sour cream, ½ cup sugar, lemon juice, and 1½ teaspoons vanilla, mixing well; gently spread over top of cheesecake. Bake at 475° for 5 minutes. Let cool to room temperature on a wire rack; refrigerate 8 hours. Remove sides of springform pan; sprinkle additional chocolate morsels around top edge and in center of cheesecake, if desired. Yield: 10 to 12 servings. *Grace Bravos,*
Timonium, Maryland.

CHOCOLATE CHIP PIE

¼ cup plus 2 tablespoons butter or margarine, softened
1 cup sugar
1 teaspoon vanilla extract
2 eggs
½ cup all-purpose flour
1 (6-ounce) package semisweet chocolate morsels
¾ cup chopped pecans
½ cup flaked coconut
1 unbaked 9-inch pastry shell

Combine butter, sugar, and vanilla in a medium mixing bowl; beat well. Add eggs, and beat well. Stir in flour. Gradually stir in chocolate morsels, pecans, and coconut. Pour mixture into pastry shell. Bake at 350° for 35 to 40 minutes. Yield: one 9-inch pie. *Pam Wright,*
Bowling Green, Kentucky.

CHOCOLATE TRUFFLES

1 (6-ounce) package semisweet chocolate morsels
3 tablespoons unsalted butter
3 tablespoons powdered sugar
3 egg yolks
1 tablespoon rum
Cocoa

Place chocolate morsels in top of a double boiler; bring water to a boil. Reduce heat to low; cook until chocolate melts. Add butter and powdered sugar, stirring until sugar dissolves. Remove from heat.

Add egg yolks, one at a time, beating with an electric mixer after each addition. Stir in rum. Pour mixture into a bowl; cover, and let sit for 12 to 24 hours in a cool, dry place. (Do not refrigerate mixture.)

Shape mixture into 1-inch balls; roll in cocoa. Freeze 1 hour. Store in an airtight container in refrigerator. Yield: about 2 dozen. *Thelma Peedin, Newport News, Virginia.*

CHOCOLATE CHIP-BANANA LOAF

1¾ cups all-purpose flour
¾ teaspoon baking soda
1¼ teaspoons cream of tartar
½ cup chopped walnuts
½ cup semisweet chocolate morsels
¾ cup sugar
½ cup vegetable oil
2 eggs
2 ripe bananas, sliced
½ teaspoon vanilla extract
¼ teaspoon ground cinnamon

Combine flour, soda, cream of tartar, walnuts, and chocolate in a large bowl; mix well, and set aside.

Combine remaining ingredients in container of electric blender; process at medium speed 20 seconds. Stir into flour mixture, mixing well.

Pour batter into a greased 9- x 5- x 3-inch loafpan. Bake at 350° for 50 minutes or until a wooden pick inserted in center comes out clean. Yield: 1 loaf.
Lorene Carlisle, Columbus, Georgia.

CHOCOLATE CHIP-SOUR CREAM CAKE

½ cup butter or margarine, softened
1 cup sugar
2 eggs
2 cups all-purpose flour
1 teaspoon baking powder
1 teaspoon baking soda
1 (8-ounce) carton commercial sour cream
1 teaspoon vanilla extract
1 (6-ounce) package semisweet chocolate morsels
1 cup chopped pecans
¼ cup firmly packed brown sugar

Cream butter; gradually add 1 cup sugar, beating at medium speed of an electric mixer until light and fluffy. Add eggs, one at a time, beating after each addition.

Combine flour, baking powder, and soda; add one-third of dry ingredients to creamed mixture, stirring with a spoon until blended. Add half of sour cream, stirring until blended. Repeat procedure, ending with flour mixture. Stir in vanilla.

Combine chocolate morsels, pecans, and brown sugar; mix well, and set mixture aside.

Spoon half of batter into a well-greased and floured 10-inch tube pan. Sprinkle with half of chocolate morsel mixture. Spoon remaining batter into pan, and top with remaining chocolate morsel mixture. Bake at 350° for 50 minutes. Yield: one 10-inch cake.
Gail G. Hines, Mississippi State, Mississippi.

OATMEAL KRISPIES

1 cup shortening
1 cup firmly packed brown sugar
1 cup sugar
2 eggs
1 teaspoon vanilla extract
1½ cups all-purpose flour
1 teaspoon baking soda
1 teaspoon salt
3 cups quick-cooking oats, uncooked
1 (6-ounce) package semisweet chocolate morsels
½ cup flaked coconut
½ cup chopped pecans

Cream shortening; gradually add sugar, beating until fluffy. Add eggs and vanilla, beating well. Combine flour, soda, and salt; add to creamed mixture, beating well. Stir in the remaining four ingredients.

Drop dough by heaping teaspoonfuls onto greased cookie sheets; bake at 350° for 10 to 12 minutes. Cool slightly on cookie sheets; remove to wire racks. Yield: about 8 dozen. *Debra Murphy, Tyler, Texas.*

CHOCOLATE CRISPY COOKIES

½ cup butter or margarine, softened
1 cup sugar
1 egg
1 teaspoon vanilla extract
1¼ cups all-purpose flour
½ teaspoon baking soda
¼ teaspoon salt
2 cups crisp rice cereal
1 (6-ounce) package semisweet chocolate morsels

Cream butter; gradually add sugar, beating until light and fluffy. Add egg and vanilla, beating well. Combine flour, soda, and salt; add to creamed mixture, beating well. Stir in the rice cereal and chocolate morsels.

Drop dough by heaping teaspoonfuls onto lightly greased cookie sheets. Bake at 350° for 13 minutes. Cool slightly on cookie sheets; remove to wire racks. Yield: 3½ dozen. *Doris Lee, Langdale, Alabama.*

These Dishes Spotlight Celery

Celery is a well-known ingredient in salads, casseroles, and many different entrées, but this nutritious vegetable can stand on its own just as well. Crisp and crunchy, it has a distinctive texture and flavor and is a nice change from other vegetables.

Try Celery Almondine instead of your usual green vegetable, and you'll see what we mean. The celery is cooked in butter and chicken bouillon with other seasonings for subtle taste and tenderness. Then wine and almonds are added, and fresh parsley is sprinkled on for extra eye appeal.

Celery Oriental also features almonds, but they're sautéed with mushrooms. Don't let the name fool you; the simplicity of this dish makes it good with a variety of menus.

Stuffed Celery Trunks are a good addition to a snack or relish tray. With pimiento-stuffed olives in the Cheddar cheese stuffing, they're more colorful than most stuffed celery and have a sharper bite. You may want to try a garnish using part of this same recipe. Keep the leaves on two celery stalks, and put the stalks together after stuffing, standing them upright to resemble a tree. This adds a finishing touch to a salad or sandwich platter.

STUFFED CELERY TRUNKS

1 cup (4 ounces) shredded Cheddar cheese
½ cup mayonnaise
2 tablespoons chopped pimiento-stuffed olives
6 stalks celery, cut into 4-inch pieces

Combine Cheddar cheese, mayonnaise, and chopped olives, mixing well. Stuff celery pieces with cheese mixture. Yield: about 1 dozen.

CELERY ALMONDINE

1 chicken-flavored bouillon cube
½ cup boiling water
2 tablespoons butter or margarine, divided
½ cup slivered almonds
4 cups diagonally sliced celery (½-inch slices)
Pinch of garlic powder
¼ teaspoon salt
2 teaspoons dried onion flakes or 2 tablespoons minced onion
2 tablespoons dry white wine
1 tablespoon finely chopped fresh parsley

Dissolve bouillon cube in boiling water; set aside. Melt 1 tablespoon butter over low heat; add almonds, and sauté until golden brown. Set aside.

Melt remaining tablespoon of butter in a large saucepan; add celery, bouillon mixture, garlic powder, salt, and onion. Cover and cook 5 minutes or until celery is crisp-tender. Add wine and sautéed almonds; cook 3 minutes. Sprinkle with parsley. Yield: 6 servings.

Mrs. Roy Nieman,
Dunnellon, Florida.

CELERY ORIENTAL

8 stalks celery, diagonally sliced
1 cup sliced mushrooms
¼ cup butter or margarine, melted
¼ cup sliced almonds, toasted
Salt to taste

Cook celery in a small amount of boiling water 4 minutes or until crisp-tender; drain well.

Sauté mushrooms in butter until tender; add celery, almonds, and salt. Cook celery until thoroughly heated. Yield: 4 to 6 servings.

Mrs. Robert M. Neumann,
Bartlesville, Oklahoma.

More Punch, Please!

Graduation parties, bridal showers, and all kinds of festivities make May a busy month for party giving. And nothing makes the party more festive than a sparkling punch with a refreshing, new taste. With that in mind, we've gathered a variety of recipes that fit the bill. Why not try one of these instead of your old standby the next time you entertain?

Citrus-Tea Punch combines tea and three kinds of fruit juice; ginger ale is added just before serving. With tea as a base, even people who don't normally care for punch will like this one. You can serve it plain or dress it up as we did with orange and lemon slices and swirls of lemon rind.

Perky Rum Punch also has tea and fruit juice in it, but a cup of rum in the mixture adds an unmistakable difference. Be sure to note the freezing and thawing instructions; it is best to serve this punch somewhat slushy.

Consider Coffee-and-Cream Punch if you want to offer a non-alcoholic drink at an adult party. This version is probably different from other coffee punches you've tasted; it has ice milk in it as well as ice cream and ginger ale. The result is a creamy, delectable beverage with an unusual flavor.

Strawberry-Lemonade Punch is a good choice no matter what the age group. It features pink lemonade, frozen strawberries, strawberry ice cream, and peppermint flavoring. For an adult party, you may want to garnish each serving with a fresh strawberry and a sprig of mint. For children, add peppermint sticks instead.

STRAWBERRY-LEMONADE PUNCH

½ cup sugar
2 teaspoons peppermint flavoring
2 cups boiling water
2 (10-ounce) packages frozen strawberries
5 cups water
2 (6-ounce) cans frozen pink lemonade concentrate, thawed and undiluted
½ gallon strawberry ice cream

Combine first 3 ingredients; stir to dissolve sugar, and let stand 5 minutes. Add strawberries, stirring until thawed. Press strawberry mixture through a strainer, and discard pulp. Add water and lemonade, stirring well. Chill thoroughly. Spoon ice cream into punch just before serving. Yield: 4½ quarts.

Miriam C. Colimore,
Cockeysville, Maryland.

CITRUS-TEA PUNCH

1½ cups water
1 tea bag
1½ cups orange juice
1½ cups pineapple juice
½ cup lemon juice
1 cup sugar
3 cups ginger ale, chilled
Orange and lemon slices (optional)
Lemon rind strips (optional)

Bring water to a boil in a large saucepan; add tea bag. Remove from heat; cover and let stand 5 minutes. Remove tea bag. Add fruit juices and sugar, stirring until sugar dissolves. Chill.

Stir in ginger ale just before serving. Add orange and lemon slices and lemon rind strips, if desired. Yield: 2 quarts.

Mrs. H. D. Baxter,
Charleston, West Virginia.

PERKY RUM PUNCH

1 (6-ounce) can frozen orange juice concentrate, thawed and undiluted
1 (6-ounce) can frozen lemonade concentrate, thawed and undiluted
4½ cups hot water
1 cup rum
1 cup sugar
1 teaspoon instant tea
2 (33.8-ounce) bottles lemon-lime carbonated beverage

Combine all ingredients except lemon-lime beverage, stirring until sugar dissolves. Freeze overnight.

Remove from freezer; let thaw 30 minutes. (Mixture should be slushy.) Combine with lemon-lime beverage, stirring well. Serve immediately. Yield: about 4 quarts.

Becky May,
Nederland, Texas.

COFFEE-AND-CREAM PUNCH

2 quarts brewed strong coffee, chilled
½ gallon vanilla ice cream, softened
½ gallon vanilla ice milk, softened
1 (33.8-ounce) bottle ginger ale, chilled

Combine coffee, ice cream, and ice milk in a large mixing bowl or punch bowl; stir gently with a wire whisk until almost smooth. (Some chunks of ice cream may remain.) Stir in ginger ale, and serve immediately. Yield: about 5½ quarts.

Vera Stevens,
Garden City Beach, South Carolina

Bake A One-Layer Cake

Since sheet cakes involve only one baking pan and a smaller amount of frosting than layer cakes, you'll find them easy to prepare. Another advantage is that sheet cakes travel well and can be cut into squares and served right from the pan.

Our Spicy Fruited Carrot Cake is a little different from other carrot cakes—a whole can of fruit cocktail is stirred into the batter. After baking, leave the cake in the pan, and top with frosting.

A birthday or office party might call for a fully frosted cake such as Lemon-Coconut Sheet Cake. The cake is removed from the pan; then the top and sides are frosted with Lemon-Butter Cream Frosting.

A rich butter cream frosting covers our Lemon-Coconut Sheet Cake, which is garnished with lemon slices to make an eye-catching dessert for any occasion.

SPICY FRUITED CARROT CAKE

2 cups all-purpose flour
1 cup sugar
¼ teaspoon salt
2 teaspoons baking soda
½ teaspoon ground cloves
½ teaspoon ground allspice
1 (30-ounce) can fruit cocktail, drained
¼ cup vegetable oil
3 eggs, slightly beaten
2 cups shredded carrots
1 cup chopped pecans
Nutty Cream Cheese Frosting

Combine flour, sugar, salt, soda, cloves, and allspice; stir in fruit cocktail. Add oil, eggs, carrots, and pecans; stir gently until mixed well. Pour into a greased and floured 13- x 9- x 2-inch baking pan; bake at 350° for 35 to 40 minutes or until a wooden pick inserted in center comes out clean. Cool in pan completely. Spread top with Nutty Cream Cheese Frosting. Yield: one 13- x 9- x 2-inch cake.

Nutty Cream Cheese Frosting:

3 tablespoons butter or margarine, softened
2 (3-ounce) packages cream cheese, softened
3 cups sifted powdered sugar
Dash of salt
1½ teaspoons vanilla extract
¼ cup plus 2 tablespoons chopped pecans

Cream butter and cream cheese until fluffy. Add remaining ingredients except chopped pecans; beat until smooth. Stir in pecans. Yield: enough for one 13- x 9- x 2-inch cake. *Maxine Compton, Lampasas, Texas.*

LEMON-COCONUT SHEET CAKE

1 cup butter or margarine, softened
2 cups sugar
5 eggs
2½ cups all-purpose flour
1 teaspoon baking powder
1 teaspoon baking soda
¼ teaspoon salt
1 cup buttermilk
1 cup grated coconut
½ teaspoon lemon extract
½ teaspoon coconut flavoring
Lemon-Butter Cream Frosting
Lemon slices (optional)

Cream butter; gradually add sugar, beating well with electric mixer. Add eggs, one at a time, beating well after each addition.

Combine flour, baking powder, soda, and salt; add to creamed mixture alternately with buttermilk, beginning and ending with flour mixture. Stir in grated coconut and flavorings.

Pour batter into a greased and floured 13- x 9- x 2-inch baking pan.

Bake at 350° for 35 to 40 minutes or until a wooden pick inserted in center comes out clean. Cool in pan 10 minutes. Remove cake from pan, and place on a serving tray. Allow cake to cool completely.

Spread Lemon-Butter Cream Frosting on top and sides of cake. Garnish with lemon slices, if desired. Yield: one 13- x 9- x 2-inch cake.

Lemon-Butter Cream Frosting:

½ cup butter or margarine, softened
4 cups sifted powdered sugar
3 tablespoons milk
2 tablespoons lemon juice
1 teaspoon grated lemon rind
½ teaspoon vanilla extract
½ teaspoon butter flavoring

Cream softened butter; add the remaining ingredients, beating until smooth. Yield: enough frosting for one 13- x 9- x 2-inch cake.

Billie Taylor, Afton, Virginia.

BANANA WALDORF CAKE

½ cup butter or margarine, softened
1½ cups firmly packed brown sugar
3 eggs
2¼ cups all-purpose flour
2 teaspoons baking powder
1 teaspoon baking soda
1⅓ cups mashed banana
¼ cup milk
1 teaspoon vanilla extract
1 cup chopped walnuts
Cream Cheese Frosting

Cream butter and sugar, beating well with electric mixer. Add eggs, one at a time, beating well after each addition.

Combine flour, baking powder, and soda; add to creamed mixture alternately with banana and milk, beginning and ending with flour mixture. Mix well after each addition. Stir in the vanilla and chopped walnuts.

Pour batter into a greased and floured 13- x 9- x 2-inch baking pan. Bake at 350° for 35 minutes or until a wooden pick inserted in center comes out clean; cool completely. Frost top with Cream Cheese Frosting. Yield: one 13- x 9- x 2-inch cake.

Cream Cheese Frosting:

2 (3-ounce) packages cream cheese, softened
3 tablespoons butter or margarine, softened
1½ teaspoons vanilla extract
3 cups sifted powdered sugar

Cream softened cream cheese, butter, and vanilla; gradually add sugar, beating until light and fluffy. Yield: enough frosting for one 13- x 9- x 2-inch cake.

*Tomi Babb,
Oklahoma City, Oklahoma.*

BUTTER BRICKLE CAKE

2 cups all-purpose flour
1¼ cups sugar
1 tablespoon plus ¼ teaspoon baking powder
1 teaspoon salt
1 cup milk
½ cup shortening
1½ teaspoons vanilla extract
3 egg whites
¼ cup butter
2 cups sifted powdered sugar
2 tablespoons half-and-half
2 tablespoons hot water
1½ teaspoons vanilla extract

Combine flour, sugar, baking powder, and salt in a large mixing bowl. Add

milk, shortening, and 1½ teaspoons vanilla; beat at medium speed of an electric mixer until well blended. Add egg whites (at room temperature), and beat 2 minutes.

Pour batter into a greased and floured 13- x 9- x 2-inch baking pan. Bake at 350° for 20 to 25 minutes or until a wooden pick inserted in center comes out clean. Cool.

Melt butter in a heavy saucepan. Cook over low heat until butter turns a golden brown. Remove from heat. Add powdered sugar, half-and-half, water, and 1½ teaspoons vanilla. Beat 3 minutes at medium speed of an electric mixer. Spread evenly over top of cake. Yield: one 13- x 9- x 2-inch cake.

*Debbie Baskin,
Shreveport, Louisiana.*

PRUNE CAKE AND SAUCE

1½ cups sugar
1 cup vegetable oil
3 eggs
1½ teaspoons baking soda
1 cup buttermilk
2 cups all-purpose flour
1 teaspoon ground cinnamon
1 teaspoon ground nutmeg
1 teaspoon ground allspice
1 teaspoon vanilla extract
1 cup cooked, chopped prunes
1 cup chopped pecans
1 cup sugar
½ cup buttermilk
¼ cup plus 1 tablespoon butter or margarine
1 tablespoon light corn syrup
½ teaspoon vanilla extract

Combine sugar, oil, and eggs in a mixing bowl; beat on medium speed of an electric mixer 1 minute. Dissolve soda in buttermilk; set aside.

Combine flour and spices; add to sugar mixture alternately with buttermilk mixture, beginning and ending with flour mixture. Mix well after each addition. Stir in 1 teaspoon vanilla, prunes, and pecans.

Pour batter into a greased and floured 13- x 9- x 2-inch baking pan. Bake at 350° for 35 minutes or until a wooden pick inserted in center comes out clean; cool.

Combine remaining ingredients in a medium saucepan; bring to a boil. Boil 1 minute or until sugar dissolves; pour over cake while sauce is hot. Yield: one 13- x 9- x 2-inch cake.

*Dorothy Martin,
Woodburn, Kentucky.*

Tempting Party Appetizers

If you're looking for an appetizer with pizazz, search no more. Choose one of these delicious and colorful concoctions that your guests will enjoy.

CHICKEN-CURRY CHEESE BALL

1 (8-ounce) package cream cheese, softened
1 cup chopped cooked chicken
¾ cup chopped almonds, toasted
⅓ cup mayonnaise
2 tablespoons chopped chutney
1 tablespoon curry powder
Chopped parsley
Almond slices (optional)

Combine cream cheese, chicken, ¾ cup chopped almonds, mayonnaise, chutney, and curry powder; chill at least 2 hours. Shape mixture into a ball, and coat with parsley. Garnish with almond slices, if desired. Serve with crackers. Yield: 1 cheese ball. *Jean McKnight, Abbeville, Alabama.*

PÂTÉ-STUFFED MUSHROOMS

12 large fresh mushrooms
3 tablespoons vegetable oil
2 teaspoons grated onion
1 (2¾-ounce) can liver pâté
2 tablespoons fresh minced parsley
3 cherry tomatoes, quartered

Clean mushrooms with damp paper towels. Remove mushroom stems, and dice; set caps aside.

Heat oil in a large skillet. Add mushroom caps; sauté 3 minutes on each side. Place caps on a serving plate.

Add diced stems and onion to skillet; sauté until tender. Stir in liver pâté and parsley. Spoon mixture into caps. Garnish each mushroom with tomato; chill. Yield: 1 dozen. *Mrs. L. D. Howell, Hendersonville, North Carolina.*

Tip: When preparing finger sandwiches in advance, keep them from drying out by placing them in a shallow container lined with a damp towel and waxed paper. Separate sandwich layers with waxed paper, and cover with another layer of waxed paper and a damp towel; refrigerate.

Tea In The Teapot, Dainties On The Table

How would you like to take a break from work for an hour or so tomorrow afternoon? You could nibble on dainty sandwiches and sweets, sip a cup of tea, and visit with a few close friends. It is known as "afternoon tea" in England, where the idea originated. And the popularity of this leisurely way of entertaining now spans the South.

Tradition allows some flexibility in the timing of tea. A formal afternoon tea can begin anywhere from 3 to 5 p.m., so plan your party to accommodate your guests. This type of tea rarely lasts more than an hour or so—it's intended to be a prelude to evening plans.

Since afternoon tea is usually a fancy event, bring out your prettiest china and laciest linens to dress the table. We suggest both sweet and savory food offerings, all delicately sized and garnished.

Offer freshly brewed tea for the event, counting on about two cups per person. Milk, rather than cream, and lemon slices instead of wedges traditionally accompany tea. Float a slice or two of lemon in the cup rather than actually squeezing it into the tea; too much juice overpowers the delicate flavor.

Honey, granulated sugar, or sugar cubes are all appropriate to sweeten tea. For extra frills, you can pipe tiny Royal Icing flowers atop several sugar cubes to garnish the sugar bowl. Consider fresh mint or cinnamon-stick stirrers to further flavor the tea. (See "From Our Kitchen to Yours," beginning on page 120, for information on making a good pot of tea.)

TEATIME PETITS FOURS

2 eggs, separated
2 tablespoons sugar
¼ teaspoon vanilla extract
2 tablespoons sugar
¼ cup plus 2 tablespoons all-purpose flour
½ teaspoon baking powder
⅛ teaspoon salt
⅓ cup apricot jam
1 egg white
1 tablespoon powdered sugar
Quick Pour Frosting
Additional powdered sugar
Red paste food coloring

Grease a 15- x 10- x 1-inch jellyroll pan with vegetable oil, and line with waxed paper. Grease waxed paper lightly with vegetable oil, and set aside.

Beat egg yolks until light and lemon colored; gradually add 2 tablespoons sugar and vanilla, stirring well. Set mixture aside.

Beat 2 egg whites (at room temperature) until foamy in a large mixing bowl; gradually add 2 tablespoons sugar, 1 tablespoon at a time, beating until stiff but not dry. Fold in yolk mixture. Combine flour, baking powder, and salt; fold into egg mixture. Spread batter evenly into prepared pan. Bake at 350° for 8 to 10 minutes or until a wooden pick inserted in center comes out clean. Invert cake onto wire rack; peel away waxed paper, and let cool completely.

Place cake on a cutting board; slice cake crosswise into 3 equal pieces. Heat jam over low heat until melted, stirring often; press jam through a sieve to remove large pieces. Spread half of jam on top of one portion; top with second layer. Spread remaining jam on top of second layer, and top with remaining cake layer.

Cover cake with waxed paper; then wrap securely in plastic wrap. Weight the cake down with a book, and let stand overnight.

Beat 1 egg white (at room temperature) until frothy and slightly thickened. Add 1 tablespoon powdered sugar, mixing well. Brush egg white mixture lightly over top of cake. Using an electric knife, trim sides of cake stack to make edges even. Then slice cake into 1½-inch squares.

Arrange squares 2 inches apart on a wire rack; place rack in a large shallow pan. Cover and set aside about ½ cup Quick Pour Frosting for piping top decoration. Quickly pour remaining warm frosting over cakes, completely covering the top and sides.

Spoon up all frosting that drips through rack, and reheat, if necessary, to maintain original consistency. Continue pouring and reheating until cake squares are smoothly and evenly coated. (This may take 2 or 3 coatings.)

Place cakes on a cutting board, and trim away any surplus frosting from bottom edge of each cake square using a sharp knife.

Stir a little powdered sugar into reserved frosting, if necessary, to make frosting a piping consistency. Stir a small amount of food coloring into frosting to color it pale pink. Spoon frosting into decorating bag fitted with No. 2 or 3 round tip. Pipe simple designs as desired on petits fours. Yield: 1½ dozen.

Quick Pour Frosting:

6 cups sifted powdered sugar
½ cup water
2 tablespoons light corn syrup
1 teaspoon light rum

Combine all of the ingredients in a saucepan; cook over low heat, stirring constantly, until the frosting reaches a good pouring consistency, about 110°. Yield: enough frosting for 1½ dozen petits fours.

CHICKEN-SALAD FINGER SANDWICHES

1 cup chopped cooked chicken
¼ cup plus 2 tablespoons finely chopped celery
2 hard-cooked eggs, finely chopped
2 tablespoons sweet pickle relish
¼ teaspoon salt
⅛ teaspoon pepper
¼ cup plus 2 tablespoons mayonnaise
1 (1-pound) loaf unsliced sandwich bread
3 tablespoons butter or margarine, softened
1 (4-ounce) container whipped cream cheese, softened
8 tomato roses made from large cherry tomatoes
Sprigs of fresh dill
8 small green onion fans
8 strips of pimiento
3 whole canned pimientos
Green onion tops

Combine chicken, celery, eggs, relish, salt, and pepper, tossing well. Stir in mayonnaise; cover and chill.

Trim crust from loaf of bread, making bread an even rectangle. Slice loaf horizontally into 8 (⅓-inch) slices. Lightly spread softened butter on one side of each slice. Spread chicken salad evenly over butter on 4 slices; top with remaining slices of bread, buttered side down. Spread cream cheese evenly on tops of sandwiches. Slice each large sandwich rectangle into 6 finger sandwiches. Cover with a damp paper towel, then plastic wrap; chill sandwiches until ready to serve.

Just before serving, garnish tops of 8 sandwiches with cherry tomato roses and sprigs of fresh dill; tops of 8 with small green onion fans and strips of pimiento; and tops of remaining 8 with pimiento flowers cut from whole pimiento using canapé cutters. (Use green onion tops for stems and leaves.) Yield: 2 dozen.

CUCUMBER PINWHEEL SANDWICHES

1 medium cucumber, unpeeled
1 (3-ounce) package cream cheese, softened
1 ounce blue cheese, crumbled
1 tablespoon milk
¼ teaspoon dried whole dillweed
1 (1-pound) loaf unsliced sandwich bread
2 tablespoons butter or margarine, softened
1 small cucumber

Shred cucumber; pat shredded cucumber between absorbent paper towels to remove excess moisture. Combine cucumber, cream cheese, blue cheese, milk, and dillweed, mixing well.

Trim crust from loaf of bread, making an even rectangle. Slice bread horizontally into 6 even slices. Roll each slice with a rolling pin to flatten. Spread one side of each slice with 1 teaspoon butter, and spread cucumber filling evenly over butter. Roll up tightly, jellyroll fashion, beginning at short end. Wrap in plastic wrap, and chill at least 8 hours. When ready to serve, cut chilled rolls into ½-inch slices.

Score small cucumber with the tines of a fork. Cut 9 (¼-inch) slices from cucumber, and cut slices into quarters. Reserve remaining cucumber for other uses. Insert a cucumber wedge, point side down, in top center of each sandwich for garnish. Yield: 3 dozen.

ALMOND TEA TARTS

1 egg
2 tablespoons plus 2 teaspoons sugar
½ teaspoon grated orange rind
2 tablespoons plus 2 teaspoons orange juice
⅛ teaspoon almond extract
Tea Tart Shells
3 tablespoons sliced almonds, lightly toasted
3 tablespoons apricot preserves
About 5 maraschino cherries, quartered

Beat egg at medium speed of an electric mixer until thick and lemon colored. Add sugar, orange rind, juice, and almond extract, mixing until blended. Spoon mixture into prepared Tea Tart Shells. Bake at 350° for 15 minutes or until top is firm. Let cool in tart pans 5 minutes. Remove from pans.

Arrange sliced almonds in a ring, flower fashion, on top of filling.

Heat apricot preserves over low heat until melted, stirring often; press preserves through a sieve to remove large pieces. Spoon warm preserves evenly over almonds. Top each with a cherry quarter. Yield: 1½ dozen tarts.

Tea Tart Shells:

⅔ cup all-purpose flour
¼ teaspoon salt
¼ cup shortening
1½ to 2 tablespoons cold water

Combine flour and salt; cut in shortening with pastry blender until mixture resembles coarse meal. Sprinkle cold water (1 tablespoon at a time) evenly over surface; stir with a fork until dry ingredients are moistened. Shape into a ball; chill.

Divide dough into 18 equal portions. Gently press dough into 1¾-inch tart pans. Bake at 375° for 8 to 10 minutes or until lightly browned. Let cool 5 minutes. Yield: 1½ dozen.

STRAWBERRIES 'N LEMON CREAM

½ cup whipping cream
3 tablespoons powdered sugar
½ cup commercial sour cream
2 tablespoons lemon juice
Mint leaves
2 pints fresh strawberries

Beat whipping cream until foamy; gradually add powdered sugar, beating until soft peaks form. Combine sour cream and lemon juice; fold into whipped cream. Garnish with mint leaves. Serve with strawberries. Yield: 1¼ cups.

SNOW-CAPPED MADELEINES

3 eggs
⅛ teaspoon salt
½ cup sugar
1 cup all-purpose flour
1 teaspoon grated orange rind
½ cup butter, melted and cooled
Powdered sugar

Beat eggs and salt until foamy. Gradually add sugar, and beat 15 minutes at high speed of an electric mixer or until thick and lemon colored. Gently fold in flour, 2 tablespoons at a time, and orange rind. Fold in butter, 1 tablespoon at a time. Spoon batter evenly into greased and floured madeleine molds. Bake at 400° for 6 to 8 minutes or until lightly browned. Remove from molds, and cool on a wire rack, flat side down. Lightly sprinkle with powdered sugar. Yield: 2 dozen.

From Our Kitchen To Yours

Hot or cold, plain or spiced, tea is popular in the South. Since there are so many varieties, we'd like to answer some of your questions about the types of tea and the terms often seen on tea packages. We also have some tips on brewing and storing tea.

What's the difference between teas? Black, green, and oolong are the three main types. All these tea leaves come from the same plants, but the processing varies, giving each type a distinct taste and color.

Black tea results from partially drying the tea leaves and then crushing them in a roller machine to release their juices. Then the leaves ferment and dry in a controlled environment until they turn a brownish black. The fermentation time determines the strength of the tea. Black tea is hearty and strong and is the most popular. Darjeeling, Keemun, and Ceylon are all varieties of black tea.

The leaves of *green* tea are steamed, preventing them from fermenting and changing colors. Then the leaves are crushed and dried for packaging. Green tea is usually a light color when brewed. When the leaves are rolled into tiny pellets after steaming, the result is called gunpowder tea.

Oolong tea is the king of the teas. It's semi-fermented, so it's between a black and green tea. After processing, these leaves turn greenish brown, and oolong brews light in color.

What is meant by pekoe? Pekoe, a word used to grade black teas, indicates size and grade of the tea leaf and has nothing to do with flavor or quality.

Is herbal tea a black tea? A true herbal tea doesn't have any caffeine, so black tea is not an ingredient. Herbal teas are usually made from a combination of natural ingredients, such as spices, plant leaves, seeds, roots, and flowers. Herbal teas are more delicate than black teas and are light in color. Since they're a special blend, they usually have a flowery or spicy aroma.

How can I brew the best pot of tea? Always start with cold tap water because it's fresh and full of oxygen. The cold water will bring out the true flavor of the tea, whereas hot water has lost most of its oxygen and will make tea flat and stale. Next, bring the water to a full rolling boil. If the water is not hot enough, the tea will not brew fully; if you boil water too long, it will become flat and lose its freshness.

While the water is coming to a boil, preheat your teapot. It's best to use a porcelain, glass, stainless steel, or silver teapot rather than aluminum. Fill the teapot with hot water, and let it stand a few minutes. Empty the teapot, and add your tea bags or loose tea; then pour boiling water over the top.

If you're using loose tea leaves, it's best to use an infuser, which is a silver or stainless steel container with a mesh surface that holds the tea leaves. If you don't have an infuser, just strain the tea after it's brewed. Use one teaspoon of loose tea or one tea bag for every cup of water. Cover your teapot to hold in the heat, and let it brew three to five minutes.

During this brewing time, the flavor, color, and body are coming out. Remember to brew for only the recommended time, or the tea will be bitter. After brewing, take out the tea bag or infuser. If you use tea bags, squeeze them well; they absorb a lot of water. If you like weaker tea, add boiling water after the brewing time.

What can I do to prevent cloudy tea? If you refrigerate tea after it's brewed, it may become cloudy. To clear it up, try adding a little boiling water.

How long will tea keep? If tea bags or tea leaves are stored properly, they should last a year. Tea is delicate; it absorbs moisture and odors easily. For that reason, store it away from garlic or other strong spices. Also keep in mind that any bright light or heat will damage tea. Store it on a dark shelf in an enameled tin can that has a tight-fitting lid.

Macaroni Salad Stars Shrimp

Are you looking for a main-dish salad that's filling, easy to make, and attractive enough to serve your special luncheon guests? Macaroni-Shrimp Salad may be your answer.

The base is macaroni, but there's plenty of shrimp to round it out and make it satisfying. With chopped eggs, English peas, and other vegetables in the mixture, it's a meal-in-one for light eaters. You could also serve hot rolls or croissants with it.

You can prepare this meal ahead; in fact, it is important to allow time for the salad to chill before serving. This step improves the taste considerably; that's because the flavors have time to blend and become more pronounced.

MACARONI-SHRIMP SALAD

4½ cups water
1½ pounds unpeeled medium shrimp
2 cups cooked elbow macaroni
1 cup frozen English peas, thawed
2 hard-cooked eggs, chopped
1 medium-size green pepper, chopped
¼ cup chopped pimiento-stuffed olives
2 tablespoons chopped pimiento
1 tablespoon chopped onion
1 cup mayonnaise or salad dressing
½ teaspoon salt
⅛ teaspoon pepper
Lettuce leaves
Tomato wedges (optional)

Bring water to a boil; add shrimp, and cook 3 to 5 minutes. Drain well; rinse with cold water. Chill. Peel and devein shrimp.

Combine shrimp, macaroni, peas, eggs, green pepper, olives, pimiento, and onion; toss well. Combine mayonnaise, salt, and pepper; pour over shrimp mixture, tossing gently. Chill. Serve salad on lettuce leaves; garnish with tomato wedges, if desired. Yield: 4 servings.   *Rublelene Singleton,*
Scotts Hill, Tennessee.

Whip Up A Batch Of Cupcakes

If there's a child at your house, you probably already know about the virtues of cupcakes. They're easy to make, easy to serve, and what's more, children love them. They're a natural choice for school parties, birthdays, or any other occasion that involves children.

Cupcakes are also ideal for an after-school snack or a quick family dessert. For example, try Golden Vanilla Cupcakes when you want to make a home-baked sweet in a hurry.

Don't wait until Halloween to sample Pumpkin Cupcakes; since they're made with canned pumpkin, they're appropriate any time of the year. The rich pumpkin flavor and cream cheese frosting make them popular with both adults and children.

GOLDEN VANILLA CUPCAKES

⅓ cup butter or margarine, softened
¾ cup sugar
1 egg
1¾ cups all-purpose flour
2½ teaspoons baking powder
½ teaspoon salt
¾ cup milk
1 teaspoon vanilla extract
Commercial frosting

Cream butter; gradually add sugar, beating at medium speed of an electric mixer until light and fluffy. Add egg, beating well. Combine flour, baking powder, and salt; add to creamed mixture alternately with milk, beginning and ending with flour mixture. Mix well after each addition. Stir in vanilla.

Spoon batter into paper-lined muffin pans, filling one-half full. Bake at 350° for 18 minutes. Frost with commercial frosting. Yield: 1½ dozen.
Mildred Tipton,
Edna, Texas.

PUMPKIN CUPCAKES

4 eggs
1 cup vegetable oil
2 cups sugar
2 cups all-purpose flour
1 tablespoon pumpkin pie spice
2 teaspoons baking soda
1½ cups canned pumpkin
Cream Cheese Frosting

Beat eggs in a large mixing bowl; add all ingredients except frosting, and mix well with an electric mixer. Spoon batter into paper-lined muffin pans, filling three-fourths full. Bake at 350° for 25 to 30 minutes. Let cool; frost with Cream Cheese Frosting. Yield: 2 dozen.

Cream Cheese Frosting:

½ (8-ounce) package cream cheese, softened
3 tablespoons butter or margarine, softened
2½ cups sifted powdered sugar
2 teaspoons vanilla extract

Combine cream cheese and butter; beat until light and fluffy. Add remaining ingredients; beat until smooth. Yield: enough for 2 dozen cupcakes.
Jeri Rieken,
Lubbock, Texas.

This Quiche Is Hot And Spicy

If you're a quiche fan but have grown tired of the usual egg-and-cheese combinations, try Jalapeño-Corn Quiche. It's guaranteed to liven up any meal, but it's especially good for a brunch or luncheon menu.

Chopped jalapeño peppers provide a pungent contrast to the cream-style corn in the filling. You can make it as hot as you like, depending on how many jalapeños you use.

JALAPEÑO-CORN QUICHE

1 unbaked 9-inch pastry shell
3 slices bacon
½ cup chopped onion
1 (17-ounce) can cream-style corn
1 or 2 jalapeño peppers, seeded and finely
   chopped
2 eggs, beaten
¼ cup half-and-half
½ cup (2 ounces) shredded Cheddar
   cheese
1 tablespoon all-purpose flour
¼ teaspoon salt
⅛ teaspoon pepper
Jalapeño slices (optional)

Line a 9-inch quiche dish with pastry; trim excess pastry around edge. Prick bottom and sides of pastry with fork. Bake at 400° for 3 minutes; remove from oven, and gently prick with fork. Bake 5 minutes. Let cool on rack.

Cook bacon in a skillet until crisp; remove bacon, reserving 1 tablespoon drippings in the skillet. Crumble bacon, and set aside.

Sauté onion in bacon drippings until tender; drain well. Combine onion, corn, peppers, egg, half-and-half, cheese, flour, salt, and pepper, mixing well; pour into pastry shell. Sprinkle with bacon. Bake at 375° for 45 minutes or until set. Garnish with jalapeño slices, if desired. Yield: one 9-inch quiche.
Doris Curls,
Anniston, Alabama.

Sweet Strawberry Treats

When Louise Jones of Lithia Springs, Georgia, spots the first strawberries of the season, she knows it's time for her favorite dessert—Strawberry Shortcake Squares. Louise sweetens the plump berries and then sandwiches them between pieces of shortcake. More berries and whipped cream make it taste as luscious as it looks.

Another way to enjoy fresh strawberries is in Claire Buquoi's Stuffed Strawberries With Walnuts, as an appetizer or dessert. Each berry is scooped out and filled with a rich walnut and cream cheese mixture.

STRAWBERRY SHORTCAKE SQUARES

4 cups strawberries, hulled and sliced
¼ cup sugar
2 cups all-purpose flour
¼ cup sugar
1 tablespoon baking powder
¼ teaspoon salt
½ cup butter or margarine
⅔ cup half-and-half
1 egg, beaten
2 cups sweetened whipped cream
6 additional strawberries (optional)

Combine sliced strawberries and ¼ cup sugar; chill.

Combine flour, sugar, baking powder, and salt; cut in butter with a pastry blender until mixture resembles coarse meal. Combine half-and-half and egg, stirring well; add to flour mixture, stirring just until moistened. Spread mixture in a lightly greased 8-inch square baking pan. Bake at 450° for 15 minutes or until golden brown. Cool 5 minutes; turn out onto a wire rack.

Cut shortcake into 6 pieces; slice each piece crosswise in half. Place bottom half of shortcake, cut side up, on an individual serving plate; top with a dollop of whipped cream and 2½ tablespoons of strawberry mixture. Add second layer of shortcake, cut side down; top with a dollop of whipped cream and 2½ tablespoons of strawberry mixture. Garnish with an additional dollop of whipped cream. Add a strawberry, if desired. Repeat for each of remaining five shortcake squares. Yield: 6 servings.
Louise Jones,
Lithia Springs, Georgia.

STUFFED STRAWBERRIES WITH WALNUTS

18 extra-large strawberries
¾ cup whipped cream cheese
2 tablespoons finely chopped walnuts
1½ teaspoons powdered sugar
½ to 1½ teaspoons milk

Cut a thin slice from the stem end of strawberries, allowing the berries to stand upright. Cut ¼ inch off tip end of berries, reserving tips.

Carefully scoop out about half of the pulp from each berry, leaving shells intact. Combine pulp with cream cheese, walnuts, sugar, and milk, mixing well. Add extra milk if needed to make a creamy consistency. Spoon mixture into a decorating bag fitted with a large tip. Pipe mixture into strawberries, and top with reserved strawberry tips. Yield: 1½ dozen.
Claire Buquoi,
New Orleans, Louisiana.

STRAWBERRY-YOGURT PIE

1 envelope unflavored gelatin
¼ cup boiling water
1 (3-ounce) package cream cheese,
   softened
¼ cup sifted powdered sugar
1 teaspoon vanilla extract
1 cup whipping cream
¾ cup plain yogurt
1 (9-inch) graham cracker crust
2 cups strawberries, hulled and halved
⅓ cup strawberry jelly, melted

Dissolve gelatin in boiling water, and set aside.

Combine cream cheese, sugar, and vanilla; beat until light and fluffy. Add whipping cream; beat until soft peaks form. Add yogurt and gelatin mixture, mixing until smooth.

Spoon filling into graham cracker crust. Chill at least 4 hours. Arrange strawberries on top of pie; drizzle melted jelly over strawberries. Yield: one 9-inch pie.
Helen Maurer,
Christmas, Florida.

Tip: It is best to store most fruit in the refrigerator. Allow melons, avocados, and pears to ripen at room temperature; then refrigerate. Berries should be sorted to remove imperfect fruit before refrigerating; then wash and hull just before serving.

June

Pair Herbs And Vinegar For Flavor

Combine a handful of garden herbs and vinegar, and you'll have a fresh tasting seasoning you can use all year long. Just pour hot vinegar over herbs in a jar, and let stand two weeks. It's that easy.

You can use any fresh herb or combination of herbs. We tried some blends of two or more in our kitchens to take the guesswork out of teaming flavors. If you want to come up with your own combinations, keep in mind that strong herbs, such as basil, sage, and rosemary, need to be mixed with milder flavored ones.

Use the flavored vinegars in recipes other than those for salad dressings and marinades. For example, you'll find Garlic-Basil Vinegar adds a fabulous taste to hot fresh green beans. Try Tarragon-Dill Vinegar in place of lemon or lime juice in a seviche marinade or to season cold smoked salmon. If you enjoy the tangy lemon flavor of chicken or veal piccata, add some Spicy Oregano-Lemon Vinegar to the thin slices of sautéed meat. Also, you can sprinkle it over hot, buttered broccoli. Just a hint of mint is what you detect when you mix Lemon-Mint Vinegar with vegetable oil and toss it with a fresh fruit salad. Or add Five-Herb Vinegar to a fresh vegetable soup or stew.

SPICY OREGANO-LEMON VINEGAR

1 lemon, quartered
¼ teaspoon white mustard seeds
1 teaspoon peppercorns
3 whole cloves
½ cup fresh oregano, crushed
2 cups white wine vinegar (5% acidity)
Additional sprigs of fresh oregano (optional)

Place lemon, mustard seeds, peppercorns, cloves, and oregano in a large widemouthed jar.

Place vinegar in a medium saucepan; bring to a boil. Pour vinegar over ingredients in jar; cover with lid. Let stand at room temperature two weeks.

Strain vinegar into decorative jars, discarding lemon, herb, and spice residue; add additional sprigs of fresh oregano, if desired. Seal jars with a cork or other airtight lid. Yield: 2 cups.

LEMON-MINT VINEGAR

1 lemon
¼ cup chopped fresh mint
2 cups white wine vinegar (5% acidity)
Additional sprigs of fresh mint (optional)
Lemon rind strips (optional)

Cut a continuous spiral of rind from lemon, and place in a large widemouthed jar. Reserve remainder of lemon for other uses. Add mint to jar.

Place vinegar in a medium saucepan and bring to a boil. Pour vinegar over mint and lemon rind; cover with lid. Let stand at room temperature two weeks.

Strain vinegar into decorative jars, discarding lemon and herb residue; add additional sprigs of fresh mint and lemon rind, if desired. Seal jars with a cork or other airtight lid. Yield: 2 cups.

FIVE-HERB VINEGAR

½ cup chopped fresh rosemary
¼ cup chopped chive blossoms
½ cup chopped fresh thyme
¼ cup chopped fresh oregano
1 sprig fresh parsley, chopped
4 shallots, thinly sliced
12 peppercorns
3¾ cups white wine vinegar (5% acidity)
Additional sprigs of fresh rosemary, oregano, and thyme (optional)

Place herbs, shallots, and peppercorns in a large widemouthed jar.

Place vinegar in a medium saucepan; bring to a boil. Pour vinegar over ingredients in jar; cover with lid. Let stand at room temperature two weeks.

Strain vinegar into decorative jars, discarding herb residue; add additional sprigs of fresh rosemary, oregano, and thyme, if desired. Seal jars with a cork or other airtight lid. Yield: 4 cups.

GARLIC-BASIL VINEGAR

½ cup fresh basil
1 clove garlic, crushed
2 cups white vinegar (5% acidity)
Additional sprigs of fresh basil (optional)

Slightly bruise basil, and place in a large widemouthed jar with garlic.

Place vinegar in a medium saucepan; bring to a boil. Pour vinegar over basil and garlic; cover with lid. Let stand at room temperature two weeks.

Strain vinegar into decorative jars, discarding basil and garlic residue; add additional sprigs of basil, if desired. Seal jars with a cork or other airtight lid. Yield: 2 cups.

TARRAGON-DILL VINEGAR

⅓ cup fresh tarragon leaves
¼ cup fresh dill
2 cups white wine vinegar (5% acidity)
Additional sprigs of tarragon and dill (optional)

Slightly bruise tarragon and dill, and place in a large widemouthed jar.

Place vinegar in a medium saucepan, and bring to a boil. Pour vinegar over herbs; cover with lid. Let stand at room temperature two weeks.

Strain vinegar into decorative jars, discarding herb residue. Add additional sprigs of fresh dill and tarragon, if desired. Seal jars with a cork or other airtight lid. Yield: 2 cups.

Surprise Cakes Start In Jellyroll Pans

On the outside, Jellyroll Layer Cake looks like any other cake, but slicing reveals vertical, not horizontal, layers. It sounds tricky to make, but it's actually as simple as a jellyroll. The layers are baked in a jellyroll pan, sliced, and rolled in the traditional manner, adding a new strip where the rolled strip ends.

Six-Layer Black Forest Cake has its beginnings in a jellyroll pan, too. Once baked, the two jellyroll layers are sliced into three crosswise strips; then they're stacked, with whipped cream and cherries between each layer. The result? Six stately, rectangular-shaped layers.

The slicing technique for Chocolate Triangle Cake is a little trickier, but we think you'll be proud of the end result. For this cake, two layers are stacked on top of each other; next, they're sliced into seven strips of varied widths. The strips are frosted and stacked by graduated sizes into two halves of a triangle. The stacks are weighted down to compress the layers and make them adhere; they're then joined into a triangle and frosted. A garnish of crystallized violets finishes the cake beautifully. (Check with caterers or food specialty shops in your area if you'd like to buy these candied flowers.)

Before you reach the garnishing stage, however, you'll need to keep in mind some important points about baking and slicing these jellyroll layers. For instance, when baking in jellyroll pans, grease pans and line with waxed paper. This helps keep the thin layers from sticking and will prevent tearing when you invert the cake layers.

Because jellyroll layers are so thin, the recipes call for short baking times. Bear in mind that baking too long can make them dry and tough.

When the layers are done, don't let them cool in the pan for 10 minutes as you may often do with cake layers. Immediately invert them, and carefully peel away the waxed paper while the cake is still warm. Then proceed as the recipe directs.

Since each of these cakes depends on precise slicing techniques for the novel end result, it's important that you measure each cut accurately—keep a ruler handy. And you'll get cleaner, neater slices if you use a long knife with serrated edges. If your slices are even, your cake layers should fit together like the pieces of a puzzle. (See photograph of these jellyroll cakes on page IV.)

JELLYROLL LAYER CAKE

6 eggs
1⅔ cups sugar
2 cups self-rising flour
⅔ cup water
2 teaspoons vanilla extract
1 teaspoon ground cinnamon
½ teaspoon ground nutmeg
¼ teaspoon ground allspice
Powdered sugar
English Toffee Frosting
Chocolate curls (optional)

To make Jellyroll Layer Cake, slice both jellyroll layers into three lengthwise strips, and spread with frosting; then roll layers like a giant jellyroll, adding a new cake strip where the previously rolled strip ends. Frost entire cake with remaining frosting.

Grease two 15- x 10- x 1-inch jellyroll pans, and line with waxed paper; grease and flour waxed paper. Set aside.

Beat eggs at high speed of an electric mixer until foamy. Gradually add 1⅔ cups sugar, beating until mixture is thick and lemon colored (about 5 to 6 minutes). Fold flour, water, vanilla, and spices into egg mixture. Spread batter evenly into prepared pans. Bake at 375° for 8 minutes.

Sift powdered sugar in a 15- x 10-inch rectangle on each of 2 towels. When cakes are done, immediately loosen from sides of pan, and turn each out on a sugared towel. Peel off waxed paper. Trim ⅛ inch from edges of each cake using a long serrated knife. Roll up towel; chill.

Carefully unroll chilled cakes; cut each cake lengthwise into 3 equal strips. Spread each cake strip with English Toffee Frosting; set aside remaining frosting. Gently roll up one cake strip jellyroll fashion starting at short end. Set roll upright in center of serving plate. Starting where roll ends, wind second cake strip around first roll. Repeat until all 6 strips are used.

Frost top and sides of cake with remaining frosting. Arrange chocolate curls on top of cake, if desired. Chill cake several hours before serving. Yield: one 8-inch cake.

English Toffee Frosting:

5 (1⅛-ounce) English toffee-flavored candy bars, crushed
1½ tablespoons amaretto or other almond-flavored liqueur
3 tablespoons flaked coconut, toasted
1 (12-ounce) carton frozen whipped topping, thawed

Gently fold crushed candy bars, amaretto, and coconut into whipped topping. Yield: about 4½ cups.

SIX-LAYER BLACK FOREST CAKE

¾ cup all-purpose flour
½ cup cocoa
1¼ teaspoons baking powder
½ teaspoon salt
6 eggs, separated
1¼ cups sugar
¾ teaspoon vanilla extract
Whipped Cream Frosting
1 (20-ounce) can cherry pie filling

Grease two 15- x 10- x 1-inch jellyroll pans, and line with waxed paper; grease and flour waxed paper. Set aside.

Sift flour, cocoa, baking powder, and salt together; set mixture aside.

For Six-Layer Black Forest Cake, cut both jellyroll layers into three crosswise strips, and stack them on the serving platter, spreading cream and cherries between layers.

Beat egg whites (at room temperature) at high speed of an electric mixer until foamy. Gradually add sugar, beating until soft peaks form. Set aside.

Beat egg yolks until thick and lemon colored; stir in vanilla. Fold egg yolk mixture into egg white mixture; gently fold in flour mixture. Spread batter evenly into prepared jellyroll pans; bake at 350° for 10 to 12 minutes.

When layers are done, immediately loosen from sides of pans, and turn out onto wire racks to cool. Peel off waxed paper. When cool, cut each cake crosswise into 3 equal strips.

Set aside about 1 cup Whipped Cream Frosting for piping. Stack cake layers on serving plate, spreading about ¼ cup Whipped Cream Frosting and ¼ cup pie filling between each layer. Spread additional frosting on top and sides of cake.

Spoon reserved frosting into a decorating bag fitted with No. 5 or 6B large fluted tip. Pipe frosting around top border of cake. Spoon remaining cherry pie filling on top of cake within piped frosting. Chill cake several hours before serving. Yield: 12 servings.

Whipped Cream Frosting:

2½ cups whipping cream
½ teaspoon vanilla extract
⅔ cup sifted powdered sugar

Beat whipping cream and vanilla at high speed of an electric mixer until foamy; gradually add powdered sugar, beating mixture until soft peaks form. Yield: 5 cups.

CHOCOLATE TRIANGLE CAKE

4 eggs, separated
¾ cup sugar, divided
1 teaspoon vanilla extract
¾ cup all-purpose flour
¾ teaspoon baking powder
¼ teaspoon salt
Satiny Chocolate Frosting
Crystallized violets (optional)

Grease two 15- x 10- x 1-inch jellyroll pans, and line with waxed paper; grease and flour waxed paper. Set aside.

Beat egg yolks at medium speed of an electric mixer until thick and lemon colored. Gradually add ¼ cup sugar, beating constantly. Beat in vanilla.

Chocolate Triangle Cake requires precise measuring. Stack the jellyroll layers on top of each other; then carefully cut strips into widths specified in the recipe.

Join layers of Chocolate Triangle Cake in graduating sizes to make two halves of the triangle cake, spreading frosting between each layer; cover layers with foil, and weight down for about an hour. Later, join the triangle halves, and spread cake with remaining frosting.

Beat egg whites (at room temperature) at high speed of electric mixer until foamy. Gradually add remaining ½ cup sugar, 1 tablespoon at a time, beating until stiff peaks form. Fold egg yolk mixture into egg whites. Combine flour, baking powder, and salt; gently fold flour mixture, one-third at a time, into egg mixture. Spread batter evenly into prepared pans; bake at 400° for 5 to 7 minutes. When cake is done, immediately loosen from sides of pans, and turn out onto wire racks to cool. Peel off waxed paper.

Stack the two layers on top of each other to allow even slicing. Using a long serrated knife, slice layers crosswise into strips of the following widths: 3½ inches, 3 inches, 2½ inches, 2 inches, 1½ inches, 1 inch, and ½ inch.

Spread one side of both of the 3½-inch strips with a thin layer of Satiny Chocolate Frosting. Top each with a 3-inch strip, keeping edges even on one lengthwise side. Forming two stacks, repeat spreading thin layers of frosting and topping with successively smaller cake strips, keeping edges even, until all cake strips are used. (Stacks will be slanted on one side, with layers running horizontal; each stack represents half of the triangle.)

Turn stacks onto jellyroll pan, even edges down. (Layers now run vertical.) Cover cake stacks with aluminum foil, and place a weight (packages of cake or pancake mix work well) on the slanted side of each stack. Refrigerate cake stacks about 1 hour.

Remove weights and foil. Spread a thin layer of frosting against the 3½-inch side of one of the stacks, and join stacks to make a triangle.

Carefully transfer cake to platter, using wide spatulas. Spread remaining frosting over cake. Arrange crystallized violets down sides and peak of cake, if desired. Yield: 12 to 15 servings.

Satiny Chocolate Frosting:

3 (1-ounce) squares unsweetened chocolate
¼ cup plus 2 tablespoons butter or
    margarine
3¾ cups sifted powdered sugar
¼ cup plus 2 tablespoons milk
¾ teaspoon vanilla extract

Combine chocolate and butter in top of a double boiler; bring water to a boil. Reduce heat to low; cook until chocolate melts. Remove from heat, and cool.

Add powdered sugar and milk to chocolate mixture; beat at low speed of an electric mixer until smooth. Stir in vanilla. Yield: 2 cups.

Summer Entrées Beat The Heat

With summer here, the heat can take its toll on the appetite; the usual foods just aren't as appealing. For a refreshing change, try our warm-weather entrées. They're light and tasty and designed to make cooking easier in the months ahead.

Consider Lemon-Herb Chicken, for example, when you want something spicy. It's marinated in a flavorful olive oil-lemon juice mixture before baking. Then it's served with fresh oregano and lemon slices for extra color.

Stir-fry dishes are a nice alternative to heavy fried foods during the summer. Most of the preparation for Walnut Chicken is done ahead; the actual stir-frying takes only a few minutes.

WALNUT CHICKEN

3 tablespoons vegetable oil
1 cup chopped celery
1 cup chopped onion
2 tablespoons vegetable oil
2 cups walnut halves
3 tablespoons vegetable oil
1 pound boneless chicken breasts, skinned
    and cubed
1 tablespoon cornstarch
1 (8-ounce) can bamboo shoots, drained
1 (8-ounce) can sliced water chestnuts,
    drained
¼ cup chicken broth
3 tablespoons soy sauce
2 tablespoons sherry
1 tablespoon cornstarch
1 teaspoon sugar
Hot cooked rice

Pour 3 tablespoons oil into a preheated wok; heat at medium high (325°) for 2 minutes. Add celery and onion; stir-fry 2 to 3 minutes or until tender. Remove vegetables; set aside.

Heat 2 tablespoons oil in wok. Add walnuts, and stir-fry 2 to 3 minutes or until toasted. Remove from wok; set aside. Wipe wok with paper towel.

Heat 3 tablespoons oil in wok. Coat chicken with 1 tablespoon cornstarch; add chicken to wok, and cook 3 minutes. Add onion-celery mixture, bamboo shoots, and water chestnuts.

Combine remaining ingredients except rice; stir well. Add mixture to wok. Cook, stirring constantly, until thickened. Stir in walnuts. Serve chicken over rice. Yield: 6 servings.

Carol L. Haggett,
Norfolk, Virginia.

LEMON-HERB CHICKEN

1 (3½-pound) broiler-fryer, cut up and
    skinned
½ cup olive oil
¼ cup lemon juice
2 small garlic cloves, crushed
3 tablespoons chopped fresh oregano or 1
    tablespoon dried whole oregano
⅛ teaspoon salt
⅛ teaspoon pepper
Fresh oregano (optional)
Lemon slices (optional)

Place chicken, meaty side down, in a
13- x 9- x 2-inch baking pan. Combine
olive oil, lemon juice, garlic, oregano,
salt, and pepper, mixing well. Pour mixture over chicken; marinate in refrigerator 2 hours, turning occasionally.

Bake, uncovered, at 350° for 30 to 40
minutes. Turn chicken over; broil 6
inches from heat for 5 minutes or until
lightly browned. Garnish with fresh
oregano and lemon slices, if desired.
Yield: about 4 servings.
Mrs. Clayton Turner,
De Funiak Springs, Florida.

POACHED RED SNAPPER

1 (3-ounce) package crab and shrimp boil
¼ cup chopped celery
¼ cup chopped onion
¼ cup chopped green pepper
⅛ teaspoon salt
1 (1½- to 2-pound) dressed red snapper

Place crab and shrimp boil in a fish
poacher, and pour in water 3 to 4
inches deep; bring to a boil.
Combine celery, onion, green pepper,
and salt; place in fish cavity. Wrap fish
with cheesecloth; tie securely with
string. Place in boiling water; cover, reduce heat, and simmer 20 minutes or
until fish flakes easily when tested with
a fork. Remove fish from poacher; unwrap and serve. Yield: 2 to 3 servings.
Mrs. Karl Koenig,
Dallas, Texas.

GROUPER MACADAMIA

1 (8-ounce) can tomato sauce
½ cup chopped onion
1 stalk celery with leaves, chopped
1 clove garlic, minced
1 bay leaf
⅛ teaspoon salt
⅛ teaspoon pepper
1 (1¾- to 2-pound) fresh grouper fillet
3 tablespoons butter or margarine, melted
¼ cup coarsely chopped macadamia nuts

Combine tomato sauce, onion, celery,
garlic, bay leaf, salt, and pepper in a
medium saucepan; bring to a boil. Reduce heat, and simmer 30 minutes.
Strain sauce, and keep warm.
Place fillet on a lightly greased broiling rack, and brush with butter. Bake at
400° for 20 to 30 minutes or until fish
flakes easily when tested with a fork.
Remove from oven; top with sauce,
and sprinkle with nuts. Broil 6 inches
from heat for 2 minutes or until macadamia nuts begin to brown. Serve
grouper immediately. Yield: 4 servings.
Rinne Ashcraft,
Dunedin, Florida.

From Our Kitchen To Yours

Poaching is a moist-heat cooking
method using liquid to gently simmer
food until it's tender. Foods that have
been poached are usually light and non-
greasy, because fats are not used in the
cooking process. Consider poaching not
only for cooking eggs, but also in preparing other fragile foods, such as fruit
and fish.

To poach eggs, start by bringing several inches of water to a boil in a saucepan or skillet. (You'll want to be sure
to have enough liquid to cover the eggs
when cooking.) Reduce the heat, and
let the water simmer. Start with fresh,
high-quality eggs so they'll keep their
shape; break each egg into a measuring
cup or saucer. Gently slip one egg at a
time into the simmering water, being
sure not to overcrowd them.

If eggs are not fresh, they'll have
thinner whites, so you may want to add
a pinch of salt or about 2 teaspoons of
vinegar to the water. This speeds up
coagulation and cooking time and also
helps the eggs keep their shape. Eggs
should be done in 3 to 5 minutes. Then
quickly remove them from water with a
slotted spoon or spatula. Be careful not
to overcook; the whites will get tough
and the yolks mealy.

If milk is used for the poaching liquid, save it and pour over the eggs
when served on toast.

To make cooking this way even easier, you can use an egg poacher. It's a
saucepan with a metal frame that holds
three to four cups. The eggs are placed
in greased cups (use vegetable cooking
spray), then covered and cooked over
simmering water until done. With a
poacher, cooking time is not shortened,
but the eggs have a more perfect shape.

Poaching is a good cooking method
for firm fruits, such as pears or apples.
The most commonly poached fruit is the
pear, which is peeled and dipped in
lemon juice before cooking to keep it
from darkening. It's simmered in water,
a little sugar, and sometimes wine and
spices. Both sugar and acid help fruit
keep its shape and not become mushy
as it cooks. (Often wine is added because it contains sugar and acid.)
Poaching a pear takes about 20 to 25
minutes. If the fruit is going to be
served as compotes, it's often cooled in
the poaching liquid.

Fish can be poached whole or in fillets or steaks. Like eggs and fruit, fish
needs to be placed in enough liquid to
completely cover it as it cooks. You can
use salted water, broth, cream, or a
wine-fish stock. What you decide on depends on the flavor and degree of
whiteness you want. If you want to taste
the true flavor of fish, use salted water.
Adding some acid, such as vinegar, to
the poaching liquid will help the fish
stay firmer and whiter. The liquid
should be kept barely simmering; if it
boils, the fish will tear apart. Poaching
fish takes 5 to 8 minutes per pound. To
keep from overcooking, remove it from
the liquid immediately after it's done.

In cooking a whole fish, a poacher
works best, but a large skillet can also
be used. If you use a poacher, the fish
is held together better and transferred
more easily to a serving platter because
of the steamer tray. But if you're
poaching in a skillet, you may need to
wrap fish in muslin or cheesecloth to
help keep the fish basted and intact.
The muslin also helps in removing the
fish from the skillet.

*Tip: You should not thaw fish at room
temperature or in warm water; it will
lose moisture and flavor. Instead, place
the fish in the refrigerator to thaw.
Keep in mind that you should allow 18
to 24 hours for thawing a 1-pound
package. Of course, you should never
refreeze thawed fish.*

Jams, Jellies, And More To Spread

A sweet, fruity fragrance lingers in the air, and pretty jelly jars glisten like jewels on the kitchen counter. Listen closely, and you'll hear the lids pop as they seal—the reassuring sound of a job well done. These are the smells, sights, and sounds of summer, as Southerners put up tasty fruit spreads destined to lather homemade bread, to be sandwiched with peanut butter, or to be enjoyed in a slice of jam cake.

Preferences often follow family traditions. Some lean toward sparkling gelatin-like **jellies,** the result of cooking sugar and fruit juice together, or less-firm **jams,** which use crushed or chopped fruit rather than juice. And **preserves,** slightly jellied syrup-type spreads suspending chopped or whole fruit, are popular. **Marmalades** offer a tangy bite; traditionally, these soft products contain citrus fruit and peel.

The mixture doesn't need to jell for spreads such as **butters** and **honeys.** Butters consist of fruit pulp and sugar cooked until thick, usually livened up with some cinnamon or nutmeg. If they're cooked a little longer without the spices, they become fruit honeys; these have the syrupy consistency of real honey.

Ingredients

You don't need much to make these tasty summer treats—only fruit, sugar, acid, and fruit pectin. For the best jellied product, three-fourths of the fruit should be just ripe and the remaining one-fourth slightly underripe.

The proper amount of sugar is important for achieving a good jell, so never reduce the recommended amount. Sugar contributes to the taste of the product and also acts as a preservative. You can substitute mild-flavored honey or light corn syrup for some of the sugar, but then adjustments are sometimes necessary in other ingredients. If you use another sweetener, be sure to check with your county Extension agent for advice.

Acid and pectin, contained in the fruit itself, are necessary for formation of jelly, as well. Fruit contains varying amounts of both, depending on the type of fruit and the degree of ripeness. Pectin is at its highest quality in just-ripe fruit, and acid content is higher in underripe fruit. Keep in mind that if the fruit is naturally low in acid, lemon juice may be added.

Some guesswork as to acidity level and doneness of the cooked mixture can be eliminated by using commercial pectin. A disadvantage to adding pectin is that the natural fruit flavor may be masked to some extent, since more sugar is needed with these products.

Equipment

Check to see that you have these items: an 8- to 10-quart heavy flat-bottomed kettle; a jelly bag or cheesecloth; a jelly, candy, or deep-fat thermometer; a timer; a jar filler or funnel; jelly jars with metal rings and new lids; a boiling-water bath canner with a rack and lid. Jars need to be sterilized, since they won't be processed in the water bath 15 minutes. To sterilize, place in boiling water 15 minutes.

Making Jelly

Here are general directions for making a cooked jelly, with and without using added pectin. Keep in mind that there are exceptions for products, such as uncooked freezer jellies. (Our step-by-step photographs offer directions on how to make freezer jelly.)

Be sure to follow recipe directions exactly, and never double the recipe. Each batch should start with no more than 4 to 6 cups juice.

Extracting Juice: Place fruit in a large kettle; add just enough water to grapes and berries to keep them from scorching and enough water to apples and other hard fruit to cover them. Crush soft fruit to start juices flowing. Place over high heat; bring to a boil, stirring constantly. Reduce heat, and cook berries and grapes 10 minutes or less and hard fruit 20 to 25 minutes or until soft. Be careful not to overcook.

Pour fruit into a damp jelly bag or four thicknesses of damp cheesecloth, and allow juice to drip into a bowl. Jelly is clearer when allowed to drip instead of being squeezed or pressed from the bag. If using a fruit press, strain juice again.

At this point, you may want to see if the juice contains enough acid and pectin to form a jell if you're using a recipe without added pectin. You can use the following tests.

—Test for Acid: Combine 1 teaspoon lemon juice, 3 tablespoons water, and ½ teaspoon sugar; mix well. Taste the lemon juice mixture and the fruit juice. If fruit juice is not as tart as lemon juice mixture, add 1 tablespoon lemon juice for each cup of juice.

—Test for Pectin: Combine ⅓ cup juice and ¼ cup sugar in a small saucepan. Heat slowly, stirring constantly, until sugar dissolves. Bring to a boil, and boil until mixture "sheets" from a spoon. Pour into a small bowl, and let cool. If cooled mixture jells, fruit juice will jell.

To make Grape-Burgundy Freezer Jelly (page 130), heat ripe grapes for 15 minutes; use a potato masher to crush fruit.

Strain crushed fruit through a jelly bag or cheesecloth, and discard pulp. Stir wine and sugar into grape juice; let stand 10 minutes.

Using a **jelmeter** is another method of finding a rough estimate of the amount of pectin in the juice and the amount of sugar needed. This instrument measures the rate juice flows through a graduated glass tube. Contact your local food editor, Extension agent, or other food preservation specialist for information on ordering a jelmeter.

After you know that the juice will jell, determine the cooking method by whether or not the jelly recipe uses commercial pectin. The powdered and liquid forms are not interchangeable. Use the following directions for cooking with and without pectin.

To Make Jelly With Powdered Pectin: Use manufacturer's directions for determining amount of sugar to use per cup of juice. Combine juice and powdered pectin in a large kettle; bring to a rapid boil. Add sugar all at once; stir and return to a boil. Boil 1 minute, stirring constantly. Remove mixture from heat, skim off foam, and pour into hot sterilized jars, leaving ¼-inch headspace. Cover jars at once with metal lids, and screw on bands. Process in a boiling-water bath 5 minutes.

To Make Jelly With Liquid Pectin: Combine juice and sugar in a large kettle. Bring to a rapid boil. Add liquid pectin, and return to a boil. Boil 1 minute, stirring constantly. Remove mixture from heat, skim off foam, and pour into hot sterilized jars, leaving ¼-inch headspace. Cover at once with metal lids, and screw on bands. Process in a boiling-water bath 5 minutes.

If the jelly—using either form of added pectin—is too soft after cooling 24 hours, use ¼ to ½ cup less juice in the next batch. If jelly is too firm, use ¼ to ½ cup more juice.

To Make Jelly Without Added Pectin: Combine ¾ cup sugar to each cup juice in a large kettle. Bring to a rapid boil, and continue to boil, stirring constantly, until thermometer reaches 220° F (or 8° above the boiling point of water).

To test for doneness, dip a cool metal spoon into boiling jelly and lift spoon out of steam so syrup runs off. When two drops form together and "sheet" off the spoon, the point of jelling has been reached.

For another doneness check, spoon a small amount of boiling jelly on a saucer, and place in the freezer a few minutes. If it jells, the mixture should be done. Remove the rest of the mixture from heat during the test.

When jelly is done, remove from heat, skim off foam, and pour the mixture into hot sterilized jars, leaving ¼-inch headspace. Cover at once with metal lids, and screw on bands. Process in a boiling-water bath 5 minutes.

If the jelly is too firm after cooling 24 hours, cook the next batch to a lower temperature. For firmer jelly, cook to a higher temperature.

Making Jams and Other Fruit Spreads

Fruit spreads other than jellies contain fruit that has been cut into chunks and require cooking to a slightly higher temperature. Here's how to do it.

Combine fruit and sugar in a large kettle. Cook over low heat, stirring occasionally, until sugar dissolves. Then bring to a rapid boil, stirring constantly. Boil until thermometer reaches 221° F (or 9° above the boiling point of water). Cook to a higher temperature for firmer product, to a lower temperature for softer product.

When the mixture is done, skim off foam, and pour into hot sterilized jars. Process in a boiling-water bath 5 minutes for honeys and butters, 10 minutes for jams and marmalades, and 15 minutes for preserves.

Commercial pectin can be used with fruit spreads other than butters and honeys. If you add pectin, follow the manufacturer's directions.

Processing Fruit Spreads

Processing in a boiling-water bath is now recommended for all jellies and fruit spreads except for freezer fruit spreads. Place jars on the rack in a water-bath canner with the water hot to gently boiling, and covering the tops of the jars by 1 to 2 inches. Cover and begin to count processing time when

Combine water and powdered fruit pectin in saucepan. Boil 1 minute, stirring constantly, and add to grape juice mixture.

After adding pectin mixture to grape juice mixture, stir constantly for 3 minutes. (A few crystals will remain in mixture.)

Pour jelly into hot sterilized jars, and screw on bands. Let stand at room temperature 24 hours, and store in the freezer.

water returns to a boil. If no time is given in the recipe, process 5 minutes.

Tips for Preserving Fruit

—Runny jelly or jam can be remade with the addition of lemon juice or commercial pectin. Call an Extension agent for proportions and directions.

—Jellied products should keep at least a year if they are stored in a cool, dark, dry place. But use as soon as possible, since flavor and quality begin to decrease within a few months.

—Mold on jellied products results from imperfect sealing. Discard whole jar if mold is extensive. If mold only slightly covers top, remove it and ½ inch of product underneath.

GRAPE-BURGUNDY FREEZER JELLY

3 pounds ripe Concord grapes
¼ cup Burgundy wine
5¾ cups sugar
¾ cup water
1 (1¾-ounce) package powdered pectin

Remove stems from grapes; wash and drain thoroughly. Place grapes in a Dutch oven, adding just enough water to keep grapes from scorching; cover and cook over low heat 15 minutes. Remove from heat; mash grapes thoroughly. Strain through a damp jelly bag or 4 layers of damp cheesecloth, reserving 2¾ cups juice. Discard pulp.

Stir wine and sugar into juice; let stand 10 minutes. Combine water and pectin in a small saucepan. Bring to a boil; boil 1 minute, stirring constantly. Stir pectin mixture into grape juice mixture; stir constantly for 3 minutes. (A few crystals will remain.)

Quickly pour jelly into hot sterilized jars or frozen food containers leaving ½-inch headspace; cover at once with metal lids, and screw on bands. Let stand at room temperature 24 hours. Store in freezer. To serve, remove from freezer, and allow to come to room temperature. Yield: 6 to 7 half pints.

PEACH-PLUM FREEZER JAM

¾ pound fresh plums
1 pound fresh peaches, peeled and chopped
2 tablespoons lemon juice
½ teaspoon ascorbic-citric powder
4 cups sugar
¾ cup water
1 (1¾-ounce) package powdered pectin

Remove pits from plums (do not peel), and grind fruit finely. Measure 1¼ cups peaches and 1 cup ground plums. Combine fruit, lemon juice, and ascorbic-citric powder in a large bowl.

Add sugar to fruit, mixing well; let stand 10 minutes. Combine water and pectin in a small saucepan. Bring to a boil, and boil 1 minute, stirring constantly. Pour over fruit mixture, and stir 3 minutes.

Pour quickly into hot sterilized jars or frozen-food containers, leaving ¼-inch headspace. Cover at once with metal lids, and screw on bands. Let stand at room temperature 24 hours, and store in freezer. To serve, remove from freezer, and allow to come to room temperature. Yield: about 6 half pints.

HONEYED PEACH PRESERVES

3 pounds peaches, peeled and quartered
4 cups sugar
1 cup honey
½ medium-size orange, quartered
½ teaspoon salt
¼ teaspoon almond extract

Combine peaches, sugar, and honey in Dutch oven. Cover and let stand for 45 minutes.

Position knife blade in food processor bowl. Add orange, and top with cover. Process until finely chopped. Measure chopped orange, and add an equal amount of water. Cook covered, about 10 minutes or until orange peel is soft. Set aside.

Bring peaches slowly to a boil, stirring frequently until sugar dissolves. Bring to a rapid boil, and cook 15 minutes, stirring constantly. Add orange mixture, return to a boil, and cook about 25 minutes or until mixture registers 221° on candy thermometer; stir mixture frequently. Remove from heat; stir in salt and almond extract. Skim off foam with a metal spoon.

Quickly pour preserves into hot jars, leaving ¼-inch headspace; cover at once with metal lids, and screw on bands. Process in boiling-water bath 15 minutes. Yield: 5 half pints.

BLUEBERRY JAM

4½ cups slightly crushed fresh blueberries
7 cups sugar
2 tablespoons lemon juice
2 (3-ounce) packages liquid pectin

Combine blueberries, sugar, and lemon juice in a large Dutch oven; bring to a rolling boil. Boil 1 minute, stirring constantly. Remove from heat, and immediately stir in pectin. Stir, and alternately skim off foam with a metal spoon for 5 minutes.

Quickly pour into hot sterilized jars, leaving ¼-inch headspace; cover at once with metal lids, and screw on bands. Process in boiling-water bath 10 minutes. Yield: 9 half pints.

PEAR BUTTER

18 to 20 medium-size, ripe pears (about 5 pounds), quartered and cored
1 cup water
4 cups sugar
1 teaspoon grated orange rind
⅓ cup orange juice
½ teaspoon ground nutmeg

Combine pears and water in a large, heavy Dutch oven. Cover and cook over medium-low heat 30 to 40 minutes or until pears are soft, stirring occasionally. Drain. Press pears through a sieve or food mill; measure 2 quarts of puree. Combine 2 quarts puree with remaining ingredients in a Dutch oven. Cook over medium heat, stirring frequently, for 15 minutes or until mixture thickens. Remove from heat, and skim off foam.

Pour hot pear mixture into hot sterilized jars, leaving ¼-inch headspace. Cover at once with metal lids, and screw on bands. Process in boiling-water bath 10 minutes. Yield: 5 pints.

STRAWBERRY-PINEAPPLE MARMALADE

1 medium-size fresh pineapple
1 teaspoon grated orange rind
2½ cups chopped orange sections
7 cups sugar
1½ quarts fresh strawberries, hulled

Remove leaves and stem end from pineapple. Peel pineapple, and trim out eyes; remove core. Chop pineapple, and measure 2½ cups.

Combine pineapple, orange rind, oranges, and sugar in a large Dutch oven. Bring to a boil; cook over medium-high heat about 15 minutes, stirring until sugar dissolves. Add strawberries, and continue to cook about 35 minutes or until mixture registers 221° on candy thermometer; stir frequently. Remove from heat, and skim off foam.

Quickly pour marmalade into hot sterilized jars, leaving ¼-inch headspace; cover jars at once with metal lids, and screw on bands. Process in boiling-water bath 10 minutes. Yield: 7 half pints.

This is the second in a four-part series on food preservation. See the May section for canning, the July section for pickling, and the August section for freezing fruits and vegetables.

Appetizers Say Cheese

For a zesty appetizer, welcome your guests with Double Cheese Twists or Parmesan Rounds. Both have rich cheese flavor yet are light and crispy, just right for cocktails or a snack.

Double Cheese Twists are rolled out and cut into strips before baking; then just give a couple of twists, and they're ready for the oven.

PARMESAN ROUNDS

¾ cup grated Parmesan cheese
½ cup all-purpose flour
⅛ teaspoon red pepper
¼ cup butter or margarine, softened
2 tablespoons cold water
2 tablespoons finely chopped walnuts
1 tablespoon parsley flakes

Combine Parmesan cheese, flour, and red pepper; cut in butter with a pastry blender until mixture resembles coarse meal. Sprinkle cold water (1 tablespoon at a time) evenly over surface; stir with a fork until dry ingredients are moistened. Shape dough into a 1½-inch-thick log, and set aside.

Combine walnuts and parsley in a shallow pan; roll log in mixture to coat evenly. Cut log with a serrated knife into ¼-inch slices; place on ungreased baking sheet. Bake at 375° for 12 minutes or until lightly browned; cool on a wire rack. Store crackers in a tightly covered container. (These crackers will freeze well.) Yield: 24 crackers.
Cynda A. Spoon,
Broken Arrow, Oklahoma.

DOUBLE CHEESE TWISTS

⅔ cup all-purpose flour
¼ cup yellow cornmeal
½ teaspoon salt
⅔ cup shredded Cheddar cheese
2 tablespoons shortening
3½ to 4 tablespoons cold water
¼ cup plus 2 tablespoons grated Parmesan cheese

Combine flour, cornmeal, and salt, mixing well; cut in Cheddar cheese and shortening with a pastry blender until mixture resembles coarse meal. Add water, stirring until dry ingredients are moistened. Shape dough into a ball.

Roll dough out between 2 sheets of waxed paper into a 12- x 10-inch rectangle. Cut dough into 3- x ½-inch strips. Twist each strip 2 or 3 times, and place on ungreased baking sheets, pressing down end of each strip to prevent curling. Bake at 425° for 5 to 7 minutes or until strips begin to brown. Remove and roll in Parmesan cheese. Cool. Yield: 6 dozen.
Melissa Walker Parks,
Maryville, Tennessee.

Serve These Satisfying Green Salads

Now's the time of year to accent meals with a cool, crisp green salad. The variety of salad greens and other ingredients now available sparked the imaginations of our readers to create these great salads. And they're not only inviting, but also quick to make.

Festive Pear-and-Spinach Salad is an attractive and light combination. Arrange pear halves atop a bed of fresh spinach and grapefruit sections; then sprinkle with crisp, crumbled bacon. Serve with Lime-Parsley Dressing for a real taste of summer.

You'll also want to try our Watercress-Tomato Salad, which has a graceful look. It uses some of summer's best produce and is covered with a simple tarragon vinegar-and-oil dressing.

Enjoy the contrast of pineapple tidbits and sharp Cheddar cheese in our Simply Good Salad. Fresh spinach leaves and iceberg lettuce provide the base for this tossed green salad, which is topped with a commercial buttermilk-style salad dressing.

SIMPLY GOOD SALAD

4 cups torn spinach
4 cups torn iceberg lettuce
2 cups (8 ounces) shredded sharp Cheddar cheese
2 hard-cooked eggs, chopped
2 small green onions, chopped
1 (20-ounce) can unsweetened pineapple tidbits, drained
Commercial buttermilk-style salad dressing

Combine all ingredients except salad dressing in a large salad bowl; toss gently. Serve with salad dressing. Yield: 10 to 12 servings. *Neal Johnson,*
Richmond, Virginia.

FESTIVE PEAR-AND-SPINACH SALAD

4 cups torn spinach
1 grapefruit, peeled and sectioned
½ cup thinly sliced green onion
1 (29-ounce) can pear halves
3 slices bacon, cooked and crumbled
Lime-Parsley Dressing

Combine spinach, grapefruit, and onion; toss well, and set aside.

Drain pears, reserving ¼ cup juice for dressing. Arrange pears on spinach mixture; sprinkle with bacon. Serve with Lime-Parsley Dressing. Yield: 6 servings.

Lime-Parsley Dressing:

¼ cup pear juice
¼ cup white wine vinegar
¼ cup vegetable oil
1 tablespoon chopped parsley
¼ teaspoon grated lime rind
1 tablespoon lime juice
½ teaspoon salt
Dash of red pepper

Combine all ingredients in a jar; cover tightly, and shake vigorously until well blended. Yield: ¾ cup.
Cathy Darling,
Grafton, West Virginia.

WATERCRESS-TOMATO SALAD

2 bunches fresh watercress, torn
3 tomatoes, peeled and cut into wedges
2 tablespoons tarragon vinegar
½ cup vegetable oil
½ teaspoon salt
½ teaspoon pepper

Arrange watercress and tomatoes on a platter. Combine remaining ingredients in a jar. Cover tightly, and shake vigorously until well blended. Pour dressing over salad, and serve immediately. Yield: 6 servings. *Rita Hastings, Edgewater, Maryland.*

COMBINATION SALAD BOWL

¾ cup mayonnaise
1 to 1½ tablespoons prepared horseradish
1 teaspoon cider vinegar
¼ teaspoon dry mustard
¼ teaspoon Worcestershire sauce
Dash of hot sauce
2 cups torn spinach
2 cups torn Bibb lettuce
2 cups torn red leaf lettuce
¾ cup diced Cheddar cheese
½ cup diced celery
½ cup diced purple onion
3 hard-cooked eggs, chopped

Combine mayonnaise, horseradish, vinegar, mustard, Worcestershire sauce, and hot sauce in a small bowl, and mix well. Refrigerate for several hours. Combine remaining ingredients in a large bowl.

Just before serving, pour the dressing over the salad; toss gently. Serve immediately. Yield: 8 to 10 servings.
Mrs. Robert M. Neumann, Bartlesville, Oklahoma.

Rediscover Yogurt

No doubt you've tried one of the many varieties of yogurt now available in the store. But have you cooked with it? Yogurt's creamy texture makes it an ideal substitute for its higher calorie counterpart, sour cream. And its tangy flavor lends a distinctive taste to food— from appetizers to desserts.

Use plain yogurt in our Curry Dip. It's made spicy with a sprinkling of curry powder, chili powder, ground ginger, and turmeric. Enjoy the flavorful dip with vegetable nibblers picked fresh from the garden.

When you want a main dish with a Mideastern flair, make Lamb Meatballs With Yogurt Sauce. Cucumber, garlic, and dillweed give a cool, pleasing lift to this sauce. If you have trouble finding pine nuts for the meatballs, you can substitute almonds.

Create a trendy dessert with Nectarines Royale. Honey and orange-flavored liqueur make up the marinade for the nectarines. Top the nectarine slices with an irresistible vanilla yogurt and whipped-cream mixture.

Yogurt is a marvel of food chemistry. Specific bacteria are added to milk, creating an acid condition that turns the milk into a thick, creamy curd. Milk solids are added to commercial yogurt, making it even more nutrition-packed with calcium, riboflavin, and protein.

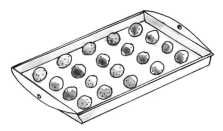

LAMB MEATBALLS WITH YOGURT SAUCE

1 (8-ounce) carton plain yogurt
½ cup diced cucumber
1 clove garlic, minced
¼ teaspoon dried whole dillweed
2 pounds ground lamb
1 cup soft breadcrumbs
⅓ cup chopped pine nuts
⅓ cup chopped parsley
1 egg, beaten
½ teaspoon salt
¼ teaspoon pepper

Combine yogurt, cucumber, garlic, and dillweed; mix well. Cover the mixture and refrigerate.

Combine remaining ingredients; mix well. Shape into 1-inch meatballs; place on greased broiler pan. Bake at 350° for 20 minutes. Serve meatballs warm with yogurt sauce. Yield: 8 servings.
Tammy Smith, Talbott, Tennessee.

CURRY DIP

1 (8-ounce) carton plain yogurt
½ cup mayonnaise
1½ teaspoons curry powder
¼ teaspoon chili powder
¼ teaspoon ground ginger
¼ teaspoon turmeric
⅛ teaspoon salt

Combine all ingredients; mix well. Serve dip with fresh vegetables. Yield: 1½ cups. *Mrs. D. R. Heun, Louisville, Kentucky.*

YOGURT-APRICOT PIE

2 eggs, beaten
1 cup sugar
2 tablespoons all-purpose flour
1 teaspoon almond extract
1 (8-ounce) carton plain yogurt
1 (6-ounce) package dried apricots, chopped
1 cup flaked coconut
1 unbaked 9-inch pastry shell
2 tablespoons flaked coconut, toasted

Combine eggs, sugar, flour, and almond extract, mixing well. Stir in yogurt, apricots, and 1 cup coconut. Pour mixture into pastry shell. Bake at 350° for 35 minutes or until filling is set. Sprinkle with toasted coconut. Yield: one 9-inch pie. *Ila Ellington, Greensboro, North Carolina.*

NECTARINES ROYALE

3 tablespoons honey
2 tablespoons Cointreau or other orange-flavored liqueur
6 medium nectarines, unpeeled and sliced
½ cup whipping cream
1 tablespoon powdered sugar
1 (8-ounce) carton vanilla yogurt

Combine honey and Cointreau; pour over nectarines. Chill.

Beat whipping cream until foamy; gradually add sugar, beating until stiff peaks form. Stir yogurt with whisk until smooth; fold into whipped cream. Top each serving of nectarines with a dollop of yogurt mixture. Yield: 8 servings.
Pat Boschen, Ashland, Virginia.

Right: *Familiar cream puffs take on new fillings in these recipes: Front to back, Luncheon Shrimp Puffs, Appetizer Chicken Puffs, and Giant Fruit Puff (page 72).*

Page 134: *Pretty garnishes dress these foods for a pretty tea: (from front) Cucumber Pinwheel Sandwiches, Chicken-Salad Finger Sandwiches, Almond Tea Tarts, and Snow-Capped Madeleines (recipes on pages 119 and 120).*

Spectacular Sandwich Spreads

If you start with a few flavorful ingredients and quickly stir them together, you'll have the fixings to turn two pieces of bread into a feast. Creating your own sandwich spread is easy because the ingredients, including olives, eggs, vegetables, fruits, cheese, and mayonnaise, are often on hand.

But don't be afraid to experiment, either. Open a small can of shrimp for a tasty seafood sandwich. Or try adding spicy Italian salad dressing mix to cream cheese and chopped pimiento.

Most of these spreads can be made ahead and refrigerated. Just keep plenty of your favorite bread on hand, and assemble the sandwiches as needed.

SHRIMP SPREAD

1 (4¼-ounce) can shrimp, drained, rinsed, and chopped
½ cup finely chopped celery
1 green onion with tops, finely chopped
12 pimiento-stuffed olives, chopped
1 hard-cooked egg, chopped
1 teaspoon lemon juice
Dash of lemon-pepper seasoning
¼ cup plus 1 tablespoon mayonnaise

Combine all ingredients; mix well. Serve on bread. Yield: 1½ cups.
Maureen Dolan,
Dallas, Texas.

VEGETABLE SANDWICH SPREAD

1½ teaspoons unflavored gelatin
2 tablespoons cold water
2 tablespoons boiling water
1 tomato, peeled and finely chopped
¾ cup finely chopped cucumber
½ cup finely chopped celery
⅓ cup finely chopped green pepper
⅓ cup finely chopped onion
½ cup plus 2 tablespoons mayonnaise
½ teaspoon salt

Soften unflavored gelatin in cold water; add boiling water, stirring until gelatin dissolves. Cool.

Drain vegetables on paper towels and set aside.

Combine mayonnaise and salt; fold in gelatin mixture. Gently stir in vegetables. Chill before serving on bread. Yield: 2 cups. *Mrs. H. W. Carmichael,*
Dyersburg, Tennessee.

ITALIAN SPREAD

1 (8-ounce) package soft cream cheese
1 (4-ounce) jar sliced pimientos, chopped
½ cup mayonnaise
⅓ cup parsley flakes
2½ teaspoons Italian salad dressing mix

Combine all ingredients, mixing well. Chill mixture before serving on bread. Yield: 2 cups. *Susie M. E. Dent,*
Saltillo, Mississippi.

FRUIT SPREAD

1 (8-ounce) package cream cheese, softened
1 tablespoon milk
2 teaspoons lemon juice
1 cup finely chopped apple
½ cup chopped pitted dates

Combine cream cheese, milk, and lemon juice; beat until smooth. Stir in fruit. Serve on bread. Yield: 1¾ cups.
Sharon Bramlett,
Clyde, North Carolina.

Savvy Ways With Summer Squash

Get ready for the annual crop of summer squash. Whether you grow your own or buy it at a farmers' market, you'll find tender yellow crookneck, zucchini, and pattypan squash abundantly available.

Mild-flavored summer squash lends itself to a variety of preparation methods, and each dish takes on character all its own, depending on how it's seasoned. Enjoy the convenience of this popular vegetable in some of our readers' favorite recipes.

Make the most of two types of summer squash in South-of-the-Border Zucchini. Yellow crookneck and zucchini team up with corn, tomato, and green pepper in this garden combo. The trio of colors will brighten any meal.

Yellow Squash Casserole gets its rich taste from the addition of cream of shrimp soup and water chestnuts. Savor the home-style goodness of this dish with your favorite pot roast.

You'll welcome the fresh-picked taste of Stuffed Pattypan Squash. It's filled with mushrooms, green onions, and rice, and seasoned with chicken broth.

The scalloped edge of this squash adds a decorative flair.

Summer squash is not only delicious, but nutritious and inexpensive as well. It's high in vitamin A content, especially the yellow and green varieties, and there's little waste; the skin, flesh, and seeds are all edible. When buying squash, let tenderness be your guide. Avoid oversized summer squash and those with a hard rind. And when cooking, remember that summer squash has a high water content. Use little cooking liquid to help retain the most nutrients and flavor.

SOUTH-OF-THE-BORDER ZUCCHINI

1 medium onion, diced
2 small green peppers, diced
¼ cup olive oil
2 cups fresh corn, cut from cob
2 zucchini, thinly sliced
2 yellow squash, thinly sliced
1 tomato, chopped
½ cup water
½ teaspoon salt
¼ teaspoon pepper

Sauté onion and green pepper in oil in a Dutch oven 2 to 3 minutes. Add remaining ingredients, and bring to a boil. Cover, reduce heat, and simmer 8 to 10 minutes or until vegetables are tender. Yield: 8 servings.
Shelley Bennett,
Amarillo, Texas.

YELLOW SQUASH CASSEROLE

2 pounds yellow squash, cut into ½-inch cubes
1 large onion, chopped
2 tablespoons butter or margarine, melted
1 (10¾-ounce) can cream of shrimp soup, undiluted
1 (8-ounce) can water chestnuts, drained
¾ teaspoon salt
¼ teaspoon pepper
1 cup soft breadcrumbs
2 tablespoons butter or margarine, melted

Sauté squash and onion in 2 tablespoons butter in a large skillet 5 minutes or until tender. Stir in soup, water chestnuts, salt, and pepper; pour mixture into a lightly greased 2-quart shallow baking dish.

Combine breadcrumbs and 2 tablespoons butter; mix well. Sprinkle over top of casserole; bake at 350° for 30 minutes. Yield: 6 to 8 servings.
Mrs. Jack Land,
Live Oak, Florida.

SUMMER SQUASH SOUP

1 medium onion, chopped
¼ cup butter or margarine, melted
6 medium-size yellow squash, sliced
2 cups chicken broth
½ teaspoon poultry seasoning
¼ teaspoon salt
¼ teaspoon pepper
1 cup half-and-half
Chopped chives (optional)

Sauté onion in butter in a large skillet until tender. Add squash; cover and simmer 5 minutes. Add chicken broth and seasonings; cover and simmer an additional 15 minutes.

Place squash mixture in container of an electric blender; process until smooth. Return mixture to skillet. Stir in half-and-half; cook just until thoroughly heated. (Do not boil.) Garnish with chives, if desired. Serve hot or cold. Yield: 6 cups.

Mrs. James S. Stanton,
Richmond, Virginia.

STUFFED PATTYPAN SQUASH

4 medium pattypan squash
1 cup chopped fresh mushrooms
¼ cup chopped green onion
¼ cup butter or margarine, melted
1½ cups cooked rice
2 tablespoons chicken broth
¼ teaspoon pepper
1 tablespoon butter or margarine
Paprika

Remove a slice from stem end of squash. Scoop out pulp, leaving a ¼-inch shell; repeat procedure for remaining squash. Chop pulp.

Sauté mushrooms, green onions, and squash pulp in ¼ cup butter in a large skillet for 8 minutes. Add rice, chicken broth, and pepper; mix well.

Place squash shells in an 8-inch square baking dish; spoon rice mixture into shells. Dot with remaining butter. Pour water ½ inch deep into dish; cover, and bake at 350° for 50 minutes or until tender. Sprinkle with paprika. Yield: 4 servings. *Kay Shaplow,*
Baltimore, Maryland.

Tip: Use a stiff vegetable brush to scrub vegetables rather than peel them. Peeling is not necessary for many vegetables and causes a loss of vitamins found in and just under the skin.

Relishes
To Rave About

Let chilled relishes replace rich, heavy sauces on your menus. Our tangy meat and seafood accompaniments are easy to make and add a welcome flair to meals. Unlike relishes that you can and process, these recipes yield a smaller amount and can be stored in the refrigerator up to three or four days.

Hot Mexican Salsa combines red, ripe tomatoes with green onions, jalapeño peppers, and cumin for a snappy taste. Simply place all ingredients in a food processor bowl, and pulse until chunky. And for a savvy new way with pork, try Peach Relish. It's spicy and a little bit tart, a tempting combination served with cold sliced ham.

When the fisherman at your house brings in the catch, fry it up, and serve with our Sauerkraut Relish instead of coleslaw. This calico delight is dotted with cucumber, carrot, green onions, celery, and pimientos. It's also good when served with assorted cold cuts.

For a tasty change of pace, spoon Colorful Beet Relish alongside cold, sliced roast beef. This bright-pink relish is spiked with horseradish and sour cream, a classic condiment duo for beef.

HOT MEXICAN SALSA

3 large tomatoes, coarsely chopped
3 canned or fresh jalapeño peppers
3 tablespoons chopped green onions with tops
1 tablespoon chopped fresh parsley
1 clove garlic, crushed
1½ tablespoons cider vinegar
½ teaspoon salt
¼ teaspoon ground cumin
⅛ teaspoon sugar

Position knife blade in food processor bowl; add all ingredients. Top with cover; pulse 5 to 6 times or until mixture is chunky. Cover and chill. Serve with beef patties. Yield: 3 cups.

Patricia Pashby,
Memphis, Tennessee.

CORN RELISH

1 (16-ounce) can whole kernel corn
1½ cups sweet pickle relish
2 teaspoons sugar
2 teaspoons celery seeds
3 tablespoons diced pimiento

Drain corn, reserving ¼ cup liquid. Set corn aside.

Combine liquid, pickle relish, sugar, and celery seeds in a medium saucepan; bring to a boil. Boil 1 minute. Add corn and pimiento; simmer 10 minutes, stirring occasionally. Let cool, and chill. Serve with poultry. Yield: 2⅔ cups.

Mrs. Earl Faulkenberry,
Lancaster, South Carolina.

SAUERKRAUT RELISH

1 (16-ounce) jar sauerkraut, drained and chopped
1 small cucumber, unpeeled and finely shredded
1 small carrot, scraped and finely shredded
¼ cup sugar
¼ cup diced green onions with tops
2 tablespoons diced celery
2 tablespoons diced green pepper
2 tablespoons vinegar
2 tablespoons vegetable oil
1 tablespoon chopped pimiento
½ teaspoon caraway seeds
⅛ teaspoon paprika
⅛ teaspoon white pepper

Combine all ingredients in a large bowl; mix well. Cover and chill. Serve with fish or cold cuts. Yield: 3½ cups.

Dorothy Krell,
Rosenberg, Texas.

COLORFUL BEET RELISH

1 (8-ounce) carton commercial sour cream
3 tablespoons prepared horseradish
2 tablespoons red wine vinegar
2 teaspoons sugar
½ teaspoon dry mustard
¼ teaspoon salt
¼ teaspoon white pepper
1 (16-ounce) can cut beets, drained and diced

Combine all ingredients except beets, mixing well. Fold in beets. Cover and chill. Serve with roast beef. Yield: 2 cups. *Eileen Jenkins,*
Lenoir, North Carolina.

PEACH RELISH

1 (29-ounce) can peach halves, drained and coarsely chopped
½ cup cider vinegar
⅓ cup golden raisins
⅓ cup firmly packed brown sugar
⅓ cup honey
⅛ teaspoon ground mace
6 whole cloves
1 (3-inch) stick cinnamon, broken

Combine peaches, vinegar, raisins, brown sugar, honey, and mace in a saucepan. Tie cloves and cinnamon in a cheesecloth bag; add to peach mixture.

Bring to a boil; reduce heat, and simmer 30 minutes, stirring occasionally. Remove spice bag. Cover relish, and chill. Serve with ham. Yield: 2 cups.

Mildred Sherrer,
Bay City, Texas.

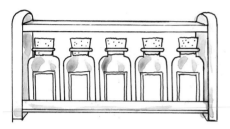

COOKING LIGHT®

Season Peas And Beans Lightly

If you're a true Southerner, you've probably eaten your share of fresh green beans, black-eyed peas, and limas. Remember how your grandmother cooked them for a long time until the beans were tender and soaked up a lot of good bacon flavor?

Unfortunately, there's a problem with this traditional Southern way of cooking. Valuable vitamins and minerals are lost when vegetables are overcooked. What's more, the addition of bacon or ham hock increases the calorie and salt content of an otherwise low-calorie, low-sodium vegetable.

In our test kitchens, we tried our hand at capturing that old-fashioned flavor without extra, unwanted calories. For instance, we used some of the very lean packaged ham now on the market instead of fatty ham hock to season Southern Peas and Ham. We found that a little chopped onion and freshly ground pepper provide additional flavor to the vegetables.

You may not think a slice of bacon added to peas would make much difference in calories. But the next time you cook bacon, notice how much grease accumulates in the skillet. Each tablespoon of the grease contains around 100 calories. When bacon or any other fatty meat is added to vegetables during cooking, the grease coats the vegetables and raises the calorie count.

Instead of seasoning with bacon grease or ham hock, we tried beef-flavored bouillon cubes in Seasoned Black-Eyed Peas and in Peas-and-Corn Medley. Each bouillon cube provides only 6 calories, but adds a lot of flavor to cooked vegetables. It's important to remember that since bouillon cubes are quite salty, you don't need to add any more salt to the vegetables.

Margie Livengood of Georgetown, Kentucky, has learned the secret of using herbs in place of salt when cooking vegetables. Basil and pepper are her choices for Green Beans With Tomatoes. You might also experiment with bay leaves, dill, oregano, savory, or thyme when preparing green beans. Marjoram, sage, and savory are possibilities for limas.

For a different twist, try fresh green beans and lima beans for cold summer salads. Lima Bean-Tomato Salad and Marinated Bean Salad are both on the recommended list for dieters since they're made without sugar or oil, as are many marinated salads.

Marinated Bean Salad calls for white grape juice and vinegar mixed with seasonings, while Italian reduced-calorie salad dressing serves as the marinade in our Lima Bean-Tomato Salad.

LIMA BEAN-TOMATO SALAD

2 cups shelled fresh lima beans
8 medium tomatoes
1 tablespoon chopped fresh parsley
1 small onion, grated
¼ cup finely chopped celery
¼ teaspoon freshly ground pepper
½ cup Italian reduced-calorie salad dressing

Cook lima beans, covered, in boiling water to cover 15 to 20 minutes or until tender; drain and set aside to cool.

Cut off top of each tomato; scoop out pulp, leaving shells intact. Invert shells on paper towels to drain; chop pulp. Combine tomato pulp, lima beans, and remaining ingredients; toss gently. Fill tomato shells with bean mixture, and chill. Yield: 8 servings (about 81 calories per serving).

LIMA BEANS CREOLE

3½ cups shelled fresh lima beans
1 chicken-flavored bouillon cube
Vegetable cooking spray
¼ cup finely chopped onion
2 tablespoons chopped green pepper
1 (16-ounce) can whole tomatoes, undrained
⅛ teaspoon pepper

Place lima beans and bouillon cube in a large saucepan. Add boiling water to cover, and cook, covered, 20 minutes or until tender; drain. Return lima beans to saucepan; set aside.

Coat a small skillet with cooking spray; place over medium heat until hot. Add onion and green pepper; sauté until tender. Add sautéed vegetables, tomatoes, and pepper to lima beans; cover and simmer 15 to 20 minutes. Yield: 8 servings (about 100 calories per serving).

MARINATED BEAN SALAD

3 cups cut fresh green beans
1 medium-size green or red pepper, thinly sliced
½ cup chopped green onions
2 medium tomatoes, unpeeled and sliced into wedges
½ cup unsweetened white grape juice
½ cup cider vinegar
½ teaspoon pepper
¼ teaspoon dry mustard
¼ teaspoon dried whole basil

Cook green beans, covered, in a small amount of boiling water 10 to 12 minutes or until crisp-tender. Drain beans, and set aside to cool.

Combine beans, green pepper, green onions, and tomatoes in a large shallow container. Combine remaining ingredients in a jar; cover tightly, and shake vigorously. Pour over bean mixture; cover and chill salad overnight. Yield: 12 servings (about 23 calories per ½-cup serving).

GREEN BEANS WITH TOMATOES

1 pound fresh green beans
1 small onion, chopped
½ cup chopped celery
¼ cup chopped green pepper
½ teaspoon dried whole basil
¼ teaspoon pepper
2 cups coarsely chopped tomatoes

Wash beans; trim ends, and remove strings. Cut beans into 1½-inch pieces. Cook beans, onion, celery, green pepper, basil, and pepper in a small amount of boiling water 10 to 12 minutes or until tender. Add tomatoes, and cook until thoroughly heated. Yield: 8 servings (about 32 calories per ½-cup serving). *Margie Livengood, Georgetown, Kentucky.*

PEAS-AND-CORN MEDLEY

2 cups shelled purple-hull peas
1 cup fresh corn cut from cob
⅓ cup chopped onion
⅓ cup chopped celery
1 beef-flavored bouillon cube
¼ teaspoon dried whole savory
¼ teaspoon freshly ground pepper
2 cups water
Celery leaves (optional)

Combine vegetables, bouillon cube, savory, pepper, and water in a medium saucepan; bring to a boil. Cover, reduce heat, and cook 30 to 35 minutes or until peas are tender. To serve, garnish vegetable dish with celery leaves, if desired. Yield: 7 servings (about 77 calories per ½-cup serving).

SEASONED BLACK-EYED PEAS

4 cups shelled fresh black-eyed peas
2 cups water
1 medium onion, chopped
2 beef-flavored bouillon cubes
½ teaspoon ground red pepper
1 bay leaf
Pimiento strips (optional)

Combine all ingredients except pimiento in saucepan. Bring to a boil; cover, reduce heat, and simmer 30 minutes or until tender. Add water, if necessary. Remove bay leaf before serving. Garnish with pimiento, if desired. Yield: 8 servings (about 99 calories per ½-cup serving).

SOUTHERN PEAS AND HAM

3 cups shelled fresh purple-hull peas or
**   crowder peas**
2 cups water
2 ounces cubed cooked lean ham (⅓ cup)
½ cup chopped onion
½ teaspoon freshly ground pepper
¼ teaspoon salt

Combine all ingredients in a saucepan; bring to a boil. Cover, reduce heat, and simmer 30 to 45 minutes or until peas are tender. Yield: 7 servings (about 93 calories per ½-cup serving).

Try Foil For Cooking

You're probably familiar with using aluminum foil in grilling or barbecuing, but there's no need to fire up the grill to cook these tasty recipes; they're cooked in the oven.

William Biggs of Stevensville, Maryland, uses this method to prepare Red Snapper in Wine Sauce, which is as elegant as it is easy.

Cooking in foil is an excellent way of preparing wild game because this method keeps the meat from drying out during the cooking process.

You'll notice that there are two sets of instructions for folding the foil packets. The one used most often is the drugstore wrap. It's used for large pieces of meat and all-around baking. The other type of wrap is a pyramid wrap that folds together in a triangle shape; it's used for dishes that consist of many small pieces or contain a lot of liquid. Both are easier to handle with a cookie sheet under them.

QUAIL WITH MUSHROOMS

6 slices bacon
6 quail, dressed
½ teaspoon salt
⅛ teaspoon pepper
½ pound mushroom caps
1 bunch green onions with tops, chopped
3 tablespoons butter or margarine, melted
1 (12-ounce) jar orange marmalade
2 tablespoons prepared mustard
¼ to ½ teaspoon ground ginger

Wrap a slice of bacon around each quail; sprinkle with salt and pepper. Place quail in center of a large sheet of heavy-duty aluminum foil; set aside.

Sauté mushroom caps and green onions in butter in a large skillet until tender; pour over quail. Using pyramid-wrap method, bring 4 corners of foil together in a triangle shape; fold open edges together in loosely locked folds, allowing for heat circulation and expansion. Place packet on a baking sheet, and bake at 325° for 1 hour and 20 minutes to 1½ hours. Open foil, and broil 6 inches from heat until browned.

Combine orange marmalade, mustard, and ginger; mix well. Serve with quail. Yield: 6 servings.

Marlene Gaither,
Albertville, Alabama.

RED SNAPPER IN WINE SAUCE

2 (1½-pound) dressed red snappers
Juice of 1 lemon
2 tablespoons butter or margarine, melted
2 tablespoons grated onion
1 tablespoon chopped fresh parsley
1 tablespoon Worcestershire sauce
¼ teaspoon salt
¼ teaspoon pepper
½ cup Chablis or other dry white wine
Additional chopped parsley (optional)
Lemon slices (optional)

Place fish in center of a large sheet of heavy-duty aluminum foil; set aside.

Combine lemon juice, butter, onion, parsley, Worcestershire sauce, salt, and

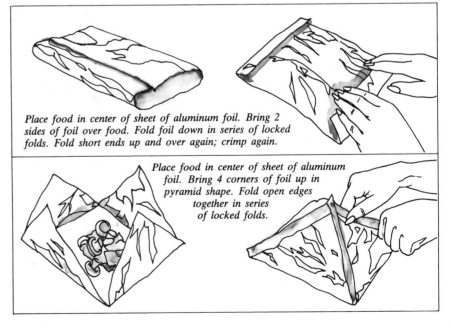

Place food in center of sheet of aluminum foil. Bring 2 sides of foil over food. Fold foil down in series of locked folds. Fold short ends up and over again; crimp again.

Place food in center of sheet of aluminum foil. Bring 4 corners of foil up in pyramid shape. Fold open edges together in series of locked folds.

pepper; stir well. Using pyramid-wrap method, bring 4 corners of foil together in a triangle shape; pour sauce mixture over fish. Fold open edges together in a series of locked folds, allowing for heat circulation and expansion. Place packet on a baking sheet; bake at 425° for 20 minutes. Open foil slightly, and slowly pour wine over fish. Reseal, and bake an additional 15 minutes. Open foil and bake, uncovered, for 10 minutes or until fish flakes easily when tested with a fork. Garnish with parsley and lemon slices, if desired. Yield: 4 servings.

William E. Biggs,
Stevensville, Maryland.

GINGER CARROTS

1 pound carrots, scraped and sliced ¼ inch thick
1½ tablespoons butter or margarine
1½ teaspoons powdered ginger

Place carrots in center of a large sheet of heavy-duty aluminum foil. Dot with butter, and sprinkle with ginger.

Using drugstore-wrap method, bring 2 sides of foil up over carrots; fold down in a series of locked folds, allowing space for heat circulation and expansion. Fold short ends up and over again; crimp to seal. Place packet on a baking sheet, and bake at 350° for 45 to 50 minutes or until carrots are tender. Yield: 4 servings.

Mrs. H. Maxcy Smith,
St. Petersburg, Florida.

SWEET-HOT ONIONS

3 large onions, cut into ¼-inch slices
2 tablespoons honey
½ teaspoon dry mustard
½ teaspoon salt
½ teaspoon pepper
½ teaspoon paprika

Place onion in center of a large sheet of heavy-duty aluminum foil; set aside.

Combine honey and mustard; drizzle over onion. Sprinkle onion with remaining ingredients. Using the drugstore-wrap method, bring 2 sides of foil up over onion; fold down in a series of locked folds, allowing space for heat circulation and expansion. Fold short ends up and over again; crimp to seal. Place packet on a baking sheet, and bake at 350° for 40 minutes or until tender. Yield: 6 servings.

Ann Elsie Schmetzer,
Madisonville, Kentucky.

Try A New Way With Coleslaw

Nothing is better than cool, crisp coleslaw for warm-weather menus. You can rely on it to add pizzazz to hot or cold main dishes. Everyone seems to have a favorite coleslaw recipe, but our readers have offered so many flavorful variations, you may change your mind.

Fruited Coleslaw combines two kinds of cabbage with toasted walnuts and sliced apples. It is tossed with a buttermilk salad dressing. Serve it with any hot or spicy barbecued meat.

For an exotic change of pace, try Curried Coleslaw. This spicy salad is embellished with a sprinkling of raisins and crumbled bacon. You're sure to enjoy it with sliced chicken or turkey.

Cucumbers, peanuts, and prepared horseradish make Peanut Slaw an unusual yet tasty treat. With fried fish, it's sure to be a winner.

FRESH CABBAGE SLAW

4 cups shredded cabbage
1 (8-ounce) can crushed pineapple, drained
½ cup mayonnaise
1 tablespoon sugar
1 teaspoon cider vinegar
½ teaspoon prepared horseradish
½ teaspoon salt
¼ teaspoon white pepper

Combine cabbage and pineapple in a large bowl. Combine remaining ingredients; mix well. Add to cabbage mixture; toss well. Cover and refrigerate. Yield: 6 servings.   *Pearl A. Johnson, Hobson, Texas.*

CURRIED COLESLAW

3½ cups shredded cabbage
¼ cup raisins
2 tablespoons diced onion
½ cup mayonnaise
1 tablespoon cider vinegar
1 teaspoon sugar
½ teaspoon curry powder
4 slices bacon, cooked and crumbled

Combine cabbage, raisins, and onion in a large bowl; set aside.

Combine mayonnaise, vinegar, sugar, and curry, mixing well. Spoon over cabbage mixture; toss well. Cover and chill. Stir in bacon just before serving. Yield: 4 to 6 servings. *Mrs. J. David Stearns, Mobile, Alabama.*

PEANUT SLAW

3½ cups shredded cabbage
¾ cup chopped celery
½ cup peeled and chopped cucumber
½ cup chopped cocktail peanuts
3 tablespoons diced onion
½ cup mayonnaise
½ cup commercial sour cream
¾ teaspoon prepared horseradish
¼ teaspoon prepared mustard
Dash of salt and pepper

Combine cabbage, celery, cucumber, peanuts, and onion in a large bowl. Set mixture aside.

Combine remaining ingredients; mix well. Add to cabbage mixture; toss well. Cover and chill. Yield: 6 servings.

Mrs. R. L. Lyerly,
Mocksville, North Carolina.

HOT-AND-SOUR CHINESE SLAW

4 cups shredded cabbage
¾ cup shredded carrot
¼ cup vegetable oil
¼ cup cider vinegar
3 tablespoons sugar
¼ teaspoon ground ginger
⅛ teaspoon red pepper

Combine cabbage and carrot in a large bowl; set aside.

Combine oil and vinegar in a small saucepan; stir in remaining ingredients. Cook over low heat, stirring constantly, until sugar dissolves. Immediately pour hot mixture over vegetables; toss well. Chill overnight. Yield: 4 to 6 servings.

Lynda Cable,
Hixson, Tennessee.

FRUITED COLESLAW

1 (1-ounce) package buttermilk-style salad dressing mix
½ medium-size green cabbage, shredded
1 cup shredded red cabbage
1 cup coarsely chopped walnuts, toasted
2 red apples, unpeeled and sliced

Prepare salad dressing mix according to the package directions. Refrigerate for 30 minutes.

Combine remaining ingredients in a large bowl. Add 1 to 1½ cups salad dressing; toss well. (Reserve remaining salad dressing for other uses.) Cover and chill. Yield: 10 servings.

Cathy Darling,
Grafton, West Virginia.

Fry A Scoop
Of Ice Cream

With a few scoops of ice cream and some cookie crumbs, you can fry up one of the most spectacular desserts yet. Hot and crisp on the outside, and cool and creamy inside, the fried ice cream variations below are easy to make and even allow you to do most of the preparation the day before. Our recipes call for vanilla ice cream, but you can substitute your favorite flavor.

To make Coconut Fried Ice Cream, Patsy Gowen of Amherst, Virginia, dips scoops of ice cream in beaten eggs, then dredges them in a mixture of coconut cookie crumbs and flaked coconut. She freezes the ice cream balls and dips them again for an extra thick coating. Once the ice cream and the crust are frozen firm, the ice cream is fried for 30 seconds. That's just long enough to crisp the cookie coating and leave the ice cream slightly soft, but still cool on the inside.

Carrie Bartlett of Gallatin, Tennessee, says she serves her Fried Ice Cream Puffs for company or at special family meals. It's a little different from most fried ice cream recipes; Carrie fills baked cream puffs with vanilla ice cream, freezes them, and fries just before serving. To make them for your guests, follow our easy step-by-step instructions pictured here. To serve, top each puff with raspberry syrup.

A scoop of ice cream is encased in each golden cream puff for Fried Ice Cream Puffs. After frying frozen cream puffs, top with raspberry syrup, and serve immediately.

Step 1: For Fried Ice Cream Puffs, cook water, butter, and flour into a batter ball. Remove from heat, and beat in eggs.

Step 2: Drop cream puff batter by one-third cupfuls onto baking sheets. Bake pastry at 350° until puffed and golden.

Step 3: After cooling the cream puffs, slice the top from each one. Remove and discard the doughy center from each puff.

FRIED ICE CREAM PUFFS

1 cup water
½ cup butter or margarine
1½ cups all-purpose flour
5 eggs
3⅓ cups vanilla ice cream
Vegetable oil
Commercial raspberry or other
  fruit-flavored syrup

Combine water and butter in a medium saucepan; bring mixture to a boil. Reduce heat to low and add flour, stirring vigorously until mixture leaves sides of pan and forms a smooth ball. Remove saucepan from the heat, and allow mixture to cool slightly.

Add eggs, one at a time, beating with a wooden spoon after each addition; beat until batter is smooth.

Drop batter by scant one-third cupfuls about 3 inches apart on lightly greased baking sheets. Bake at 350° for 40 minutes or until golden brown and puffed. Cool puffs on wire racks away from drafts.

Cut off top of each puff; pull out and discard soft dough inside. Fill bottom halves with vanilla ice cream, and cover with top halves. Wrap in aluminum foil and freeze.

Fry ice cream puffs in deep hot oil (350°) for 30 to 40 seconds or until golden brown. Drain on paper towels, and serve immediately with commercial raspberry syrup. Yield: about 10 servings.

Carrie B. Bartlett,
Gallatin, Tennessee.

COCONUT FRIED ICE CREAM

1 quart vanilla ice cream
2 eggs, beaten
½ teaspoon vanilla extract
4 cups coconut-flavored cookie crumbs
½ cup flaked coconut

Place 8 scoops of ice cream on a cookie sheet; freeze at least 1 hour or until firm.

Combine eggs and vanilla; mix well, and divide in half. Cover half of egg mixture, and chill. Combine cookie crumbs and coconut; divide mixture in half. Set half of crumb mixture aside.

Dip each ice cream ball in egg mixture, and dredge in crumb mixture. Place on a cookie sheet, and freeze at least 1 hour or until firm. Remove from freezer; dip in remaining egg mixture, and dredge in remaining crumb mixture. Return to cookie sheet; cover and freeze several hours or until firm. Fry ice cream balls in deep hot oil (375°) for 30 seconds or until golden brown. Drain on paper towels, and serve immediately. Yield: 8 servings.   *Patsy Gowen,*
Amherst, Virginia.

FRENCH-FRIED ICE CREAM

1 quart vanilla ice cream
1 (3-ounce) package slivered almonds,
  finely ground
2 eggs, beaten
¾ cup graham cracker crumbs
Cinnamon-Fudge Sauce

Place 10 scoops ice cream on a cookie sheet; freeze ice cream balls at least 1 hour or until firm.

Roll each ice cream ball in ground almonds, coating well. Dip in beaten eggs, and dredge in graham cracker crumbs until thoroughly coated. Place on a cookie sheet; then cover and freeze for several hours.

Fry ice cream balls in deep hot oil (375°) for 20 to 30 seconds or until golden brown. Drain on paper towels, and serve immediately with Cinnamon-Fudge Sauce. Yield: 10 servings.

Cinnamon-Fudge Sauce:

2 (1-ounce) squares unsweetened chocolate
1 tablespoon butter or margarine
⅓ cup boiling water
1 cup sugar
¼ teaspoon ground cinnamon
1 tablespoon corn syrup
1 teaspoon vanilla extract

Combine chocolate, butter, and water in a heavy saucepan; cook over low heat until chocolate melts, stirring constantly. Add sugar, cinnamon, and corn syrup; mix well. Bring mixture to a boil; reduce heat and simmer, uncovered, 7 minutes without stirring. Remove from heat, and stir in vanilla. Allow to cool before serving. Yield: 1¼ cups.

Bake The Best Beans

When it comes to making baked beans, everybody has a recipe. Some like them sweet and spicy, while others prefer them tart. But Rhonda Cox of Shawnee, Oklahoma, combines both tastes in her Easy Baked Beans.

EASY BAKED BEANS

1 (28-ounce) can pork and beans
1 cup firmly packed brown sugar
½ cup chopped celery
½ cup chopped onion
1 tablespoon prepared mustard
2 slices bacon

Combine all ingredients except bacon; stir well. Spoon mixture into a lightly greased 10- x 6- x 2-inch baking dish. Arrange bacon slices on top. Bake, uncovered, at 350° for 1 hour. Yield: 6 servings.   *Rhonda Cox,*
Shawnee, Oklahoma.

Step 4: Fill each pastry puff with vanilla ice cream, and replace the pastry top. Wrap each puff in aluminum foil and freeze.

Step 5: Just before serving, remove puffs from foil, and deep-fry in hot oil for 30 seconds or until they're golden brown.

BEEFY BAKED BEANS

1 pound ground beef
1 small green pepper, chopped
½ cup chopped onion
1 (16-ounce) can pork and beans
½ cup catsup
2 tablespoons brown sugar
2 tablespoons vinegar
2½ teaspoons chili powder
½ teaspoon salt
½ teaspoon pepper

Combine ground beef, green pepper, and onion in a large skillet; cook until meat is browned, stirring to crumble. Drain. Stir in remaining ingredients. Spoon into a lightly greased 10- x 6- x 2-inch baking dish. Bake, uncovered, at 350° for about 30 minutes. Yield: 4 to 6 servings.
Brenda P. Kidd,
Wingina, Virginia.

BEANS AND FRANKS

2 (16-ounce) cans pork and beans
1 (16-ounce) package frankfurters, cut
  into ½-inch pieces
1 medium onion, chopped
½ cup catsup
½ cup light corn syrup
2 tablespoons brown sugar

Combine all ingredients; stir well. Spoon mixture into a lightly greased 8-inch square baking dish. Bake, uncovered, at 350° for 1 hour. Yield: 6 to 8 servings.
Vera Anderson,
Moultrie, Georgia.

PICNIC BAKED BEANS

1 (31-ounce) can pork and beans
1 cup chopped onion
¾ cup chopped green pepper
½ cup catsup
¼ cup commercial chili sauce
2 tablespoons brown sugar
2 tablespoons prepared mustard
2 tablespoons molasses

Combine all ingredients; stir well. Spoon mixture into a lightly greased shallow 2-quart baking dish. Bake uncovered, at 350° for 1 hour. Yield: 6 servings.
Alice G. Pahl,
Raleigh, North Carolina.

Tip: Every time the door is opened to the oven, the temperature drops 25 to 30 degrees. Use the oven window so not to waste energy.

SPICED BAKED BEANS

2 (16-ounce) cans pork and beans
½ cup chopped onion
⅓ cup firmly packed brown sugar
2 tablespoons catsup
2 tablespoons Worcestershire sauce
1 tablespoon prepared mustard
¼ teaspoon ground cinnamon
2 slices bacon

Combine all ingredients except bacon; stir well. Spoon mixture into a lightly greased shallow 2-quart baking dish. Arrange bacon slices on top. Bake the beans, uncovered, at 375° for 1 hour. Yield: 6 servings.
Mrs. Doyle Register,
Columbus, Georgia.

MICROWAVE COOKERY

The Quickest Way To Cook Vegetables

Fresh vegetables are at their best when cooked in the microwave oven. Besides faster preparation, this method helps retain more of each vegetable's natural color, nutrients, and flavor.

When fresh vegetables are microwaved, only a small amount of water is usually added—the natural moisture of the vegetables provides most of the liquid. If you cover the vegetables with heavy-duty plastic wrap before microwaving, the steam and heat will be retained as the vegetables cook.

Always remember to remove the plastic wrap covering cooked vegetables by lifting from the far side first. This will allow the steam to escape without burning your hands or face.

Keep in mind that fresh vegetables cook much faster in the microwave than they do conventionally. It may, in fact, be necessary to stir the vegetables as they microwave to avoid overcooking the outer portions.

SIMPLE SQUASH TOSS

2 pounds (about 8) medium-size yellow
  squash
1 (2-ounce) jar diced pimiento, drained
2 tablespoons water
2 tablespoons butter or margarine
¼ teaspoon dried whole basil
¼ teaspoon garlic powder
Salt and pepper to taste

Wash squash, and cut into ½-inch-thick slices; place in a 2-quart casserole. Sprinkle with pimiento. Add water, and dot with butter; sprinkle with basil and garlic powder. Cover with heavy-duty plastic wrap, and microwave at HIGH for 12 minutes, stirring every 4 minutes. Let stand, covered, 10 minutes before serving. Yield: 6 servings.

GARDEN HARVEST

3 medium ears fresh corn
1 small onion, chopped
¼ cup chopped green pepper
1 medium zucchini, sliced
¼ cup butter or margarine, softened
2 teaspoons sugar
¾ teaspoon salt
¼ teaspoon dried whole basil
⅛ teaspoon pepper
1 medium tomato, chopped

Cut corn from cobs. Place corn in a 1½-quart casserole. Add onion and green pepper. Cover with heavy-duty plastic wrap, and microwave at HIGH 2 minutes. Add remaining ingredients, except tomato. Cover and microwave at HIGH for 7 to 8 minutes, stirring once. Add tomato. Cover and microwave at HIGH for 1½ to 2 minutes or until thoroughly heated. Yield: 4 servings.

TANGY GREEN BEANS

1 pound fresh green beans
2 slices bacon, chopped
1 medium onion, chopped
⅓ cup water
1 tablespoon sugar
2 tablespoons vinegar
½ teaspoon celery salt
Dash of pepper

Wash beans; trim ends, and remove strings. Cut into 1½-inch pieces. Set beans aside.

Place bacon in a 1-quart glass casserole; cover with a paper towel, and microwave at HIGH for 3 to 3½ minutes. Remove bacon, and set aside, reserving drippings.

Add onion, beans, and water to bacon drippings. Cover with heavy-duty plastic wrap, and microwave at HIGH for 9 to 12 minutes or until the beans are tender, stirring twice.

Combine sugar, vinegar, celery salt, and pepper, stirring well; add to beans. Cover and microwave at HIGH for 1 minute or until heated. Gently stir beans, and sprinkle with crisp bacon. Yield: 4 servings.

ZUCCHINI BOATS

4 small zucchini (about 7 inches long)
2 tablespoons chopped onion
½ cup (2 ounces) shredded Cheddar cheese
¼ cup mayonnaise
2 tablespoons fine, dry breadcrumbs
½ teaspoon dried whole tarragon
¼ teaspoon salt
⅛ teaspoon pepper
1 medium tomato, chopped
2 teaspoons minced fresh parsley

Wash squash, trimming ends. Arrange squash in a circle on a platter. Microwave at HIGH for 4½ to 5 minutes or until hot, rearranging once. Let stand 5 minutes. Cut in half lengthwise. Scoop out pulp into a 2-cup glass measure, leaving ¼-inch zucchini shells. Invert shells; set aside.

Chop pulp, and add onion. Microwave at HIGH for 3 minutes, stirring once. Drain. Add cheese, mayonnaise, breadcrumbs, tarragon, salt, and pepper, stirring well. Gently stir in tomato. Arrange shells, cut side up, on serving platter. Spoon filling into shells, mounding slightly. Microwave at HIGH for 2 to 4 minutes or until hot, rotating once. Sprinkle with parsley. Yield: 8 servings.

Lively Main Dishes For Breakfast

If you want to make your breakfast extra special, fill the menu with these appetizing main dishes. Liven up eggs by serving them poached over bacon and English muffins; Parmesan Cheese Sauce adds the crowning touch. Or gently simmer eggs until done in a mixture of green pepper, tomato sauce, and mushrooms for Skillet Eggs Creole.

For a simple but attractive main dish, serve wine-flavored Mushrooms and Eggs in Patty Shells. If hominy is a favorite with your family, they'll like Bacon, Eggs, and Hominy.

BACON, EGGS, AND HOMINY

4 slices bacon
1 (16-ounce) can hominy, drained
4 eggs, beaten
½ teaspoon salt
Dash of pepper

Cook bacon in a large skillet until crisp; remove bacon, reserving 2 tablespoons drippings in skillet. Crumble bacon, and set aside.

Cook hominy in the reserved drippings until golden.

Combine eggs, salt, and pepper; add to hominy. Cook over low heat, stirring gently, until eggs are set but still moist. Sprinkle with bacon; serve immediately. Yield: 4 servings.   *Lorraine Keener, San Angelo, Texas.*

BACON-AND-EGG DELIGHT

3 English muffins, split, buttered, and toasted
6 slices bacon, cooked and cut in half
6 poached eggs
Parmesan Cheese Sauce
Paprika

Top each muffin half with 2 pieces of bacon and a poached egg. Spoon Parmesan Cheese Sauce over eggs, and sprinkle with paprika. Serve immediately. Yield: 3 servings.

Parmesan Cheese Sauce:

2 tablespoons butter or margarine
2 tablespoons instant-blending flour
1 cup milk
½ cup grated Parmesan cheese
¼ teaspoon salt
Dash of seasoned pepper

Melt butter in a heavy saucepan over low heat; add flour, and stir until smooth. Cook 1 minute, stirring constantly. Gradually add milk; cook over medium heat, stirring constantly, until thickened and bubbly. Add Parmesan cheese, salt, and a dash of seasoned pepper; stir until blended. Yield: about 1¼ cups.   *Nancy M. Pohl, Gainesville, Georgia.*

Tip: Burned food can be removed from an enamel saucepan by using the following procedure: Fill the pan with cold water containing 2 to 3 tablespoons salt, and let stand overnight. The next day, cover the pan, and bring water to a boil.

MUSHROOMS AND EGGS IN PATTY SHELLS

6 frozen patty shells
½ pound fresh mushrooms, sliced
2 tablespoons chopped onion
2 tablespoons butter or margarine, melted
¼ cup butter or margarine
3 tablespoons all-purpose flour
1½ cups milk
½ teaspoon salt
⅛ teaspoon red pepper
6 hard-cooked eggs
3 tablespoons dry white wine

Bake patty shells according to package directions; set aside.

Sauté mushrooms and onion in 2 tablespoons melted butter until tender, and set aside.

Melt ¼ cup butter in a heavy saucepan over low heat; add flour, stirring until smooth. Cook 1 minute, stirring constantly. Gradually add milk; cook over medium heat, stirring constantly, until mixture is thickened and bubbly. Stir in salt and red pepper.

Chop 5 eggs; stir chopped eggs, mushroom mixture, and wine into sauce. Cook until thoroughly heated. Spoon into patty shells. Cut remaining egg into 6 wedges; place 1 wedge on each patty shell. Yield: 6 servings.

Susan Kamer-Shinaberry, Charleston, West Virginia.

SKILLET EGGS CREOLE

½ small onion, chopped
½ small green pepper, chopped
1 tablespoon vegetable oil
1 (8-ounce) can tomato sauce
1 (4-ounce) can sliced mushrooms, undrained
⅛ teaspoon dried whole thyme
Salt and pepper to taste
2 eggs
1 English muffin, split and toasted

Sauté onion and green pepper in oil until tender; add tomato sauce, mushrooms, and seasonings. Cook over low heat until thoroughly heated.

Break eggs, one at a time, into a custard cup. Hold the lip of the cup close to tomato sauce mixture, and gently slip egg into sauce. Cover and simmer over low heat 10 minutes or until eggs reach desired degree of doneness. Spoon eggs and sauce over English muffin halves. Yield: 1 to 2 servings.

Mrs. Carl Costello, Plaquemine, Louisiana.

Cook With Smoke For Rich Flavor

Catch a whiff of pungent hickory smoke coming from your neighbor's grill on a breezy summer day. If you weren't hungry before, you're probably ready to invite yourself to dinner or put on some steaks of your own. It's that same tantalizing aroma of smoldering wood that adds extra flavor to food.

The next time you use the smoker or grill, toss in a handful of dampened wood chips, and experiment with using wood smoke for seasoning steaks, chicken, fish, vegetables, and more. Some folks even like to add a pan of nuts or cheese to whatever they're grilling to create savory smoked appetizers.

The type of wood to use is a matter of preference; many outdoor cooks claim they can name the kind used for cooking just by tasting the food. Basically, any hardwood will work well for smoking. Never use wood from trees with needles, such as pine, fir, spruce, or cedar, since pitch from the wood adds an unpleasant taste to food.

Precut wood chips are available in grocery stores, but you can use whatever you might find in nearby woods or your backyard. Hickory, oak, apple, maple, and mesquite are all popular woods to use for smoking. Twigs or thin slices from a fallen branch work as well as the chips. Fresh or green wood is best since it doesn't catch on fire easily.

You'll need to soak the wood in water before adding it to the hot coals or heat source. Most sources recommend soaking at least 1 hour before using. This is necessary so the wood will smolder and smoke rather than flame.

If you like a strong smoke flavor, then you'll enjoy Smoked Brisket With Barbecue Sauce. It's actually smoke-cooked in a covered grill or smoker for several hours. When it's done, the meat may still be somewhat pink inside, but this is quite typical of smoked meat.

If your grill is large enough or your smoker has several racks, you may want to cook vegetables right along with the meat. Try our Hickory-Smoked Corn or Herbed-Smoked Vegetables. Since they don't take as long to cook as most meat, add them later so all the food will be done about the same time. If you use a covered grill, remember that cooking time will be shorter than for a smoker since there is less space to heat.

In Lubbock, Texas, Gene Eads found a quick way to add smoke flavor to his specialty—Grilled Steaks With Green Chiles. He marinates rib-eye steaks for an hour and then grills them for less than 20 minutes. Gene claims that using mesquite chips over the hot coals is the key to their special taste. For more smoke flavor, he skips the charcoal and builds the fire with mesquite.

GRILLED STEAKS WITH GREEN CHILES

3 (1½-inch-thick) rib-eye steaks
¼ teaspoon salt-free herb and spice seasoning
½ cup plus 2 tablespoons teriyaki sauce
2 tablespoons Worcestershire sauce
1 tablespoon browning and seasoning sauce
1 (4-ounce) can whole green chiles, sliced in strips

Soak mesquite wood chips in water 1 to 24 hours.

Place steaks in a shallow dish; sprinkle one side of each with herb and spice seasoning. Combine sauces, and pour over meat. Marinate 1 hour.

Prepare charcoal fire in grill; let burn 15 to 20 minutes. Cover coals with soaked mesquite chips. Remove steaks from marinade. Grill over medium-hot coals 6 to 8 minutes; turn, placing 3 strips of green chiles on each steak. Grill an additional 6 to 8 minutes or until desired degree of doneness. Yield: 3 servings.
Gene Eads,
Lubbock, Texas.

SMOKED BRISKET WITH BARBECUE SAUCE

1 (5- to 6-pound) beef brisket, rolled
1 cup catsup
1 cup water
¼ cup firmly packed brown sugar
¼ cup cider vinegar
¼ cup finely chopped onion
1 tablespoon Worcestershire sauce
1 teaspoon dry mustard
Salt and pepper to taste

Soak oak wood chips in water for 1 to 24 hours.

Prepare charcoal fire in smoker, and let burn 10 to 15 minutes or until the flames disappear. Then add 6 to 8 pieces of soaked oak chips to coals.

Place water pan in smoker, and fill with hot water. Place brisket on rack; cover with smoker lid, and cook 5 to 6 hours or until tender.

Combine remaining ingredients in a medium saucepan. Bring mixture to a boil; reduce heat, and simmer 20 minutes. Serve sauce with smoked brisket. Yield: 12 to 15 servings.
Katherine Zettner,
Wetmore, Texas.

BARBECUED CHICKEN

2 cups vinegar
½ cup plus 2 tablespoons shortening
½ cup butter or margarine
3 tablespoons black pepper
2 tablespoons red pepper
1½ tablespoons salt
8 chicken breast halves

Soak hickory wood chips in water for 1 to 24 hours.

Combine all ingredients except chicken in a saucepan; bring to a boil, and cook until shortening and butter melt. Remove from heat.

Prepare charcoal fire in grill; let burn 15 to 20 minutes. Cover coals with soaked hickory chips. Coat chicken breast halves with sauce. Grill chicken over medium coals 45 to 55 minutes, turning and basting every 10 minutes. (Refrigerate any leftover sauce to use with other meats.) Yield: 8 servings.
Kathryn Geralds,
Tompkinsville, Kentucky.

SMOKED FISH LOG

1 (1½-pound) Spanish mackerel
Vegetable oil
Salt
1 (8-ounce) package cream cheese, softened
2 tablespoons grated onion
1 tablespoon lemon juice
1 teaspoon prepared horseradish
¼ teaspoon salt
1 cup chopped pecans
¼ cup chopped parsley

Soak hickory wood chips in water for 1 to 24 hours.

Brush fish liberally with vegetable oil on both sides; sprinkle with salt. Refrigerate fish while preparing grill.

Prepare charcoal fire by piling charcoal in one corner of grill; let burn 15 to 20 minutes or until flames disappear and coals are white. Add 6 to 8 pieces of soaked hickory to coals.

Arrange fish away from coals on opposite side of grill; cover with grill hood. Open air vents halfway.

Cook 35 to 45 minutes or until fish flakes easily with a fork. Cool.

Remove skin and bones from mackerel; flake fish with a fork. Combine fish, cream cheese, onion, lemon juice, horseradish, and salt; mix well. Shape mixture into a 12- x 1½-inch log; chill several hours.

Combine pecans and parsley; roll log in mixture. Serve with crackers. Yield: 3 cups.
Vicky Murphy,
Dunwoody, Georgia.

HERBED-SMOKED VEGETABLES

2 teaspoons butter or margarine, melted
12 medium-size fresh mushrooms, sliced
3 medium zucchini, sliced ¼-inch thick
3 medium tomatoes, chopped
1 tablespoon finely chopped onion
¾ teaspoon dried whole basil
¾ teaspoon dried whole oregano
½ teaspoon garlic salt
1 tablespoon butter or margarine
3 tablespoons water

Soak apple or oak wood chips in water 1 to 24 hours.

Make a 2½-inch-deep tray from heavy-duty aluminum foil. Place 2 teaspoons melted butter in tray, and coat bottom evenly.

Combine vegetables, basil, oregano, and garlic salt; place in foil tray. Dot with 1 tablespoon butter, and sprinkle with water. Cover loosely with foil; set tray aside.

Prepare charcoal fire in smoker or on one side of a covered grill. Let burn 10 to 15 minutes or until flames disappear. Add 6 pieces of soaked wood chips to coals. Place vegetables on grill. (Place on opposite side from coals if using covered grill.) Cover and cook 1 hour and 20 minutes in smoker or 1 hour in covered grill. Yield: 6 to 8 servings.

HICKORY-SMOKED CORN

3 ears fresh corn
¼ cup butter or margarine, softened
6 cloves garlic, unpeeled

Soak hickory wood chips in water for 1 to 24 hours.

Remove husks and silks from corn; cut in half. Spread 2 teaspoons butter on each half. Place each of the 6 pieces of corn on small sheets of heavy-duty aluminum foil; wrap loosely, leaving ends open. Set aside.

Prepare charcoal fire in smoker or on one side of covered charcoal grill. Let burn 10 to 15 minutes or until flames disappear. Add garlic and 6 to 8 pieces of soaked hickory to coals.

Place corn on grill (place on opposite side from coals if using covered grill). Cover with lid, and cook corn 2 hours in smoker or 1 hour in covered grill. Yield: 6 servings.

No-Knead Yeast Rolls Are Easy

You don't have to be an experienced baker to have success making these yeast rolls. We've eliminated the 8- to 10-minute kneading period called for in most recipes. Kneading helps develop the gluten in flour, which gives the bread structure and a fine-grained texture. Yeast breads that aren't kneaded often have a coarse texture, but not so with these recipes.

There's whole grain goodness in our Bran Rolls and Petite Whole Wheat Rolls. A hint of sweetness in the Bran Rolls makes them adaptable as a breakfast bread as well as a dinner roll. Try Petite Whole Wheat Rolls at your next luncheon buffet when guests are tempted with a variety of foods and don't want to fill up on bread.

Super Potato Rolls modernize an age-old recipe. Instant mashed potato flakes replace the need to cook potatoes from scratch. These rolls have a smooth texture and a mild taste.

SUPER POTATO ROLLS

2 packages dry yeast
½ cup warm water (105° to 115°)
1½ cups warm milk (105° to 115°)
¾ cup instant mashed potato flakes
½ cup butter or margarine, softened
½ cup sugar
1 teaspoon salt
2 egg yolks, slightly beaten
About 4½ cups all-purpose flour, divided
1½ tablespoons butter or margarine, melted

Dissolve yeast in warm water in a large bowl; let stand 5 minutes. Combine milk, potato flakes, butter, sugar, and salt; mix well. Add to yeast mixture, stirring well. Stir in egg yolks and ½ cup flour. Cover and let rise in a warm place (85°), free from drafts, for 30 minutes. (Batter will look spongy.) Gradually stir in enough of the remaining flour to make a soft dough. Cover and let rise in a warm place (85°), free from drafts, 1 hour, or until dough is doubled in bulk.

Punch dough down; turn onto a lightly floured surface, and roll out to ¼-inch thickness. Cut into 2½-inch circles; brush with melted butter. Make a crease across each circle, and fold over; gently press edges to seal. Place on greased cookie sheets, and let rise in a warm place (85°), free from drafts, 20 minutes, or until dough is doubled in bulk. Bake at 400° for 10 minutes or until golden brown. Yield: about 4 dozen.
Mrs. Guy Burnette,
Lynch Station, Virginia.

BRAN ROLLS

2 cups shreds of wheat bran cereal
1 cup butter or margarine
¾ cup sugar
1½ cups boiling water
2 teaspoons salt
2 packages dry yeast
½ cup warm water (105° to 115°)
2 eggs, beaten
About 5 cups all-purpose flour, divided

Combine bran cereal, butter, sugar, 1½ cups boiling water, and salt, mixing well; cool to lukewarm (105° to 115°). Dissolve yeast in warm water in a large bowl; let stand 5 minutes. Add bran mixture, eggs, and 2 cups flour; beat at medium speed of an electric mixer 1 minute. Add remaining flour; beat mixture until combined. Cover dough and refrigerate 2 hours.

Punch dough down; turn onto a lightly floured surface, and shape into 2-inch balls. Place balls in greased muffin pans. Cover and let rise in a warm place (85°), free from drafts, 1 hour or until doubled in bulk. Bake at 375° for 20 minutes. Yield: 3 dozen.
Janet Soefje Bozeman,
New Braunfels, Texas.

Tip: If you grease more muffin cups than you need, fill the empty cups with water to keep grease from baking on.

PETITE WHOLE WHEAT ROLLS

3 packages dry yeast
⅓ cup warm water (105° to 115°)
1¼ cups shortening
1 cup boiling water
1 cup sugar
1 teaspoon salt
3 eggs, beaten
About 3½ cups all-purpose flour
About 3½ cups whole wheat flour
¼ cup butter or margarine, melted

Dissolve yeast in warm water; set mixture aside.

Combine shortening, boiling water, sugar, and salt in a large bowl; stir until shortening melts. Cool to lukewarm, (105° to 115°). Add eggs and yeast mixture, stirring well. Add 3 cups of each flour, mixing well; stir in remaining flour. Place dough in a well-greased bowl, turning to grease top. Cover and chill 3 hours or overnight.

Divide dough in half. Roll half of dough out to ¼-inch thickness on a lightly floured surface; cut into 2-inch circles, and brush with butter. Make a crease across each circle, and fold over; gently press edges to seal. Place on ungreased baking sheets. Repeat procedure with remaining dough. Bake at 400° for 8 to 10 minutes or until golden brown. Yield: about 12 dozen.

Note: Rolls may be stored in airtight freezer bags, and frozen up to 3 months before baking. Remove from freezer 30 minutes before baking.

Rebecca Ann Walton,
Lafayette, Alabama.

Take Advantage Of Leftover Rice

Leftover rice is a bonus when you consider the different ways you can use it. Smart cooks have been adding it to soups and salads for years. They know it makes good nutritional sense and helps stretch the food dollar, too. And many families have their own version of "sweet rice," an old standby that usually consists of leftover rice heated with a little milk and butter and sprinkled with cinnamon and sugar. It still comes in handy as a quick, last-minute solution when someone asks, "What's for dessert?"

Our readers have demonstrated that cooked rice can be used in many other ways as well. For example, it's a main ingredient in Oriental Rice, a savory dish with ground chuck and Chinese vegetables. It helps round out the filling in Beef-Stuffed Peppers, a chili-flavored main dish that features ground beef and cottage cheese.

Leftover rice has new possibilities as a side dish when it's combined with other ingredients. Spinach Rice is a delicious example; spinach and rice are baked with milk, eggs, cheese, and herbs in a flavorful casserole. Mexican Rice, which also cooks in the oven, is a spicy blend of rice, green chiles, cumin, celery soup, sour cream, and two kinds of cheese.

Rice Pancakes are a good idea when you have just a little bit of rice left over. Stiffly beaten egg whites folded into the batter make them surprisingly light. The rice adds a slight crunchiness as well as extra nutrition.

Think about Old-Fashioned Rice Pudding when you want a special dessert with a home-style touch. This version uses cooked rice and has a hint of lemon; buttered breadcrumbs are sprinkled on top before baking.

Cooked rice can be kept six to seven days in the refrigerator or frozen for up to four months. Use your imagination and come up with ideas for using this versatile ingredient. What started out as a leftover can easily become the base of tomorrow's menu.

BEEF-STUFFED PEPPERS

6 large green peppers
1 pound ground beef
½ cup diced onion
2 cups cooked rice
1 egg, beaten
½ cup small curd cottage cheese
¼ cup chili sauce
1 teaspoon dry mustard
½ teaspoon salt
¼ teaspoon pepper

Cut off tops of green peppers; remove seeds. Cook peppers 5 minutes in boiling salted water; drain and set aside.

Cook ground beef and onion in a skillet until browned; drain well. Stir in remaining ingredients. Stuff peppers with beef mixture. Place peppers in a 13- x 9- x 2-inch baking dish, and pour water 1 inch deep into dish. Bake at 350° for 30 minutes. Yield: 6 servings.

Claire Wash,
Greenwood, South Carolina.

ORIENTAL RICE

1 tablespoon vegetable oil
1 pound ground chuck
¼ teaspoon garlic salt
¼ cup soy sauce
¼ teaspoon pepper
1 cup shredded cabbage
¾ cup chopped green pepper
1 cup chopped celery
1 medium onion, chopped
1½ cups sliced carrots
½ pound fresh mushrooms, sliced
1 (5-ounce) can bamboo sprouts, drained
1 (5-ounce) can sliced water chestnuts, drained
2 cups cooked rice
1 (6-ounce) package frozen Chinese pea pods, thawed and drained

Heat oil in a large Dutch oven. Add ground chuck and garlic salt, and cook, stirring to crumble until meat is browned. Drain. Stir in remaining ingredients except rice and pea pods; cover and simmer 20 minutes, stirring occasionally. Stir in rice and pea pods; simmer 5 minutes. Yield: 6 servings.

Joyce Petrochko,
St. Albans, West Virginia.

SPINACH RICE

1 (10-ounce) package frozen chopped spinach, thawed
1 cup cooked rice
1 cup (4 ounces) shredded sharp Cheddar cheese
½ cup minced onion
¼ cup plus 2 tablespoons milk
2 eggs, beaten
½ teaspoon dried whole thyme
½ teaspoon dried whole rosemary leaves
½ teaspoon Worcestershire sauce
⅛ teaspooon salt
⅛ teaspoon pepper
1 tablespoon butter or margarine

Drain thawed spinach, and squeeze out excess moisture between paper towels. Combine spinach and remaining ingredients except butter; mix well. Spoon mixture into a greased 1-quart casserole; dot with butter. Bake at 350° for 25 to 30 minutes or until thoroughly heated. Yield: 4 servings. *Jane Noe,*
Sandia, Texas.

Tip: When grains, such as rice, are served together with dried beans or peas, the two dishes complement each other, providing a good source of high quality protein.

MEXICAN RICE

2 cups cooked rice
1 (10¾-ounce) can cream of celery soup, undiluted
1 (4-ounce) can chopped green chiles, drained
½ cup (2 ounces) shredded sharp Cheddar cheese
½ cup (2 ounces) shredded Monterey Jack cheese
½ cup commercial sour cream
¾ teaspoon garlic powder
½ teaspoon ground cumin
Additional shredded sharp Cheddar cheese

Combine all ingredients except final ingredient; mix well. Spoon mixture into a greased 1½-quart baking dish. Bake, uncovered, at 325° for 20 minutes. Top with cheese; bake an additional 5 minutes. Yield: 6 servings.

Deanne Anthony,
Poteau, Oklahoma.

CURRIED RICE SALAD

1 (10-ounce) package frozen English peas
1½ cups cooked rice
1 cup chopped celery
¼ cup minced onion
½ cup mayonnaise or salad dressing
2 tablespoons vegetable oil
1 tablespoon vinegar
¾ teaspoon curry powder

Cook peas according to package directions; drain. Cool.
Combine peas and remaining ingredients; mix well. Cover and chill 1 to 2 hours. Yield: 4 to 6 servings.

Mrs. Borden Gray, Sr.,
Snyder, Texas.

RICE PANCAKES

1 cup all-purpose flour
1 teaspoon baking powder
½ teaspoon salt
1 tablespoon sugar
2 eggs, separated
1 cup milk
2½ tablespoons vegetable oil
¾ cup cooked rice

Combine flour, baking powder, salt, and sugar in a large bowl. Combine egg yolks, milk, and oil; stir into dry ingredients. Stir in rice, and set aside.
Beat egg whites (at room temperature) until stiff but not dry; gently fold beaten egg whites into batter.

For each pancake, pour about ¼ cup batter onto a hot, lightly greased griddle. Turn pancakes when tops are covered with bubbles and edges are browned. Serve pancakes with syrup, if desired. Yield: 12 (4-inch) pancakes.

Martha Kubecka,
Palacios, Texas.

OLD-FASHIONED RICE PUDDING

2 eggs, beaten
1⅓ cups milk
¼ cup sugar
1 tablespoon butter or margarine, softened
1 teaspoon vanilla extract
⅛ teaspoon salt
2 cups cooked rice
⅓ cup raisins
½ teaspoon grated lemon rind
1 teaspoon lemon juice
3 tablespoons soft breadcrumbs
1 tablespoon butter or margarine, melted

Combine eggs, milk, sugar, butter, vanilla, and salt, mixing well. Stir in rice, raisins, lemon rind, and juice. Spoon into a lightly greased 1-quart baking dish. Combine breadcrumbs and butter; sprinkle breadcrumbs over top. Bake at 325° for 40 to 45 minutes or until set. Yield: 4 to 6 servings.

Irene Payne,
Columbus, Georgia.

Fresh Ideas For Green Beans

With green beans in plentiful supply this month, why not try cooking them a new way? They are great simmered with ham hocks or bacon drippings, but our readers have shared some other ideas.
Carol S. Noble of Burgaw, North Carolina, suggests Stir-Fried Green Beans; rapid cooking and a sweet glaze make them delicious. Or try them layered in a casserole and sprinkled with herbs, as in Italian Green Beans; it may turn out to be your favorite way to cook this fresh green vegetable.

GREEN BEANS WITH BACON DRESSING

1½ pounds fresh green beans
8 slices bacon
2 eggs
½ cup water
⅓ cup vinegar
3 tablespoons sugar
¼ teaspoon salt
3 tablespoons diced pimiento

Wash beans; trim ends, and remove strings. Cut into 1½-inch pieces. Cook beans, covered, in boiling salted water to cover 20 minutes or until tender; drain and keep warm.
Cook bacon until crisp; crumble bacon. Drain off drippings, reserving 2 tablespoons in skillet. Combine eggs, water, vinegar, sugar, and salt, stirring well. Stir into bacon drippings; cook over medium heat, stirring constantly, until smooth and thickened.
Place beans in serving dish; pour dressing over top. Sprinkle with bacon and pimiento. Yield: 6 servings.

Laura F. Plyler,
Lancaster, South Carolina.

ITALIAN GREEN BEANS

1½ pounds fresh green beans
1 cup water
1 tablespoon bacon drippings
¼ teaspoon salt
¼ teaspoon pepper
1 onion, diced
1 clove garlic, crushed
2 tablespoons olive oil
2 small tomatoes, chopped
¼ teaspoon dried whole oregano, divided
¼ teaspoon dried whole basil, divided
¼ teaspoon dried whole rosemary, divided
2 tablespoons grated Parmesan cheese

Wash beans; trim ends, and remove strings. Cut into 1½-inch pieces.
Combine beans, water, bacon drippings, salt, and pepper in a large saucepan; bring to a boil. Cover, reduce heat, and simmer 25 to 30 minutes. Drain and set aside.
Sauté onion and garlic in olive oil until onion is tender.
Layer half each of beans, onion mixture, and chopped tomatoes in a lightly greased 1½-quart baking dish; sprinkle with ⅛ teaspoon of each herb. Repeat procedure. Sprinkle top with grated Parmesan cheese; cover and bake at 350° for 15 minutes. Yield: 4 to 6 servings.

Marybryan Espinoza,
San Marcos, Texas.

STIR-FRIED GREEN BEANS

1 pound fresh green beans
1 to 2 tablespoons vegetable oil
¾ cup chicken broth
1 teaspoon sugar
1 teaspoon cornstarch
2 tablespoons water

Wash beans; trim ends, and remove strings. Cut into 1½-inch pieces.

Pour oil around top of preheated wok or large skillet; allow to heat at medium high (325°) for 2 minutes. Add green beans; stir-fry 3 minutes. Add chicken broth and sugar; cover, reduce heat, and cook 10 minutes. Combine cornstarch and water, stirring well; add to wok. Cook beans, stirring constantly, until thickened. Yield: 4 servings.
Carol S. Noble,
Burgaw, North Carolina.

SIMPLE SNAP BEANS

1½ pounds fresh green beans
2 slices bacon, diced
¼ cup diced onion
1 tablespoon all-purpose flour
¾ cup hot water
½ teaspoon salt
⅛ teaspoon pepper
1 tablespoon vinegar

Wash beans; trim ends, and remove strings. Cut into 1-inch pieces. Cook beans, covered, in a small amount of boiling salted water 10 to 15 minutes or until crisp-tender; drain and set aside.

Cook bacon in a heavy skillet over medium heat; add onion, and sauté until tender. Add flour, stirring until smooth. Cook 1 minute, stirring constantly. Gradually add water; cook over medium heat, stirring constantly, until thickened. Stir in salt, pepper, vinegar, and green beans. Cook until thoroughly heated, stirring occasionally. Yield: 4 to 6 servings. *Deborah Alford,*
Independence, Kentucky.

Spoon On The Sauce

For some people, broccoli isn't broccoli unless it's served with hollandaise sauce. Emmie Lou Tucker of Milton, Florida, says, "In my family, hollandaise was a must—broccoli was indecent without it." She goes on to give us her mother's foolproof recipe for Tangy Hollandaise, which follows a somewhat different procedure from most hollandaise sauce recipes.

TANGY HOLLANDAISE

½ cup butter or margarine, cut into 8 pieces
2 egg yolks, broken
2 tablespoons lemon juice
⅛ teaspoon white pepper

Place all ingredients in top of a double boiler; let stand 30 minutes. Bring water to a boil. (Water in bottom of double boiler should not touch top pan.) Reduce heat to low; cook, stirring constantly with a wooden spoon, until butter melts and sauce thickens (about 5 minutes). Serve over hot cooked vegetables. Yield: ⅔ cup.
Emmie Lou Tucker,
Milton, Florida.

ONION-PARSLEY SAUCE

1 small onion, finely chopped
2 tablespoons butter or margarine, melted
1½ tablespoons all-purpose flour
1¼ cups milk
1 egg yolk
1 tablespoon minced parsley
¼ teaspoon salt
⅛ teaspoon pepper

Sauté onion in butter in a heavy saucepan until tender. Add flour, stirring until smooth; cook 1 minute, stirring constantly. Gradually add milk; cook over medium heat, stirring constantly, until thickened. Remove from heat. Beat egg yolk; gradually stir about one-fourth of hot mixture into yolk. Add to remaining hot mixture, stirring constantly. Return to heat 1 minute, stirring constantly. Add remaining ingredients. Serve over hot vegetables. Yield: ¾ cup. *Mrs. Ernest Harmon,*
Elk Park, North Carolina.

MUSTARD SAUCE

2 tablespoons chopped onion
¼ cup butter or margarine, melted
¼ cup all-purpose flour
¾ cup milk
¾ cup chicken broth
1½ tablespoons lemon juice
1½ tablespoons prepared mustard
1 teaspoon sugar
½ teaspoon salt

Sauté onion in butter in a medium saucepan until tender. Add flour, stirring until smooth; cook 1 minute, stirring constantly. Gradually add milk and chicken broth; cook over medium heat,

stirring constantly, until mixture is thickened and bubbly. Stir in remaining ingredients, and serve over hot cooked vegetables. Yield: 1¾ cups.
Dorothy K. Brick,
Marion, Arkansas.

Tabbouleh Is No Ordinary Salad

When Lillian Resha of Birmingham has guests, they always expect her to serve Tabbouleh. This Lebanese salad, which is filled with parsley, wheat, and tomatoes, is a wonderful substitute for tossed salad.

Lillian tells us there are several secrets to making Tabbouleh taste just right. She recommends thoroughly drying the parsley and lettuce before shredding. "Be sure to squeeze as much water as you can out of the wheat. Otherwise, it will be too soggy," she adds.

TABBOULEH

2 small bunches fresh parsley
½ medium head iceberg lettuce
½ cup bulgur wheat
2 large tomatoes, diced
1 small onion, finely chopped
Juice of 2 to 3 lemons
1 tablespoon olive oil
1 tablespoon vegetable oil
¾ to 1 teaspoon salt
¾ teaspoon pepper
¼ teaspoon dried mint flakes
Lemon slices (optional)

Rinse parsley and lettuce under cold water; drain well. Dry thoroughly with paper towels. Chop parsley and shred lettuce; set aside.

Place wheat in a saucepan, and cover with water; bring to a boil. Reduce heat, and simmer 15 minutes. Drain well, and cool.

Squeeze excess water from wheat with hands; place wheat in a large bowl. Add parsley, lettuce, and remaining ingredients except lemon; mix thoroughly. Garnish with lemon, if desired. Yield: 10 to 12 servings.

Tip: Plastic bags that have been used to wrap dry foods, vegetables, and fruits can often be washed and reused.

July

Serve Summer Turkey Chilled

Some cooks rely on turkey for traditional holiday meals but forget about the tasty meat the rest of the year. Our Galantine of Turkey, however, is especially suited for warm-weather months—it's served chilled.

"Galantine" refers to any type of meat, fish, or poultry that's boned, stuffed, rolled, and served chilled. Originally filled with forcemeat (finely chopped and highly seasoned meat used as stuffing), the famous dish has come to take on a variety of flavors, such as our English pea and green onion combination. Galantines often sport a clear or white aspic coating, as well as adornments of cut vegetables or nuts that give the entrée (or elegant appetizer) a striking appearance in a buffet menu, as the photograph of the Galantine of Turkey on page 97 shows.

To make our galantine, ask your butcher for a boneless turkey breast of about 3 pounds. Then follow our recipe directions to prepare the turkey roll.

Once you have completed all the stages of preparation, gently place the turkey roll in an oval Dutch oven or poacher, and pat the roll with your hands to make its form even. (The shape of the roll is somewhat malleable before cooking but is firm and cannot be reshaped after cooking.) If the shape is noticeably uneven after cooking, you can slice away any bulges to make it more uniform.

A galantine is rather time consuming to make; it requires at least eight hours of chilling at one point. Because of this, you can prepare it a couple of days ahead of time, reserving last-minute garnishing for the day you plan to serve it. (For instructions on making garnishes, such as green onion fans, see the Appendices of this book.)

GALANTINE OF TURKEY

1 (16-ounce) package frozen English peas, thawed
2 tablespoons all-purpose flour
3 tablespoons whipping cream or milk
2 eggs
¼ cup chopped green onions
2 tablespoons chopped fresh parsley
½ teaspoon salt
⅛ teaspoon white pepper
⅛ teaspoon ground nutmeg
1 (3-pound) boneless turkey breast
½ pound cooked ham, cut into ⅜-inch strips
1 (10¾-ounce) can chicken broth, undiluted
2 bay leaves
1 stalk celery, cut into 1-inch pieces
1 large carrot, sliced
1 teaspoon whole peppercorns
White Aspic Coating
2 whole canned pimientos
1 green onion fan
Fresh Italian or regular parsley sprigs

Position knife blade in food processor bowl; add peas to processor bowl, and process 30 seconds or until pureed. Add flour, whipping cream, eggs, onions, chopped parsley, salt, pepper, and nutmeg to peas; process 1 minute or until smooth, scraping sides of bowl occasionally. Pour mixture in top of a double boiler; bring water to a boil. Reduce heat to medium; cook pea mixture, stirring frequently, 12 minutes or until thick. Remove from heat, and let cool.

Lay turkey breast flat on waxed paper or aluminum foil, skin side up. Carefully slice away skin, tendons, and excess fat, keeping meat intact. Turn turkey breast over. From center of turkey breast, slice horizontally through thickest part of each side of breast almost to outer edge; flip the cut piece and breast fillets over to enlarge breast and make a more even thickness. To fill in shallow area between breast halves, slice meat from thicker parts of breast, and lay slices in shallow area. Pound breast to ½-inch thickness.

Spread half of pea mixture over turkey breast, leaving a 1½-inch border at sides. Lay strips of ham lengthwise down turkey breast, about 1 inch apart, and spoon remaining pea mixture over ham, spreading evenly. Fold in short sides of turkey ½ to 1 inch, to make ends even. Roll turkey breast jellyroll fashion over filling, starting at long side. (Roll will be about 12 inches long.) Secure seam with wooden picks.

Wrap turkey breast securely in several thicknesses of cheesecloth; tie ends

Step 1: *Lay turkey breast flat; slice from center through thickest part of each side almost to outer edge. Flip cut pieces over to enlarge breast; pound to an even thickness.*

Step 2: *Spread half the pea mixture over turkey breast. Lay ham strips down length of turkey breast, and cover with remaining pea mixture, spreading evenly.*

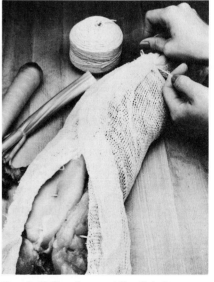

Step 3: *Roll turkey up jellyroll fashion over filling, starting at long side. Secure seam with wooden picks, and wrap roll in cheesecloth. Tie ends tightly with twine.*

tightly with twine. Place turkey in a large oval Dutch oven or fish poacher, seam side down. Add broth and enough water to cover two-thirds of the turkey. Add bay leaves, celery, carrot, and peppercorns. Bring mixture to a boil; cover, reduce heat, and simmer 1 hour or until turkey is just firm to the touch. Cool slightly in broth. Remove, cool to lukewarm, and wrap with plastic wrap. Chill 8 hours or overnight.

Carefully remove plastic wrap, cheesecloth, and wooden picks. Place turkey on a wire rack, seam side down. Working as quickly as possible, spoon or pour about half the White Aspic Coating over turkey. (Coating mixture dries quickly, so do not stop spooning until entire turkey is covered, or coating may not be smooth. The first coating will not be very smooth; the second coating should be smoother and more even.) Refrigerate 5 minutes for coating to set thoroughly.

Spoon remaining coating mixture over turkey roll; refrigerate 5 minutes. Trim aspic drippings from turkey base with knife, if necessary; transfer turkey roll to serving platter.

Cut four triangles from pimientos, and dry on paper towels; arrange pimientos on turkey. Slice green onion fan into 1½-inch lengths, making curly, thin strips; sprinkle green onion strips over each pimiento triangle. Chill until aspic is firm. Then cover loosely with plastic wrap; chill until serving. Arrange parsley sprigs around galantine before serving. Yield: 10 to 12 servings.

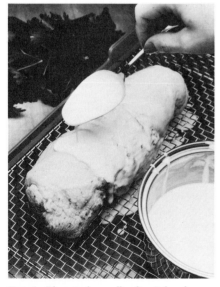

Step 4: *Place turkey roll, after it has been cooked and chilled, on a wire rack, and spoon aspic mixture over top; continue until roll is covered with aspic coating.*

White Aspic Coating:
⅓ cup cold water
1 tablespoon vinegar
¼ teaspoon chicken-flavored bouillon granules
1 envelope unflavored gelatin
1 cup mayonnaise

Combine water, vinegar, and bouillon granules in a small saucepan. Sprinkle gelatin over vinegar mixture; let stand 5 minutes. Cook over low heat until gelatin dissolves, stirring constantly.

Remove from heat; stir in mayonnaise with a wire whisk until the mixture is smooth. Tap pan lightly on surface to remove air bubbles. Use immediately. (If mixture stands too long before using, it will cool and become too thick to spoon properly. To soften, reheat the mixture slightly over low heat.) Yield: 1¼ cups.

MICROWAVE COOKERY

Quick Sauces To Top Pasta

If you're in a hurry for dinner, try making one of these sauces in the microwave to serve over pasta. Using the conventional cooking method, you may spend hours on a sauce, but we've come up with some tasty toppers you can microwave in just 10 minutes. Since you don't save time by cooking pasta in the microwave, cook it conventionally while you prepare the sauce.

We offer two choices with tomato bases. While tomatoes are in season, use their fresh flavor with other vegetables and spices for Herbed Fresh Tomato Sauce. Quick Crab Marinara Sauce has a simple tomato base made from canned tomato paste and sauce. You can omit the crabmeat for an easy tomato sauce to make year-round.

Cream sauces are easy in the microwave. To make the base, melt butter in a glass container; add flour, and stir until smooth. Stir in liquid gradually; then microwave a few minutes, stopping to stir several times. If you add cheese, stir it in at the last minute, and microwave just until it melts. This will keep it from being too tough or stringy.

To adapt your own pasta sauce recipes to the microwave, remember that the liquid will not cook down as in the

conventional saucepan method. You may need to reduce the liquid and thickening ingredient, such as flour or cornstarch, for a successful product.

QUICK CRAB MARINARA SAUCE
1 tablespoon olive oil
½ cup chopped onion
1 (8-ounce) can tomato sauce
1 (6-ounce) can tomato paste
½ cup water
2 tablespoons chopped fresh parsley
½ teaspoon dried whole basil, crushed
½ teaspoon salt
¼ teaspoon white pepper
1 (6½-ounce) can crabmeat, drained and rinsed

Combine olive oil and onion in a 12- x 8- x 2-inch, microwave-safe baking dish. Cover and microwave at HIGH for 3 minutes or until onion is tender, stirring once. Stir in remaining ingredients except crabmeat. Cover and microwave at HIGH for 4 to 5 minutes or until sauce thickens, stirring after 2 minutes. Stir in crabmeat. Serve over hot cooked pasta. Yield: 2⅔ cups.

HERBED FRESH TOMATO SAUCE
1 tablespoon butter or margarine
2 cups sliced fresh mushrooms
¼ cup chopped green onions
1 clove garlic, minced
3 fresh tomatoes, peeled and coarsely chopped
1 teaspoon lemon juice
1½ teaspoons dried whole oregano
½ teaspoon dried whole basil
⅛ teaspoon dried whole thyme
⅛ teaspoon celery salt
¼ teaspoon salt
¼ teaspoon pepper

Combine butter, mushrooms, green onions, and garlic in a 12- x 8- x 2-inch microwave-safe baking dish. Cover and microwave at HIGH for 4 to 5 minutes, stirring once. Stir in remaining ingredients. Microwave at HIGH for 6 to 7 minutes or until thoroughly heated, stirring twice. Serve over hot cooked pasta. Yield: 3½ cups.

Tip: Adding 1 or 2 tablespoons of vegetable oil to the cooking water keeps pasta separated.

VEGETABLE-CHEESE SAUCE

2 tablespoons butter or margarine
1 cup sliced fresh mushrooms
1 small zucchini, coarsely chopped
2 cloves garlic, crushed
¼ cup all-purpose flour
1 cup chicken broth
1 cup half-and-half
¾ cup freshly grated Parmesan cheese
⅛ teaspoon white pepper

Combine first 4 ingredients in a 1½-quart casserole. Cover and microwave at MEDIUM HIGH (70% power) for 5 minutes or until tender, stirring once. Add flour, stirring until smooth. Gradually add broth and half-and-half, stirring well. Microwave at HIGH for 4½ to 6 minutes, stirring at 2-minute intervals, until thick and bubbly. Stir in cheese and pepper; microwave at HIGH for 30 seconds or until cheese melts. Serve over hot cooked pasta. Yield: 3 cups.

SHERRIED CREAM SAUCE

½ cup pine nuts or slivered almonds
3 tablespoons butter or margarine
3 tablespoons all-purpose flour
1 cup evaporated milk
½ cup chicken broth
3 tablespoons dry sherry
2 tablespoons minced fresh parsley
¼ teaspoon ground nutmeg
⅛ teaspoon salt

Spread pine nuts evenly in a glass pieplate; microwave at HIGH for 4 minutes. Set aside.

Place butter in a 1-quart glass measure. Microwave at HIGH for 50 seconds or until melted. Add flour, stirring until smooth. Combine milk and broth; gradually add to flour mixture, stirring well. Microwave at HIGH for 2 minutes; stir well. Microwave at HIGH for 2½ minutes, stirring at 1-minute intervals until thickened. Stir in nuts and remaining ingredients. Serve over hot cooked pasta. Yield: 2⅓ cups.

Serve Sweet Blueberries

Southerners are heading to the berry patch to find plump, ripe blueberries. While berries are in season, use our recipes to enhance the sweet flavor.

Purchase or pick plenty of extra berries to freeze and use later. Place them in one layer on a tray, and freeze until hard. Then package in freezer containers. The blueberries will then be easy to pour and measure when you need them.

FRESH BLUEBERRY PIE

4 cups fresh blueberries
1 tablespoon lemon juice
Pastry for double-crust 9-inch pie
1 cup sugar
⅓ cup all-purpose flour
¼ teaspoon ground cinnamon
⅛ teaspoon ground nutmeg
Dash of ground cloves
2 tablespoons butter or margarine
1 egg yolk
1 tablespoon water

Sprinkle blueberries with lemon juice; set aside.

Roll half of crust to ⅛-inch thickness, and fit into a 9-inch pieplate.

Combine sugar, flour, and spices; stir well. Add flour mixture to berries, stirring well. Pour into pastry-lined pieplate. Dot filling with butter.

Roll out remaining pastry to ⅛-inch thickness. Cover pie with crust. Trim pastry; seal and flute edges. Cut slits in crust top for steam to escape. Combine egg yolk and water; lightly brush pastry top with mixture. Bake at 400° for 40 to 45 minutes or until golden brown. Cool before serving. Yield: one 9-inch pie.

Mary Kay Menees,
White Pine, Tennessee.

BLUEBERRY FRITTERS

2 tablespoons all-purpose flour
1 cup fresh blueberries
1 cup all-purpose flour
2½ teaspoons baking powder
¼ cup sugar
Pinch of salt
1 egg, beaten
⅓ cup milk
Vegetable oil
Powdered sugar

Combine 2 tablespoons flour and blueberries; toss lightly. Set aside.

Combine 1 cup flour, baking powder, ¼ cup sugar, and salt in mixing bowl; mix well. Combine egg and milk; gradually add milk mixture to flour mixture; stir until smooth. Fold in blueberries.

Heat 3 to 4 inches of oil to 375° in a Dutch oven; drop 3 to 4 scant ¼ cupfuls of batter at a time. Cook 3 minutes or until golden brown on 1 side; turn

and cook 3 minutes. Drain on paper towels. Sprinkle with powdered sugar. Yield: about 1 dozen. *Sandra Russell, Gainesville, Florida.*

BLUEBERRY PANCAKES

1 cup all-purpose flour
1 teaspoon baking powder
½ teaspoon salt
1 egg, beaten
1 cup buttermilk
1 tablespoon commercial sour cream
1 tablespoon molasses
¾ cup fresh blueberries

Combine flour, baking powder, and salt; set aside. Combine egg, buttermilk, sour cream, and molasses; slowly stir into dry ingredients. Fold in ¾ cup blueberries.

For each pancake, pour about ¼ cup batter onto a hot, lightly greased griddle. Turn pancakes when tops are covered with bubbles and edges are browned. Serve with syrup. Yield: nine 4-inch pancakes. *Mrs. Harlan J. Stone, Ocala, Florida.*

ALMOND-BLUEBERRY COFFEE CAKE

¾ cup butter or margarine, softened
1 cup sugar
4 eggs
2 teaspoons lemon juice
1¾ cups all-purpose flour
2 teaspoons baking powder
2 cups fresh blueberries
2 teaspoons lemon juice
Almond Topping

Cream softened butter; gradually add sugar, beating until light and fluffy. Add eggs, one at a time, beating well after each addition. Next, stir in 2 teaspoons lemon juice.

Combine flour and baking powder; stir into creamed mixture, mixing well.

Spread batter evenly in a greased and floured 13- x 9- x 2-inch glass baking dish; sprinkle with blueberries and 2 teaspoons lemon juice. Sprinkle with Almond Topping. Bake at 325° for 40 to 45 minutes. Yield: 15 servings.

Almond Topping:

1 cup all-purpose flour
¼ cup sugar
½ cup slivered almonds, toasted
¼ cup butter or margarine

Combine flour, sugar, and almonds; cut in butter until mixture resembles coarse meal. Yield: about 1½ cups.

Gayle Wallace,
Kingwood, Texas.

summer Suppers.

A Roundup For Outdoor Fun

We don't need a calendar to know when it's summer. The temperatures rise, and days get longer, bringing everyone outdoors to enjoy baseball, swimming, and best of all—eating.

And summertime food is unique. With this, our ninth annual *Summer Suppers* special section, come many ideas for all your outdoor favorites. We suggest pretty salads and new ways to serve cold pasta. We include a light menu for the weight conscious and so many ways to fry chicken that you're bound to find one you like.

But first, we'll stop in Texas for one of the most exciting outdoor parties we've ever seen.

Welcome to Renderbrook-Spade Ranch

South of Colorado City, Texas, Bob and Charlotte Northcutt, managers of the Renderbrook-Spade Ranch, are throwing a party. In this part of the state, it's not unusual to drive hundreds of miles for a party, so once a year Charlotte issues an invitation to ranchers to gather and discuss the cattle business and share the latest news.

On the day of the party, everyone gets an early start. By the time the sun begins to rise, Charlotte and her helpers are busy squeezing fresh juice. "There's nothing like fresh fruit juice. Since there's so much citrus in Texas, I wouldn't consider making margaritas or the punches without it.

"My party menus usually include tamales and enchiladas," says Charlotte. "Texas was once a part of Mexico, so our food has that influence, plus some influence from New Mexico. I'm serving Miniature Tamales today; they make a good appetizer."

During the early afternoon, pickup trucks are loaded with food, and we take off for the party site—a tree-covered creek that runs through the ranch. Soon, beans in large, cast-iron pots are simmering over an open fire, and tables are set up.

"I like each table to have a different theme. One will look Spanish, another Western, and another Indian," says Charlotte. The food is served from one of the original ranch chuckwagons and several reproductions. Bowls of punch help quench parched throats and are accompanied by Toasted Chili Pecans, olives, Miniature Tamales, and pistachio nuts to munch on.

Bob begins the process of grilling the steaks. As might be expected of a rancher, he likes his steaks big and thick. "Mesquite wood gives them their great smoked taste," he says. "Always let your wood burn down to good, even coals." He also tells us that the type barbecue pit you use will determine the distance steaks should be placed from the coals.

When guests begin to arrive, they are met at the gate of the ranch by the hosts, who tie different-colored ribbons around guests' wrists or arms. To locate a dinner partner, each guest must find the person with the matching ribbon. "This helps get the ball rolling," says Charlotte.

Down by the creek, a mandolin player has found a guitar picker, and together they're making lively foot-tapping music. When the dinner bell rings, everyone gets in line to fill plates with Charlotte's specialties.

After the main course, everyone gathers around the fire to watch Charlotte and Bob pat out dough for Fry Bread. "The main thing is to cook the bread until it's golden and puffy, and then toss it in cinnamon and sugar," says Charlotte. To accompany the Fry Bread, she serves fresh fruit and Kahlúa Chocolate Sauce—a delightful way to end the meal before loading everything up for the trip back home.

Tart Margaritas
Champagne Punch
Fresh Citrus Punch
Toasted Chili Pecans
Miniature Tamales
Olives   Pistachio nuts
Mesquite-Grilled Steaks
Cheese Enchiladas
Trailride Pinto Beans
Avocado with commercial red sauce
Fresh fruit with
Kahlúa Chocolate Sauce
Cheese
Fry Bread
Beer

TART MARGARITAS

Lime wedges
Salt
2 cups fresh lime juice
1½ cups tequila
½ cup Triple Sec or other orange-flavored liqueur
Cracked ice

Rub rims of 8 cocktail glasses with lime wedges. Place salt in saucer; spin rim of each glass in salt. Set prepared glasses aside.

Combine remaining ingredients, shaking well. Pour into prepared glasses. Yield: 8 servings.

CHAMPAGNE PUNCH

4 cups fresh orange juice, chilled
1 cup fresh grapefruit juice, chilled
½ cup fresh lemon juice, chilled
½ cup fresh lime juice, chilled
2 (25.4-ounce) bottles champagne, chilled

Combine fruit juice in a punch bowl. Just before serving, stir in champagne. Yield: 3 quarts.

FRESH CITRUS PUNCH

3 cups fresh orange juice, chilled
2 cups fresh grapefruit juice, chilled
1 cup fresh lemon juice, chilled
1 cup fresh lime juice, chilled
½ to ¾ cup sugar
1 cup sparkling mineral water, chilled
Fresh strawberries (optional)
Canned pineapple chunks (optional)

Combine fruit juice and sugar, stirring until sugar dissolves. Add mineral water. Serve over ice, if desired. Garnish punch with strawberries and pineapple chunks on skewers, if desired. Yield: 8 cups.

TOASTED CHILI PECANS

2 cups pecan halves
2 tablespoons butter or margarine, melted
1 teaspoon chili powder
⅛ teaspoon salt

Toss pecans in butter in a 13- x 9- x 2-inch pan. Bake at 350° for 20 to 25 minutes, stirring occasionally. Sprinkle with chili powder and salt; toss to coat. Yield: 2 cups.

MINIATURE TAMALES

1 (1½-pound) shoulder or chuck roast
2 cloves garlic
½ teaspoon salt
About 1½ dozen cornhusks
3 large, dried chiles
2 teaspoons shortening
1½ teaspoons all-purpose flour
¾ teaspoon ground cumin
¾ teaspoon salt
3 cups instant corn masa
1 teaspoon salt
½ cup plus 1 tablespoon shortening

Combine roast, garlic, and salt in a Dutch oven. Add water to cover; bring to a boil. Cover, reduce heat, and simmer 1 hour or until meat is done. Drain meat, reserving broth; set broth aside. Shred meat with a fork; set aside.

Cover dried cornhusks with hot water; let stand several hours or until softened. Drain well. Tear the wide husks in half lengthwise. (If some husks are too narrow to tear in half, tear off only a portion; you will need about 2 dozen husks to fill.)

Remove and discard seeds from chiles; place in a saucepan, and cover with water. Bring to a boil; reduce heat, and simmer 20 to 25 minutes or until chiles are tender. Drain chiles, reserving ¾ cup water; place softened chiles in container of electric blender. Add reserved water, and blend 1 minute or until smooth; set aside.

Melt 2 teaspoons shortening in a small saucepan; add flour and cumin, stirring until smooth. Cook 1 minute, stirring constantly. Remove from heat, and stir in ½ cup chile mixture and ¾ teaspoon salt; add to shredded meat, mixing well. Set aside.

Bring reserved beef broth to a boil. Combine corn masa, 1 teaspoon salt, and ½ cup plus 1 tablespoon shortening in a large bowl. Stir in 1 cup plus 2 to 3 tablespoons hot beef broth to make a stiff dough. Add the remaining chile mixture to the dough, mixing well.

Place 1½ to 2 tablespoons masa dough (depending on size of husk) in the center of each husk, spreading to within 1 inch of edge. Place 1 tablespoon meat mixture in center. Fold short ends of husks to center. Fold one long side of husk to center, enclosing filling; roll up from same side. Tie with string or strip of softened cornhusk.

Place a cup in center of a steaming rack or metal colander inside a large pot. Add enough water to fill pot below rack level and keep tamales above water. Stand tamales on folded ends around the cup. Bring water to a boil. Cover and steam 1 hour or until tamale dough pulls away from husk; add more water as necessary. Yield: about 2 dozen miniature tamales.

Note: Steamed tamales may be frozen. Allow to cool; place in a plastic bag, or wrap securely in aluminum foil, and put in freezer. To reheat, follow steaming procedure until tamales are thoroughly heated.

Tip: Ice will be clearer if you boil the water and let it cool before freezing.

MESQUITE-GRILLED STEAKS

8 (1½-inch-thick) T-bone steaks
2 to 2½ teaspoons seasoned salt
1⅓ cups beer
8 large cloves garlic, minced
Freshly ground black pepper (optional)

Soak mesquite wood chips in water 1 to 24 hours.

Trim fat around steaks to ¼ to ½ inch thick. Sprinkle each side of steaks evenly with salt, beer, and garlic. Pierce steaks with a fork on each side. Cover steaks and let stand at room temperature 1 hour.

Heat coals; place mesquite chips directly on hot coals. Grill steaks over hot coals 8 to 10 minutes on each side or until desired degree of doneness. Sprinkle with pepper, if desired. Yield: 8 servings.

CHEESE ENCHILADAS

16 corn tortillas
Vegetable oil
⅓ cup minced onion
3 cups (12 ounces) shredded Monterey Jack cheese
2½ cups (10 ounces) shredded Longhorn cheese

Fry tortillas, one at a time, in ¼ cup hot oil for 3 to 5 seconds on each side or just until softened. Add more oil if necessary. Drain tortillas thoroughly on paper towels.

Sprinkle 1 teaspoon onion down the center of each tortilla; top with about 1 tablespoon each of Monterey Jack and Longhorn cheese. Roll up each tortilla; place seam side down in a lightly greased 13- x 9- x 2-inch baking dish. Sprinkle with remaining cheese. Bake at 350° for 20 minutes. Serve immediately. Yield: 6 to 8 servings.

TRAILRIDE PINTO BEANS

4 cups pinto beans
10 cloves garlic
1 gallon water
Salt to taste

Sort and wash beans. Combine beans, garlic, and water in a large Dutch oven;

bring to a boil over medium heat. Reduce heat to low and cook, uncovered, 2 hours or until beans are tender, adding more water, if necessary. Add salt to taste. Yield: 10 to 12 servings.

KAHLÚA CHOCOLATE SAUCE

6 (1-ounce) squares semisweet chocolate
½ cup Kahlúa or other coffee-flavored
   liqueur
1 tablespoon powdered sugar
Fresh fruit

Place chocolate in top of a double boiler; bring water to a boil. Reduce heat to low; cook until chocolate melts. Remove from heat; gradually stir in Kahlúa and sugar, stirring until smooth. Let sauce cool to room temperature; serve with fresh fruit. Yield: ¾ cup.

FRY BREAD

1 (25-ounce) package frozen roll dough,
   thawed
Vegetable oil
¼ cup sugar
1 tablespoon ground cinnamon

Flatten each roll to a 3½-inch diameter; place a few at a time in deep hot oil (375°). Fry about 2 minutes or until golden brown, turning once. Drain on paper towels.
Combine sugar and cinnamon, stirring well; gently toss fry bread in sugar mixture. Serve fry bread immediately. Yield: 2 dozen.

A Menu Fresh From The Garden

All-vegetable menus are a special treat this time of year when the best flavors of summer come from the garden or the produce stand. The following menu makes use of fresh summer bounty for a hearty meal.

Note the light seasonings in these recipes; avoid overpowering the fresh taste of vegetables with other flavors. Since vegetables retain more nutrients when cooked just until done, recipes like Fresh Vegetable Medley and Green Beans Amandine require only short cooking times.
When assembling the whole menu, you can make Chocolate-Zucchini Cake and Marinated Tomatoes a day in advance. The next day, bake Pepper Bread, and put Favorite Corn Soup on to simmer first. Then you'll still have plenty of time to prepare the remainder of the menu.

Favorite Corn Soup
Fresh Vegetable Medley
Green Beans Amandine
Marinated Tomatoes
Cheesy New Potatoes
Pepper Bread
Chocolate-Zucchini Cake
Iced tea

FAVORITE CORN SOUP

6 medium ears fresh corn
1 large onion, chopped
¼ cup butter or margarine, melted
1 bay leaf
2 whole cloves
Pinch of dried whole rosemary
Pinch of dried whole thyme
6 cups chicken broth
Dash of ground nutmeg
Dash of pepper
1 cup whipping cream
2 tablespoons cornstarch
Fresh parsley sprigs (optional)

Cut corn from cob, scraping cob to remove pulp. Set aside.
Sauté chopped onion in butter in a Dutch oven until tender. Add 2 cups corn, and cook 3 minutes.
Tie bay leaf, cloves, rosemary, and thyme in a cheesecloth bag. Add cheesecloth bag, broth, nutmeg, and pepper to sautéed mixture, stirring well. Simmer, uncovered, 45 minutes.
Remove and discard cheesecloth bag. Strain soup mixture, reserving liquid;

spoon strained vegetables into container of electric blender, and process 30 seconds or until smooth. Add pureed mixture to strained liquid, and stir in remaining corn. Bring soup to a boil. Reduce heat and simmer, uncovered, 10 minutes.
Combine whipping cream and cornstarch; stir into soup. Cook just until thickened. Transfer soup to serving bowl; garnish with parsley, if desired. Yield: 8 cups. *Mrs. James S. Stanton, Richmond, Virginia.*

FRESH VEGETABLE MEDLEY

½ cup water
2 tablespoons butter or margarine
½ teaspoon salt
¼ teaspoon pepper
⅛ teaspoon garlic powder
3 medium carrots, scraped and diagonally
   cut into ¼-inch slices
2 medium-size green peppers, cut into
   ½-inch pieces
1 large onion, cut into 8 wedges
2 medium-size yellow squash, cut into
   ¼-inch slices
2 medium zucchini, cut into ¼-inch slices
1 pound fresh mushrooms, sliced
1 cup (4 ounces) shredded Cheddar cheese

Combine water, butter, salt, pepper, and garlic powder in a Dutch oven; bring to a boil. Add carrots; cover, reduce heat, and simmer 5 minutes. Add green pepper, onion, yellow squash, and zucchini; cover and simmer 10 minutes. Stir in mushrooms; cover and simmer 3 to 4 minutes. Drain.
Place vegetables in a lightly greased 13- x 9- x 2-inch baking dish; sprinkle with cheese. Broil just until cheese melts. Yield: 8 servings.
Mrs. J. Lane Sauls, De Ridder, Louisiana.

GREEN BEANS AMANDINE

3 cups water
½ teaspoon salt
2 pounds fresh green beans, french cut
½ cup slivered almonds
3 tablespoons butter or margarine, melted
1 tablespoon lemon juice
½ teaspoon salt
Lemon twist (optional)

Combine water and ½ teaspoon salt; bring to a boil. Add beans; return to a boil. Cover, reduce heat, and simmer 20 minutes; drain.

Sauté almonds in butter until golden. Reduce heat; stir in lemon juice and ½ teaspoon salt. Toss with beans. Garnish with a lemon twist, if desired. Yield: 8 servings.   *Harriet O. St. Amant,*
Fayetteville, North Carolina.

MARINATED TOMATOES

4 large tomatoes, sliced
⅓ cup olive oil
¼ cup red wine vinegar
2 teaspoons parsley flakes
1 teaspoon chopped onion
1 teaspoon Italian seasoning
1 teaspoon salt
½ teaspoon sugar
¼ teaspoon garlic salt
¼ teaspoon coarsely ground pepper

Arrange tomato slices in a shallow container. Combine remaining ingredients; mix well, and pour over tomatoes. Cover and marinate in refrigerator several hours or overnight. Yield: 8 servings.   *Lynne Teal Weeks,*
Columbus, Georgia.

CHEESY NEW POTATOES

12 medium-size new potatoes, unpeeled
    and cut in cubes
½ cup butter or margarine, melted
¼ teaspoon pepper
1 cup fully cooked real bacon pieces
2 cups (8 ounces) sharp process American
    cheese
¼ cup chopped fresh parsley

Cover potatoes with salted water, and bring to a boil; reduce heat, and cook

about 15 minutes or until tender. Drain potatoes, and cool slightly. Stir in butter and pepper; toss lightly.

Spoon half of potato mixture into a lightly greased, 3-quart casserole. Top with half each of bacon and cheese. Repeat layers. Bake at 350° for 20 minutes or until bubbly. Garnish with parsley. Yield: 8 to 10 servings.
Carolyn Robertson,
Houston, Texas.

PEPPER BREAD

2 eggs, slightly beaten
1 cup buttermilk
2 cups self-rising cornmeal
⅔ cup vegetable oil
⅓ cup chopped onion
⅓ cup chopped green pepper

Combine eggs and buttermilk; stir in cornmeal just until moistened. Add remaining ingredients; pour mixture into a greased 8½- x 4½- x 3-inch loafpan. Bake at 350° for 1 hour. Serve warm. Yield: 1 loaf.   *Mrs. E. E. Woodruff,*
Charlottesville, Virginia.

CHOCOLATE-ZUCCHINI CAKE

½ cup plus 1 tablespoon butter or
    margarine, softened
2 cups sugar
3 (1-ounce) squares unsweetened chocolate,
    melted and cooled
3 eggs
½ cup milk
2 teaspoons grated orange rind
2 teaspoons vanilla extract
2 cups coarsely grated unpeeled zucchini
2½ cups all-purpose flour
2½ teaspoons baking powder
1½ teaspoons baking soda
½ teaspoon salt
1 teaspoon ground cinnamon
2 tablespoons powdered sugar
½ teaspoon ground cinnamon
Whole fresh strawberries (optional)

Cream butter; gradually add 2 cups sugar, beating until light and fluffy. Beat in chocolate. Add eggs, one at a time, beating well after each addition. Beat in milk, orange rind, vanilla, and zucchini.

Combine flour, baking powder, soda, salt, and 1 teaspoon cinnamon; add to creamed mixture, mixing well. Pour batter into a greased and floured 10-inch Bundt pan. Bake at 350° for 1 hour or until a wooden pick inserted in center comes out clean. Cool cake in pan 10 to 15 minutes; remove from pan, and place on a wire rack.

Combine powdered sugar and ½ teaspoon cinnamon; sift over warm cake. Cool completely. Fill center of cake with strawberries, if desired. Yield: one 10-inch cake.   *Janet M. Filer,*
Arlington, Virginia.

COOKING LIGHT®

Lighten Calories At The Cookout

Get out your grill, and fire up the coals. It's time for a cookout! While everyone knows cookouts are fun, they can also be suprisingly good for a dieter. When meat is cooked on a grill, excess fat drips out onto hot coals, leaving meat with fewer calories and a delicious, smoky flavor.

Grilling, however, is a dry-heat method of cooking, and lean cuts of meat, fish, and poultry can become tough and dry. This can be avoided by tenderizing the meat beforehand with a marinade containing wine, vinegar, pineapple juice, lemon juice, or another acidic liquid. Also, brushing the marinade over the meat during grilling helps prevent drying.

The entrées in both of our low-calorie cookout menus are grilled. A marinade made with reduced-sodium soy sauce is used to tenderize, flavor, and moisten cubes of chicken breast for Hawaiian Kabobs.

Served over a bed of rice, the kabobs contain fruit, vegetables, and chicken, so all you'll need to round out the main course is a green salad and bread. A

Melon Ball Compote is a perfect dessert for this meal.

Our second entrée, Seasoned Burgers, is a flavorful version of an all-time favorite. Although Seasoned Burgers are made with ground chuck instead of the more fatty ground beef, there's still some extra fat, which cooks out during grilling.

You can cook the side dish, Grilled Tomatoes, at the same time as Seasoned Burgers. Serve the burgers and tomatoes with Cauliflower-Vegetable Salad, a refreshing, low-calorie alternative to traditional potato salad. It's made by tossing several high-fiber vegetables with reduced-calorie mayonnaise. For dessert, try Instant Fruit Sherbet; each serving provides only 58 calories.

Hawaiian Kabobs
Green salad with
Spring Garden Dressing
Commercial French bread
Melon Ball Compote

HAWAIIAN KABOBS

½ cup reduced-sodium soy sauce
½ cup unsweetened pineapple juice
¼ cup vegetable oil
1 tablespoon brown sugar
1 teaspoon garlic powder
2 teaspoons ground ginger
1 teaspoon dry mustard
¼ teaspoon freshly ground pepper
1½ pounds boneless chicken breasts, skinned and cut into 1-inch cubes
1 (15¼-ounce) can unsweetened pineapple chunks, drained
1 large green pepper, cut into 1-inch pieces
12 medium-size fresh mushrooms
18 cherry tomatoes
3 cups hot cooked rice

Combine first 8 ingredients in a saucepan; bring to a boil. Reduce heat, and simmer 5 minutes; let cool. Pour mixture into a shallow dish; add chicken, tossing gently to coat. Cover and marinate at least 1 hour in the refrigerator, stirring mixture occasionally.

Remove chicken from marinade, reserving marinade. Alternate chicken,

pineapple, green pepper, mushrooms, and tomatoes on 12 (7-inch) skewers. Grill over hot coals 20 minutes or until done, turning and basting frequently with marinade. Serve over hot cooked rice. Yield: 6 servings (about 239 calories per serving plus 90 calories per ½ cup cooked rice).

Marsha R. Braunstein,
Silver Spring, Maryland.

SPRING GARDEN DRESSING

1 (8-ounce) carton plain low-fat yogurt
½ cup reduced-calorie mayonnaise
¼ teaspoon salt
Dash of pepper
¼ cup diced green onions
¼ cup diced radishes
¼ cup diced green pepper
¼ cup diced cucumber
1 clove garlic, minced

Combine yogurt, mayonnaise, salt, and pepper; stir well. Stir in remaining ingredients, and chill thoroughly. Serve

over green salad. Yield: 2 cups (about 16 calories per tablespoon).

Note: Dressing may be used as a dip with raw vegetables.   *Becky Slagle,*
Hopewell, Virginia.

MELON BALL COMPOTE

1 cup unsweetened apple juice
1 tablespoon arrowroot
¾ teaspoon anise seeds
6 cups cantaloupe balls

Combine apple juice, arrowroot, and anise seeds in a small saucepan; stir until arrowroot dissolves. Bring to a boil; reduce heat and simmer, stirring constantly, until slightly thickened. Remove from heat; strain. Cool.

Place cantaloupe balls in a shallow bowl; pour sauce over top. Cover and chill 4 to 6 hours or overnight. Yield: 6 servings (about 73 calories per serving).   *Patra Collins Sullivan,*
Columbia, South Carolina.

Chicken, vegetables, and fruit are combined on skewers for Hawaiian Kabobs. By using short skewers, each person can enjoy two kabobs over rice, along with a green salad and Spring Garden Dressing, French bread, and Melon Ball Compote. Calories for the complete meal are about 520.

Seasoned Burgers
Grilled Tomatoes
Cauliflower-Vegetable Salad
Instant Fruit Sherbet

SEASONED BURGERS

1 pound ground chuck
2 tablespoons chopped green pepper
1 tablespoon dried onion flakes
1 tablespoon prepared horseradish
2 teaspoons Worcestershire sauce
2 teaspoons prepared mustard
½ teaspoon chili powder
¼ teaspoon salt
⅛ teaspoon pepper
4 whole wheat hamburger buns
Lettuce leaves
4 (⅔-ounce) slices low-fat process Cheddar
   cheese

Combine first 9 ingredients; mix well.
Shape into 4 patties. Place patties on
grill over medium coals, and grill 4 to 5
minutes on each side or until desired
degree of doneness. Serve in hamburger
buns with lettuce leaves and cheese
slices. Yield: 4 servings (about 372 calories per serving). *Cathy Lancaster,*
Virginia Beach, Virginia.

GRILLED TOMATOES

4 small ripe tomatoes
2 tablespoons reduced-calorie margarine,
   melted
Freshly ground pepper
1 tablespoon plus 1 teaspoon Parmesan
   cheese

Cut each tomato into 6 sections, leaving stem ends intact. Brush insides of
tomatoes with margarine; sprinkle with
pepper and Parmesan cheese. Place
each on a piece of aluminum foil; fold
foil securely around each tomato. Cook
tomatoes on grill over medium coals 10
to 15 minutes or until tomatoes are
tender. Yield: 4 servings (about 57 calories per serving).

CAULIFLOWER-VEGETABLE
SALAD

1 small cauliflower, broken into flowerets
½ cup chopped cucumber
½ cup chopped green pepper
½ cup chopped celery
½ cup chopped green onions with tops
2 tablespoons finely chopped dill pickle
¼ teaspoon celery seeds
¼ teaspoon instant minced onion
¼ teaspoon pepper
¼ cup reduced-calorie mayonnaise
Lettuce leaves
Ground paprika
1 hard-cooked egg, quartered

Cook cauliflower, covered, in a small
amount of boiling water 5 minutes or
until crisp-tender; drain well. Add cucumber, green pepper, celery, green
onions, pickle, celery seeds, instant
onion, pepper, and mayonnaise; toss
gently. Cover and refrigerate 8 hours or
overnight. Spoon onto lettuce leaves,
and sprinkle with paprika; garnish with
egg. Yield: 4 servings (about 89 calories
per serving). *Nancy Hubner,*
Marietta, Georgia.

INSTANT FRUIT SHERBET

1 (16-ounce) can mixed fruit in light
   syrup, undrained
6 (½-inch) slices honeydew melon, cut
   in half

Position knife blade in food processor
bowl. Place fruit in processor container;
top with cover. Process 1 minute or
until pureed. Pour fruit into shallow
container, and freeze until almost frozen. Return to processor bowl, and process until consistency of soft sherbet;
freeze until firm.
Place honeydew slices in individual
dessert dishes; top with fruit sherbet.
Yield: 4 servings (about 58 calories per
serving). *Ruby Kirkes,*
Tuskahoma, Oklahoma.

*Tip: Plan your picnic menu according
to the distance you'll travel to the site;
for long distances, plan to use less perishable foods.*

Fire Up The Grill
For Flavorful Meat

It's that "cooked outdoors" flavor
that draws Southerners, bearing skewers
of meat and platters of thick burgers, to
the grill in summer. The smoky aroma
penetrates the air, tempting the neighbors to grill out, too, and even prompt-
ing friendly conversation between
outdoor chefs.
If you'd like something other than the
usual grilled entrée, you can impress
guests with recipes like Marinated
Shrimp Kabobs or Hawaiian Grilled
Pork Chops. The pineapple makes both
recipes different.
The shrimp kabobs are ideal for a
quick-to-cook meal. After marinating
the shrimp, thread them on skewers
with green pepper and pineapple, and
place kabobs on the grill. They cook in
a matter of minutes. Serve over rice,
and heat leftover marinade to go with
it. A salad and some crusty bread are
all you need to complete the meal.
For something a little different from a
plain hamburger, try our Stuffed
Burgers. One bite reveals a delicious
surprise—a slice of cheese between
layers of meat.

MARINATED SHRIMP KABOBS

1 pound large unpeeled fresh shrimp
1 (15¼-ounce) can pineapple chunks,
   undrained
1 (8-ounce) bottle Italian salad dressing
1 (8-ounce) can tomato sauce
2 tablespoons brown sugar
1 teaspoon prepared mustard
1 medium-size green pepper, cut into
   1-inch cubes
Hot cooked rice

Peel and devein shrimp; set aside.
Drain pineapple chunks, reserving ¼
cup juice. Set pineapple aside. Combine
reserved pineapple juice, Italian dressing, tomato sauce, sugar, and mustard
in a shallow dish; mix well. Add
shrimp, tossing gently to coat. Cover
and marinate 2 hours in the refrigerator, stirring occasionally.
Remove shrimp from marinade, reserving marinade. Alternate shrimp,

pineapple, and green pepper on 4 skewers. Grill over medium-hot coals 3 to 4 minutes on each side or until done, basting with marinade. Serve over rice with hot marinade. Yield: 4 servings.

Margot Foster,
Hubbard, Texas.

MARINATED BEEF KABOBS

1 pound lean boneless sirloin steak
1 (8-ounce) bottle Russian salad dressing
2 tablespoons lemon juice
1 tablespoon Worcestershire sauce
⅛ teaspoon pepper
⅛ teaspoon garlic powder
About 10 slices bacon, cut in half
2 medium-size green peppers, cut into
  1-inch squares
1 large onion, cut into 2-inch pieces
½ pound fresh mushrooms
1 pint cherry tomatoes

Trim fat from sirloin steak; cut into 1½-inch cubes. Place meat in a shallow container.

Combine salad dressing, lemon juice, Worcestershire sauce, pepper, and garlic powder; pour over meat. Cover and marinate in the refrigerator 8 hours. Drain, reserving the marinade.

Wrap bacon around meat; secure with a wooden pick. Alternate meat and vegetables on four skewers. Grill kabobs over medium-hot coals for 15 minutes or until meat reaches desired degree of doneness, turning and basting frequently with reserved marinade. Yield: 4 servings. *Mrs. Brickford Faucette,*
Knoxville, Tennessee.

STUFFED BURGERS

1½ pounds ground beef
1 (1.25-ounce) envelope onion soup mix
⅓ cup water
6 (1-ounce) slices process American cheese
6 slices bacon
Toasted hamburger buns

Combine ground beef, soup mix, and water; mix well, and shape into 12 thin patties. Place a cheese slice on each of 6 patties; top each with one of the remaining patties, and seal edges. Wrap bacon around edge of each patty, and secure with a wooden pick.

Place hamburgers on grill 5 inches from hot coals. Cook about 10 minutes on each side or to desired doneness. Serve on toasted buns. Yield: 6 servings. *Leigh Ann Shepard,*
Memphis, Tennessee.

HAWAIIAN GRILLED PORK CHOPS

1 (20-ounce) can pineapple slices,
  undrained
6 (1-inch-thick) pork chops
½ cup soy sauce
⅓ cup vegetable oil
¼ cup minced onion
1 clove garlic, minced
1 tablespoon brown sugar

Drain pineapple, reserving ¼ cup juice. Set pineapple aside.

Place chops in a large shallow dish. Combine reserved pineapple juice, soy sauce, oil, onion, garlic, and sugar, mixing well. Pour over chops; cover and marinate in refrigerator about 2 hours.

Remove chops, reserving marinade. Grill over medium coals 40 to 45 minutes, turning frequently and basting with marinade. Place a pineapple ring on each chop during last few minutes of cooking time. Yield: 6 servings.

Susan Laubacher,
Marietta, Georgia.

BARBECUED RIBS

10 pounds pork ribs
2 teaspoons garlic salt
2 teaspoons pepper
1 tablespoon prepared mustard
½ cup diced onion
2 tablespoons butter or margarine, melted
½ cup firmly packed brown sugar
¼ cup lemon juice
¼ cup steak sauce
2 tablespoons vinegar
2 tablespoons Worcestershire sauce
1 tablespoon chili powder

Cut ribs into serving-size pieces; place in a large Dutch oven. Cover ribs with water. Bring water to a boil; cover, reduce heat, and simmer 20 minutes. Drain well.

Sprinkle ribs with garlic salt and pepper, and baste with mustard. Sauté diced onion in butter in a saucepan; add remaining ingredients, and simmer mixture 5 minutes.

Prepare charcoal fire in grill; let burn 15 to 20 minutes. Grill ribs, 5 inches from heat, 25 to 30 minutes or until desired degree of doneness, turning frequently. Brush ribs with sauce during last 5 to 8 minutes. Serve with remaining sauce. Yield: 10 servings.

Tomi Babb,
Oklahoma City, Oklahoma.

LAMB KABOBS

1½ pounds boneless lamb, cut into 1-inch
  cubes
¼ cup plus 2 tablespoons white wine
  vinegar
¼ cup plus 2 tablespoons water
2 tablespoons dry sherry
1½ tablespoons sugar
2 tablespoons chopped fresh parsley
1 tablespoon dried whole rosemary,
  crushed
½ teaspoon salt
¼ teaspoon pepper
4 large, fresh mushroom caps, fluted

Place lamb in a large shallow dish. Combine remaining ingredients except mushrooms, mixing well. Pour over lamb; cover and marinate in refrigerator at least 2 hours.

Remove lamb from marinade; place on 4 skewers. Reserve ½ cup marinade; set aside. Grill kabobs 15 to 20 minutes over medium coals, turning and basting frequently with remaining marinade.

Combine reserved ½ cup marinade and mushrooms in a saucepan, and bring to a boil. Reduce heat, and simmer 4 to 5 minutes. Drain. Place a mushroom cap on each skewer with lamb. Yield: 4 servings.

Elnora Broady,
Fayetteville, North Carolina.

SMOKY GRILLED CHICKEN

½ cup vinegar
½ cup soy sauce
2 tablespoons lime juice
1 clove garlic
1 (2½- to 3-pound) broiler fryer, cut up
1 large onion, halved, then quartered

Soak 6 to 8 pieces of hickory wood chips in water 24 hours.

Combine vinegar, soy sauce, lime juice, and garlic in a blender; process 10 seconds. Place chicken in a large shallow baking dish; pour vinegar mixture over meat, and cover. Refrigerate overnight, turning chicken once.

Prepare charcoal fire in grill; let burn 15 to 20 minutes. Cover coals with soaked hickory chips and place onion on chips. Grill chicken over hot coals 50 minutes or until tender, turning and basting every 10 minutes. Yield: 8 servings.   *Karen Dickson,*
Fayetteville, Arkansas.

Treat Your Friends To Fried Chicken

Keep your next summer party casual by making fried chicken the center of attention. Nutty Oven-Fried Chicken is one of the variations we recommend. It fries up golden in the oven—chopped pecans give added interest.

You don't have to limit fried chicken to the main course; for a change, offer it as bite-size appetizers. Chicken Nuggets Supreme are seasoned with Parmesan cheese and herbs.

For French-Fried Chicken Bites, simply dredge chicken pieces in cracker crumbs before frying. The result is a crispy appetizer your guests will love.

NUTTY OVEN-FRIED CHICKEN

1 cup biscuit mix
2 teaspoons paprika
½ teaspoon salt
½ teaspoon poultry seasoning
½ teaspoon rubbed sage
⅓ cup finely chopped pecans
1 (2½- to 3-pound) broiler-fryer, cut up
½ cup evaporated milk
⅓ cup butter or margarine, melted

Combine biscuit mix, seasonings, and pecans; mix well. Dip chicken in milk; coat generously with pecan mixture.

Place in a lightly greased 13- x 9- x 2-inch baking pan. Drizzle butter over chicken; bake, uncovered, at 350° for 1 hour or until done. Yield: 4 servings.
Mrs. George Lance,
Madison, Tennessee.

CURRIED FRIED CHICKEN

½ cup all-purpose flour
¼ cup plus 2 tablespoons cornmeal
½ teaspoon salt
¾ teaspoon curry powder
½ teaspoon paprika
1 egg
1½ tablespoons milk
6 chicken breast halves
Vegetable oil

Combine flour, cornmeal, salt, curry powder and paprika; mix well, and set aside. Combine egg and milk in a shallow dish, and beat until blended. Dip chicken in egg mixture, and dredge in the flour mixture.

Fry chicken in hot oil (350°) 10 to 15 minutes on each side or until golden brown. Drain chicken on paper towels. Yield: 6 servings.   *Mrs. J. P. Weber,*
Corpus Christi, Texas.

FRENCH-FRIED CHICKEN BITES

1 pound boneless chicken breasts, cut into bite-size pieces
½ teaspoon salt
1 egg
½ cup all-purpose flour
¼ cup milk
1 cup cracker crumbs
Vegetable oil

Sprinkle chicken breasts with salt, and set aside.

Combine egg, flour, and milk, stirring until smooth. Dip chicken in egg mixture; roll in cracker crumbs. Fry chicken in 1 inch hot oil (325°) until golden brown. Drain on paper towels. Yield: about 3 dozen appetizers.
Louise Womack,
Oceana, West Virginia.

CHICKEN NUGGETS SUPREME

¼ cup all-purpose flour
¼ cup grated Parmesan cheese
1 teaspoon paprika
½ teaspoon salt
½ teaspoon dried whole oregano
¼ teaspoon dry mustard
4 chicken breast halves, skinned, boned, and cut into bite-size pieces
¼ cup milk
Vegetable oil

Combine flour, Parmesan cheese, paprika, salt, oregano, and dry mustard, stirring well. Dip chicken in milk, and dredge in flour mixture.

Heat 1 inch of oil in a large skillet to 325°; add chicken, and fry 5 minutes on each side. Drain on paper towels. Yield: 2 dozen appetizers. *Jean Voan,*
Shepherd, Texas.

Serve A Spirited Dessert

For summer entertaining, consider serving simple desserts delicately flavored with liqueurs or other alcoholic beverages. We offer several that have the casual sophistication that's just right for the season.

For example, try Strawberries Jamaica when you want an unusual ending to a festive meal. This luscious dish features a creamy dip that's laced with Grand Marnier and served with fresh

strawberries. Supply plenty of party picks, and let your guests help themselves. This unconventional dessert is fun and adds to the party atmosphere.

Chocolate-Crème de Menthe Parfaits couldn't be easier; they're layered with a mixture of chocolate syrup and crème de menthe, vanilla ice cream, and whipped topping. Garnished with mint leaves and served in tall, frosty glasses, they're a classic summer delight.

Still another unusual dessert is Amaretto Cream Tortoni, a frozen concoction with the distinctive taste of amaretto in a crunchy macaroon cookie and whipped cream mixture.

STRAWBERRIES JAMAICA

1 (3-ounce) package cream cheese, softened
½ cup firmly packed brown sugar
1½ cups commercial sour cream
2 tablespoons Grand Marnier
1 quart fresh strawberries

Beat cream cheese at medium speed of an electric mixer until smooth. Add sugar, sour cream, and Grand Marnier; beat 1 minute or until smooth. Cover and chill. Serve as a dip with strawberries. Yield: about 10 to 12 servings.

Sara Arnold,
Lewisville, Texas.

AMARETTO CREAM TORTONI

2 cups coarsely crushed coconut macaroon cookies
3 egg yolks
1 egg
¼ cup sugar
¼ cup amaretto
½ cup whipping cream, whipped
Additional whipped cream for garnish (optional)
Sliced almonds, toasted (optional)

Spread cookie crumbs on a cookie sheet; bake at 300° for 8 minutes. Cool.

Combine egg yolks, egg, and sugar in a medium mixing bowl; beat at high speed of an electric mixer 6 minutes or until sugar is dissolved and mixture is thickened. Reduce mixer speed to low; gradually add amaretto. Fold in

whipped cream. Spoon 2 tablespoons cookie crumbs into each of 8 dessert dishes. Top with ⅓ cup amaretto mixture. Sprinkle remaining crumbs equally around outer edge of each dish. Freeze until firm. Top with a dollop of whipped cream and almonds, if desired. Yield: 8 servings.

Frances Berga-Rigsby,
Daphne, Alabama.

CHOCOLATE-CRÈME DE MENTHE PARFAITS

3 tablespoons chocolate syrup
3 tablespoons crème de menthe
1 quart vanilla ice cream
Frozen whipped topping, thawed
Mint leaves (optional)

Combine chocolate syrup and crème de menthe in a small bowl; mix well. Spoon 1½ teaspoons chocolate mixture into each of six (6-ounce) chilled parfait glasses; spoon in ⅓ cup ice cream. Repeat layers. Cover and freeze until firm. Remove parfaits several minutes before serving; top with a dollop of whipped topping. Garnish them with mint leaves, if desired. Yield: 6 servings.

Mrs. Harold A. Wagner,
Hendersonville, North Carolina.

PEACH-PRALINE SAUCE

1 cup peeled fresh peach slices
⅓ cup praline-flavored liqueur
¼ cup firmly packed brown sugar
2 tablespoons butter or margarine
½ cup chopped pecans

Combine peach slices, liqueur, sugar, and butter in a small saucepan; bring mixture to a boil, stirring constantly. Reduce heat; cook 1 minute. Set aside to cool slightly.

Spoon sauce over vanilla ice cream; top with pecans. Serve immediately. Yield: 1¼ cups.

Iced Tea With Added Flavor

When summer days heat up the South, nothing is more refreshing than a cold glass of iced tea. This year, cool off while you're sunbathing or mowing the lawn with one of our recipes for iced tea. Each offers a twist that's a little different.

LEMONADE WITH FROZEN TEA CUBES

Juice of 4 medium lemons (about ¾ cup)
½ cup sugar
2 cups cold water
Frozen tea cubes (recipe follows)
Lemon slices (optional)

Combine lemon juice, sugar, and water, stirring until sugar dissolves. To serve, place several frozen tea cubes in each glass. Pour lemonade mixture over cubes, and garnish with lemon slices, if desired. Yield: 3 cups.

Frozen Tea Cubes:

1½ cups water
10 whole cloves
2 (2-inch) sticks cinnamon
4 regular tea bags
1½ cups cold water
Lemon slices (optional)

Combine 1½ cups water, cloves, and cinnamon sticks in a saucepan; bring to a boil. Reduce heat, and simmer 5 minutes; remove from heat. Pour over tea bags; cover and let stand 10 minutes. Discard tea bags and spices; add 1½ cups cold water to tea mixture. Pour tea into ice cube tray; freeze. Yield: about 2 dozen cubes. *Mrs. Hugh F. Mosher,*
Huntsville, Alabama.

Tip: Save lemon and orange rinds. Store in the freezer, and grate as needed for pies, cakes, breads, and cookies. Or the rinds can be candied for holiday uses.

LEMON-MINT TEA

2 cups water
6 regular tea bags
3 lemons, cut into ½-inch-thick slices
1 cup mint leaves, crushed
2 (46-ounce) cans pineapple juice
4 cups water
1 cup sugar
1½ teaspoons vanilla extract
1½ teaspoons almond extract

Bring water to a boil, and pour over tea bags. Add lemons and mint; cover and let stand 20 minutes. Strain.

Combine tea mixture and remaining ingredients. Serve over ice. Yield: about 3 quarts. *Mrs. Blair Cunnyngham, Cleveland, Tennessee.*

ICED CITRUS TEA

3 tablespoons loose tea
6 fresh mint leaves
2 quarts boiling water
1 cup sugar
Juice of 3 medium oranges (about 1 cup)
Juice of 5 medium lemons (about 1 cup)

Combine tea and mint in a large container. Add boiling water, cover and let stand 7 minutes. Strain tea and mint leaves; add remaining ingredients, stirring well. Serve over ice. Yield: 2½ quarts. *Mrs. W. Judd Wyatt, Columbia, Missouri.*

Just a few ingredients make an exciting presentation in Asparagus-Artichoke Salad. It has an herb-vinaigrette dressing that's poured on just before serving.

SUMMER TEA

1 quart water
6 regular tea bags
1 cup sugar
½ cup lemon juice
½ cup white grape juice
1 quart water

Bring 1 quart water to a boil, and pour over tea bags. Remove from heat; cover and let stand 5 minutes. Discard tea bags. Add remaining ingredients, stirring until sugar dissolves. Serve over ice. Yield: 9 cups. *Mrs. Bob Nester, Charleston, West Virginia.*

Picture-Perfect Salads

When you're planning a summer menu, don't forget the salad. Instead of putting something together at the last minute or preparing an old standby, plan ahead and serve an eye-catching salad with fresh appeal.

Asparagus-Artichoke Salad is a striking example. It features frozen asparagus spears and canned artichokes; these ingredients make quite an impact arranged in a spoke pattern over a bed of lettuce and sliced tomatoes.

ASPARAGUS-ARTICHOKE SALAD

½ cup vegetable oil
¼ cup white wine vinegar
1 teaspoon finely chopped chives
1 teaspoon finely chopped parsley
½ teaspoon dried salad herbs
½ teaspoon salt
⅛ teaspoon pepper
2 (10-ounce) packages frozen asparagus spears
Lettuce leaves
3 large tomatoes, sliced
1 (14-ounce) can artichoke bottoms, chilled, drained, and cut into strips
1 hard-cooked egg, sieved
Additional chopped chives

Combine oil, vinegar, chives, 1 teaspoon parsley, dried herbs, salt, and pepper in a jar. Cover tightly, and shake vigorously. Chill dressing.

Cook asparagus according to package directions; drain and chill.

Line a round serving platter with lettuce. Arrange tomatoes in a circle around outer edge of serving plate. Arrange asparagus and artichoke bottoms in spoke pattern over tomatoes and lettuce. Mound egg in center, and top with additional chopped chives. Pour dressing over the salad, and serve immediately. Yield: 10 to 12 servings.

Norma Patelunas,
St. Petersburg, Florida.

MANDARIN SPINACH SALAD

8 cups washed, torn spinach
1 cup diagonally sliced celery
2 green onions with tops, chopped
1 (11-ounce) can mandarin oranges, drained
1 (2-ounce) package slivered almonds, toasted
Sweet-and-sour dressing (recipe follows)

Combine spinach, celery, and green onions; toss gently. Place on a large serving platter; arrange mandarin oranges and toasted almonds in desired pattern on spinach mixture. Serve with the sweet-and-sour dressing. Yield: 6 to 8 servings.

Sweet-and-Sour Dressing:
¼ cup vegetable oil
2 tablespoons vinegar
2 tablespoons sugar
5 drops of hot sauce
1 teaspoon chopped fresh parsley
1 teaspoon salt
Dash of pepper

Combine all ingredients in a jar. Cover jar tightly, and shake vigorously. Yield: about ½ cup. *Joyce Dantzler, Fairfax, Virginia.*

Tip: Sand and dirt can be removed from fresh vegetables by soaking in warm salted water 5 minutes.

COTTAGE-TOMATO SALAD

About ¾ pound fresh green beans
2 cups large-curd cottage cheese
⅓ cup mayonnaise or salad dressing
½ cup shredded carrots
¼ cup salted, chopped peanuts
2 tablespoons chopped green onions
6 medium tomatoes
Lettuce leaves
Salted whole peanuts (optional)

Wash beans; trim ends, and remove strings. Cut beans into 1½-inch pieces. Cook beans in boiling water 15 minutes or until crisp-tender. Drain and plunge into cold water; drain again.

Combine cottage cheese and mayonnaise, mixing well. Add green beans, carrots, peanuts, and green onions; mix well. Set aside.

Remove stems from tomatoes. Place stem side down, and cut almost through each tomato, making 6 wedges. Place tomatoes on lettuce leaves on salad plates; stuff with cottage cheese mixture. Garnish top with whole peanuts, if desired. Yield: 6 servings.

Note: For a special touch, "fringe" tomato wedges by carefully peeling back skin from the upper quarter of each tomato wedge and curling it under.

Mary Mae Herring,
Eureka, Kansas.

Tray Dining
For Casual Meals

When the sun starts beaming down, tray dining makes it easy to pick up your meal and head to the nearest shade. With either of these menus, the trays will look just as as pretty and colorful as your summer garden.

If the occasion calls for a small, intimate gathering, serve Salmon Steaks With Dill Sauce. Tomatoes, salad, and fruit round out the menu.

Casual diners may prefer our soup-and-sandwich combination. Gazpacho, a favorite for summer vegetable lovers, is served with Tangy Ham-and-Swiss Sandwiches and Melons in Mint Sauce.

Rice-Pea Salad
Marinated Tomatoes
Salmon Steaks With Dill Sauce
Fresh fruit
Wine

RICE-PEA SALAD

¾ cup uncooked regular rice
⅓ cup frozen English peas
¾ cup chopped celery
⅓ cup mayonnaise
2 tablespoons minced onion
1 teaspoon lemon juice
¼ teaspoon salt
¼ teaspoon white pepper
Lettuce leaves (optional)
Pimiento strips (optional)

Cook rice according to package directions, omitting salt; set aside.

Cook peas according to package directions, omitting salt and butter; drain, reserving 3 tablespoons liquid.

Combine rice, peas, and celery; chill. Combine reserved pea liquid, mayonnaise, onion, lemon juice, salt, and pepper, mixing well. Toss with rice mixture. If desired, serve on lettuce leaves, and garnish with pimiento strips. Yield: 4 to 6 servings. *Sara H. Davis, Sherrill's Ford, North Carolina.*

MARINATED TOMATOES

⅓ cup vegetable oil
2 tablespoons wine vinegar
2 tablespoons thinly sliced onion
2 tablespoons chopped fresh parsley
½ teaspoon salt
¼ teaspoon dried whole marjoram
⅛ teaspoon pepper
3 medium tomatoes, peeled and quartered

Combine all ingredients except tomatoes in a jar. Cover tightly, and shake vigorously. Pour over tomatoes; cover and marinate 6 to 8 hours. Yield: 4 to 6 servings. *Mrs. Rudolph F. Watts, Glasgow, Kentucky.*

SALMON STEAKS WITH DILL SAUCE

4 (1-inch-thick) salmon steaks (1½ to 2 pounds)
1 small onion, sliced
½ lemon, sliced
1 bay leaf
¼ teaspoon salt
¾ cup milk
1 tablespoon all-purpose flour
2 teaspoons Dijon mustard
½ to ¾ teaspoon dillseeds
¼ teaspoon grated lemon rind
¼ teaspoon salt
Dash of white pepper
1 egg yolk, beaten
1 tablespoon lemon juice
Fresh sprigs of dillweed (optional)

Place salmon steaks in a 10-inch skillet; add enough water to cover. Top with onion, lemon slices, and bay leaf; sprinkle with ¼ teaspoon salt, and bring to a boil. Cover, reduce heat, and simmer 8 minutes or until fish flakes easily when tested with a fork.

Combine milk and flour in a saucepan, stirring well. Add mustard, dillseeds, lemon rind, ¼ teaspoon salt, and pepper; cook over medium heat, stirring constantly, until thickened. Gradually stir about one-fourth of hot milk mixture into egg yolk; add to remaining hot milk mixture, stirring constantly. Cook 1 minute, stirring constantly. Add lemon juice, mixing well.

Remove salmon steaks from skillet, reserving lemon slices; spoon sauce over salmon. Garnish with reserved lemon slices and sprigs of dillweed, if desired. Yield: 4 servings.

Mrs. James A. Tuthill,
Virginia Beach, Virginia.

Tip: Fresh meat, poultry, and fish should be loosely wrapped and refrigerated; use in a few days. Loosely wrap fresh ground meat, liver, and kidneys; use in one or two days. Wieners, bacon, and sliced sandwich meats can be stored in original wrappings in the refrigerator. Store all meat in the coldest part of the refrigerator.

Gazpacho
Tangy Ham-And-Swiss Sandwiches
Melons In Mint Sauce
Wine

GAZPACHO

3 hard-cooked eggs
2 tablespoons olive oil
1 teaspoon dry mustard
1 clove garlic, crushed
1 teaspoon Worcestershire sauce
2 medium cucumbers, peeled, seeded, and chopped
1 medium tomato, peeled and chopped
1 small onion, diced
½ cup diced green pepper
6 cups tomato juice
3 tablespoons lemon or lime juice
¼ teaspoon pepper
⅛ teaspoon sugar
⅛ teaspoon celery salt
Lemon slices (optional)

Separate egg yolks from egg whites; press hard-cooked egg whites through a sieve, and set aside.

Mash egg yolks with olive oil to make a smooth paste; stir in mustard, garlic, and Worcestershire sauce. Add vegetables, mixing well. Stir in juice, pepper, sugar, and celery salt; cover and chill at least 3 hours. Stir well; garnish with egg whites and lemon slices, if desired. Yield: about 11 cups.

Margaret Cowdery,
Atlanta, Georgia.

TANGY HAM-AND-SWISS SANDWICHES

¾ cup mayonnaise
3 tablespoons sweet-pickle salad cubes
1½ tablespoons Dijon mustard
1½ tablespoons tangy mustard-mayonnaise-flavored sandwich sauce
12 slices rye bread, toasted
12 (1-ounce) slices ham
12 (1-ounce) slices Swiss cheese
6 lettuce leaves

Combine first 4 ingredients; mix well. Spread mayonnaise mixture on one side of each slice of bread. Top half of bread slices with 2 slices ham, 2 slices cheese, and a lettuce leaf. Cover with remaining bread slices. Cut each sandwich into quarters. Yield: 6 servings.

Beverly Nevins,
Birmingham, Alabama.

MELONS IN MINT SAUCE

1 small canteloupe
1 small honeydew
½ cup sugar
1 cup water
6 to 8 fresh mint leaves, coarsely chopped

Scoop out melons with melon ball cutter; set aside. Combine remaining ingredients in a small saucepan; bring to a boil, stirring constantly. Reduce heat, and simmer 5 minutes. Remove from heat, and let cool. Strain. Pour syrup over melon balls; chill 2 to 3 hours. Yield: 6 servings.

Charlotte Ann Pierce,
Greensburg, Kentucky.

Toss A Pasta Salad

When a light dish appeals to you, think cold pasta salad. Macaroni Salad Véronique is refreshing with its combination of grapes and ham. And it's just one of eight tempting recipes.

MACARONI SALAD VÉRONIQUE

1¾ cups uncooked shell macaroni
2 cups cubed cooked ham
2 cups seedless green grapes, halved
½ cup sliced green onions
Dressing (recipe follows)

Cook macaroni according to package directions; drain. Rinse with cold water; drain again.

Combine macaroni, ham, grapes, and onions; add dressing. Toss lightly until well coated. Chill 6 hours or overnight. Yield: 4 to 6 servings.

Dressing:

½ cup mayonnaise
½ cup commercial sour cream
2 tablespoons cider vinegar
1½ tablespoons Dijon mustard
1 teaspoon sugar
½ teaspoon white pepper
¼ to ½ teaspoon dried whole dillweed
¼ teaspoon seasoned salt

Combine all ingredients in a small bowl, mixing well. Yield: 1¼ cups.

Mrs. J. C. Harville, Jr.,
Grenada, Mississippi.

KIDNEY BEAN-SALAMI PASTA TOSS

1 cup uncooked elbow macaroni
1 (19-ounce) can red kidney beans, rinsed and drained
1 cup chopped celery
¾ cup slivered salami
⅔ cup chopped purple onion
¼ cup cider vinegar
2 tablespoons olive oil
¼ teaspoon garlic salt
⅛ teaspoon pepper
Celery leaves (optional)

Cook macaroni according to package directions; drain. Rinse with cold water; drain again.

Combine macaroni and remaining ingredients except celery leaves in a large bowl, tossing lightly until macaroni mixture is well coated. Chill 6 hours or overnight. Garnish with celery leaves, if desired. Yield: 4 to 6 servings.

Charlotte Watkins,
Lakeland, Florida.

FESTIVE MACARONI-SHRIMP SALAD

5 cups water
1½ pounds unpeeled fresh shrimp
3¾ cups uncooked corkscrew macaroni
1 (6-ounce) package frozen Chinese pea pods or 1 (10-ounce) package frozen English peas
½ cup sliced water chestnuts, drained
½ to 1 cup mayonnaise
2 tablespoons chopped parsley
1½ tablespoons chopped pimiento
⅛ teaspoon salt
⅛ teaspoon coarsely ground pepper

Bring water to a boil; add shrimp, and cook 3 to 5 minutes. Drain well; rinse with cold water. Chill. Peel and devein shrimp; set aside.

Cook macaroni according to package directions; drain. Rinse with cold water; drain again.

Cook pea pods according to package directions; drain. Set aside.

Combine shrimp, macaroni, pea pods, and remaining ingredients in a large bowl; toss lightly until well coated. Chill 6 hours. Yield: 6 servings.

Jene M. Harner,
Towson, Maryland.

SHRIMP ROTELLE

3 cups water
1 pound unpeeled fresh shrimp
2 cups rotelle macaroni
1 medium onion, finely chopped
1 medium cucumber, peeled and chopped
½ cup chopped celery
¼ cup chopped radishes
1 carrot, scraped and grated
½ cup commercial Italian dressing
3 tablespoons commercial hot taco sauce
2 tablespoons lemon juice
1 tablespoon Worcestershire sauce
Salt and pepper to taste
Hard-cooked egg wedges (optional)

Bring water to a boil; add shrimp, and return to a boil. Reduce heat, and simmer 3 to 5 minutes. Drain; rinse with cold water. Chill. Peel and devein shrimp.

Cook macaroni according to package directions; drain. Rinse with cold water; drain again.

Combine shrimp, macaroni, and remaining ingredients except egg wedges; chill at least 1 hour. Garnish with hard-cooked egg wedges, if desired. Yield: 6 servings.

Sydney Wood Sivertsen,
Bartlesville, Oklahoma.

Tip: Keep in mind that you cook pasta only until it's tender and slightly firm to the bite; overcooking makes it soft and mushy.

TACO MACARONI SALAD

2 cups uncooked corkscrew macaroni
1 pound ground round
1 (1¼-ounce) package taco seasoning mix
½ cup commercial French dressing
½ head lettuce, shredded
1 pint cherry tomatoes, halved
1 cup (4 ounces) shredded sharp Cheddar cheese
½ cup chopped green onions
½ cup chopped green pepper

Cook macaroni according to package directions; drain. Rinse with cold water; drain. Chill at least 1 hour.

Cook ground round in a large skillet until browned, stirring to crumble; drain off drippings. Stir in taco seasoning and French dressing; cool.

Combine macaroni, beef mixture, and remaining ingredients in a large bowl, tossing well. Serve salad immediately. Yield: about 8 servings.

Cynthia Kannenberg,
Brown Deer, Wisconsin.

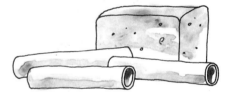

ZITI-CHEDDAR SALAD

3 cups uncooked ziti macaroni
1 (12-ounce) package sharp Cheddar cheese, cubed
2 cups sliced radishes
1 medium-size green pepper, chopped
¾ cup mayonnaise
⅓ cup milk
¾ teaspoon dried whole dillweed
¼ teaspoon salt
¼ teaspoon pepper
Radish fans (optional)

Cook macaroni according to package directions; drain. Rinse with cold water; drain again.

Combine remaining ingredients except radish fans in a large bowl, mixing well. Fold in macaroni; toss lightly until well coated. Chill 6 hours or overnight. Garnish with radish fans, if desired. Yield: 8 to 10 servings.

Bonnie Ramsburg,
Frederick, Maryland.

CRUNCHY PASTA SALAD

3½ cups uncooked rotelle macaroni
1 cup chopped celery
¾ cup chopped green pepper
¾ cup chopped cucumber
3 hard-cooked eggs, chopped
¼ teaspoon salt
Dressing (recipe follows)
Tomato wedges (optional)

Cook macaroni according to package directions; drain. Rinse with cold water; drain again.

Combine macaroni, celery, green pepper, cucumber, eggs, and salt; add dressing. Toss lightly until well coated. Chill 6 hours or overnight. Garnish with tomato wedges, if desired. Yield: 4 to 6 servings.

Dressing:

2 tablespoons butter or margarine
1 egg, beaten
¼ cup cider vinegar
1 teaspoon all-purpose flour
¼ teaspoon salt
1 cup mayonnaise

Melt butter in saucepan over medium heat; add egg, vinegar, flour, and salt. Cook, stirring constantly, until mixture thickens. Cool slightly. Add mayonnaise; stir until well blended. Yield: About 1 cup.   *Evelyn Milam,*
Knoxville, Tennessee.

SWEET-AND-SOUR MACARONI SALAD

1 (8-ounce) package uncooked elbow
   macaroni
3 medium carrots, scraped and diced
2 stalks celery, diced
1 medium onion, chopped
1 medium cucumber, peeled and chopped
1 large tomato, peeled and chopped
½ cup vegetable oil
½ cup cider vinegar
⅓ cup sugar
1 teaspoon salt
½ teaspoon pepper

Cook macaroni according to package directions; drain. Rinse with cold water; drain again.

Combine macaroni, carrots, celery, onion, cucumber, and tomato.

Combine remaining ingredients; mix well. Pour over macaroni mixture; toss gently. Cover; chill 8 hours. Yield: 8 servings.   *Michele Hawa Raeuber,*
Jacksonville, Florida.

Centerpieces That Steal The Show

Fill the container with pasta, and top with flowers. These may sound like directions from an exotic recipe, but in this case the combination isn't for cooking. Instead, the ingredients make a unique arrangement of fresh flowers and uncooked pasta—one that is likely to be as popular as the meal itself.

The obvious time to create such a centerpiece is when you're serving pasta, such as in the salads beginning on

Long spaghetti provides a strong vertical accent for stems of lilies and tulip buds.

page 164. But this unique presentation should be a hit just about anytime.

The basis of each arrangement is simple—show off the pasta in the vase that holds the flowers. The pasta provides an anchor for the stems. Seashells, bow ties, and other large pasta shapes are perfect for filling a big container. Elbow shapes are well suited to a smaller vase, while long pasta, such as linguine and spaghetti, is ideal for a tall vase. No matter what size you choose, always use a container of clear glass or the effect of the pasta will be lost.

The most important thing to remember is that if you take special care, you can lengthen the life of the arrangement. Adding water directly to the container would soften the pasta, so we've offered some alternatives that will keep these arrangements looking fresh.

Set a small bowl filled with water within a larger one, and arrange flowers in a block of florist foam. Or put each flower stem in a special tubelike holder called a water vial, available from a florist or florist's supply store. This provides water for each stem while the pasta stays dry.

If you plan to use the arrangement over a period of several days, add a preservative to the water. An ingredient in Sprite® also acts as a floral preservative; just add 1 part Sprite® to 5 parts water. Changing the water every other day and trimming about an inch off the stems will also help keep the flowers looking fresh.

Most flowers that you purchase have been conditioned so that they remain fresh for several hours. So even without water, your centerpiece, if it's arranged at the last minute, can make it through a party. However, it is unlikely that roses will stay in good shape.

If you cut flowers from your garden, condition them by placing the freshly cut stems in tepid water for a couple of hours. Then refrigerate the flowers for about an hour before arranging them.

Right: Varied pasta shapes add interest to these dishes: (front to back) Festive Macaroni-Shrimp Salad, Macaroni Salad Véronique, and Ziti-Cheddar Salad. (Recipes begin on page 164.)

Far left: *Summertime means making fresh peach desserts like Spicy Peach Cobbler* (*left*) *and Peach Dumplings* (*right*), *two favorites in our test kitchens.* (*Recipes begin on page 177.*)

Left: *Strawberries Jamaica* (*front*) *and Chocolate-Crème de Menthe Parfaits* (*back*) *are easy but elegant. Both offer cool refreshment for summer dining* (*page 161*).

Below: *Guests will enjoy Lemon-Orange Pie* (*page 172*) *with a whipped cream topping and a chiffon filling.*

Above: *Our seasoned vinegars feature garden fresh herb flavor: (left to right) Five-Herb Vinegar, Tarragon-Dill Vinegar, Garlic-Basil Vinegar, Lemon-Mint Vinegar, and Spicy Oregano-Lemon Vinegar (recipes on page 124).*

Right: *Experience a range of sweet-and-sour flavor when you sample crisp pickle slices, vegetable relishes, fruit pickles, and more. (Pickling information and recipes begin on page 174.)*

When You're Hungry, Reach For Cookies

School is out, and it's a great time to invite friends over for a relaxing afternoon in the sun. And just in case everyone is hungry for sweets, be prepared with a tempting snack. Here you'll find sweets that can take the heat. They also pack and travel well since there are no messy frostings or gooey fillings to crush or melt.

Vanilla Slice-and-Bake Cookies are ready when you are. The dough can be stored in the refrigerator for several days or in the freezer for up to 3 months. You will love the convenience of these flavorful treats.

For a rich, spicy taste, bite into Sour Cream-Nutmeg Cookies. Plenty of pecans add texture to this cookie.

Saucepan Pretzel Brownies are different yet delectable. Just as you may have guessed, part of the flour has been replaced with finely crushed pretzels for an interesting taste change. And best of all, these pretzel brownies make cleanup a breeze since you mix them up in a saucepan.

VANILLA SLICE-AND-BAKE COOKIES

½ cup butter or margarine, softened
1 cup sugar
1 egg
2 teaspoons vanilla extract
1¾ cups all-purpose flour
½ teaspoon baking soda
½ teaspoon salt
½ cup chopped pecans

Cream butter; gradually add sugar, beating well. Add egg and vanilla; beat well. Combine flour, soda, and salt; add to creamed mixture, beating well. Stir in chopped pecans.

Shape dough into 2 long rolls, 1 inch in diameter; wrap rolls in waxed paper, and chill for 2 hours or until firm.

Unwrap rolls, and cut into ¼-inch slices. Place on ungreased cookie sheets, and bake at 400° for 8 to 10 minutes. Cool cookies slightly on cookie sheets; remove to wire racks. Yield: about 6½ dozen.

Note: Dough may be frozen for up to 3 months. *Gwen Templeton, Albertville, Alabama.*

SOUR CREAM-NUTMEG COOKIES

½ cup butter or margarine, softened
1 cup firmly packed brown sugar
1 egg
½ cup commercial sour cream
1 cup all-purpose flour
1 cup sifted cake flour
2 teaspoons baking powder
½ teaspoon baking soda
½ teaspoon salt
½ teaspoon ground nutmeg
1 cup chopped pecans

Cream butter; gradually add sugar, beating well. Add egg and sour cream, and beat well. Combine flour, baking powder, soda, salt, and nutmeg; add to creamed mixture, beating well. Stir in pecans.

Drop dough by heaping teaspoonfuls onto lightly greased cookie sheets. Bake at 350° for 8 to 10 minutes. Cool slightly on cookie sheets; remove to wire racks. Yield: 5 dozen. *Sarah Watson, Knoxville, Tennessee.*

SAUCEPAN PRETZEL BROWNIES

⅔ cup shortening
4 (1-ounce) squares unsweetened chocolate
4 eggs, beaten
2 cups sugar
1 cup all-purpose flour
1 teaspoon baking powder
1 cup finely crushed pretzels
1 cup coarsely chopped walnuts

Melt shortening and chocolate in a large saucepan over low heat. Combine eggs and sugar, mixing until blended. Add to chocolate mixture, beating until smooth. Add remaining ingredients, mixing well. (Batter will be very stiff.)

Spread mixture in a well-greased 13- x 9- x 2-inch baking pan. Bake at 350° for 30 minutes or until center is firm. Cool in pan on wire rack. Cut into squares. Yield: 32 squares. *Madze Hay, Dunedin, Florida.*

COCOA KISS COOKIES

1 cup butter or margarine, softened
⅔ cup sugar
1 teaspoon vanilla extract
1⅔ cups all-purpose flour
¼ cup cocoa
1 cup coarsely ground walnuts
1 (9-ounce) package milk chocolate kisses, unwrapped

Cream butter; gradually add sugar, beating until light and fluffy. Add vanilla, mixing well. Add flour and cocoa, mixing well. Stir in walnuts. Chill dough 2 hours or until firm.

Wrap 1 tablespoon of dough around each chocolate kiss, and roll to form a ball. Place on ungreased cookie sheets, and bake at 375° for 12 minutes. Cool slightly on cookie sheets; remove to wire racks. Yield: about 4 dozen. *Barbara Rogers, Cleveland, Tennessee.*

OATMEAL-PEANUT BUTTER COOKIES

1 cup butter or margarine, softened
2 cups sugar
3 eggs
½ cup peanut butter
3½ cups regular oats, uncooked
1 cup all-purpose flour
¾ teaspoon baking soda
½ teaspoon salt
1½ teaspoons ground cinnamon
1 cup raisins

Cream butter; gradually add sugar, beating well. Add eggs and peanut butter, and beat well. Combine oats, flour, soda, salt, and cinnamon; add to creamed mixture, beating well. Stir in raisins.

Drop dough by heaping teaspoonfuls onto lightly greased cookie sheets. Bake at 350° for 10 to 11 minutes. Cool slightly on cookie sheets; remove to wire racks. Yield: 9 dozen. *Maxine M. Ballew, Columbia, Missouri.*

Chill The Summer Dessert

Summer nights—sometimes we wish they could go on forever. Good friends, good food, good conversation; the magic is all there. When the meal is over and it's time to bring out dessert, serve something in keeping with the season. Present your guests with one of these chilled desserts.

Strawberry Cake Roll is a delectable example. It has a strawberry-whipped cream filling that's rolled up inside a soft, spongy cake layer. The surface is brushed with corn syrup and jam and garnished with whipped cream and strawberries.

Lemon-Orange Pie pairs two citrus flavors for tangy, cool refreshment. The filling is chilled in a baked pastry shell and the top swirled with sweetened whipped cream.

STRAWBERRY CAKE ROLL

4 eggs, separated
¾ cup sugar
1 teaspoon vanilla extract
¾ cup sifted cake flour
¾ teaspoon baking powder
¼ teaspoon salt
Powdered sugar
1 cup whipping cream
3 tablespoons sugar
¼ teaspoon vanilla extract
1 (10-ounce) package frozen sliced
   strawberries, drained
¼ cup strawberry jam
¼ cup light corn syrup

Grease a 15- x 10- x 1-inch jellyroll pan, and line with waxed paper. Grease and flour waxed paper; set aside.

Beat egg yolks until thick and lemon colored; gradually add ¾ cup sugar, beating well. Stir in 1 teaspoon vanilla. Combine flour and baking powder; gradually add to sugar mixture, beating just until blended. Beat egg whites (at room temperature) and salt until stiff peaks form; stir one-fourth of egg white mixture into flour mixture. Repeat with remaining egg white mixture, stirring in one-third of mixture at a time.

Spread batter evenly in prepared pan. Bake at 375° for 10 to 12 minutes.

Sift powdered sugar in a 15- x 10- x 1-inch rectangle on a towel. When cake is done, immediately loosen from sides of pan, and turn out onto powdered sugar. Peel off waxed paper. Starting at narrow end, roll up cake and towel together; cool cake on a wire rack, seam side down.

Beat whipping cream until foamy; gradually add 3 tablespoons sugar, beating until soft peaks form. Add ¼ teaspoon vanilla; beat until blended. Fold in strawberries. Unroll cake, and remove towel. Spread cake with strawberry filling, and reroll. Place on serving plate, seam side down. Combine jam and corn syrup in a small saucepan; bring to a boil, stirring constantly. Remove from heat; brush mixture over cake roll. Chill until serving time. Yield: 8 to 10 servings.
Derrell H. Sears,
Anderson, South Carolina.

LEMON-ORANGE PIE

4 eggs, divided
½ cup sugar
⅓ cup lemon juice
3 tablespoons orange juice
½ teaspoon salt
1 envelope unflavored gelatin
¼ cup cold water
1 teaspoon grated lemon rind
½ teaspoon grated orange rind
¼ cup sugar
1 (9-inch) baked pastry shell
1 cup whipping cream
¼ cup plus 2 tablespoons sifted powdered
   sugar
Lemon and orange slices (optional)
Fresh mint sprig (optional)

Combine egg yolks, ½ cup sugar, lemon juice, orange juice, and salt in top of a double boiler; mix well. Bring water in bottom of double boiler to a boil; reduce heat, and cook egg mixture over hot water, stirring constantly, until mixture thickens.

Combine gelatin and cold water; let stand 1 minute. Add to hot mixture, and stir until gelatin dissolves. Stir in grated lemon rind and grated orange rind. Chill until mixture mounds when dropped from a spoon.

Beat egg whites (at room temperature) until foamy; gradually add ¼ cup sugar, 1 tablespoon at a time, beating until stiff peaks form. Carefully fold into lemon mixture. Pour into baked pastry shell; chill.

Beat whipping cream until foamy; gradually add powdered sugar, beating until soft peaks form. Spread whipped cream over filling. Garnish with lemon and orange twists and mint sprig, if desired. Yield: one 9-inch pie.
Mrs. Herbert W. Rutherford,
Baltimore, Maryland.

CHOCOLATE-COFFEE FROZEN DESSERT

2 cups vanilla wafer crumbs, divided
¼ cup butter or margarine, melted
2½ (1-ounce) squares unsweetened
   chocolate
½ cup butter or margarine
2 cups sifted powdered sugar
1 teaspoon vanilla extract
3 eggs, separated
1 cup coarsely chopped pecans
2 quarts coffee ice cream, softened

Combine 1¾ cups vanilla wafer crumbs and ¼ cup melted butter, mixing well. Press mixture into a 13- x 9- x 2-inch pan. Set aside.

Combine chocolate and ½ cup butter in a heavy saucepan; cook over low heat until melted. Remove from heat. Add powdered sugar and vanilla; beat 2 minutes at medium speed of electric mixer. Add egg yolks, beating mixture until smooth.

Beat egg whites (at room temperature) until stiff peaks form; fold into chocolate mixture. Spread mixture over crumbs, and sprinkle with pecans. Cover and freeze until firm.

Spread ice cream over pecan layer; sprinkle with remaining ¼ cup crumbs. Cover and freeze overnight or until ice cream is firm. Yield: 15 to 18 servings.
Nancy Swinney,
Tallahassee, Florida.

Holiday Lights For Southern Nights

Luminarias have long been popular in Mexico and the Southwest during the Christmas season. These festive lights—made with paper bags, sand, and votive candles—are also a natural decoration for outdoor entertaining.

We've designed three adaptations of luminarias; they're all inexpensive and easy to make, and they're guaranteed to add a special touch to summer parties. Following are instructions and the materials you'll need to make them.

The yellow luminarias with scalloped tops (below) are colored lunch bags, available at discount stores. Of our three examples, these are the simplest to make. This quality, as well as their low cost (a package of 40 bags costs under $1), makes these luminarias ideal for lighting a big area.

To make a luminaria, fold a bag vertically into three equal portions. Draw an arc across the top of the folded bag

White lunch bags, pierced with an ice pick in geometric designs, help to light the dark steps of a deck in a festive way.

Simple flower cutouts make these luminarias an attractive centerpiece that gives a soft glow to a summer table.

with a compass. Next, cut through the folded bag along the arc to create a scalloped effect. Use this bag as a pattern for the rest of the bags.

There are other designs that can be used. Luminarias decorated with geometric designs are shown in the photograph directly above. These lights are made from white lunch bags found at grocery or discount stores. To make the designs, simply pencil dots on a bag, using a compass and/or ruler to form a geometric pattern. Then lay the bag on a piece of wood, and punch out the dots with an ice pick and hammer. (The holes can be enlarged by holding the bag up and running the ice pick through them.) Finally, turn the top of the bag down a couple of times to stiffen it and create a finished look.

The luminarias with flower cutouts (above) are made from gift bags of heavyweight stock. These are available at stationery, gift, and variety shops. Trace each flower design (see patterns below) onto a piece of stencil paper or thin cardboard, and cut it out with a sharp hobby knife. Position the design on the bag. While holding it steady with one hand, cut it out with the other. (Before cutting out the design, slip a piece of cardboard into the bag to protect the back. Don't tape the stencil to the bag while you are cutting; this will mar the bag's finish.) Trim the top of the bag into a wide arc.

After you have decorated all your bags, add three cups of sand to each one, and place a votive candle firmly in the sand.

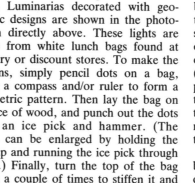

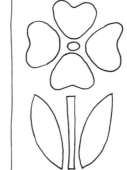

Luminarias used along a walkway cast a welcoming glow. They're made with inexpensive colored lunch bags, sand, and votive candles.

Putting Up Pickles

Crock jars filled with cucumbers and salt water rest in a cool spot in the cellar. A boiling syrup of vinegar, sugar, and spices stings the air with a sharp scent, and knives rhythmically rap on cutting boards, leaving piles of chopped vegetables, ready for making into relish.

It's time for pickling and for showing off blue-ribbon results to friends, neighbors, and county fair judges. And the pantry becomes a canvas, painted with jars of red-speckled relishes, bright green pickle slices, and golden peaches in a rosy syrup.

Produce is at its best now—just right for restocking your shelves with the best tasting pickles and relishes. If you've never attempted making them before, or if you just need to update favorite recipes to new standards, read on for all the details.

Types of Pickles

Consider the amount of time you have when deciding on which pickles to make. **Fresh-pack or quick-process pickles,** such as our Cucumber Chips or Sour Cucumber Pickles, are the best bet if you're short on time; they can be prepared in one to two days. The cucumbers are covered with a boiling vinegar-and-spice mixture and allowed to stand several hours. Even though these types of pickles are quick to make, the flavor is best if, after processing, you let them sit in the jars for a period of three to four weeks.

Brined pickles require several weeks to prepare, and during that time they must be checked daily. The cucumbers soak in a brine (salt-water solution) and go through a curing process. The fermentation produces lactic acid, which aids in preservation. The cucumbers change from a bright green to a dark olive or yellow-green color, and the flavor that develops is delicate and not too sour, salty, or spicy.

If you have an abundance of cucumbers to pickle right away, you may want to make the **brined, unfermented type,** like our recipe for Sweet Icicle Pickles. The process used for brining is not as particular as that for fermenting cucumbers. The salt content of the brine is too high to allow fermentation, but a cured flavor develops. After brining, the cucumbers must be desalted by soaking in several changes of fresh water. Then they must be prepared like fresh-pack pickles, since the cucumbers never develop a high acidity during brining.

Chopped, seasoned, and pickled vegetables and fruit are traditionally known as **pickle relishes.** The pickling process is similar to that of fresh-pack pickles, but more time is required in preparation because the vegetables must be chopped. A food processor, of course, is a great timesaver.

Fruit pickles are made from whole or sliced fruit simmered in a spicy, sweet-sour syrup. Peaches, pears, figs, crabapples, green tomatoes, and watermelon rind are popular Southern fruit often used for pickling.

Equipment

You'll need the same utensils for processing pickles as you do for jams, jellies, and high-acid canned goods: a water-bath canner with rack, standard canning jars, new metal lids, metal bands, jar filler or funnel, timer, jar lifter, and a slotted spoon. Since pickles are usually processed in a water bath for under 15 minutes, the canning jars need to be sterilized by boiling in water 15 minutes.

For fresh-pack pickles, be sure to use containers of unchipped enamelware, stainless steel, aluminum, or glass for heating the vinegar solution. You should use only a crock, stone, or glass jar or plastic container intended for use with food for brining pickles. Other materials, such as copper, brass, galvanized steel, or iron may affect the pickle product or be unsafe.

Household scales are also helpful, especially for making sauerkraut (a brined pickle product). The proper proportions of salt and cabbage are necessary for successful results.

Ingredients

Always start with just-ripe **produce** that is free from deformities, bruises, and blemishes. It's best to begin pickling within 24 hours after fruit or vegetables are picked. If you can't start pickling right away, store the produce, unwashed, in the refrigerator, or spread it in a cool, ventilated area. Cucumbers will deteriorate quickly when left at room temperature.

Be sure to select a pickling variety of cucumber; your local Extension office can help you determine the one most available in your area. If you plan to pickle them whole, choose unwaxed cucumbers since pickling solutions won't penetrate the wax.

Wash cucumbers well, especially around the stem end, since it can harbor undesirable bacteria that affect the pickles. Be sure to remove the blossom

To make brined, unfermented pickles, use a glass, stoneware, or crock jar. Place a glass plate on top of cucumbers to keep them submerged in the salt solution. Cover jar with a clean cloth.

end because enzymes stored there cause pickles to soften.

Vinegar and **salt** are essential for making pickles, and amounts should never be reduced. Vinegar provides the acidity necessary for preservation of fresh-pack pickles. Always use vinegar between 4% and 6% acidity. (It's listed on the label.) You may use cider or white vinegar for making pickles, but cider vinegar can darken light-colored vegetables and fruit.

Be sure to use granulated uniodized pickling or canning salt. Table salt contains anti-caking ingredients, which may leave a white sediment in the pickles or cloud the brine.

Most pickling recipes call for some **sugar,** since it helps to plump the pickles and keep them crisp. Unless the recipe specifies brown sugar, use the regular white granulated kind.

Spices give pickles their distinctive flavor—dill, garlic, cinnamon, mustard seeds, and cloves are just a few typically used. It's best to start with fresh whole spices; powdered ones may darken and cloud the pickle product. Tie spices in a cheesecloth bag so they may be removed easily.

The type of **water** in your area may affect your pickles. If you have hard water, soften it by boiling 15 minutes. Cover and let set for 24 hours. Remove any scum that forms, and slowly pour water from the container without disturbing the sediment. Discard sediment. Distilled water may be used for making pickles, but it's expensive.

Lime and **alum** are additives that have been used to ensure crisp pickles, but they are no longer recommended or needed in the procedure. If you follow up-to-date methods for pickling and always start with good quality ingredients, pickles will be crisp.

Brined Pickle Pointers

Directions for brined or fermented pickles may vary with recipes, but keep the following basic tips in mind.

—Use only a clean crock or jar that has never held milk or fat.

—Keep cucumbers submerged in the liquid during the brining process. Place a glass plate on top of cucumbers. Weight the plate down with a water-filled jar, if necessary. Cover top of crock with a clean cloth so that carbon dioxide can escape.

—When making sauerkraut, the cabbage should be submerged in the brine, but no air should be allowed to reach the brine surface. Place a glass plate on top of cabbage to submerge it; then fill a heavy-duty plastic bag with water. Seal tightly, and place on top of the plate. Check to see that the bag touches the inside wall completely.

—Check daily for gray scum that may form on top of the brine, and remove it. If left on the pickles, acidity and preservation quality may be destroyed.

—Fermentation is complete when bubbles no longer rise to the top of the brine. To be sure the process is complete, tap the side of the container to release any trapped bubbles.

Packing the Pickles

When pickles are ready, firmly place them in sterilized canning jars without packing too tightly. Then cover pickles with boiling syrup or brine, leaving recommended headspace.

The brine for fermented pickles is usually cloudy as a result of the fermentation process. Although it is preferable to pack the pickles in this same brine for added flavor, you may prepare a fresh brine for packing. If using the original brine, be sure to strain it before heating to boiling. Make fresh brine with ½ cup salt, 4 cups vinegar, and 1 gallon water.

After adding boiling liquid to pickles, run a rubber spatula around the inside edge of jars to remove air bubbles. Don't use a metal utensil, since it may scratch the glass and cause the jar to break during processing.

Always buy new metal lids, and follow the manufacturer's directions on the package to prepare them for use. You may use metal bands as many times as you wish, as long as they aren't rusted or misshapen.

Tightening the band onto the jar is an important step. If it is too loose, the larger amounts of liquid will be lost during processing, and the seal will be weak. Bands screwed on too firmly may cause the lid to collapse, leaving a weak seal. The correct tightness can be achieved with the following method: Screw the band on with your fingertips until tight; then give another turn, just until the band is snug. Using a jar opener or continuing to turn the band with all your strength is probably too tight. Bands should be removed after jars are processed and cooled.

Processing Pickles

Water-bath processing for all pickles is necessary to destroy yeasts, molds, and bacteria that cause spoilage. Processing also inactivates enzymes that can change color, flavor, and texture.

Most pickle products—**relishes,** most **fresh-pack pickles,** and **fruit pickles**—will require processing by the standard water-bath method. Put the jars into the canner filled with simmering water. The water should cover the jar tops by 1 to 2 inches. Start to count processing time when water starts to boil. If no processing time is given, process 10 minutes for pints and quarts. Relishes and pickles made from vegetables other than cucumbers and cabbage may require longer processing times.

For fresh-pack dill pickles, brined cucumbers, and sauerkraut, place filled jars in a canner of boiling water. You should begin to count processing time as soon as pickles are placed in the water. Process pints and quarts 10 minutes if no time is given.

Now that you're ready to start pickling, try one—or all—of our recipes on the following pages. You'll find a generous selection from which to choose.

After brining and desalting cucumbers, prepare a vinegar-and-sugar syrup for pickling. Tie fresh whole spices in cheesecloth, and add to syrup. Allow cucumbers to stand in syrup several days.

To pack pickles for processing, place in hot sterilized jars (being careful not to pack too tightly), and cover with boiling syrup, leaving recommended headspace. Cover with metal lids, and screw on bands.

To process, place pickles in a boiling-water bath, and process 10 minutes. For brined pickles (and fresh-pack dill pickles and sauerkraut), start to count processing time as soon as jars are placed in boiling water.

CUCUMBER CHIPS

24 small cucumbers (about 4 to 5 inches),
   sliced ¼ inch thick
½ cup pickling salt
3 cups vinegar (5% acidity)
1 quart water
1 tablespoon ground turmeric
1 quart vinegar (5% acidity)
1 cup water
2 cups sugar
2 (3-inch) cinnamon sticks
1 (1-inch) piece fresh gingerroot
1 tablespoon mustard seeds
1 teaspoon whole cloves
2 cups firmly packed brown sugar

Place cucumbers in a large bowl; sprinkle with salt. Cover and let stand 3 hours. Drain well.

Combine 3 cups vinegar, 1 quart water, and turmeric in a large Dutch oven; bring to a boil, and pour over cucumbers. Cover and let stand until cooled to room temperature. Drain and rinse cucumbers. Drain again.

Combine 1 quart vinegar, 1 cup water, and 2 cups sugar in a Dutch oven. Tie spices in a cheesecloth bag, and add to vinegar mixture. Bring to a boil, and simmer, uncovered, 15 minutes. Pour mixture over cucumbers. Cover and let stand at least 12 hours or overnight in a cool place.

Drain syrup from cucumbers into a Dutch oven. Add brown sugar and heat to boiling.

Pack cucumbers into hot sterilized pint jars, leaving ¼-inch headspace. Pour hot syrup over cucumbers, leaving ¼-inch headspace. Remove air bubbles with a rubber spatula. Cover at once with metal lids, and screw on bands. Process in boiling-water bath 10 minutes. Yield: 4 pints.

SOUR CUCUMBER PICKLES

40 to 50 medium cucumbers
1 gallon cider vinegar (5% acidity)
1 quart water
1 cup pickling salt
1 cup sugar
1 cup whole mustard seeds

Wash cucumbers; remove ¼ inch from ends. Pack cucumbers into hot sterilized quart jars, leaving 1-inch headspace.

Combine remaining ingredients in a Dutch oven; bring to a boil. Pour hot vinegar mixture over cucumbers, leaving ½-inch headspace.

Cover at once with metal lids, and screw on bands. Process in boiling-water bath 10 minutes. Yield: 8 quarts.

Pickle Problem Chart

Problems	Possible Causes
Soft or slippery pickles	blossom ends not removed vinegar of too low acidity used not enough salt in brine cucumbers not completely submerged in brine improper processing
Hollow pickles	cucumbers too large too much time between picking and brining improper brining process
Shriveled pickles	brine or vinegar too strong syrup too heavy overcooking or overprocessing too much time between picking and brining dry weather during vegetable growth
Dark or discolored pickles	hard water used spices left in pickles iodized salt used ground spices used
Spoilage	unsterilized jars used processing time too short canning jars and/or new lids not used ingredients not measured accurately vinegar that has lost strength used

CUCUMBER RELISH

2 quarts chopped cucumbers
2 cups chopped green peppers
2 cups chopped red peppers
1 cup chopped onion
1 tablespoon ground turmeric
½ cup pickling salt
2 quarts cold water
1½ cups firmly packed brown sugar
1 quart vinegar (5% acidity)
2 (3½-inch) cinnamon sticks
1 tablespoon whole mustard seeds
2 teaspoons whole allspice
2 teaspoons whole cloves

Combine cucumbers, peppers, and onion; sprinkle with turmeric. Dissolve salt in 2 quarts water; pour over vegetables, and let stand 3 to 4 hours. Drain. Cover vegetables with cold water, and let stand 1 hour. Drain thoroughly.

Combine sugar and vinegar in a large saucepan. Tie cinnamon sticks, mustard seeds, allspice, and cloves in a cheesecloth bag; add to vinegar mixture, and bring to a boil. Pour over vegetables. Cover and let stand 12 hours or overnight in a cool place.

Remove spice bag. Bring mixture to a boil. Fill hot sterilized pint jars, leaving ¼-inch headspace. Cover at once with metal lids, and screw on bands. Process in boiling-water bath 10 minutes. Yield: about 6 pints.

SWEET ICICLE PICKLES

20 medium cucumbers, quartered
2 cups pickling salt
1 gallon water
5 cups sugar
5 cups vinegar (5% acidity)
1½ tablespoons mixed pickling spices

Place quartered cucumbers in a large crock or a glass or stainless steel container; set aside.

Combine salt and water, and bring to a boil; pour over cucumbers. Place a dinner plate or saucer on cucumbers; place a weight on the plate to submerge cucumbers in brine. Cover crock with a clean cloth; let cucumbers stand one week in a cool, dark place. Remove any scum from the top of brine each day.

Drain cucumbers, and rinse thoroughly. Cover cucumbers with boiling water, and let stand 24 hours. Drain. Again cover with boiling water; then let stand an additional 24 hours. Drain.

Combine sugar and vinegar in a Dutch oven. Tie pickling spices in a cheesecloth bag; add to vinegar mixture. Bring to a boil, and simmer 5 minutes or until sugar dissolves. Pour syrup over cucumbers; cover and let stand 24 hours. Drain syrup; bring syrup to a boil, and pour over cucumbers. Let stand 24 hours. Repeat this procedure four more times.

Pack pickles into hot sterilized quart jars, leaving ¼-inch headspace. Remove spice bag, and bring syrup to a boil. Pour hot syrup over pickles, leaving ¼-inch headspace. Remove air bubbles. Cover at once with metal lids, and screw on bands. Process in boiling-water bath 10 minutes. Yield: about 3 quarts.

PEACH PICKLES

3 quarts cold water
¾ teaspoon ascorbic acid
8 pounds small- to medium-size, firm, ripe
    peaches, peeled
6¾ cups sugar
1 quart vinegar (5% acidity)
4 (3-inch) cinnamon sticks
2 tablespoons whole cloves
1 (1-inch) piece fresh gingerroot

Combine water and ascorbic acid in a large container. Drop peaches into water mixture; set aside.

Combine sugar and vinegar in a large Dutch oven; bring to a boil, and cook 5 minutes. Tie remaining ingredients in a cheesecloth bag, and add to syrup.

Drain peaches, and add to syrup mixture. Cook, uncovered, about 3 minutes, just until peaches can be pierced with a fork. Remove from heat. Cover peaches and let stand at room temperature 24 hours.

Bring peaches to a boil; pack into hot sterilized pint jars, leaving ½-inch headspace. Pour hot syrup over peaches, leaving ½-inch headspace. Remove air bubbles with a rubber spatula. Cover at once with metal lids, and screw on bands. Process in boiling-water bath 15 minutes. Yield: 6 pints.

This is the third in a four-part series on food preservation. See May section for canning, June section for making jams and jellies, and August section for freezing fruits and vegetables.

Enjoy The Bounty Of Southern Peaches

When it comes to peaches, more than one Southern state has a claim to fame. Drive across the South any time in July, and along the way, you'll see baskets of fresh peaches adorning roadside stands with reddish-gold splendor. In fact, the U.S. Department of Agriculture says that the South produces about half the fresh peaches in the entire nation.

So it's not surprising that Southern cooks also have a wealth of delicious recipes for preparing this sweet, juicy fruit. We've picked some of the best to share with you.

Rublelene Singleton of Scotts Hill, Tennessee, sent us the recipe for Peach Dumplings. They're made with an unusual almond pastry and served with a spicy whipped cream topping. Or you might try topping the dumplings with a scoop of vanilla ice cream.

Spicy Peach Cobbler has generous amounts of cinnamon and ginger to make it extra flavorful. It bakes in a deep dish and has a double crust; the latticework crust on top gives it a traditional look.

When you're selecting peaches, take a tip from Gwen Bulman of Cash Farms, a family-owned peach operation near Cowpens, South Carolina. She says, "Check first of all for good maturity; never buy peaches that are underripe. Look for a soft-yellow background color. The blush (reddish color) will vary from one variety to the next, but a yellow undercolor usually indicates ripeness in all varieties."

For information about canning and freezing peaches, see our home preservation series in the May through August sections of *Annual Recipes*.

PEACH DUMPLINGS

⅓ cup apricot-pineapple preserves
⅓ cup sugar
2 teaspoons quick-cooking tapioca
¼ teaspoon ground nutmeg
2½ cups sliced fresh peaches
Almond Pastry
Spicy Cream Topping

Combine apricot-pineapple preserves, sugar, tapioca, and ground nutmeg; mix well. Add fresh peaches; stir to coat. Set aside.

Roll Almond Pastry out onto a lightly floured surface into an 18- x 12-inch rectangle; cut into six 6-inch squares. Spoon about ½ cup peach mixture into center of each square. Moisten edges of pastry with water, and fold opposite corners to center. Press edges together to seal. Carefully transfer dumplings to a lightly greased baking sheet; bake at 375° for 40 minutes or until golden.

Transfer dumplings to individual serving dishes while warm; spoon Spicy Cream Topping over each dumpling. Yield: 6 servings.

Almond Pastry:

2 cups all-purpose flour
½ cup ground almonds
1 teaspoon salt
⅔ cup shortening
7 to 8 tablespoons cold water

Combine flour, almonds, and salt; cut in shortening with pastry blender until mixture resembles coarse meal. Sprinkle cold water (1 tablespoon at a time) evenly over surface; stir with a fork until dry ingredients are moistened. Shape into a ball. Yield: enough for 6 dumplings.

Spicy Cream Topping:

1 cup whipping cream
1 tablespoon powdered sugar
⅛ teaspoon ground cinnamon
⅛ teaspoon ground nutmeg

Beat whipping cream until foamy; gradually add sugar and spices, beating until soft peaks form. Chill until serving time. Yield: about 2 cups.

Rublelene Singleton,
Scotts Hill, Tennessee.

CREAMY PEACH ICE CREAM

1 cup sugar
¼ cup all-purpose flour
¼ teaspoon salt
3 eggs, beaten
1 cup milk
1½ tablespoons vanilla extract
3 cups peeled, chopped peaches
½ cup sugar
2 cups whipping cream
2 cups half-and-half

Combine 1 cup sugar, flour, and salt in a heavy saucepan; mix well. Stir in eggs and milk; cook over medium heat, stirring constantly, until mixture is thickened and bubbly. Remove saucepan from heat; stir in vanilla. Cool mixture completely.

Combine peaches and ½ cup sugar; mix well, and let stand 5 minutes.

Combine cooked mixture, peach mixture, whipping cream, and half-and-half; mix well. Pour into freezer can of a 1-gallon hand-turned or electric freezer. Freeze according to manufacturer's instructions, using one part rock salt to six parts ice. Let ice cream ripen at least 1 hour. Yield: 2½ quarts.

Mrs. Joe Pegourie,
Louisville, Kentucky.

SPICY PEACH COBBLER

8 large ripe peaches, peeled and sliced
2 tablespoons lemon juice
¾ cup sugar
¼ cup all-purpose flour
1 teaspoon ground cinnamon
1 teaspoon ground ginger
Pastry for double-crust 9-inch pie

Combine sliced peaches and lemon juice; toss. Combine sugar, flour, cinnamon, and ginger; add to peaches, mixing lightly. Set the mixture aside.

Roll half of pastry onto a lightly floured surface to ⅛-inch thickness; fit into a 9-inch square baking dish. Spoon peach mixture evenly into prepared pastry shell. Roll out remaining pastry to ⅛-inch thickness; cut into ½-inch strips. Lay half the strips across the filling, spacing them about ¾ inch apart. Repeat with remaining strips, arranging them in opposite direction to form latticework. Bake at 425° for 10 minutes; reduce heat to 350°, and bake an additional 40 minutes. Yield: 6 servings.

GRENADINE-PEACH COBBLER

1 cup sugar
3 tablespoons all-purpose flour
2 tablespoons cornstarch
⅛ teaspoon ground nutmeg
6 cups sliced fresh peaches
2 tablespoons grenadine syrup
1 tablespoon lemon juice
2 tablespoons butter or margarine
Pastry for 9-inch pie

Combine sugar, flour, cornstarch, and nutmeg; mix well. Add peaches, grenadine syrup, and lemon juice; toss gently. Let stand 5 minutes. Pour into a lightly greased 8-inch square baking dish; dot with butter.

Roll pastry out on a lightly floured surface into an 8-inch square; place over peach mixture, sealing edges to sides of dish. Cut slits in pastry. Bake at 350° for 55 minutes or until golden brown. Yield: 6 servings. *Caroline Quoyeser, Lafayette, Louisiana.*

EASY PEACH FRIED PIES

¾ cup sugar
3 tablespoons cornstarch
¾ cup water
3 peaches, peeled and diced
¼ teaspoon almond extract
1 (10-ounce) can flaky refrigerator biscuits
Vegetable oil

Combine sugar, cornstarch, and water in a small saucepan; mix well. Cook over low heat, stirring constantly, until smooth and thickened. Remove from heat; stir in peaches and almond extract. Set mixture aside.

Roll each biscuit out on a lightly floured surface to ⅛-inch thickness. Spoon about ¼ cup peach mixture on half of each dough circle. To seal pies, moisten edges of circles and fold in half, making sure edges are even. Using a fork dipped in flour, firmly press dough edges together.

Cook pies in 1-inch-deep hot oil (360°) until golden, turning once. Drain pies on paper towels, and serve warm. Yield: 10 pies. *Janice Fields, Rutherfordton, North Carolina.*

QUICK PEACH DESSERT

4½ cups sliced fresh peaches
½ cup sugar
½ cup butter or margarine, softened
½ cup sugar
1 cup self-rising flour
1 egg
1 teaspoon vanilla extract

Place peaches in a lightly greased 8-inch square baking dish. Sprinkle with ½ cup sugar.

Cream butter and ½ cup sugar, beating well. Add self-rising flour and egg; mix well. Stir in vanilla. Spoon mixture over sugared peaches. Bake at 350° for 30 to 35 minutes or until golden brown. Yield: 6 servings. *Nina L. Andrews, Tappahannoch, Virginia.*

FRESH PEACH CAKE

½ cup vegetable oil
1½ cups sugar
2 eggs
2 cups all-purpose flour
1 teaspoon baking soda
1 teaspoon salt
1 teaspoon ground cinnamon
1½ cups mashed peaches
½ cup chopped pecans

Combine oil and sugar, beating well. Add eggs, one at a time, beating well after each addition.

Combine flour, soda, salt, and cinnamon; mix well. Gradually add to creamed mixture, mixing just until blended. Stir in peaches and pecans.

Spoon batter into a greased and floured 13- x 9- x 2-inch baking pan; bake at 325° for 40 to 45 minutes or until a wooden pick inserted in center comes out clean. Yield: 15 servings. *Maggie Hatley, Sikeston, Missouri.*

MINCEMEAT PEACHES

4 peaches, peeled, seeded, and halved
½ cup mincemeat, divided
2 tablespoons plus 2 teaspoons butter or margarine, divided

Place peach halves, cut side up, in a 12- x 8- x 2-inch baking dish. Fill each cavity with 1 tablespoon mincemeat, and dot with 1 teaspoon butter. Broil 6 to 7 inches from heat 3 to 5 minutes or until bubbly. Serve peaches warm. Yield: 8 servings. *Patricia Murphree, Pensacola, Florida.*

PERFECT PICKLED PEACHES

½ cup cider vinegar
⅓ cup sugar
¼ teaspoon ground ginger
1 (3-inch) stick cinnamon
⅛ teaspoon ground cloves
3 large, firm, ripe peaches, peeled, seeded, and quartered

Combine vinegar, sugar, and spices in a heavy saucepan; bring to a boil. Reduce heat, and simmer, uncovered, 5 minutes. Add peaches; return to a boil. Reduce heat, and simmer 10 minutes. Let stand 30 minutes. Serve peaches warm or chilled. Yield: 6 servings. *Gwen Louer, Roswell, Georgia.*

Tip: Always measure accurately. Level dry ingredients in a cup with a knife edge or a spoon handle. Measure liquids in a cup so that the fluid is level with the top of the measuring line. Measure solid shortening by packing it firmly in a graduated measuring cup.

Recipes With A Handful Of Ingredients

If you flip the page when you see a recipe with a long list of ingredients, the entrée recipes here are just for you. You can whip up some of them in just a few minutes; others, such as our roast recipes, take a few hours. But all of them feature five major ingredients or less. (We're not counting water, butter, salt, or pepper, since these items are usually on hand.)

Tahiti Burgers are a busy person's solution to dinner for four in less than 20 minutes. Ground beef patties are cooked in a skillet and topped with pineapple rings and Swiss cheese. They're served without buns, so the flavor combination is easier to taste.

Chicken Rollups bake about an hour, but the recipe is quick to put together. Mix cream cheese, green onions, and garlic powder; then place in the center of flattened chicken breast halves, roll up, and top each one with bacon. You can prepare the rest of the meal while the chicken bakes.

TAHITI BURGERS

1 pound ground beef
2 tablespoons soy sauce
2 tablespoons water
4 (1-ounce) slices Swiss cheese
4 slices canned pineapple

Shape ground beef into 4 patties; set aside. Combine soy sauce and water in a skillet over medium heat. Place patties in skillet; cover and simmer about 5 minutes. Turn patties; top each patty with a cheese slice and a pineapple slice. Cover and simmer an additional 10 minutes or until desired degree of doneness. Yield: 4 servings.
Diane Poythress,
Birmingham, Alabama.

ORANGE MARINATED CHUCK ROAST

1 cup orange juice
¼ cup soy sauce
2 tablespoons vinegar
1 (3-pound) boneless chuck roast

Combine orange juice, soy sauce, and vinegar in a large, shallow dish; add roast. Cover and marinate several hours or overnight in refrigerator, turning roast occasionally.

Remove roast from marinade; place in a roasting pan or a Dutch oven. Bake, uncovered, at 375° for 30 minutes. Pour marinade over roast; cover and bake at 350° for 2½ hours or until done. Yield: 6 servings.
Peggy Blackburn,
Winston-Salem, North Carolina.

CHICKEN ROLLUPS

6 chicken breast halves, skinned and boned
1 (8-ounce) package cream cheese, softened
4 green onions, chopped
⅛ teaspoon garlic powder
6 slices bacon, cut in half

Place each chicken breast half on a sheet of waxed paper. Flatten to ¼ inch thickness using a meat mallet.
Combine cream cheese, green onions, and garlic powder; mix well. Shape mixture into 6 equal-size balls; place one in center of each chicken breast half. Fold long sides of chicken over filling. Then fold ends of chicken over, and secure with wooden picks.
Top each piece of chicken with 2 bacon slices. Place in a lightly greased 12- x 8- x 2-inch baking dish. Bake at 350° for 50 to 60 minutes. Yield: 6 servings.
Edith Askins,
Greenville, Texas.

SKILLET VEGETABLE PORK CHOPS

4 (¾-inch-thick) pork chops
Salt and pepper
1 teaspoon vegetable oil
1 (16-ounce) can whole tomatoes, undrained
½ cup uncooked quick-cooking rice
4 green pepper rings

Lightly sprinkle pork chops with salt and pepper. Heat oil in a skillet over medium-high heat; brown pork chops on both sides. Reduce heat. Drain tomatoes, and add liquid to pork chops. Coarsely chop tomatoes, and add to pork chops; stir in rice. Place a green pepper ring on each chop. Cover and simmer 40 to 45 minutes or until chops are tender. Yield: 4 servings.
Mrs. L. A. Hutchinson,
Montgomery, Alabama.

ZESTY PORK ROAST

1 (5-pound) pork shoulder roast
8 small green onions, cut 5 to 6 inches long
8 small cayenne peppers
8 cloves garlic
Salt
1 (8-ounce) bottle Italian salad dressing

Make 24 slits lengthwise all the way through to the bone in roast. Insert one green onion, pepper, or garlic clove into each of the 24 slits. Sprinkle pork with salt, and place in a shallow dish. Pour dressing over pork. Cover and marinate in refrigerator 10 to 12 hours, turning occasionally.
Drain roast well. Insert meat thermometer into pork, making sure thermometer does not touch bone or fat. Bake at 325° for 3 to 3½ hours or until thermometer registers 170°. Yield: 8 servings.
Lora Blocker,
Dade City, Florida.

HAM SKILLET DINNER

3 cups chopped cooked ham
1 cup chopped onion
1 tablespoon butter or margarine, melted
1 (16-ounce) can tomatoes, undrained
2 cups cooked rice
2 tablespoons Worcestershire sauce

Sauté ham and onion in butter in a large skillet; add remaining ingredients, stirring well. Reduce heat, cover, and simmer 20 minutes or until thoroughly heated. Yield: 4 to 6 servings.
Dorothy R. Bender,
Holiday, Florida.

FISH AMANDINE

⅓ cup all-purpose flour
¼ teaspoon salt
⅛ teaspoon pepper
4 (6- to 8-ounce) trout fillets
⅔ cup milk
¼ cup butter or margarine, melted
¼ cup slivered almonds

Combine flour, salt, and pepper; set aside. Dip fillets in milk, and coat with flour mixture. Sauté fish in butter 2 to 3 minutes on each side or until fish flakes when tested with a fork. Transfer fish to a warm platter. Sauté almonds in pan drippings until browned; sprinkle over fish. Yield: 4 servings. *Patrick Greer,*
Meridian, Mississippi.

Hook Into Fish For Light Eating

If you've given up fried fish as part of an effort to keep the bathroom scales friendly, don't despair. You're not destined to eat plain broiled fish for the duration of your diet. Indulge in our collection of light fish recipes that even waistline watchers can afford.

Fish has surged in popularity as a staple for dieters who have become more weight conscious and concerned about fat in the diet, and with good reason. Its high protein and low calorie content makes it a light, nutritious choice that is hard to beat.

Fish is classified as either lean (having an oil content of less than 5%) or fat (having an oil content of more than 5%). Find your favorites on the chart. Fat fish will be slightly higher in calories than lean fish. But the good news is that the fat in all fish is largely polyunsaturated, a real plus for those trying to modify the amount of saturated fat in their diets.

As a general rule, the color of fat fish tends to be darker than that of lean fish. If you plan to interchange the two in a recipe, note that the flavor of fat fish is stronger than lean fish. Either type, however, can be baked, broiled, poached, steamed, or grilled for lighter eating. But when lean fish is cooked by a dry-heat method, frequent basting may be required to keep the fish from drying out.

Stuffed Flounder Rolls With Citrus Sauce is an entrée you'll want to try even if you aren't watching your weight. A delicate blend of rice, carrots, and dillweed is nestled inside fillets that are topped with an orange-lemon sauce and baked to perfection. And best of all, we've kept the calories to a mere 196 per serving, plus 16 calories per tablespoon of sauce.

If a light recipe that's not time consuming is more to your liking, try Honey-Curried Snapper. An unusual combination of Dijon mustard, honey, lemon juice, and curry powder adorns fillets that cook in less than 20 minutes. And at only 191 calories per serving, it's a dish you'll serve often.

For the spicy flavor of the Old South, make Creole-Style Flounder your choice. Fillets are smothered in a rich sauce consisting of green onions, green pepper, tomatoes, thyme, and bay leaf. Enjoy this delightful fare with only 153 calories per serving. If you feel like splurging, serve it over a half cup of rice for an additional 90 calories.

Prepare fish so that it's moist and flaky. Fish is naturally tender and requires only a short amount of cooking time. It is done when the flesh becomes opaque and flakes easily when tested with a fork.

Be adventurous, and try some of the new fish species now available in the market. You'll be pleasantly surprised how much lesser known varieties, such as tilefish, amberjack, redfish, and others, taste like those that are more familiar to you. And best of all, they may be available at a lower price.

Fat Fish	Lean Fish
amberjack	black sea bass
butterfish	bluegill
carp	cod
freshwater catfish	crappie
king mackerel	croaker
lake trout	dolphin
mullet	flounder
rainbow trout	grouper
sablefish	haddock
salmon	halibut
sea herring	ocean catfish
shad	ocean perch
Spanish mackerel	permit
tuna	pike
whitefish	plaice
	pollock
	pompano
	porgy
	red snapper
	redfish
	rockfish
	scamp
	scrod
	shark
	sheepshead
	sole
	speckled sea trout
	spot
	swordfish
	tilapia
	tilefish
	triggerfish
	turbot
	walleye
	white sea trout
	whiting

CREOLE-STYLE FLOUNDER

1 cup sliced green onions with tops
1 large green pepper, sliced into thin strips
1½ tablespoons margarine, melted
1 (16-ounce) can whole tomatoes, undrained
1 (8-ounce) can tomato sauce
1 bay leaf
½ teaspoon dried whole thyme
6 flounder fillets (about 1½ pounds)
Vegetable cooking spray
¼ teaspoon salt
⅛ teaspoon pepper
3 cups hot cooked rice (cooked without fat)

Sauté green onions and green pepper strips in margarine in a medium saucepan until tender. Add liquid from tomatoes; chop tomatoes, and add to saucepan. Stir in tomato sauce, bay leaf, and thyme; bring to a boil. Reduce heat, and simmer, uncovered, for 20 minutes; remove bay leaf.

Place fish in a 13- x 9- x 2-inch baking dish coated with cooking spray; sprinkle fish with salt and pepper. Spoon sauce over fish; cover and bake at 350° for 20 minutes or until fish flakes when tested with a fork. Serve sauce over rice. Yield: 6 servings (about 153 calories per serving plus 90 calories per ½ cup cooked rice). *Elizabeth Koen, New Orleans, Louisiana.*

STUFFED FLOUNDER ROLLS WITH CITRUS SAUCE

¾ cup cooked regular rice (cooked without fat)
½ cup chopped cooked carrots
1½ teaspoons chopped fresh dillweed
1½ teaspoons chopped fresh parsley
¼ teaspoon salt
2 tablespoons margarine, melted and divided
6 flounder fillets (2¼ pounds)
Vegetable cooking spray
Citrus Sauce
Fresh dillweed sprigs (optional)

Combine rice, carrots, dillweed, parsley, salt, and 1 tablespoon margarine; mix well. Spoon about 3 tablespoons rice mixture onto each fillet; carefully roll up, and secure with a wooden pick. Place in a 12- x 8- x 2-inch baking dish coated with cooking spray. Brush remaining margarine over top of rolls.

Bake, uncovered, at 350° for 20 to 25 minutes or until fish flakes easily when tested with a fork. Serve with Citrus Sauce. Garnish with dillweed sprig, if desired. Yield: 6 servings (about 196 calories per serving plus 16 calories per tablespoon of sauce).

Citrus Sauce:

1½ cups unsweetened orange juice
¼ cup lemon juice
1½ tablespoons cornstarch
2 tablespoons margarine

Combine orange juice, lemon juice, and cornstarch; stir until cornstarch dissolves. Set aside.

Melt margarine in a heavy saucepan; stir in juice mixture. Cook mixture over medium heat, stirring constantly, until smooth and thickened. (Do not boil.) Yield: 1⅔ cups.
Cheryl Edmond,
Valdosta, Georgia.

SOLE VÉRONIQUE

3 sole fillets (about 12 ounces)
½ teaspoon salt
¼ teaspoon white pepper
Vegetable cooking spray
½ cup dry white wine
1½ teaspoons lemon juice
1 tablespoon margarine
1 tablespoon all-purpose flour
¾ cup skim milk
½ cup seedless green grapes, halved

Sprinkle fish with salt and pepper; place in a baking dish coated with cooking spray. Add wine and lemon juice. Cover and bake at 350° for 15 minutes or until fish flakes easily when tested with a fork. Remove fish to platter; reserve liquid.

Melt margarine in a heavy saucepan over low heat; add flour, stirring until smooth. Cook 1 minute, stirring constantly. Gradually add milk; cook over medium heat, stirring constantly, until mixture is thickened and bubbly. Add reserved liquid; mix well. Pour over fish; top with grapes. Yield: 3 servings (about 206 calories per serving).
Judy Warren,
Charlotte, North Carolina.

BAKED SNAPPER À L'ORANGE

2 (2-pound) whole-dressed red snappers
Vegetable cooking spray
8 small slices onion
¼ cup frozen orange juice concentrate, undiluted
2 tablespoons margarine, melted
1 tablespoon soy sauce
⅛ teaspoon garlic powder
⅛ teaspoon pepper

Place fish in an aluminum foil-lined shallow baking pan coated with cooking spray. Cut four ½-inch-deep slashes in each fish; place an onion slice in each of the slashes.

Combine remaining ingredients, stirring well. Brush mixture over fish. Bake, uncovered, at 350° for 30 minutes, basting frequently. Yield: 6 servings (about 206 calories per serving).
Maryse H. Rose,
Mary Esther, Florida.

HONEY-CURRIED SNAPPER

1 tablespoon Dijon mustard
2 teaspoons honey
2 teaspoons lemon juice
⅛ teaspoon curry powder
⅛ teaspoon salt
2 red snapper fillets (¾ pound)
Vegetable cooking spray
⅛ teaspoon paprika
2 teaspoons chopped fresh parsley

Combine mustard, honey, lemon juice, curry powder, and salt; mix well.

Place fish in a 9-inch square baking dish coated with cooking spray; pour mustard sauce over top. Cover and bake at 350° for 15 minutes or until fish flakes easily when tested with a fork. Uncover and broil 2 minutes. Sprinkle with paprika and parsley. Yield: 2 servings (about 191 calories per serving).
Ruth A. Colosimo,
Copperas Cove, Texas.

From Our Kitchen To Yours

This is the time of year to take advantage of the tomato crop. Whether stewed, sliced for salads or sandwiches, or used for juice, this versatile summer staple is readily available now. To help in your selection and preparation, here are some tips.

Picking the Best

By growing your own tomatoes, you're at an advantage, because the best ones are those that ripen completely on the vine. Let tomatoes stay on the vine until they turn red. This extra time helps the tomatoes develop flavor and possibly more vitamin C.

If tomatoes are bought, you'll most likely be selecting them at an earlier stage of ripeness. Since they're so fragile and perishable, they are picked and shipped when still green or only slightly blushed. Thus when buying, look for firm tomatoes, almost ripened, without cuts, soft spots, or shriveled skin.

Small tomatoes work best for sauces and casseroles; the medium-size and large-size ones are much better for slicing, stuffing, and marinating. For a more flavorful sauce, overripe tomatoes often work best.

Ripening

If tomatoes are picked from the vine or bought at the market before ripening, you'll need to finish the process at home. Don't put them in the refrigerator, because they will not ripen. Instead, place the tomatoes in a bowl or on a table in a room where the temperature is ranging between 65° and 75°.

If the room temperature where they are stored is too cold, they will either redden slowly or become soft without turning red. A little sunlight is fine, but high heat is harmful.

If the room temperature is above 85°, tomatoes will lose quality quickly. Under the right conditions, the ripening process usually takes one to three days. Placing tomatoes in a paper sack with small air vents cut into the sides can be used to speed up the process.

Storage

After tomatoes are fully ripened, keep them in a cool, dark place. The stem end is the most sensitive, so to prevent bruising, store tomatoes stem end up.

It's best to wash tomatoes just before you're ready to use them. Long refrigeration will cause tomatoes to lose flavor as well as nutritive value, so remember to refrigerate tomatoes for only about two or three days.

Since they have such a high water content, raw tomatoes don't freeze well. However, you can freeze cooked tomatoes, sauces, soups, and casseroles that contain cooked tomatoes.

Tomato Preparation

—Slicing: It's best to use a serrated knife when slicing; this helps to cut through the skin more easily without squeezing out the natural juice.

—Peeling: If you're peeling just a few tomatoes, try pressing the dull side of the knife over the skin until it wrinkles; then the tomato skin should peel away more easily.

To peel a lot of fresh tomatoes, drop them in boiling water for 15 to 30 seconds, and then quickly transfer them to cold water; the skins should then slip off very easily.

Peeling is usually not necessary unless you're cooking tomatoes. When they're cooked unpeeled, the heat will cause the peel to slip away from the tomato. When marinating and tossing in salads, leave unpeeled so the tomato will keep its shape and not lose water.

—Seeding: For homemade catsup or tomato juice, our recipes often recommend seeding the tomatoes. To do this, just slice the tomato in half so you can see the seed pockets, and then squeeze the tomato half to force seeds out. If you have an overripe tomato, cut it in half, and scrape the seeds away with a knife or a spoon.

—Stuffing: If you're using the tomato as a natural shell, we suggest that after you scoop out the seeds and pulp, turn the shells upside down on a paper towel to drain. This keeps the tomato liquid from diluting the flavor of the filling.

Turn plain produce baskets into attractive serving containers, individual picnic baskets, friendship gifts, and even placecard holders.

For Summertime, Serve It In A Basket

Don't throw away those produce baskets when you come home from the farmers' market. Every container—no matter what the shape and size—can be used creatively when you entertain or want to give a gift.

Take a look at some of the following ideas for using baskets to hold unexpected surprises for casual parties, gifts, or a little something extra for an overnight guest.

Entertaining Ideas

—Let party guests garnish their drinks with fruit-filled skewers. Line a mushroom basket with plastic wrap, and fill with ice. Then nestle an orange in the ice, anchoring it with skewers, if necessary. Arrange colorful skewers of fruit in the orange, and scatter lemon and lime wedges around it. (See photograph for ideas.)

—Use a basket instead of a bowl when it's time to serve the coleslaw. Even green pint-size baskets (like the ones strawberries come in) are excellent for serving condiments. Place plastic wrap in the bottom of each to prevent leakage; then line with lettuce leaves.

Scoop relish, mustard, catsup, or pickles onto leaves.

—Use produce baskets instead of paper plates for a summertime meal. Pick a small to medium basket, depending on what you plan to serve. Line with lacy paper doilies for a summery look and to protect the baskets so that you can use them again. Chips, pickles, and hot dogs will all fit into one basket. Tie fresh summer flowers onto the handle for a colorful accent. Baskets for a ladies' luncheon or a bridal shower become more elegant when a crisp white linen or roll cover lines each one.

—Save crate-like produce containers, and arrange a display and holder for paper goods and flatware you'll use for an outdoor party. Guests can find cups, plates, napkins, and everything else they will need all in one place. For a dressier look, tack a garland of ivy and flowers to the basket rim. Or red, white, and blue ribbons woven through the basket would add just the right touch to carry out the theme of a Fourth of July gathering.

Baskets on the Go

—Create a special surprise for a friend or new neighbor with a produce basket of goodies. A sick friend will enjoy a sunshine basket filled with a magazine and a container or jar of homemade soup or juice.

—Pack a picnic lunch for yourself and a friend in a basket tied with a colorful piece of fabric. Include a bottle of wine, cheese, fruit, and crackers.

—Give a bride and groom a going-away basket decorated in white. Fill it with fresh homemade bread, a jar of preserves, freshly squeezed orange juice, and two glasses. For a final touch, add a bottle of champagne.

For a Little Something Extra

—Set a tiny produce basket filled with after-dinner mints beside each place setting at your next party. Attach a placecard for a personal touch.

—Put a special chocolate in a small basket on the bedside table for an overnight guest. Substitute a single flower if your guest would rather skip the sweets.

August

Freeze Produce Now To Enjoy Later

One of the best things about summer is the pleasure of sitting down to a vegetable dinner fresh from the garden. And for dessert, there's probably a hot blackberry cobbler or a fresh blueberry pie made from berries picked that morning. When the harvest is too plentiful to enjoy all at once, you can put these wonderful summer flavors on your winter table too, thanks to the freezer.

If your schedule is busy, bear in mind that freezing is the easiest method of food preservation. You'll find too that this is a quick way to put up fresh produce without much special equipment.

Just remember that the key to putting up the best frozen produce is selecting top-quality vegetables and fruit, freezing as quickly as possible, and using the proper containers. Also, the sooner the produce is prepared and frozen after harvesting, the better the flavor will be. Follow the directions below for freezing each type of vegetable and fruit.

Equipment

Whether you're freezing vegetables or fruit, you'll need the following items on hand for preparing the produce: knife, cutting board, colander, large measuring container, kitchen scales, freezer containers, freezer paper, freezer tape, labels, and marking pen. To freeze vegetables, you'll also need equipment for blanching, such as a blancher or a large Dutch oven or saucepan with a wire-mesh basket, and a timer. It's also handy to have another large container to fill with ice water for cooling the vegetables after blanching.

Freezer containers come in many forms. Rigid containers made of plastic or glass are especially good for food packed in liquid. Select those intended for use in the freezer with straight sides and flat tops for easy stacking. Wide-mouth containers are most convenient for easy removal of partially thawed food. Lids for rigid containers should be tight fitting and can be reinforced with freezer tape, if necessary.

Plastic freezer bags are the best flexible packaging for dry-packed vegetables and fruit. They may also be used for liquid packs. Waxed freezer cartons used with the bags provide extra protection against tearing during storage, but do not use the cartons without freezer bags. See chart on this page to determine the headspace recommended for each type of container.

Headspace For Filled Freezer Containers

Type of Pack	Wide-Mouth Containers		Narrow-Mouth Containers	
	Pint	Quart	Pint	Quart
Liquid pack for vegetables or fruit packed in juice, sugar, syrup, or water	½ inch	1 inch	¾ inch	1½ inches
Dry pack for vegetables or fruit packed without added sugar or liquid	½ inch	½ inch	½ inch	½ inch

Freezing Vegetables

Start with just-harvested vegetables at the peak of flavor, and prepare amounts to fill only a few containers at a time. Discard damaged produce. Wash and drain before peeling or shelling, and prepare according to directions.

For the best quality frozen product, most vegetables require **blanching** (exposure to boiling water or steam for a few minutes) to inactivate natural enzymes that cause loss of flavor, color, and texture. Blanching also gives vegetables a brighter color, helps retain nutrients, and destroys microorganisms on the surface.

It's important to follow the recommended blanching time for each vegetable. Overblanching causes a loss of color, flavor, and nutrients, while underblanching stimulates rather than inactivates the enzymes in the vegetables.

Vegetables need to be cooled immediately after blanching to stop the cooking process. Then, before packing, drain the vegetables well to eliminate extra moisture, which can cause a noticeable loss of quality during freezing.

Follow these directions for blanching: Heat 1 gallon of water to boiling for each pound of prepared vegetables. (Use 2 gallons per pound for leafy green vegetables.) Place vegetables in a blanching basket, and submerge in boiling water. Cover, and begin timing when water returns to a boil.

To stop the cooking process, plunge the basket in ice water, using 1 pound of ice for each pound of vegetables, or hold the vegetables under cold running water. Cool the vegetables in ice water or under cold running water for the same number of minutes recommended for blanching. Drain well.

To blanch vegetables for freezing, submerge prepared produce in boiling water; cover vegetables, and immediately begin to count the recommended blanching time.

Next, immediately plunge hot vegetables in ice water to stop the cooking process. Then drain the vegetables, and package them in proper containers for freezing.

Vegetable Freezing Chart

Vegetable	Preparation	Blanching Time
Beans (butter, lima, and pinto)	Choose tender beans with well-filled pods. Shell and wash; then sort according to size.	Small beans, 2 minutes; medium beans, 3 minutes; large beans, 4 minutes
Beans (green, snap, and waxed)	Select tender, young pods. Wash beans, and cut off tips. Cut lengthwise or in 1- or 2-inch lengths.	3 minutes
Corn (on the cob)	Husk corn, and remove silks; trim and wash.	Small ears, 7 minutes; medium ears, 9 minutes; large ears, 11 minutes
Corn (whole kernel, blanched on the cob)	Blanch ears first. Then cut kernels from cob about ⅔ depth of kernels.	4 minutes
Corn (cream-style)	Blanch ears first. Cut off tips of kernels. Scrape cobs with back of a knife to remove juice and hearts of kernels.	4 minutes
Greens (beet, chard, collards, mustard, spinach, turnip)	Select tender, green leaves. Wash thoroughly, and remove woody stems.	Collards, 3 minutes; other greens, 2 minutes
Okra	Select tender green pods. Wash and sort according to size. Remove stems at end of seed cells. After blanching, leave pods whole or slice crosswise.	Small pods, 3 minutes; large pods, 4 minutes
Peas (black-eyed and field)	Select pods with tender, barely mature peas. Shell and wash peas; discard the hard, immature, and overly mature ones.	2 minutes
Peas (English)	Select tender young peas. Shell and wash.	1½ minutes
Peppers (green and sweet red)	Select crisp, tender, green or red pods. Wash peppers; cut off tops; remove seeds and membrane. Dice peppers; cut in halves, or cut in ½-inch strips or rings. Pack raw, or blanch, if desired.	(Blanching is optional.) Pepper halves, 3 minutes; strips or rings, 2 minutes
Peppers (hot)	Wash peppers; remove stems. Place in containers leaving no headspace.	Not required
Squash (summer)	Select young squash with small seeds and tender rind. Wash and cut into ½-inch slices.	3 minutes
Tomatoes	**Raw:** Dip tomatoes in boiling water 30 seconds to loosen skins. Core and peel. Chop or quarter tomatoes, or leave whole. Pack, leaving 1-inch headspace.	**Stewed:** Remove stem end and core from tomatoes; peel and quarter. Cover and cook until tender (10 to 20 minutes). Place pan containing cooked tomatoes in cold water to cool. Pack, leaving recommended headspace for liquid pack.

Blanching can be done in the microwave oven or by steaming, but these methods aren't as good as boiling. Research shows that enzymes may not be inactivated in microwave blanching. However, if you plan to use the microwave method, work with small quantities, and use the directions that were designed for your microwave oven.

After blanching, freeze vegetables in a **dry pack** or a **tray pack.** For a dry pack, place cooled vegetables in freezer containers, leaving the recommended headspace, and freeze.

In a tray pack, vegetables are frozen individually so that they remain loose in the package. Simply spread the vegetables in a single layer on a shallow tray, and freeze until firm, checking every 10 minutes after 1 hour.

Package, leaving no headspace, and freeze. For preparation directions and blanching times for individual vegetables, see chart at left.

Freezing Fruit

Wash and drain fruit before peeling, shelling, pitting, or capping, and do not soak the fruit.

Since fruit is naturally acidic, avoid galvanized, copper, or iron utensils in preparation. These materials can react with the acid and make the fruit unsafe.

Enzymes in some fruit, such as apples, peaches, pears, plums, figs, and persimmons, cause browning and loss of vitamin C when the fruit is exposed to air. This can be controlled with ascorbic acid (vitamin C) or a commercial mixture called ascorbic-citric powder.

Ascorbic acid is most effective in controlling browning. It's available in powder, crystalline, or tablet forms and can be found in some drugstores. Use according to the instructions included for each type of fruit pack listed. For crushed and pureed fruit, stir dissolved ascorbic acid directly into fruit.

Ascorbic-citric powder, a commercial mixture of ascorbic acid, sugar, and citric acid, also prevents darkening of fruit. Use the powder according to the manufacturer's directions.

Citric acid and lemon juice are occasionally used to prevent discoloration. But they aren't as effective as ascorbic acid and may mask natural fruit flavors.

Fruit may be frozen in one of three ways: unsweetened, with sugar, or in syrup. Sugar and syrup packs give the fruit the best texture and flavor. Unsweetened packs usually lack plump texture and good color. Berries, blanched apples, rhubarb, and figs freeze well unsweetened. Directions for each type

When using a syrup pack, place crumpled waxed paper between the fruit and the container lid to keep fruit submerged. Using commercial ascorbic-citric powder in the syrup helps prevent darkening of fruit.

of pack follow this paragraph. Preparation instructions and recommended packs for individual fruit are listed in the fruit freezing chart facing this page.

Syrup pack: While a 40% sugar syrup is recommended for most fruit (see sugar syrups chart, below), a lighter syrup may be used for mild-flavored fruit to keep from masking the flavor. A heavier, sweeter syrup may be needed for tart fruit, such as sour cherries.

Use the sugar syrups chart for proportions and directions for making.

Use just enough cold syrup to cover the fruit—usually ½ to ⅔ cup for each pint. Stir dissolved ascorbic acid into syrup just before using to prevent darkening, if necessary. When using rigid containers, place crumpled waxed paper between the top of fruit and the lid to submerge fruit in the syrup. Seal, label, and freeze.

Sugar Syrups
For Freezing Fruit

Type of Syrup	Sugar (Cups)	Water (Cups)	Yield (Cups)
30%	2	4	5
35%	2½	4	5⅓
40%	3	4	5½
50%	4¾	4	6½

Directions: Combine the sugar and warm water, mixing until the sugar dissolves. Chill.

Sugar pack: Spread fruit in a shallow tray, and sprinkle with ascorbic acid dissolved in water to prevent darkening, if necessary. Sprinkle fruit with recommended amount of sugar, and let stand 10 to 15 minutes to draw out juices and allow the sugar to dissolve. Stir gently to coat fruit, and package with juices. Seal, label, and freeze.

Unsweetened packs: For a **liquid pack,** fruit may be frozen unsweetened in water containing ascorbic acid, if needed, or in unsweetened juice. Package the fruit, as for syrup pack, using chilled liquid.

For unsweetened **dry pack,** place fruit in containers, leaving recommended headspace, and freeze. Ascorbic acid dissolved in water may be sprinkled over fruit before packing, if necessary. Fruit pieces can be frozen separately in a **tray pack,** making it easy to measure fruit without thawing. To prepare a tray pack, spread fruit in a single layer; sprinkle with dissolved ascorbic acid, if necessary. Place tray in freezer, and freeze just until fruit is firm; package, leaving no headspace. Seal, label, and return to freezer.

Puree: Press fruit pulp through a sieve; then puree in a blender or food processor. Purees may be packed with or without sugar. To prevent browning, dissolve ascorbic acid in a small amount of water, and stir into the puree. Rigid containers are usually best for packing.

Fruit that's juicy, such as strawberries, or fruit that's intended for cooking purposes freezes well in a sugar pack. Sprinkle sugar over fruit on a tray, and let stand 10 to 15 minutes. Stir gently to coat fruit and dissolve sugar; then pack the coated fruit in freezer containers.

Package, leaving recommended headspace; seal, label, and freeze.

Packaging: Food will be more convenient to use if packed in amounts to be used for a single meal or recipe. Freezer containers should be no larger than ½-gallon capacity; food packed in larger containers freezes too slowly for a quality product.

Have all the food cooled before packing to help speed freezing. Be sure syrup or juice for liquid packs is chilled before using. Pack food tightly in the containers to leave as little air as possible, but leave recommended headspace to allow for expansion during freezing.

With freezer bags, press all the air from the bag starting at the bottom, working your way to the opening. Twist tightly, and double back the top of the bag. Secure with a rubber band, string, or twist tie.

When sealing rigid containers, keep the edge free from food or moisture for a good seal. The lids should be tight fitting and may be reinforced with freezer tape, if necessary.

Freezing Tips

—Freeze food as soon as it is packaged and sealed. Be sure to label container with the date frozen, package contents, and amount.

—Place in the freezer only the amount of food that will freeze in 24 hours (about 2 or 3 pounds of food per cubic foot of freezer space). Food is best frozen quickly, and overloading slows the freezing rate.

—Place packages in contact with the surface in the coldest part of the freezer. Leave some space between packages for good air circulation. After freezing, the packages may be stacked up or stored close together.

—Freeze food at 0° or lower. For rapid freezing, set the temperature at -10° a day in advance. Once food is frozen, return temperature setting to 0°.

—Accidentally thawed vegetables may be refrozen only if ice crystals are still present, or if the freezer temperature is 40° or below.

—Accidentally thawed fruit may be refrozen if it shows no signs of spoilage. You may want to use it for cooking or making jams, jellies, and sauces.

—Vegetables and most fruit retain good quality in the freezer for eight to twelve months; citrus fruit keeps for four to six months.

Freezing is the last of a four-part series on food preservation. See the May section for canning, June for making jams and jellies, and July for pickling.

Fruit Freezing Chart

Fruit	Preparation	Type of Pack (syrup, sugar, unsweetened, puree)	Remarks
Apples	Wash, peel, and core. Apples may be steam blanched 1½ to 2 minutes to retain shape and color.	**Syrup:** 40% **Sugar:** use ½ cup sugar/1 quart apples	To prevent browning, use ½ teaspoon ascorbic acid per quart of syrup for syrup pack. Sprinkle ¼ teaspoon ascorbic acid mixed with ¼ cup water over each quart for sugar pack.
Blackberries, Dewberries, Raspberries	Select fully ripe berries. Wash quickly; remove caps and drain.	**Syrup:** 40% **Sugar:** use ¾ cup sugar/1 quart berries **Unsweetened:** dry pack **Puree:** 1 cup sugar/1 quart pureed berries	These freeze well in unsweetened tray packs.
Blueberries, Huckleberries	Select fully ripe berries. For unsweetened pack, do not wash. Prepare as for blackberries for puree.	**Unsweetened:** dry pack **Puree:** 1 cup sugar/1 quart pureed berries	Wash berries frozen in unsweetened pack before using.
Cantaloupe, Honeydew, Watermelon	Cut melons in half; remove seeds and rind. Cut into slices or cubes, or use melon ball cutter.	**Syrup:** 30% **Unsweetened:** dry pack	Best results with syrup pack.
Figs	Select soft-ripe figs. Make sure they are not sour in centers. Sort, wash, and cut off stems; do not peel. Halve or leave whole.	**Syrup:** 35% **Unsweetened:** dry or liquid pack	To prevent browning, use ¾ teaspoon ascorbic acid per quart of syrup for syrup pack or per 1 quart water for unsweetened liquid pack. May use ½ cup lemon juice per quart syrup instead of ascorbic acid.
Peaches, Nectarines	Select firm, ripe peaches. Peel; halve or slice.	**Syrup:** 40% **Sugar:** use ⅔ cup sugar/1 quart peaches **Unsweetened:** liquid pack **Puree:** use 1 cup sugar/1 quart pureed peaches	To prevent browning, use ½ teaspoon ascorbic acid per quart of syrup for syrup pack or 1 teaspoon ascorbic acid per quart of water for unsweetened pack. Sprinkle ¼ teaspoon ascorbic acid mixed with ¼ cup water over each quart for sugar pack. Use ⅛ teaspoon ascorbic acid per quart of puree.
Pears	Peel pears; cut in halves or quarters, and remove cores. Heat pears in boiling syrup 1 to 2 minutes. Drain and cool. Chill the syrup.	**Syrup:** 40%	To prevent browning, use ¾ teaspoon ascorbic acid per quart of cold syrup.
Persimmons	Select orange-colored, soft-ripe persimmons. Peel, cut into quarters, and remove seeds. Press pulp through a sieve to puree.	**Sugar:** use 1 cup sugar/1 quart puree **Unsweetened:** dry pack	To prevent browning, use ⅛ teaspoon ascorbic acid per quart of puree.
Plums	Select firm, ripe plums soft enough to yield to slight pressure. Sort and wash. Leave whole or cut into halves or quarters; remove pits.	**Syrup:** 40% to 50%	To prevent browning, use 1 teaspoon ascorbic acid per quart of syrup.
Rhubarb	Select firm, tender, well-colored stalks with few fibers. Wash, trim, and cut into lengths to fit package.	**Syrup:** 40% **Unsweetened:** dry pack	Rhubarb may be heated in boiling water 1 minute and cooled quickly to retain color and flavor.
Strawberries	Select fully ripe, firm, deep-red strawberries. Wash a few at a time; drain and remove caps.	**Syrup:** 50% **Sugar:** use ¾ cup sugar/1 quart whole berries	Strawberries may be crushed or sliced for sugar pack.

Capture Fresh Tomato Flavor

Summer's tomato crop has arrived in full glory, blazing with color and brimming with juice. Tomatoes are delicious sliced for sandwiches, tossed with greens, eased under the broiler, or stuffed with a variety of salads. But if you still have more than you're able to use, try them in one of these recipes and enjoy the flavor longer.

To use up large quantities of excess tomatoes, make a batch of Homemade Catsup or Spicy Tomato Juice. You'll be able to capture the flavor of juicy tomatoes by cooking them down and adding just the right amount of spices.

From Banks, Arkansas, comes Wilma Hamaker's Chunky Chili Sauce. It's thick with bits of tomato, onion, and green pepper. According to Wilma, "There are lots of chili sauce recipes, but mine's different because it's sweetened with honey."

When the tomato crop isn't large, just cook Refrigerator Tomato Sauce. It's easy to store and doesn't require processing in a boiling-water bath.

You'll probably notice that some of the following recipes call for a lot of salt. The salt is added for flavor, but it also acts as a preservative; thus, it shouldn't be left out.

Peeling large quantities of tomatoes can be a difficult task. To make it easier, we suggest placing whole tomatoes in boiling water for 15 to 30 seconds. The skins will then slip off easily.

HOMEMADE CATSUP

23 pounds medium tomatoes (about 46), sliced
3 medium onions, coarsely chopped
3 (3-inch) sticks cinnamon
1 tablespoon whole cloves
3 cloves garlic, chopped
3 cups vinegar (5% acidity)
1½ cups sugar
1 tablespoon salt
1 tablespoon paprika
⅛ teaspoon red pepper

Combine tomatoes and onion in two large kettles. Bring to a boil; reduce heat, and simmer, uncovered, 45 minutes, stirring frequently. Remove tomato mixture from heat; put tomato mixture through a food mill or sieve, reserving tomato juice.

Tie cinnamon sticks, cloves, and garlic in a cheesecloth bag; add to vinegar

in a small saucepan. Bring to a boil; reduce heat, and simmer, uncovered, 30 minutes. Remove spices; set vinegar mixture aside.

Cook reserved tomato juice, uncovered, in a large kettle over medium-high heat 1 hour and 20 minutes or until volume is reduced by half, stirring frequently. Add vinegar mixture and remaining ingredients. Cook, uncovered, 30 to 40 minutes or until mixture is thickened.

Quickly pour mixture into hot jars, leaving ½-inch headspace; cover at once with metal lids, and screw on bands. Process in boiling-water bath 20 minutes. Yield: 4 pints.

Mrs. Earl L. Faulkenberry,
Lancaster, South Carolina.

CHUNKY CHILI SAUCE

10 pounds medium tomatoes (about 19)
2 cups chopped onion
2 cups chopped green pepper
2 small hot peppers, minced
1 cup honey
3 tablespoons salt
3 tablespoons mixed pickling spices
1 tablespoon celery seeds
1 tablespoon mustard seeds
2 cups vinegar (5% acidity)

Peel, core, and chop tomatoes. Combine tomatoes, chopped onion, chopped green pepper, hot peppers, honey, and salt in a large Dutch oven. Bring mixture to a boil; reduce heat, and simmer, uncovered, 45 minutes.

Tie pickling spices, celery seeds, and mustard seeds in a cheesecloth bag; add to tomato mixture. Simmer, uncovered, 45 minutes, stirring often. Stir in vinegar; simmer, uncovered, an additional 2 hours. Remove spice bag.

Quickly spoon sauce into hot jars, leaving ½-inch headspace; cover at once with metal lids, and screw on bands. Process in boiling-water bath 35 minutes. Yield: 3 pints.

Wilma L. Hamaker,
Banks, Arkansas.

REFRIGERATOR TOMATO SAUCE

3 pounds medium tomatoes (about 6)
1 medium onion, quartered
2 medium carrots, scraped and cut into 1-inch pieces
1 large celery stalk with leaves, cut into ½-inch pieces
2 cloves garlic, minced
⅓ cup chopped fresh parsley
5 to 6 leaves fresh basil, or ½ teaspoon dried whole basil
1 teaspoon salt
¾ teaspoon pepper

Peel, core, and quarter tomatoes. Combine all ingredients in a Dutch oven; cook, uncovered, over low heat 1 hour and 15 minutes to 1½ hours, or until thickened.

Pour mixture into food processor bowl or container of electric blender; process 30 seconds or until grainy in texture. Store in refrigerator up to 4 days. Yield: 2¼ cups. *Harris Simpson, Atlanta, Georgia.*

TOMATO RELISH

16 pounds medium tomatoes (about 32)
12 medium onions, finely chopped
3 red peppers, finely chopped
3 green peppers, finely chopped
3 tablespoons salt
2 cups firmly packed brown sugar
2 cups vinegar (5% acidity)
1 tablespoon ground cinnamon
1½ teaspoons ground allspice
1½ teaspoons ground cloves

Peel, core, and chop tomatoes. Combine tomatoes, onion, peppers, and salt in a large kettle. Bring to a boil; reduce heat to medium, and cook, uncovered, 25 minutes. Add remaining ingredients; reduce heat, and simmer, uncovered, 1½ to 2 hours or until thickened.

Quickly pack into hot jars, leaving ½-inch headspace; cover at once with metal lids, and screw on bands. Process in boiling-water bath 20 minutes. Yield: 12 pints. *Ruth Teague, Lincolnton, North Carolina.*

Tip: If power to your freezer is interrupted, do not open the door unnecessarily. Food in a full freezer will stay frozen 2 days, and food in a half-filled freezer about one day. If power is not resumed within this time, use dry ice to prevent spoilage, or move your food to a locker plant nearby.

SPICY TOMATO JUICE

20 pounds medium tomatoes (about 40)
2 tablespoons lemon juice
2 tablespoons prepared horseradish
1 tablespoon plus ½ teaspoon seasoned
   salt
1½ teaspoons Worcestershire sauce
1 teaspoon hot sauce

Core and quarter tomatoes. Place in two large Dutch ovens; cook over medium heat 45 minutes, stirring occasionally, until soft. Remove from heat; press through a food mill or sieve, reserving tomato juice. Return juice to a Dutch oven, and stir in remaining ingredients; simmer until thoroughly heated. Quickly pour into hot jars, leaving ½-inch headspace; cover at once with metal lids, and screw on bands. Process in boiling-water bath 35 minutes. Yield: 9 pints.
*Mrs. W. P. Chambers,
Louisville, Kentucky.*

Plain Dessert? Not With These Sauces

Most of us have served ice cream, fruit, pound cake, or angel food cake for dessert. But when the occasion calls for something more unusual than these favorite standbys, try adding a spectacular topping to them.

Praline Ice Cream Sauce is full of all the South's favorite things—toasted pecans, brown sugar, and lots of caramel flavor. This thick sauce is perfect served warm over vanilla ice cream. We also found it could be made ahead and reheated just before serving.

We're certain chocolate fans will find Chocolate Sauce Supreme to be the best sauce they have ever tasted. Its robust chocolate flavor is enhanced with sugar, corn syrup, and a splash of crème de cacao. You might want to consider packaging a bottle of the chocolate sauce to share as a gift with friends.

If you like thick, chunky sauces, then Creamy Peach Sauce and Tasty Cranberry Jubilee are for you. Each one of these sauces is filled with plump bits of fruit. The peach sauce is great over cake, while the cranberry sauce brightens up ice cream.

For something that's smoother and fluffier, serve Coconut-Orange Sauce. This melt-in-your-mouth nectar is a treat served over fresh fruit desserts or salads as well as angel food cakes.

TASTY CRANBERRY JUBILEE

1 cup sugar
1½ cups water
2 cups fresh cranberries
¼ cup brandy
Vanilla ice cream

Combine sugar and water in a saucepan. Bring mixture to a boil, stirring occasionally; boil 5 minutes, stirring often. Add cranberries, and return to a boil; boil an additional 5 minutes, stirring occasionally. Remove from heat.

Place brandy in a small, long-handled saucepan; heat just until warm (do not boil). Ignite brandy, and pour over cranberries; stir until flames die down. Serve immediately over ice cream. Yield: 2 cups sauce. *Alice McNamara,
Eucha, Oklahoma.*

COCONUT-ORANGE SAUCE

1 cup sugar
1 tablespoon all-purpose flour
4 egg yolks, beaten
½ cup orange juice
2 tablespoons flaked coconut
1 tablespoon grated orange rind
1 cup whipping cream, whipped
Angel food cake

Combine sugar and flour in top of a double boiler; stir in egg yolks. Gradually add orange juice, stirring constantly; bring the water to a boil. Reduce heat to low. Cook, stirring constantly, until the mixture is thickened.

Remove from heat; stir in flaked coconut and grated orange rind. Cool. Fold in whipped cream. Serve over angel food cake. Yield: 2⅔ cups.
*Edna Earle Moore,
Hueytown, Alabama.*

PRALINE ICE CREAM SAUCE

1½ cups chopped pecans
¼ cup butter or margarine
1¼ cups firmly packed light brown sugar
¾ cup light corn syrup
3 tablespoons all-purpose flour
1 (5.33-ounce) can evaporated milk

Spread pecans on a baking sheet; bake at 300° for 15 minutes. Set aside.

Melt butter in a medium saucepan; add sugar, corn syrup, and flour, stirring well. Bring to a boil; reduce heat, and simmer, stirring constantly, 5 minutes. Remove from heat, and let cool to lukewarm. Gradually stir in milk and pecans. Serve warm over ice cream. Yield: 3 cups. *Carolyn Webb,
Jackson, Mississippi.*

CREAMY PEACH SAUCE

1 (29-ounce) can sliced peaches, undrained
¼ cup sugar
1 tablespoon cornstarch
¼ teaspoon salt
1½ teaspoons grated lemon rind
1 tablespoon lemon juice
1½ tablespoons butter or margarine
1 cup evaporated milk

Drain peaches, reserving 1 cup juice; set peaches aside.

Combine sugar, cornstarch, and salt in a heavy saucepan; mix well. Add reserved peach juice, lemon rind, lemon juice, and butter; stir well. Bring to a boil; reduce heat to low, and simmer 10 minutes, stirring often.

Remove from heat; cool 10 minutes. Stir in milk and peaches; serve warm or cool over cake. Yield: 3¼ cups.
*Stacy Skoog,
Woodsboro, Texas.*

CHOCOLATE SAUCE SUPREME

1 (6-ounce) package semisweet chocolate
   morsels
¼ cup butter or margarine
1 cup sifted powdered sugar
½ cup light corn syrup
¼ cup crème de cacao liqueur
¼ cup water
1 teaspoon vanilla extract
Dash of salt

Combine chocolate morsels and butter in top of a double boiler; bring water to a boil. Reduce heat to low; cook until chocolate melts. Stir in remaining ingredients. Cook over medium heat, stirring until sugar dissolves and sauce is smooth. Serve sauce hot or cold over ice cream. Yield: 2 cups.
*Patsy Hull,
Florence, Alabama.*

CHOCOLATE-CHERRY SAUCE

½ cup pitted fresh sweet cherries
½ cup chocolate syrup

Combine cherries and chocolate syrup in container of electric blender; process on high 15 seconds. Serve over vanilla ice cream. Yield: about 1 cup.

LEMON SAUCE

½ cup sugar
2 tablespoons cornstarch
⅛ teaspoon salt
1 cup water
2 teaspoons grated lemon rind
⅓ cup lemon juice
1 tablespoon butter or margarine

Combine sugar, cornstarch, salt, and water in a small saucepan, stirring until smooth. Cook over medium heat, stirring constantly, until smooth and thickened. Add remaining ingredients; cook until thoroughly heated. Serve warm over cake or date nut bread. Yield: about 1½ cups.   *Mrs. Jesse Lanham, Middleburg, Kentucky.*

These Dishes Are Delightfully Lemon

Slice a fresh juicy lemon, and you'll get an idea of the wonderful effect this tart fruit has on summer menus. The sharp fragrance that fills the air creates a cool and inviting atmosphere.

We've included a wide range of recipes to give you a sampling of the many ways lemons can be used in cooking. For example, try Golden Lemon Tarts or Old-Fashioned Lemon Layer Cake when you want a special dessert.

The zesty taste of lemon is a winner in main dishes, too. Flounder Thermidor has a creamy cheese sauce that contains lemon juice, parsley, and paprika. Baked Lemon Chicken is seasoned with garlic as well as lemon.

Lemony Green Beans and Lemon Spinach With Feta are two savory vegetable dishes. In fact, lemon juice is a great seasoning for almost any vegetable. Try substituting it for vinegar in salad dressings, or just squeeze it over cooked vegetables for a classic light touch in seasoning.

Lemons are also versatile when it comes to garnishes and food styling. A simple lemon slice or some grated lemon rind makes a colorful accent for a variety of dishes. If you want to be a bit more creative, hollow out lemon halves and use them as containers for ice cream or custard.

With all their uses, it's a good idea to always keep some lemons on hand. You can store them at room temperature for a week to ten days or in a plastic bag in the refrigerator for about a month.

FLOUNDER THERMIDOR

4 flounder fillets (about 1 pound)
1½ cups milk
¼ teaspoon pepper
3 tablespoons butter or margarine, melted
3 tablespoons all-purpose flour
1 cup (4 ounces) shredded Cheddar cheese
¼ cup lemon juice
1 tablespoon chopped fresh parsley
1 teaspoon paprika
Hot cooked rice

Cut fillets in half lengthwise; roll up, and secure with wooden picks. Place fillets in a lightly greased 12- x 8- x 2-inch baking dish. Pour milk in dish; sprinkle fillets with pepper. Cover and bake at 350° for 30 minutes or until fish flakes easily when tested with a fork. Remove from oven; drain, reserving liquid.

Melt butter in a heavy saucepan over low heat; add flour, stirring until smooth. Cook 1 minute, stirring constantly. Gradually add reserved liquid; cook over medium heat, stirring constantly, until mixture is thickened and bubbly. Add cheese; stir until melted. Stir in lemon juice; pour over fish. Sprinkle with parsley and paprika. Place under broiler 6 inches away from heat; cook 2 to 3 minutes or until lightly browned. Serve over hot cooked rice. Yield: 4 servings.   *Beckie Webster, Roanoke, Virginia.*

BAKED LEMON CHICKEN

4 chicken breast halves, skinned
¼ cup plus 2 tablespoons lemon juice
½ cup butter or margarine, melted
1 teaspoon garlic powder
1 teaspoon poultry seasoning
½ teaspoon salt
¼ teaspoon pepper
Hot cooked rice (optional)

Place chicken in a lightly greased 12- x 7- x 2-inch baking dish. Combine remaining ingredients except rice; pour over chicken. Bake, uncovered, at 350° for 1 hour or until chicken is tender, basting frequently. Serve with hot cooked rice, if desired. Yield: 4 servings.   *Sharon McClatchey, Muskogee, Oklahoma.*

Tip: When you use fresh lemons for cooking, remember that one medium lemon will yield 2 to 4 tablespoons juice and 1 tablespoon grated rind.

LEMONY GREEN BEANS

1 large lemon
1 pound fresh green beans
3 cups water
½ teaspoon salt
1 small onion, sliced and separated into rings
3 tablespoons butter or margarine, melted
1 teaspoon brown sugar

Cut 3 thin slices from lemon. Squeeze remaining lemon; set juice aside.

Remove strings from green beans, and wash thoroughly. Cut green beans into 1½-inch pieces. Combine water and salt in a large saucepan; bring to a boil. Add green beans, and cover. Reduce heat, and simmer 30 minutes or until tender. Drain beans.

Sauté onion in butter 2 to 3 minutes. Add beans, lemon juice, and brown sugar; heat thoroughly. Garnish with lemon slices. Yield: 4 servings.   *Evelyn Snellings, Richmond, Virginia.*

LEMON SPINACH WITH FETA

1½ pounds fresh spinach
¾ cup water
⅓ cup crumbled feta cheese
⅛ teaspoon salt
⅛ teaspoon pepper
2 tablespoons olive oil
Juice of 1 lemon

Remove stems from spinach; wash leaves well. Place spinach in a large Dutch oven. Add water; cover and cook over medium heat 10 minutes. Drain spinach well.

Combine spinach, cheese, salt, and pepper; toss lightly. Combine oil and lemon juice. Pour over spinach mixture; toss well. Yield: 4 servings.   *Mary Pappas, Richmond, Virginia.*

BLUEBERRY-LEMON BREAD

¼ cup plus 2 tablespoons butter or margarine, softened
1 cup sugar
2 eggs
1½ cups all-purpose flour
1 teaspoon baking powder
Pinch of salt
½ cup milk
2 teaspoons grated lemon rind
1 cup fresh blueberries
2 teaspoons all-purpose flour
⅓ cup sugar
3 tablespoons lemon juice

Cream butter; gradually add 1 cup sugar, beating at medium speed of an electric mixer until well blended. Add eggs, one at a time, beating well after each addition.

Combine 1½ cups flour, baking powder, and salt; add to creamed mixture alternately with milk, beginning and ending with flour mixture. Stir in grated lemon rind. Dredge blueberries in 2 teaspoons flour; fold into batter.

Pour batter into a greased 8- x 4- x 3-inch loafpan. Bake at 350° for 55 minutes or until a wooden pick inserted in center comes out clean.

Combine ⅓ cup sugar and lemon juice in a small saucepan; heat until sugar dissolves. Puncture top of bread in several places with a wooden pick; pour lemon juice mixture over warm bread, allowing mixture to soak into bread. Cool bread in the pan 30 minutes. Yield: 1 loaf. *Janet Filer, Arlington, Virginia.*

OLD-FASHIONED LEMON LAYER CAKE

1 cup plus 2 tablespoons butter or margarine, softened
2¼ cups sugar
6 eggs, separated
3¼ cups all-purpose flour
1 tablespoon baking powder
⅛ teaspoon salt
1 cup plus 2 tablespoons milk
¾ teaspoon grated lemon rind
1¾ teaspoons lemon juice
Lemon filling (recipe follows)
Additional grated lemon rind (optional)
Lemon twist (optional)

Cream butter; gradually add sugar, beating well at medium speed of an electric mixer. Add egg yolks, one at a time, beating well after each addition.

Combine flour, baking powder, and salt; add to creamed mixture alternately with milk, beginning and ending with flour mixture. Mix well after each addition. Stir in lemon rind and juice. Beat egg whites (at room temperature) until stiff peaks form; fold into batter.

Pour batter into 3 greased and floured 9-inch round cakepans. Bake at 350° for 25 to 30 minutes or until a wooden pick inserted in center comes out clean. Cool in pans 10 minutes. Remove layers; cool completely.

Split each layer in half horizontally. Spread lemon filling between layers and on top; garnish with additional lemon rind and lemon twist, if desired. Yield: one 9-inch layer cake.

Lemon Filling:

2¼ cups sugar
¼ cup plus 1½ tablespoons all-purpose flour
2 tablespoons grated lemon rind
½ cup lemon juice
1 egg, beaten
2 tablespoons butter or margarine

Combine all ingredients except butter in a heavy saucepan; cook over medium heat, stirring constantly, until smooth and thickened. Remove from heat. Add butter; stir until melted. Cool. Yield: about 2½ cups. *Cheryl Daniel, Austin, Texas.*

MELTING MOMENTS

1 cup butter or margarine, softened
⅓ cup sifted powdered sugar
1¼ cups all-purpose flour
½ cup cornstarch
Lemon frosting (recipe follows)

Cream butter; add sugar, and beat well. Gradually add flour and cornstarch, beating until smooth. Drop mixture by level teaspoonfuls onto ungreased cookie sheets.

Bake at 350° for 10 to 12 minutes. (Cookies do not brown on top.) Cool slightly on cookie sheets; remove cookies to wire racks to cool completely. Frost with lemon frosting. (These cookies are fragile.) Yield: about 7 dozen.

Lemon Frosting:

¼ cup butter or margarine, softened
1½ cups sifted powdered sugar
2 tablespoons lemon juice
1 tablespoon grated lemon rind

Cream butter; gradually add powdered sugar and lemon juice, beating until smooth. Stir in lemon rind. Yield: 2 cups. *Sally Smith, Rustburg, Virginia.*

GOLDEN LEMON TARTS

½ cup butter or margarine
1 cup sugar
1 tablespoon cornstarch
3 eggs, beaten
½ cup lemon juice
Double-crust pastry (recipe follows)
Whipped cream (optional)

Place butter in top of a double boiler; bring water to a boil. Reduce heat to low, and cook until butter melts.

Combine sugar and cornstarch, stirring well; add to butter, and stir until smooth. Stir in eggs, and cook 5 minutes, stirring constantly. Add lemon juice; cook 3 to 4 minutes longer or until mixture thickens, stirring constantly. Cool.

Spoon a rounded tablespoon of lemon filling into each baked, cooled tart shell. Before serving, top each lemon tart with a small dollop of whipped cream, if desired. Yield: 22 tarts.

Double-Crust Pastry:

2 cups all-purpose flour
½ teaspoon salt
⅔ cup shortening
5 to 6 tablespoons cold water

Combine flour and salt; cut in shortening with pastry blender until mixture resembles coarse meal. Sprinkle cold water evenly over surface; stir with a fork until all dry ingredients are moistened. Shape dough into a ball; chill.

Roll dough to ⅛-inch thickness on a lightly floured surface; cut into 3¼-inch rounds. Fit each pastry round into 3-inch tart pans. Prick with a fork. Bake at 400° for 10 to 12 minutes; cool. Yield: 22 tart shells. *Katherine Mabry, Athens, Alabama.*

TART LEMON SAUCE

1 cup sugar
½ cup butter or margarine
1 to 2 tablespoons grated lemon rind
⅓ cup lemon juice
2 eggs, beaten

Combine sugar, butter, lemon rind, and lemon juice in top of double boiler; bring water to a boil. Reduce heat to low, and cook until butter melts and sugar dissolves, stirring occasionally. Stir in eggs, and cook, stirring constantly, for 5 to 7 minutes or until sauce thickens and coats a metal spoon. Remove from heat. Serve on pound cake or gingerbread. Yield: 1⅔ cups.

Jo F. Johnston, St. Simons Island, Georgia.

It's Hot Dog Time Again

Hot dogs are a natural for summer menus. With warm weather, the pace is a bit slower, and casual meals that don't involve a lot of fuss seem particularly appealing. Hot dogs also lend themselves well to a favorite summer activity—eating outdoors. It doesn't have to be a full-fledged picnic; hot dogs are great served on the deck or at a backyard picnic table.

For some new versions of this old favorite, try a couple of recipes from our readers, such as Corn Relish Dogs and Barbecued Franks. Both of these have a zesty barbecue flavor that gives them an edge on ordinary hot dogs.

If you're a chili fan, you'll want to try Sloppy Joe Dogs. As the name implies, these have a spicy chili-meat sauce that is served over frankfurters instead of open-face hamburger buns.

BARBECUED FRANKS

½ medium onion, chopped
½ green pepper, chopped
¼ cup chopped celery
1 tablespoon butter or margarine, melted
¾ cup catsup
½ cup water
2 tablespoons lemon juice
1½ tablespoons vinegar
2 teaspoons Worcestershire sauce
1½ tablespoons sugar
¾ teaspoon ground mustard
8 frankfurters
8 hot dog buns

Sauté onion, green pepper, and celery in butter in a Dutch oven until tender; add catsup, water, lemon juice, vinegar, Worcestershire sauce, sugar, and mustard. Cook over medium heat 10 minutes, stirring occasionally. Add frankfurters; simmer an additional 5 minutes or until franks are thoroughly heated. To serve, place in buns, and spoon sauce on top. Yield: 8 servings.
Debbie Whitlock,
Liberty, South Carolina.

Tip: Onions offer outstanding nutritive value. They are a good source of calcium and vitamins A and C. They contain iron, riboflavin, thiamine, and niacin; have a high percentage of water; and supply essential bulk. They are low in calories and have only a trace of fat.

CORN RELISH DOGS

¾ cup commercial barbecue sauce
¼ cup chopped green pepper
¼ cup chopped onion
1 (12-ounce) can whole kernel corn, drained
8 frankfurters
8 hot dog buns

Combine barbecue sauce, green pepper, and onion in a saucepan; simmer, uncovered, 10 minutes. Add corn and frankfurters; cover and simmer 10 minutes. Place frankfurters in buns; spoon on corn mixture. Yield: 8 servings.
A. A. Goodman,
Knoxville, Tennessee.

SLOPPY JOE DOGS

½ pound ground beef
1 medium onion, chopped
2 (8-ounce) cans tomato sauce
1 teaspoon chili powder
1 teaspoon steak sauce
⅛ teaspoon salt
⅛ teaspoon ground cumin
8 frankfurters, cooked
8 hot dog buns

Cook beef and onion in a large skillet until meat is browned, stirring to crumble. Drain off pan drippings. Stir in tomato sauce, chili powder, steak sauce, salt, and cumin; bring to a boil. Reduce heat, and simmer 30 minutes. Serve immediately over frankfurters in buns. Yield: 8 servings. *Sandra Ramsey,*
Wilson, North Carolina.

From Our Kitchen To Yours

The home economists in our test kitchens are frequently asked questions about how to measure ingredients. Since recipe results depend on using the right proportion of ingredients and accurate measuring, we'd like to answer some typical questions about measuring.

What's the difference between dry and liquid measuring cups, and how are they used to accurately measure ingredients? Dry measuring cups are usually metal or plastic and come in sets of 1 cup, ½ cup, ⅓ cup, and ¼ cup. They're used for measuring dry or solid ingredients. To measure accurately, you need to use the cup that holds the exact amount called for in the recipe. Fill the cup to the very top, and then level off with a flat edge or knife.

Liquid measuring cups are glass or clear plastic with a rim above the last cup level to prevent spilling. Each cup also has a spout for pouring. Liquid measures are available in 1-cup, 2-cup, and 4-cup sizes.

To measure liquids correctly, put the cup on a level surface. (You may need to use a cutting board to work on if your counter top is ceramic tile.) Then get eye level with the marking you want to read, and fill the cup to that line. It's best not to pick up the cup and bring it to your eye level to measure, because you may be not be able to hold it level.

How do I accurately measure flour? Does it need to be sifted? We just stir flour before measuring to lighten it. Next, we gently spoon it into the exact-size dry measuring cup needed and level off the top with a spatula or knife. Remember to be careful not to shake the cup when spooning flour in, or it may pack down. Because today most brands of all-purpose flour are pre-sifted, our home economists don't sift it again before measuring.

What ingredients need to be sifted before measuring? Both powdered sugar and cake flour are very light and have a tendency to pack down easily. For that reason, they need to be sifted and then lightly spooned into the right-size dry measuring cup.

What do you mean by firmly packed brown sugar? We call for firmly packed brown sugar when using a cup measurement. To measure brown sugar accurately, we pack it into the measuring cup firmly enough that the sugar keeps the shape of the cup when it's turned out. All the lumps are pressed out as it is packed into the measuring cup.

How do I measure solid shortening or butter? Shortening, like brown sugar, should be packed into the right-size dry measuring cup, but be sure all the air bubbles are out. To do this, use a spatula to cut through the shortening in the cup, pack it again, and then level off the top.

Butter or margarine is often already measured. For ½ cup, use a stick (quarter of a pound); for ¼ cup, use a half stick. If a different amount is needed, each stick is usually marked on the wrapper to help you measure the butter accurately. Remember when using butter or margarine, whipped margarine is not an equal substitute for regular stick margarine.

More on Measuring

—If you're unsure about the cup measurement of a baking dish, pour measured amounts of water into the dish until it's full.

—When measuring dry or liquid ingredients in amounts of less than ¼ cup, use measuring spoons (⅛ cup equals 2 tablespoons).

—To measure honey or syrup more accurately, grease your measuring cup to make it easy to remove the measured amount.

—To prevent a mistake, measure each ingredient in a utensil by itself, instead of in a container with any other measured ingredients.

—A dash in recipes is equal to about 1/16 teaspoon.

COOKING LIGHT®

International Entrées With Appeal

You don't have to travel around the world to discover the joy of international food. The South's melting-pot cuisine is rich with the heritage of other countries.

Hot and spicy Creole and Cajun cooking, so popular in Louisiana, is a direct influence of the French Acadians and others who settled the land. In Florida, a variety of fresh fruit and seafood dishes have a Caribbean flair. And to Texans, the food of Old Mexico is as familiar as fried chicken. Our light international entrées are no exception. Readers have added a bit of Southern ingenuity and made these dishes lower in calories or sodium.

Cheesy Beef Burritos are bursting with color and excitement. We made our recipe light in a number of innovative ways. Wafer-thin unleavened tortillas have less sodium than most bread, and we kept the amount of salt low in the beef mixture, letting cumin, oregano, garlic, and onion provide the flavor. If you use "no added salt" canned tomatoes, the sodium content can be cut even more. By substituting lean ground chuck for refried beans and sausage, two common ingredients in classic burrito recipes, we shaved off additional calories. By using Neufchâtel cheese, instead of the more familiar Monterey Jack cheese, and plain low-fat yogurt

for sour cream topping, we reduced the amount of fat and calories.

Grains, such as wheat used in tortillas, are low in one of the essential amino acids that make up proteins. But when combined with a small amount of animal protein, such as the beef and cheese mixture in our burritos, the essential amino acid gap is filled. This rounds out and improves the protein quality of the grain.

The versatility and convenience of Oriental stir-frying can't be beat as a method for cooking light. Our Walnut Chicken and Vegetables recipe uses this technique in which food is stirred and tossed in a small amount of oil over high heat. This low-fat, quick method of preparation cuts calories and, at the same time, helps retain nutrients.

Sweet-and-Sour Pork is one of the most popular Chinese main courses. Our recipe calls for pork tenderloin, a leaner cut that is lower in calories than the pork shoulder traditionally used. Instead of frying the pork in an egg and flour batter, we trimmed calories even more by simply browning the meat in a skillet coated with vegetable cooking spray. Calories from sugar were reduced by using unsweetened pineapple and by cutting in half the amount of brown sugar ordinarily called for in similar recipes. Reduced-sodium soy sauce, which contains 40% less sodium than regular soy sauce, helps keep the sodium content down. Enjoy this dish for only 228 calories per serving, plus 90 calories per ½ cup of rice.

Italian food is the number-one favorite foreign food in the South. We all know the satisfying taste of thick tomato sauces, rich cheese, and various pastas familiar to this cuisine. But if you can't afford the calories that usually accompany them, you'll appreciate Zucchini Lasagna. It's rich and spicy but lighter in calories because lean ground chuck was substituted for fattier Italian sausage commonly used, and we reduced the amount of cheese. The surprise in this entrée is fresh sliced zucchini, which replaces lasagna noodles, saving about 784 calories, yet retaining a unique texture that pasta lovers crave. Zucchini Lasagna has only 212 calories per serving.

The Greeks have their own version of pasta casseroles, and one of their favorites is Pastichio. Elbow macaroni is layered with a spicy beef mixture and a creamy, browned topping. You'll never miss the salt we reduced in our version because a touch of cinnamon, cloves, and allspice—common spices used in Greek cookery—add flavor. We also

substituted skim milk for regular milk and egg whites for whole eggs in the topping, making this entrée lower in saturated fat as well as calories. Feast on a serving for only 321 calories.

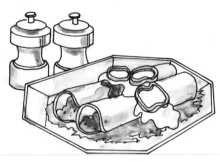

CHEESY BEEF BURRITOS

1 pound ground chuck
½ cup chopped onion
3 ounces Neufchâtel cheese, softened
¼ teaspoon salt
½ teaspoon dried whole oregano
½ teaspoon ground cumin
¼ teaspoon garlic powder
10 (6-inch) flour tortillas
Vegetable cooking spray
5 cups shredded lettuce
Tomato sauce (recipe follows)
Plain low-fat yogurt
Sliced fresh green chiles (optional)

Combine ground chuck and onion in a large skillet; cook until beef is browned. Drain off pan drippings. Add cheese and seasonings; stir until combined. Fill each tortilla with ¼ cup beef mixture. Roll up; place seam side down in a 12- x 7- x 2-inch baking dish coated with cooking spray. Cover and bake at 350° for 20 minutes.

Place each burrito on ½ cup shredded lettuce; top with tomato sauce and a dollop of yogurt. Garnish with fresh chiles, if desired. Yield: 10 servings (about 233 calories per serving plus 4 calories per tablespoon of sauce, and 9 calories per tablespoon of yogurt).

Tomato Sauce:

1 (16-ounce) can whole tomatoes, undrained
1 (4-ounce) can diced green chiles, drained
1 teaspoon cornstarch
1 teaspoon sugar
1 teaspoon ground coriander

Combine all ingredients in container of blender; process until smooth. Pour mixture into a saucepan; bring to a boil. Reduce heat. Simmer 2 minutes; stir occasionally. Yield: 2 cups. *Betty Quillen, Rogers, Arkansas.*

PASTICHIO

1 pound ground chuck
1 cup chopped onion
2 (8-ounce) cans tomato sauce
½ teaspoon salt
¼ teaspoon ground cinnamon
¼ teaspoon ground cloves
¼ teaspoon ground allspice
1 (8-ounce) package elbow macaroni
Vegetable cooking spray
3 tablespoons margarine
3 tablespoons all-purpose flour
⅛ teaspoon salt
2 cups skim milk
2 egg whites

Combine ground chuck and onion in a skillet; cook until meat is browned and onion is tender. Drain and pat dry.

Return meat mixture to skillet; add tomato sauce and seasonings. Simmer, uncovered, 5 minutes, stirring mixture occasionally.

Cook macaroni, omitting salt; drain.

Layer half of macaroni in a 2½-quart casserole coated with cooking spray; top macaroni with meat sauce and remaining macaroni.

Melt margarine in a saucepan; add flour and salt, stirring until smooth. Cook 1 minute, stirring constantly. Gradually add milk; cook, stirring constantly, until mixture is thickened. Beat egg whites slightly. Gradually stir one-fourth of hot mixture into whites; add to remaining hot mixture, stirring constantly. Cook 1 minute. Pour sauce over macaroni. Bake, uncovered, at 350° for 45 minutes. Place casserole under broiler 2 to 3 minutes or until browned. Yield: 8 servings (about 321 calories per serving).   *Jean Kabasan,*
Sanford, North Carolina.

ZUCCHINI LASAGNA

1 pound ground chuck
2 (16-ounce) cans whole tomatoes, undrained and chopped
2 bay leaves
2 cloves garlic, crushed
1 (6-ounce) can tomato paste
⅓ cup chopped onion
¼ cup chopped fresh parsley
¼ teaspoon salt
¼ teaspoon pepper
¼ teaspoon dried whole thyme
¼ teaspoon dried whole basil
6 medium zucchini (about 2½ pounds), unpeeled and thinly sliced
1 cup (4 ounces) shredded mozzarella cheese
Vegetable cooking spray

Cook beef in a skillet until browned, stirring to crumble; drain off pan drippings. Stir in tomatoes, bay leaves, garlic, tomato paste, onion, parsley, and seasonings; bring to a boil. Reduce heat, and simmer, uncovered, 30 minutes or until thickened, stirring occasionally. Remove bay leaves.

Layer half each of zucchini, meat sauce, and cheese in a 13- x 9- x 2-inch baking dish coated with cooking spray; repeat layers, except cheese. Bake, uncovered, at 375° for 35 minutes. Top with remaining cheese, and bake 5 minutes. Let stand 10 minutes. Yield: 8 servings (about 212 calories per serving).   *Anita Cox,*
Fort Worth, Texas.

SWEET-AND-SOUR PORK

1 (1-pound) pork tenderloin
Vegetable cooking spray
¼ cup water
1 (20-ounce) can unsweetened pineapple tidbits, undrained
¼ cup firmly packed brown sugar
2 tablespoons cornstarch
¼ cup cider vinegar
2 tablespoons reduced-sodium soy sauce
¾ cup thinly sliced green pepper strips
¼ cup thinly sliced onion
3 cups hot cooked rice (cooked without fat)

Trim fat from pork; cut into 2- x ½-inch strips. Coat skillet with cooking spray; place over medium heat. Add pork; cook until browned. Add water; cover, reduce heat, and simmer 30 minutes. Drain.

Drain pineapple, reserving juice; set pineapple aside. Combine sugar and cornstarch in a saucepan; stir in reserved juice, vinegar, and soy sauce. Cook over medium heat, stirring constantly, until thickened. Pour mixture over pork; let stand 15 minutes.

Stir in reserved pineapple, green pepper, and onion; simmer, uncovered, 8 to 10 minutes. Serve over rice. Yield: 6 servings (about 228 calories per serving plus 90 calories per ½ cup cooked rice).   *Bernard Lauritsen,*
Rock Port, Missouri.

WALNUT CHICKEN AND VEGETABLES

1 pound boneless chicken breast, skinned
1 egg white
1 tablespoon cornstarch
¼ cup reduced-sodium soy sauce
¼ cup dry sherry
2 tablespoons water
1 tablespoon red-wine vinegar
½ teaspoon sugar
1 tablespoon cornstarch
¼ cup vegetable oil
½ teaspoon minced garlic
1½ cups broccoli flowerets
1½ cups cauliflower flowerets
1 small onion, sliced and separated into rings
1 small green pepper, cut into thin strips
1 small sweet red pepper, cut into thin strips
½ cup walnut pieces
3 cups hot cooked rice (cooked without fat)

Cut chicken into strips. Combine egg white and 1 tablespoon cornstarch; beat until smooth. Add chicken, tossing to coat well. Cover chicken and refrigerate 30 minutes.

Combine soy sauce, sherry, water, vinegar, sugar, and 1 tablespoon cornstarch; stir until cornstarch dissolves. Set aside.

Pour oil into a preheated wok; heat to medium high (325°) for 2 minutes. Add garlic; stir-fry 1 minute. Add chicken to wok; stir-fry 2 to 3 minutes or until lightly browned. Add broccoli and cauliflower; stir-fry 2 minutes. Add onion and pepper; stir-fry 2 minutes. Add walnuts.

Pour cornstarch mixture over chicken mixture. Cook, stirring constantly, until slightly thickened. Serve over rice. Yield: 6 servings (about 320 calories per serving plus 90 calories per ½ cup cooked rice).   *Edna Hanks,*
Woodlawn, Virginia.

Tip: Read labels to learn the weight, quality, and size of food products. Don't be afraid to experiment with new brands. Store brands can be equally good in quality and nutritional value, yet lower in price. Lower grades of canned fruit and vegetables are as nutritious as higher grades. Whenever possible, buy most foods by weight or cost per serving rather than by volume or package size.

Our Chocolate Mousse Baked Alaska hides frozen chocolate cake and creamy chocolate filling beneath a layer of meringue.

Serve A Mousse-Filled Baked Alaska

In Austin, Texas, Debbie Brown whips up a dessert that fulfills any chocoholic's dreams. She calls it Chocolate Mousse Baked Alaska, a frozen chocolate cake filled with a rich chocolate mixture and frosted with meringue.

To assemble this dessert, Debbie lines a large bowl with thin pieces of chocolate cake and brushes them with a sweet Cognac syrup. Then she pours in a creamy filling flavored with two types of chocolate and coffee, topping it with the remaining cake layer. She stores this in the freezer until serving time.

After unmolding the cake, Debbie caps it with snowy meringue and bakes just until it browns. This dessert can also be frosted with two-thirds of the meringue and, using a pastry bag, the remaining one-third piped over it in decorative designs.

CHOCOLATE MOUSSE BAKED ALASKA

¼ cup all-purpose flour
¼ cup cocoa
3 eggs
½ cup superfine sugar
¼ cup butter or margarine, melted
½ teaspoon vanilla extract
¼ cup sugar
½ cup water
¼ cup Cognac or brandy
12 (1-ounce) squares semisweet chocolate
4 (1-ounce) squares unsweetened chocolate
6 eggs, separated
½ cup superfine sugar
3 tablespoons Cognac
1½ tablespoons brewed strong coffee
1 cup whipping cream
5 egg whites
¼ teaspoon cream of tartar
¾ cup superfine sugar
½ teaspoon vanilla extract
Pecan halves

Grease three 8-inch round cakepans; line bottoms with waxed paper. Grease and flour waxed paper; set aside.

Combine flour and cocoa; mix well and set aside.

Combine 3 eggs and ½ cup superfine sugar in a medium-size mixing bowl; beat about 5 minutes or until thick and lemon colored. Fold in cocoa mixture; then fold in butter and ½ teaspoon vanilla. Pour batter into pans; bake at 350° for 15 minutes or until a wooden pick inserted in center comes out clean. Remove pans from oven; immediately invert onto racks. Remove waxed paper, and cool.

Combine ¼ cup sugar and water in a small saucepan; cook over medium heat, stirring constantly, until mixture boils. Boil 3 minutes. Remove from heat; cool. Stir in ¼ cup Cognac; set mixture aside.

Place chocolate in top of a double boiler; bring water to a boil. Reduce heat to low; cook until chocolate melts. Remove from heat.

Combine 6 egg yolks and ½ cup superfine sugar in a large mixing bowl; beat until thick and lemon colored. Stir in 3 tablespoons Cognac and coffee. Fold in melted chocolate. Beat 6 egg whites (at room temperature) until stiff peaks form; fold into chocolate mixture. Beat whipping cream until stiff peaks form; fold into chocolate mixture. Chill 30 minutes.

Line a 2½-quart mixing bowl (about 9 inches in diameter) with plastic wrap, leaving an overhang around the edges. Cut 2 layers of the cake into pieces to line bowl completely.

Brush cake with about two-thirds of Cognac syrup; spoon in chocolate filling. Top with remaining cake layer; brush with remaining syrup. Pull edges of plastic wrap over top to cover; freeze 24 hours.

Remove from freezer; invert bowl of mousse onto an ovenproof wooden board or serving dish, leaving plastic wrap intact. Remove bowl; place mousse in freezer.

Beat 5 egg whites (at room temperature) and cream of tartar until foamy. Gradually add ¾ cup superfine sugar, 1 tablespoon at a time, beating until stiff peaks form. Add ½ teaspoon vanilla; beat until blended. Remove frozen mousse from freezer, and peel off plastic wrap. Quickly spread meringue over entire surface of mousse, making sure edges are sealed.

Bake at 450° for 5 minutes or until meringue peaks are browned. Garnish with pecan halves. Serve immediately. Yield: 14 to 16 servings.

Note: After meringue is sealed, the dessert can be frozen for up to 1 week and baked just before serving.

Okra: Fry The Pods Whole

Catherine O'Quin of Tylertown, Mississippi, says that her Okra Fingers are a hit with all her neighbors. Catherine likes to pick young, tender okra from her garden and fry the pods whole rather than slice them.

After she soaks the okra pods in buttermilk, she rolls them in flour and cornmeal and fries them until they're crisp. "The fried pods taste just like popcorn," she tells us. You can be sure that's why this is one way to serve okra that the whole family will enjoy.

OKRA FINGERS

20 small fresh okra pods
1 cup buttermilk
¾ cup all-purpose flour
¼ cup cornmeal
1 teaspoon baking powder
½ teaspoon salt
Dash of pepper
Vegetable oil

Wash okra; trim stems. Drain well, and place in a shallow container. Pour buttermilk over okra. Set aside.

Combine flour, cornmeal, baking powder, salt, and pepper, mixing well. Remove each okra pod from buttermilk and carefully roll in cornmeal mixture. Drop into deep hot oil (375°); fry 3 to 5 minutes, turning once. Drain on paper towels. Yield: 4 servings.

Potatoes Can Be A Dinner Favorite

You may think of potatoes as just an everyday vegetable, but add a few extra ingredients, and suddenly they're fancy fare. Rather than serving them only when in a pinch, you may decide they are your favorite side dish.

The whole family will love Garlic Potatoes. Cut into cubes, these potatoes are baked with chopped onion, celery, garlic, and fresh parsley.

Soufflé Potatoes are perfect for formal meals. This recipe starts with packaged potato flakes, but sour cream, cottage cheese, and eggs give it rich flavor and soufflé-like texture.

GARLIC POTATOES

4 large baking potatoes, peeled and cubed
2 stalks celery, finely chopped
1 small onion, finely chopped
2 to 3 cloves garlic, minced
½ cup butter or margarine, melted
3 tablespoons chopped fresh parsley
½ teaspoon salt
½ teaspoon pepper

Combine all ingredients; place in a greased 12- x 8- x 2-inch baking dish. Bake at 350° for 1 hour and 15 minutes or until potatoes are tender. Yield: 6 to 8 servings. *Charlotte Watkins, Lakeland, Florida.*

POTATOES WITH FETA CHEESE

5 medium baking potatoes
10 pimiento-stuffed olives, thinly sliced
1¼ cups crumbled feta cheese
⅓ cup half-and-half
2 tablespoons butter or margarine, melted
¼ teaspoon white pepper
⅛ teaspoon garlic salt
1 medium-size green pepper, cut into rings
2 tablespoons butter or margarine, melted

Cook potatoes in boiling salted water 25 to 30 minutes or until tender; drain well, and cool. Peel potatoes, and cut into 1-inch cubes.

Combine potatoes, olives, cheese, half-and-half, 2 tablespoons butter, pepper, and garlic salt; gently toss. Spoon into a lightly greased 10- x 6- x 2-inch baking dish.

Sauté green pepper in 2 tablespoons butter; arrange around edge of baking dish. Bake at 350° for 20 minutes. Yield: 6 servings. *Ella C. Stivers, Abilene, Texas.*

HOT DEVILED POTATOES

4 medium-size red potatoes, peeled and cubed
1 (8-ounce) carton commercial sour cream
2 tablespoons chopped green onions
2 to 3 teaspoons prepared mustard
¼ teaspoon salt
¼ teaspoon white pepper
Paprika

Cook potatoes in boiling salted water for about 20 minutes or until tender. Drain them well, and then mash.

Combine potatoes and remaining ingredients except paprika, mixing well. Spoon mixture into a lightly greased 1-quart casserole; sprinkle with paprika. Cover and bake at 350° for 15 minutes. Yield: 4 servings. *Michele Zenon, Alexandria, Virginia.*

FLUFFY POTATOES

2 cups mashed potatoes
½ cup milk
2 tablespoons butter or margarine, softened
1 teaspoon salt
Dash of pepper
2 eggs, separated
½ cup (2 ounces) shredded sharp Cheddar cheese

Combine potatoes, milk, butter, salt, and pepper; beat at medium speed of electric mixer until smooth. Beat egg yolks until thick; stir yolks and cheese into potato mixture. Beat egg whites (at room temperature) until stiff but not dry; gently fold into potato mixture. Spoon into a greased 1-quart casserole. Cover and bake at 350° for 20 to 25 minutes. Yield: 4 servings. *Margot Foster, Hubbard, Texas.*

SOUFFLÉ POTATOES

1 (2.7-ounce) package mashed potato flakes
1 (8-ounce) carton commercial sour cream
1 cup cream-style cottage cheese
3 tablespoons minced onion
1 teaspoon parsley flakes
¼ teaspoon garlic salt
¼ teaspoon pepper
3 eggs, separated

Prepare potatoes according to package directions, using 1 cup water. Combine potatoes and remaining ingredients except eggs; stir well.

Beat egg yolks until thick and lemon colored; stir into potato mixture.

Beat egg whites (at room temperature) until stiff but not dry. Gently fold into potato mixture. Spoon into a lightly greased 1½-quart casserole. Bake at 350° for 1 hour and 5 minutes or until puffed and lightly browned. Serve immediately. Yield: 6 servings. *Mrs. W. J. Nichol, Knoxville, Tennessee.*

Tips For Better Defrosting And Reheating

If you have a busy household, you'll profit from knowing about two important benefits of the microwave oven—defrosting and reheating. The defrost setting makes it a simple matter to reduce thawing time. And reheating in the microwave oven can save you time as well as dishes.

Careful attention must be given to food while it is defrosting in the microwave. Most of these ovens have a defrost setting. However, the actual power level assigned to the defrost setting may vary from oven to oven. We've found that the most common defrost setting is MEDIUM LOW (30% power). At reduced power settings, the microwave oven will cycle on and off; during the off periods, heat has time to equalize throughout the food. If the power level is too high, food will begin to cook as it defrosts, resulting in a tough, overcooked product.

Similarly, when you are reheating in the microwave oven, care must be taken to avoid additional cooking. It appears that the best results from reheating are obtained when MEDIUM (50% power)

Microwave frozen blocks of soup until partially thawed, breaking apart with a fork.

to LOW (10% power) settings are used. Although many kinds of food can be reheated in only a minute or two on HIGH power, others turn out better if they are gradually reheated on lower settings.

Techniques for Defrosting

—To defrost frozen fruit juice, empty the solid concentrate into a large glass measuring cup or heat-proof pitcher. Microwave in short periods for a total of several minutes or until nearly thawed, breaking apart the concentrate several times with a fork. Stir in cold water if using as a beverage.

—When defrosting meat, place it in the original plastic or paper-wrapped package on a microwave rack in a shallow baking dish. Microwave at MEDIUM LOW (30% power), removing the package and wrappings as soon as possible. Cover loosely with waxed paper after half the time, turning the meat over on the rack. With newer oven models, shield the edges of the meat with aluminum foil to help prevent overcooking. Foil shouldn't be used in older models. If thawing a roast, continue microwaving until a skewer can be inserted into the center.

—Test meat often as it defrosts. If warm to the touch, the meat has started to cook and should be prepared immediately. If you are defrosting for later use, we suggest partially defrosting in the microwave, and then placing the meat in the refrigerator.

—Always put poultry and fish on a microwave rack for defrosting so the

bottom of the food doesn't start to cook in the liquid that drains off. When it is partially thawed, plunge poultry or fish into cool water.

—Place frozen blocks of soup in a casserole or soup bowl. Cover and microwave until partially thawed, gradually breaking apart with a fork.

Techniques for Reheating

—Individual plates of food reheat best at lower power settings. Arrange thick or dense foods to the outside of the plate. Softer, more delicate foods should be placed toward the center. Cover with waxed paper or plastic wrap to hold in heat and moisture.

—Never reheat meat at HIGH power; this will cause it to toughen. Most refrigerated main dishes should be reheated at MEDIUM (50% power).

—Bread can be reheated in just seconds; it will become tough if heated too long. Always wrap bread in a paper towel to absorb moisture.

—Wedges of quiche or egg casserole can be reheated satisfactorily, but scrambled eggs cook so quickly in the microwave that it's best to start over, rather than to reheat.

—To reheat rice, just add several tablespoons of water, and microwave at MEDIUM HIGH (70% power) for a few minutes. Fluff the hot rice with a fork before serving.

As frozen fish fillets defrost on low (10% power), gently break them apart with a spatula or fork. As soon as they can be separated, plunge them into cold water to finish thawing.

When defrosting roast, shield edges with aluminum foil, and secure with wooden picks. This helps prevent edges from starting to cook while defrosting.

Fresh Ideas For Vegetables

After you've fried, steamed, baked, and sautéed vegetables, it's time for a change. Why not enjoy them in a crisp, cool vinaigrette salad?

Cauliflower-Olive Toss combines the vegetable's flowerets with ripe olives, pimiento, and parsley. Red wine vinegar, which has a snappy flavor similar to the wine, and olive oil, with its nutty taste, give this colorful dish just the right amount of zest.

Try Cucumber-Vinaigrette Oriental for the subtle flavor of fresh ginger spiked with the sharp, tart taste of white distilled vinegar. You'll find that this type of vinegar goes well with light-colored vegetables to help them keep their natural color.

Two types of vinegar combine with green beans and garbanzo beans in Sweet-and-Sour Bean Salad. Cider vinegar provides a smooth, mellow flavor while tarragon-wine vinegar adds a lively herb taste.

SWEET-AND-SOUR BEAN SALAD

2 pounds green beans
1 (15-ounce) can garbanzo beans, drained
1 medium-size purple onion, thinly sliced
1 (4-ounce) jar diced pimiento, drained
⅔ cup sugar
½ cup vegetable oil
½ cup cider vinegar
½ cup tarragon-wine vinegar
1 clove garlic, crushed
½ teaspoon salt
½ teaspoon lemon-pepper seasoning

Remove strings from green beans; wash. Cut green beans into 1½-inch pieces. Cook, covered, in a small amount of water 8 to 10 minutes; drain. Toss green beans with garbanzo beans, sliced onion, and pimiento.

Combine remaining ingredients in a jar. Cover tightly, and shake vigorously. Pour over vegetables, tossing gently. Chill 8 hours, stirring occasionally. Yield: 10 to 12 servings.
Maude Crenshaw,
Lehigh Acres, Florida.

Tip: Steaming fresh vegetables over boiling water preserves more vitamins than cooking in boiling water.

CAULIFLOWER-OLIVE TOSS

1 small head cauliflower, cut into flowerets
½ cup sliced ripe olives
1 (2-ounce) jar diced pimiento, drained
3 tablespoons chopped fresh parsley
⅓ cup olive oil
¼ cup red wine vinegar
1 teaspoon sugar
¼ teaspoon salt
⅛ teaspoon pepper

Arrange cauliflower on a steaming rack. Place over boiling water; cover and steam 5 to 6 minutes or until crisp-tender. Drain and cool.

Combine cauliflower, olives, pimiento, and parsley in a bowl.

Combine olive oil, vinegar, sugar, salt, and pepper in a jar. Cover tightly, and shake vigorously. Pour over vegetables, tossing gently. Chill 8 hours, stirring occasionally. Yield: 4 servings.
Betty J. Moore,
Belton, Texas.

CUCUMBER-VINAIGRETTE ORIENTAL

2 large cucumbers, peeled and thinly sliced
⅓ cup white distilled vinegar
1 tablespoon plus 1 teaspoon sugar
½ teaspoon salt
1½ teaspoons minced fresh ginger

Place cucumbers in a bowl. Combine remaining ingredients in a jar. Cover tightly, and shake. Pour over cucumbers; toss gently. Chill 8 hours; stir occasionally. Yield: 6 servings.
Carole May,
Valley, Alabama.

Energy Beverages To Perk You Up

A great way to cool down on a warm afternoon is to sip one of these thirst-quenching energy beverages. They're perfect for after-school snacks or anytime your appetite needs a lift.

The blender makes it simple to whip up Peanut Butter Milkshakes. Just combine all the ingredients, and blend until smooth and creamy. The nutty flavor will make it a favorite.

MALT SPECIAL

4 cups milk
½ cup chocolate-flavored instant malted milk
2 ripe bananas, mashed

Combine all ingredients in container of an electric blender; process until smooth. Yield: about 5 cups.
Sandra Bowlin,
Morristown, Tennessee.

PEANUT BUTTER MILKSHAKES

1 quart vanilla ice cream
1½ cups milk
1 tablespoon cocoa
1 tablespoon instant orange-flavored breakfast drink
2 tablespoons peanut butter

Combine all ingredients in container of an electric blender; process until smooth. Yield: 5½ cups. *Sue Yatzy,*
Ellsinore, Missouri.

TROPICAL REFRESHER

1 (8¼-ounce) can pineapple tidbits, chilled and drained
1 (8-ounce) carton plain yogurt
1 banana

Combine all ingredients in container of an electric blender; process mixture until smooth. Yield: 2½ cups.
Mrs. Fred H. Lofland,
Williston, Florida.

PEACH COOLER

1 pint vanilla ice cream
1 cup fresh or canned peach slices
1 (8-ounce) carton peach yogurt
⅓ cup orange juice concentrate, undiluted
⅓ cup water
Mint sprigs (optional)

Combine all ingredients except mint sprigs in container of an electric blender; process mixture until smooth. Garnish with mint sprigs, if desired. Yield: 3½ cups. *Vickie Dubois,*
Erath, Louisiana.

September

Cornbread Like Mama Used To Make

Johnnycake. Hoecake. Ashcake. Corn pone. Spoonbread. Corn sticks. No matter which name you use, it's still cornbread, made from one of our country's native ingredients—cornmeal.

Oven-fresh, steaming, or smothered with butter, cornbread has always been an important part of Southern cooking. In the 1901 edition of *The Picayune's Creole Cook Book,* it was noted "The further you go South of Mason and Dixon's line, the better the corn bread, corn cakes, corn muffins, that will be offered you."

But just ask a group of cooks how to make the best cornbread, and you're certain to set off controversy. Some like to start with yellow cornmeal, even though tradition has it that most Southern cooks use only white. The batter of one might include buttermilk or eggs, while another may have sugar and flour. Now if all this is confusing, don't despair. Basically, most cornbreads are just fancier versions of the original cornbread that was called johnnycake.

How did the first cornmeal, salt, and water johnnycake come about? No one seems to know for sure. One explanation is that it may have been an Indian food known as Shawnee cakes. Another theory suggests they were called journey cakes because travelers often took them along on trips. Whatever the origin, these cornmeal cakes gradually became known as johnnycakes.

Besides the variety in ingredients, another thing about cornbread that has changed over the years is the way it is cooked. Early Americans and Indians fried their bread on improvised surfaces, such as shovels or hoes. Thoreau described his method for cooking hoecakes during a stay at Walden Pond by saying, "I baked before my fire out of doors on a shingle or the end of a stick of timber sawed off in building my house."

Eventually, the metal or cast-iron skillet came into being. At first, it was heated over open fires—later, on the wood-burning stove. Today's cooks still swear by these heavy skillets. Seasoned with bacon drippings or shortening and heated in the oven, they cause a delicate crust to appear on the bottom and sides of the bread.

We recently asked our readers to send us their family's favorite recipe for cornbread. The hundreds of letters we received made it clear that cornbread has a special place in the hearts of Southern cooks.

June Hudgins of Roanoke, Virginia, tells us, "I found my recipe for Skillet Cornbread when I first married. I've changed it a bit, but it's still my favorite. Now my daughters use it too."

"My grandmother used to bake Crackling Cornbread, especially in the fall after hog-butchering time," claims Barbara Carson of Hollywood, Florida. "She never measured ingredients when she baked, so I had to experiment to come up with the amounts." According to Barbara, one reason her grandmother's cornbread tasted so good was that the bread was cooked on a wood-burning stove.

Sally Frederickson of Birmingham shares her recipe for Favorite Corn Sticks. "When I grew up, these corn sticks were an everyday item. Mother cooked with this same recipe until she was 94."

"We never had homemade soup without having my Grandmother McDowell's Cornmeal Waffles. They're light and delicious, and my family still enjoys them," says Eleanor H. McIntyre of Starkville, Mississippi. The buttermilk-rich waffles are equally good served with butter and honey or syrup for breakfast.

Regardless of which type cornbread you grew up on, we think you'll enjoy trying some other favorites. You may even want to start a new cornbread tradition in your family. If the recipe calls for cornmeal, you can use either yellow or white. Just be sure to remember that cornmeal mix has the leavening added and should not be substituted for plain cornmeal.

JALAPEÑO CORNBREAD

3 cups cornbread mix
2 tablespoons sugar
3 eggs, beaten
2 cups milk
½ cup vegetable oil
6 slices bacon, cooked and crumbled
1½ cups (6 ounces) shredded sharp
   Cheddar cheese
1 large onion, diced
1 (8¾-ounce) can cream-style corn
1 (4-ounce) jar diced pimiento, drained
2 tablespoons minced jalapeño peppers

Combine cornbread mix and sugar in a large bowl. Add eggs, milk, and oil, mixing well. Stir in remaining ingredients. Pour batter into a greased 13- x 9- x 2-inch baking pan. Bake at 400° for 40 to 45 minutes or until done. Yield: 12 servings.

CRACKLING CORNBREAD

2 cups cornmeal
1 teaspoon baking soda
½ teaspoon salt
2 eggs, beaten
2 cups buttermilk
¼ cup bacon drippings
1 cup cracklings

Combine cornmeal, soda, and salt, mixing well. Add eggs, buttermilk, and bacon drippings; stir until smooth. Stir in cracklings.

Place a well-greased 9-inch square baking pan in a 450° oven for 3 to 5 minutes or until hot. Remove pan from oven; pour batter into pan. Bake at 450° for 25 minutes or until golden brown on top. Yield: 9 servings.

Barbara Carson,
Hollywood, Florida.

SKILLET CORNBREAD

1 cup self-rising cornmeal
1 cup self-rising flour
1½ cups buttermilk
¼ cup vegetable oil
2 eggs, beaten
2 tablespoons brown sugar

Combine cornmeal and flour, mixing well. Combine remaining ingredients, mixing well; add to dry mixture, stirring until smooth.

Pour the batter into a well-greased 10-inch cast-iron skillet. Bake at 450° for 20 to 25 minutes. Remove from heat, and invert on a plate. Yield: 8 to 10 servings.

June Hudgins,
Roanoke, Virginia.

CORNBREAD LOAF

1½ cups cornmeal
1 cup all-purpose flour
½ cup sugar
1 tablespoon baking powder
1 teaspoon salt
1½ cups half-and-half
⅓ cup shortening, melted
¼ cup butter or margarine, melted
2 eggs, beaten

Combine cornmeal, flour, sugar, baking powder, and salt in a large bowl, mixing well. Combine remaining ingredients, mixing well; add to dry mixture, stirring until smooth.

Pour into a greased 9- x 5- x 3-inch loafpan. Bake at 350° for 55 minutes or

Whether you use your grandmother's recipe or try a new one, nothing can match the oven-fresh aroma and traditional goodness of cornbread: (front to back) Cornmeal Waffles, Cornbread Loaf, Skillet Cornbread, and Southern Cornbread Muffins.

until a wooden pick inserted in center comes out clean. Cool loaf in pan 10 minutes; remove from pan. Serve warm or cool completely on wire rack. Yield: 1 loaf.

Edna H. Clyburn,
Kershaw, South Carolina.

CORNMEAL WAFFLES

1½ cups cornmeal
¾ cup all-purpose flour
2 tablespoons sugar
1 tablespoon baking powder
½ teaspoon salt
½ teaspoon baking soda
1¾ cups buttermilk
2 eggs, separated
3 tablespoons vegetable oil

Combine cornmeal, flour, sugar, baking powder, salt, and soda in a medium bowl, mixing well. Combine buttermilk, egg yolks, and oil, mixing well; add to dry ingredients, stirring until smooth.

Beat egg whites (at room temperature) until stiff peaks form; gently fold into batter.

Spread about 1 cup batter onto greased, hot waffle iron. Bake 3 to 4 minutes or until steaming stops. Repeat procedure until all the batter is used. Yield: 16 (4-inch) waffles.

Eleanor H. McIntyre,
Starkville, Mississippi.

Tip: Beware—a wet potholder used on a hot utensil may cause a steam burn.

SOUTHERN CORNBREAD MUFFINS

2 cups cornmeal
⅓ cup all-purpose flour
2 tablespoons sugar
1 teaspoon salt
1 teaspoon baking soda
1¾ cups buttermilk
1 egg, beaten
2 tablespoons butter or margarine, melted

Combine cornmeal, flour, sugar, salt, and soda in a large bowl, mixing well. Combine buttermilk, egg, and butter, mixing well. Add to dry ingredients, stirring just until moistened. Spoon into greased muffin pans. Bake at 425° for 15 minutes or until edges begin to brown. Yield: 1 dozen.

Lorraine Mitchell,
Gainesville, Texas.

OZARK SPOONBREAD

½ cup cornmeal
½ teaspoon salt
2 cups milk
1 tablespoon butter or margarine
1 teaspoon baking powder
3 eggs, separated
1 tablespoon butter or margarine

Combine cornmeal, salt, milk, and butter in a heavy saucepan; cook over medium heat, stirring constantly, until smooth and thickened. Remove from heat; stir in baking powder.

Beat egg yolks until thick and lemon colored; stir into cornmeal mixture. Beat egg whites (at room temperature) until stiff peaks form; fold into cornmeal mixture.

Place 1 tablespoon butter in a 1½-quart casserole; heat dish at 350° for 3 to 5 minutes or until hot. Remove from oven; pour batter into dish. Bake at 350° for 30 minutes or until golden. Yield: 4 to 6 servings.

Mrs. Woodrow Edwards,
Cedar Bluff, Alabama.

FAVORITE CORN STICKS

1¼ cups cornmeal
¾ cup all-purpose flour
1 tablespoon plus 1 teaspoon baking
  powder
1 tablespoon sugar
¾ teaspoon salt
2 eggs, slightly beaten
1 cup milk
¼ cup vegetable oil

Combine cornmeal, flour, baking powder, sugar, and salt, mixing well. Combine the remaining ingredients, mixing well; add to dry ingredients, stirring until smooth.

Place a well-greased cast-iron corn stick pan in a 425° oven for 3 minutes or until hot. Remove pan from oven; spoon batter into pan, filling two-thirds full. Bake at 425° for 12 minutes or until lightly browned. Yield: about 2 dozen corn sticks.

Sally Frederickson,
Birmingham, Alabama.

Oatmeal–Not Just For Breakfast

Good cooks have been adding oatmeal to their recipes for years. It's rich in vitamins, minerals, and fiber—and it adds as much taste and texture as it does good nutrition. And because it keeps well if stored in a cool, dry place, it's also a staple in most pantries. Here are some new ways you can use it.

CRUNCHY OATMEAL COOKIES

2 cups all-purpose flour
2 teaspoons baking soda
1 teaspoon baking powder
½ teaspoon salt
1 cup shortening
1 cup sugar
1 cup firmly packed brown sugar
2 eggs
1 teaspoon vanilla extract
2 cups quick-cooking oats, uncooked
2 cups corn flakes

Combine flour, soda, baking powder, and salt, and set aside.

Cream shortening and sugar; beat in eggs and vanilla. Add flour mixture, mixing well. Stir in oats and corn flakes.

Drop by heaping tablespoonfuls onto lightly greased cookie sheets. Bake at 325° for 12 to 14 minutes. (Cookies will sink and flatten when they are removed from the oven.) Cool slightly on cookie sheets; remove to wire racks to cool completely. Yield: 4 dozen.

Alice G. Liles,
Muleshoe, Texas.

COCONUT GRANOLA BARS

2¼ cups quick-cooking oats, uncooked
1 cup flaked coconut
¼ cup wheat germ
¼ cup butter or margarine
¼ cup firmly packed brown sugar
¼ cup honey
¼ cup peanut butter
1½ teaspoons vanilla extract
½ cup chopped unsalted peanuts
½ cup raisins

Combine oats, coconut, and wheat germ in a greased 9-inch square baking pan. Bake at 325° for 25 minutes, stirring occasionally. Set aside.

Combine butter, sugar, and honey in a medium saucepan; cook over medium heat, stirring occasionally, until butter

melts and sugar dissolves. Remove from heat, and add peanut butter and vanilla, stirring until peanut butter melts. Pour over oats mixture. Add peanuts and raisins, and stir well. (Mixture will seem dry at first; continue mixing until moist.)

Press mixture firmly into pan with greased fingertips. Bake at 350° for 12 minutes. Yield: 2 dozen bars.

Sandra Russell,
Gainesville, Florida.

ORANGE-OATMEAL MUFFINS

2 tablespoons brown sugar
2 teaspoons all-purpose flour
1 teaspoon butter or margarine, melted
¼ teaspoon ground cinnamon
1 cup all-purpose flour
1 cup quick-cooking oats, uncooked
½ cup chopped pecans
¼ cup sugar
2 teaspoons grated orange rind
2 teaspoons baking powder
½ teaspoon salt
½ cup orange juice
¼ cup milk
3 tablespoons vegetable oil
1 egg, beaten

Combine brown sugar, 2 teaspoons flour, butter, and cinnamon, mixing until crumbly; set aside.

Combine 1 cup flour, oats, pecans, sugar, orange rind, baking powder, and salt in a medium mixing bowl, stirring well. Make a well in center of mixture. Combine orange juice, milk, oil, and egg. Add to dry ingredients; stir just until moistened.

Spoon mixture into greased muffin pans, filling three-fourths full. Sprinkle with cinnamon mixture, and bake at 425° for 15 minutes. Yield: 1 dozen.

T. O. Davis,
Waynesboro, Mississippi.

Right: *New Mexican Flat Enchiladas (front) and Chimachangas (back) are two spicy Southwestern specialties that make good use of a ristra, a string of dried red chiles. Both dishes call for these chiles, but they are used in different ways (pages 244 and 245).*

Page 204: *Enjoy the bounty of winter squash and sweet potatoes: (from front to back) Savory Butternut Sauté, Sweet Potato-Apricot Bake, Butternut Squash Puff, and Sweet Potatoes in Apple Shells. (Recipes begin on page 205.)*

Try Two Really Versatile Vegetables

Winter squash and sweet potatoes were here long before Columbus stepped foot on American soil, yet in comparison to their more familiar relatives—summer squash and white potatoes—they seem almost like exotic newcomers.

Fall is the peak season for both types of vegetables; however, keep in mind that sweet potatoes and some varieties of winter squash are available almost year-round. Winter squash are distinguished from summer squash by the fact that they ripen later, have fully developed seeds, and are covered with hard skins or shells.

Once the squash are cooked, the hard shells offer some interesting serving possibilities; they're ideal for holding a number of different fillings. For example, Apple-Stuffed Squash has a maple-flavored stuffing made of chopped apples and cashews.

Butternut Squash Puff uses squash in a different way. It starts with cooked squash, mashed and mixed with other ingredients to make a delicately flavored casserole with a soufflé-like texture. Savory Butternut Sauté features rings of butternut squash sautéed with brown sugar and basil.

Baked and candied sweet potatoes are long-time favorites in the South, but the possibilities for this unusual vegetable don't end there. Try Sweet Potato-Apricot Bake as an alternative; pecan halves on top add a special touch. Sweet potatoes and apples make a nice combination in Sweet Potatoes in Apple Shells. The filling is a creamy mixture of sweet potatoes, apples, and whipping cream; the shells are garnished with apple wedges.

SUNSHINE SQUASH

1 (2-pound) butternut squash
¾ cup orange juice
1½ teaspoons cornstarch
1½ teaspoons grated fresh gingerroot
1 tablespoon butter or margarine
¼ teaspoon salt
⅛ teaspoon pepper

Cut squash in half lengthwise, and remove seeds. Place squash cut side down in a large Dutch oven; pour in boiling water 1 inch deep. Cover and cook 15 minutes or until tender. Drain squash, and allow to cool slightly.

Combine orange juice, cornstarch, and gingerroot in a medium saucepan over medium heat. Bring to a boil, and boil 1 minute. Add butter to mixture, and stir well.

Peel and cube squash. Add squash, salt, and pepper to orange juice mixture, tossing lightly. Yield: 4 servings.

Marion M. Jones,
Whispering Pines, North Carolina.

SAVORY BUTTERNUT SAUTÉ

1 (2-pound) butternut squash, peeled and cut into ¼-inch-thick slices
12 to 14 fresh basil leaves, chopped
2 tablespoons brown sugar
⅛ to ¼ teaspoon salt
2 to 3 tablespoons butter or margarine
Additional fresh basil leaves (optional)
Cinnamon stick (optional)

Place squash in a single layer on a large platter or baking sheet. Sprinkle with chopped basil, sugar, and salt; let stand for 30 minutes.

Melt butter in a skillet; add squash, turning pieces to coat with butter. Cover and cook over low heat 15 to 20 minutes or until tender.

Before serving, garnish with additional fresh basil leaves and cinnamon stick, if desired. Yield: 4 servings.

Jean Pridgen,
Fayetteville, North Carolina.

BUTTERNUT SQUASH PUFF

3 cups mashed cooked butternut squash
2 eggs, beaten
¼ cup half-and-half
2 tablespoons butter or margarine, melted
1 tablespoon grated orange rind
½ teaspoon grated lemon rind
2 tablespoons all-purpose flour
1 tablespoon sugar
¼ teaspoon salt
⅛ teaspoon pepper
Pecan halves (optional)

Combine all ingredients except pecans; mix well. Spoon into a greased 1½-quart casserole; place casserole in a 13- x 9- x 2-inch baking pan. Pour hot water into pan ½ inch deep; bake at 350° for 50 minutes or until set. Garnish with pecan halves, if desired. Yield: 6 servings. *Mrs. James S. Stanton,*
Richmond, Virginia.

BAKED BUTTERNUT SQUASH

1 medium butternut squash
2 tablespoons brown sugar
1 teaspoon lemon juice
¼ teaspoon salt
Paprika to taste
1½ tablespoons butter or margarine

Cut squash in half lengthwise, and remove seeds. Place cut side up in a shallow baking dish; pour in water ½ inch deep. Sprinkle squash halves with sugar, lemon juice, salt, and paprika; dot with butter. Cover and bake at 375° for 30 minutes. Uncover and bake an additional 30 minutes. Yield: 4 servings.

Myrtle C. Clark,
Plant City, Florida.

ACORN SQUASH WITH MOLASSES AND PECANS

3 medium acorn squash
¾ cup chopped pecans
¼ cup molasses
3 tablespoons butter or margarine, melted
1 tablespoon grated orange rind
½ teaspoon salt

Cut squash in half lengthwise, and remove seeds. Place cut side down in a shallow baking dish, and pour in boiling water 1 inch deep. Bake, uncovered, at 375° for 35 minutes.

Turn squash cut side up. Combine remaining ingredients; mix well, and spoon into squash cavities. Bake squash, uncovered, at 375° for 25 to 30 minutes. Yield: 6 servings.

Rose Naquin,
Melville, Louisiana.

MAPLE-FLAVORED STUFFED SQUASH

3 small acorn squash
¼ cup plus 1 tablespoon maple-flavored syrup
3 tablespoons butter or margarine, melted
½ teaspoon ground nutmeg
⅓ cup miniature marshmallows

Cut squash in half lengthwise, and remove seeds. Place cut side down in a shallow baking dish, and pour in boiling water ½ inch deep. Bake at 375° for 35 minutes.

Cool squash; carefully scoop out pulp, leaving shells intact. Mash pulp; add syrup, butter, and nutmeg, stirring well. Spoon mixture into shells; top with marshmallows. Bake at 350° for 20 minutes. Yield: 6 servings.

Ruth J. Hoskings,
Maysville, Kentucky.

APPLE-STUFFED SQUASH

3 small acorn squash
2 apples, peeled, cored, and diced
½ cup coarsely chopped cashews
¼ cup butter or margarine, melted
¼ cup maple-flavored syrup

Cut squash in half lengthwise, and remove seeds. Place squash, cut side down, in a steamer rack over boiling water in a large Dutch oven. Steam squash about 20 minutes; transfer to two 9-inch square baking dishes, turning squash upright. Set aside.

Combine remaining ingredients; mix well, and spoon into squash cavities. Pour hot water ½ inch deep into dishes. Cover and bake at 400° for 25 minutes. Yield: 6 servings.   *Lynn R. Koenig,*
Charleston, South Carolina.

STUFFED BAKED SQUASH

3 medium acorn squash
¼ teaspoon pepper
½ teaspoon curry powder
⅛ teaspoon ground nutmeg
1 cup chopped onion
1 cup chopped green pepper
1 cup chopped celery
1 cup sliced fresh mushrooms
3 tablespoons butter or margarine, melted
3 cups chopped cooked ham
1 cup sliced ripe olives
2 tablespoons chopped walnuts

Cut squash in half lengthwise, and remove seeds. Place cut side down in a shallow baking dish, and pour in boiling water ½ inch deep. Cover and bake at 400° for 45 minutes or until squash is tender; drain. Cool squash slightly; remove pulp, leaving a firm shell. Mash pulp with pepper, curry powder, and nutmeg; set aside.

Sauté onion, green pepper, celery, and mushrooms in butter until vegetables are crisp-tender. Stir in ham, sliced ripe olives, and seasoned squash pulp; cook until thoroughly heated. Spoon mixture into squash shells; sprinkle with chopped walnuts. Cover and bake at 350° for 20 minutes. Yield: 6 servings.
Pamela W. Copenhauer,
Springfield, Illinois.

GLAZED SWEET POTATOES

2 pounds sweet potatoes
¼ cup butter or margarine
½ cup firmly packed brown sugar

Peel potatoes, and cut into 1-inch cubes. Cover with water, and bring to a boil. Cover, reduce heat, and simmer 10 to 12 minutes or until tender. Drain potatoes well.

Melt butter in skillet; add sugar and cook, stirring until sugar melts. Add potatoes; cook 10 minutes; stir occasionally. Yield: 8 servings.
Mrs. Bernie Benigno,
Gulfport, Mississippi.

SWEET POTATO-APRICOT BAKE

3 small sweet potatoes (about 1½ pounds),
   peeled and halved lengthwise
¾ cup firmly packed brown sugar
1½ tablespoons cornstarch
¼ teaspoon salt
⅛ teaspoon ground cinnamon
1 teaspoon grated orange rind
1 (16-ounce) can apricot halves
2 tablespoons butter or margarine
½ cup pecan halves

Place sweet potato halves in a lightly greased 10- x 6- x 2-inch baking dish; set aside.

Combine sugar, cornstarch, salt, cinnamon, and orange rind in a heavy saucepan; mix well. Drain apricots, reserving liquid, and set aside.

Add enough water to apricot liquid to make 1 cup. Gradually stir into dry mixture; cook over medium heat, stirring constantly, until smooth and thickened. Remove from heat. Add butter; stir until butter melts. Add apricots and pecans; stir gently. Pour over sweet potatoes; cover and bake at 375° for 50 to 55 minutes or until potatoes are tender. Yield: 6 servings.   *Marjorie Henson,*
Benton, Kentucky.

SWEET POTATOES
IN APPLE SHELLS

3 large red baking apples
¼ cup plus 2 tablespoons firmly packed
   brown sugar, divided
3 cups mashed cooked sweet potatoes
¼ cup butter or margarine, melted and
   divided
3 tablespoons whipping cream
6 small apple wedges with peel (optional)

Cut apples in half crosswise; remove core. Place apples in a shallow baking dish; sprinkle each with 1½ teaspoons brown sugar. Pour 1 cup water into bottom of baking dish. Bake apples at 400° for 25 minutes or until just tender.

Scoop out apple pulp, leaving a ½-inch border of shells intact. Chop pulp.

Combine apple pulp with sweet potatoes, 2 tablespoons butter, and whipping cream; beat mixture with electric mixer until well blended.

Spoon potato mixture into apple shells; sprinkle with remaining sugar, and drizzle with remaining butter. Place the stuffed shells in a shallow baking dish, and bake at 400° for 10 to 15 minutes or until thoroughly heated. Garnish with apple wedges, if desired. Yield: 6 servings.   *Doris S. Bissett,*
Baltimore, Maryland.

Get Ready For A Football Brunch

Get your gang ready for that big football game by inviting them to a pre-game brunch. Our choice of appetizer, entrée, and dessert is hearty enough to supply guests with lots of energy to cheer their team to victory.

For starters, serve your guests Golden Punch and Bourbon Frankfurter Appetizers; both are economical and easy to prepare. Everyone can then enjoy eating Fruit Salad With Pineapple Dressing, Simple Crab Quiche, and Marinated Broccoli.

The bread can be left up to you, but we suggest Whole Wheat Raisin Muffins. And before the fans dash off to the stadium, tell them to grab a dish of ice cream topped with Classic Chocolate Sauce. It's sure to be a popular way to end your gathering and send everyone off with thoughts of victory.

Golden Punch
Bourbon Frankfurter Appetizers
Fruit Salad
With Pineapple Dressing
Simple Crab Quiche
Marinated Broccoli
Whole Wheat Raisin Muffins
Ice Cream
With Classic Chocolate Sauce

GOLDEN PUNCH

1 (6-ounce) can frozen orange juice
concentrate, thawed
1 (6-ounce) can frozen lemonade
concentrate, thawed
1 (12-ounce) can apricot nectar
1 (46-ounce) can pineapple juice
1 (12-ounce) can lemon-lime carbonated
beverage, chilled

Prepare orange juice and lemonade
according to directions on can. Add
apricot nectar and pineapple juice; chill
well. To serve, stir in carbonated beverage and pour over ice. Yield: 1 gallon.
Mrs. Charles Hellem,
Columbia, Missouri.

BOURBON FRANKFURTER
APPETIZERS

1½ cups catsup
¾ cup bourbon
½ cup firmly packed brown sugar
1 teaspoon minced onion
½ teaspoon dried whole oregano
½ teaspoon dried whole rosemary
2 (1-pound) packages frankfurters, cut
into 1-inch pieces

Combine all ingredients except frankfurters in a Dutch oven; mix well. Stir
in frankfurters. Bring to a boil; reduce
heat, and simmer 20 minutes. Serve
with wooden picks. Yield: about 16 appetizer servings. *Carol Allen,*
Dallas, Texas.

FRUIT SALAD
WITH PINEAPPLE DRESSING

1 (15¼-ounce) can unsweetened pineapple
chunks, undrained
½ cup sugar
1 tablespoon plus 1½ teaspoons cornstarch
¼ cup lemon juice
1 (11-ounce) can mandarin oranges,
drained
1¼ cups seedless white grapes
2 large bananas, sliced
1 avocado, peeled and cut into wedges

Drain pineapple, reserving juice; set
pineapple aside.

Combine reserved pineapple juice,
sugar, cornstarch, and lemon juice in a
heavy saucepan. Cook mixture over low
heat, stirring constantly, until thickened. Let cool.

Combine pineapple and remaining ingredients except avocado. Pour dressing
over fruit, tossing gently. Garnish with
avocado wedges before serving. Yield: 6
servings. *Mary Andrew,*
Winston-Salem, North Carolina.

SIMPLE CRAB QUICHE

Pastry for a 9-inch deep-dish pie
1 (6-ounce) can lump crabmeat, drained
1 cup (4 ounces) shredded Swiss or
mozzarella cheese
⅓ cup minced green onions
1 tablespoon minced fresh parsley
4 eggs, beaten
2 cups half-and-half
½ teaspoon salt
⅛ teaspoon red pepper
Parsley sprigs (optional)

Line a 9-inch quiche dish or deep-dish
pieplate with pastry. Trim excess
around edges. Prick bottom and sides of
pastry with a fork; bake at 425° for 5
minutes. Cool.

Sprinkle crabmeat, cheese, green
onions, and 1 tablespoon parsley evenly
into pastry shell. Combine eggs, half-
and-half, salt, and red pepper, stirring
well; pour over crabmeat mixture. Bake
at 325° for 35 to 40 minutes or until set.
Let stand 10 minutes before serving.
Garnish with parsley sprigs, if desired.
Yield: one 9-inch quiche.
Carolyn Brantley,
Greenville, Mississippi.

MARINATED BROCCOLI

1 (1-pound) bunch broccoli
⅓ cup vegetable oil
2 tablespoons tarragon vinegar
1 teaspoon dried whole oregano
1 teaspoon onion salt
1 teaspoon garlic salt
1 teaspoon dry mustard
½ teaspoon dried whole thyme
½ teaspoon pepper
2 hard-cooked eggs, coarsely chopped

Trim off large leaves of broccoli. Remove tough ends of lower stalks and
wash broccoli; cut into spears. Cook
broccoli, covered, in a small amount of
boiling water 15 minutes. Drain well;
place in a shallow dish.

Combine remaining ingredients except eggs in a jar. Cover tightly, and
shake vigorously. Pour dressing over
broccoli. Cover and refrigerate 8 hours
or overnight. Sprinkle broccoli with
chopped eggs before serving. Yield: 6
servings. *Ripple Rausch,*
Meridian, Mississippi.

WHOLE WHEAT RAISIN MUFFINS

1 cup whole wheat flour
1 cup all-purpose flour
2½ teaspoons baking powder
½ teaspoon salt
1 egg, beaten
¾ cup milk
⅓ cup vegetable oil
⅓ cup honey
¾ cup raisins

Combine flour, baking powder, and
salt in a mixing bowl. Make a well in
center. Combine egg, milk, oil, and
honey; add to dry ingredients, stirring
just until moistened. Stir in raisins.
Spoon into greased muffin pans. Bake
at 400° for 15 minutes. Yield: 14
muffins. *Susan C. Hall,*
Russellville, Arkansas.

CLASSIC CHOCOLATE SAUCE

2 (1-ounce) squares unsweetened chocolate
¼ cup butter or margarine
1¼ cups sugar
½ teaspoon salt
¾ cup evaporated milk
½ teaspoon vanilla extract

Melt chocolate and butter in top of a
double boiler; stir in remaining ingredients, except vanilla. Cook over medium heat, stirring until sugar dissolves
and sauce is smooth. Stir in vanilla.
Serve sauce warm over ice cream.
Yield: 2 cups. *Susan Bellows,*
Birmingham, Alabama.

*Tip: Chocolate must be treated deli-
cately. It should always be stored at a
temperature under 75°. If a gray color
develops, this is a sign that the cocoa
butter has risen to the surface. Flavor
and quality will not be lessened, and
the gray color will disappear when the
chocolate is melted.*

You'll Cheer For These Snacks

Cheering for your favorite team takes a lot of energy, so we are providing some tasty snack ideas to keep you going through the fourth quarter. Crunchy Corn Brittle and Nutty Popcorn are great take-along snacks. If tailgating is your style, enjoy these snacks before the game, or pack a bag of goodies for munching on in the stands.

In your home, when you've invited the whole gang for a televised game, serve our Shrimp-Cheese Ball. Or prepare colorful Cheese-Bean Dip as an appetizer. An avocado mixture, tomatoes, cheese, olives, and green onions arranged over bean dip make it look as good as it tastes.

SHRIMP-CHEESE BALL

3 cups water
1 pound medium-size fresh shrimp
1 (8-ounce) package cream cheese, softened
1 tablespoon prepared horseradish
1 tablespoon lemon juice
2 teaspoons grated onion
1 teaspoon liquid smoke
¼ cup chopped pecans
2 tablespoons chopped fresh parsley

Bring water to a boil; add shrimp, and cook 3 to 5 minutes. Drain and rinse with cold water. Chill.

Peel shrimp, and chop. Combine with cream cheese, horseradish, lemon juice, onion, and liquid smoke; mix well. Shape into a ball, and chill.

Combine chopped pecans and parsley; roll cheese ball in pecan mixture. Chill several hours or overnight. Yield: 1 cheese ball. *Barbara Woodward, Ocean Springs, Mississippi.*

CHEESE-BEAN DIP

2 medium avocados
1 tablespoon lemon juice
½ cup chopped tomatoes
2 tablespoons minced onion
⅛ teaspoon salt
Dash of pepper
1 (10½-ounce) can bean dip
½ cup (2 ounces) shredded Cheddar cheese
½ cup (2 ounces) shredded Monterey Jack cheese
3 tablespoons chopped ripe olives
Chopped tomatoes (optional)
Chopped green onions with tops (optional)

Mash avocados; stir in lemon juice, ½ cup chopped tomatoes, minced onion, salt, and pepper. Set aside.

Spread bean dip in a shallow 9-inch round dish. Spread avocado mixture over bean dip. Alternate cheese over top in sections resembling pie wedges (wheel-spoke fashion). Sprinkle top with ripe olives. Sprinkle edges with chopped tomatoes and green onions, if desired. Serve with king-size corn chips. Yield: 4 cups. *Patsy Layer, Galveston, Texas.*

NUTTY POPCORN

12 cups popped corn, unsalted
1 cup whole almonds, toasted
1 cup pecan halves, toasted
½ cup butter or margarine
½ cup firmly packed brown sugar
½ teaspoon salt

Combine popped corn, almonds, and pecans in a large bowl; set aside.

Melt butter in a small saucepan; add sugar and salt. Cook about 30 seconds, stirring constantly. Pour sugar mixture over popcorn mixture, stirring until evenly coated. Spread mixture in a 15- x 10- x 1-inch jellyroll pan. Bake at 350° for 10 minutes, stirring only once. Store in a covered container. Yield: 14 cups. *Brenda Heupel, Florence, Alabama.*

CRUNCHY CORN BRITTLE

1 cup firmly packed brown sugar
¼ cup light corn syrup
½ cup water
1 teaspoon salt
¾ cup salted peanuts
2 tablespoons butter or margarine
¼ teaspoon baking soda
5 cups crispy corn cereal squares

Combine sugar, syrup, water, and salt in a heavy Dutch oven. Cook over medium heat, stirring occasionally, until mixture reaches hard ball stage (250°). Add peanuts. Reduce heat to low, and cook, stirring constantly, until mixture reaches 285°. Remove from heat; stir in butter and soda. Quickly stir in cereal.

Working rapidly, spread mixture evenly onto a buttered 15- x 10- x 1-inch jellyroll pan. Let cool; break into pieces. Yield: about 1 pound. *Debra Leckie, Shreveport, Louisiana.*

Make Molds From Your Own Cheese

Don't shy away from making cheese at home because you think it might be too difficult. And after you've made the cheese, it's just one more easy step to shape it into molds.

Start with our recipe for Cream-Style Cheese, which has only four basic ingredients. Then flavor and shape it as you desire. The most difficult part of the recipe is waiting two or three days for it to drain before you can sample it.

Homemade cream cheese has a mild flavor and buttery texture that closely resembles the commercial product. But the consistency may vary from batch to batch, depending on variations in room temperature and how long it drains.

Using Cream-Style Cheese as your base, take your pick of Garlic-Chive Cheese Mold or Blue Cheese Mold, both of which can be shaped in any smooth-sided mold you have on hand. Even a mixing bowl will work.

For a unique look, shape Pot-of-Herb Cheese in a clean clay pot. Carefully remove it from the pot just before serving, and place it on a small clay saucer; add a large one underneath for crackers. Sprinkle coarsely ground pepper on top, and insert a sprig of fresh dill so it looks as if it's growing out the top.

Appropriately named, Pot-of-Herb Cheese blends fresh dill, basil, and garlic with homemade Cream-Style Cheese. It's molded in a clay pot and served in the saucer.

Serve Heavenly Dessert Cheese Molds as a surprise ending to a meal. Spread the cheese on apple wedges or not-so-sweet cookies; then top it with the orange sauce.

You can even serve cheese for dessert. Heavenly Dessert Cheese Molds has a slightly sweetened cheese base, and includes whipped cream. The mixture is spooned into individual molds (we used brioche pans) and refrigerated until firm. Molds are then inverted onto dessert plates, and fresh orange sauce is spooned around them. Serve cheese molds with apple wedges or not-so-sweet cookies for an unusual dessert.

Whether you're making the cheese molds for an appetizer or dessert, you'll appreciate their make-ahead quality. The cheese will stay fresh in the refrigerator about five days, and you can even freeze it as long as a month with just minimal texture changes.

If you'd like to make the cheese molds but don't have the time for homemade cheese to drain, you can substitute commercial cream cheese. Directions are given with each recipe. Cheese molds made with commercial cheese may be a little firmer than those with homemade cheese.

CREAM-STYLE CHEESE

3 cups half-and-half
¾ cup whipping cream
1½ tablespoons cultured buttermilk
¼ teaspoon plus ⅛ teaspoon salt

Combine half-and-half and whipping cream in a heavy saucepan. Cook over low heat until mixture reaches 90°. Stir in buttermilk. Pour mixture into a large glass or ceramic bowl; cover with plastic wrap. Wrap a large towel around entire bowl, and place bowl in an oven with light on or in a warm place, about 85°, for 28 hours or until mixture is consistency of soft yogurt.

Cut several thicknesses of cheesecloth large enough to line a large colander and extend 4 inches over edges. Rinse cheesecloth, and squeeze out excess moisture; line colander with cheesecloth. Place colander in sink. Pour cream mixture into colander, and let drain 20 minutes.

Place colander in a container to drain completely. Cover colander and container tightly with enough plastic wrap to make an airtight seal. Refrigerate 12 hours or until well drained. Spoon cheese mixture into a bowl, and stir in salt. If the cheese is to be flavored and molded according to the following recipes, then do so at this point.

If cheese is to be molded unflavored, cut 4 (8-inch-square) pieces of cheesecloth; rinse cheesecloth, and squeeze out excess moisture. Smooth out wrinkles of cheesecloth, and stack layers on top of each other. Spoon cheese mixture in center of cheesecloth. Wrap cheesecloth around cheese mixture, and tie ends securely. Pat cheesecloth-wrapped cheese into an oval or round shape. (Cheese can also be shaped in desired mold. Line mold with cheesecloth, and spoon in cheese mixture, pressing with the back of a spoon to smoothly and firmly pack mixture.)

To make homemade cheese, let the milk mixture stand at 85° until it's the consistency of soft yogurt.

Place cheesecloth-wrapped cheese (or invert mold) over a wire rack in a shallow pan. Cover pan with enough plastic wrap to make an airtight seal. Refrigerate 1 to 2 days or until firm and well drained. Unmold cheese, and remove cheesecloth just before serving. Cheese will keep in the refrigerator up to 5 days. Yield: about 2 cups.

HEAVENLY DESSERT CHEESE MOLDS

½ recipe Cream-Style Cheese
⅔ cup sifted powdered sugar
½ teaspoon vanilla extract
1 cup whipping cream, whipped
Fresh Orange Sauce

Combine Cream-Style Cheese, powdered sugar, and vanilla, mixing well. Fold whipped cream into mixture.

Line six 3½-inch brioche pans or other molds with 4 thicknesses of dampened cheesecloth large enough to extend over edges. Spoon cheese mixture evenly into molds, pressing firmly with the back of a spoon. Gather edges of cheesecloth, and tie securely. Invert molds on a wire rack set in a shallow pan. Cover pan with enough plastic wrap to make an airtight seal. Refrigerate 1 to 2 days or until firm and well drained.

Unmold cheese and remove cheesecloth just before serving. Place each cheese mold on an individual dessert plate. Spoon Fresh Orange Sauce on plates around molds. Serve with apple wedges or cookies. Yield: six ½-cup cheese molds.

Fresh Orange Sauce:

⅓ cup sugar
1 tablespoon cornstarch
1 cup orange juice
⅓ cup water
1 tablespoon butter or margarine
2 teaspoons grated orange rind

Combine sugar, cornstarch, orange juice, and water in a small saucepan, stirring until smooth. Cook over medium heat, stirring constantly, until smooth and thickened. Add remaining ingredients; cook until butter melts. Chill. Yield: 1½ cups.

Note: One 8-ounce package commercial cream cheese, softened, can be substituted for ½ recipe Cream-Style Cheese. If using commercial cream cheese, omit salt and add 1 tablespoon plus 1 teaspoon milk. Mold cheese as directed. No drainage is necessary.

POT-OF-HERB CHEESE

1 recipe Cream-Style Cheese
2 cloves garlic, crushed
2 tablespoons chopped fresh basil or 2
    teaspoons dried whole basil
1 tablespoon chopped fresh dill or 1
    teaspoon dried whole dill
2 teaspoons caraway seeds
1 tablespoon coarsely ground pepper
Sprigs of fresh dill or basil

Combine Cream-Style Cheese, crushed garlic, basil, dill, and caraway seeds, mixing well.

Line a new 4-inch clay flower pot with 4 thicknesses of dampened cheesecloth large enough to extend over edges. Spoon cheese mixture into pot, pressing firmly with the back of a spoon. Gather edges of cheesecloth, and tie securely. Invert pot on a wire rack in a shallow pan. Cover pan with enough plastic wrap to make an airtight seal. Refrigerate 1 to 2 days or until firm and well drained.

Unmold cheese, and remove cheesecloth just before serving. Set cheese upright on clay saucer to look like a flower pot. Sprinkle coarsely ground pepper on top of cheese to look like soil. Insert several sprigs of fresh dill or basil for garnish on top of cheese pot. Serve with crackers. Yield: one 2-cup cheese mold.

Note: Two 8-ounce packages commercial cream cheese, softened, can be substituted for 1 recipe Cream-Style Cheese. If using commercial cream cheese, omit salt and add 2 tablespoons plus 2 teaspoons milk. Mold cheese as directed. No drainage is necessary.

BLUE CHEESE MOLD

½ recipe Cream-Style Cheese
½ pound blue cheese, crumbled
¼ cup plus 2 tablespoons butter or
    margarine, softened
1 tablespoon coarsely chopped onion
1 small clove garlic, cut in half
Dash of coarsely ground pepper
1 tablespoon diced, drained pimiento

Spoon Cream-Style Cheese into food processor bowl with knife blade attached. Add blue cheese, butter, onion, garlic, and pepper; process just until smooth. Remove knife blade, and gently stir in pimiento.

Line a 3-cup smooth-sided mold with 4 thicknesses of dampened cheesecloth large enough to extend over edges. Spoon cheese mixture into mold, pressing firmly with the back of a spoon.

Gather edges of cheesecloth, and tie securely. Invert mold on a wire rack in a shallow pan. Cover pan with enough plastic wrap to make an airtight seal. Refrigerate 1 to 2 days or until firm and well drained.

Unmold cheese, and remove cheesecloth just before serving. Serve with crackers or apple wedges. Yield: one 2-cup cheese mold.

Note: One 8-ounce package commercial cream cheese, softened, can be substituted for ½ recipe Cream-Style Cheese. If using commercial cream cheese, omit salt and add 1 tablespoon plus 1 teaspoon milk. Mold cheese as directed. No drainage is necessary.

GARLIC-CHIVE CHEESE MOLD

1 recipe Cream-Style Cheese
2 cloves garlic, crushed
2 tablespoons chopped fresh chives

Combine Cream-Style Cheese, garlic, and chives, stirring until blended.

Line a smooth-sided 1½-cup mold with 4 thicknesses of dampened cheesecloth large enough to extend over edges. Spoon cheese mixture into mold, pressing firmly with the back of a spoon. Gather edges of cheesecloth, and tie securely. Invert mold on a wire rack in a shallow pan. Cover pan with enough plastic wrap to make an airtight seal. Refrigerate 1 to 2 days or until mixture is firm and well drained.

Unmold and remove cheesecloth before serving. Serve with crackers. Yield: one 1½-cup cheese mold.

Note: Two 8-ounce packages commercial cream cheese, softened, can be substituted for 1 recipe Cream-Style Cheese. If using commercial cream cheese, omit salt and add 2 tablespoons plus 2 teaspoons milk. Mold cheese as directed. No drainage is necessary.

From Our Kitchen To Yours

Chances are that some of your favorite dishes include cheese. Keeping this in mind, the home economists in our test kitchens are constantly testing recipes with different types of cheese, as you'll find in the preceding article

"Make Molds From Your Own Cheese," beginning on page 208. Here are some helpful ideas about cheese that we would like to pass on to you.

Buying

Before you buy cheese, it's ideal to be able to do some sampling. As you taste test, look for a smooth nonbutter flavor. If tasting isn't possible, check the wrapper; avoid a wet and sticky wrapper or a cheese that has shrunken from the rind. To pick the freshest, check the date on unripened soft cheese, such as ricotta, cream cheese, or Neufchâtel. When buying cheese with blue or green veins, such as blue or Roquefort, avoid pieces with browning near the veins. Semi-firm cheese, such as Swiss, Monterey Jack, or mozzarella, should look moist, not dry or cracked.

Storing

If you buy freshly cut cheese, you may want to rewrap it tightly in plastic wrap to prevent it from drying out. Keeping air out will lengthen the storage life. Strong-smelling cheese should be kept in a plastic container with a tight lid so that other foods aren't affected. The coldest part of the refrigerator is the best place to store it. Fresh unripened cheese should be used soon after it's bought, but natural and processed cheese will stay fresh for several months if wrapped well and refrigerated. Some cheese will mold as it's stored, but don't discard it; just cut or scrape the mold off before using.

Cooking With Cheese

—Because cheese is already cooked, it just needs enough heat to melt evenly or blend in well. Low heat works best; high heat or overcooking can make cheese tough and stringy.

—When adding cheese to a sauce, it's best to grate, shred, or dice cheese so that it will melt and blend quickly.

—To make shredding and grating easier, chill cheese well. Processed cheese works better diced; in fact, it's often too soft to shred.

—If you're topping a casserole with cheese, our home economists recommend adding the cheese during the last 5 minutes of baking time; that way the cheese won't harden.

Serving

Soft cheese should be served chilled, but most cheese tastes best when it's served at room temperature. To bring cheese to this temperature, take out just the amount you'll need about 30 minutes before serving. The microwave oven can also be used to warm cheese; for 1 ounce, microwave on high for 15 seconds, and let stand 1 minute.

Freezing

Certain types of cheese can be frozen without significant changes in flavor or texture. Hard and semi-hard cheese, if unopened, can be frozen for 6 weeks to 2 months. If the original package has been opened and rewrapped tightly, the cheese can be kept frozen for a maximum of 6 weeks.

To freeze, cut cheese into pieces of 1 pound or less (not over 1-inch thick), and wrap tightly in plastic wrap to keep moisture in and air out. To thaw, take cheese from the freezer, and refrigerate 24 hours. It's best to use frozen cheese soon after thawing.

Soft and soft-curd cheese don't freeze well; they may become crumbly and break down in texture.

MICROWAVE COOKERY

These Recipes Say Cheese

Whether it's the tangy taste of sharp Cheddar, nutty-tasting Swiss, or creamy Monterey Jack, cheese adds rich flavor to appetizers, side dishes, and entrées. Cooking with cheese requires caution, however, since cheese can be overcooked easily—especially in the microwave oven.

To prevent tough, stringy cheese which can result from overcooking, microwave food containing cheese at MEDIUM (50% power) if you are converting a conventional recipe or if no other directions are given. If the recipe must be cooked longer than 2 or 3 minutes, stir frequently to keep the cheese from toughening.

In our recipe for Broccoli-Swiss Cheese Casserole, the cheese is combined with cooked vegetables and other ingredients; it's then microwaved at MEDIUM HIGH (70% power) for 10 to 12 minutes. Since it cooks so long, it must be stirred every 3 minutes. Layering the cheese between other ingredients also helps to protect it from overcooking.

If possible, add cheese to the recipe last. When a recipe calls for topping with cheese, sprinkle it on after the food is cooked. Heat from the food will help melt the cheese without additional cooking. If necessary, you can microwave the dish at MEDIUM for a few seconds until the cheese melts.

BROCCOLI-SWISS CHEESE CASSEROLE

8 slices bacon
2 (10-ounce) packages frozen chopped broccoli, thawed
¼ cup chopped onion
¼ cup water
1 (8¾-ounce) can whole kernel corn, drained
1½ cups (6 ounces) shredded Swiss cheese
1 tablespoon butter or margarine
2 cups cottage cheese
2 eggs
¼ cup all-purpose flour
¼ teaspoon salt
4 drops of hot sauce
⅓ cup dry, seasoned breadcrumbs

Place bacon on a rack in a 12- x 8- x 2-inch baking dish; cover with paper towels. Microwave at HIGH for 8 to 9 minutes or until bacon is crisp. Drain bacon; crumble and set aside.

Place broccoli, onion, and water in a shallow 2-quart casserole. Cover with heavy-duty plastic wrap, and microwave at HIGH for 8 to 9 minutes, stirring once. Drain. Stir in corn and shredded Swiss cheese. Set aside.

Place butter in a microwave-safe glass measure. Microwave at HIGH for 35 seconds or until melted. Combine butter, cottage cheese, eggs, flour, salt, and hot sauce in container of an electric blender; process until smooth. Stir into vegetable mixture.

Pour vegetable mixture into a lightly greased 8-inch square baking dish. Cover with waxed paper, and microwave at MEDIUM HIGH (70% power) for 10 to 12 minutes, stirring every 3 minutes. Combine breadcrumbs and bacon; sprinkle over top. Cover and microwave at MEDIUM HIGH for 2 to 3 minutes. Let stand 5 minutes. Yield: 8 servings.

MONTEREY JACK CHEESE SOUP

½ cup diced onion
½ cup peeled, diced tomato
2 canned green chiles, seeded and chopped
1 small clove garlic, minced
¼ cup chicken broth
¼ cup all-purpose flour
3 cups milk, divided
1½ tablespoons butter or margarine
¼ teaspoon salt
Dash of pepper
1½ cups (6 ounces) shredded Monterey Jack cheese
Chopped green onion tops (optional)

Combine onion, tomato, chiles, garlic, and chicken broth in a 2½-quart casserole. Cover and microwave at HIGH 3½ to 4 minutes or until vegetables are tender. Combine flour and ¼ cup milk, stirring until smooth. Stir flour mixture, remaining milk, butter, and seasonings into vegetable mixture. Microwave, uncovered, at HIGH for 5 to 6 minutes, stirring twice. Add cheese, stirring until melted. Cover and microwave at MEDIUM (50% power) for 1½ minutes. Top with chopped green onions, if desired. Yield: 4 cups.

TORTILLA PIE

6 (6-inch) flour tortillas
1 cup chopped tomato
½ cup chopped onion
1 (4-ounce) can chopped green chiles, drained
½ cup sliced ripe olives
½ cup (2 ounces) shredded Cheddar cheese
½ cup (2 ounces) shredded Monterey Jack cheese
3 eggs, beaten
¾ cup half-and-half
½ teaspoon chili powder
¼ teaspoon salt
Commercial taco sauce

Line bottom and sides of a well-greased, 9½-inch quiche dish with tortillas. Top with tomato, onion, chiles, olives, and shredded cheese.

Combine eggs, half-and-half, chili powder, and salt, stirring until smooth. Pour mixture into quiche dish. Microwave at MEDIUM HIGH (70% power) for 8 minutes. Give dish a half turn; microwave at MEDIUM HIGH for 9 to 10 minutes or until knife inserted in center comes out clean. (Center will be slightly soft.) Let stand 10 minutes before serving. Serve with taco sauce. Yield: one 9½-inch pie.

HOT ARTICHOKE SEAFOOD DIP

1 (14-ounce) can artichoke hearts, drained and chopped
1 cup mayonnaise
1 cup grated Parmesan cheese
1 (6-ounce) package frozen crabmeat with shrimp, thawed, drained, and flaked
2 tablespoons dry seasoned breadcrumbs
1 tablespoon finely chopped fresh parsley

Combine artichoke hearts, mayonnaise, cheese, and crabmeat with shrimp, mixing well. Spoon mixture into a lightly greased shallow 1-quart casserole. Microwave at MEDIUM (50% power) for 1½ minutes; stir well. Microwave at MEDIUM for 6 to 7 minutes, stirring mixture every 1½ minutes, until hot.

Combine breadcrumbs and parsley, and sprinkle over top. Microwave at MEDIUM for 30 to 45 seconds. Serve dip hot with unsalted crackers. Yield: 2½ cups.

Gather Grapes For This Dessert

Grapes are great for eating fresh and for making jelly, but have you ever tried them in a pie? Lillian Holt of Bluefield, Virginia, makes her double-crust Grape Pie every fall when Concord grapes are at their peak season. She says the recipe has been in her family for generations, and she can remember her mother and grandmother making this pie when she was young. Now you can enjoy a slice of this sweet-tart dessert with a cup of coffee or a tall glass of iced tea.

GRAPE PIE

Pastry for a double-crust 9-inch pie
5 cups fresh Concord grapes
¾ cup sugar
2 tablespoons quick-cooking tapioca
1 tablespoon grated lemon rind
1½ tablespoons lemon juice

Line a 9-inch pieplate with half of pastry; set aside.

Wash grapes thoroughly, and remove seeds. Place grapes in a large saucepan. Bring to a boil; cover, and reduce heat. Cook 15 minutes or until grapes are soft. Remove from heat; stir in sugar, tapioca, lemon rind, and lemon juice.

Spoon mixture into pastry-lined pieplate. Cover with top pastry. Trim edges of pastry; seal and flute edges. Cut slits in top of pastry to allow steam to escape.

Bake at 450° for 10 minutes; reduce heat to 350°, and bake an additional 30 minutes. Yield: one 9-inch pie.

Dinner Party Finales

For a dinner party you want a special dessert—something that's as unusual as it is delicious. Even though the dessert may be the last thing on the menu, your guests will be looking forward to it all during dinner. It's worth a little extra consideration.

Southern cooks are known for their spectacular desserts, so we had no trouble finding some sent in by our readers. Mrs. Peter Rosato III of Memphis offers the recipe for Rum Cream Pie, which has a delectable rum-and-whipped cream filling. Garnished with grated chocolate and chocolate curls, it's an elegant dessert that's worthy of any gathering.

Varniece Warren of Hermitage, Arkansas, serves her Coconut Soufflé warm from the oven with a sherry-flavored whipped cream topping. She says, "I've made this dessert for company often and always received compliments on it." We liked it too; it's a rich dessert, but it has the light, airy texture of a soufflé. It's a sophisticated ending for a special meal.

If your menu calls for a frozen dessert, consider Chocolate-Walnut Cups. A delightful cross between chocolate mousse and cupcakes, they're sprinkled lightly with graham cracker crumbs and frozen in shiny foil baking cups for extra glamour. Your guests will enjoy the novelty as well as the luscious taste.

Frosty Strawberry Parfaits make another frozen dessert that's ideal for company. Each parfait is layered with streusel-like crumbs; a rich mixture of egg whites, whipping cream, and strawberries; and more crumbs. Parfait glasses are a must for showing them off.

RUM CREAM PIE

1½ cups chocolate wafer crumbs
¼ cup plus 2 tablespoons butter or margarine, melted
1½ teaspoons unflavored gelatin
¼ cup water
3 egg yolks
½ cup sugar
¼ cup light rum
1 cup whipping cream, whipped
Coarsely grated chocolate (optional)
Chocolate curls (optional)

Combine chocolate wafer crumbs and butter, mixing well. Place crumb mixture in a 9-inch pieplate, and press onto bottom and sides to form an even crust. Chill crust 1 hour.

Combine gelatin and water in a small saucepan; let stand 1 minute. Cook over medium heat, stirring constantly, about 1 minute or until gelatin dissolves; set aside to cool.

Beat egg yolks and sugar until thick and lemon colored. Gradually stir gelatin mixture into yolk mixture; beat well. Stir in rum; fold in whipped cream. Pour mixture into chilled pastry. Chill pie until firm. Top with grated chocolate and chocolate curls, if desired. Yield: one 9-inch pie.

Mrs. Peter Rosato III,
Memphis, Tennessee.

COCONUT SOUFFLÉ

⅓ cup quick-cooking tapioca
⅓ cup sugar
2 cups milk
1 (3½-ounce) can flaked coconut, divided
2 tablespoons butter or margarine
¾ teaspoon lemon extract
3 eggs, separated
¼ teaspoon salt
1 cup whipping cream
¼ cup sifted powdered sugar
1 tablespoon dry sherry

Lightly butter bottom of a 1-quart soufflé dish; set aside.

Combine tapioca and sugar in top of a double boiler; gradually stir in milk. Bring water to a boil; reduce heat to low, and cook, stirring constantly, 10 minutes or until thickened. Remove from heat.

Set aside 3 tablespoons coconut. Add remaining coconut, 2 tablespoons butter, and lemon extract to tapioca mixture; stir until butter melts. Cool.

Beat egg yolks until thick and lemon colored; fold into coconut mixture. Beat egg whites (at room temperature) and salt until stiff peaks form; fold into coconut mixture. Carefully spoon into prepared soufflé dish. Sprinkle reserved coconut on top; bake at 350° for 50 to 55 minutes or until puffed and set.

Combine whipping cream, powdered sugar, and sherry; beat until stiff peaks form. Serve immediately with warm soufflé. Yield: 6 servings.

Varniece Warren,
Hermitage, Arkansas.

graham cracker crumbs into each of 12 foil baking cups placed in muffin pans; spoon in chocolate mixture. Lightly sprinkle remaining crumbs on top. Freeze until firm. Yield: 12 servings.

Leah Brock,
Stone Mountain, Georgia.

Combine potatoes, eggs, pickle, pimiento, ¼ cup chopped olives, and onion in a large bowl; toss lightly, and set aside.

Combine salad dressing, pickle juice, and seasonings; stir until blended. Add to potatoes, stirring well. Chill thoroughly. Garnish with olive slices, parsley, and gherkin fan. Yield: 8 to 10 servings.

Mrs. Harry Zimmer,
El Paso, Texas.

Pep Up Potato Salad

Wherever there's a cookout, family reunion, or church supper, you're bound to find a bowl of potato salad. Mustard, spices, and sweet or sour pickles give variety to standard versions, but the recipes included here have ingredients that make them unique.

Start with all the usual ingredients when you make Sweet Pickle-Potato Salad; then stir in pimiento and chopped olives for attractive flecks of red and green. Corned beef, shredded carrot, and chopped fruit make some of the other recipes different.

Take advantage of colorful ingredients when you garnish these salads. Pimientos, olives, pickle slices, shredded carrot, green onions, green pepper rings, or fruit slices make the potato salad look more interesting as well as give a preview of what is inside. (See our special garnishing section in the appendices of this book.)

When selecting potatoes, choose round red, round white, or long white potatoes for the best texture. The home economists in our test kitchens prefer the sweeter flavor of red or new potatoes. They have found that baking potatoes tend to have a mealier texture when used for salads.

FROSTY STRAWBERRY PARFAITS

1 cup butter or margarine, melted
2 cups all-purpose flour
½ cup firmly packed brown sugar
1 cup chopped pecans
2 egg whites
1 cup sugar
1 (16-ounce) package frozen sliced
    strawberries, slightly thawed and
    drained
3 tablespoons lemon juice
1 cup whipping cream, whipped

Combine butter, flour, brown sugar, and pecans; mix well. Pat out evenly in a 13- x 9- x 2-inch baking pan. Bake at 350° for 10 minutes. Stir and bake an additional 10 minutes. Cool. Remove one-third of crumbs for topping; spoon remaining crumbs evenly into 12 parfait glasses.

Beat egg whites (at room temperature), sugar, strawberries, and lemon juice at high speed of an electric mixer until stiff peaks form. Fold in whipped cream. Spoon mixture into parfait glasses, and top with remaining crumbs. Freeze 6 hours. Yield: 12 servings.

Jean Clayton,
Birmingham, Alabama.

CHOCOLATE-WALNUT CUPS

1 cup butter or margarine, softened
2 cups sifted powdered sugar
3 eggs, separated
3 (1-ounce) squares unsweetened chocolate,
    melted
1 teaspoon vanilla extract
½ cup chopped walnuts
About 3 tablespoons graham cracker
    crumbs

Cream butter; gradually add powdered sugar, beating well. Add egg yolks and chocolate, and beat until smooth. Stir in vanilla and walnuts.

Beat egg whites (at room temperature) until stiff peaks form. Fold into chocolate mixture. Sprinkle ½ teaspoon

SWEET PICKLE-POTATO SALAD

6 cups cubed cooked potatoes
4 hard-cooked eggs, chopped
1 cup chopped sweet pickle
1 (2-ounce) jar diced pimiento, drained
¼ cup chopped pimiento-stuffed olives
¼ cup finely chopped onion
1 cup salad dressing or mayonnaise
2 tablespoons sweet pickle juice
½ teaspoon celery seeds
¼ teaspoon paprika
Salt and pepper to taste
Pimiento-stuffed olive slices
Fresh parsley sprig
Gherkin fan

CORNED BEEF-POTATO SALAD

4 to 5 medium potatoes
2 tablespoons vinegar
2 teaspoons sugar
1 teaspoon celery seeds
1 teaspoon mustard seeds
½ teaspoon salt
1 (12-ounce) can corned beef, flaked
2 cups shredded cabbage
¼ cup chopped dill pickle
¼ cup chopped onion
1 cup salad dressing or mayonnaise

Cook potatoes in boiling water 20 to 25 minutes or until tender. Drain and cool slightly. Peel potatoes, and cut into ½-inch cubes while warm.

Combine vinegar, sugar, celery seeds, mustard seeds, and salt; add to potatoes, tossing gently.

Add corned beef, cabbage, pickle, and onion to potato mixture; toss gently. Chill at least 8 hours. Add salad dressing just before serving, and toss gently. Yield: 8 servings.

Dorothy Martin,
Woodburn, Kentucky.

DILL POTATO SALAD

¾ to 1 cup salad dressing
½ cup commercial sour cream
1 teaspoon salt
½ teaspoon dill seeds
Dash of pepper
6 cups cubed cooked potatoes
1 medium cucumber, sliced
1 cup shredded carrot, divided
1 tablespoon minced fresh chives

Combine salad dressing, sour cream, salt, dill seeds, and pepper; mix well. Set aside. Combine potatoes, cucumber, ¾ cup carrot, chives, and salad dressing mixture; toss gently. Garnish with remaining shredded carrot. Cover and chill salad 1 to 2 hours. Yield: 8 to 10 servings.

Pauline B. Vann,
Fort Oglethorpe, Georgia.

FRUITY POTATO SALAD

8 small new potatoes (about 2 pounds)
2 hard-cooked eggs, chopped
¾ cup chopped apple
¾ cup seedless green grapes, halved
¼ cup chopped onion
¼ cup chopped green pepper
½ cup mayonnaise
2 tablespoons lemon juice
¼ teaspoon salt
⅛ teaspoon pepper

Cook potatoes in boiling water to cover 20 minutes or until tender. Drain well, and let cool. Peel potatoes, and slice into ½-inch-thick slices.

Combine potatoes, eggs, apple, grapes, onion, and green pepper in a large bowl; toss gently.

Combine remaining ingredients; spoon over potato mixture, stirring gently to coat. Chill thoroughly. Yield: 8 servings.   *Dorothy Krell,*
Rosenberg, Texas.

Enjoy Those Green Tomatoes

As summer comes to an end, you still have time to bring in some green tomatoes for a true Southern favorite—Fried Green Tomatoes. Mrs. Robert L. Humphrey of Palestine, Texas, calls for simply dipping the green slices in egg and milk before coating them with a mixture of cornmeal and flour.

While fried is probably the most common way Southerners eat green tomatoes, this vegetable is also good baked. Top green tomato halves with a mixture of Parmesan cheese and herbs for Herb-Baked Green Tomatoes. Or bake green tomatoes with commercial spaghetti sauce for another delicious version called Italian-Sauced Green Tomatoes.

FRIED GREEN TOMATOES

1 egg, beaten
½ cup milk
½ cup cornmeal
¼ cup all-purpose flour
1 teaspoon salt
½ teaspoon pepper
4 medium-size green tomatoes, cut into ⅓-inch slices
3 to 4 tablespoons vegetable oil

Combine egg and milk; set aside. Combine cornmeal, flour, salt, and pepper. Dip tomatoes in egg mixture; dredge in cornmeal mixture.

Heat 3 tablespoons oil in a large skillet over medium heat. Arrange a single layer of tomato slices in skillet, and cook until golden brown on each side; set aside. Repeat with remaining slices, adding additional oil, if needed. Yield: 6 servings. *Mrs. Robert L. Humphrey,*
Palestine, Texas.

HERB-BAKED GREEN TOMATOES

4 medium-size green tomatoes, cut in half crosswise
¼ cup grated Parmesan cheese
2 tablespoons fine dry breadcrumbs
2 tablespoons minced fresh parsley
¾ teaspoon dried whole basil
¾ teaspoon dried whole oregano
¼ teaspoon salt
¼ teaspoon freshly ground pepper
3 tablespoons margarine, melted

Place tomato halves on a lightly greased baking sheet. Combine remaining ingredients; mix well, and spoon over cut surface of each tomato. Bake at 350° for 15 minutes or until tomato is thoroughly heated. Yield: 8 servings.

ITALIAN-SAUCED GREEN TOMATOES

6 medium-size green tomatoes, peeled and cut into ¼-inch slices
2 eggs, beaten
1¼ cups dry breadcrumbs
¼ to ½ cup butter or margarine
1 (15½-ounce) jar spaghetti sauce
¼ cup grated Parmesan cheese

Dip tomato slices in eggs; coat with breadcrumbs. Melt ¼ cup butter in a large skillet over medium heat. Arrange a single layer of tomato slices in skillet, and cook until browned on both sides. Drain on paper towels; set aside. Repeat with remaining tomato slices, adding additional butter, if needed.

Spoon half of spaghetti sauce into a greased 12- x 8- x 2-inch baking dish. Arrange tomato slices over sauce; top with remaining sauce. Bake, uncovered, at 350° for 15 minutes. Sprinkle with cheese; bake an additional 5 to 10 minutes or until heated. Yield: 8 servings.

COOKING LIGHT®

Spice Up Your Diet With A Snack

You don't have to pass up snacks just because you're dieting. And you don't have to feel guilty about reaching for a between-meal pick-me-up. Many popular snack foods have gained a bad reputation because of their high-fat, sugar, or sodium content, but the idea that all snacks are empty-calorie "junk foods" just isn't so. All foods can contribute to a healthy diet if you eat a variety of them in moderation. Just make sure your diet doesn't become a "junk diet"—eating foods low in nutrition at the exclusion of those high in nutrition—thus limiting variety.

Snacking can actually be an aid to dieters when it introduces new foods and missing nutrients in the diet. After all, attaining and maintaining your ideal body weight is not a matter of how frequently you eat, but rather what you eat compared to the number of calories used in physical activity. The key is choosing snacks as carefully as those foods you serve at mealtime. Make them a planned part of your daily diet plan. Our light snacks offer variety, good nutrition, and fewer calories.

Nutritious Vegetable Pockets use halved pita bread rounds chock-full of vegetables and contain a sprinkling of cheese, raisins, and walnuts. Each is topped with Yogurt Dressing and can be enjoyed as a late-night snack.

If you're limiting the amount of sodium in your diet, feel free to nibble on Toasted Cereal Snack. With only 187 calories and 3 milligrams of sodium per serving, you can easily afford the luxury of this savory treat. It combines bite-size shredded wheat biscuits with peanuts and a variety of seasonings. Or let our low-sodium Pineapple-Banana Shake quench your thirst. Norah Cooney of Dalzell, South Carolina, processes crushed pineapple, bananas, skim milk, and ice in an electric blender for this smooth, refreshing beverage. And at only 114 calories and 44 milligrams of sodium per serving, you won't be going overboard with calories or sodium.

Apple-Oatmeal Cookies offer yet another type of snacking option. The natural sugar in a can of unsweetened apple juice concentrate provides all the sweetness needed to make these dainties delicious. Oats, raisins, and sunflower kernels add texture and make these spicy cookies high in dietary fiber.

For a super snack you can make ahead of time, try chilled Vegetable Garden Dip. The low-fat cottage cheese and plain low-fat yogurt make it lower in calories than sour cream- or cream cheese-based dips. Grated carrot, onion, green pepper, and garlic flavor this zesty dip. Keep it in the refrigerator alongside a colorful assortment of crisp, low-calorie, fresh vegetable dippers for a handy after-school snack.

VEGETABLE POCKETS

½ cup coarsely shredded lettuce
½ cup alfalfa sprouts
½ cup (2 ounces) shredded Cheddar
  cheese
½ cup shredded carrots
¼ cup raisins
¼ cup chopped walnuts
2 (6-inch) pita bread rounds
Yogurt Dressing

Combine lettuce, alfalfa sprouts, cheese, carrots, raisins, and walnuts, tossing gently.

Cut pita bread rounds in half; spoon vegetable mixture into bread, and top with Yogurt Dressing. Serve immediately. Yield: 4 servings (about 215 calories per serving plus 16 calories per tablespoon dressing).

Yogurt Dressing:

¼ cup plain low-fat yogurt
2 teaspoons lemon juice
2 teaspoons honey

Combine all ingredients; mix until well blended. Yield: ⅓ cup.
Ann Manke,
Cape Coral, Florida.

LOW-CALORIE PIMIENTO
CHEESE SPREAD

1 (8-ounce) package low-fat process
  American cheese
⅓ cup skim milk
1 (4-ounce) jar diced pimiento, drained
1 tablespoon cider vinegar
½ teaspoon dry mustard
Dash of red pepper

Combine cheese and milk in top of a double boiler; bring water to a boil. Reduce heat to low; cook until cheese melts. Add remaining ingredients, stirring well. Cover and chill. Yield: 1½ cups (about 20 calories per tablespoon). *Frances Christopher,*
Iron Station, North Carolina.

SPICY APPLE SALAD

¼ cup plus 2 tablespoons plain low-fat
  yogurt
⅛ teaspoon ground cinnamon
⅛ teaspoon ground allspice
3 cups unpeeled, chopped apple
½ cup sliced celery
3 tablespoons chopped dates
3 tablespoons raisins

Combine yogurt, cinnamon, and allspice; mix well. Add remaining ingredients; toss gently. Cover and chill. Yield: 6 servings (about 67 calories per ½-cup). *Miriam Maddox,*
Chatsworth, Georgia.

VEGETABLE GARDEN DIP

½ cup low-fat cottage cheese
1 cup plain low-fat yogurt
1 tablespoon finely grated carrot
2 teaspoons finely grated onion
1 teaspoon finely grated green pepper
⅛ teaspoon garlic powder

Place cottage cheese in container of an electric blender; process until smooth. Transfer cottage cheese to a bowl; stir in remaining ingredients. Cover and chill; serve with raw vegetables. Yield: 1⅓ cups (about 12 calories per tablespoon). *Irene Pankey,*
Richmond, Virginia.

TOASTED CEREAL SNACK

⅓ cup plus 1 tablespoon unsalted
  margarine
1½ teaspoons dried whole oregano
1¼ teaspoons dried whole basil
½ teaspoon garlic powder
½ teaspoon onion powder
4 cups bite-size shredded wheat biscuits
½ cup unsalted peanuts

Melt margarine in a 15- x 10- x 1-inch jellyroll pan in a 350° oven. Remove pan from oven; stir in seasonings. Add cereal and peanuts, mixing well. Bake at 350° for 15 minutes, stirring occasionally. Let cool in pan. Yield: about 4½ cups (about 187 calories and 3 milligrams sodium per ½ cup).
Jodie McCoy,
Tulsa, Oklahoma.

Tip: Keep all dry foods in their original containers or airtight ones.

PINEAPPLE-BANANA SHAKE

1 (8-ounce) can unsweetened crushed
  pineapple, undrained
1 cup skim milk
1 medium banana, cut into chunks
½ teaspoon vanilla extract
2 ice cubes
Whole fresh strawberries (optional)

Drain pineapple, reserving ¼ cup juice; set aside.

Combine pineapple, reserved juice, milk, banana, and vanilla in container of an electric blender; process until smooth. Add ice cubes; process until frothy. Garnish with whole fresh strawberries, if desired. Serve immediately. Yield: 3 cups (about 114 calories and 44 milligrams sodium per cup).
Norah Cooney,
Dalzell, South Carolina.

APPLE-OATMEAL COOKIES

¼ cup margarine, softened
1 egg
1 (6-ounce) can frozen unsweetened apple
  juice concentrate, thawed and
  undiluted
1 cup all-purpose flour
1 cup regular oats
1 teaspoon baking powder
1 teaspoon ground cinnamon
½ teaspoon ground nutmeg
¼ cup unsalted sunflower kernels
¼ cup raisins
Vegetable cooking spray

Cream margarine; add egg and apple juice concentrate, beating well. Combine flour, oats, baking powder, cinnamon, and nutmeg; add to creamed mixture, mixing well. Stir in sunflower kernels and raisins.

Drop dough by rounded teaspoonfuls onto cookie sheets coated with cooking spray. Bake at 350° for 10 to 12 minutes or until lightly browned. Yield: 3 dozen (about 53 calories per cookie).
Kathy Henry,
Jefferson City, Tennessee.

Create A Fancy Chicken Salad

Chicken salad can be a whole lot more than chunks of chicken tossed with mayonnaise, celery, and pickle relish. And to prove it, here are four new and fancy ways to enjoy one of the South's favorite luncheon dishes.

It's hard to top Chicken Salad Ambrosia for eye appeal or taste. Chicken is combined with celery, mandarin oranges, grapes, and toasted pecans; then it's tossed with a sour cream-and-Italian salad-dressing mix. Served in individual Cheese Pastry Tart Shells, it's sure to be a hit the next time you invite friends over for a casual yet impressive meal.

Fried rice sticks add crunch to Oriental Chicken Salad. Fresh ginger, sesame seeds, and a vinaigrette dressing also make this salad entrée different from the rest.

If you like fruit in your chicken salad, try our Tropical Chicken Salad for a different taste. Pineapple, mandarin oranges, and cashews provide texture, while a combination of peach yogurt and mayonnaise makes the dressing.

ORIENTAL CHICKEN SALAD

6 chicken breast halves
1 (1-inch-thick) slice fresh ginger
3 tablespoons sugar
2 teaspoons salt
½ teaspoon pepper
¼ cup vinegar
½ cup vegetable oil
1 small head lettuce, shredded
4 cups fried rice sticks
4 green onions, thinly sliced
1 (2-ounce) package slivered almonds, toasted
¼ cup sesame seeds, toasted

Cook chicken and ginger in boiling water to cover for 30 minutes or until chicken is tender. Drain; discard ginger. Cool chicken; then skin, bone, and shred chicken.

Combine sugar, salt, pepper, and vinegar in a small saucepan; cook over low heat, stirring until sugar dissolves. Remove from heat; cool. Add oil to mixture; mix well.

Combine chicken, vinegar mixture, and remaining ingredients in a large bowl; toss gently to mix. Serve immediately. Yield: 10 servings.   *Patsy Hull, Florence, Alabama.*

CHICKEN SALAD IN AVOCADOS

3 cups chopped cooked chicken
½ cup diced celery
½ cup mayonnaise
¼ cup diced onion
2 hard-cooked eggs, chopped
2 tablespoons chopped fresh parsley
2 tablespoons lemon juice
1 tablespoon capers, drained
Dash of salt
⅛ teaspoon pepper
4 medium avocados, peeled and halved
Lemon juice
Paprika
Lettuce leaves
Tomato wedges (optional)

Combine chicken, celery, mayonnaise, onion, eggs, parsley, lemon juice, capers, salt, and pepper in a mixing bowl; mix well.

Brush avocado halves with lemon juice; spoon chicken mixture evenly into avocado cavities. Sprinkle with paprika. Serve on lettuce-lined plates, and garnish with tomato wedges, if desired. Yield: 8 servings.   *Barbara E. Bach, Clearwater, Florida.*

CHICKEN SALAD AMBROSIA

2 cups chopped cooked chicken breast
1 cup chopped celery
1 (11-ounce) can mandarin oranges, drained
½ cup seedless green grapes, halved
½ cup chopped pecans, toasted
¼ cup mayonnaise
¼ cup commercial sour cream
1½ teaspoons Italian salad dressing mix
Cheese Pastry Tart Shells
Green grape halves (optional)

Combine chicken, celery, mandarin oranges, grapes, and pecans; set aside.

Combine mayonnaise, sour cream, and salad dressing mix; mix well. Pour over chicken mixture, and toss gently to mix. Cover and chill 2 to 3 hours; serve in baked Cheese Pastry Tart Shells. Garnish with green grape halves, if desired. Yield: 10 servings.

Cheese Pastry Tart Shells:

¼ cup butter or margarine, softened
1 (3-ounce) package cream cheese, softened
1 cup (4 ounces) shredded Cheddar cheese
1 cup all-purpose flour

Combine butter, cream cheese, and Cheddar cheese; mix well. Add flour; stir until mixture forms a ball. Divide dough into 10 pieces; press each piece into an ungreased tart pan, and place on a baking sheet. Bake at 350° for 10 to 12 minutes; cool. Remove from pans. Yield: 10 shells.

Mary Evelyn Hollaway, Hanceville, Alabama.

TROPICAL CHICKEN SALAD

4 cups chopped cooked chicken
1 (15¼-ounce) can pineapple tidbits, drained
1 (11-ounce) can mandarin oranges, drained
¾ cup chopped celery
1 (2-ounce) jar diced pimiento, drained
2 tablespoons chopped green pepper
1 teaspoon grated onion
½ cup unsalted cashews
½ cup peach yogurt
½ cup mayonnaise

Combine chicken, pineapple, mandarin oranges, celery, pimiento, green pepper, onion, and cashews; set aside. Combine yogurt and mayonnaise. Add to chicken mixture; toss. Chill 2 to 3 hours. Yield: 6 to 8 servings.

Gayle Wallace, Kingwood, Texas.

Start With Fish Fillets

If you're lucky enough to have someone at your house who loves fishing, you already know the benefits of having fish fillets on hand. They're like money in the bank when it comes to preparing quick, nutritious meals. But with the availability of fish in markets, anyone can take advantage of this natural convenience food.

There are several ways to purchase fish fillets. You can buy them already frozen, or you can buy a fresh fish and fillet it yourself. In many cities, you can select a live fish from a tank and have it cleaned and filleted while you wait.

Flounder and fresh vegetables star in Flounder-Vegetable Medley. The fillets are layered with mushrooms, zucchini, onion, and parsley, and they are then topped with bacon slices before baking. The result is a savory dish that combines the vegetables and main course all in one.

RED SNAPPER CHOWDER

¼ cup chopped salt pork
1 (6½-ounce) can minced clams, undrained
1 pound fresh red snapper fillets, cut into bite-size pieces
1 cup diced potatoes
½ cup chopped onion
¼ teaspoon salt
⅛ teaspoon white pepper
2 cups milk
Minced parsley (optional)

Fry salt pork in a Dutch oven until crisp. Add remaining ingredients except milk and parsley. Bring to a boil; cover, reduce heat, and simmer 15 minutes or until potatoes are tender. Stir in milk; cook over medium heat, stirring frequently, until thoroughly heated. Sprinkle each serving with parsley, if desired. Yield: 5 cups.   *Maryse H. Rose,*
Mary Esther, Florida.

RED SNAPPER LOUISIANE

1 egg, beaten
1 cup milk
4 red snapper fillets (about 2½ pounds)
2 tablespoons butter or margarine, melted
Salt and pepper
½ cup all-purpose flour
1 cup vegetable oil
1 (14-ounce) can artichoke hearts, drained and quartered
4 large fresh mushrooms, sliced
¼ cup butter or margarine, melted
1 teaspoon Worcestershire sauce
1 teaspoon lemon juice
1 teaspoon tarragon vinegar
⅓ cup sliced almonds, toasted

Combine egg and milk; mix well. Brush fillets with 2 tablespoons butter, and sprinkle with salt and pepper. Dip fish in egg mixture, and dredge in flour. Fry fish in hot oil until golden brown. Drain well, and transfer to a serving platter; keep warm.

Sauté artichoke hearts and mushrooms in ¼ cup butter. Add Worcestershire sauce, lemon juice, and vinegar; simmer 1 minute. Spoon mixture over fish, and sprinkle with almonds. Yield: 4 servings.   *Peggy Blackburn,*
Winston-Salem, North Carolina.

FLOUNDER-VEGETABLE MEDLEY

½ pound fresh mushrooms, thinly sliced
1 medium zucchini, thinly sliced
1 medium onion, thinly sliced and separated into rings
¼ teaspoon salt, divided
¼ teaspoon pepper, divided
1 tablespoon minced parsley, divided
¼ cup butter or margarine, divided
4 flounder fillets (about 1½ pounds)
1 tablespoon lemon juice
5 to 6 slices bacon

Layer mushrooms, zucchini, and onion in a greased 13- x 9- x 2-inch baking dish. Sprinkle with half each of salt, pepper, and parsley. Dot with 2 tablespoons butter. Lay fillets over vegetables; top with remaining salt, pepper, parsley, and butter. Sprinkle with lemon juice, and top with bacon slices. Bake, uncovered, at 425° for 30 minutes or until fish flakes easily when tested with a fork. Yield: 4 to 6 servings.
Mrs. Peter Rosato III,
Memphis, Tennessee.

FLOUNDER NICOLE

¼ pound fresh mushrooms, sliced
1 medium onion, chopped
1 clove garlic, minced
¼ teaspoon dried whole basil
1 tablespoon vegetable oil
¾ cup chopped, peeled tomato
3 tablespoons lemon juice
2 flounder fillets (about ¾ pound)
Salt and pepper
1 pound fresh spinach
Lemon slices (optional)

Sauté mushrooms, onion, garlic, and basil in oil until onion is tender; remove from heat. Stir in tomato and lemon juice. Set aside.

Sprinkle flounder with salt and pepper, and place in a greased 12- x 8- x 2-inch baking dish. Top with vegetable mixture; cover and bake at 350° for 20 to 25 minutes or until fish flakes easily when tested with a fork.

Remove stems from spinach; wash leaves in lukewarm water. Place spinach in Dutch oven (do not add water); cover and cook 3 to 5 minutes. Drain spinach well; chop and arrange on serving platter. Gently transfer fish and vegetables to platter; garnish with lemon slices, if desired. Yield: 2 to 3 servings.   *Jill Rorex,*
Dallas, Texas.

CREAMY BAKED FISH FILLETS

2 pounds trout fillets
¼ teaspoon salt
¼ teaspoon pepper
¼ teaspoon paprika
Juice of 1 lemon
2 tablespoons butter or margarine
2 tablespoons all-purpose flour
1½ teaspoons dry mustard
1 cup milk
¼ teaspoon salt
¼ teaspoon pepper
½ cup soft breadcrumbs
2 tablespoons butter or margarine, melted
1 tablespoon minced parsley
Lemon wedges (optional)
Additional parsley for garnish (optional)

Arrange fillets in a lightly greased 13- x 9- x 2-inch baking dish; sprinkle with ¼ teaspoon salt, ¼ teaspoon pepper, paprika, and lemon juice.

Melt 2 tablespoons butter in a heavy saucepan over low heat; add flour and mustard, stirring until smooth. Cook 1 minute, stirring constantly. Gradually add milk; cook over medium heat, stirring constantly, until mixture is thickened and bubbly. Stir in ¼ teaspoon salt and ¼ teaspoon pepper. Pour mixture over fillets.

Combine breadcrumbs and 2 tablespoons melted butter; sprinkle over fillets. Sprinkle with 1 tablespoon minced parsley. Bake, uncovered, at 350° for 30 minutes or until fish flakes easily when tested with a fork. Garnish with lemon and additional parsley, if desired. Yield: 6 servings.   *Mrs. E. L. Warstler,*
Kill Devil Hill, North Carolina.

CRUNCHY BAKED FISH FILLETS

⅓ cup butter or margarine
1 small clove garlic, minced
¾ teaspoon fine herbs
2 (1-pound) packages frozen perch fillets, thawed
1½ cups crushed potato chips (about 4 cups potato chips), divided
3 tablespoons grated Parmesan cheese

Melt butter in a small saucepan. Stir in garlic and herbs; remove from heat.

Place fillets in a greased 15- x 10- x 1-inch jellyroll pan; brush with half the butter mixture. Sprinkle with half the crushed potato chips; turn fillets, and repeat procedure. Top with cheese; bake at 400° for 10 to 15 minutes or until fish flakes easily when tested with a fork. Yield: 8 servings.
Mrs. Hugh F. Mosher,
Huntsville, Alabama.

FAST FISH BAKE

1 large onion, thinly sliced
2 pounds fish fillets
½ cup mayonnaise
2 tablespoons lemon juice
2 teaspoons Worcestershire sauce
¼ cup grated Parmesan cheese

Line a greased 13- x 9- x 2-inch baking dish with half the onion; top with fish fillets and remaining onion. Combine mayonnaise, lemon juice, and Worcestershire sauce, and spread mixture evenly over onion; sprinkle with cheese. Bake at 350° for 35 minutes or until fish flakes easily when tested with a fork. Yield: 4 to 6 servings.

Elizabeth W. Dean,
Alexandria, Virginia.

This Dessert Has Carob

When company comes to Wanda Edwards' home in Fayetteville, North Carolina, guests ask for Carob-Pecan Torte. This lusciously rich, spongy cake is a favorite with family and friends.

If you're allergic to chocolate, this recipe is for you. Carob, also called St. John's bread or locust bean, is a large dried bean-like pod from an evergreen tree native to the eastern Mediterranean area. The major use of carob today is as an extender or substitute for cocoa powder. The two have similar tastes, but carob has less fat and a higher sugar content than cocoa.

CAROB-PECAN TORTE

5 eggs, separated
¾ cup sugar
3 tablespoons all-purpose flour
2 tablespoons rum
1 teaspoon baking powder
Pinch of salt
2 cups ground pecans
Carob Frosting
Additional ground pecans (optional)
Pecan halves (optional)

Grease two 8-inch round cakepans; line them with waxed paper. Grease the waxed paper, and then set pans aside.

Beat egg yolks and sugar at medium speed of an electric mixer 5 minutes or until thick and lemon colored. Add flour, rum, baking powder, and salt, mixing well. Stir in 2 cups ground pecans; set mixture aside.

Beat egg whites (at room temperature) until stiff but not dry; fold into egg yolk mixture. Pour into prepared pans. Bake at 350° for 25 to 30 minutes or until a wooden pick inserted in center comes out clean. Cool in pans 8 minutes; remove from pans, and cool completely on wire racks.

Spread Carob Frosting between layers and on top and sides of torte. Gently press additional ground pecans onto sides of torte, and garnish top with pecan halves, if desired. Yield: one 2-layer torte.

Carob Frosting:

¾ cup unsweetened carob morsels
3 tablespoons half-and-half
3 tablespoons butter or margarine, softened
2¼ cups powdered sugar
2 tablespoons commercial sour cream
½ teaspoon vanilla extract

Combine carob and half-and-half in top of a double boiler; bring water to a boil. Reduce heat to low; cook mixture until carob melts.

Cream butter; blend in carob mixture and remaining ingredients. Beat until smooth. Yield: enough frosting for one 8-inch layer torte.

Make It With Macaroni

Mix macaroni with any type of meat, seafood, herbs, or spices, and it magically takes on a wonderful new flavor. We've used it in the recipes here to help you stretch your meat dollar without cutting back on taste.

Use macaroni in a casserole as Marcella Winters does in Corryton, Tennessee. Marcella says she usually divides her Chicken-Macaroni Casserole into two smaller containers and freezes one to serve later. Her recipe uses 3½ cups of chopped chicken, which is about the amount we've found you can get from a whole chicken.

For a quick skillet dinner, Helen McKey of Edna, Texas, prepares Ground Beef and Macaroni. She stirs in okra, onion, tomatoes, and green pepper, making it a tasty one-dish meal.

Since macaroni is bite-size, it's ideal for popular pasta salads. You'll fancy our Macaroni-Ham Salad served in tomato cups. It can be chilled if you prefer an easy make-ahead salad.

When serving macaroni chilled, be sure to rinse it with cold water after cooking, and drain well to keep it from tasting pasty or starchy. There is no need to rinse pasta if you plan to serve it hot.

GROUND BEEF AND MACARONI

3 cups water
1 teaspoon salt
1 cup uncooked elbow macaroni
1 pound ground beef
2 cups sliced okra
1 medium-size green pepper, chopped
1 medium onion, chopped
1 (28-ounce) can whole tomatoes, undrained and chopped
1 teaspoon chili powder
½ teaspoon salt
¼ teaspoon pepper

Combine water and 1 teaspoon salt in a Dutch oven; bring to a boil. Gradually add macaroni; cook, uncovered, 6 to 8 minutes, stirring occasionally. (Do not drain.)

Brown ground beef in a skillet, stirring to crumble; drain well. Add to macaroni. Add remaining ingredients; stir well. Cover and bring to a boil. Reduce heat; simmer 15 minutes or until vegetables are tender. Yield: 6 servings.

Helen McKey,
Edna, Texas.

MACARONI-HAM SALAD

6 small tomatoes
1 cup cooked elbow macaroni
½ cup cooked cubed ham
½ cup peeled, chopped cucumber
1½ teaspoons diced onion
1½ teaspoons chopped fresh parsley
2½ tablespoons mayonnaise
⅛ to ¼ teaspoon salt
⅛ teaspoon pepper
¼ cup plus 2 tablespoons (1½ ounces) shredded Cheddar cheese

Cut off top of each tomato; scoop out pulp, leaving shells intact. (Reserve pulp for other uses.) Invert tomato shells on paper towels to drain.

Combine remaining ingredients except cheese; mix well. Fill tomato shells with macaroni-ham salad; sprinkle each with 1 tablespoon cheese. Yield: 6 servings.

Irene Murry,
Herculaneum, Missouri.

CHICKEN-MACARONI CASSEROLE

½ cup chopped onion
3 tablespoons butter or margarine, melted
2 (10¾-ounce) cans cream of chicken soup, undiluted
2 cups (8 ounces) shredded Cheddar cheese, divided
1 cup milk
3½ cups chopped cooked chicken
2½ cups cooked macaroni
¼ cup round buttery cracker crumbs

Sauté onion in butter in a large skillet until tender. Add soup and 1½ cups cheese; gradually stir in milk. Cook over medium heat until cheese melts. Stir in chicken and macaroni.

Pour mixture into a greased 2½-quart casserole; sprinkle with cracker crumbs. Bake at 350° for 30 minutes or until thoroughly heated. Top with remaining ½ cup cheese, and bake an additional 5 minutes. Yield: 8 servings.

Marcella C. Winters,
Corryton, Tennessee.

SHRIMP-MACARONI SALAD

3 cups water
1 pound medium-size fresh shrimp
1 (8-ounce) package elbow macaroni, cooked, drained, and rinsed
1 cup chopped celery
½ cup sliced green onions
¼ cup chopped green pepper
⅔ cup mayonnaise
1 tablespoon lemon juice
1 teaspoon sugar
¼ teaspoon celery seeds
¼ teaspoon salt
¼ teaspoon freshly ground pepper
Lettuce leaves

Bring water to a boil; add shrimp, and cook 3 to 5 minutes. Drain well; rinse with cold water. Cool shrimp; peel and devein. Combine shrimp, macaroni, celery, green onions, and green pepper; toss well.

Combine remaining ingredients except lettuce; mix well. Stir into shrimp mixture; chill. Serve over lettuce leaves. Yield: 6 to 8 servings.

Jeannette Shedd,
Roswell, Georgia.

Tip: Reheat cooked pasta or rice in a metal strainer or colander over a pan of steaming water. Cover strainer with foil and steam 15 minutes.

Cook Liver So They'll Like It

If liver has the reputation of being a dull dish at your house, try these recipes. Sliced fairly thin and smothered with gravy, vegetables, or creole or Italian sauce, liver could easily become a favorite with your family.

Still another flavor comes through when barbecue sauce is added to liver. With Patsy M. Smith's recipe, you mix your own spicy barbecue sauce, and pour it over the liver before baking.

An excellent source of protein and iron, liver will also help stretch your meat budget. Once purchased, liver can be kept in the refrigerator for one or two days, or it can be frozen for up to six months.

BARBECUED LIVER

3 tablespoons all-purpose flour
¾ teaspoon salt
¾ teaspoon pepper
1 pound thinly sliced beef liver
1 tablespoon vegetable oil
⅓ cup water
¼ cup catsup
2 tablespoons brown sugar
1 tablespoon Worcestershire sauce
1 tablespoon vinegar
Dash of garlic powder

Combine flour, salt, and pepper. Dredge liver in flour mixture, and brown in hot oil. Combine remaining ingredients, and pour over liver. Cover and simmer 20 minutes or until tender. Yield: about 4 servings.

Patsy M. Smith,
Lampasas, Texas.

CALF'S LIVER WITH VEGETABLES

¼ cup all-purpose flour
¾ teaspoon salt
⅛ teaspoon pepper
1¾ pounds thinly sliced calf's liver
¼ cup vegetable oil
6 green onions, cut into 3-inch pieces
4 stalks celery, cut into 3- x ¼-inch strips
2 bay leaves
½ to 1 teaspoon dried whole thyme
2 dozen cherry tomatoes
1 tablespoon vegetable oil

Combine flour, salt, and pepper. Dredge liver in flour mixture. Heat ¼ cup oil in a large skillet. Cook liver in hot oil about 4 minutes, turning once. Remove liver and keep warm.

Add green onions, celery, bay leaves, and thyme to skillet; cook until vegetables are crisp-tender. Return liver to skillet; cover and cook over low heat 5 minutes. Remove liver and vegetables to a serving platter, discarding bay leaves.

Sauté tomatoes in 1 tablespoon oil for 3 to 5 minutes, stirring often; spoon over liver. Yield: 6 servings.

Mary Kay Menees,
White Pine, Tennessee.

LIVER ITALIANO

2 tablespoons all-purpose flour
½ teaspoon garlic salt
½ pound thinly sliced beef liver
2 tablespoons vegetable oil
1 (8-ounce) can tomato sauce
1 medium green pepper, cut into strips
1 small onion, sliced and separated into rings
4 ounces hot cooked spaghetti
2 tablespoons grated Parmesan cheese

Combine flour and garlic salt. Dredge liver in flour mixture, and brown in hot oil. Add tomato sauce, green pepper, and onion; cover and simmer 10 minutes. Serve over spaghetti, and sprinkle with cheese. Yield: 4 servings.

Patricia Andrews,
McAlester, Oklahoma.

CREOLE LIVER

4 slices bacon
1 medium onion, chopped
¼ cup all-purpose flour
⅛ teaspoon red pepper
1 pound thinly sliced beef liver
1 (16-ounce) can whole tomatoes, undrained and chopped
⅓ cup chopped green pepper
½ teaspoon salt
½ teaspoon sugar
¼ teaspoon chili powder

Cook bacon in a large skillet until crisp; remove bacon, reserving 2 tablespoons drippings in skillet. Crumble bacon, and set aside. Sauté onion in drippings until tender; push to one side in skillet.

Combine flour and red pepper. Dredge liver in flour mixture, and brown in bacon drippings. Add bacon and remaining ingredients; cover and simmer 40 to 45 minutes. Yield: 4 servings.

Suzanne Weisman,
Hampton, Virginia.

September   **219**

Add A Dash Of Curry

It may come as a surprise to know that curry is actually a blend of several spices—not just one. Ginger, turmeric, red pepper, and coriander are just a few of the spices that give curry its distinctive flavor.

If you've never used curry before, remember that the flavor can vary from mild to hot. It might be wise to start by adding just a small amount to your recipes; more can be added later.

To help discover whether mild or hot curry is your style, try experimenting with these recipes. Our selections range from a colorful rice salad to an interesting pita bread sandwich filled with curry-flavored beef and vegetables.

Curry powder gives Curried Rice Salad a spicy flavor and bright-yellow color. The salad is especially attractive when garnished with English peas.

CURRIED BEEF PITAS

1 pound ground beef
1 medium onion, chopped
1 clove garlic, minced
1 tablespoon curry powder
1 medium zucchini, chopped
½ teaspoon salt
¼ teaspoon pepper
1 medium tomato, chopped
Leaf lettuce
4 (6-inch) pita bread rounds, cut in half

Combine ground beef, onion, garlic, and curry powder in a large skillet; cook over medium heat until meat is browned, stirring to crumble. Drain off pan drippings. Stir in zucchini, salt, and pepper. Cover and simmer 15 minutes or until zucchini is tender. Add tomato; cook until thoroughly heated.

Line each bread half with lettuce; spoon meat mixture into each with a slotted spoon. Yield: 4 servings.

Martha Edington,
Knoxville, Tennessee.

CURRIED SWISS BITES

1 (8-ounce) can water chestnuts, drained and chopped
1 (6-ounce) can lump crabmeat, drained and flaked
1 cup (4 ounces) shredded Swiss cheese
½ cup mayonnaise
1½ tablespoons sliced green onions
½ teaspoon curry powder
1 teaspoon lemon juice
2 (10-ounce) packages refrigerated biscuits

Combine all ingredients except biscuits; mix well. Separate each biscuit into 2 halves; place on ungreased baking sheets. Spoon 1 rounded teaspoon of crabmeat mixture on each biscuit; bake at 400° for 10 to 12 minutes or until lightly browned. Yield: 40 appetizer servings.

Kay C. Cooper,
Burke, Virginia.

CURRIED RICE SALAD

1 cup uncooked regular rice
¼ teaspoon curry powder
1½ cups diced celery
1 cup frozen English peas, thawed
¼ cup diced onion
½ cup vegetable oil
3 tablespoons soy sauce
2 tablespoons vinegar
1 teaspoon curry powder
½ teaspoon sugar
½ teaspoon celery seeds
¼ teaspoon salt
¼ cup slivered almonds, toasted
Additional English peas, thawed (optional)
Celery leaves (optional)
Pimiento strips (optional)

Cook rice according to package directions, adding ¼ teaspoon curry powder; cool. Stir in celery, peas, and onion; set mixture aside.

Combine oil, soy sauce, vinegar, curry powder, sugar, celery seeds, and salt; mix well. Add to rice mixture; stir well. Sprinkle almonds on top; cover and chill 2 to 3 hours.

Garnish with additional English peas, celery leaves, and pimiento strips, if desired. Yield: 6 to 8 servings.

Mrs. Clayton Turner,
De Funiak Springs, Florida.

CHICKEN CURRY

2 medium apples, peeled and chopped
1 large onion, chopped
1 cup chopped celery
⅓ cup butter or margarine, melted
¼ cup plus 1 tablespoon all-purpose flour
1 tablespoon curry powder
1¾ cups milk
¾ cup chicken broth
¼ cup cream of coconut
3 cups chopped cooked chicken
1 teaspoon salt
¼ teaspoon pepper
Hot cooked rice

Sauté apples, onion, and celery in butter in a Dutch oven for 5 minutes or until crisp-tender. Add flour and curry powder, stirring well. Cook 1 minute, stirring constantly. Gradually stir in milk, chicken broth, and cream of coconut; cook over medium heat, stirring frequently, until mixture is thickened and bubbly. Stir in chicken and seasonings. Serve mixture over rice. Yield: 6 servings.
Brenda Clark,
Auburn, Alabama.

Offer Eggplant More Often

What can be used as a main dish, side dish, or soup? Eggplant. This versatile vegetable, with its exotic shape and regal color, is mysterious to some. But adventurous cooks know that both its economy and mild flavor make it an ideal selection for meals. This vegetable is also a source of iron and potassium in the diet.

When you shop for an eggplant, choose one that is firm and heavy for its size. Blemishes, scars, shriveling, and softness indicate poor quality. You can plan for one pound of eggplant to yield about 2½ cups when diced.

EGGPLANT SUPPER SOUP

1 pound ground beef
2 (14-ounce) cans beef broth
1 (28-ounce) can whole tomatoes, undrained and chopped
1 medium eggplant, peeled and diced
1 medium onion, chopped
½ cup chopped carrot
½ cup chopped celery
1 clove garlic, minced
½ teaspoon salt
½ teaspoon pepper
½ teaspoon ground nutmeg
½ cup uncooked elbow macaroni
2 tablespoons chopped fresh parsley

Brown ground beef in a Dutch oven; drain. Add remaining ingredients except macaroni and parsley; cover and simmer 30 minutes. Add macaroni, and simmer an additional 12 minutes or until done. Stir in parsley. Yield: 2½ quarts.
Lenore Partlow,
Louisville, Kentucky.

EGGPLANT PIZZA

½ pound ground beef
1 medium eggplant, peeled and cut into ½-inch thick slices
1¼ cups commercial pizza sauce
1 cup (4 ounces) shredded mozzarella cheese
¼ cup grated Parmesan cheese

Cook ground beef until browned, stirring to crumble; drain, and set aside.

Place eggplant on greased baking sheets; broil 5 to 6 inches from heat until lightly browned, turning once. Remove from oven; spread eggplant slices with a thin layer of pizza sauce. Top each slice with 2 to 3 tablespoons ground beef and cheese.

Broil 1 to 2 minutes or until cheese melts. Serve pizza immediately. Yield: 8 to 10 servings.
Patsy Layer,
Galveston, Texas.

EGGPLANT JULIENNE

5 slices bacon
½ cup chopped onion
1 medium eggplant, peeled and cut into julienne strips
1 (16-ounce) can whole tomatoes, undrained and chopped
1 teaspoon sugar
¾ teaspoon dried whole basil
½ teaspoon salt
Dash of pepper
2 tablespoons chopped fresh parsley

Cook bacon until crisp; drain and crumble, reserving 2 tablespoons drippings in skillet. Set bacon aside.

Sauté onion in drippings until tender; add eggplant, tomatoes, sugar, basil, salt, pepper, and bacon. Bring to a boil; cover. Reduce heat, and simmer 10 minutes, stirring occasionally. Sprinkle with parsley. Yield: 6 servings.
Margaret G. Quaadman,
Roswell, Georgia.

EGGPLANT-SAUSAGE BAKE

3 large eggplant, peeled and cubed
½ pound bulk hot pork sausage
1 cup chopped celery
1 cup chopped onion
3 green onions with tops, chopped
1 (6¼-ounce) package stuffing mix
½ teaspoon pepper
2 cups (8 ounces) shredded sharp Cheddar cheese

Cook eggplant, covered, in a small amount of water 10 minutes or until tender. Drain, and set aside.

Sauté sausage, celery, and onion in a skillet until the sausage is cooked and vegetables are tender. Drain and set mixture aside.

Prepare stuffing mix according to package directions. Combine stuffing, eggplant, sausage mixture, and pepper; mix well. Spoon into a greased 13- x 9- x 2-inch baking dish. Cover and bake at 350° for 10 to 15 minutes; uncover, top with cheese, and bake an additional 5 minutes or until cheese melts. Yield: 10 to 12 servings.
Dixie Delaney,
Beaumont, Texas.

Pick Pears Now For Flavor

Fresh pears, sweet and juicy, are at the peak of flavor during the fall season. Our recipes will help you savor this fruit at its best. It's a natural in salads as well as desserts.

Most of the pears you'll find at the grocery store are slightly underripe. Since the flavor is best in fully ripe pears, buy the fruit a few days in advance, and leave at room temperature until ripe.

PEAR CRUMBLE

6 medium pears, peeled, cored, and sliced
⅓ cup port wine
1 tablespoon lemon juice
1 cup firmly packed brown sugar
¾ cup all-purpose flour
½ teaspoon ground cinnamon
½ teaspoon ground nutmeg
⅓ cup butter or margarine
Whipped cream (optional)

Arrange pears in a greased 8-inch square baking dish; pour wine and lemon juice over pears.

Combine sugar, flour, cinnamon, and nutmeg; cut in butter with pastry blender. Spoon sugar mixture on top of pears; pat firmly. Bake at 375° for 40 minutes or until pears are tender. Serve warm, and top with whipped cream, if desired. Yield: 6 to 8 servings.
Lorraine Brownell,
Salisbury, North Carolina.

CHILLED FRUIT WITH DRESSING

1 (8-ounce) can pineapple chunks,
  undrained
2 apples
2 pears
2 bananas
2 tangerines, peeled and sectioned
1 (10-ounce) package frozen strawberries,
  thawed and undrained
¼ cup frozen orange juice concentrate,
  thawed and undiluted
2 to 3 tablespoons cream sherry
1 tablespoon lemon juice
¼ cup sugar
1 teaspoon all-purpose flour
1 egg, beaten
¼ cup whipping cream, whipped

Drain pineapple, reserving ¼ cup juice; set aside.

Cut apples and pears into bite-size chunks; slice bananas and add to apple mixture. Combine apple mixture with pineapple, tangerines, strawberries, orange juice concentrate, sherry, and lemon juice in a large bowl. Toss mixture well. Refrigerate fruit mixture up to 3 hours.

Combine sugar and flour in a small saucepan; stir in egg, mixing well. Add reserved ¼ cup pineapple juice and cook, stirring constantly, over low heat 4 to 5 minutes or until thickened; cool. Fold in whipped cream.

Serve fruit in compotes topped with dollops of whipped cream sauce. Yield: 8 to 10 servings.   *Janet M. Filer,*
Arlington, Virginia.

FRUITED CHEF SALAD

1 (8-ounce) can pineapple chunks,
  undrained
1 teaspoon lemon juice
2 bananas
2 pears
2 nectarines
2 plums
¾ cup seedless green grape halves
Dressing (recipe follows)
3 cups chopped cooked chicken
Salad greens
2 cups (8 ounces) shredded Swiss cheese
¼ cup slivered almonds, toasted

Combine pineapple and lemon juice in a large bowl. Cut remaining fruit into bite-size chunks, and add to pineapple mixture, tossing to coat fruit. Drain; pour prepared dressing over fruit and set aside.

For each serving, place ½ cup chicken on a bed of salad greens, and sprinkle with cheese. Spoon fruit mixture over cheese, and top with almonds. Yield: 6 servings.

Dressing:

⅓ cup vegetable oil
3 tablespoons wine vinegar
3 tablespoons orange juice
1 teaspoon Dijon mustard
1 teaspoon seasoning salt
¼ teaspoon dried whole basil
⅛ teaspoon pepper

Combine all ingredients in a jar. Cover tightly, and shake vigorously. Chill dressing several hours. Yield: about ¾ cup.   *Mrs. James Tuthill,*
Virginia Beach, Virginia.

Try These Unusual Loaf Breads

If you're looking for a special bread to serve with a meal, consider these loaf bread recipes from our readers. Each adds a distinctive touch to a menu.

Loaf breads take on extra glamour if they are served in baskets lined with pretty tea towels or napkins; the covering also helps keep the bread warm. For a casual meal, it's sometimes fun to pass the loaf around on a small bread board, restaurant-style.

PULL-APART MAPLE WHEAT BREAD

1¼ cups water
¾ cup maple-flavored syrup
⅓ cup vegetable oil
3 cups all-purpose flour
2 packages dry yeast
1 teaspoon salt
1 teaspoon ground cinnamon
2 eggs, beaten
1 cup raisins
3 to 3½ cups whole wheat flour
1 tablespoon butter or margarine, melted

Combine water, syrup, and oil in a small saucepan; heat until very warm (120° to 130°). Set aside.

Combine all-purpose flour, yeast, salt, and cinnamon in a large mixing bowl; stir in syrup mixture and eggs, mixing well. Stir in raisins and enough whole wheat flour to make a soft dough.

Turn dough out onto a lightly floured surface, and knead about 5 minutes or until smooth and elastic. Place in a greased bowl, turning to grease top. Cover and let rise in a warm place (85°), free from drafts, 1 hour.

Punch dough down; divide into 20 pieces, and shape each piece into a ball. Place 10 balls, in rows of 5, in each of two greased 9- x 5- x 2-inch loafpans. Brush each loaf with melted butter. Cover and let rise in a warm place (85°), free from drafts, 45 minutes.

Bake at 375° for 30 minutes or until loaves sound hollow when tapped. Remove loaves from pan, and cool on wire racks. Yield: 2 loaves.

Deborah Alford,
Independence, Kentucky.

HERBED FRENCH BREAD

1 (1.6-ounce) package buttermilk-style
  salad dressing mix, divided
5 to 6 cups all-purpose flour, divided
2 packages dry yeast
1 tablespoon plus 2 teaspoons sugar
½ teaspoon salt
1½ cups buttermilk
½ cup water
¼ cup shortening
1 egg
Melted butter or margarine

Set aside 1 teaspoon salad dressing mix. Combine 2 cups flour, yeast, remaining salad dressing mix, sugar, and salt in a large mixing bowl. Set aside.

Combine buttermilk, water, and shortening in small saucepan; cook over low heat until very warm (120° to 130°). Gradually add buttermilk mixture to flour mixture, mixing at low speed of an electric mixer. Add egg; beat 3 minutes at medium speed. Stir in enough remaining flour to make a soft dough.

Turn dough out onto a lightly floured surface, and knead until smooth and elastic (5 to 10 minutes). Place in a greased bowl, turning to grease top. Cover and let rise in a warm place (85°), free from drafts, 45 minutes or until doubled in bulk.

Punch dough down, and divide in half. Place dough on a lightly floured surface. Roll each half into a 12- x 7-inch rectangle. Starting at long end, roll up each rectangle jellyroll fashion; pinch edges together to seal. Place dough seam side down on a greased cookie sheet; turn ends under. Cut diagonal slashes, 2 inches apart, in top of each loaf. Brush with butter, and sprinkle each loaf with ½ teaspoon salad dressing mix. Cover and let rise in a warm place (85°), free from drafts, 30 minutes or until doubled in bulk.

Bake at 375° for 30 to 40 minutes or until golden brown. Yield: 2 loaves.

Martha Edington,
Knoxville, Tennessee.

PIMIENTO-CHEESE BREAD

3 tablespoons all-purpose flour
2 tablespoons butter or margarine, melted
1 tablespoon sugar
1 teaspoon salt
½ teaspoon ground marjoram
¼ teaspoon ground thyme
1 cup milk
⅓ cup (1½ ounces) shredded sharp
   Cheddar cheese
¼ cup finely chopped pimiento
1 package dry yeast
2 tablespoons warm water (105° to 115°)
3¼ to 3¾ cups all-purpose flour
1 tablespoon butter or margarine, melted

Combine first 6 ingredients in a medium saucepan; gradually stir in milk. Cook over medium heat, stirring constantly, until smooth and thick. Remove from heat; add cheese and pimiento, stirring until cheese melts. Cool to lukewarm (105° to 115°).

Dissolve yeast in warm water; add to cooled cheese mixture. Gradually add 3 cups flour, beating at medium speed of an electric mixer until smooth. Stir in enough remaining flour to form a stiff dough.

Turn dough out onto a lightly floured surface, and knead 5 to 10 minutes until smooth and elastic. Place in greased bowl, turning to grease top. Cover and let rise in a warm place, free from drafts, 1 hour or until doubled in bulk.

Punch dough down, and shape into a loaf. Place in a greased 9- x 5- x 3-inch loafpan. Cover and let rise in a warm place, free from drafts, 1 hour or until doubled in bulk.

Brush top with 1 tablespoon melted butter. Bake at 350° for 35 to 40 minutes or until loaf sounds hollow when tapped. Remove loaf from pan, and cool on a wire rack. Yield: 1 loaf.

Mary M. Hoppe,
Kitty Hawk, North Carolina.

Prunes For Good Eating

Prunes begin as plums—royal purple and with an amber-colored seed. But not all plums can be prunes. It's a special type, a prune plum, that lends itself to producing such a tasty treat. Once harvested, a dehydration process removes enough water from the fruit to make it stable without refrigeration. You can enjoy prunes for their fruity,

sweet taste and high-quality nutrition. They're a good source of potassium, iron, and vitamin A.

If you enjoy prunes for breakfast, try our Miniature Prune Muffins or Orange-Spiced Prunes. The muffins have a hint of cinnamon, and they almost melt in your mouth.

Prunes are plumped in a spicy mixture of orange juice concentrate, cinnamon, cloves, orange rind, and honey for the great taste of Orange-Spiced Prunes. Top each serving with a dollop of plain yogurt and chopped pecans.

Or if you prefer, serve prunes in a dessert. Brandied Prune Tarts carry a faint taste of orange and brandy, but neither overpowers the fruit. It's an ideal choice for a make-ahead dessert, since the individual servings are refrigerated and ready when you are.

MINIATURE PRUNE MUFFINS

1⅓ cups all-purpose flour
¼ cup sugar
1½ teaspoons baking powder
¼ teaspoon salt
1 egg, beaten
½ cup milk
⅓ cup vegetable oil
1 cup chopped prunes
¼ cup sugar
¼ teaspoon ground cinnamon
2 tablespoons butter or margarine, melted

Combine flour, ¼ cup sugar, baking powder, and salt in a bowl; make a well in center. Combine egg, milk, and oil. Add to dry ingredients; stir just until moistened. Stir in prunes.

Spoon batter into greased miniature muffin pans, filling three-fourths full. Bake at 375° for 15 minutes. Combine ¼ cup sugar and ¼ teaspoon cinnamon in a small bowl; dip tops of warm muffins in butter and then in sugar mixture. Yield: 3 dozen. *Sudie Lovorn,*
Atlanta, Georgia.

BRANDIED PRUNE TARTS

1 cup finely chopped pitted prunes
⅓ cup brandy
⅓ cup water
2 tablespoons sugar
½ teaspoon cornstarch
1 teaspoon grated orange rind, divided
2 (3-ounce) packages cream cheese,
   softened
3 tablespoons orange juice
8 (3-inch) tart shells, baked

Combine prunes, brandy, and water in a saucepan; bring to a boil. Reduce heat, and simmer, uncovered, 5 minutes. Combine sugar and cornstarch; add to prunes. Cook, stirring constantly, until thickened. Add ½ teaspoon orange rind; set aside.

Beat cream cheese until smooth; add orange juice and remaining ½ teaspoon orange rind, beating well. Place 2 teaspoons cream cheese mixture in bottom of each tart shell; top with prune mixture. Pipe remaining cream cheese mixture around edges and in middle of tarts. Yield: 8 servings.

Mrs. James L. Twilley,
Macon, Georgia.

PRUNE CAKE

¾ cup shortening
1¾ cups sugar
3 eggs
2¼ cups all-purpose flour
1 teaspoon baking soda
1 teaspoon salt
1¼ teaspoons ground cinnamon
1 teaspoon ground nutmeg
¼ teaspoon ground allspice
1 cup buttermilk
1½ cups chopped cooked prunes
1 cup chopped walnuts
1½ teaspoons grated lemon rind
1 teaspoon vanilla extract
Powdered sugar

Cream shortening; gradually add sugar, beating well. Beat in eggs.

Combine flour, soda, salt, and spices; add to creamed mixture alternately with buttermilk, beginning and ending with flour mixture; mix until ingredients are moistened. Stir in prunes, walnuts, lemon rind, and vanilla.

Pour batter into a greased and floured 13- x 9- x 2-inch baking pan. Bake at 350° for 40 to 45 minutes or until a wooden pick inserted in center comes out clean.

Cool and sprinkle with powdered sugar. Yield: 15 to 18 servings.

Gladys Tucker,
Vinton, Louisiana.

ORANGE-SPICED PRUNES

1 cup water
1 (3-inch) stick cinnamon
4 whole cloves
⅓ cup frozen orange juice concentrate, thawed and undiluted
⅓ cup honey
1 teaspoon grated orange rind
1 (12-ounce) package pitted prunes
2 small oranges, peeled, sliced, and quartered
Vanilla yogurt
Chopped pecans

Combine water, cinnamon, and cloves in a small saucepan. Bring to a boil; reduce heat, and simmer 5 minutes. Add orange juice concentrate, honey, and orange rind; return to a boil. Immediately remove mixture from heat, and pour over prunes and oranges. Cover and chill 24 hours. Serve in individual compotes, topped with a dollop of yogurt and sprinkled with pecans. Yield: 4 to 6 servings.

Try Savory Sauces For Meat

When there isn't time to cook, consider reaching for a fully cooked ham or deli meats. Sound boring? It doesn't have to be if you add one of our delectable hot sauces.

Royal Cherry Sauce goes well with ham or poultry. Its rich, regal color is topped only by its delicious flavor. And no one will ever know you made it in minutes.

Turn unadorned roast beef into something to rave about with Mild Mustard Sauce. Even people who aren't mustard fans will enjoy its delicate flavor.

Deli corned beef will never be the same once you serve it with our distinct but mild Horseradish Sauce.

ROYAL CHERRY SAUCE

1 (16-ounce) can pitted dark cherries
3 tablespoons brown sugar
2 tablespoons cornstarch
½ cup Sauterne wine or other dry white wine
1 teaspoon lemon juice
2 teaspoons grated orange rind

Drain cherries, reserving liquid. Set cherries aside. Combine sugar, cornstarch, and reserved cherry liquid in a saucepan; stirring until smooth. Add wine, lemon juice, and orange rind. Cook over medium heat, stirring occasionally, until mixture thickens. Stir in cherries; cook until thoroughly heated. Serve hot with ham or poultry. Yield: 2 cups. *Mrs. Earl L. Faulkenberry, Lancaster, South Carolina.*

MILD MUSTARD SAUCE

1 tablespoon butter or margarine
1½ teaspoons all-purpose flour
¼ teaspoon salt
1 cup evaporated milk
1 tablespoon plus 1 teaspoon prepared mustard
1 tablespoon diced pimiento
½ teaspoon lemon juice

Melt butter in a heavy saucepan over low heat. Add flour and salt, stirring until smooth. Cook 1 minute, stirring constantly. Gradually add milk; cook over medium heat, stirring constantly, until mixture thickens. Stir in remaining ingredients; cook until thoroughly heated. Serve hot with roast beef or ham. Yield: about 1 cup. *Janis Moyer, Farmersville, Texas.*

HORSERADISH SAUCE

¼ cup butter or margarine
¼ cup all-purpose flour
¼ teaspoon salt
⅛ teaspoon pepper
Dash of red pepper
2 cups milk
3 to 4 tablespoons prepared horseradish
1 tablespoon lemon juice

Melt butter in a large saucepan over low heat; add flour, salt, and both peppers, stirring until smooth. Cook 1 minute, stirring constantly. Gradually add milk; cook over medium heat, stirring constantly, until mixture is thickened and bubbly. Stir in horseradish and lemon juice; cook until sauce is thoroughly heated. Serve hot with corned beef or roast beef. Yield: 2 cups.
Mrs. Bernie Benigno, Gulfport, Mississippi.

ONION-MUSHROOM SAUCE

½ clove garlic
¼ cup butter or margarine, melted
1 (¾-ounce) package brown gravy mix
½ cup water
½ cup Burgundy or other dry red wine
Pinch of pepper
½ pound mushrooms, sliced
1 cup thinly sliced green onions

Sauté garlic in butter in a large skillet. Add gravy mix, water, wine, and pepper; bring to a boil. Cook over medium heat, stirring constantly, until smooth and thickened. Add mushrooms and green onions; cook until thoroughly heated. Serve hot with beef patties or steak. Yield: about 3 cups.
Maggie Cates, Orlando, Florida.

CRANBERRY JUICE SAUCE

1 cup firmly packed brown sugar
1½ tablespoons cornstarch
¼ teaspoon ground allspice
1 cup cranberry juice
1 tablespoon lemon juice
½ cup golden raisins

Combine sugar, cornstarch, and allspice in a small saucepan. Stir in cranberry juice and lemon juice; cook over medium heat, stirring constantly, until thickened. Stir in raisins. Serve sauce hot with ham or pork. Yield: 1½ cups. *Mrs. Thomas Lee Adams, Kingsport, Tennessee.*

Tip: Evaporated milk and sweetened condensed milk are two of the forms in which milk is sold. They are different and cannot be interchanged within a recipe. Evaporated milk is unsweetened milk thickened by removing some of its water content. Sweetened condensed milk is sweetened with sugar and thickened by evaporation of some of its water content.

October

It's Easy To Make Onion Soup

If you think all onion soups are alike, take a look at the recipes here. It's true that most versions include onions, broth, cheese, and toasted bread, but you can change the flavors to suit your own tastes. Just use mild, sweet onions and soft, mild-flavored cheese.

For some recipes, you might like to make your own croutons if you have slightly stale fine-textured bread on hand. Just remove the crust, and cut into cubes or other desired shapes. Bake at 300° for 30 minutes or until the croutons are crisp. To add extra flavor, brown the croutons in melted seasoned butter before baking.

You might want to keep some homemade broth in the freezer. It's simple to make with a beef soup bone or bony chicken pieces, such as the back, neck, and wings. Cover with water, and simmer several hours until meat can be easily pulled from the bones. Remove the bones and meat, and strain. To remove fat, chill the broth—the fat will rise to the top and solidify. Remove fat, and freeze the broth.

For handy storage and easy use, freeze the broth in the cups of a muffin pan or an ice tray; then remove and store together in a freezer bag. Broth will keep in the freezer about three to four months. To use frozen broth, let it thaw at room temperature, or heat it gently in the top of a double boiler.

EASY ONION SOUP

3 large onions (about 2 pounds), thinly sliced
¼ cup butter or margarine, melted
5 cups boiling water
1 tablespoon chicken bouillon granules
2 teaspoons beef bouillon granules
½ teaspoon salt
Dash of pepper
1 tablespoon sugar (optional)
½ teaspoon browning and seasoning sauce
6 (¾-inch-thick) slices French bread, toasted
6 (4- x ⅛-inch) slices Swiss cheese

Separate onions into rings, and sauté in butter in a Dutch oven until tender. Add water to onions. Combine bouillon granules, salt, pepper, and sugar, if desired; add to onions. Stir in browning and seasoning sauce. Bring mixture to a boil; reduce heat, and simmer, uncovered, 1 hour.

Place 6 ovenproof individual serving bowls on a baking sheet. Place 1 slice of bread in each bowl; ladle soup over bread. Top each with 1 slice cheese; broil 6 inches from heat until cheese melts. Yield: 6 cups. *Marie B. Curry, Chunchula, Alabama.*

FRENCH ONION SOUP

10 medium onions (about 2½ pounds), thinly sliced
¼ cup butter or margarine, melted
¼ cup sherry
5 cups water
2 (12-ounce) cans beer
2 tablespoons Worcestershire sauce
3 tablespoons chopped parsley
9 beef-flavored bouillon cubes
2 cloves garlic, pressed
1 teaspoon salt
½ teaspoon pepper
½ teaspoon dry mustard
½ teaspoon dried whole dillweed
½ teaspoon celery seeds
⅛ teaspoon marjoram leaves
1 bay leaf
2 cups croutons
2 cups (8 ounces) shredded Swiss cheese

Separate onions into rings; cook in butter in a large Dutch oven over medium heat 25 to 30 minutes, stirring frequently. Add sherry to onions; cook 5 minutes. Add remaining ingredients except croutons and cheese, and bring to a boil. Cover, reduce heat, and simmer 1 hour. Remove bay leaf.

Place desired number of ovenproof bowls on baking sheet. Ladle 1 cup soup into each bowl; top each with 2 tablespoons croutons. Sprinkle 2 tablespoons cheese over croutons. Broil 6 inches from heat until cheese melts. Yield: 4 quarts.

Note: Soup (without cheese and croutons) may be refrigerated for up to 2 days. *Kay Castleman Cooper, Burke, Virginia.*

RICH ONION SOUP

¼ cup plus 2 tablespoons butter or margarine, melted
2 tablespoons corn oil
3 large onions (about 2 pounds), thinly sliced
½ teaspoon sugar
½ teaspoon dry mustard
3 tablespoons all-purpose flour
4 (14½-ounce) cans beef broth, undiluted
1½ cups dry white wine
3 cups (12 ounces) shredded Gruyère cheese
French bread slices, toasted (optional)

Combine butter and oil in a large Dutch oven. Separate onions into rings, and add to Dutch oven. Cook over medium heat 30 minutes, stirring frequently. Stir in sugar and mustard; cook 30 minutes, stirring occasionally. Sprinkle flour over onions; cook 2 minutes, stirring constantly. Add broth and wine. Bring to a boil; cover. Reduce heat, and simmer 30 minutes.

Place desired number of ovenproof individual bowls on a baking sheet; ladle in soup. Sprinkle cheese over hot soup. Broil 6 inches from heat until cheese melts. Serve soup with French bread, if desired. Yield: about 9 cups.
Paula Causey, Byron, Georgia.

Step 1: *To make Easy Onion Soup, slice onions thin, and separate into rings. Sauté in butter in a Dutch oven until tender.*

Step 2: *Add water to onions; stir in bouillon granules and seasonings. Bring to a boil, reduce heat, and simmer 1 hour.*

DOUBLE-CHEESE ONION SOUP

2 large onions (about 1⅓ pounds), thinly
    sliced
¼ cup butter or margarine, melted
3 cups beef broth
2 cups chicken broth
2 cups water
¼ teaspoon pepper
½ cup cooking sherry
2 cups (¾-inch) French bread cubes,
    toasted
Grated Parmesan cheese
7 (4- x ⅛-inch) slices mozzarella cheese

Separate onions into rings, and sauté
in butter in a large Dutch oven until
tender. Add broth, water, and pepper;
bring to a boil. Reduce heat, and simmer, uncovered, 30 minutes. Remove
from heat, and stir in sherry.

Place 7 ovenproof individual serving
bowls on a baking sheet. Ladle soup
into each bowl. Top each with bread
cubes, about 1 teaspoon Parmesan
cheese, and 1 slice mozzarella cheese.
Broil 6 inches from heat until cheese
melts. Yield: 7 cups.　*Carolyn Baker,*
Kingsport, Tennessee.

Our Easy Onion Soup is prepared the traditional way—it hides a slice of toasted French bread beneath the flavorful broth and melted Swiss cheese.

Pass The Biscuits!

"The biscuits are ready" can bring
more folks to the table than a dinner
bell. Everyone knows these fresh-baked
treats are best with a pat of butter
spread on them while they're still fresh
from the oven.

WHOLE WHEAT BISCUITS

1 cup all-purpose flour
½ cup whole wheat flour
2 tablespoons sugar
2½ teaspoons baking powder
½ teaspoon salt
½ cup milk
3 tablespoons vegetable oil

Combine flour, sugar, baking powder,
and salt, mixing well. Combine milk
and oil; stir into dry ingredients just
until moistened.

Turn dough out onto a lightly floured
surface, and knead 3 or 4 times. Roll
dough to ½-inch thickness; cut with a
2½-inch biscuit cutter. Place biscuits on
an ungreased baking sheet. Bake at 400°
for 12 to 15 minutes or until golden
brown. Yield: 8 biscuits.

Sandra Teston,
Hattiesburg, Mississippi.

Step 3: *Place ovenproof bowls on baking sheet; put a toasted French bread slice in each bowl. Spoon soup over bread.*

Step 4: *Top each bowl of onion soup with a slice of Swiss cheese, and broil the soup just until the cheese melts.*

BRAN BISCUITS

1⅓ cups all-purpose flour
2½ teaspoons baking powder
¾ teaspoon salt
⅓ cup butter or margarine
½ cup shreds of wheat bran cereal
¾ cup skim milk

Combine flour, baking powder, and salt in a medium bowl; cut in butter with a pastry blender until mixture resembles coarse meal. Set aside.

Combine bran cereal and milk in a small bowl; let stand 2 minutes. Add bran mixture to flour mixture, stirring until dry ingredients are moistened.

Turn dough out onto a lightly floured surface, and knead 3 or 4 times. Roll dough to ½-inch thickness; cut with a 3-inch biscuit cutter. Place biscuits on an ungreased baking sheet. Bake at 425° for 12 to 15 minutes or until biscuits are golden brown. Yield: ½ dozen.

Nancy Swinney,
Tallahassee, Florida.

CORNMEAL BISCUITS

2 cups all-purpose flour
¾ cup coarsely ground cornmeal
1 tablespoon baking powder
1 teaspoon salt
½ teaspoon baking soda
½ cup butter or margarine
1 cup buttermilk

Combine flour, cornmeal, baking powder, salt, and soda; stir well. Cut in butter with a pastry blender until mixture resembles coarse meal. Add buttermilk to mixture, stirring until dry ingredients are moistened. Turn dough out onto a floured surface, and knead lightly 3 or 4 times.

Roll dough to ½-inch thickness; cut with a 2½-inch biscuit cutter. Place biscuits on a lightly greased baking sheet. Bake at 450° for 10 to 12 minutes or until lightly browned. Yield: about 2 dozen. *Mrs. John A. Eckhart,*
Rocksprings, Texas.

HERBED BISCUITS

2 teaspoons grated Parmesan cheese
2 teaspoons parsley flakes
1 teaspoon onion flakes
¾ teaspoon celery flakes
¼ teaspoon dried whole dillweed
1 (10-ounce) package refrigerated biscuits
2 to 3 tablespoons butter or margarine, melted

Combine Parmesan cheese and herbs in a small bowl; set aside. Place biscuits in a 9-inch square baking pan; bake at 400° for 6 minutes.

Remove from oven; brush each biscuit with butter, and sprinkle with ½ teaspoon herb mixture. Return to oven, and bake an additional 6 to 8 minutes or until biscuits are golden brown. Yield: 10 to 12 biscuits.

Mrs. J. David Stearns,
Mobile, Alabama.

When They Entertain, He Cooks

From Texas to Tennessee, men are finding their way to the kitchen and discovering they like it. Take a look as we visit in three homes where the host takes the compliments for the meal. In Atlanta, Georgia, we feature an expert at grilling; in Jonesborough, Tennessee, a host who specializes in homegrown food and regional delicacies; and in Victoria, Texas, a man with a flair for the unusual.

Grilling a Fish Specialty

Don Childress enjoys playing the role of the host. More often than not, a dinner invitation to the Childresses' home means Don will be planning the menu, selecting the wine from his wine cellar, and preparing the food.

Jill Childress says she gladly surrenders the kitchen to her husband. "We make a pretty good team. He does the food, and I decorate."

As he starts one of his favorite outdoor recipes—Grilled Trout With Ginger and Soy Sauce—Don talks about how easy it is to grill fish when you use a wire basket. "Whole fish work best because they won't slip around in the basket like fillets." And we see this is especially important because the basket is flipped several times as the fish are basted and cooked. Basting with the ginger and soy sauce mixture gives the fish a distinct flavor. "It adds a little bit of bite," laughs Don.

The most valuable advice this cook gives to grillers is to watch the fish closely as they cook. "It doesn't take long to grill fish—I like mine slightly under-cooked. If you wait until they're flaky, they're probably overcooked."

Back inside, Don assembles his dinner guests and the remainder of his menu. A crisp Bibb lettuce salad with herb dressing starts the meal, followed by fresh steamed asparagus, a saffron-yellow rice dish called Risotto alla Milanese, and the trout.

One of Don's other specialties is saved for dessert—Zuppa Inglese. Also known as tipsy cake, Zuppa Inglese was a fairly complicated recipe that originally came from a friend.

"I decided to modify it by using a cake mix and vanilla pudding mix rather than making cake and custard from scratch," explains Don. These shortcuts save time but don't cheat you of taste, as seen when guests proclaim this coffee-and-rum-flavored dessert a hit.

GRILLED TROUT WITH GINGER AND SOY SAUCE

6 (12-ounce) lake trout
¼ cup plus 2 tablespoons butter or margarine
¼ cup plus 2 tablespoons lime juice
¼ cup plus 2 tablespoons soy sauce
1 teaspoon ground ginger
¾ teaspoon cracked pepper
Vegetable cooking spray
Lemon slices
Parsley sprigs

Dress fish, leaving heads on. Cut several diagonal slashes on both sides of each fish; rinse and pat dry.

Combine butter, lime juice, soy sauce, ginger, and pepper in a small saucepan; cook over medium heat, stirring often, until hot. Remove from heat. Brush internal cavities of fish with soy sauce mixture, reserving remainder. Spray a fish basket with cooking spray; place fish in basket.

Cook fish over medium hot coals 3 to 5 minutes on each side or until fish is light golden and flakes easily, brushing often with reserved soy sauce mixture. Remove fish from grill; transfer to a serving platter. Garnish with lemon and parsley. Yield: 6 servings.

RISOTTO ALLA MILANESE

1 medium onion, chopped
1½ cups uncooked regular rice
2 tablespoons olive oil
2 cups chicken broth, diluted
¼ teaspoon salt
¼ teaspoon ground saffron
½ cup pine nuts or slivered almonds
½ cup raisins
Parsley sprigs (optional)

Sauté onion and rice in olive oil in a skillet over medium heat until onion is tender. Add broth, salt, and saffron; bring to a boil. Cover, reduce heat, and simmer 20 minutes or until liquid is absorbed. Stir in nuts and raisins. Garnish with parsley sprigs, if desired. Yield: 6 to 8 servings.

ZUPPA INGLESE

1 (18.5-ounce) butter-flavored cake mix
1 (6-ounce) package vanilla pudding mix
1 (3-ounce) package vanilla pudding mix
2 cups whipping cream
2 tablespoons instant coffee granules
1 teaspoon hot water
¼ cup rum, divided
Shaved sweet chocolate

Prepare cake mix according to package directions; pour into two greased and floured 9-inch round cakepans. Bake at 350° for 25 to 30 minutes or until a wooden pick inserted in center comes out clean. Cool in pans 10 minutes; remove from pans, and cool completely on a wire rack.

Prepare both packages pudding mix, using half of the milk called for in package directions; cool completely. Cover pudding and chill.

Beat whipping cream until stiff peaks form; fold into pudding. Divide pudding mixture in half; set aside.

Stir coffee granules into hot water; cool. Fold into half of pudding mixture.

Split each cake layer horizontally; place bottom layer of cake on a cake plate; brush with 1 tablespoon rum. Spread half of coffee-flavored pudding over rum. Top with second layer; brush with 1 tablespoon rum. Spread about ¼ of plain pudding over rum. Top with third layer; brush with 1 tablespoon rum. Spread remaining coffee-flavored pudding over rum. Top with fourth layer; brush with 1 tablespoon rum. Frost top and sides of cake with remaining plain pudding. Sprinkle top with shaved chocolate; cover and chill before serving. Yield: one 9-inch cake.

Serving Homegrown Food

Dinner guests of Jay and LeVenia Allen know that they'll be treated to a bountiful buffet. Most of the food he prepares, from entrée to dessert, is grown on the Allens' farm.

Jay says he enjoys planning menus that reflect food typical of the East Tennessee region. Pork, apples, pears, and vegetables, such as sweet potatoes, are usually included. His succulent Stuffed Pork Roast, glazed with homemade cherry preserves and stuffed with a sausage dressing, has proven popular with guests. Vegetables from the Allens' garden, along with homemade pickles and relishes, accompany the roast.

For dessert, Jay serves an old family favorite, Tennessee Pear Pie. "It's kind of a tradition to have pear pie in the fall when the pears are getting ripe," he says. "It's very good to eat by itself, but my family prefers it topped with whipped cream and a little nutmeg."

Jay's reputation as a cook has grown, and friends often call on his expertise for a church or neighborhood pig roast, to cater a party, or to request a recipe.

Jay sees sharing his talents and ideas and growing his own food as more than just a hobby; he says that it's preserving an aspect of Southern heritage. He grew up where people shared a spirit of hard work and giving, and he hopes to pass these qualities on to his children. "It also gives the children a good heritage to know how to become self sufficient, if it becomes necessary," he adds.

STUFFED PORK ROAST

¼ pound bulk pork sausage
2 cups herb-seasoned stuffing mix
1 cup peeled, chopped, tart apple
¾ cup hot water
½ cup diced celery
½ cup raisins
1 tablespoon diced onion
½ teaspoon salt
½ teaspoon sage
⅛ teaspoon pepper
1 (4- to 6-pound) boneless, rolled pork loin roast
½ teaspoon salt, divided
½ teaspoon pepper, divided
½ teaspoon ground coriander, divided
6 slices bacon
1 (10-ounce) jar cherry preserves
2 tablespoons orange marmalade
Fresh watercress
Orange twists
Cherry tomatoes
Concord grapes

Cook sausage until slightly pink; drain well. Combine sausage and next 9 ingredients; set aside.

Separate pork into two pieces, and sprinkle flat sides with ¼ teaspoon each of salt, pepper, and coriander. Spoon stuffing mixture lengthwise over one piece of pork. Top with remaining pork; turn under ends. Tie securely with heavy string at 2- to 3-inch intervals. Sprinkle outside with remaining ¼ teaspoon each of salt, pepper, and coriander. Place roast in a lightly greased shallow roasting pan. Place bacon lengthwise over roast. Insert meat thermometer into thickest part of roast.

Bake roast at 325° for 1 hour. Remove bacon. Combine cherry preserves and orange marmalade; stir well. Brush roast with preserve mixture. Bake an additional 30 minutes to 1½ hours (30 to 35 minutes per pound) or until meat thermometer registers 170°, basting often. Place roast on a bed of watercress; garnish with orange twists, cherry tomatoes, and Concord grapes. Yield: 10 to 12 servings.

SOUTHERN SWEET POTATO BAKE

8 medium-size sweet potatoes
Vegetable oil
1 egg, beaten
1 (8-ounce) can crushed pineapple, drained
⅓ cup firmly packed brown sugar
½ cup chopped pecans
3 tablespoons butter or margarine
2 tablespoons grated orange or lemon rind
1 teaspoon salt
1 teaspoon ground cinnamon
½ teaspoon vanilla extract
Pecan halves

Wash sweet potatoes, and rub with vegetable oil. Bake at 375° for 1 hour or until done.

Slice away skin from top of each potato; carefully scoop out pulp, leaving shells intact. Mash pulp; add remaining ingredients except pecan halves, and mix well. Spoon potato mixture into shells. Place on baking sheet, and top with pecan halves. Bake at 375° for 20 minutes. Yield: 8 servings.

Tip: When buying sweet potatoes, select well-shaped, firm potatoes with smooth, bright colored skins. Avoid those with cuts and holes.

SQUASH À L'ORANGE

1 cup sliced carrots
1 cup orange juice
2 leaves fresh mint, chopped
¼ cup olive oil
1½ pounds small yellow squash, sliced
1 pound small zucchini, sliced
½ cup chopped onion
1 cup diced celery
Salt and pepper to taste
¼ cup almond slices, toasted
Orange slices
Fresh mint sprigs

Place carrots, orange juice, mint, and oil in a large saucepan. Bring to a boil; cover, reduce heat, and simmer 5 minutes. Add yellow squash, zucchini, onion, and celery; cover and simmer 5 to 8 minutes or until vegetables are crisp-tender. Uncover and cook over high heat 2 to 3 minutes to reduce liquid; add salt and pepper. Transfer to serving dish; sprinkle almonds over top. Garnish with orange slices and mint sprigs. Yield: 8 servings.

TENNESSEE PEAR PIE

Pastry for double-crust 9-inch pie
4 large pears, peeled, cored, and thinly sliced
1 cup water
¾ cup sugar
2 tablespoons cornstarch
½ teaspoon ground nutmeg
½ teaspoon ground cinnamon
½ teaspoon ground allspice
2 tablespoons honey
1 tablespoon lemon juice
2 tablespoons butter or margarine, melted
1 tablespoon sugar
Whipped cream (optional)
Ground nutmeg (optional)

Roll half of pastry to ⅛-inch thickness on a lightly floured surface; fit into a 9-inch pieplate.

Combine pears and water in a saucepan over high heat. Bring water to a boil, reduce heat, and simmer 10 minutes. Drain, reserving ½ cup liquid; set pears and liquid aside.

Combine ¾ cup sugar, cornstarch, and spices in a large mixing bowl. Combine reserved pear, liquid, honey, and lemon juice, mixing well; stir into sugar mixture. Add cooked pears, stirring well to coat; pour pear mixture into pastry shell.

Roll out remaining pastry to ⅛-inch thickness, and place over filling. Trim edges; seal and flute. Cut slits to allow steam to escape. Brush top of pie evenly with butter; sprinkle with 1 tablespoon sugar. Bake at 425° for 30 to

35 minutes. (Cover edges with foil to prevent overbrowning, if necessary.) Serve warm or cool. Top slices with whipped cream and nutmeg, if desired. Yield: one 9-inch pie.

Serving The Unusual

When the weather's nice, Chip and Mary Cox begin their dinner parties with drinks on the front porch of their Victorian home. Despite the nostalgic setting, this couple's style of entertaining is anything but traditional. For openers, guests sip—not mint juleps—but Cajun martinis, a concoction of gin with a splash of jalapeño juice and a slice of jalapeño. Chip says, "The secret is chilling the gin and the martini glasses beforehand; they must be ice cold, or it just doesn't work."

After a round of Cajun martinis, everyone gathers in the kitchen around the large cooking island, and they all have a hand in preparing Coconut-Beer Shrimp. Chip has all the ingredients ready, including the Spicy Orange Dip. It's ladled out as soon as the first shrimp are cooked so the appetizers can be enjoyed while they're hot.

Although their dinner parties are basically informal, Chip and Mary like to serve the main course in the graciously appointed dining room. There the menu features Fillets With Horseradish Sauce and Curried Bananas along with a mixed green salad and hot bread.

After the meal, the group moves to the living room for coffee and dessert. Chip serves French Bread Pudding warm from the oven and topped with Brown Sugar-Rum Sauce. It's an appropriate finale for an unusual menu.

COCONUT-BEER SHRIMP

1 pound medium-size fresh shrimp
2¼ teaspoons red pepper
1⅛ teaspoons salt
1 teaspoon pepper
¾ teaspoon paprika
½ teaspoon garlic powder
½ teaspoon onion powder
½ teaspoon ground thyme
½ teaspoon ground oregano
¾ cup plus 2 tablespoons all-purpose flour
¼ cup plus 2 tablespoons beer
1 egg, beaten
½ teaspoon baking powder
1 (7-ounce) package flaked coconut
Vegetable oil
Spicy Orange Dip

Peel and devein shrimp, leaving tails on; rinse well, and set aside.

Combine seasonings in a small bowl, mixing well; set aside. Combine flour, beer, egg, and baking powder in a medium bowl; mix well.

Dip shrimp into seasoning mixture; shake off excess mixture. Dip seasoned shrimp into beer batter; dredge batter-coated shrimp in coconut. Fry shrimp, 5 or 6 at a time, in deep, hot oil (350°) about 45 seconds on each side or until shrimp are golden brown. Drain shrimp on paper towels, and serve immediately with Spicy Orange Dip. Yield: 8 appetizer servings.

Spicy Orange Dip:

1 (10-ounce) jar orange marmalade
3 tablespoons prepared horseradish
3 tablespoons spicy brown mustard
½ teaspoon grated lemon rind

Combine all ingredients in a small bowl; mix well. Yield: 1¼ cups.

FILLETS WITH HORSERADISH SAUCE AND CURRIED BANANAS

1½ teaspoons salt
1½ teaspoons pepper
1 teaspoon garlic powder
⅛ teaspoon paprika
Pinch of red pepper
8 (1- to 1½-inch-thick) beef tenderloin steaks
3 tablespoons green jalapeño sauce
1 cup whipping cream
1 (6-ounce) bottle prepared horseradish
Pinch of salt
Pinch of white pepper
1 cup butter or margarine, divided
8 small bananas
½ to ¾ teaspoon curry powder
Cherry tomato halves (optional)
Parsley (optional)

Combine 1½ teaspoons salt, 1½ teaspoons pepper, garlic powder, paprika, and red pepper in a small bowl; mix well, and set aside. Brush steaks with jalapeño sauce, and sprinkle each steak with ½ teaspoon seasoning mixture. Let steaks stand at room temperature for 30 minutes.

Bring whipping cream to a boil in a small saucepan; reduce heat, and simmer 10 minutes or until cream has been reduced to ⅔ cup. Stir in horseradish and a pinch of salt and pepper; cook until thoroughly heated. Set sauce aside, and keep warm.

Melt 2 tablespoons butter in a large heavy skillet. Cook half the steaks in skillet over medium-high heat about 5 minutes on each side or until steaks reach desired degree of doneness. Repeat with an additional 2 tablespoons butter and remaining steaks. (Steaks may also be grilled over hot coals 5 to 7 minutes on each side or until meat reaches desired degree of doneness.)

Melt remaining ¾ cup butter in a 13- x 9- x 2-inch baking dish. Peel bananas, and slice in half lengthwise. Place bananas in butter, turning to coat each side. Sprinkle banana halves with curry powder, and bake at 350° for 3 to 5 minutes or until slightly soft.

To serve, spoon a heaping tablespoon horseradish sauce on each plate. Place steaks on top of sauce, and add two banana halves to each plate. Garnish with cherry tomato halves and parsley, if desired. Yield: 8 servings.

FRENCH BREAD PUDDING

½ cup chopped pecans
½ cup butter or margarine, softened
1 cup sugar
4 eggs
1¾ cups milk
1½ teaspoons ground cinnamon
1½ teaspoons freshly grated nutmeg
1½ teaspoons vanilla extract
5 cups (1-inch) French bread cubes
⅓ cup raisins
Brown Sugar-Rum Sauce
Freshly grated nutmeg (optional)

Spread pecans on a baking sheet; bake at 350° for 8 minutes or until slightly roasted. Set aside.

Cream butter; gradually add sugar, beating well. Add eggs, and beat well. Stir in milk, cinnamon, 1½ teaspoons nutmeg, and vanilla, mixing well. Stir in pecans, bread cubes, and raisins, stirring just until bread is moistened. Spoon into a greased 8-inch square baking dish. Let stand at room temperature 15 minutes. Cover and bake at 350° for 45 minutes; uncover and bake 10 minutes. Serve warm or cold with Brown Sugar-Rum Sauce. Sprinkle with nutmeg, if desired. Yield: 8 servings.

Brown Sugar-Rum Sauce:

1 egg, separated
3 tablespoons brown sugar, divided
½ cup whipping cream
1 tablespoon rum

Beat egg yolk until thick and lemon colored; add 1 tablespoon brown sugar, and beat well. Set aside.

Beat egg white (at room temperature) until foamy; gradually add remaining brown sugar, and beat until soft peaks form. Fold egg yolk mixture into beaten egg whites; set aside.

Beat whipping cream until soft peaks form; stir in rum. Fold whipped cream into egg mixture. Cover and store in refrigerator up to 4 hours. Yield: 1 cup.

Note: To prepare bread pudding a day in advance, cover and refrigerate overnight after spooning into baking dish. Let pudding stand at room temperature 30 minutes before baking.

Bring Autumn's Flavors To The Table

The air is crisp and the leaves are changing, heralding autumn's harvest. Roadside stands, fresh-air markets, and produce counters are awash with the deep, rich hues of fall—pumpkin orange, cranberry, apple red, and the green and rose of blushing, two-toned pears. Pecans and peanuts add browns and muted golds.

It's a sure sign of autumn when homemade signs advertising "Boil'd p-nuts" appear along sides of highways. Boiling is only one way to enjoy this Southern crop; roasting nuts in or out of the shell turns them into crunchy snacks with a toasted flavor.

To roast them at home, spread the peanuts one or two layers deep in a large shallow pan. Bake at 300° for 30 to 45 minutes. Shell a few after 30 minutes, and test for doneness. The skins should slip off easily, and the nuts should be a toasted beige color. If the nuts are already shelled, roast at 300° for 30 to 45 minutes.

Whether you call them "PEE cans" or "p'KAHNS," these tasty tree-grown nuts find their way into everything from appetizers to desserts. In our test kitchens, we found that toasting pecans before using them in sauces, pies, candies, and other recipes added a richer flavor. To toast pecans, spread the nuts in a shallow pan and bake at 400° for 5 to 8 minutes. If the recipe calls for chopped pecans, chop before toasting.

Even though you can enjoy apples all year, you'll find their flavor is best this time of year. For a fresh dessert, try our recipe for Old English Caramel Apples. Chunks of fresh apples are drizzled with a rich caramel-pecan sauce. Select eating varieties, such as Red or Golden Delicious or Jonathan, for the sweetest, juiciest apple. For Maple-Baked Apples, you'll find that cooking varieties, such as Rome Beauty, York Imperial, or Stayman, will provide a good texture after baking.

When you're looking for a quick entrée, you'll want to keep some fresh Cranberry-Pear Relish in the refrigerator. We enjoyed it cold over a slice of chilled ham for a colorful, fruity-tasting sauce. It can be used to baste ham during the last few minutes of baking.

You may have heard oldtimers say that persimmons just aren't any good until after the first frost. Whether the saying is true or not, it's important to be certain the golden orange fruit is soft and ripe before using. You can speed ripening by storing in a paper bag with apples for a few days. Use one apple for every six persimmons. Traditionally, persimmons have been used and enjoyed most in desserts.

For more information about selecting and cooking persimmons, pumpkins, and pears, see "From Our Kitchen to Yours" on page 233.

OLD ENGLISH CARAMEL APPLES

½ cup sugar
½ cup firmly packed brown sugar
1 tablespoon cornstarch
½ cup half-and-half
½ cup butter or margarine
¼ cup chopped pecans, toasted
½ teaspoon vanilla extract
3 medium apples

Combine sugar and cornstarch in a medium saucepan. Gradually stir in half-and-half and butter; mix well. Cook over medium heat, stirring constantly. Bring to a boil; boil 1 minute. Stir in pecans and vanilla; cool 15 minutes. Core and cube apples; place in individual serving bowls. Pour ¼ cup sauce mixture over each apple serving. Yield: 6 servings. *Mrs. James L. Twilley, Macon, Georgia.*

MAPLE BAKED APPLES

2 medium-size cooking apples
2 tablespoons raisins
2 tablespoons chopped pecans
½ teaspoon ground cinnamon
½ cup maple syrup
2 tablespoons butter or margarine, divided
¼ cup water

Core apples; peel top third of each. Place apples in a shallow baking dish. Combine raisins, pecans, and cinnamon; fill cavities of apples with mixture. Pour maple syrup over apples; top each with 1 tablespoon butter. Pour water into bottom of dish. Cover and bake at 350° for 45 to 50 minutes. Yield: 2 servings. *Shirley Draper, Winter Park, Florida.*

APPLE RINGS

1½ cups all-purpose flour
½ teaspoon salt
½ cup shortening
4 to 5 tablespoons ice water
4 to 6 apples, peeled, cored, and shredded
¾ cup sugar
¼ cup firmly packed brown sugar
½ cup butter or margarine, melted
2 cups water
Ground cinnamon
Whipped cream or ice cream (optional)

Combine flour and salt in a mixing bowl; cut in shortening with a pastry blender until mixture resembles coarse meal. Sprinkle ice water evenly over surface; stir with a fork until dry ingredients are moistened. Shape into a ball; chill 1 hour. Roll dough out onto a lightly floured surface to a 12- x 8-inch rectangle. Spread apples on top of dough, leaving a ½-inch margin. Roll up jellyroll fashion, starting at long side. Pinch seams and ends together. Slice into 1½-inch rings. Set aside.

Combine sugar, butter, and 2 cups water in a 12- x 8- x 2-inch baking dish; bake at 400° until mixture is hot and bubbly. Place apple rings in mixture, and sprinkle with cinnamon. Bake at 400° for 45 minutes. Serve with whipped cream or ice cream, if desired. Yield: 8 servings. *Marie Harris, Sevierville, Tennessee.*

Tip: Bent or dented measuring utensils give inaccurate measures. Use only standard measuring cups and spoons that are in good condition.

CRANBERRY-PEAR RELISH

1 orange, unpeeled
1 lemon, unpeeled
2 fresh pears, unpeeled
4 cups fresh cranberries
2 cups sugar
1 teaspoon ground ginger

Position knife blade in food processor bowl. Quarter orange and lemon, remove seeds, and place fruit in processor. Pulse 2 times. Quarter pears; add to processor, and pulse until fruit is coarsely ground. Transfer ground fruit to a large mixing bowl. Set aside. Place cranberries in processor bowl; pulse until coarsely ground.

Add cranberries and remaining ingredients to fruit mixture; mix well. Chill. Store in an airtight container in refrigerator. Yield: 1½ quarts.

Kathleen Stone, Houston, Texas.

BAKED PEAR MERINGUES

3 large Anjou pears, peeled, halved lengthwise, and cored
¼ cup plus 2 tablespoons sugar, divided
1 tablespoon grated lemon rind, divided
¼ cup lemon juice
2 egg whites
⅛ teaspoon cream of tartar
Pinch of salt
¼ cup plus 2 tablespoons sifted powdered sugar
¼ teaspoon almond extract

Place pears cut side up in a 12- x 8- x 2-inch baking dish. Sprinkle each pear half with 1 tablespoon sugar and ½ teaspoon lemon rind. Pour lemon juice over pears. Cover and bake at 300° for 25 minutes. Baste and continue baking 20 minutes. Put pear halves in a lightly greased 8-inch square baking dish, reserving liquid.

Beat egg whites (at room temperature) at high speed of an electric mixer until foamy. Sprinkle cream of tartar and salt over egg whites; continue beating until soft peaks form. Gradually add powdered sugar, 1 tablespoon at a time, beating until stiff peaks form (2 to 4 minutes). Stir in almond extract.

Spread meringue over each pear half, mounding the meringue in center and smoothing to edges of each half. Bake at 300° for 10 to 15 minutes or until golden brown.

Cook reserved liquid in a small saucepan until thickened. Pour syrup over warm pears. Serve at room temperature. Yield: 6 servings. *Carrie Bartlett, Gallatin, Tennessee.*

PERSIMMON-RAISIN COOKIES

½ cup butter or margarine, softened
1 cup sugar
1 egg
1½ cups all-purpose flour
½ teaspoon ground cinnamon
½ teaspoon ground nutmeg
¼ teaspoon ground cloves
¼ teaspoon salt
1 cup persimmon pulp
1 teaspoon baking soda
1 cup raisins
1 cup chopped pecans

Cream butter; gradually add sugar, beating well. Add egg, and beat well.

Combine flour, spices, and salt; add to creamed mixture, mixing well. Combine persimmon pulp and soda; stir well, and add to creamed mixture. Stir in raisins and pecans.

Drop dough by level tablespoonfuls onto greased cookie sheets. Bake at 350° for 12 to 15 minutes or until done. Yield: 3 dozen. *Mary Mays, Lebanon, Kentucky.*

HARVEST PUMPKIN LOAF

½ cup butter or margarine, softened
1 cup sugar
2 eggs
1¾ cups all-purpose flour
1 teaspoon baking soda
½ teaspoon salt
1 teaspoon ground cinnamon
½ teaspoon ground nutmeg
¼ teaspoon ground ginger
¼ teaspoon ground cloves
¾ cup cooked, mashed pumpkin
¾ cup semisweet chocolate morsels
¾ cup chopped pecans, divided
Glaze (recipe follows)

Cream butter; gradually add sugar, beating well. Add eggs, one at a time, beating well after each addition.

Combine flour, soda, salt, and spices; add to creamed mixture alternately with pumpkin, beginning and ending with flour mixture. Stir in chocolate morsels and ½ cup pecans. Spoon mixture into a 9- x 5- x 3-inch greased and floured loafpan. Sprinkle top with remaining pecans. Bake at 350° for 1 hour and 5 minutes or until a wooden pick inserted in center comes out clean. Cool in pan 10 minutes; remove from pan, and cool on a wire rack. Drizzle top of loaf with glaze. Yield: 1 loaf.

Glaze:

½ cup sifted powdered sugar
1 tablespoon half-and-half
⅛ teaspoon ground nutmeg
⅛ teaspoon ground cinnamon

Combine all ingredients, stirring until smooth. Yield: ¼ cup.

Frances Robison,
Mobile, Alabama.

PUMPKIN-PECAN PIE

4 eggs, slightly beaten
2 cups cooked, mashed pumpkin
1 cup sugar
½ cup dark corn syrup
1 teaspoon vanilla extract
½ teaspoon ground cinnamon
¼ teaspoon salt
1 unbaked 9-inch pastry shell
1 cup chopped pecans
Orange rind strips
Pecan halves

Combine eggs, pumpkin, sugar, syrup, vanilla, cinnamon, and salt in a medium bowl; stir until well blended. Pour into pastry shell; sprinkle with pecans. Bake at 350° for 1 hour and 10 minutes or until pie is firm in center. Let cool completely. Before serving, garnish with orange rind strips and pecan halves. Yield: one 9-inch pie.

Evelyn Milam,
Knoxville, Tennessee.

ROASTED PECAN CLUSTERS

3 tablespoons butter or margarine
3 cups pecan pieces
¾ pound (6 squares) chocolate or almond bark

Melt butter in a 15- x 10- x 1-inch jellyroll pan. Spread pecans evenly in pan. Bake at 300° for 30 minutes, stirring every 10 minutes.

Melt bark squares in top of a double boiler; remove from heat, and stir until smooth. Cool 2 minutes; add pecans, and stir until well coated. Drop by rounded teaspoonfuls onto waxed paper. Before serving, let cool completely. Yield: about 3½ dozen.

Margaret Haegelin,
Hondo, Texas.

PEANUT DIVINITY

2½ cups sugar
½ cup light corn syrup
½ cup water
2 egg whites
1 teaspoon orange extract
1 cup unsalted roasted peanuts

Combine sugar, syrup, and water in a heavy saucepan; cook mixture over low heat, stirring constantly, until sugar dissolves. Cook over high heat, without stirring, until mixture reaches hard ball stage (260°).

Beat egg whites (at room temperature) in a large mixing bowl until stiff peaks form. Pour hot sugar mixture in a very thin stream over egg whites while beating constantly at high speed of an electric mixer. Add orange extract, and continue beating 3 to 4 minutes until mixture holds its shape. Stir in 1 cup unsalted peanuts.

Quickly drop mixture by heaping teaspoonfuls onto waxed paper. Cool. Yield: about 4 dozen.

Lois Cavenaugh,
Tifton, Georgia.

From Our Kitchen To Yours

It's the peak season for persimmons, pumpkins, and pears, so we're offering a variety of recipes using them in "Bring Autumn's Flavors to the Table," beginning on page 231. And to help you make the most of these popular fall fruits, here is additional information on selection, storage, and preparation.

Persimmons

Persimmons need to be fully ripened before they're eaten, or they will have a bitter flavor. When they're ready to eat, they will be soft and a little darker in color. Because persimmons are very perishable, you'll need to freeze them or keep them refrigerated and use within several days after ripening.

Before using persimmons, just wash and drain; soaking them may cause a loss of flavor. If you need persimmon pulp, as in the Persimmon-Raisin Cookies on page 232, just cut the skin of each persimmon and push it back to show the pulp. Scoop the pulp out with a small spoon, discarding the skin, seeds, and stem. Use a blender or food mill to puree the pulp.

Persimmons can be frozen either whole or pureed, although freezing may cause some loss in flavor. If you're freezing pureed persimmons, add 1 tablespoon lemon juice for every 2 cups of puree. Fill the storage container up to 1 inch from the top, leaving some room for the fruit to expand. To freeze slices of persimmons, use a sugar syrup and lemon juice to cover the fruit.

Pumpkins

When you're buying a pumpkin to eat, remember the biggest may not be the best. Smaller pumpkins usually have more tender and edible flesh. Look for a pumpkin with a bright orange color and an attached stem. If the stem is off, the inside may dry out and rot.

To prepare a fresh pumpkin for cooking, first slice in half crosswise and remove seeds. Put the halves, cut side down, on a jellyroll pan, and bake at 325° for 45 minutes or until the pumpkin is tender. When it's cool, just remove the peeling and mash the pulp. A 5-pound pumpkin will yield about 4½ cups of cooked, mashed pulp. If you're using a microwave, peel and cut the pumpkin into 1½- to 2-inch chunks. Then place chunks in a baking dish; cover and microwave at HIGH 8 minutes or until tender.

You'll find that pumpkins aren't as perishable as persimmons; they'll keep about 1 to 2 months at room temperature and as long as 3 months if refrigerated. If pumpkins are frozen after they have been cubed or pureed, they should last up to 6 months.

Pears

When choosing pears, avoid bruised, blemished, and hard ones. The skin should not be shriveled or dull looking.

Pears will have better flavor and texture when they're allowed to ripen off the tree. To test for ripeness, press gently at the stem end of the pear; it should give to gentle pressure. When judging ripeness of a pear, you can't go by its color, because the color varies with variety. If pears need to be ripened at home, let them sit at room temperature for a few days until ripe. To speed up the ripening process, place pears in a paper sack.

When cooking with pears, use firm ones that are slightly underripe. If you peel or cut pears, brush with lemon juice to prevent browning.

Versatile Round Steak

Round steak is the ideal cut of meat to serve when you're watching the budget. It's versatile and flavorful, as well as very tender when cooked properly.

For Marinated Beef on a Stick, the meat is cut into thin strips and marinated overnight to tenderize tough fibers. Pounding the meat with a mallet before cooking, as is done in Oven Swiss Steak, also makes it more tender.

The moist-heat method of cooking is the secret to Beef Roulades. In this recipe, tiny beef bundles simmer with consomme and herbs until the meat is tender and flavorful.

OVEN SWISS STEAK

1½ pounds boneless round steak
2 tablespoons all-purpose flour
¼ teaspoon salt
¼ cup vegetable oil
2 tablespoons all-purpose flour
1 (16-ounce) can tomatoes, undrained and chopped
½ cup chopped celery
½ cup chopped carrots
½ cup chopped onion
½ teaspoon soy sauce

Pound steak to ¼-inch thickness; cut into serving-size pieces.

Combine 2 tablespoons flour and salt. Dredge steak in flour mixture; brown in hot oil in a large skillet. Remove from skillet, and place in a lightly greased 13- x 9- x 2-inch baking dish; set aside.

Add 2 tablespoons flour to pan drippings; cook over medium heat 1 minute, stirring constantly. Add tomatoes, celery, carrots, and onion; cook until thickened, stirring constantly. Stir in soy sauce. Pour mixture over steak. Cover and bake at 350° for 1 hour and 15 minutes or until steak is tender. Yield: 6 servings.
Cindy Murphy,
Cleveland, Tennessee.

MARINATED BEEF ON A STICK

1½ pounds boneless round steak
½ cup soy sauce
2 tablespoons olive oil
2 tablespoons honey
2 tablespoons wine vinegar
1 clove garlic, minced
½ teaspoon ground ginger
⅛ teaspoon pepper
Hot cooked parslied rice (optional)

Partially freeze steak; slice into 4- x ¼-inch strips, and set aside.

Combine remaining ingredients except rice in a shallow dish; add steak, stirring to coat. Cover and marinate overnight in the refrigerator.

Remove steak from marinade. Using 7-inch skewers, thread 3 to 4 pieces of steak on each skewer. Place on grill over hot coals. Cook 2 to 3 minutes on each side or to desired degree of doneness, basting frequently with marinade. Serve on bed of rice, if desired. Yield: 6 to 8 servings or 20 appetizer servings.
Mrs. David A. Gibson,
Martin, Tennessee.

BEEF PARMIGIANA

1½ pounds boneless round steak
⅓ cup fine, dry breadcrumbs
⅓ cup grated Parmesan cheese
1 egg, well beaten
2 to 3 tablespoons vegetable oil
1 medium onion, chopped
1 (6-ounce) can tomato paste
2 cups water
½ teaspoon ground marjoram
½ teaspoon salt
¼ teaspoon pepper
3 (6- x 3-inch) slices mozzarella cheese, halved

Pound steak to ¼-inch thickness; cut into 6 serving-size pieces. Combine breadcrumbs and Parmesan cheese. Dip steak in egg, and coat with breadcrumb mixture.

Brown steak in hot oil in a large skillet. Remove from skillet, and place in a lightly greased 13- x 9- x 2-inch baking dish; set aside.

Add onion to pan drippings; sauté until tender, adding more oil, if necessary. Add tomato paste, water, marjoram, salt, and pepper. Bring to a boil. Cook, uncovered, 5 minutes, stirring frequently; pour over steak. Cover and bake at 350° for 50 minutes. Remove from oven; uncover and place a slice of cheese on each piece of steak. Return to oven; bake 10 minutes or just until cheese melts. Yield: 6 servings.
Kathryn Di Fiore,
Cary, North Carolina.

BEEF ROULADES

1½ pounds boneless round steak
4 slices bacon
2 tablespoons butter or margarine
1 medium onion, sliced
1 (10½-ounce) can beef consommé, undiluted
1 bay leaf
1 teaspoon minced fresh parsley
¼ teaspoon pepper
1½ tablespoons all-purpose flour
1½ tablespoons water
Hot cooked noodles

Pound steak to ¼-inch thickness; cut into 12 (4- x 1½-inch) pieces. Cut each bacon slice into 3 equal pieces. Lay a piece of bacon in center of each piece of steak. Roll up tightly, and secure with a wooden pick. Set aside.

Melt butter in a Dutch oven; add steak and brown on all sides. Remove steak, and set aside. Add onion to pan drippings, and sauté until tender. Add steak, consommé, bay leaf, parsley, and pepper. Cover and simmer 45 minutes or until tender. Remove bay leaf.

Combine flour and water, stirring until smooth. Gradually stir flour mixture into steak mixture; cook until thickened. Serve over hot cooked noodles. Remove wooden picks before serving. Yield: 4 servings. *Jane Cleary,*
Burlington, North Carolina.

COOKING LIGHT®

Enjoy Starchy Vegetables On Your Diet

Potatoes, corn, and peas grace the tables of most Southerners as frequently as iced tea. But lately, since many individuals are in a battle to lose weight, these vegetables may not appear on the menu as often as in the past. You've probably heard that they are fattening.

The truth is that you don't have to shun starchy vegetables while everyone else enjoys them. These foods have a lot fewer calories than most dieters think. For example, one ounce of plain baked potato has only one-third the calories of the same amount of broiled lean T-bone steak. Adding lots of butter, sour cream, other fats, or sugar to starchy vegetables is what makes them so high in calories. But when you are aware of these limits, you can say "pass the potatoes" with a clear conscience at your next diet meal.

Starchy vegetables are nutritious, and smart cooking and seasoning makes them delicious. Complex carbohydrates, they are good sources of energy and dietary fiber. In addition, some of these vegetables, such as beans and peas, are good sources of protein, calcium, and iron. Others, such as sweet potatoes and winter squash, contain high amounts of vitamin A.

Stuffed baked potatoes and baked potatoes with toppings are a current food trend here in the South. But most dieters wouldn't think of indulging in such a high-calorie craze. We offer a solution with our Vegetable-Topped Stuffed Potatoes. They're filled with flavor instead of calories, and a tangy marinated vegetable topping helps keep the potatoes at a surprisingly low 170 calories per serving.

Our Scalloped Potatoes and Turnips recipe uses skim milk and part-skim mozzarella cheese to add flavor with fewer calories than the whole milk and Cheddar cheese commonly used. Sliced turnips, green pepper, and pimiento perk up the taste and texture. At only 101 calories per serving, this casserole is sure to please, especially when it's served with lean ham or pork chops.

The rich color and flavor of Sweet Potato Puff may fool you. It's similar in taste to a traditional sweet potato casserole, but without the hundreds of extra calories hidden in sugar, butter, nuts, and coconut. Instead, orange juice and a minimal amount of margarine and sugar make up the dish. Accent it with vanilla butter-and-nut flavoring or coconut extract.

SCALLOPED POTATOES AND TURNIPS

2 cups peeled, thinly sliced potatoes
2 cups peeled, thinly sliced turnips
Vegetable cooking spray
¼ cup chopped green pepper
¼ cup chopped onion
1 (2-ounce) jar diced pimiento, drained
¼ teaspoon salt
¼ teaspoon white pepper
2 tablespoons chopped fresh parsley, divided
¾ cup skim milk
½ cup (2 ounces) shredded mozzarella cheese
1 tablespoon seasoned breadcrumbs

Combine potatoes and turnips; layer half of mixture in a 1¾-quart baking dish coated with cooking spray.

Combine green pepper, onion, pimiento, salt, pepper, 1 tablespoon parsley, and milk; stir until blended. Pour half of mixture over potatoes and turnips; repeat layers. Top with cheese. Cover and bake at 350° for 45 minutes.

Combine breadcrumbs and remaining 1 tablespoon parsley; sprinkle over vegetable mixture. Bake, uncovered, an additional 15 minutes or until vegetables are tender. Yield: 6 servings (about 101 calories per serving). *Lisa Lindsey, Daytona Beach, Florida.*

VEGETABLE-TOPPED STUFFED POTATOES

6 small baking potatoes (about 2 pounds)
⅔ cup chopped onion
⅔ cup coarsely shredded radishes
⅔ cup unpeeled, chopped cucumber
2 tablespoons rice or cider vinegar
½ teaspoon dried whole dillweed
1 cup plain, low-fat yogurt
¼ cup plus 2 tablespoons grated Parmesan cheese
¼ cup skim milk
½ teaspoon butter-flavored salt
½ teaspoon white pepper

Scrub potatoes; bake at 400° for 50 to 60 minutes or until done. Combine onion, radishes, cucumber, vinegar, and dillweed, tossing well; set aside.

Allow potatoes to cool to touch. Cut a 1-inch strip lengthwise from top of each potato; carefully scoop pulp from shell. Reserve shells.

Mash potato pulp with a fork; add yogurt, cheese, milk, salt, and pepper, stirring well. Stuff potato mixture into potato shells. Bake at 375° for 10 to 12 minutes or until thoroughly heated. Top with vegetable mixture. Yield: 6 servings (about 170 calories per serving).

SWEET POTATO PUFF

2½ to 3 pounds unpeeled sweet potatoes
½ cup unsweetened orange juice
1 tablespoon margarine, melted
1 tablespoon sugar
¼ teaspoon vanilla butter-and-nut flavoring or coconut extract
⅛ teaspoon grated orange rind
⅛ teaspoon pumpkin pie spice
2 eggs, separated

Cook sweet potatoes in boiling water 20 to 25 minutes or until tender. Let cool to touch; peel and mash with a fork. Combine 3 cups mashed potatoes and remaining ingredients except eggs, stirring well.

Beat egg yolks until thick and lemon colored; stir into potato mixture.

Beat egg whites (at room temperature) until stiff, but not dry. Gently fold into potato mixture. Spoon into an ungreased 1-quart soufflé dish.

Bake at 375° for 40 minutes or until puffed and lightly browned. Serve immediately. Yield: 6 servings (about 204 calories per serving).

FRUITED ACORN SQUASH

1 small acorn squash (about 1 pound)
¾ cup unpeeled, chopped cooking apple
¼ cup chopped orange sections
1 tablespoon unsweetened orange juice
2 teaspoons brown sugar
2 teaspoons reduced-calorie margarine, melted

Cut squash in half lengthwise; remove seeds. Place cut side down in a shallow baking pan, and add boiling water to a depth of ½ inch. Cover and bake squash at 350° for 35 minutes. Turn cut side up, and set aside.

Combine remaining ingredients; spoon into squash cavities. Cover and bake an additional 15 minutes. Yield: 2 servings (about 154 calories per serving). *Pati Wilson, Tulsa, Oklahoma.*

TURNIP SALAD

2 large turnips, peeled
1 large cucumber, unpeeled
1 small onion, chopped
2 tablespoons cider vinegar
2 tablespoons vegetable oil
½ to 1 teaspoon dried whole dillweed
⅛ teaspoon salt

Slice turnips into julienne strips (2 x ⅛ inches). Cut cucumber lengthwise into quarters, and slice.

Combine turnips, cucumber, and onion in a medium bowl. Add remaining ingredients, and toss gently. Cover and chill 3 hours. Yield: 8 servings (about 47 calories per serving). *Deborah Newman, Haymarket, Virginia.*

ENGLISH PEA MEDLEY

½ cup water
½ teaspoon chicken-flavored bouillon
  granules
1 (16-ounce) package frozen English peas
⅓ cup sliced green onions
¼ cup thinly sliced celery
⅔ cup sliced mushrooms
1 tablespoon reduced-sodium soy sauce

Bring water to a boil in a saucepan; add bouillon granules, stirring until dissolved. Add peas and remaining ingredients. Bring to a boil; cover, reduce heat, and simmer 5 minutes. Yield: 4 servings (about 100 calories per serving).
Therese M. Golden,
Wheaton, Maryland.

CORN SALAD

1 (16-ounce) package frozen whole
  kernel corn
½ cup plain low-fat yogurt
3 tablespoons reduced-calorie Italian
  salad dressing
1 tablespoon cider vinegar
¼ teaspoon dry mustard
⅛ teaspoon celery salt
⅛ teaspoon white pepper
½ cup sliced mushrooms
⅓ cup unpeeled, chopped cucumber
3 tablespoons thinly sliced green onions
3 tablespoons chopped green pepper
3 tablespoons chopped red pepper

Cook corn according to package directions; drain and cool.
Combine yogurt, salad dressing, vinegar, mustard, salt, and pepper in a medium bowl; mix well. Add corn and remaining ingredients; toss gently. Cover and chill 3 to 4 hours. Yield: 6 servings (about 82 calories per serving).

Halloween Means
A Party

Whether your Halloween party is for little ghosts and goblins or for grown-ups, you'll want to offer your guests some of these festive recipes. They'll be sure to gobble up every bite.
For a Halloween theme, we cut Frosted Cutout Cookies into owls and pumpkins and tinted the frosting brown and orange. You can use strips of licorice, raisins, currants, or sugar sprinkles

to decorate them. Or if you're handy with a decorating bag, the vanilla frosting is thick enough to pipe out any designs you would like.
Guests won't be squeamish about trying our Chocolate Spiders, a tasty mixture of chow mein noodles, peanuts, and chocolate. It's best to keep these flavorful treats chilled until serving time to prevent them from becoming sticky.
Be sure to have plenty of Pizza-Flavored Popcorn on hand for a switch from the traditional sweets. Just stir Parmesan cheese, garlic salt, Italian herb seasoning, and paprika into freshly popped corn for a spicy snack.

FROSTED CUTOUT COOKIES

¾ cup butter or margarine, softened
1 cup sugar
2 eggs
1 tablespoon milk
1 teaspoon vanilla extract
2¾ cups all-purpose flour
1 teaspoon baking powder
½ teaspoon salt
Vanilla frosting (recipe follows)
Black licorice (optional)

Cream butter; gradually add sugar, beating until light and fluffy. Add eggs, milk, and vanilla, beating well. Combine flour, baking powder, and salt; add to creamed mixture, stirring well. Cover and chill at least 4 hours.
Work with one-fourth of dough at a time; store remainder in refrigerator. Place dough on a lightly greased cookie sheet; roll out to ⅛- to ¼-inch thickness. Cut dough with floured cookie cutters, leaving 1 inch between each cookie. Remove excess dough; combine with remaining dough in refrigerator. Repeat rolling and cutting procedure with remaining dough.
Bake at 350° for 8 to 10 minutes. Cool slightly on cookie sheets; remove to wire racks, and cool completely. Spread cookies with vanilla frosting. Decorate with licorice, if desired. Yield: 6 dozen.

Vanilla Frosting:

3 cups sifted powdered sugar
2½ tablespoons milk
2 tablespoons butter or margarine,
  softened
1½ teaspoons vanilla extract
Paste food coloring (optional)

Combine all ingredients except food coloring in mixing bowl; beat until smooth. Stir in food coloring, if desired. Yield: 1⅓ cups.
Barbara S. Dobbs,
Lampasas, Texas.

CHOCOLATE SPIDERS

1½ cups semisweet chocolate morsels
1 (5-ounce) can chow mein noodles
1 cup salted peanuts

Place chocolate morsels in top of double boiler; bring water to a boil. Reduce heat to low; cook until chocolate melts. Add noodles and peanuts, stirring well. Drop chocolate mixture by teaspoonfuls onto greased baking sheets. Refrigerate 8 hours or overnight. Keep chilled until ready to serve. Yield: about 3 dozen.
Mrs. David Curl,
Collierville, Tennessee.

PIZZA-FLAVORED POPCORN

2 tablespoons grated Parmesan cheese
1 teaspoon garlic salt
1 teaspoon Italian herb seasoning
1 teaspoon paprika
3 quarts freshly popped corn, unsalted

Combine Parmesan cheese, garlic salt, herb seasoning, and paprika in a small bowl; mix well. Sprinkle mixture over popcorn, tossing until evenly coated. Store in an airtight container. Yield: 3 quarts.
Mildred Bickley,
Bristol, Virginia.

PINEAPPLE-ORANGE PUNCH

½ gallon orange sherbet
1 (46-ounce) can pineapple juice, chilled
1 (33.8-ounce) bottle ginger ale, chilled
3 cups orange-flavored drink, chilled
3 cups lemon-lime carbonated beverage,
  chilled

Place sherbet in a large punch bowl; add remaining ingredients, and stir well. (Chunks of orange sherbet will remain in the punch.) Yield: 5 quarts.
Lynn Bartlett,
Jacksonville, Florida.

Right: This bountiful buffet was prepared from homegrown food. Stuffed Pork Roast, Squash à l'Orange (left), and Southern Sweet Potato Bake (back) are all special recipes that feature Southern favorites (pages 229 and 230). Colorful cooked vegetable combinations (right), fresh bread, and a selection of homemade pickles and relishes round out this menu.

Above: *Fall flavor is at its best in (left to right) Harvest Pumpkin Loaf, Pumpkin-Pecan Pie, Roasted Pecan Clusters, Peanut Divinity, and Cranberry-Pear Relish. (Recipes begin on page 231.)*

Right: *Serve Chilled Fruit With Dressing (page 222) in individual compotes, and top with pineapple-flavored dressing. Fresh pears and other fruit are tossed with cream sherry and juices for extra flavor.*

Remember Oldtime Sorghum Syrup?

Remember sorghum syrup? This Southern treat, made from the boiled-down juice squeezed from sweet sorghum cane, is used less today than it was fifty years ago now that granulated sugar is so popular. But those who know sorghum's distinct flavor probably recall drizzling it over pancakes and eating it with butter and biscuits.

If you've never had the pleasure of trying this prized syrup, you can look forward to a delicious taste that's slightly stronger than honey, but not as strong as molasses. Here are some new ideas for using and enjoying sorghum syrup down to the very last drop.

Give a lift to beef and vegetables by adding a little sorghum syrup to Brown Stew. Seasoned with lemon, Worcestershire sauce, allspice, garlic, onion, and bay leaves, it's a different way to use the syrup.

Instead of topping your waffles with sorghum syrup, put it in the batter for a change. That's just what we did with Sorghum-Ginger Waffles. Made with buttermilk, these breakfast favorites are topped with warm applesauce.

Besides adding just the right sweet taste, sorghum syrup is a good source of carbohydrate in the diet, and it contains significant amounts of calcium, potassium, and iron. Like honey, it may crystallize as it gets older. To liquefy, loosen the lid and place the container on a rack in a pan of warm water until the crystals disappear.

BROWN STEW

1 (2-pound) boneless chuck roast, cut into
    1-inch cubes
1 tablespoon vegetable oil
1 quart water
2 tablespoons sorghum syrup
1 tablespoon lemon juice
1 tablespoon Worcestershire sauce
1 medium onion, sliced
1 clove garlic, minced
2 bay leaves
1 teaspoon salt
½ teaspoon paprika
½ teaspoon pepper
⅛ teaspoon ground allspice
6 medium carrots, scraped and cut into
    thirds
4 medium potatoes, peeled and quartered
1½ tablespoons cornstarch
1½ tablespoons cold water

Brown meat in hot oil in a large Dutch oven. Stir in 1 quart water, sorghum syrup, lemon juice, Worcestershire sauce, onion, garlic, bay leaves, and seasonings; cover, reduce heat, and simmer 2 hours.

Add carrots and potatoes; cover and cook an additional 20 minutes or until tender. Remove bay leaves.

Combine cornstarch and 1½ tablespoons cold water, stirring until smooth. Gradually add to stew, stirring constantly. Cook, uncovered, until thickened and bubbly, stirring constantly. Yield: about 6½ cups. *Burleen Miller, Boaz, Alabama.*

SORGHUM-GINGER WAFFLES

2 cups all-purpose flour
1 teaspoon baking powder
1 teaspoon baking soda
1 teaspoon ground ginger
2 eggs, separated
½ cup vegetable oil
½ cup sorghum syrup
½ cup buttermilk
Vegetable oil
Warm applesauce

Combine flour, baking powder, soda, and ginger; set aside. Combine egg yolks, ½ cup vegetable oil, sorghum syrup, and buttermilk in a medium mixing bowl. Add dry ingredients, stirring until smooth.

Beat egg whites (at room temperature) until stiff peaks form; gently fold into batter. (Batter will be stiff.)

Brush an 8-inch square waffle iron with vegetable oil; allow to preheat. Pour a heaping cup of batter onto hot waffle iron, spreading batter to edges. Bake about 3 minutes or until steaming stops. Repeat procedure until all the batter is used. Serve with warm applesauce. Yield: 12 (4-inch) waffles.

SORGHUM CAKE

¾ cup shortening
¾ cup sugar
2 eggs
1 cup chunky applesauce
1 cup sorghum syrup
2½ cups all-purpose flour
1½ teaspoons baking soda
1 teaspoon salt
1 teaspoon ground cinnamon
½ teaspoon ground cloves
½ teaspoon ground nutmeg
Frosting (recipe follows)

Cream shortening and sugar until light and fluffy. Add eggs, one at a time, beating after each addition. Add applesauce and sorghum syrup to mixture; beat well.

Combine flour, soda, salt, cinnamon, cloves, and nutmeg; stir into batter. Pour batter into 3 greased and floured 8-inch round cakepans.

Bake at 350° for 20 to 25 minutes or until a wooden pick inserted in center comes out clean. Cool in pans 10 minutes. Remove layers from pans; cool completely on wire racks.

Frost between layers and on top of cake. Yield: one 3-layer cake.

Frosting:

¼ cup butter or margarine, softened
3 cups sifted powdered sugar
3 tablespoons milk

Combine butter and powdered sugar; cream until light and fluffy. Add milk, 1 tablespoon at a time, beating until spreading consistency. Yield: enough for one 3-layer cake. *Mrs. Bob Renfro, Louisville, Kentucky.*

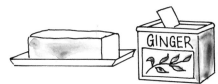

SORGHUM TEA CAKES

1 cup butter or margarine, softened
1 cup sugar
3 eggs
1 cup sorghum syrup
2 tablespoons buttermilk
6 to 6½ cups all-purpose flour
1 teaspoon baking soda
1 teaspoon ground ginger
1 teaspoon ground cloves
1 teaspoon ground cinnamon
Additional sugar

Cream butter; gradually add 1 cup sugar, beating at medium speed of an electric mixer until light and fluffy. Add eggs, one at a time, beating well after each addition. Add sorghum syrup and buttermilk; mix well.

Combine flour, soda, and spices; stir dry ingredients into creamed mixture. Chill 3 hours or overnight.

Roll dough to ¼-inch thickness on a lightly floured board; cut with a 1½-inch cookie cutter.

Place cookies on greased cookie sheets; sprinkle lightly with additional sugar. Bake at 375° for 8 to 10 minutes; cool on wire racks. Yield: 9 dozen.

Katie Harville, Grenada, Mississippi.

Enjoy A Shrimp Entrée

Linda Tompkins's Shrimp Casserole is quickly finding its way onto the dinner tables of many of Linda's friends in Birmingham. Raves and requests for the recipe are common whenever she serves this dish.

If you don't have au gratin dishes, Linda suggests preparing it all in a casserole dish.

SHRIMP CASSEROLE

9 cups water
3 pounds medium-size fresh shrimp
1 tablespoon lemon juice
½ cup chopped green pepper
¼ cup chopped onion
2 tablespoons butter or margarine, melted
1 (10¾-ounce) can cream of celery soup, undiluted
1 cup half-and-half
¼ cup dry sherry
½ teaspoon salt
½ teaspoon white pepper
3 cups cooked rice
Paprika
Fresh parsley sprigs

Bring water to a boil; add shrimp, and cook 3 to 5 minutes. Drain well; rinse with cold water. Chill. Peel and devein shrimp. Set 6 shrimp aside for garnish.

Combine shrimp and lemon juice; set aside. Sauté green pepper and onion in butter in a small skillet until tender.

Combine soup, half-and-half, sherry, salt, and pepper. Stir in shrimp, vegetables, and rice. Spoon into lightly greased individual au gratin dishes. Bake at 350° for 15 to 20 minutes or until bubbly. Garnish with paprika, reserved shrimp, and parsley. Yield: 6 servings.

Get A Headstart On The Salad

Salads add interest to the menu, but they often take a lot of time to assemble. Why not make them in advance?

You probably can't think of make-ahead salads without congealed salads coming to mind. Minted Pineapple

Mold offers cool, sweet flavor that tastes just right with beef or lamb. Lemon-Cheese Salad looks pretty and tastes refreshing served on crisp lettuce leaves.

For advance preparation, marinated salads are a natural choice. Parslied Potato Salad is tossed with lemon juice and oil rather than mayonnaise. Cauliflower Salad, on the other hand, boasts a seasoned dressing that consists of mayonnaise and Italian salad dressing.

PARSLIED POTATO SALAD

4 large potatoes (about 2 pounds)
3 green onions, diced
⅓ to ½ cup chopped fresh parsley
¼ cup olive or vegetable oil
¼ cup lemon juice
1 teaspoon salt
Dash of garlic powder
Dash of pepper

Cook potatoes in boiling water 20 to 25 minutes or until tender. Drain and cool. Peel potatoes, and cut into ½-inch cubes. Combine potatoes, green onions, and parsley in a large bowl.

Combine remaining ingredients; pour over potato mixture, tossing gently. Chill at least 3 hours. Yield: 8 servings. *Nancy Oglesby, Wilmington, Delaware.*

CAULIFLOWER SALAD

1 medium head cauliflower
5 green onions, chopped
3 stalks celery, chopped
¼ cup sliced pimiento-stuffed olives
½ cup chopped green pepper
⅓ cup salad dressing or mayonnaise
⅓ cup commercial Italian salad dressing
1 teaspoon sugar
½ teaspoon salt
¼ teaspoon pepper

Separate cauliflower into flowerets; cut into bite-size pieces. Combine cauliflower, green onions, celery, olives, and green pepper in a large bowl; set aside.

Combine remaining ingredients; mix well, and pour over vegetables. Toss gently; cover and chill 3 to 4 hours. Yield: 8 servings. *Sharon Cotton, Rogersville, Missouri.*

LEMON-CHEESE SALAD

1 (20-ounce) can crushed pineapple, undrained
1 (3-ounce) package lemon-flavored gelatin
1 cup boiling water
½ cup mayonnaise
1½ cups (6 ounces) shredded sharp Cheddar cheese
Lettuce leaves (optional)

Drain pineapple, reserving juice. Add enough water to juice to make ¾ cup; set aside. Dissolve gelatin in 1 cup boiling water; stir in pineapple juice mixture. Beat in mayonnaise with a wire whisk, stirring until lumps are removed. Stir in pineapple and cheese; pour into an 8-inch square dish. Chill. Serve on lettuce leaves, if desired. Yield: 9 servings. *Laura Hartman, College Station, Texas.*

MINTED PINEAPPLE MOLD

1 (20-ounce) can crushed pineapple, undrained
1 envelope unflavored gelatin
⅓ cup mint-flavored apple jelly
1 cup whipping cream
1 teaspoon powdered sugar

Drain pineapple, reserving ½ cup juice. Soften gelatin in juice in a small saucepan; cook over medium heat, stirring constantly, until gelatin dissolves. Remove from heat. Add jelly; stir until melted. Stir in pineapple; chill until consistency of unbeaten egg white.

Combine whipping cream and powdered sugar; beat until stiff peaks form. Fold into gelatin mixture; spoon into a lightly oiled 5-cup mold. Chill until firm. Yield: 8 servings.
Perle J. Caldwell, Knoxville, Tennessee.

Tip: To serve a congealed salad, invert the mold on a serving dish; then wrap the mold with a hot towel. The salad will slip out easily.

Southerners Keep Cooking In Cast Iron

In the South, a legacy of crisp-crusted cornbread, thin-layered stack cakes, and crunchy fried chicken is enough to keep at least one piece of cast-iron cookware in even the most sophisticated cook's kitchen. And more than likely, the skillet, corn stick pan, or Dutch oven has been handed down from generation to generation—still slick on the inside from years of use and seasoning.

The heavy coal-black utensils can reach a high heat and hold it, which results in the characteristic brown crust on cornbread baked in cast iron. This quality also makes cast iron ideal for browning and braising meat or simmering soups. The more it's used, the more seasoned it becomes, offering a smoother cooking surface.

Cast iron requires more care than the newer versions of cookware. If you own some of the hand-me-down pieces, you're fortunate to benefit from a coating layered from each loaf of cornbread, batch of fried okra, or pot of soup.

Once you've cooked in it, wipe it out with a clean cloth or wash in hot water with a little soap, if necessary. Never let cast iron soak. Be sure to dry thoroughly to prevent rusting. One of the best ways to dry the utensil is to place it in a hot oven just until dry.

You can continue to season your cast-iron cookware by preparing some of these traditional favorites we've listed here. Our recipe for Firecracker Corn Sticks with crushed red pepper adds a spicy twist to the oldtime version. Or mix up a pot of Garden Soup, and cook it on low heat in a cast-iron Dutch oven until the seasonings blend.

If you live in an area with hard water, the cookware may develop rust or a whitish deposit. Remove deposits by washing thoroughly, and pop popcorn in the skillet or pan to reseason it. Harsh detergents should never be used on cast-iron utensils.

If you would like to add old black cast-iron cookware to your collection, look for it at flea markets, estate sales, and yard sales. In addition to the more popular skillets, griddles, and corn stick pans, look for unusual pieces, such as cookie molds, tea kettles, chicken fryers, and long-handled pans.

New cast iron is usually lighter in color than the older pieces and can be purchased in hardware and department stores and through mail-order companies. It comes coated with a sticky substance, which needs to be removed before you can season it. To remove the sticky substance and season cast iron, follow these simple instructions:

—Scrub new cast-iron cookware with a sponge and mild cleanser to remove the sticky coating. Rinse cookware and dry thoroughly.

—Spread a thick layer of unsalted vegetable shortening on the inside, including the underside of the lid. (Do not use vegetable oil since it will leave a sticky coating.)

—Place the lid on the pot, and bake at 250° for 1½ to 2 hours. Wipe grease around the interior occasionally to keep the surfaces evenly coated.

—Remove the utensil from the oven, and cool. Wipe out excess grease, and buff with a soft cloth until the surface develops a sheen.

FRIED CHICKEN WITH CREAM GRAVY

1 (13-ounce) can evaporated milk
1 tablespoon Worcestershire sauce
1 (2½- to 3-pound) broiler-fryer, cut up
¾ cup all-purpose flour
¾ cup plain cornmeal
¾ teaspoon salt
Dash of pepper
Vegetable oil
1 tablespoon butter or margarine
2 tablespoons all-purpose flour
½ cup water
½ teaspoon salt
¼ teaspoon pepper

Combine evaporated milk and Worcestershire sauce; mix well. Place chicken in a shallow dish, and pour milk mixture over top. Cover and refrigerate 3 hours or overnight.

Combine ¾ cup flour, cornmeal, ¾ teaspoon salt, and dash of pepper; mix well. Drain chicken, reserving ½ cup milk mixture; dredge chicken in flour mixture. Let stand 5 minutes.

Heat ½ inch oil in a large cast-iron skillet to 325°; add chicken, and fry 30 to 35 minutes, turning once. Drain chicken well on paper towels, reserving 1½ tablespoons drippings in skillet.

Add butter to drippings; melt over low heat. Add 2 tablespoons flour, stirring until smooth. Cook 1 minute, stirring constantly. Gradually add reserved ½ cup milk mixture and water; cook over medium heat, stirring constantly, until the mixture is thickened and bubbly. Stir in ½ teaspoon salt and ¼ teaspoon pepper. Serve gravy with chicken. Yield: 4 servings. *Mary Pike, Marietta, Georgia.*

FIRECRACKER CORN STICKS

2 cups self-rising cornmeal
2 teaspoons sugar
1½ to 2 teaspoons crushed red pepper
1 egg, beaten
¼ cup butter or margarine, melted
1 cup milk
¼ cup buttermilk

Combine dry ingredients; mix well. Add remaining ingredients, and stir until batter is smooth.

Place 2 well-greased cast-iron corn stick pans in a 450° oven for 5 minutes or until very hot. Remove pans from oven; spoon batter into pan, filling two-thirds full. Bake at 450° for 12 to 15 minutes or until lightly browned. Yield: 14 corn sticks. *Thelma Peedin, Newport News, Virginia.*

GARDEN SOUP

2 (14½-ounce) cans chicken broth, undiluted
2 (12-ounce) cans tomato juice
1½ cups chopped cooked chicken
1 (12-ounce) can whole kernel corn, drained
1 (10-ounce) package frozen lima beans, thawed
2 small potatoes, peeled and chopped
1 medium onion, chopped
½ cup finely chopped celery
½ cup finely chopped carrots
1½ tablespoons Worcestershire sauce
1 bay leaf
¾ teaspoon garlic salt
½ teaspoon pepper
Croutons (optional)

Combine all ingredients except croutons in a cast-iron Dutch oven. Bring to a boil. Cover, reduce heat, and simmer 1 hour, stirring occasionally. Remove bay leaf. Top with croutons, if desired. Yield: 11 cups. *Martha Ann Rabon, Stapleton, Alabama.*

DRIED APPLE STACK CAKE

½ cup shortening
½ cup sugar
½ cup molasses
½ cup buttermilk
1 egg, beaten
1 teaspoon vanilla extract
3 to 3½ cups all-purpose flour
1 teaspoon ground ginger
½ teaspoon baking soda
½ teaspoon salt
Dried Apple Filling

Cream shortening; gradually add sugar and molasses, beating until smooth. Add buttermilk, egg, and vanilla; mix well. Combine flour, ginger, soda, and salt. Gradually add to creamed mixture, beating just until blended.

Divide dough into 6 portions, and pat 1 portion into the bottom of a lightly greased 9-inch cast-iron skillet. (Chill remaining dough.) Bake at 350° for 8 to 9 minutes. Carefully remove to cooling rack. Repeat with remaining dough.

Stack layers, spreading Dried Apple Filling between each. Store overnight in refrigerator before serving. Yield: one 9-inch cake.

Dried Apple Filling:

4 cups dried apple slices
3½ cups water
1½ cups sugar
½ teaspoon ground cinnamon
½ teaspoon ground nutmeg

Combine apples and water in a large saucepan. Bring to a boil; cover, reduce heat, and simmer 30 minutes or until tender. Stir in sugar and spices. Yield: about 2½ cups.   *Edith M. Seeley,*
London, Kentucky.

SKILLET PINEAPPLE
UPSIDE-DOWN CAKE

¼ cup butter or margarine
1 cup firmly packed brown sugar
½ cup chopped pecans
1 (15¼-ounce) can pineapple slices, undrained
3 eggs, separated
1 cup sugar
1 cup all-purpose flour
1 teaspoon baking powder
1 teaspoon salt
6 or 7 maraschino cherries

Melt butter in a 9-inch cast-iron skillet. Add brown sugar and pecans; mix well. Drain pineapple, reserving ¼ cup plus 1 tablespoon pineapple juice; set

juice aside. Arrange pineapple slices in a single layer over brown sugar mixture; set skillet aside.

Beat egg yolks until thick and lemon colored; gradually add sugar, beating well. Combine flour, baking powder, and salt; add to egg mixture. Stir in reserved pineapple juice.

Beat egg whites (at room temperature) until stiff peaks form; fold into flour mixture. Spoon batter evenly over pineapple slices. Bake at 375° for 30 to 35 minutes. Immediately invert cake onto a serving plate. Place cherries in centers of pineapple rings. Yield: one 9-inch cake.   *Phyllis Goodwin,*
Rocky Mount, North Carolina.

Fill Up
On Hot Soups
And Sandwiches

Add variety to lunch or supper with one of these hot soup-and-sandwich ideas. Accompany each with a serving of potato chips, green onions, or pickles, and you'll have a nourishing meal.

The ingredients in our hearty Corned Beef Sandwiches are served in hot dog buns for easy eating. A bowl of Corn Soup makes the perfect accompaniment.

If you occasionally find yourself with leftover chicken, perhaps you'll enjoy Toasted Chicken-and-Cheese Sandwiches and Cream of Chicken Soup. If seafood is your preference, try our open-faced Shrimp-Cheese Sandwiches. They have pimiento-stuffed olives and green pepper, along with shrimp and Cheddar cheese.

TOASTED CHICKEN-AND-CHEESE
SANDWICHES

4 slices white or whole wheat bread
2 teaspoons prepared mustard
¼ pound thinly sliced cooked chicken
2 (1-ounce) slices Swiss cheese
1 egg, beaten
1 tablespoon milk
2 tablespoons butter or margarine, melted

Spread one side of each slice of bread with mustard. Place equal amounts of chicken and cheese on two slices of bread; top with remaining bread slices.

Combine egg and milk in a shallow dish, beating well. Dip each side of sandwiches in egg mixture. Cook in butter over medium heat in a skillet until golden brown, turning once. Yield: 2 servings.   *Louise Osborne,*
Lexington, Kentucky.

SHRIMP-CHEESE SANDWICHES

3 cups water
1 pound medium shrimp
1 cup (4 ounces) shredded Cheddar cheese
¼ cup milk
¼ teaspoon dried whole basil
¼ cup diced green pepper
2 tablespoons diced onion
1 tablespoon diced pimiento-stuffed olives
2 tablespoons butter or margarine, softened
8 slices bread, cut into 3-inch rounds

Bring water to a boil; add shrimp, and cook 3 to 5 minutes. Drain well; rinse with cold water. Chill. Peel, devein, and chop shrimp; set aside.

Combine cheese, milk, and basil; beat at medium speed of an electric mixer until smooth. Add shrimp, green pepper, onion, and olives; mix well. Set mixture aside.

Spread butter on one side of bread rounds; place on baking sheet. Broil 5 to 6 inches from heat until golden, turning once. Remove from oven. Spread about ¼ cup shrimp mixture on buttered side of each toasted bread round; return to baking sheet. Broil 3 to 4 minutes or until bubbly. Serve immediately. Yield: 8 sandwiches.

Lenah Miller Elliott,
Destin, Florida.

CORNED BEEF SANDWICHES

1 (12-ounce) can corned beef
2 cups (8 ounces) shredded Cheddar cheese
2 hard-cooked eggs, diced
¼ cup diced onion
¼ cup chili sauce or catsup
3 tablespoons mayonnaise
12 hot dog buns

Combine all ingredients except buns; mix well. Fill buns with mixture; wrap each sandwich in aluminum foil. Bake at 400° for 15 minutes or until cheese melts. Serve immediately. Yield: 12 servings.   *Mrs. Bruce Drinnen, Jr.,*
Knoxville, Tennessee.

CREAM OF CHICKEN SOUP

1¾ pounds chicken pieces
4 cups water
2 medium carrots, minced
2 stalks celery, minced
1 teaspoon salt
½ teaspoon pepper
1 cup milk
3 tablespoons all-purpose flour

Combine chicken and water in a Dutch oven; bring to a boil. Cover, reduce heat, and simmer 20 to 25 minutes. Remove chicken and let cool, reserving 3½ cups broth. Bone chicken, and chop meat.

Combine chicken, reserved broth, carrots, celery, salt, and pepper in a Dutch oven. Bring to a boil; cover, reduce heat, and simmer 1 hour. Combine milk and flour, stirring until smooth. Gradually add to soup mixture, stirring well. Simmer, uncovered, an additional 15 minutes or until thickened, stirring occasionally. Yield: 5 cups.

Minna Hill,
Montgomery, Alabama.

CORN SOUP

1 medium onion, diced
2 tablespoons butter or margarine, melted
1 (10¾-ounce) can cream of mushroom soup, undiluted
2⅔ cups milk
1 (17-ounce) can cream-style corn
¼ teaspoon salt
¼ teaspoon pepper

Sauté onion in butter in a large saucepan; set aside. Combine soup and milk, stirring until blended. Add soup mixture, corn, salt, and pepper to onion mixture, stirring well. Cook over low heat, stirring constantly, just until thoroughly heated. (Do not boil.) Yield: 4 cups.

Mrs. Theron L. Trimble,
Pensacola, Florida.

Make Pizza At Home

Pizza lovers are everywhere and include all ages; chances are there's at least one at your house. If you're like most folks, you satisfy the craving by eating out or picking up a pizza to go. But you can make this popular dish at home, too. We've found just the recipes to inspire you.

If you're looking for a speedy supper entrée, Quick Hamburger Pizza is a simple version that offers a few shortcuts. It has a biscuit-like crust and uses commercial spaghetti sauce.

Deep-Dish Vegetarian Pizza is another delectable possibility. In addition to the usual vegetable toppings—mushrooms, olives, and green pepper—it has sliced broccoli and green onions. For a thicker crust, it's baked in a cast-iron skillet instead of a pizza pan.

Thick 'n' Crusty Pepperoni Pizza offers still a third variation. We think it rivals restaurant pizzas in both taste and appearance. Because it starts with a yeast dough and has a homemade sauce, it takes a little while to make, but the result is definitely worth it. The tomato-base sauce, made with red wine and fresh parsley, is topped with pepperoni, green pepper, mushrooms, and onion and sprinkled with mozzarella and Parmesan cheeses.

QUICK HAMBURGER PIZZA

¾ pound ground beef
¼ teaspoon salt
1 (8-ounce) jar chunky spaghetti sauce
Pizza crust (recipe follows)
1 cup (4 ounces) shredded mozzarella cheese

Combine ground beef and salt in a skillet; cook over medium heat until meat is browned, stirring to crumble. Drain well.

Spread half of sauce evenly over each pizza crust. Sprinkle meat over sauce; top with cheese. Bake at 450° for 12 to 15 minutes. Yield: two 10-inch pizzas.

Pizza Crust:

1 cup all-purpose flour
1½ teaspoons baking powder
¼ teaspoon salt
¼ teaspoon garlic powder
2 tablespoons shortening
About ⅓ cup milk

Combine flour, baking powder, salt, and garlic powder; cut in shortening with pastry blender until mixture resembles coarse meal. With a fork, stir in enough milk to make a soft dough. Turn dough out onto a floured surface; knead lightly 4 or 5 times. Lightly grease hands, and pat dough evenly into 2 (10-inch) pizza pans. Yield: two 10-inch pizza crusts.

Becky Braddock,
West Columbia, Texas.

DEEP-DISH VEGETARIAN PIZZA

1 (10¾-ounce) can tomato puree
1 clove garlic, crushed
2 tablespoons thinly sliced green onions
1 tablespoon chopped fresh parsley
½ teaspoon dried whole oregano
¼ teaspoon dried whole basil
¼ teaspoon sugar
⅛ teaspoon pepper
Pizza crust (recipe follows)
½ pound fresh mushrooms, sliced
2 tablespoons butter or margarine, melted
1 cup thinly sliced fresh broccoli
1 medium-size green pepper, cut into strips
2 tablespoons sliced green olives
2 tablespoons sliced ripe olives
¼ cup grated Italian-blend cheese
2 cups (8 ounces) shredded mozzarella cheese

Combine tomato puree, garlic, green onions, parsley, oregano, basil, sugar, and pepper in a saucepan; simmer 15 minutes, stirring occasionally. Remove from heat, and let stand 30 minutes. Spread the tomato sauce evenly over the pizza crust.

Sauté mushrooms in butter, and drain well. Arrange mushrooms, broccoli, strips of green pepper, and olives over tomato sauce. Sprinkle with grated Italian-blend cheese.

Bake at 425° for 10 minutes. Sprinkle with shredded mozzarella cheese, and bake an additional 5 minutes. Yield: one 10-inch pizza.

Pizza Crust:

1 package dry yeast
¼ cup warm water (105° to 115°)
2 cups all-purpose flour
1 teaspoon sugar
1 teaspoon salt
1 tablespoon vegetable oil
½ to ¾ cup milk
About ½ cup all-purpose flour

Dissolve yeast in warm water in a large bowl; let stand 5 minutes.

Combine 2 cups flour, sugar, and salt; stir in yeast mixture and oil. Add enough milk to make a soft dough. Cover and let rise 15 minutes.

Turn dough out onto a floured surface; knead 5 to 8 times, working in about ½ cup additional flour. Pat dough evenly into bottom and up sides of a lightly greased 10-inch cast-iron skillet. Line crust with aluminum foil; place a 9-inch cakepan on foil.

Bake crust at 425° for 5 minutes. Remove cakepan and foil; bake crust an additional 3 minutes. Yield: one 10-inch pizza crust.

Lorre Grimes,
Hoover, Alabama.

THICK 'N' CRUSTY PEPPERONI PIZZA

¼ cup warm water (105° to 115°)
1 package dry yeast
4¼ to 4½ cups all-purpose flour, divided
1¼ cups warm water (105° to 115°)
2 teaspoons vegetable oil
1 teaspoon salt
1 teaspoon sugar
Tomato Sauce (recipe follows)
1 (3½-ounce) package sliced pepperoni
1 medium-size green pepper, diced
1 cup sliced fresh mushrooms
1 small onion, thinly sliced
4 cups (16 ounces) shredded mozzarella
    cheese
Grated Parmesan cheese
Green pepper rings (optional)

Combine ¼ cup warm water and yeast in a large bowl; stir until yeast dissolves. Let stand 5 minutes. Add 2 cups flour, 1¼ cups warm water, oil, salt, and sugar. Beat until smooth. Stir in enough remaining flour to make a soft dough.

Turn dough out onto a lightly floured surface, and knead about 3 minutes. Place in a greased bowl, turning to grease top. Cover; let rise in a warm place (85°), free from drafts, 15 minutes. Punch dough down; divide in half. Lightly grease hands; pat dough evenly into 2 lightly greased 12-inch pizza pans. Spread Tomato Sauce over each crust. Top each with half of pepperoni, diced green pepper, mushrooms, and onion. Bake at 450° about 22 minutes. Top with cheese; bake additional 5 minutes or until cheese melts. Garnish with green pepper rings, if desired. Yield: two 12-inch pizzas.

Tomato Sauce:

1 (8-ounce) can tomato sauce
1 (6-ounce) can tomato paste
2 tablespoons dry red wine
2 tablespoons minced fresh parsley
1 tablespoon vegetable oil
1 tablespoon water
1 clove garlic, chopped
½ teaspoon salt
½ teaspoon sugar
½ teaspoon dried whole oregano
¼ teaspoon freshly ground pepper

Combine all ingredients in a medium saucepan. Bring to a boil; cover, reduce heat, and simmer 15 to 20 minutes. Yield: 1½ cups.

Note: Unbaked pizzas may be frozen. To serve, remove from freezer for 15 minutes. Bake at 450° for 35 minutes or until crust is browned. Add cheese, and bake an additional 5 minutes or just until cheese melts.   *Susan Hall, Alpharetta, Georgia.*

Ristras Are For Cooking, Too

The glistening strings of dried red chiles that entice us with decorating possibilities are right at home in the kitchen. Not only do the chiles add a wonderful earthy touch, but they also have a rich culinary heritage.

Ristras (ree-struhs) are made of ripe chiles that are strung together on cords of various lengths and hung to dry. They gradually turn from a bright red to a deep crimson. Dried, the chiles last for months and can be plucked from the string as needed. They're unequaled as seasoning for hot, spicy dishes.

Unfortunately, ristras rarely come with instructions, so the dried chiles are more likely to gather dust than to be used in cooking. If you would like to try your hand at cooking with a ristra, here are some recipes and general guidelines.

First, it should be noted that some ristras on the market have a shellac or acrylic coating. These usually include dried materials other than chiles and are meant for purely decorative purposes; they should never be used for cooking. Humidity is another consideration; moist climates can cause the chiles to mold. Moths can also be a problem; therefore, it's always a good idea to inspect the chiles closely before you start to use them.

If you take chiles from the top of the string and work your way down, the basic appearance of your ristra will be unchanged, and it can still be used for decorating. Discontinue using it for cooking after it's a year old or when discolored areas start appearing—a sure sign the chiles are past their prime.

The simplest way to use ristra chiles is to wash them, remove the stems and seeds, and add them whole to soups, stews, or side dishes. Keep in mind that simmering brings out their pungent flavor. Chiles vary considerably in hotness, so be conservative when you're deciding on how many to add. Be sure to remove the remains of the chiles before the dish is served.

You can also grind dried chiles into Red Chile Powder and keep it on hand to use in many Southwestern dishes. This product is much different from commercial chili powder, which has cumin and other spices in it. If you have a *molcajete* (mortar) and *tejolote* (pestle), you can grind the chiles the old-fashioned way. We used a blender to save time and found the results more than satisfactory in New Mexican Flat Enchiladas.

Ristras, which have long been common signs of fall in the Southwest, are now showing up all over the South.

A third way of using a ristra requires soaking the chiles and blending them with some of the soaking liquid to make a paste that can then be used in sauces and other mixtures. This paste is often referred to as *chile caribe*. Some people feel it adds a superior flavor as compared to powdered red chiles. We used this method to make the sauce in our Chimachangas.

A word of caution: Be careful in working with dried chiles; they can be as irritating as fresh chiles to your eyes and skin. Keep your hands away from your face while you're handling them, and wash your hands thoroughly with warm, soapy water afterward. If you want to be on the safe side, wear rubber gloves.

CHIMACHANGAS (FRIED BURRITOS)

1 (2½-pound) boneless chuck or rump
    roast
Red Chile Sauce
½ teaspoon salt
⅛ teaspoon pepper
½ teaspoon ground cumin
½ teaspoon ground oregano
12 (10-inch) flour tortillas
Vegetable oil
1 (8-ounce) carton commercial sour cream
1 (6-ounce) carton frozen guacamole,
    thawed
1 (2.2-ounce) can sliced ripe olives,
    drained

Place roast in a roasting pan; add 2 cups water. Cover and bake at 325° for 2 to 3 hours or until tender. Let roast cool. Cut beef into ½-inch cubes with an electric knife.

Combine cubed beef, 2½ cups Red Chile Sauce, and seasonings, stirring well; set aside.

Wrap tortillas tightly in aluminum foil; bake at 350° for 15 minutes.

Place a scant ½ cup of meat mixture just below center of each tortilla. Fold in left and right sides of tortilla to partially enclose filling. Fold up bottom edge of tortilla to partially cover filling; roll up, and secure with a wooden pick.

Gently place filled tortillas, 1 or 2 at a time, in deep hot oil (375°); fry 1 to 2 minutes or until golden brown, turning once. Drain on paper towels. Remove wooden picks.

Garnish with sour cream, guacamole, and olives. (Chimachangas may also be topped with chopped tomatoes and served on a bed of shredded lettuce, if desired.) Serve immediately. Yield: 12 servings.

Red Chile Sauce:

4 large dried red chiles
2¾ cups water
¼ cup shortening
¼ cup plus 2 tablespoons all-purpose flour
¾ teaspoon salt

Wash chiles, and place in a medium saucepan; add 2¾ cups water. Cover and bring to a boil. Remove from heat, and let stand, covered, 45 minutes or until softened. Drain chiles, reserving soaking liquid. Pull off stems, slit chiles open, and rinse away seeds under running water. Place chiles and ½ cup of soaking liquid in blender; process chiles until pureed.

Press pureed mixture through a sieve with back of a spoon. Rinse blender with remaining soaking liquid, and pour over remainder of pulp in sieve; add result to pureed chile mixture. Discard any unprocessed bits of peel left in sieve. Set aside pureed mixture.

Melt shortening in a heavy saucepan over low heat; add flour and salt, stirring until smooth. Continue cooking 5 minutes, stirring constantly, or until mixture is light golden brown. Gradually add chile mixture; cook over low heat, stirring frequently, 15 to 20 minutes or until thickened to gravylike consistency. (Add extra water if mixture is too thick.) Yield: about 2½ cups.

Note: Burritos may also be baked, if desired. Prepare burritos, making 2 recipes of Red Chile Sauce. Instead of frying, place burritos on ovenproof plates,

and top with the extra recipe of Red Chile Sauce and shredded Monterey Jack cheese. Bake at 325° for 10 to 15 minutes. Serve immediately.

NEW MEXICAN FLAT ENCHILADAS

12 corn tortillas
Vegetable oil
About 2½ cups Red Chile Enchilada Sauce
½ cup sliced green onions
3 cups (12 ounces) shredded Monterey Jack cheese

Fry tortillas, one at a time, in ¼ inch hot oil in a skillet 5 seconds on each side or just until softened. Drain on paper towels.

Spoon about 2 tablespoons Red Chile Enchilada Sauce on each of 4 ovenproof plates; top with tortilla. Place about 2½ tablespoons Red Chile Enchilada Sauce, 2 teaspoons green onions, and ¼ cup cheese on top of tortilla; repeat with 2 additional layers, ending with cheese. Bake at 350° for 10 minutes or until cheese melts. Serve enchiladas immediately. Yield: 4 servings.

Red Chile Enchilada Sauce:

2 cloves garlic, minced
2 tablespoons bacon drippings
2 tablespoons all-purpose flour
2 tablespoons Red Chile Powder (see recipe)
½ teaspoon salt
Pinch of ground oregano
Dash of ground cumin
½ cup tomato sauce
2 cups cold water

Sauté garlic in hot bacon drippings in a medium saucepan over low heat. Add flour, and cook 1 minute, stirring constantly. Stir in seasonings. Gradually add tomato sauce and water, and simmer about 15 minutes, stirring occasionally. Yield: about 2½ cups.

Note: Enchiladas may be garnished with shredded lettuce, if desired.

RED CHILE POWDER

12 dried red chiles

Rinse chiles with cold water; dry well.

Place chiles in a single layer on a baking sheet; bake at 350° about 2 minutes or until outsides of chiles are stiffened, turning frequently. (Chiles burn easily.) Cool.

Remove and discard stems, seeds, inner veins, and any dark spots. Place

chiles in container of electric blender; process at high speed until ground. Sieve powder to remove large unground flakes, if desired. Store powder in a cool, dark place, or freeze. Use to season soups, stews, vegetables, and meats or use to make New Mexican Flat Enchiladas. Yield: about ½ cup.

Note: Use caution in preparing and handling Red Chile Powder; protect your eyes, nose, face, and hands.

Serve Bite-Size Corn Dogs

If you're a corn dog fan, take a tip from a savvy Texas cook and try this miniversion as an appetizer or snack. Mrs. David A. Bennett of Dallas cuts frankfurters into sections before dipping them into batter and deep frying. The result is Corn Dog Bites, a tasty treat that's a hit with all ages.

CORN DOG BITES

1 cup all-purpose flour
⅔ cup cornmeal
1 tablespoon sugar
1½ teaspoons baking powder
1 teaspoon salt
2 tablespoons melted bacon drippings
1 egg, beaten
1 to 1¼ cups buttermilk
½ teaspoon baking soda
1 pound frankfurters
Vegetable oil
Prepared mustard, catsup, picante sauce (optional)

Combine flour, cornmeal, sugar, baking powder, and salt; stir in bacon drippings. Combine egg, buttermilk, and soda; mix well. Stir into flour mixture, mixing well. Cut each frankfurter into 10 pieces. Dip frankfurter sections into batter, covering completely. (Wooden picks work well for dipping.) Drop into 3 to 4 inches deep hot oil (375°), and cook until golden, turning once; drain on paper towels.

Insert party picks, and serve immediately. Serve with mustard, catsup, or picante sauce, if desired. Yield: about 10 servings.

Note: If whole corn dogs are desired, insert wooden sticks or skewers into frankfurters; dip frankfurters into batter, and fry in deep hot oil until golden.

Classic Beef Stew In Less Time

With the help of the microwave oven, you can serve steaming bowls of Beef Stew With Parsley Dumplings in less time than most conventionally made beef stews. In fact, this recipe will probably cut about an hour from the total cooking time.

It's important that the beef and vegetables for this stew be cut into small, uniform pieces to ensure that they cook completely. Just as in conventional beef stew, the meat in this stew will be browned first. We tell you how to do this in a microwave browning skillet rather than on the stove.

For best results, most thick mixtures need to be stirred all along as they cook in the microwave oven. This is also true with this recipe.

Parsley dumplings are easy to make when you use a biscuit mix. You'll find the dumplings have a very light, fluffy texture when microwaved.

Step 1: *Dredge pieces of beef in a mixture of flour, salt, and pepper. Brown meat on all sides in melted butter in a 10-inch microwave browning skillet.*

Step 2: *Place meat in a 3-quart casserole before continuing to microwave. Add water, onion rings, and seasonings. Cover and microwave at medium low for 30 minutes.*

Step 3: *Add potatoes, quartered onions, carrots, and celery. Cover and microwave at medium low for 40 to 50 minutes, stirring every 10 minutes, until vegetables are tender.*

Step 4: *Make dumplings by combining biscuit mix, egg, milk, and parsley and stirring just until moistened. Drop batter by tablespoonfuls onto hot stew.*

BEEF STEW WITH PARSLEY DUMPLINGS

¼ cup plus 2 tablespoons all-purpose flour
1 teaspoon salt
½ teaspoon pepper
1¾ pounds boneless beef chuck, cut into ¾-inch pieces
3 tablespoons butter or margarine
2½ cups water
1 small onion, sliced and separated into rings
1 clove garlic, minced
1 bay leaf
1½ teaspoons Worcestershire sauce
2 medium potatoes, peeled and cut into twelfths
4 small onions, quartered
3 medium carrots, thinly sliced
2 stalks celery, cut into ½-inch pieces
1 cup biscuit mix
1 egg, beaten
3 tablespoons milk
1 tablespoon minced fresh parsley

Combine flour, salt, and pepper. Dredge meat in flour mixture; set aside. Place a 10-inch microwave browning skillet in microwave. Preheat, uncovered, at HIGH for 3 minutes. Add butter, tilting to coat surface. Place meat in skillet, and stir well; microwave at HIGH for 3 minutes. Stir well. Microwave 2 minutes or until meat is browned, stirring well after 1 minute.

Remove meat to a 3-quart casserole. Add water, onion, garlic, bay leaf, and Worcestershire sauce; cover and microwave at HIGH for 5 minutes. Reduce power to MEDIUM LOW (30% power), and microwave 30 minutes. Stir in potatoes, onion, carrots, and celery. Cover and microwave at MEDIUM LOW for 40 to 50 minutes, stirring every 10 minutes, until meat and vegetables are tender. Remove bay leaf.

Combine biscuit mix and remaining ingredients; stir until moistened. Drop batter by tablespoonfuls onto stew. Cover and microwave at HIGH for 3½ to 4 minutes. Let stand 5 to 10 minutes before serving. Yield: 2½ quarts.

Step 5: *Cover casserole dish, and microwave dumplings on high for 3½ to 4 minutes. Then allow stew with dumplings to stand 5 to 10 minutes before serving.*

Caramel Makes It Delicious

If you like caramel, we've chosen some mouth-watering treats just for you—cookies, candy, popcorn, and even a pie. They all have the flavor of luscious caramel.

OATMEAL-CARAMEL BARS

1 (14-ounce) package caramels
⅓ cup milk
2 cups all-purpose flour
2 cups regular oats, uncooked
1½ cups firmly packed brown sugar
1 teaspoon baking soda
½ teaspoon salt
1 egg, slightly beaten
1 cup butter or margarine, softened
1 (12-ounce) package semisweet chocolate morsels
1 cup chopped pecans

Combine caramels and milk in a saucepan; cook over low heat, stirring constantly, until caramels melt. Set mixture aside.

Combine flour, oats, sugar, soda, and salt. Add egg and butter, stirring until mixture is crumbly. Press half of mixture into a greased 13- x 9- x 2-inch baking pan. Bake at 350° for 10 minutes. Sprinkle with chocolate morsels and pecans; pour caramel mixture evenly on top. Sprinkle on remaining crumbs. Bake at 350° for 20 to 25 minutes. Cool and cut into bars. Chill 8 hours. Yield: about 3 dozen.
Mrs. Charles De Haven,
Owensboro, Kentucky.

CARAMEL-PEANUT SQUARES

1 (12-ounce) package semisweet chocolate morsels
2 tablespoons vegetable shortening
1 (14-ounce) package caramels
¼ cup plus 1 tablespoon butter or margarine
1 cup coarsely chopped salted peanuts

Combine chocolate morsels and shortening in top of a double boiler; bring water to a boil. Reduce heat to low; cook until chocolate melts. Pour half of chocolate mixture into a greased 8-inch square pan, spreading chocolate to edges of pan. Return remaining chocolate mixture to low heat. Chill mixture in pan about 15 minutes or until firm.

Combine caramels and butter in a heavy saucepan over low heat; cook, stirring occasionally, until caramels melt. Stir in peanuts. Spoon mixture evenly over chocolate layer, and spread to edges of pan. Chill about 15 minutes or until partially cool. Pour remaining chocolate mixture evenly over caramel filling. Chill 8 hours. Let sit at room temperature 5 minutes; cut into squares. Serve immediately. Yield: about 3 dozen.
Frances Robison,
Mobile, Alabama.

CARAMEL-PECAN APPLE PIE

Pastry for double-crust 9-inch pie
6 cups peeled and thinly sliced apples
¾ cup sugar
2 tablespoons all-purpose flour
¼ teaspoon salt
2 tablespoons butter or margarine
⅓ cup commercial caramel ice cream topping
2 teaspoons chopped pecans

Roll half of pastry onto a lightly floured surface to ⅛-inch thickness; fit pastry into a 9-inch pieplate. Chill remaining pastry.

Combine apples, sugar, flour, and salt; toss gently to coat. Spoon mixture into pastry shell; dot with butter.

Roll out remaining pastry to ⅛-inch thickness, and place over filling. Trim edges; seal and flute. Cut several slits in top crust. Bake pie at 425° for 35 to 40 minutes. Remove from oven; immediately drizzle caramel topping over top. Before serving, sprinkle with pecans. Serve warm or at room temperature. Yield: one 9-inch pie. *Shirley Draper,*
Winter Park, Florida.

CRISPY CARAMEL POPCORN

½ cup sugar
¼ cup butter or margarine
¼ cup dark corn syrup
¼ teaspoon vanilla extract
¼ teaspoon salt
2 quarts freshly popped corn, unsalted

Combine all ingredients except popped corn in a saucepan; bring to a boil. Reduce heat, and simmer 5 minutes, stirring constantly. Remove mixture from heat; pour over popcorn, and mix well.

Spread mixture in a 15- x 10- x 1-inch jellyroll pan. Bake at 250° for 1 hour, stirring every 15 minutes. Remove from oven; stir immediately. Stir occasionally while mixture cools. Store in an airtight container. Yield: 2 quarts.
Mrs. Joe M. Campbell,
Spartanburg, South Carolina.

Select A Strata Or Soufflé

While stratas and soufflés may be similar in some ways, they are also very different. Both rely on eggs to give them a lift as they bake. However, most stratas are packed with bread and so many other ingredients that they won't rise as high as traditional soufflés. Stratas were originally created to use up leftover bread and cheese.

We think you'll agree that our Egg-and-Bacon Casserole is a particularly good strata to serve for breakfast or brunch. As a bonus, some stratas, such as Smoked Sausage-Egg Bake and Cheesy Breakfast Casserole, can be made the night before they are served.

Most hot soufflés can be temperamental if you aren't careful. In making the Spinach Soufflé, be sure to drain the spinach thoroughly, and grease only the bottom of the dish. This helps the mixture cling to the sides as it bakes and rises. Guests will enjoy this side dish when you bring it directly to the table from the oven.

CHEESY BREAKFAST CASSEROLE

3 slices white bread, quartered
2 cups small-curd cottage cheese
6 eggs
¼ teaspoon salt
⅛ teaspoon pepper
1 cup (4 ounces) shredded Cheddar cheese
4 (1-ounce) slices Swiss cheese
Grated Parmesan cheese
Paprika

Line a lightly greased 12- x 8- x 2-inch baking dish with bread. Spread cottage cheese over bread.

Combine eggs, salt, and pepper; beat well. Stir in Cheddar cheese; pour over cottage cheese. Arrange Swiss cheese over egg mixture. Sprinkle with Parmesan cheese and paprika. Bake at 325° for 30 minutes. Yield: 6 servings.
Pat Dail,
Radford, Virginia.

SMOKED SAUSAGE-EGG BAKE

1 pound smoked sausage, chopped
1 cup sliced fresh mushrooms
6 slices white bread, cut into ½-inch
  cubes
2 cups (8 ounces) shredded Cheddar
  cheese
6 eggs
2 cups milk
1 teaspoon dry mustard
½ teaspoon celery seeds
1 teaspoon dried whole oregano

Combine sausage and mushrooms in a large skillet; sauté until mushrooms are tender. Drain well.

Place bread cubes in a lightly greased 12- x 8- x 2-inch baking dish. Top with sausage and mushroom mixture and Cheddar cheese.

Combine remaining ingredients; beat well. Pour over cheese; cover and refrigerate 8 hours or overnight.

Bake, uncovered, at 325° for 40 to 45 minutes or until golden brown. Serve immediately. Yield: 6 to 8 servings.

Pankey Kite,
Macon, Georgia.

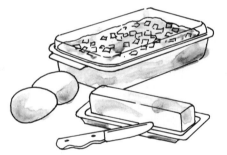

EGG-AND-BACON CASSEROLE

¼ cup butter or margarine
4 cups unseasoned croutons
2 cups (8 ounces) shredded Cheddar
  cheese
2 cups milk
8 eggs, beaten
½ teaspoon dry mustard
1 (12-ounce) package bacon, cooked and
  crumbled

Place butter in an 11- x 7- x 1½-inch baking dish. Heat butter in a 325° oven 5 minutes or until melted, tilting to coat dish; remove from oven. Pour croutons over butter; sprinkle cheese over croutons, and set aside.

Combine milk, eggs, and mustard; mix well. Pour egg mixture over cheese, and sprinkle with bacon. Bake at 325° for 40 to 50 minutes or until set. Let casserole stand at room temperature 5 to 10 minutes before serving. Yield: 6 to 8 servings.

SPINACH SOUFFLÉ

1 (10-ounce) package frozen chopped
  spinach
3 tablespoons chopped green onions
  with tops
¼ cup butter or margarine, melted
¼ cup plus 1 tablespoon all-purpose flour
1½ cups milk
1 cup (4 ounces) shredded sharp Cheddar
  cheese
¼ teaspoon salt
½ teaspoon white pepper
¼ teaspoon dried whole basil
2 dashes of hot sauce
4 eggs, separated
⅛ teaspoon cream of tartar

Cook spinach according to package directions, omitting salt. Drain and squeeze dry with paper towels.

Lightly grease the bottom of a 5-cup soufflé dish. Cut a piece of foil long enough to circle the dish, allowing a 1-inch overlap. Fold foil lengthwise into thirds, and lightly butter one side. Wrap buttered side of foil against dish, so it extends 3 inches above rim. Secure foil with string.

Sauté green onions in butter in a large saucepan until tender. Add flour, and cook 1 minute, stirring constantly. Gradually add milk; cook over medium heat, stirring constantly, until thickened. Add cheese, salt, pepper, basil, and hot sauce. Stir until cheese melts. Add spinach; mix well.

Beat egg yolks; stir a small portion of spinach mixture into yolks. Return to remaining spinach mixture; stir well.

Beat egg whites (at room temperature) and cream of tartar until stiff peaks form; fold into spinach mixture. Pour into prepared dish; bake at 350° for 50 to 55 minutes. Serve immediately. Yield: 6 servings.

Help Yourself To Brownies

Brownies still warm from the oven and milk ice cold from the refrigerator are probably remembered as a favorite snack from childhood. It's hard to believe that Mother's or Grandmother's version of brownies could be matched, but the recipes our readers have shared may change your mind.

The secret to making the best brownies is not to overbake them. When they're done, a wooden pick inserted in the center will come out clean but still have a small amount of moisture on it, and the edges of the brownies will begin to pull away from the pan slightly.

BLONDIE SWIRLS

½ cup butter or margarine
1½ cups firmly packed brown sugar
2 eggs
1 teaspoon vanilla extract
1½ cups all-purpose flour
2 teaspoons baking powder
½ teaspoon salt
½ cup chopped walnuts
1 (6-ounce) package semisweet chocolate
  morsels, divided

Melt butter in a heavy saucepan; add brown sugar, and stir until combined. Remove from heat, and cool. Add eggs, one at a time, beating after each addition. Stir in vanilla.

Combine flour, baking powder, and salt; add to sugar mixture, stirring well. Stir in walnuts and ¼ cup chocolate morsels.

Spread batter in a greased and floured 13- x 9- x 2-inch baking pan. Sprinkle with remaining chocolate morsels. Bake at 350° for 3 minutes; remove from oven, and gently swirl batter with a knife. Return to oven, and bake an additional 20 minutes. Cool and cut into bars. Yield: about 2½ dozen.

Dana Donaldson,
Hallsville, Missouri.

BUTTERSCOTCH BROWNIES

⅔ cup butter or margarine, softened
1½ cups firmly packed brown sugar
2 eggs
2 teaspoons vanilla extract
2 cups all-purpose flour
1 teaspoon baking powder
¼ teaspoon baking soda
1 teaspoon salt
1 (6-ounce) package butterscotch morsels
½ cup chopped pecans

Cream butter; add brown sugar, beating well. Add eggs and vanilla to mixture, beating well.

Combine flour, baking powder, soda, and salt; add to creamed mixture, stirring well.

Pour batter into a greased 13- x 9- x 2-inch baking pan. Sprinkle with butterscotch morsels and pecans. Bake at 350° for 30 minutes. Cool and cut into bars. Yield: 2½ dozen. *Susan Watkins,*
Raleigh, North Carolina.

BUTTERMILK BROWNIES

1 cup water
½ cup butter or margarine
½ cup vegetable oil
2 cups all-purpose flour
2 cups sugar
¼ cup cocoa
½ cup buttermilk
1 teaspoon baking soda
2 eggs, beaten
Buttermilk Frosting
½ cup chopped peanuts

Combine water, butter, and oil in a small saucepan; bring to a boil.

Combine flour, sugar, and cocoa in a mixing bowl; add hot mixture, stirring well. Combine buttermilk and soda; stir until soda dissolves. Add buttermilk mixture and eggs to batter; mix well. Spoon mixture into a greased 15- x 10- x 1-inch jellyroll pan. Bake at 400° for 15 minutes.

Frost brownies with Buttermilk Frosting while warm; sprinkle with peanuts. Cool. Cut into squares. Yield: about 3½ dozen.

Buttermilk Frosting:

½ cup butter or margarine
⅓ cup buttermilk
¼ cup cocoa
1 (16-ounce) package powdered sugar, sifted
½ teaspoon vanilla extract

Combine butter, buttermilk, and cocoa in a medium saucepan; bring to a boil. Add powdered sugar and vanilla; blend until smooth. Yield: enough for a 15- x 10- x 2-inch pan of brownies.

Mrs Ken Altizer,
Waxhaw, North Carolina.

CHEESECAKE BROWNIES

½ cup butter or margarine, softened
1 (8-ounce) package cream cheese, softened
1½ cups sugar
3 eggs
1 teaspoon instant coffee granules
1½ teaspoons hot water
¾ cup all-purpose flour
½ cup cocoa
½ teaspoon baking powder
½ teaspoon salt
1½ teaspoons vanilla extract
1 cup chopped pecans

Cream butter and cream cheese; gradually add sugar, beating well. Add eggs, one at a time, beating well after each addition. Dissolve coffee granules in hot water, and add to mixture.

Combine flour, cocoa, baking powder, and salt; add to cream cheese mixture, mixing well. Stir in vanilla and chopped pecans.

Pour batter into a greased 9-inch square baking pan. Bake at 350° for 30 to 35 minutes. Cool and cut into squares. Yield: 20 brownies.

Roseanna Stevens,
Jacksonville, Florida.

Perk Up
Sack Lunches

If sack lunches have become a bore, spice them up with some of the recipes you'll find here. All are suitable to carry along to school, to work, or to picnics in the park.

Give school kids a treat with peanut butter sandwiches made with our Banana-Apple Bread. The moist bread is tasty eaten by the slice, but sturdy enough for sandwiches.

For lunch, adults will enjoy chilled Ham-Noodle Salad. We suggest packing it in a green pepper or tomato shell—just replace the top, and wrap in foil or plastic wrap—and you won't have a food container to take home. You'll note that the dressing for this salad contains mayonnaise, which makes the mixture less likely to spoil when you travel with it. Contrary to what many people think, the acid in commercial mayonnaise actually helps prevent spoilage of meat salads and sandwiches. Of course, it's still important to keep perishable meat items chilled.

If you're stuck on new ideas for sack lunches, try some of these suggestions:

—Make a unique sandwich by rolling cold cuts in a flour tortilla.

—For a fruit-and-cheese lunch, pack bite-size pieces of fruit and cubes of cheese in separate containers.

—On cold days, store chili or vegetable soup in a thermos to keep it hot. Or in warmer weather pack a thermos with chilled soup.

—Line a pita bread pocket with lettuce, and then fill with chopped marinated vegetables.

—Slice off the top of an apple, and carve out the core. Stuff with a mixture of peanut butter and raisins. Replace the top, and wrap the apple in foil or plastic wrap.

HAM-NOODLE SALAD

4 cups cooked macaroni, rinsed and chilled
½ pound cooked ham, cubed
2 cups chopped celery
1 cup (4 ounces) shredded Cheddar cheese
¼ cup chopped green onions
⅔ cup commercial sour cream
⅓ cup mayonnaise or salad dressing
2 teaspoons prepared mustard
½ teaspoon salt
¾ cup sliced radishes
Green pepper shells

Combine macaroni, ham, celery, Cheddar cheese, and chopped green onions in a large bowl.

Combine sour cream, mayonnaise, mustard, and salt; stir into macaroni mixture, mixing well. Chill 1 hour. Stir in radishes. Spoon into pepper shells to serve. Yield: 8 servings.

Sharon McClatchey,
Muskogee, Oklahoma.

BROCCOLI SALAD

1 large head broccoli (about 1½ pounds)
10 slices bacon, cooked and crumbled
5 green onions, sliced
½ cup raisins
1 cup mayonnaise
2 tablespoons vinegar
¼ cup sugar

Trim off large leaves of broccoli. Remove the tough ends of lower stalks, and wash broccoli thoroughly; cut the flowerets and stems into bite-size pieces. Place in a large bowl. Add bacon, green onions, and raisins.

Combine remaining ingredients, stirring well. Add dressing to broccoli mixture, and toss gently. Cover and refrigerate 2 to 3 hours. Yield: 6 servings. *Victoria M. Carpenter,*
Sarasota, Florida.

MEATY CHILI WITH BEANS

1½ pounds ground beef
2 large onions, finely chopped
1 stalk celery, finely chopped
1 large clove garlic, minced
1 (19-ounce) can kidney beans, undrained
1 (10¾-ounce) can tomato soup, undiluted
½ cup water
2 tablespoons chili powder
1 teaspoon salt
½ teaspoon ground cumin
½ teaspoon pepper
3 drops of hot sauce

Combine ground beef, onion, celery, and garlic in a Dutch oven; cook until beef is browned, stirring to crumble meat. Drain. Add remaining ingredients; cover, reduce heat, and simmer 1 hour, stirring frequently. Yield: about 8 cups.   *Carolyne M. Carnevale,*
Trumbull, Connecticut.

HIGH-FIBER MUFFINS

½ cup unprocessed bran
½ cup boiling water
1 egg, slightly beaten
½ cup firmly packed brown sugar
¼ cup vegetable oil
1½ teaspoons vanilla extract
1 cup buttermilk
1¼ teaspoons baking soda
¾ cup raisins
⅓ cup chopped pecans
1¼ cups whole wheat flour
¾ cup unprocessed bran
¼ teaspoon salt

Combine ½ cup bran and boiling water in a small bowl; set aside.
Combine egg, brown sugar, oil, and vanilla in a medium mixing bowl. Combine buttermilk and soda, stirring well; add buttermilk mixture, raisins, and chopped pecans to brown sugar mixture, mixing well.
Combine whole wheat flour, ¾ cup bran, and salt in a large mixing bowl. Add buttermilk mixture and bran and water mixture, stirring just until moistened. Spoon into greased muffin pans. Bake at 400° for 20 minutes. Yield: about 1½ dozen.   *Cheryl Daniel,*
Austin, Texas.

Tip: If muffins are done ahead of serving time, loosen them from their cups, tilt slightly, and slide the pan back into the oven to stay warm. This keeps the muffins from steaming on the bottom.

BANANA-APPLE BREAD

½ cup shortening
1 cup sugar
2 eggs
1 cup peeled and finely chopped apple
1 cup mashed banana
1½ cups all-purpose flour
1 teaspoon baking soda
½ teaspoon salt
Peanut butter (optional)

Cream shortening; gradually add sugar, beating well. Add eggs, one at a time, beating well after each addition. Stir in apple and banana.
Combine flour, soda, and salt; add to the creamed mixture, stirring just until blended.
Spoon batter into a greased and floured 9- x 5- x 3-inch loafpan. Bake at 350° for 1 hour or until a wooden pick inserted in center comes out clean. Cool in pan 10 minutes; remove from pan, and cool completely on a wire rack. Serve with peanut butter, if desired. Yield: 1 loaf.   *Mary Brooke Casad,*
Gainesville, Georgia.

MOCHA CUPCAKES

½ cup shortening
1 cup sugar
1 egg
1 teaspoon vanilla extract
2 teaspoons coffee powder
½ cup hot water
1⅓ cups all-purpose flour
½ cup cocoa
1 teaspoon baking powder
½ teaspoon baking soda
¼ teaspoon salt
½ cup milk
Sifted powdered sugar

Position knife blade in food processor bowl; add shortening and 1 cup sugar. Top with cover; process 2 to 3 minutes. Add egg and vanilla; cover, and process 30 seconds or until well mixed.
Combine coffee powder and water; mix well, and set aside.
Combine flour, cocoa, baking powder, soda, and salt; mix well. Add to creamed mixture; top with cover. Add milk and coffee gradually through food chute with the processor running; process just until smooth.
Fill paper-lined muffin pans two-thirds full; bake at 375° for 15 to 20 minutes or until a wooden pick inserted in center comes out clean. Remove from pans, and cool on wire racks; sprinkle lightly with powdered sugar. Yield: 1½ dozen.   *Lynn Gossett,*
Sugar Hill, Georgia.

OLD-FASHIONED OATMEAL COOKIES

1 cup raisins
½ cup chopped walnuts
¼ cup all-purpose flour
1 cup shortening
1 cup sugar
1 cup firmly packed brown sugar
2 eggs
1¼ cups all-purpose flour
1 teaspoon baking soda
½ teaspoon salt
1 teaspoon ground cinnamon
¼ teaspoon ground nutmeg
⅛ teaspoon ground cloves
3 cups regular oats, uncooked
1 teaspoon vanilla extract

Combine raisins, walnuts, and ¼ cup flour; toss well to coat, and set aside.
Cream shortening; gradually add sugar, beating well. Add eggs, beating well after each addition.
Combine 1¼ cups flour, soda, salt, and spices; stir into creamed mixture. Stir in oats. (Dough will be stiff.) Stir in raisin mixture and vanilla. Drop dough by rounded teaspoonfuls onto lightly greased cookie sheets. Bake at 350° for 12 to 15 minutes. Cool cookies on wire racks. Yield: 6 dozen.
Jenny Heinzmann,
Lothian, Maryland.

Follow These Steps To Easy Boudin

You don't have to be Cajun or even live in Louisiana to enjoy the great taste of boudin. Therea Blount of Baton Rouge, Louisiana, sent us her creative recipe for making Old-Fashioned Boudin, a highly seasoned rice dressing stuffed into casings. Enjoy this ethnic favorite the same as you would other sausages—with biscuits for breakfast or as an appetizer served with crackers.

OLD-FASHIONED BOUDIN

2 cups uncooked regular rice
3 cups water
1¾ pounds ground pork
¼ pound beef liver, ground
1 cup chopped fresh parsley
1 cup diced green onions with tops
½ cup diced onion
½ cup diced green pepper
2 tablespoons creole seasoning
8 to 10 feet pork casings

Cook rice according to package directions, omitting salt; set aside.

Combine remaining ingredients except pork casings in a large Dutch oven; mix well. Bring to a boil; reduce heat, and simmer 30 minutes or until liquid is absorbed, stirring occasionally. Add rice, stirring well, set aside.

Rinse pork casings thoroughly with warm water; drain. Tie one end of each casing securely with cotton string. Attach stuffing tube to electric meat grinder. Slip open end of casing over end of stuffing tube until the entire length of casing is over the end of the tube. Fill top of stuffing tube attachment with sausage mixture. Turn on machine; press sausage mixture into casing. Do not overstuff. Twist filled casings into links 4 to 5 inches long; tie at end of links with cotton string. Carefully cut between strings to the separate the links.

Pierce each link 3 or 4 times, using a straight pin or other small sharp object. Drop links into boiling water to cover. Cover, reduce heat, and simmer 20 minutes. Remove from heat; drain. Yield: 5½ pounds (about 18 links).

Note: If an electric meat grinder is not available, a hand grinder or food processor may be used. Links may be stuffed using a pastry bag. Insert a large wide-mouth tip into a large pastry bag. Fill bag with sausage mixture. Slip open end of casing over tip of bag. Press sausage mixture into casing, using hand to force mixture evenly into casings. Twist into desired links, and tie with cotton string. Cut between strings to separate links.

Depend On Versatile Chicken Breasts

The entrée doesn't have to be time consuming or expensive when the menu features one of these chicken breast recipes. Each one is tasty and different—proof that this piece of chicken has many uses.

SUNSHINE CHICKEN ROLLUPS

¼ cup pineapple juice
¼ cup prepared mustard
1 tablespoon brown sugar
4 chicken breast halves, skinned and boned
8 slices bacon

Combine juice, mustard, and sugar, mixing well.

Cut each chicken breast in half crosswise. Roll each piece up lengthwise; wrap with a slice of bacon, and secure with a wooden pick.

Place chicken on grill over medium coals; baste with mustard mixture, and grill 25 minutes or until done, turning and basting frequently. Yield: 4 servings.
Cheryl L. Blakney,
Sandersville, Georgia.

SAN ANTONIO-STYLE CHICKEN BUNDLES

4 chicken breast halves, skinned and boned
¼ teaspoon salt
2 canned whole green chiles, halved or 4 jalapeño peppers, seeded
2 (1-ounce) slices Monterey Jack cheese, cut into 8 strips
½ cup all-purpose flour
1 egg, beaten
1 tablespoon milk
1 cup soft breadcrumbs
Vegetable oil

Place each chicken breast on a sheet of waxed paper. Flatten chicken to ¼-inch thickness using a meat mallet or rolling pin. Sprinkle with salt.

Place a halved green chile and 2 strips cheese in center of each piece of chicken; roll up lengthwise, tucking edges inside. Secure roll with a wooden pick.

Dredge chicken in flour. Combine egg and milk; dip chicken in egg mixture, and roll in breadcrumbs. Fry chicken in deep hot oil (375°) about 8 minutes or until golden brown. Drain thoroughly on paper towels, and serve immediately. Yield: 4 servings.
Marge Clyde,
San Antonio, Texas.

CHAMPAGNE CHICKEN

2 tablespoons all-purpose flour
½ teaspoon salt
Dash of pepper
4 chicken breast halves, skinned and boned
2 tablespoons butter or margarine, melted
1 tablespoon olive oil
¾ cup champagne or dry white wine
¼ cup sliced fresh mushrooms
½ cup whipping cream

Combine flour, salt, and pepper. Lightly dredge chicken in flour mixture.

Heat butter and oil in a large skillet; add chicken, and sauté about 4 minutes on each side. Add champagne; cook over medium heat about 12 minutes or until chicken is done. Remove chicken, and set aside. Add mushrooms and whipping cream to skillet; cook over low heat, stirring constantly, just until thickened. Add chicken, and cook until heated. Yield: 4 servings.
Beth R. McClain,
Grand Prairie, Texas.

SPICY CHICKEN BAKE

4 chicken breast halves, skinned
1 (8-ounce) can tomato sauce
½ cup sliced fresh mushrooms
1 tablespoon Worcestershire sauce
1 teaspoon dried whole oregano
1 teaspoon seasoning blend
1 cup (4 ounces) shredded Cheddar cheese

Place chicken in a lightly greased 8-inch square baking dish. Combine remaining ingredients, except cheese, mixing well; pour over chicken. Cover and bake at 350° for 50 minutes. Sprinkle chicken with cheese; bake, uncovered, an additional 3 minutes or until cheese melts. Yield: 4 servings. *Susan Hartin,*
Montgomery, Alabama.

TANGY CHICKEN

½ cup all-purpose flour
¼ teaspoon salt
¼ teaspoon pepper
6 chicken breast halves, skinned and boned
½ cup vegetable oil
1 (12-ounce) bottle chili sauce
1 (5-ounce) bottle steak sauce

Combine flour, salt, and pepper; dredge chicken in flour mixture.

Heat oil in a large skillet; add chicken, and cook over medium heat until lightly browned, turning once. Remove chicken; place in a lightly greased 12- x 7- x 2-inch baking dish.

Combine chili sauce and steak sauce; pour over chicken. Cover and bake at 350° for 45 minutes. Yield: 6 servings.
Marge Killmon,
Annandale, Virginia.

SESAME CHICKEN

1 medium onion, chopped
¼ cup plus 2 tablespoons soy sauce
1 tablespoon sugar
3 tablespoons sherry
3 tablespoons vegetable oil
¼ teaspoon ground ginger
Dash of red pepper
6 chicken breast halves, skinned
1½ teaspoons sesame seeds

Combine onion, soy sauce, sugar, sherry, oil, ginger, and red pepper; stir well. Place chicken, meat side down, in a lightly greased 13- x 9- x 2-inch baking dish; pour sauce mixture over chicken. Cover and bake at 350° for 40 minutes. Turn chicken, and sprinkle with sesame seeds. Bake, uncovered, an additional 10 minutes or until done. Yield: 6 servings.
Cindy Zellner,
Shorter, Alabama.

One-Dish Meal Has Tex-Mex Flavor

South Texas Beans, with meat, rice, and vegetables all combined in one dish, is ideal when you want something filling that takes a minimum of fuss. Serve it with cornbread, tortillas, or your favorite hot bread.

SOUTH TEXAS BEANS AND RICE

1¼ pounds dried pinto beans
7 cups water
1 small ham hock
1 medium onion, chopped
2 cloves garlic, minced
1½ teaspoons salt
1 (1-pound) ring smoked beef and pork sausage, thickly sliced
1 (10-ounce) can tomatoes with green chiles, undrained
½ cup uncooked regular rice

Sort and wash beans. Combine beans, water, ham hock, onion, garlic, and salt in a large Dutch oven; bring to a boil. Cover, reduce heat to medium, and cook 45 minutes. Add remaining ingredients. Cover, reduce heat, and simmer 1 hour, stirring occasionally. Remove ham hock, shred ham from bone with a fork, and return ham to bean mixture. Yield: 6 servings.
Thomas Dawlearn,
El Toro, Texas.

Shape A Salad With Gelatin

Gelatin salads are pretty and flavorful, but best of all, they can be made the day before serving. Filled with your favorite fruit or vegetable, they will stand tall and firm, making a gleaming addition to any menu.

CHILI SAUCE TOMATO ASPIC

2 envelopes unflavored gelatin
3 cups tomato juice
1 cup chili sauce
¼ cup lemon juice
½ teaspoon salt
¼ teaspoon white pepper
¼ to ½ teaspoon hot sauce

Sprinkle gelatin over tomato juice in a saucepan; let stand 1 minute. Cook over low heat, stirring until the gelatin dissolves.

Add remaining ingredients; stir until blended. Pour into a lightly oiled 5-cup ring mold; chill until firm. Yield: 10 to 12 servings.
Mrs. Russell T. Shay,
Murrells Inlet, South Carolina.

MOLDED GREEN BEAN SALAD

1 (16-ounce) can French-style green beans, undrained
1 envelope unflavored gelatin
¼ cup cold water
1 (3-ounce) package lemon-flavored gelatin
2 tablespoons vinegar
1 (8-ounce) can sliced water chestnuts, drained
1 (2-ounce) jar diced pimiento, drained
½ cup minced onion
½ cup chopped celery

Drain green beans, reserving liquid. Add enough water to the bean liquid to make 3 cups. Set the beans aside.

Sprinkle unflavored gelatin over ¼ cup cold water; let stand 5 minutes.

Bring bean liquid to a boil; add unflavored gelatin mixture and lemon gelatin, stirring until dissolved. Stir in vinegar; chill until consistency of unbeaten egg white. Fold in beans and remaining ingredients; spoon into a lightly oiled 6-cup mold. Chill until firm. Yield: 8 to 10 servings.
Julia R. Clark,
Doyle, Tennessee.

ASPARAGUS-CUCUMBER MOLD

1 (3-ounce) package lime-flavored gelatin
½ cup boiling water
1 (10¾-ounce) can cream of asparagus soup, undiluted
½ cup mayonnaise
⅛ teaspoon white pepper
1 cup chopped cucumber
¼ cup chopped celery
¼ cup diced onion
¼ cup minced fresh parsley

Dissolve gelatin in boiling water; let cool. Combine soup, mayonnaise, and pepper; stir into gelatin mixture. Add remaining ingredients, mixing well. Pour into a lightly oiled 4-cup mold; chill until firm. Yield: 8 servings.
Mrs. George Sellers,
Albany, Georgia.

LEMON-ONION SALAD

1 (6-ounce) package lemon-flavored gelatin
1 cup boiling water
1½ cups cottage cheese
1 cup mayonnaise
1 cup finely chopped celery
½ cup finely chopped green pepper
½ cup grated onion

Dissolve gelatin in boiling water; set aside, and let cool.

Combine remaining ingredients, and add to gelatin mixture, stirring well. Pour mixture into a lightly oiled 6-cup mold; cover and chill until firm. Yield: 10 to 12 servings.
Mrs. M. L. Welch,
Silverton, Texas.

CONGEALED APPLE SALAD

1 (3-ounce) package lime-flavored gelatin
1 cup boiling water
½ cup cold water
½ cup mayonnaise
2 tablespoons lemon juice
1 cup diced apples
¾ cup seedless green grapes, halved
½ cup chopped pecans

Dissolve gelatin in boiling water in a large bowl; add cold water, mayonnaise, and lemon juice. Beat with a wire whisk until smooth. Chill until consistency of unbeaten egg white.

Fold in remaining ingredients. Pour into a lightly oiled 5-cup mold; chill until firm. Yield: 8 to 10 servings.
Velma McGregor,
Gretna, Virginia.

November

Taste Some Real Southern Cooking

Imagine fist-size Buttermilk Biscuits and Banana Pudding that is piled high with meringue. Consider dumplings that have just the right amount of softness and moist Sweet Potato Pie. These recipes mean we're talking about one thing—serious Southern cooking.

The South is known for its good cooks and good food. We take pride in preserving our traditional recipes and making them over and over, year after year. Mothers copy down ingredients and instructions and pass them on to their children. It's not unusual to find today's Southern newlyweds using some convenience products so that they have time left over to make their favorite treasured family recipes. Here are a few of those all-time Southern favorites.

When it's time for dinner, everyone will come running for these Southern favorites: (front to back) Buttermilk Biscuits, Down-Home Beans and Potatoes, Country Chicken and Dumplings, and Sweet Potato Pie.

COUNTRY CHICKEN AND DUMPLINGS

1 (3- to 3½-pound) broiler-fryer
2 quarts water
2 stalks celery, cut into pieces
1 teaspoon salt
2 cups all-purpose flour
2 teaspoons baking powder
½ to ¾ teaspoon salt
¼ cup butter or margarine, softened

Place chicken in a Dutch oven; add water, celery, and 1 teaspoon salt. Bring to a boil; cover, reduce heat, and simmer 1 hour or until tender. Remove chicken from broth, and cool. Discard celery. Bone chicken, and cut meat into bite-size pieces; set aside meat and ¾ cup chicken broth. Leave remaining broth in Dutch oven.

Combine flour, baking powder, and ½ teaspoon salt; cut in butter until mixture resembles coarse meal. Add ¾ cup reserved broth, stirring with a fork until dry ingredients are moistened. Turn dough out onto a well-floured surface, and knead.

Pat dough to ½-inch thickness. Cut dough in 4- x ½-inch pieces, and sprinkle with additional flour.

Bring broth to a boil. Drop dough, one piece at a time, into boiling broth, gently stirring after each addition. Reduce heat to low; cover and cook 8 to 10 minutes. Stir in chicken, and serve immediately. Yield: 4 servings.

Carolyn Webb,
Jackson, Mississippi.

DOWN-HOME BEANS AND POTATOES

1½ pounds fresh green beans
8 slices bacon, quartered
1 small onion, chopped
5 cups water
1 teaspoon salt
½ teaspoon pepper
1½ cups cubed red potatoes

Wash beans; trim ends, and remove strings. Cut beans into 1½-inch pieces, and set aside.

Fry bacon until crisp in a Dutch oven. Remove bacon, and set aside; reserve ¼ cup bacon drippings in Dutch oven. Sauté onion in drippings until tender.

Add water to onion; bring to a boil. Add bacon, beans, salt, and pepper, and return to a boil; cover and simmer 15 minutes. Add potatoes, and cook an additional 10 minutes or until potatoes are tender. Drain. Yield: 6 servings.

Corinne R. Gilder,
Crowley, Louisiana.

Tip: Keep foods such as strawberries, pork chops, diced green pepper, and bacon from sticking together in the freezer by placing in a single layer on a baking sheet and freezing until firm. Remove from the baking sheet, store in freezer containers, and use as needed.

OLD-FASHIONED TURNIP GREENS

5 pounds fresh turnip greens with roots
½ pound salt pork
6 to 8 cups water
2 teaspoons bacon drippings
Green onions (optional)

Wash turnip greens. Tear into bite-size pieces. Peel turnip roots, and slice.

Rinse salt pork, and cut into 2-inch pieces. Combine salt pork and water in a large Dutch oven; bring to a boil. Cover, reduce heat, and simmer 30 minutes. Add turnip greens; cover and cook an additional 10 minutes. Add turnip roots and bacon drippings; cover and cook an additional 15 to 20 minutes or until greens and roots are tender. Serve with green onions, if desired. Yield: 6 to 8 servings. *Mary Elizabeth Hughes, Memphis, Tennessee.*

CRUSTY CORNBREAD

1 cup cornmeal
½ cup all-purpose flour
1 tablespoon sugar
1 tablespoon baking powder
½ teaspoon baking soda
½ teaspoon salt
1 egg, beaten
1 cup buttermilk
¼ cup bacon drippings

Combine dry ingredients; mix well. Add egg and buttermilk; stir until smooth.

Place bacon drippings in a 9-inch cast-iron skillet; heat at 425° for 5 minutes. Remove skillet from oven, and pour hot drippings into batter; mix well. Quickly pour batter into skillet. Bake at 425° for 20 to 25 minutes or until golden. Yield: 8 servings. *Martha James, Batesville, Arkansas.*

BUTTERMILK BISCUITS

2½ cups all-purpose flour
1 tablespoon plus 1 teaspoon baking powder
½ teaspoon baking soda
¾ teaspoon salt
¼ cup plus 2 tablespoons shortening
1 cup buttermilk

Combine flour, baking powder, soda, and salt; mix well. Cut in shortening with a pastry blender until mixture resembles coarse meal.

Add buttermilk, stirring just until dry ingredients are moistened. Turn dough out onto a floured surface, and knead 3 or 4 times.

Roll dough to ½-inch thickness; cut with a 2½-inch biscuit cutter. Place biscuits on a greased baking sheet. Bake at 450° for 10 minutes or until tops are golden. Yield: 14 biscuits.
Rebecca Kerr, Albany, Georgia.

PECAN PIE

4 eggs, beaten
1 cup light corn syrup
⅔ cup sugar
2 tablespoons butter or margarine, melted
1 teaspoon vanilla extract
1 cup coarsely chopped pecans
1 unbaked (9-inch) pastry shell

Combine eggs, syrup, sugar, butter, and vanilla; beat with an electric mixer until blended. Stir in pecans. Pour mixture into unbaked pastry shell; bake at 350° for 50 to 55 minutes. Yield: one 9-inch pie. *Cathy Bruce, Shreveport, Louisiana.*

SWEET POTATO PIE

2 cups mashed cooked sweet potatoes
2 tablespoons butter or margarine, softened
2 eggs
1 cup sugar
1 tablespoon all-purpose flour
½ teaspoon salt
½ cup buttermilk
¼ teaspoon baking soda
1 teaspoon vanilla extract
1 unbaked (9-inch) pastry shell

Combine sweet potatoes, butter, and eggs, mixing well. Combine sugar, flour, and salt; stir into potato mixture. Combine buttermilk and soda; add to potato mixture, mixing well. Stir in vanilla. Pour filling into pastry shell. Bake at 350° for 1 hour and 10 minutes or until set. Serve warm or cool. Yield: one 9-inch pie. *Willine G. Bell, Daleville, Alabama.*

BUTTERMILK POUND CAKE

1 cup butter, softened
2 cups sugar
4 eggs
3 cups all-purpose flour
½ teaspoon baking soda
¼ teaspoon salt
1 cup buttermilk
1 teaspoon vanilla extract
1 teaspoon lemon extract

Cream butter; gradually add sugar, beating at medium speed of an electric mixer until well blended. Add eggs, one at a time, beating after each addition. Combine flour, soda, and salt; add to creamed mixture alternately with buttermilk, beginning and ending with flour mixture. Stir in flavorings. Pour batter into a greased and floured 10-inch tube pan. Bake at 325° for 1 hour or until a wooden pick inserted in center comes out clean. Cool in pan 10 minutes; remove from pan, and cool completely on a rack. Yield: one 10-inch cake.
Jacquelyn Christopher, Asheville, North Carolina.

BANANA PUDDING

½ cup sugar
3 tablespoons all-purpose flour
Dash of salt
1 egg
3 eggs, separated
2 cups milk
½ teaspoon vanilla extract
3 dozen vanilla wafers
3 large bananas, sliced
¼ cup sugar

Combine ½ cup sugar, flour, and salt in top of a double boiler; mix well. Stir in 1 egg, 3 egg yolks, and milk; mix well. Place over boiling water; cook, stirring constantly, until smooth and thickened. Remove mixture from heat; stir in vanilla.

Spread about ¼ cup pudding in a 1¾-quart casserole; arrange 1 dozen vanilla wafers over top of pudding. Top with one-third of banana slices and one-third of remaining pudding. Repeat layers twice.

Beat 3 egg whites (at room temperature) at high speed of an electric mixer 1 minute. Gradually add ¼ cup sugar, 1 tablespoon at a time, beating until stiff peaks form and sugar dissolves (2 to 4 minutes). Spread meringue over pudding, sealing to edge of casserole. Bake at 350° for 12 to 15 minutes or until golden brown. Yield: 8 servings.
Mary Swink, Campobello, South Carolina.

Spices Spark The Season

Step into many homes this time of year, and you'll know that cinnamon, allspice, cloves, and nutmeg are popular during the holiday season. Baked into sweet breads, simmered in hot fruit beverages, or mixed into bowls of potpourri, these sweet-tasting spices drift through the air with inviting aromas.

To keep your spices fragrant longer, be sure to store them properly in airtight containers in a place away from heat or light. Remember, too, that spices can be stored in the freezer.

CINNAMON UPSIDE-DOWN COFFEE CAKE

About 6 cups all-purpose flour, divided
2 packages dry yeast
½ cup sugar
1½ teaspoons salt
½ cup butter or margarine, softened
1½ cups warm water (105° to 115°)
2 eggs
¼ cup butter or margarine, softened and divided
1 cup sugar, divided
1 tablespoon plus 1 teaspoon ground cinnamon, divided
Nutty Topping

Combine 2 cups flour, yeast, ½ cup sugar, and salt in a large mixing bowl; stir well. Add ½ cup butter and warm water; beat mixture at medium speed of an electric mixer 2 minutes, scraping sides of bowl.

Beat in eggs and 2 cups flour; beat at high speed of an electric mixer 1 minute. Gradually add enough of remaining flour to make a soft dough. (Dough should remain soft and slightly sticky.)

Turn dough out onto a heavily floured surface; knead 5 minutes or until dough is smooth and elastic. Cover and let rest 10 minutes.

Shape dough into a ball; place in a well-greased bowl, turning to grease top. Cover and let rise in a warm place (85°), free from drafts, 1 to 2 hours or until doubled in bulk, or cover dough and let rise in refrigerator overnight.

Punch dough down. Divide dough in half; shape each portion into a ball. Turn one portion out onto a lightly floured surface. Roll into a 15- x 9-inch rectangle. Spread surface with 2 tablespoons butter, and sprinkle with ½ cup sugar and 2 teaspoons cinnamon. Roll up jellyroll fashion, beginning at long

side. Firmly pinch edge and ends to seal. Cut into 15 (1-inch) slices. Repeat procedure with remaining dough and ingredients.

Grease two 9-inch square pans; spoon Nutty Topping into pans, spreading evenly. Place slices, cut side up, in pans. Bake at 350° for 25 to 30 minutes. Cool 2 minutes, and turn onto a serving platter. Yield: 30 rolls.

Nutty Topping:

⅔ cup butter or margarine, melted
1 cup firmly packed brown sugar
1 cup pecan halves
2 tablespoons light corn syrup

Combine all ingredients, mixing well. Yield: about 2 cups. *Lucille Robinson, Atlanta, Georgia.*

SWEET POTATO CASSEROLE

5 medium-size sweet potatoes, peeled, cooked, and mashed
⅓ cup milk
3 tablespoons light brown sugar
2 tablespoons sugar
2 tablespoons butter or margarine, melted
½ teaspoon salt
½ teaspoon ground cinnamon
¼ teaspoon ground nutmeg
¼ teaspoon ground ginger
1 cup miniature marshmallows

Combine all ingredients except marshmallows, mixing well. Spoon into a lightly greased 1½-quart casserole. Cover and bake at 375° for 30 minutes. Uncover, sprinkle with marshmallows, and bake an additional 5 minutes. Yield: 4 servings. *Bobbie Shaw, Oxford, Mississippi.*

SPICY RICE

¾ cup chopped onion
¾ cup chopped celery
1 tablespoon butter or margarine, melted
3 cups cooked regular rice
½ cup raisins
⅓ cup chopped walnuts
2 tablespoons honey
1 tablespoon lemon juice
¾ teaspoon salt
¼ teaspoon ground cinnamon
¼ teaspoon pepper

Sauté onion and celery in butter in a large skillet until crisp-tender. Stir in remaining ingredients. Spoon into a greased 2-quart casserole. Cover and bake at 350° for 25 minutes or until thoroughly heated. Yield: 6 servings.
Ella Brown, Proctor, Arkansas.

TRADITIONAL PUMPKIN PIE

1½ cups mashed cooked pumpkin
1 cup sugar
1 cup milk
2 eggs, beaten
2 tablespoons butter or margarine, melted
½ teaspoon salt
⅛ teaspoon ground nutmeg
⅛ teaspoon ground cinnamon
1 teaspoon orange extract
1 unbaked 9-inch pastry shell

Combine all ingredients except pastry shell; mix well. Pour into pastry shell; bake at 450° for 10 minutes. Reduce heat to 350°; bake an additional 30 to 35 minutes or until set. Yield: one 9-inch pie. *Marilyn Johnson, Ringgold, Georgia.*

SPICED APPLE CIDER

½ gallon apple cider
1 cup sugar
2 teaspoons whole cloves
1 whole nutmeg
2 cups orange juice
½ cup lemon juice
½ cup apple brandy (optional)
Cinnamon sticks

Combine apple cider and sugar in a Dutch oven. Tie cloves and nutmeg in a cheesecloth bag; add to cider mixture. Bring to a boil; reduce heat, and simmer 15 minutes. Remove spice bag, and add juices. Stir in brandy, if desired. Simmer until heated. Serve with cinnamon-stick stirrers. Yield: 2½ quarts.
Linda Gellatly, Winston-Salem, North Carolina.

APRICOT GLAZE FOR HAM

1 (17-ounce) can apricot halves, drained
½ cup light or dark corn syrup
¾ teaspoon ground ginger
¼ teaspoon ground cloves

Combine all ingredients in container of an electric blender; process until smooth.

To serve, brush glaze on ham during last hour of baking, basting every 15 minutes. Heat remaining glaze; serve with ham. Yield: 1⅔ cups.
Peggy H. Amos, Martinsville, Virginia.

Hurrah For The Holidays

Traditions are never more apparent than during the holidays when friends and family gather to celebrate. It's the time of year when we like to do nice things for those we love. And Southerners have always tended to express their hospitality and kindness with food.

Here is our annual special section on holiday dinners and entertaining. The following pages contain a bountiful collection of recipes, party ideas, and helpful hints for planning a variety of seasonal events. You'll find traditional favorites, such as Fresh Coconut Cake, along with the unexpected, such as Pheasant Muscatel. We'll introduce ideas that may be completely new to you, such as Pumpkin Cheesecake for a special dessert or Cinnamon Ornaments to decorate your tree or tie on your gift packages.

We show how to turn the food processor into a handy kitchen helper when your holiday schedule gets hectic. There are ideas for food gifts to share with a holiday hostess. And when you've eaten too much, and it's time to cut back, we've got just the thing—lots of low-calorie vegetables.

Our section begins with a Thanksgiving party hosted by Stacy and Kris Childs of Birmingham. We hear guests laughing as they greet each other over cups of a champagne punch. When it's time for appetizers, the Childses' younger daughter, Pilar, and one of her friends graciously offer guests Oysters in Patty Shells. Then, before the main part of the meal, guests are treated to Turkey Gumbo ladled over rice.

"Our menu features two turkeys this year. One is domestic, and the other was shot by our older daughter, Callan. So this is a very special meal for her." Other dishes completing their holiday dinner menu include several of Kris's favorites—Cranberry Relish, Brussels Sprouts With Shallots and Mustard, Glazed Carrots, Glazed Pearl Onions, Missy Potatoes, and Sour Cream Yeast Rolls. Stacy contributes a double magnum of 1966 Château Gruaud-Larose, a rare find, from his wine cellar.

Apple Strudel With Cream and Cranberry Juice Sorbet fill the dessert table. As the evening comes to an end and Stacy and Kris bid their guests farewell, each couple receives a package of Gingerbread Men to take home. There's a cookie for each member of the family, even those too young to attend this delightful dinner.

Champagne Punch
Oysters in Patty Shells
Turkey Gumbo
Smoked Turkey
Cranberry Relish
Brussels Sprouts
With Shallots and Mustard
Glazed Carrots   Glazed Pearl Onions
Missy Potatoes
Sour Cream Yeast Rolls
Apple Strudel With Cream
Cranberry Juice Sorbet
Gingerbread Men
Wine   Coffee

CHAMPAGNE PUNCH

1 ripe pineapple
1½ cups sugar
2½ cups bourbon
2 (25.4-ounce) bottles champagne, chilled

Core pineapple, and cut into bite-size pieces; add sugar and bourbon, and let mixture sit at least 24 hours in an airtight container.

Pour pineapple mixture into punch bowl; stir in champagne just before serving. Add crushed ice, as desired. Yield: 3 quarts.

OYSTERS IN PATTY SHELLS

1 tablespoon butter or margarine, melted
1 (12-ounce) container fresh oysters, drained
1½ cups chopped celery
1 pound fresh mushrooms, chopped
½ cup minced fresh parsley
4 green onions with tops, chopped
1 clove garlic, minced
½ teaspoon dried whole thyme
¼ teaspoon coarsely ground black pepper
⅛ teaspoon red pepper
1 (10¾-ounce) can cream of mushroom soup, undiluted
2 (10-ounce) packages frozen patty shells, baked

Combine butter and oysters in skillet; cook over low heat 2 minutes. Add celery, mushrooms, parsley, onions, and garlic, and cook over medium heat until celery is crisp-tender; drain. Stir in seasonings and soup; cook just until thoroughly heated. Spoon into patty shells. Serve immediately. Yield: 12 servings.

Tip: Update your file of coupons twice a year. Many coupons expire in the summer and at the end of the year.

TURKEY GUMBO

1 pound smoked sausage, cut into ½-inch
   slices
¼ cup vegetable oil
¼ cup all-purpose flour
5 stalks celery, chopped
2 medium onions, chopped
2 cups cubed cooked turkey
4 cups water
1 teaspoon gumbo filé
½ teaspoon salt
¼ teaspoon pepper
Hot cooked rice

Brown sausage slices in a large skillet,
stirring well. Drain on paper towels,
and set aside.

Combine oil and flour in a large
Dutch oven; cook over medium heat,
stirring constantly, 10 to 15 minutes or
until mixture (roux) is the color of a
copper penny. Stir in celery and onion;
cook 5 minutes, stirring occasionally.
Add sausage, turkey, and water. Bring
to a boil; reduce heat, and simmer, uncovered, 4 hours. Stir in gumbo filé,
salt, and pepper. Serve over rice. Yield:
about 2 quarts.

SMOKED TURKEY

1 (5- to 7-pound) turkey
1 tablespoon Creole seasoning, divided
1 large onion
¼ cup butter or margarine, melted

Remove giblets and neck from turkey; reserve for other uses, if desired.
Rinse turkey with cold water; pat dry.
Sprinkle cavity with 1 teaspoon Creole
seasoning. Place onion in cavity of turkey; close cavity with skewers. Tie ends
of legs to tail with cord; lift wing tips up
and over back so they are tucked under
bird. Baste turkey with butter, and
sprinkle with remaining 2 teaspoons
Creole seasoning.

Prepare charcoal fire in smoker, and
let burn 15 to 20 minutes. Soak hickory
chips in water 15 minutes. Place hickory
chips on coals. Place water pan in
smoker, and fill with water.

Place turkey on food rack. Cover
with smoker lid; cook 4 to 8 hours or
until meat thermometer reaches 180° to
185° when inserted in breast or meaty

part of thigh. (Make sure thermometer
does not touch bone.) Refill water pan,
and add charcoal as needed.

Remove turkey from food rack; cover
and refrigerate. To serve, thinly slice
turkey. Yield: 9 to 10 servings.

Note: One domestic and one wild turkey were used for the party; both types
may be smoked.

CRANBERRY RELISH

1 orange, quartered and seeded
½ lemon, halved and seeded
1 yellow Delicious apple, peeled, cored,
   and quartered
1 (12-ounce) package fresh cranberries
1 (12-ounce) jar raspberry preserves
1 cup sugar

Position knife blade in food processor
bowl; add orange and lemon, and process until finely chopped. Remove fruit.

Reposition knife blade in processor
bowl; add remaining ingredients. Process until apple and cranberries are
coarsely chopped. Combine fruit mixtures, mixing well. Chill before serving.
Yield: about 4 cups.

BRUSSELS SPROUTS WITH
SHALLOTS AND MUSTARD

2½ pounds fresh brussels sprouts
8 medium shallots, sliced
¼ cup butter or margarine, melted
½ cup coarse-grained Dijon mustard

Wash brussels sprouts thoroughly,
and remove discolored leaves. Cut off
stem ends, and slash bottom of each
sprout with a shallow X. Place sprouts
in a small amount of boiling salted
water. Cover, reduce heat, and simmer

10 minutes or until tender; drain and set
sprouts aside.

Sauté shallots in butter until tender.
Remove from heat, and stir in mustard.
Spoon mustard mixture over sprouts,
tossing gently. Serve immediately.
Yield: 12 servings.

GLAZED CARROTS

About 5 dozen baby carrots with tops
¼ cup plus 1 tablespoon butter or
   margarine, softened
¼ cup sugar
2½ tablespoons water
¾ teaspoon salt
¼ teaspoon pepper

Scrape carrots, leaving ¼ inch of
green tops, if desired.

Combine all ingredients in a skillet;
cover and bring to a boil. Reduce heat
to low, and simmer 12 to 18 minutes or
until carrots are crisp-tender. Uncover
and cook over medium heat 5 minutes
or until liquid evaporates and carrots
are glazed. Yield: 18 servings.

GLAZED PEARL ONIONS

3 cups pearl onions
¼ cup butter or margarine
¼ cup water
3 tablespoons sugar
½ teaspoon salt

Remove outer skin from onions.
Combine onions and remaining ingredients in a skillet; cover and bring to a
boil. Reduce heat to low, and simmer 5
to 8 minutes. Uncover and cook, stirring often, over medium heat an additional 3 to 5 minutes or until liquid
evaporates and onions are glazed.
Yield: 18 servings.

*Tip: If cast-iron cookware is to be
stored for any length of time, rub a
light film of oil over interior. Wipe off
film before using, and wash cookware
in clear water.*

MISSY POTATOES

1 (2-pound) package frozen hash brown
  potatoes, thawed
1 (16-ounce) carton commercial sour
  cream
1 (10¾-ounce) can cream of celery soup,
  undiluted
1 cup (4 ounces) shredded sharp Cheddar
  cheese
½ cup butter or margarine, softened
1 teaspoon salt
1 teaspoon coarsely ground black pepper
½ cup round buttery cracker crumbs

Combine all ingredients except
cracker crumbs; spoon into a lightly
greased 13- x 9- x 2-inch baking dish.
Sprinkle cracker crumbs evenly over top
of potato mixture. Bake at 350° for 40
minutes or until bubbly. Yield: 10 to 12
servings.

SOUR CREAM YEAST ROLLS

2 packages dry yeast
½ cup warm water (105° to 115°)
1 (8-ounce) carton commercial sour cream
1 cup butter or margarine, softened
2 eggs, beaten
⅓ cup sugar
1 teaspoon salt
4 cups unbleached flour

Dissolve yeast in warm water; let
stand 5 minutes.

Place sour cream in a small saucepan;
cook over low heat to 105° to 115°.
Combine sour cream, butter, eggs,
sugar, and salt in a large bowl; add
yeast mixture, and stir well. Gradually
stir in flour. Place dough in a well-
greased bowl, turning to grease top.
Cover and let rise in refrigerator at least
6 hours. (Dough may rise in refrigerator
for up to 24 hours. Dough does not
double in bulk, but it rises slightly.)

Divide dough into 4 equal parts. Roll
each part into a 12-inch circle on a
floured surface; cut each circle into 12
pie-shaped wedges. Roll up each wedge
tightly, beginning at wide end. Seal
points, and place rolls, point side down,
on greased baking sheets. Curve each
roll into a crescent shape.

Cover rolls, and let rise in a warm
place (85°), free from drafts, about 30

to 40 minutes. Place baking rack in
upper third of oven; bake at 375° for 12
minutes. Yield: 4 dozen rolls.

APPLE STRUDEL

½ cup raisins
¼ cup brandy
2 tablespoons lemon juice
4 medium apples, peeled, cored, and
  grated
1 cup sugar
½ cup all-purpose flour
¾ teaspoon ground cinnamon
¼ teaspoon ground nutmeg
5 sheets commercial frozen phyllo pastry,
  thawed
¼ cup butter or margarine, melted
1 cup fine, dry breadcrumbs, divided
¼ cup non-dairy powdered creamer
2 tablespoons butter or margarine, melted
Sifted powdered sugar
Whipped cream

Combine raisins and brandy, and let
stand overnight.

Sprinkle lemon juice over grated
apple; add sugar, flour, cinnamon, and
nutmeg, mixing well. Set aside.

Place 2 sheets of phyllo pastry on a
damp towel, keeping remaining pastry
covered. Brush with 1 tablespoon
melted butter, and sprinkle evenly with
¼ cup breadcrumbs. Top with another
sheet of phyllo pastry; brush with 1 tablespoon butter, and sprinkle with ¼
cup breadcrumbs. Repeat the procedure
with remaining pastry sheets, butter,
and breadcrumbs.

Drain apple mixture. Spread apple
mixture over breadcrumbs, leaving a ¾-
inch border on narrow ends and a 1-
inch border on one wide end. Sprinkle
with raisins and powdered creamer.
Starting with the wide end without border, roll up jellyroll fashion, and place
on a greased cookie sheet, seam side
down, tucking ends under. Brush with 2
tablespoons melted butter.

Cut ¼-inch-deep slashes, about 1 inch
apart, diagonally across top. Bake at
375° for 40 minutes or until golden
brown. Sprinkle with powdered sugar.
Serve each slice with a dollop of
whipped cream. Yield: 12 servings.

CRANBERRY JUICE SORBET

½ cup plus 1 tablespoon sugar
½ cup plus 1 tablespoon water
3⅓ cups cranberry juice

Combine sugar and water in a small
saucepan; bring to a boil. Reduce heat,
and simmer until sugar dissolves. Set
aside until cool.

Combine sugar syrup and cranberry
juice, stirring well. Pour into a 9-inch
square pan; freeze until firm.

Position knife blade in food processor
bowl; spoon in small chunks of frozen
mixture. Process just until smooth.
Serve immediately. Yield: 1 quart.

GINGERBREAD MEN

2¼ cups sugar
¾ cup water
⅓ cup dark corn syrup
1¼ tablespoons ground cinnamon
1 tablespoon ground ginger
2 teaspoons ground cloves
1 cup plus 2 tablespoons butter or
  margarine
1 tablespoon baking soda
1 tablespoon water
8 cups all-purpose flour

Combine sugar, water, syrup, and
spices in a medium saucepan; cook over
medium heat, stirring until sugar dissolves. Add butter, stirring until melted.
Dissolve baking soda in 1 tablespoon
water; add to sugar mixture. Pour sugar
mixture into a bowl; gradually add
flour, mixing well. Chill 1 hour.

Divide dough into thirds. Roll one-
third of dough to ¼- to ⅛-inch thickness on a lightly floured surface. Cut
with a 4-inch gingerbread man cutter,
and place on lightly greased cookie
sheet. Bake at 350° for 10 to 12 minutes. Cool 1 minute on pan; remove
cookies to wire racks, and cool completely. Repeat procedure with remaining dough. Yield: about 3½ dozen.

Note: Cookie molds may be used instead of cookie cutters.

Make These Side Dishes Ahead Of Time

Ease the last-minute rush of the holiday meal by selecting some foods that can be prepared ahead of time. That's just what we did with these side dishes. Each can be made the day before.

If your special meal calls for a fruit side dish, try our Warm Praline Fruit Compote. You'll love the rich flavor of this dish made Southern by the addition of toasted pecans and praline liqueur.

HOLIDAY ASPARAGUS

2 (10-ounce) packages frozen chopped asparagus
1 (10¾-ounce) can cream of mushroom soup, undiluted
2 tablespoons milk
1 teaspoon Worcestershire sauce
¼ teaspoon salt
¼ teaspoon pepper
1 (8-ounce) can sliced water chestnuts, drained
1 (4-ounce) can sliced mushrooms, drained
1 (2-ounce) jar diced pimiento, drained
1 hard-cooked egg, sliced
1 (2.8-ounce) can fried onion rings

Thaw asparagus; drain well, and set aside. Combine soup, milk, Worcestershire sauce, salt, and pepper; mix well, and set aside. Layer half each of asparagus, water chestnuts, mushrooms, pimiento, egg, and soup mixture in a greased 8-inch square baking dish. Repeat layers. Cover and refrigerate.

Remove from refrigerator; let stand 30 minutes. Sprinkle onion rings over top. Bake, uncovered, at 350° for 25 minutes. Yield: 6 to 8 servings.
Sandra Russell,
Gainesville, Florida.

Tip: In your kitchen, keep a fire extinguisher equipped to handle all kinds of home fires.

BROCCOLI-BLUE CHEESE CASSEROLE

2 (10-ounce) packages frozen broccoli spears
2 tablespoons butter or margarine, softened
2 tablespoons all-purpose flour
½ cup milk
½ cup half-and-half
¼ teaspoon salt
⅛ teaspoon pepper
1 (3-ounce) package cream cheese, softened and cubed
½ cup (2 ounces) blue cheese, crumbled
½ cup seasoned croutons

Cook broccoli in a small amount of boiling water until crisp-tender; drain and coarsely chop. Set aside.

Melt butter in a heavy saucepan over low heat; add flour, stirring until smooth. Cook 1 minute, stirring constantly. Gradually add milk and half-and-half; cook over medium heat, stirring constantly, until thickened and bubbly. Add salt, pepper, cream cheese, and blue cheese; stir until cheese melts. Add broccoli; stir gently. Spoon into a greased 10- x 6- x 2-inch baking dish; cover and refrigerate.

Remove from refrigerator; let stand 30 minutes. Sprinkle croutons over top. Bake, uncovered, at 350° for 25 to 30 minutes. Yield: 6 to 8 servings.
Mrs. Harry Zimmer,
El Paso, Texas.

CAULIFLOWER-PEA CASSEROLE

1 large cauliflower
1 (10-ounce) package frozen English peas, thawed
½ cup slivered almonds
½ teaspoon curry powder
3 tablespoons butter or margarine, melted and divided
2 tablespoons all-purpose flour
1¼ cups commercial sour cream
1½ teaspoons onion salt
⅛ teaspoon white pepper

Separate cauliflower into flowerets; cook in a small amount of unsalted boiling water 6 to 8 minutes or until crisp-tender. Drain well; place cauliflower and peas in a greased 2-quart casserole. Set aside.

Sauté almonds and curry powder in 1 tablespoon butter in a small skillet; cook, stirring constantly, until almonds are browned. Remove from heat, and set aside.

Combine remaining 2 tablespoons butter and flour in a heavy saucepan; stir until smooth. Cook 1 minute, stirring constantly. Gradually stir in sour cream; cook over low heat, stirring constantly, until thoroughly heated. Stir in salt and pepper. Pour over cauliflower mixture; sprinkle almonds over top. Cover and refrigerate.

Remove from refrigerator; let stand 30 minutes. Bake, uncovered, at 350° for 25 to 30 minutes. Yield: 6 to 8 servings.
Connie Burgess,
Knoxville, Tennessee.

WARM PRALINE FRUIT COMPOTE

1 (16-ounce) can peach slices, undrained
1 (16-ounce) can pear slices, undrained
1 tablespoon cornstarch
1 (17-ounce) can apricot halves, drained
⅓ cup coarsely chopped pecans, toasted
¼ cup golden raisins
¼ cup orange marmalade
¼ cup praline liqueur
3 tablespoons butter or margarine

Drain peaches and pears, reserving ¾ cup syrup. Add cornstarch to syrup, mixing well; set aside.

Combine peaches, pears, apricots, pecans, and raisins in a lightly greased 2-quart casserole. Combine marmalade and liqueur; pour over fruit. Pour cornstarch mixture over fruit; stir to blend. Dot with butter. Cover and refrigerate.

Remove from refrigerator; let stand 30 minutes. Bake, uncovered, at 350° for 30 minutes or until thoroughly heated. Yield: 6 servings.

Here's A Festive Meal For Two

If you're spending the holiday with someone special, you want the meal to have an air of celebration. The menu we've put together combines simplicity and portions designed for two. You'll find cleanup easier, too, since you won't have to worry about leftovers.

To save time, prepare the mushroom soup and the salad dressing the day before. Apple Cobbler for Two bakes at the same temperature as the Cornish hens, so you can put the dessert in the oven while the hens bake the last few minutes. Aloha Carrots take only a few minutes to cook, and you can toss a green salad in the meantime. Reheat the mushroom soup just before the rest of the meal is complete.

Even though it's just the two of you, remember to add some touches that will make the evening memorable. For example, decorate the table with a few fresh flowers or seasonal greenery.

Cream of Mushroom Soup
Stuffed Cornish Hens
Green salad with Italian Dressing
Aloha Carrots
Commercial rolls
Apple Cobbler for Two
Wine   Coffee

CREAM OF MUSHROOM SOUP

¼ **pound fresh mushrooms, sliced**
3 **tablespoons chopped onion**
1 **tablespoon butter or margarine, melted**
½ **cup milk**
2 **tablespoons all-purpose flour**
⅛ **teaspoon white pepper**
1 **cup chicken broth**
Fresh parsley sprigs

Sauté mushrooms and onion in butter. Cool slightly.

Position knife blade in food processor bowl; add mushrooms, onion, milk, flour, and pepper. Top with cover, and pulse 3 times. Add chicken broth to processor bowl, and pulse until mixture is blended.

Pour mixture in a saucepan; cook over medium heat, stirring until thickened. Pour into serving bowls, and garnish with parsley. Yield: 1½ cups.
Mrs. Earl L. Faulkenberry,
Lancaster, South Carolina.

STUFFED CORNISH HENS

2 **tablespoons finely chopped onion**
⅓ **cup uncooked regular rice**
2 **tablespoons butter or margarine, melted**
1 **tablespoon lemon juice**
½ **cup cream of celery soup, undiluted**
1 **teaspoon chives**
1 **teaspoon parsley flakes**
¾ **cup water**
1 **chicken bouillon cube**
2 **(1- to 1¼-pound) Cornish hens**
Salt and pepper
Melted butter or margarine

Sauté onion and rice in 2 tablespoons butter 5 minutes or until onion is transparent and rice is golden. Add lemon juice, soup, chives, parsley, water, and bouillon cube, and bring to a boil. Cover, reduce heat to medium low, and cook for 25 minutes.

Remove giblets from hens; reserve for another use. Rinse hens with cold water, and pat dry; sprinkle cavities with salt and pepper.

Stuff hens with rice mixture, and close cavities. Secure with wooden picks; truss. Place hens, breast side up, in a shallow baking pan.

Brush hens with melted butter. Cover and bake at 375° for 30 minutes. Uncover and bake 1 hour, basting frequently with butter. Yield: 2 servings.
Mary Moseley,
Birmingham, Alabama.

ITALIAN DRESSING

2 **tablespoons olive oil**
2 **tablespoons wine vinegar**
¼ **teaspoon Italian seasoning**
¼ **teaspoon sugar**
¼ **teaspoon salt**
⅛ **teaspoon garlic powder**
⅛ **teaspoon pepper**

Combine all ingredients, mixing well; chill thoroughly. Shake well before serving. Serve over tossed green salad. Yield: ¼ cup.
Michelle Joslin Vire,
Coushatta, Louisiana.

ALOHA CARROTS

1½ **cups scraped, sliced carrots**
¼ **cup water**
¼ **teaspoon salt**
1 **tablespoon brown sugar**
¼ **cup crushed pineapple, drained**
1 **teaspoon butter or margarine**

Combine carrots, water, and salt in a saucepan. Bring to a boil; reduce heat, and cook over medium heat about 10 minutes or until carrots are crisp-tender. Stir in sugar, pineapple, and butter. Yield: 2 servings.
Carolyn Epting,
Lexington, South Carolina.

APPLE COBBLER FOR TWO

3 **tablespoons brown sugar**
¼ **teaspoon ground cinnamon**
¼ **teaspoon ground nutmeg**
1 **teaspoon lemon juice**
2 **medium-size cooking apples, peeled and sliced**
⅓ **cup all-purpose flour**
2 **tablespoons sugar**
1 **teaspoon baking powder**
2 **tablespoons milk**
1 **tablespoon vegetable oil**

Combine sugar, cinnamon, nutmeg, and lemon juice; add apples, and toss well to coat. Spoon apple mixture into two 10-ounce custard cups. Set aside.

Combine flour, sugar, and baking powder in a small bowl. Combine milk and oil; stir into flour mixture until moistened. Drop dough by teaspoonfuls onto apple mixture. Bake at 375° for 15 to 20 minutes. Serve warm. Yield: 2 servings.
Paula Patterson,
Round Rock, Texas.

Wrap Up
An Elegant Crêpe

Start with a thin, delicate crêpe pancake. Wrap it around a sweet filling, and cover it with a special sauce. The end result is one of the most luscious desserts of the season.

Each of our recipes begins with either Basic Dessert Crêpes or Chocolate Dessert Crêpes. We suggest making plenty ahead of time. They will keep two or three days in the refrigerator or about four months in the freezer.

BASIC DESSERT CRÊPES

1½ cups all-purpose flour
1 tablespoon sugar
¼ teaspoon salt
2 cups milk
1 teaspoon vanilla extract
3 eggs
2 tablespoons butter or margarine, melted
Vegetable oil

Combine flour, sugar, salt, milk, and vanilla, beating until smooth. Add eggs, and beat well; stir in butter. Refrigerate 2 hours. (This allows flour particles to swell and soften so that crêpes are light in texture.)

Brush bottom of a 6-inch crêpe pan or heavy skillet with oil; place over medium heat until just hot, not smoking.

Pour 2 tablespoons batter into pan; quickly tilt pan in all directions so batter covers pan in a thin film. Cook 1 minute or until lightly browned.

Lift edge of crêpe to test for doneness. Crêpe is ready for flipping when it can be shaken loose from pan. Flip crêpe, and cook about 30 seconds on other side. (This side is rarely more than spotty brown and is the side on which the filling is placed.)

Place crêpes on a towel to cool. Stack between layers of waxed paper to prevent sticking. Repeat until all batter is used. Yield: 2 dozen (6-inch) crêpes.

Tip: Always try to match pan size with the burner size.

These Chocolate-Orange Crêpes make a delightful dessert. They wrap around a creamy filling and sport a sweet mandarin orange topping with almonds.

CRANBERRY CRÊPES

½ cup sugar
¾ cup water
1 cup fresh cranberries
½ cup whipping cream
1 tablespoon kirsch
1 quart vanilla ice cream
12 Basic Dessert Crêpes

Combine sugar and water in a small saucepan; mix well. Bring to a boil, and cook 5 minutes, stirring often. Add cranberries; return to a boil, and cook 3 to 5 minutes or until skins pop. Remove from heat; cool.

Beat whipping cream until foamy; add kirsch, beating until stiff peaks form. Set aside.

Spoon about ⅓ cup ice cream in center of each crêpe; fold sides over. Place seam side down on serving dish. Spoon cranberry sauce over crêpes; top with whipped cream. Yield: 12 crêpes.

CHOCOLATE DESSERT CRÊPES

½ cup all-purpose flour
1 tablespoon cocoa
2 teaspoons sugar
Dash of salt
¾ cup milk
¼ teaspoon almond extract
1 egg
2 teaspoons butter or margarine, melted
Vegetable oil

Combine flour, cocoa, sugar, and salt. Add milk and almond extract; beat until smooth. Add egg, and beat well; stir in butter. Refrigerate 2 hours. (This allows flour particles to swell and soften so that crêpes are light in texture.)

Brush bottom of a 6-inch crêpe pan or heavy skillet with oil; place over medium heat until the skillet is just hot, not smoking.

Pour 2 tablespoons batter into pan; quickly tilt pan in all directions so that batter covers pan in a thin film. Cook batter 1 minute or until crêpe is lightly browned.

Lift edge of crêpe to test for doneness. Crêpe is ready for flipping when it can be shaken loose from pan. Flip crêpe, and cook about 30 seconds on other side. (This side is rarely more than spotty brown and is the side on which the filling is placed.)

Place crêpes on a towel to cool. Stack between layers of waxed paper to prevent sticking. Repeat until all batter is used. Yield: 10 (6-inch) crêpes.

CHOCOLATE-ORANGE CRÊPES

1 (11-ounce) can mandarin oranges, undrained
1 cup orange marmalade, divided
2 tablespoons Grand Marnier or other orange-flavored liqueur
2½ teaspoons cornstarch
2 (3-ounce) packages cream cheese, softened
1 (8-ounce) carton commercial sour cream
1 recipe Chocolate Dessert Crêpes
⅓ cup slivered almonds, toasted

Drain oranges, reserving juice. Combine juice, ¾ cup orange marmalade, Grand Marnier, and cornstarch; mix well. Cook over medium heat, stirring constantly, until thickened and bubbly. Remove from heat; cool.

Combine cream cheese and remaining ¼ cup marmalade; beat until smooth. Stir in sour cream. Spoon about 2½ tablespoons cream cheese mixture down center of each crêpe; fold sides over, and place seam side down on serving dish. Top each crêpe with mandarin oranges, orange syrup, and almonds. Yield: 10 crêpes.

Salads That Stand Out

You may spend hours planning the perfect entrée and dessert, but don't forget the salad—it's an important part of any special menu. Glistening vegetables in a pretty arrangement or congealed salads that stand tall with fruit offer a refreshing contrast to the entrée. In addition, they add color as well as texture to your holiday buffet.

VEGETABLE ANTIPASTO

2 small green peppers
1 small cauliflower, broken into flowerets
1 pound carrots, quartered and cut into 3-inch strips
5 stalks celery, quartered and cut into 3-inch strips
¾ pound fresh mushrooms, sliced
1½ cups tarragon vinegar
¼ cup sugar
¾ cup vegetable oil
2 cloves garlic, minced
1½ teaspoons salt
1 teaspoon dried whole tarragon
1½ teaspoons prepared mustard
Pepper to taste
Lettuce leaves (optional)

Wash and seed green peppers. Cut into ¼-inch rings; then cut rings in half. Combine green peppers, cauliflower, carrots, celery, and mushrooms in a large bowl.

Combine remaining ingredients except lettuce, stirring well; pour over vegetable mixture, tossing lightly to coat. Cover vegetables, and chill 12 hours or overnight.

Drain well. Arrange vegetables on lettuce leaves, if desired, before serving. Yield: 10 servings.   *Arlene Margolis, Little Rock, Arkansas.*

HOLIDAY MINCEMEAT SALAD

1 envelope unflavored gelatin
¼ cup cold water
1 (6-ounce) package cherry-flavored gelatin
3½ cups boiling water
1 (20½-ounce) jar brandy-flavored mincemeat
1 (8-ounce) can crushed pineapple, drained
1 small apple, unpeeled and finely chopped
1 cup chopped pecans or walnuts

Soften unflavored gelatin in cold water; set aside.

Dissolve cherry-flavored gelatin in boiling water; add unflavored gelatin mixture, stirring until gelatin dissolves. Chill until consistency of unbeaten egg white. Stir in remaining ingredients; pour into a lightly oiled 8-cup mold. Chill until firm. Yield: 12 to 14 servings.   *Loretta R. Gambrill, West Columbia, South Carolina.*

CREAMY APRICOT SALAD

1 (15¼-ounce) can crushed pineapple, undrained
1 (6-ounce) package apricot-flavored gelatin
2 cups boiling water
1½ cups miniature marshmallows
2 (7¾-ounce) jars apricot baby food
1 (3-ounce) package cream cheese, softened
1 (4-ounce) container frozen whipped topping, thawed
2 cups sliced banana
½ cup chopped pecans

Drain pineapple, reserving ½ cup juice; set aside. Dissolve gelatin in boiling water. Add marshmallows, stirring until slightly melted. Stir in pineapple and apricot baby food. Chill until the consistency of unbeaten egg white.

Combine cream cheese and reserved juice, blending well. Stir in whipped topping. Fold in gelatin mixture.

Arrange banana slices in bottom of a lightly greased 12- x 8- x 2-inch dish. Spoon gelatin mixture over bananas. Top with pecans. Chill until firm. Yield: 12 servings.   *Mrs. J. Edward Ebel, Louisville, Kentucky.*

SPICY PEACH-CRANBERRY RING

1 (29-ounce) can peach halves, undrained
1 teaspoon whole cloves
1 (3-inch) stick cinnamon
¼ cup sugar
1 tablespoon vinegar
1 (3-ounce) package lemon-flavored gelatin
¼ cup brandy
Cranberry Relish
Lemon-Cream Mayonnaise

Drain peaches, reserving juice; set peaches aside. Add enough water to juice to make 1½ cups. Add cloves, cinnamon, sugar, and vinegar to juice mixture. Simmer, uncovered, about 10 minutes. Add peaches, and simmer 5 minutes.

Remove peaches; arrange cut side up in a lightly oiled 3-quart ring mold. Strain juice mixture; add boiling water to make 1½ cups. Add gelatin, stirring until gelatin dissolves; stir in brandy. Let cool.

Pour cooled gelatin mixture over peaches. Chill.

Spoon Cranberry Relish on top of peach layer. Chill until firm. Unmold and serve with Lemon-Cream Mayonnaise. Yield: 10 to 12 servings.

Cranberry Relish:

1 cup fresh cranberries
½ orange, unpeeled
⅓ cup sugar
1¾ cups boiling water
1 (3-ounce) package cherry-flavored gelatin

Wash cranberries; drain. Cut orange half into quarters. Position knife blade in food processor bowl; add cranberries and orange. Process 30 to 45 seconds on high. Stir in sugar.

Add boiling water to gelatin, stirring until gelatin dissolves. Cool. Stir in cranberry-orange mixture. Yield: about 3 cups.

Lemon-Cream Mayonnaise:

1 cup whipping cream, whipped
½ cup mayonnaise
3 tablespoons lemon juice
3 tablespoons powdered sugar
⅛ teaspoon salt

Combine all of the ingredients, and mix well. Refrigerate for 2 hours. Yield: 2½ cups.
Evelyn Weisman,
Kingsville, Texas.

PICKLED PEACH SALAD

1 (3-ounce) package orange-flavored gelatin
1 cup boiling water
1 (22-ounce) jar pickled peaches, undrained
1 (16-ounce) can seedless white grapes, drained
1 cup coarsely chopped pecans
Lettuce leaves
1 (6-ounce) carton peach yogurt

Dissolve gelatin in boiling water; set aside. Drain peaches, reserving ⅔ cup juice; set peaches aside. Add peach juice to gelatin mixture; stir well.

Coarsely chop peaches; add peaches, grapes, and pecans to gelatin mixture. Pour into a lightly oiled 8-inch square dish; chill until firm. Cut into squares, and serve on lettuce leaves. Top each salad square with a dollop of yogurt. Yield: 9 servings.
Jane A. Dowden,
Nashville, Tennessee.

Sit Down For The Appetizer

If this time of the year brings important guests to your house, you may want to try something different to begin dinner. Guests can be seated at the table and begin their meal in style with a glass of wine and one of these delightful appetizers. Serve Cold Zucchini Soup or one of our hot appetizers.

HOLIDAY OYSTER STEW

2 tablespoons butter or margarine
1½ tablespoons all-purpose flour
3 cups milk
1 cup half-and-half
1 (12-ounce) container fresh Standard oysters, undrained
2 tablespoons butter or margarine
1½ teaspoons salt
Dash of hot sauce

Melt 2 tablespoons butter in a heavy saucepan over low heat; add flour, stirring until smooth. Cook 1 minute, stirring constantly. Gradually add milk and half-and-half; cook over medium heat, stirring constantly, until mixture is bubbly. Add oysters with liquid, 2 tablespoons butter, salt, and hot sauce. Reduce heat, and simmer, stirring constantly, 5 to 8 minutes or until edges of oysters curl. Yield: about 5½ cups.
Mildred Edwards,
Hamburg, Arkansas.

DEVILISH DEVILED CRAB

½ cup chopped onion
½ cup chopped green pepper
¼ cup butter or margarine, melted
¾ pound fresh lump crabmeat, drained
¾ cup soft breadcrumbs
¼ cup milk
1½ tablespoons Dijon mustard
1½ teaspoons Worcestershire sauce
½ teaspoon salt
¼ teaspoon white pepper
¼ cup plus 2 tablespoons soft breadcrumbs
Paprika
Minced fresh parsley
Pimiento slices (optional)
Lemon slices (optional)
Green pepper strips (optional)

Sauté onion and green pepper in butter until tender. Remove from heat; add crabmeat, ¾ cup breadcrumbs, milk, mustard, Worcestershire sauce, salt, and pepper, mixing well. Spoon mixture into six (6-ounce) lightly greased individual baking shells or dishes. Sprinkle each dish with 1 tablespoon breadcrumbs; sprinkle lightly with paprika. Bake at 400° for 15 minutes. Garnish with parsley, pimiento, lemon, and green pepper, if desired. Yield: 6 servings.
Jerry L. Rhye,
Providence Forge, Virginia.

ASPARAGUS CROQUETTES

2¾ cups fine cracker crumbs, divided
2 (14½-ounce) cans cut asparagus, drained
1 (10¾-ounce) can cream of mushroom
    soup, undiluted
2 cups (8 ounces) shredded sharp Cheddar
    cheese
Vegetable oil

Combine 1¾ cups cracker crumbs, asparagus, soup, and cheese, mixing well. Shape mixture, ¼ cup at a time, into oval croquettes. Roll croquettes in the remaining 1 cup cracker crumbs.

Deep fry croquettes in hot oil (375°) for 2 to 3 minutes or until golden brown. Drain on paper towels. Serve immediately. Yield: 15 appetizer servings.   *Vicki Fioranelli,*
Cleveland, Mississippi.

COLD ZUCCHINI SOUP

½ cup chopped onion
1 large clove garlic, minced
1 tablespoon butter or margarine, melted
1 tablespoon vegetable oil
6 medium-size zucchini, chopped
¼ to ½ teaspoon freshly ground pepper
1 tablespoon all-purpose flour
2 (10¾-ounce) cans chicken broth, diluted
1 (8-ounce) carton commercial sour cream
2 tablespoons minced fresh chives or
    green onions

Sauté onion and garlic in butter and oil in a Dutch oven until onion is tender. Add zucchini and pepper; cover and cook over low heat 10 minutes or until tender. Add flour, stirring until smooth; cook 1 minute. Gradually stir in broth; cook over medium heat, stirring constantly, until bubbly. Cook 5 minutes, stirring often. Let cool.

Pour zucchini mixture into container of an electric blender; process until smooth. Stir in sour cream and chives. Cover and chill completely. Yield: about 2 quarts.   *Mrs. E. R. Sellars,*
Oklahoma City, Oklahoma.

Tip: Rub hands with fresh parsley to remove any unpleasant odors.

Quick Beverages To Start The Meal

Make the meal a memorable one by starting with a beverage fit for the season. Hot Cranberry Punch will warm you up while the spices in it fill the room with a delicious aroma. Or for a year-round pleaser, treat family and friends to a glass of Rum Punch. The recipe calls for orange juice, so you may want to squeeze the fruit yourself. It's the peak season for citrus, and nothing beats that fresh flavor.

HOT WINE PUNCH

1 quart Burgundy or other dry red wine
2 cups orange juice
½ cup lemon juice
½ cup sugar
4 whole cloves
1 (3-inch) stick cinnamon

Combine all ingredients in a large saucepan; mix well. Place over medium heat, stirring until sugar dissolves. Remove spices and discard; serve beverage hot. Yield: about 7 cups.

Mary Andrew,
Winston-Salem, North Carolina.

VODKA PUNCH

3 cups pineapple juice, divided
2 (6-ounce) cans frozen limeade
    concentrate, thawed and undiluted
2 cups water
1½ cups vodka
1 (33.8-ounce) bottle lemon-lime
    carbonated beverage, chilled
1 lime, thinly sliced

Freeze 1½ cups pineapple juice in a 2-cup ring mold or bowl. Combine remaining 1½ cups pineapple juice and remaining ingredients except lime slices in a punch bowl, stirring well. Add frozen pineapple juice and lime slices to the punch bowl just before serving. Yield: 3 quarts.   *Mildred Beckley,*
Bristol, Virginia.

RUM PUNCH

2 cups orange juice
2 cups pineapple juice
1 to 1½ cups rum
¼ cup grenadine
Fresh pineapple chunks (optional)
Orange slices (optional)
Maraschino cherries (optional)

Combine juice, rum, and grenadine; mix well, and chill. Serve over ice. Garnish each serving with pineapple, orange, and cherry, if desired. Yield: about 5 cups.   *Lana J. Tabb,*
Lakeland, Florida.

HOT CRANBERRY PUNCH

1 (48-ounce) bottle cranberry juice
    cocktail
1 cup water
½ cup firmly packed brown sugar
¾ teaspoon ground cloves
½ teaspoon ground allspice
½ teaspoon ground cinnamon
¼ teaspoon ground nutmeg
1 (46-ounce) can pineapple juice

Combine all ingredients except pineapple juice in a large saucepan; mix well. Bring to a boil, stirring occasionally. Add pineapple juice; return to a boil. Reduce heat, and simmer the punch 5 minutes. Serve hot. Yield: about 3 quarts.   *Bonnie Taylor,*
Jackson, Tennessee.

HOLIDAY CRANBERRY PUNCH

2 cups orange juice
½ cup lemon juice
½ cup sugar
1 (48-ounce) bottle cranberry juice
    cocktail
2 pints raspberry sherbet
2 (28-ounce) bottles ginger ale, chilled

Combine orange juice, lemon juice, and sugar; stir until sugar dissolves. Add cranberry juice; mix well. Chill. Spoon scoops of sherbet on top of punch. Add ginger ale; gently stir to blend. Yield: 3½ quarts.
Margaret L. Hunter,
Princeton, Kentucky.

These Food Gifts Say Thank You

When you're invited to a dinner or a special weekend at someone's home, taking along a small gift is a gracious way to show your appreciation. A food gift makes a perfect choice, especially during the holidays.

One thing to keep in mind: Be sure it's something that can be served anytime and not something the host or hostess feels obligated to fit into the menu at hand. More than likely, the meal has been carefully planned, and a surprise dish that has to be served right away may be more of a complication than a blessing.

All of our food gifts keep well, and they're also attractive and tasty. You're sure to find something that's just right for the next time you're on the receiving end of Southern hospitality.

Orange-Cranberry Bread is packed with chopped cranberries and pecans and has a rich orange flavor. The crunchy topping is a combination of sugar and orange rind. Dress it up with a doily as we did, or put it in a basket for two gifts in one.

Cranberry Conserve also makes use of fresh cranberries and pecans. These ingredients are mixed with apple, orange, and raisins to make a tangy condiment that goes well with ham, chicken, and turkey—all meats that are likely to be served during the holidays. Because the conserve is not processed, pass along instructions to refrigerate it.

Old-fashioned tins are great containers for Shortbread. You may want to start collecting tins now because this recipe is so easy you'll want to make lots of it.

Mulled Wine Spice Mix takes a little longer to make, but we think you'll find the result worthwhile. It's a flavorful mixture of orange rind, cloves, cinnamon, allspice, and nutmeg; it's simmered with Burgundy and apple juice for a robust holiday beverage. This fragrant concoction makes a nice gift all by itself in a fabric bag tied with a shiny ribbon. To make it even more special, add a bottle of Burgundy. Don't forget to include the mulled wine recipe.

CRANBERRY CONSERVE

4 cups fresh cranberries
1 cup water
1 orange
3½ cups sugar
2 cups peeled, diced apples
½ cup raisins
½ cup chopped pecans

Combine cranberries and water in a large saucepan; bring to a boil. Cover, reduce heat, and simmer 6 to 8 minutes or until cranberry skins pop.

Grate rind of orange; peel, seed, and dice orange. Add orange, rind, and remaining ingredients to cranberries; mix well. Cook, stirring often, about 30 minutes or until mixture thickens. Remove from heat, cool, and spoon into jars or refrigerator containers. Store in refrigerator. Yield: 6 cups.

Gretchen Sherrill,
Stone Mountain, Georgia.

ORANGE-CRANBERRY BREAD

1 cup sugar
2½ cups all-purpose flour
2 teaspoons baking powder
½ teaspoon baking soda
¼ teaspoon salt
½ cup chopped pecans
2 teaspoons grated orange rind
2 eggs
¾ cup orange juice
½ cup mayonnaise
1½ cups chopped cranberries
2 tablespoons sugar
½ teaspoon grated orange rind

Combine 1 cup sugar, flour, baking powder, soda, and salt in a large mixing bowl. Stir in pecans and 2 teaspoons orange rind. Set aside.

Combine eggs, orange juice, and mayonnaise in a small bowl; mix well. Stir into dry mixture until flour is just moistened. Fold in cranberries.

Spoon into a greased and floured 9- x 5- x 3-inch loafpan. Combine 2 tablespoons sugar and ½ teaspoon orange rind. Sprinkle on top of loaf.

Bake at 350° for 55 minutes. Cover with foil, and bake an additional 10 minutes. Cool on wire rack. Yield: 1 loaf.

Hazel Slucher,
Taylorsville, Kentucky.

SHORTBREAD

1 cup butter, softened
½ cup sifted powdered sugar
2 cups all-purpose flour
Sugar

Cream butter; gradually add powdered sugar, beating until light and fluffy. Stir in flour. (Mixture will be stiff.) Press onto bottom of a 15- x 10- x 1-inch jellyroll pan; prick all over with a fork. Chill 30 minutes.

Bake at 375° for 5 minutes; reduce heat to 300°, and bake an additional 25 minutes or until golden brown.

Cut into 1½-inch squares or diamond shapes while warm, and sprinkle with sugar. Yield: 6 dozen.

MULLED WINE SPICE MIX

2 oranges
8 (3-inch) sticks cinnamon, broken into small pieces
¼ cup whole cloves
¼ cup whole allspice
4 whole nutmeg, cracked and broken into small pieces
3 drops oil of cinnamon

Peel rind from oranges in ½-inch strips, cutting into white membrane as little as possible. Reserve oranges for later use. Place rind strips, outer side up, on a wire rack on a baking sheet. Bake at 200°, leaving oven door slightly open, 2 to 2½ hours or until rind is dry. Check often. Let cool. Break into small pieces.

Combine dried orange rind and remaining ingredients; mix well. Yield: about 1½ cups.

To use, combine ⅓ cup Mulled Wine Spice Mix with 1 quart Burgundy and 1 quart apple juice. Heat to boiling; cover, reduce heat, and simmer 20 to 30 minutes. Strain spices before serving. (For a non-alcoholic beverage, ⅓ cup Mulled Wine Spice Mix may be combined with ½ gallon apple cider.) Yield: ½ gallon.

COOKING LIGHT®

Light Vegetables Fit For The Feast

The vegetable dishes served at many holiday tables may include lots of butter, rich sauces, or other high-calorie ingredients. But if you're watching fat intake, you would be wise to keep the vegetables simple. Not only are they usually lower in calories, but their interesting shapes, colors, and textures also make them perfect for almost any meal.

Here's a collection of tasty vegetable side dishes to help you stick to your diet during the holiday weeks and throughout the year. We've kept calories low by limiting the use of butter, margarine, oil, and bacon drippings, and by seasoning with various herbs, spices, and other low-calorie ingredients.

Fruit juice is the special low-calorie seasoning ingredient in both Golden Carrots and Easy Orange Broccoli. Another advantage of these two recipes is that they are both made without salt and are, therefore, low in sodium.

Zucchini-Basil Delight and Acorn Squash With Nutmeg are examples of how to prepare flavorful low-calorie vegetables with herbs and spices. Savory Fresh Mushrooms benefit from the addition of sherry, while reduced-calorie salad dressing gets credit for the unique seasoning in Brussels Sprouts Medley.

See how some of our readers use low-calorie seasonings; then use your imagination to come up with other ideas.

ACORN SQUASH WITH NUTMEG

1 medium acorn squash (about 1 pound)
1 tablespoon plus 1 teaspoon brown sugar
1 tablespoon plus 1 teaspoon
   reduced-calorie margarine, melted
¼ to ½ teaspoon ground nutmeg
⅛ teaspoon pepper

Cut squash into quarters; remove seeds. Place squash, cut side up, in a shallow baking dish; add boiling water to the depth of ½ inch. Cover and bake at 400° for 30 minutes or until tender.

Combine remaining ingredients; divide among squash cavities. Bake, uncovered, at 400° an additional 10 minutes or until lightly browned. Yield: 4 servings (about 70 calories per serving).

EASY ORANGE BROCCOLI

1 (1½-pound) bunch broccoli
1 tablespoon margarine
1 tablespoon all-purpose flour
1 tablespoon grated orange rind
¾ cup unsweetened orange juice
Strips of orange rind (optional)

Trim off large leaves of broccoli. Remove tough ends of stalks, and wash broccoli thoroughly. Make lengthwise slits in thick stalks. Arrange broccoli spears in a steaming rack with stalks to center of rack. Place over boiling water; cover and steam 10 to 15 minutes or until tender. Arrange broccoli in a serving dish; keep warm.

Melt margarine in a heavy saucepan over low heat; add flour, stirring until smooth. Cook 1 minute, stirring constantly. Gradually add orange rind and orange juice. Cook over medium heat, stirring constantly, until thickened and bubbly. Pour sauce over broccoli. Garnish with strips of orange rind, if desired. Yield: 6 servings (about 53 calories per serving). *Joan Shaw, Monticello, Florida.*

BRUSSELS SPROUTS MEDLEY

1 pound brussels sprouts
1 cup water
1 chicken-flavored bouillon cube
1 cup diagonally sliced carrots
1 cup diagonally sliced celery
1 cup cauliflower pieces
½ cup reduced-calorie, herb-flavored salad dressing

Wash brussels sprouts thoroughly, and remove discolored leaves. Cut off stem ends, and slash bottom of each sprout with a shallow X. Combine sprouts, boiling water, and bouillon cube in a saucepan; bring to a boil. Cover, reduce heat, and cook 5 minutes. Add remaining vegetables; cover and cook 5 minutes or until crisp-tender; drain. Add salad dressing, and cook until heated. Yield: 8 servings (about 46 calories per serving).

GOLDEN CARROTS

4 cups thinly sliced carrots
1 cup unsweetened pineapple juice
1 cup water
2 teaspoons grated lemon rind
½ cup golden raisins
2 teaspoons reduced-calorie margarine
1 teaspoon vanilla extract
½ teaspoon ground mace

Combine carrots, pineapple juice, water, and lemon rind in a medium saucepan; bring to a boil. Cover, reduce heat, and cook 10 to 12 minutes or just until tender. Remove from heat, and drain carrots, reserving ¼ cup liquid. Stir ¼ cup liquid and remaining ingredients into carrots. Yield: 8 servings (about 73 calories per serving). *Margaret Ellen Holmes, Jackson, Tennessee.*

ZUCCHINI-BASIL DELIGHT

4 green onions with tops, chopped
1½ teaspoons margarine, melted
2 medium zucchini, cut into 2-inch julienne strips
2 medium-size yellow squash, cut into 2-inch julienne strips
¾ pound fresh mushrooms, sliced
¾ teaspoon dried whole basil
½ teaspoon salt
¼ teaspoon pepper

Sauté green onions in margarine in a large skillet for 1 minute. Add remaining ingredients; cook over medium-high heat 5 to 8 minutes or until vegetables are crisp-tender. Yield: 8 servings (about 39 calories per serving). *Sheila Cocke, Auburn, Alabama.*

SAVORY FRESH MUSHROOMS

1 pound fresh mushrooms, sliced
2 tablespoons dry sherry
1 teaspoon margarine
¼ teaspoon paprika
¼ teaspoon seasoned salt
⅛ teaspoon pepper
¼ cup chopped fresh parsley

Combine all ingredients in a large skillet. Cover and cook over medium heat 5 minutes, stirring occasionally. Yield: 4 servings (about 43 calories per serving).

STUFFED ONIONS AND WINE

4 small onions
2 tablespoons plus 2 teaspoons dry white wine
Salt
⅔ cup chopped fresh mushrooms
Vegetable cooking spray
2 tablespoons grated Parmesan cheese
2 teaspoons parsley flakes
⅛ teaspoon white pepper
Paprika (optional)
Parsley sprigs (optional)

Peel onions, and cut out a slice from top of each. Scoop out center of onions, leaving ½-inch-thick shells; reserve onion centers. Place shells in a shallow baking dish, cut side up. Add 2 teaspoons wine to each onion, and sprinkle lightly with salt. Cover and bake at 375° for 45 minutes or just until tender.

Chop reserved onion centers; sauté chopped onion and mushrooms until tender in a small skillet coated with cooking spray. Remove from heat, and stir in cheese, parsley, and pepper. Fill baked onion shells with mushroom mixture; bake, uncovered, at 375° an additional 10 minutes. Sprinkle tops lightly with paprika, and garnish with parsley sprigs, if desired. Yield: 4 servings (about 47 calories per serving).

Elena Wellinghoff,
Little Rock, Arkansas.

Dinner Breads Fresh From The Oven

If you're looking for some attractive, unusual breads to round out holiday menus, you'll be interested in these selections. We think they're special enough for any meal—from a large family gathering to a dinner party.

Honey, whole wheat flour, and cottage cheese give Honey-Wheat Bread an interesting flavor and texture. The recipe offers two possibilities—the dough can be shaped into loaves as well as rolls.

Butter-Egg Bread is brushed with an egg for a shiny brown crust and sprinkled with poppy seeds just before baking. This recipe makes three standard-size loaves; you can also braid it or bake it in the round.

Marjoram, oregano, and thyme account for the savory taste of Herb-Sour Cream Bread. It's a good choice with a mild-flavored entrée.

HONEY WHEAT BREAD

1½ cups water
½ cup honey
1 cup cream-style cottage cheese
¼ cup butter or margarine
1 egg, beaten
2 packages dry yeast
2 tablespoons sugar
2 teaspoons salt
5½ to 6 cups all-purpose flour, divided
1 cup whole wheat flour

Combine water, honey, cottage cheese, and butter in a small saucepan; heat mixture until it is very warm (120° to 130°).

Combine egg, yeast, sugar, and salt in a large mixing bowl, mixing well. Add cottage cheese mixture, 3 cups all-purpose flour, and whole wheat flour; beat at medium speed of an electric mixer 2 minutes. Gradually stir in enough remaining flour to make a soft dough. Turn dough out onto a well-floured surface, and knead about 5 minutes until smooth and elastic. Place in a well-greased bowl, turning to grease top.

Cover and let rise in a warm place (85°), free from drafts, 1 hour.

Punch dough down; let rest 5 minutes. Divide dough in half; shape each half into 18 (2-inch) balls or 1 loaf. Arrange rolls 3 inches apart on greased baking sheets; place loaf in a greased 9- x 5- x 3-inch loafpan. Cover and let rise in a warm place (85°), free from drafts, 1 hour or until doubled in bulk. Bake rolls at 350° for 20 minutes; bake loaf at 350° for 45 minutes or until loaf sounds hollow when tapped. Remove loaf from pan, and cool on wire rack. Yield: 3 dozen rolls or 2 loaves.

Kim Van Portfleet,
Lake Park, Florida.

HERB-SOUR CREAM BREAD

2 packages dry yeast
½ cup warm water (105° to 115°)
1 (8-ounce) carton commercial sour cream (at room temperature)
¼ cup plus 2 tablespoons butter or margarine, softened
⅓ cup sugar
2 eggs, beaten
1½ teaspoons salt
¾ teaspoon dried whole oregano
¾ teaspoon marjoram leaves
½ teaspoon dried whole thyme
4 to 4½ cups all-purpose flour, divided

Dissolve yeast in warm water in a large bowl. Add remaining ingredients except flour, mixing well. Add 3 cups flour; beat well about 1 minute. Stir in enough remaining flour to make a soft dough. Place in a well-greased bowl, turning to grease top. Cover; let rise in a warm place (85°), free from drafts, 50 minutes or until doubled in bulk.

Punch dough down, and divide dough in half. Shape each half into a loaf, and place in 2 greased 8- x 4- x 3-inch loafpans. Cover and let rise in a warm place (85°), free from drafts, 35 to 40 minutes or until doubled in bulk.

Bake at 350° for 30 minutes or until loaves sound hollow when tapped. Remove loaves from pans, and cool on wire racks. Yield: 2 loaves.

Joan B. Piercy,
Memphis, Tennessee.

BUTTER-EGG BREAD

2 packages dry yeast
½ cup warm water (105° to 115°)
1½ cups milk
½ cup butter or margarine, cut into 6
  pieces
3 eggs, beaten
½ cup sugar
2½ teaspoons salt
About 8 cups bread flour, divided
1 tablespoon butter or margarine, melted
1 egg yolk
2 teaspoons water
2 teaspoons poppy seeds

Dissolve dry yeast in warm water, and set aside.

Combine milk and ½ cup butter in a small saucepan; cook over low heat, and stir until butter melts. Combine eggs, sugar, salt, and yeast mixture in a large mixing bowl; stir in milk mixture. Beat in 7½ cups flour, about 2 cups at a time, at medium-low speed of an electric mixer.

Turn dough out onto a floured surface, and knead 5 to 8 minutes or until smooth and elastic, adding remaining ½ cup flour as needed. Place dough in a well-greased bowl, turning to grease top. Cover and let rise in a warm place (85°), free from drafts, 1½ hours or until doubled in bulk.

Punch dough down, and turn out onto a floured surface; let rest at room temperature 30 minutes. Knead 3 or 4 times. Divide into thirds, and shape each third into a loaf. Place loaves in three greased 9- x 5- x 3-inch loafpans. Brush tops with 1 tablespoon melted butter. Cover and let rise in a warm place (85°), free from drafts, 30 minutes or until doubled in bulk.

Combine egg yolk and 2 teaspoons water in a small bowl; stir well. Brush mixture on top of loaves. Sprinkle with 2 teaspoons poppy seeds. Bake at 350° for 25 to 30 minutes or until loaves sound hollow when tapped. Remove loaves from pans, and allow to cool on wire racks. (This dough may also be braided or shaped into round loaves and baked on greased baking sheets, if desired.) Yield: 3 loaves.

Note: This bread freezes well.
Lynda Ramage,
Lilburn, Georgia.

Make Wild Game The Entrée

Game is a delicacy to enjoy during the holiday season, whether you bring it home yourself or share in the bounty of a friend or neighbor. You'll find entrées here that are just right for fancy dinners or casual parties.

Plan more formal meals around recipes such as Pheasant Muscatel. To make the entrée look even more enticing, serve a tasty rice-and-pecan side dish in scalloped orange-shell halves.

WILD DUCK WITH PECAN STUFFING

4 (1-pound) wild ducks, dressed
4 cups soft breadcrumbs
1 cup finely chopped onion
1 cup finely chopped celery
1 cup seedless raisins
1 cup chopped pecans
2 eggs, beaten
¼ cup milk
12 slices bacon
1 cup catsup
½ cup chili sauce
¼ cup Worcestershire sauce
¼ cup steak sauce
Parsley (optional)
Orange slices (optional)
Cranberries (optional)

Rinse ducks thoroughly with water; pat dry. Combine breadcrumbs, onion, celery, raisins, pecans, eggs, and milk, mixing well. Spoon mixture into cavities of ducks; close cavities with skewers. Place ducks, breast side up, on rack in a roasting pan. Wrap 3 slices of bacon around each duck. Bake, uncovered, at 350° for 1 hour.

Combine catsup, chili sauce, Worcestershire sauce, and steak sauce; mix well. Pour over ducks, and bake an additional 15 to 30 minutes or until desired degree of doneness. Skim off fat from sauce and discard fat; serve sauce with ducks. Garnish with parsley, orange slices, and cranberries, if desired. Yield: 4 servings. *Ann Joines,*
Hickory, North Carolina.

PHEASANT MUSCATEL

6 (1- to 1¼-pound) pheasants, dressed
½ lemon
½ teaspoon salt
¼ teaspoon pepper
⅓ cup butter or margarine, softened
3 large oranges, halved
1 (14½-ounce) can chicken broth
½ cup muscatel wine
1 cup golden raisins
1 teaspoon grated lemon rind
¼ cup all-purpose flour
Nutted Rice

Rinse pheasants with cold water; pat dry. Rub with lemon; sprinkle with salt and pepper. Place pheasants in baking dish, breast side up; rub with butter.

Squeeze juice from oranges, reserving shells for Nutted Rice. Combine orange juice, broth, wine, raisins, and lemon rind; pour over pheasants. Bake, uncovered, at 350° for 50 minutes or until meat thermometer registers 185°, basting pheasants every 10 minutes.

Combine broth mixture and ¼ cup flour in a saucepan; stir until blended. Cook over medium heat, stirring constantly, until thickened. Serve with pheasant and Nutted Rice. Yield: 6 servings.

Nutted Rice:

2 cups chicken broth
1 cup uncooked regular rice
⅔ cup chopped pecans
2 tablespoons butter or margarine
2 tablespoons minced fresh parsley
⅛ tablespoon white pepper
6 orange shells, scalloped

Combine broth and rice in a saucepan. Bring to a boil and cover. Reduce heat, and simmer 20 minutes or until liquid is absorbed and rice is tender. Remove from heat, and stir in pecans, butter, parsley, and pepper. Spoon into orange shells. Yield: 3 cups.
Lorene Hubbard,
Russellville, Alabama.

Tip: When you use fresh lemons for cooking, remember that one medium lemon will yield 2 to 4 tablespoons juice and 1 tablespoon grated rind.

November   269

SOUTHERN QUAIL BREASTS

8 whole quail breasts or whole quail, dressed
½ teaspoon salt
¼ teaspoon pepper
½ cup all-purpose flour
½ cup butter or margarine, melted
½ cup finely chopped fresh mushrooms
¼ cup finely chopped onion
1 tablespoon minced fresh parsley
½ cup white wine
½ cup whipping cream
Hot cooked wild rice

Sprinkle quail with salt and pepper; dredge in flour. Brown quail on both sides in butter in a large skillet. Remove quail, and set aside.

Sauté mushrooms, onion, and parsley in pan drippings. Add quail and wine; cover, reduce heat to medium low, and cook 30 minutes, basting frequently. Add whipping cream, and cook until thoroughly heated. (Do not boil.) Serve over rice. Yield: 4 servings.

Mrs. Troy Rainwater,
Weslaco, Texas.

DOVE ENCHILADAS

8 whole dove breasts, boned and coarsely chopped
¾ cup chopped onion
2 cloves garlic, minced
2 tablespoons vegetable oil
2 (10-ounce) cans enchilada sauce
8 corn tortillas
2 tablespoons plus 2 teaspoons chopped ripe olives
1 cup (4 ounces) shredded Cheddar cheese
Whole ripe olives

Sauté dove, onion, and garlic in oil until dove is browned; set aside.

Warm enchilada sauce in a skillet; remove from heat. Place tortillas, one at a time, in sauce. Let stand 1 minute or just until tortillas are softened. Set remaining sauce aside.

Spoon dove mixture evenly over each tortilla; sprinkle each with 1 teaspoon chopped olives and 1 tablespoon cheese. Roll up tortillas, and place in a lightly greased 13- x 9- x 2-inch baking dish, seam side down. Pour remaining sauce over tortillas; bake at 350° for 15 minutes. Top with remaining cheese, and bake an additional 5 minutes. Garnish with olives. Yield: 4 servings.

Spencer L. Liles,
Abilene, Texas.

VENISON AND TOMATOES

3 slices bacon, chopped
¾ pound ground venison
½ cup chopped onion
1 teaspoon chili powder
¾ teaspoon salt
½ teaspoon paprika
¼ teaspoon pepper
1 (14½-ounce) can stewed tomatoes
Hot cooked rice

Fry bacon until crisp; add venison, onion, and seasonings. Cook over medium heat until meat is browned, stirring to crumble. Add tomatoes; cover, reduce heat, and simmer 40 minutes. Serve over rice. Yield: 4 servings.

David R. Lowery,
Birmingham, Alabama.

VENISON ROAST WITH RED WINE GRAVY

1 (3- to 5-pound) venison roast
3 cups red wine
2 large onions, thinly sliced
12 black peppercorns
6 whole allspice
12 whole cloves
1 bay leaf
3 tablespoons all-purpose flour
¼ cup water

Remove any white membrane surrounding roast. Place roast in a shallow dish. Combine wine, onion, and seasonings. Pour over roast and cover. Marinate overnight in refrigerator, turning occasionally.

Remove roast from marinade, reserving marinade. Brown roast in a Dutch oven. Add marinade to roast, and bake, uncovered, at 350° for 1½ hours or until meat thermometer registers 170°.

Remove bay leaf and discard. Remove roast, reserving marinade. Combine flour and water, stirring until smooth. Add flour mixture to marinade; cook over medium heat, stirring constantly, until thickened. Serve gravy with roast. Yield: 6 to 8 servings.

Nell Kruger,
San Antonio, Texas.

HUNTER'S STEW

1½ pounds boneless venison, cut into ½-inch cubes
½ pound smoked sausage, cut into ½-inch slices
2 tablespoons vegetable oil
½ cup chopped onion
½ cup chopped celery
2 (28-ounce) cans tomatoes, undrained and chopped
1 (12-ounce) can beer
1 teaspoon salt
1 teaspoon sugar
½ teaspoon dried rosemary, crushed
½ teaspoon dried whole basil
½ teaspoon freshly ground pepper
2 carrots, diced
2 medium potatoes, cubed

Brown venison and sausage in hot oil in a large Dutch oven. Add onion and celery; cook until tender. Add remaining ingredients except carrots and potatoes; cover, reduce heat, and simmer 30 minutes. Add carrots; cook, uncovered, 30 minutes. Add potatoes, and cook an additional 30 minutes or until done. Yield: about 2 quarts.

Mrs. Edward F. Blassy,
Burke, Virginia.

Right: All decked out in Christmas finery, these gifts of Orange-Cranberry Bread, Cranberry Conserve, and Shortbread will delight family and friends. (Recipes begin on page 266.)

Page 274: Peanut Butter Pie (page 275) takes on a touch of glamour when it's topped with chocolate shavings and presented in a silver pie holder.

Above: *The festivities are off to a great start when the fare includes (counter-clockwise from left) Caraway Spread with rye crackers, Herb-Marinated Flank Steak with horseradish sauce, commercial party rolls, and Sparkling Cranberry Punch. (Recipes begin on page 275.)*

Left: *The piquant flavors of Cheddar cheese, oregano, and basil are braided into delicious Cheese-Herb Bread (page 283).*

Far left: *Chunks of venison simmer with vegetables, sausage, and seasonings for a one-dish meal of Hunter's Stew (page 270).*

Deliciously Simple Desserts

With all the extra tasks we take on during the holidays, something has to give. Why not take a shortcut when it comes to making dessert? We offer several possibilities that are appropriate for entertaining, as well as family meals.

BRANDY PEACHES

16 canned peach halves
1 cup maple syrup
1 cup firmly packed brown sugar
⅓ cup butter or margarine, melted
Ground cinnamon
⅓ cup brandy
Vanilla ice cream

Place peach halves, cavity side up, in a lightly greased 13- x 9- x 2-inch baking dish; spoon about 1 tablespoon syrup, 1 tablespoon sugar, and 1 teaspoon butter into each cavity. Sprinkle lightly with cinnamon; bake, uncovered, at 325° for 20 minutes. Remove from oven; pour brandy over peaches.

Place each peach half in an individual serving dish; top with ice cream. Spoon sauce from baking dish over ice cream. Yield: 16 servings. *Joan Tidwell, Gilmer, Texas.*

PEANUT BUTTER PIE

1 (8-ounce) package cream cheese, softened
1 cup crunchy peanut butter
1 (16-ounce) container frozen whipped topping
1½ cups sifted powdered sugar
2 (9-inch) graham cracker crusts
Chocolate shavings (optional)

Combine cream cheese and peanut butter in a large mixing bowl; beat at medium speed of an electric mixer until light and fluffy. Gradually add whipped topping and powdered sugar, and continue beating until smooth. Spoon filling into prepared crusts. Freeze at least 8 hours or overnight. Garnish with chocolate shavings, if desired. Yield: two 9-inch pies. *Frances Ponder, Cullman, Alabama.*

SWEET POTATO PIE

1½ cups mashed cooked sweet potatoes
1½ cups sugar
2½ tablespoons butter or margarine, softened
⅔ cup evaporated milk
3 egg yolks, beaten
1 teaspoon vanilla extract
1 teaspoon ground nutmeg
3 egg whites
1 unbaked 9-inch, deep-dish pastry shell

Combine sweet potatoes, sugar, and butter; stir well. Stir in milk, egg yolks, vanilla, and nutmeg; set aside.

Beat egg whites (at room temperature) at high speed of an electric mixer until stiff peaks form. Fold beaten egg whites into sweet potato mixture. Pour mixture into unbaked pastry shell. Bake at 375° for 10 minutes; reduce heat to 350°, and bake 45 minutes or until set. Yield: one 9-inch deep-dish pie. *Karen Brown, Vienna, Georgia.*

APPLE SNACK CAKE

¼ cup butter or margarine, softened
1 cup sugar
1 egg
1 cup all-purpose flour
1 teaspoon baking soda
½ teaspoon salt
½ teaspoon ground cinnamon
½ teaspoon ground nutmeg
½ cup chopped pecans
2 cups peeled, finely chopped apple
¼ cup powdered sugar

Cream butter; gradually add sugar, beating until light and fluffy. Add egg, blending well. Combine flour, soda, salt, and spices; add to creamed mixture, stirring well. Stir in chopped pecans and apple.

Spoon batter into a greased 8-inch square baking pan. Bake at 350° for 35 minutes or until a wooden pick inserted in center comes out clean. Cool cake in pan; sprinkle top with powdered sugar. Cut into squares. Yield: 8 servings. *Charlotte Watkins, Lakeland, Florida.*

These Foods Make The Party Inviting

When it comes to party food, we expect a lot. We want it to be colorful, attractive, unusual, and delicious. We worry about having enough and selecting dishes to be made ahead.

To make it easier, we've gathered some recipes that meet the basic requirements; they also make at least ten servings, and most of the preparation can be done ahead of time.

HERB-MARINATED FLANK STEAK

1 small onion, quartered
2 tablespoons olive oil
1 tablespoon lemon juice
1½ tablespoons soy sauce
½ teaspoon dried Italian herbs
Pinch of freshly ground pepper
1 (1½-pound) flank steak

Position knife blade in food processor bowl; add all ingredients except steak. Top with cover; pulse 2 or 3 times or until onion is finely chopped.

Score steak on both sides, and place in a large shallow dish. Spoon onion mixture over steak; cover and marinate in refrigerator 8 hours, turning steak occasionally.

Remove the steak from marinade; broil 5 inches from heat 4 to 5 minutes on each side.

Slice steak diagonally across the grain into thin slices. Serve with horseradish sauce and commercial party rolls, if desired. Yield: 12 to 15 appetizer servings. *Ann Hall, Macon, Georgia.*

SWEET-AND-SOUR RIBLETS

3 to 4 pounds spareribs
⅓ cup honey
¼ cup soy sauce
¼ cup hoisin sauce
1 clove garlic, crushed
½ teaspoon dry mustard
Commercial sweet-and-sour sauce
  (optional)

Have butcher cut ribs in half crosswise to make small ribs.

Cut ribs lengthwise into serving-size pieces; place in a large Dutch oven. Add enough water to cover ribs; bring to a boil. Cover, reduce heat, and simmer 30 minutes. Drain ribs, and place in a large, shallow broiler pan.

Combine honey, soy sauce, hoisin sauce, garlic, and mustard; mix well. Brush ribs with mixture. Broil 3 minutes; turn ribs over, and brush with mixture again. Broil an additional 3 minutes. Serve with sweet-and-sour sauce, if desired. Yield: 10 to 12 appetizer servings. *Patsy Layer, Galveston, Texas.*

LIVER-CHEESE PÂTÉ

1 pound braunschweiger liver sausage
4 (3-ounce) packages cream cheese,
  softened and divided
1 teaspoon lemon juice
½ teaspoon Worcestershire sauce
½ teaspoon paprika
¼ teaspoon pepper
¼ teaspoon garlic powder
¾ teaspoon lemon juice
Pinch of salt
Chopped fresh parsley

Combine liver sausage, 2 packages cream cheese, 1 teaspoon lemon juice, Worcestershire sauce, paprika, pepper, and garlic powder in a medium mixing bowl. Beat at medium speed of an electric mixer until smooth and well blended. Shape into a ball; chill at least 1 hour.

Combine remaining 2 packages cream cheese, ¾ teaspoon lemon juice, and salt; beat at medium speed of an electric mixture until smooth. Spread cheese

mixture over ball; sprinkle with parsley. Serve with rye crackers. Yield: one 5-inch ball. *Susan W. Pajcic, Jacksonville, Florida.*

CARAWAY SPREAD

2 (3-ounce) packages cream cheese,
  softened
¼ cup butter or margarine, softened
2 anchovies, finely chopped
¼ cup finely chopped onion
1 teaspoon caraway seeds
1 teaspoon paprika
½ teaspoon pepper
⅛ teaspoon salt

Beat cream cheese and butter at medium speed of an electric mixer until smooth and fluffy; stir in remaining ingredients. Spoon mixture into a greased 10-ounce custard cup; pack well. Cover and refrigerate 8 hours; unmold. Serve spread with rye crackers, if desired. Yield: 1½ cups. *Lenah Miller Elliott, Destin, Florida.*

RUGELACH

2 cups all-purpose flour
1 tablespoon sugar
½ teaspoon salt
⅔ cup shortening
1 egg yolk
1 tablespoon grated orange rind
¼ cup orange juice
⅔ cup sugar
2 tablespoons ground cinnamon
¼ cup butter, melted
½ cup raisins
½ cup chopped pecans
1 egg yolk
1 tablespoon water

Combine flour, 1 tablespoon sugar, and salt in a large bowl; cut in shortening with pastry blender until mixture resembles coarse meal.

Stir in 1 egg yolk and orange rind, mixing well. Sprinkle orange juice, 1 tablespoon at a time, into flour mixture, stirring until dry ingredients are moistened. Divide dough in half, and shape into 2 balls. Chill at least 30 minutes.

Combine ⅔ cup sugar and 2 tablespoons cinnamon. Set aside.

A holiday party calls for a special dessert. Rugelach, a rich cinnamon-flavored pastry with a raisin-and-nut filling, fits the occasion.

Roll half the pastry into a 12- x 10-inch rectangle. Brush with half the butter; sprinkle half the sugar mixture evenly over pastry. Sprinkle with half the raisins and pecans. Roll up jellyroll fashion, starting with the short side. Pinch seam and ends together; place roll, seam side down, on a lightly greased baking sheet. Repeat procedure with remaining pastry and filling. Cut each roll into ¾-inch slices, cutting three-fourths of the way through roll with each cut.

Combine 1 egg yolk and water; brush tops of rolls with mixture. Bake at 350° for 30 minutes or until golden brown. Yield: 2 dozen. *Harriet O. St. Amant, Fayetteville, North Carolina.*

SPARKLING CRANBERRY PUNCH

1 quart cranberry juice cocktail
1 (6-ounce) can frozen orange juice concentrate, thawed and undiluted
1 (6-ounce) can frozen lemonade concentrate, thawed and undiluted
2 cups water
1¾ cups ginger ale
Orange slices (optional)

Combine first 4 ingredients; chill well. Just before serving, pour juice mixture over ice. Gently stir in ginger ale. Add the orange slices, if desired. Yield: 2½ quarts. *Shirley E. Flynn, Charleston, West Virginia.*

Gift Baskets Made In Your Kitchen

Personalize your gift giving by assembling some of your presents in the kitchen. Friends will love receiving the homemade mixes and goodies as much as you'll enjoy making them.

We suggest using baskets to package the gifts. This way you can include other items that can be served with your homemade treats.

■ Mary Gilliam of Cartersville, Virginia, sends us her recipe for Cinnamon-Pecan Topping, a crunchy nut mixture for sprinkling over ice cream desserts. Dress up a gift basket featuring the topping, and include our recipe for Peach Split, along with jars of caramel sauce and strawberry preserves, a can of peach slices, a fancy ice cream scoop, and a pair of banana split dishes.

CINNAMON-PECAN TOPPING

2 egg whites, slightly beaten
2 cups coarsely chopped pecans
¼ cup firmly packed brown sugar
1 tablespoon ground cinnamon

Combine egg whites and pecans; stir well. Combine brown sugar and cinnamon; mix well. Add to pecans; stirring until pecans are well coated. Spread evenly on a greased jellyroll pan; bake at 300° for 30 minutes. Cool; remove from pan. Store in an airtight container, or package for gift giving. Serve as a snack or use in the following recipe. Yield: 3½ cups.

PEACH SPLIT

1 (13-ounce) can sliced peaches, drained
1 pint vanilla ice cream
¼ cup commercial caramel sauce
¼ cup strawberry preserves
¼ cup Cinnamon-Pecan Topping
Frozen whipped topping, thawed

Spoon peaches into 4 individual dessert dishes. Top each with ½ cup ice cream, 1 tablespoon caramel sauce, 1 tablespoon strawberry preserves, 1 tablespoon Cinnamon-Pecan Topping, and a dollop of whipped topping. Yield: 4 servings.

■ A jar containing nine kinds of beans to be used for French Market Soup makes a colorful gift, according to Susie M. E. Dent of Saltillo, Mississippi. Attach the soup recipe to the jar of beans,

and then fill the basket with onions, fresh garlic, chili peppers, and a can of tomatoes. A soup mug, a garlic press, and a loaf of French bread make thoughtful additions.

FRENCH MARKET SOUP MIX

1 pound dried navy beans
1 pound dried pinto beans
1 pound dried Great Northern beans
1 pound dried green split peas
1 pound dried yellow split peas
1 pound dried black-eyed peas
1 pound dried lentils
1 pound dried baby limas
1 pound dried large limas
1 pound dried black beans
1 pound dried red beans
1 pound dried soybeans
1 pound barley pearls

Combine all beans. Divide into 14 (2-cup) gift packages; present with the following recipe for French Market Soup. Yield: 14 (2-cup) packages.

FRENCH MARKET SOUP

2 cups French Market Soup Mix
2 quarts water
1 ham hock
1¼ teaspoons salt
¼ teaspoon pepper
1 (16-ounce) can whole tomatoes, undrained and coarsely chopped
1 large onion, chopped
1 clove garlic, minced
1 chili pepper, coarsely chopped
¼ cup lemon juice

Sort and wash 2 cups bean mix; place in a Dutch oven. Cover with water 2 inches above beans, and soak overnight. Drain beans; add 2 quarts water, ham hock, salt, and pepper. Cover and bring to a boil; reduce heat, and simmer 1½ hours or until beans are tender. Add remaining ingredients; simmer 30 minutes, stirring occasionally. Remove ham hock from soup. Remove meat from bone, chop meat, and return to soup. Yield: 2½ quarts.

■ Kitty Lawson of Taylorsville, Kentucky, keeps a large batch of Wheat Quick Mix on hand to make pancakes, biscuits, and doughnuts in minutes. Give some of the mix as a gift to friends, and be sure to include all the recipes. Also tuck in a jar of gourmet (or homemade) jelly or preserves for the biscuits and maple syrup for the pancakes. Add a coffee mug and a spiced coffee mix to enjoy with the doughnuts. For a fancier package, include a pretty jam spreader and a linen roll cover.

WHEAT QUICK MIX

8 cups all-purpose flour
2 cups whole wheat flour
1 cup instant nonfat dry milk powder
⅓ cup baking powder
¼ cup sugar
1 tablespoon salt
2 cups shortening

Combine dry ingredients; mix well. Cut in shortening with pastry blender until mixture resembles coarse meal. Store in an airtight container at room temperature. (Mix may be stored up to 6 weeks.) Package for gift giving, and present with the following recipes. Yield: 15 cups.

WHEAT QUICK BISCUITS

1½ cups Wheat Quick Mix
⅓ cup water

Combine Wheat Quick Mix and water; stir quickly with a fork until dry ingredients are moistened. Turn dough out onto a lightly floured surface, and knead lightly 4 or 5 times.

Roll dough to ½-inch thickness, and cut with a 2-inch biscuit cutter. Place biscuits on a greased baking sheet; bake at 425° for 10 to 12 minutes or until lightly browned. Yield: 8 biscuits.

WHEAT QUICK PANCAKES

1 egg, beaten
1 cup water or milk
2 cups Wheat Quick Mix

Combine egg and water in a mixing bowl; mix well. Add Wheat Quick Mix; stir just until moistened.

For each pancake, pour ¼ cup batter onto a hot, lightly greased griddle. Turn when tops are covered with bubbles and edges are brown. Serve with syrup. Yield: eight 4-inch pancakes.

WHEAT QUICK DOUGHNUT PUFFS

2 cups Wheat Quick Mix
¼ cup sugar
½ teaspoon ground cinnamon
½ teaspoon ground nutmeg
2 eggs, beaten
⅓ cup water
1 teaspoon vanilla extract
½ cup sugar
¼ teaspoon ground cinnamon

Combine Wheat Quick Mix, ¼ cup sugar, ½ teaspoon cinnamon, and nutmeg; mix well, and set aside.

Combine eggs, water, and vanilla; mix well. Add to dry mixture; stir quickly with a fork until dry ingredients are moistened.

Carefully drop dough by rounded teaspoonfuls into deep hot oil (360°), cooking only a few at a time, turning once. Fry 2 to 3 minutes or until golden brown. Drain on paper towels.

Combine ½ cup sugar and ¼ teaspoon cinnamon; mix well. Dredge warm doughnuts lightly in the sugar mixture. Yield: 2½ dozen.

■ Your friends will warm up quickly with a container of Spicy Hot Chocolate Mix close at hand. A. A. Goodman of Knoxville suggests an option of spicing it with rum, so put a bottle of rum in the basket along with the mix. You might also include a mug and a bundle of cinnamon sticks for stirrers.

SPICY HOT CHOCOLATE MIX

½ cup sugar
¼ cup cocoa
3 tablespoons instant coffee powder
½ teaspoon ground cinnamon

Combine all ingredients. Store in an airtight container, or package for gift giving. Yield: about 1 cup mix.

SPICY HOT CHOCOLATE

2 tablespoons Spicy Hot Chocolate Mix
1 cup milk, heated
2 tablespoons rum (optional)
Whipped cream
Cinnamon stick

Spoon chocolate mix into a cup. Add the hot milk and rum, if desired; stir until well blended. Garnish with a dollop of whipped cream and a cinnamon stick. Yield: 1 serving.

■ In McKinney, Texas, Gerrie Haas makes homemade Chunky Pecan Syrup. We suggest giving it as a treat for friends. Arrange a gift container with pancake or waffle mix, a loaf of pound cake, and an ice cream scoop as ideas for serving the syrup. A crystal syrup pitcher offers a remembrance they can keep long after the syrup is gone.

CHUNKY PECAN SYRUP

1 cup light corn syrup
¼ cup water
¼ teaspoon maple flavoring
⅛ teaspoon salt
1 to 1¼ cups coarsely chopped pecans

Combine all ingredients in a heavy saucepan; mix well. Bring to a boil over medium heat, stirring constantly. Reduce heat to low; cook 5 minutes, stirring occasionally. Let cool; store in an airtight container in refrigerator. Serve warm or at room temperature over ice cream or pancakes. Yield: 1½ cups.

Add A Chilled Dish To The Menu

With cooler temperatures outside, warm, hearty foods become the mainstay in most menus. But don't forget the importance of temperature contrast when planning the meal. Hot and cold dishes served at the same meal add interest and variety.

Our chilled dishes offer ideas from appetizer to dessert. And, best of all, they can conveniently be made ahead, allowing you more time to put the final touches on the holiday dinner.

HAM PÂTÉ

2 (3-ounce) packages cream cheese, softened, divided
1 pound cooked ham, ground
1 tablespoon grated onion
2 teaspoons finely chopped pecans
1 tablespoon milk

Combine 1 package cream cheese, ham, onion, and pecans, mixing well. Line a 2-cup mold or bowl with plastic wrap; spoon mixture into mold, pressing firmly. Cover and chill 3 hours. Unmold onto a serving plate.

Beat remaining package of cream cheese and milk until smooth; spread over ham mixture. Serve with crackers. Yield: 2 cups.   *Barbara Rogers, Cleveland, Tennessee.*

EGG, SOUR CREAM, AND CAVIAR SPREAD

12 hard-cooked eggs, finely chopped
⅓ cup mayonnaise
2 tablespoons diced green onions
½ teaspoon salt
⅛ teaspoon freshly ground black pepper
4 drops of hot sauce
½ cup commeral sour cream
1 (2-ounce) jar red caviar

Combine eggs, mayonnaise, green onions, salt, pepper, and hot sauce; mix

well. Spoon into a serving bowl, spreading surface of mixture flat. Spread with sour cream, and top with caviar. Serve with crackers or toast points. Yield: 4½ cups.   *Koenia Pereira, Newark, Texas.*

CAULIFLOWER SALAD

1 medium cauliflower, broken into flowerets and thinly sliced
1 cup thinly sliced radishes
½ cup sliced black olives
½ cup chopped watercress
2 tablespoons diced green onions or scallions
1 (8-ounce) carton commercial sour cream
1½ tablespoons lemon juice
1 tablespoon vegetable oil
1 tablespoon grated Parmesan cheese
1 small clove garlic, crushed
½ teaspoon salt
⅛ teaspoon pepper
Pinch of red pepper

Combine cauliflower, radishes, olives, watercress, and green onions in a mixing bowl; toss gently, and set aside.

Combine sour cream and remaining ingredients in container of an electric blender; process until blended. Pour dressing over cauliflower mixture; toss well. Cover and refrigerate 2 hours. Yield: 6 servings.   *Mrs. John Uecke, Fort Belvoir, Virginia.*

CONGEALED GRAPEFRUIT SALAD

2 envelopes unflavored gelatin, divided
1 cup cold water
1 (16-ounce) can grapefruit sections, undrained
1 (10½-ounce) can pineapple juice
¼ cup sugar
¼ teaspoon lemon juice
¼ teaspoon Worcestershire sauce
2 drops of hot sauce
Pinch of red pepper
Lettuce leaves

Dissolve 1 envelope gelatin in cold water in a medium saucepan.

Drain grapefruit, reserving liquid. Add enough grapefruit liquid to pineapple juice to make 2¼ cups; stir into gelatin mixture. Add sugar, and bring to a boil, stirring occasionally. Add remaining envelope gelatin; stir until gelatin dissolves. Add grapefruit sections, lemon juice, and seasonings. Spoon gelatin into 8 oiled individual molds; chill until firm. Unmold onto lettuce leaves.

Serve salad with commercial Roquefort or spicy-sweet French dressing. Yield: 8 servings.   *Mrs. Karl Koenig, Dallas, Texas.*

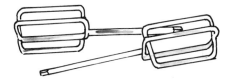

SPIKED COCONUT ANGEL CAKE

1 (14.5-ounce) package angel food cake mix
½ cup butter, softened
2 cups sifted powdered sugar
¼ cup milk
10 macaroons, crushed
1 cup chopped pecans
2 tablespoons bourbon
2 teaspoons brandy
2 cups whipping cream
2 tablespoons sifted powdered sugar
1 (6-ounce) package frozen coconut, thawed
Red and green candied cherries (optional)

Prepare angel food cake mix according to package directions; cool. Slice horizontally into 4 equal layers.

Cream butter; gradually add 2 cups powdered sugar and milk, beating well. Stir in macaroons, pecans, bourbon, and brandy. Spread filling between cake layers; refrigerate 1 hour.

Beat whipping cream until foamy; gradually add 2 tablespoons powdered sugar, beating until soft peaks form. Spread frosting on top and sides of cake. Sprinkle with coconut, and gently press into whipped cream frosting. Garnish with candied cherries, if desired. Yield: one 10-inch cake.

Mrs. Frank O'Hear, Birmingham, Alabama.

PUMPKIN CHEESECAKE

¾ cup graham cracker crumbs
½ cup ground pecans
2 tablespoons sugar
2 tablespoons brown sugar
¼ cup butter or margarine, melted
¾ cup sugar
¾ cup canned pumpkin
3 egg yolks
1½ teaspoons ground cinnamon
½ teaspoon ground mace
½ teaspoon ground ginger
¼ teaspoon salt
3 (8-ounce) packages cream cheese,
  softened
¼ cup plus 2 tablespoons sugar
1 egg
1 egg yolk
2 tablespoons whipping cream
1 tablespoon cornstarch
½ teaspoon vanilla extract
½ teaspoon lemon extract
Whipped cream (optional)
Pecan halves (optional)

Combine first 5 ingredients; mix well. Firmly press mixture into a 9-inch springform pan.

Combine ¾ cup sugar, pumpkin, 3 egg yolks, spices, and salt in a medium bowl; mix well, and set aside.

Beat cream cheese with an electric mixer until light and fluffy; gradually add ¼ cup plus 2 tablespoons sugar, mixing well. Add egg, egg yolk, and whipping cream, beating well. Add cornstarch and flavorings; beat until smooth. Add pumpkin mixture; mix well. Pour into prepared pan. Bake at 350° for 50 to 55 minutes. (Center may be soft but will firm when chilled.)

Let cool on a wire rack; chill thoroughly. Garnish with whipped cream and pecans, if desired. Yield: one 9-inch cheesecake.   *Bonnie Berry Rounds,*
                    Louisville, Kentucky.

Tip: Make certain your refrigerator or freezer is cold enough. Refrigerator temperature should be maintained at 34°F to 40°F, and freezer temperature at 0°F or lower. To allow the cold air to circulate freely, make sure that foods are not overcrowded.

CRANBERRY SUPREME

1 cup graham cracker crumbs
¼ cup butter or margarine, melted
2 cups fresh cranberries
1 cup sugar
½ cup water
¼ cup chopped pecans
2 tablespoons orange marmalade
1 (8-ounce) package cream cheese,
  softened
⅓ cup sifted powdered sugar
1 tablespoon milk
1 teaspoon vanilla extract
1 cup whipping cream, whipped

Combine graham cracker crumbs and butter; stir well. Press mixture into a greased 8-inch square dish. Chill.

Combine cranberries, sugar, and water in a saucepan; bring to a boil. Reduce heat; simmer 20 minutes. Stir in pecans and marmalade; chill.

Combine cream cheese, powdered sugar, milk, and vanilla; beat until light and fluffy. Fold in whipped cream; spread over crust. Top with cranberry mixture. Chill 8 hours. Yield: 9 servings.   *Betty E. Davis,*
                    Albuquerque, New Mexico.

Old Favorites From The Processor

As holiday time approaches, most of us are pulling out our favorite recipes for pies, cakes, dressings, and salads. If you've been making them for years, you probably work from memory. This year, think twice before you start cooking—especially if you've added a food processor to your kitchen. Take a look at your recipes, and note ways you can use the processor to save time and cleanup.

If a fresh coconut cake is part of your holiday routine, enjoy the ease of grating coconut in the processor. Use the shredding disc with the largest holes because discs for fine shredding may give the coconut a mushy texture. Besides, large shreds allow for a stronger, fresh coconut taste.

Cut time when you make dressings and stuffings by using the processor to chop vegetables and crumble bread. To prepare fine crumbs from dry bread, position the shredding disc in the processor. Tear the bread into large pieces, and process. For coarse dry crumbs or cornbread crumbs, use the knife blade.

To make coarse crumbs from fresh bread slices, position the knife blade in the processor. Tear up to four bread slices into quarters, add to the processor, and process to desired fineness.

For fine crumbs from fresh bread, use the shredding disc. Fold bread slices in half, place in food chute, and process.

To adjust your own recipes for the processor, read the recipe carefully and identify steps in the preparation or mixing of dry and liquid ingredients. Usually, the only changes you'll need to make are in the order of preparation. Chop dry ingredients first, and then mix dry ingredients; set aside. Puree or mix liquid ingredients next. For the final step, add combined dry ingredients to the liquid mixture.

CORNBREAD-SAUSAGE DRESSING

1 cup pecan halves
7½ slices toasted bread, torn
6 cups cornbread crumbs
6 chicken-flavored bouillon cubes
4 cups boiling water
1 small onion, quartered
2 green peppers, cored, seeded, and
  quartered
2 stalks celery, cut in 3-inch pieces
¼ cup butter or margarine, melted
½ pound bulk pork sausage
1 teaspoon poultry seasoning
½ teaspoon salt
¼ teaspoon pepper
4 eggs, beaten

Position knife blade in food processor bowl. Add pecans, top with cover, and pulse 10 times or until finely chopped. Remove pecans, and set aside.

Place toast pieces in processor bowl; process until coarsely crumbled. Combine with cornbread crumbs in a large bowl. Dissolve bouillon cubes in boiling water; pour over crumb mixture, and stir well.

Place onion in processor bowl, top with cover, and pulse 4 to 5 times or until coarsely chopped. Add green pepper through food chute; pulse 6 times or until onion and pepper are finely chopped. Remove knife blade, leaving vegetables in processor bowl. Position shredding disc in processor bowl, top with cover. Place celery pieces in food chute; shred celery, using medium pressure.

Remove vegetables from processor, and sauté in butter until tender; add to crumb mixture, stirring well.

Brown sausage in a heavy skillet; drain. Stir sausage and remaining ingredients into cornbread mixture. Spoon into a lightly greased 13- x 9- x 2-inch baking dish; bake at 350° for about 45 minutes. Yield: 8 to 10 servings.

JELLIED CRANBERRY SALAD

2 cups fresh cranberries
2 oranges, unpeeled, seeded, and cut into eighths
1 carrot, scraped and cut into 6 pieces
1 cup pecans or walnuts
¾ cup sugar
1 (8-ounce) can crushed pineapple, drained
2 (3-ounce) packages raspberry-flavored gelatin
1 cup boiling water
1 cup cold water
Lettuce leaves

Position knife blade in food processor bowl. Add cranberries, oranges, carrot, and pecans; top with cover, and pulse until finely chopped. Combine cranberry mixture, sugar, and crushed pineapple, stirring well.

Dissolve gelatin in boiling water; stir in cold water. Add gelatin mixture to cranberry mixture, and stir well.

Pour into a lightly oiled 6-cup mold. Chill until firm. Serve on lettuce leaves. Yield: 8 servings. *Katy Holt, Arkadelphia, Arkansas.*

APPLE-NUT BREAD

½ cup pecan halves
1 large apple, peeled and cored
⅔ cup shortening
½ cup sugar
½ cup firmly packed brown sugar
2 eggs
2 cups all-purpose flour
1 teaspoon baking powder
½ teaspoon baking soda
½ teaspoon salt
¼ cup orange juice
½ cup raisins

Position knife blade in food processor bowl. Add pecans; top with cover, and pulse 6 times or until coarsely chopped. Remove pecans, and set aside.

Cut apple into 8 pieces, and add to processor bowl. Pulse until coarsely chopped. Remove apple, and set aside.

Combine shortening, sugar, and eggs in food processor bowl; process about 10 seconds. Add remaining ingredients except raisins, and pulse 5 or 6 times, just until dry ingredients are moistened. Add pecans, apple, and raisins; process about 10 seconds. Pour mixture into a greased and floured 8½- x 4½- x 3-inch loafpan. Bake at 350° for 55 to 60 minutes or until a wooden pick inserted in center comes out clean. Let cool in pan 10 minutes. Yield: 1 loaf.
Agnes Shelton, Gretna, Virginia.

FRESH COCONUT CAKE

1 fresh coconut, cut into pieces
1½ cups sugar
3 eggs
¾ cup butter or margarine, chilled
¾ cup milk
1 teaspoon vanilla extract
2¼ cups sifted cake flour
2½ teaspoons baking powder
½ teaspoon salt
Custard filling (recipe follows)
Snow Peak Frosting
Mandarin orange sections

Position shredding disc in food processor bowl; cover with top. Peel brown skin from fresh coconut pieces; cut coconut to fit food chute and shred, using firm pressure. Remove the coconut, and set aside.

Combine sugar and eggs in processor bowl; process 1 minute. Cut butter into chunks, and add to processor bowl; process 1 minute, stopping once to scrape sides of bowl.

With processor running, pour milk and vanilla through food chute.

Combine flour, baking powder, and salt. Add to processor bowl; top with cover, and pulse 4 to 6 times or just until blended.

Pour batter into 2 greased and floured 9-inch round cakepans. Bake at 375° for 20 to 25 minutes or until a wooden pick inserted in center comes out clean. Cool in pans 10 minutes; remove from pans, and cool completely.

Split cake layers in half horizontally to make 4 layers.

Spread custard filling between layers; spread top and sides with Snow Peak Frosting, and sprinkle with coconut. Garnish with mandarin orange sections. Yield: one 4-layer cake.

Custard Filling:

2 cups milk
4 egg yolks
½ cup sugar
⅓ cup cornstarch
3 tablespoons orange-flavored liqueur or 1 teaspoon orange flavoring
1 cup grated fresh coconut

Combine milk, egg yolks, sugar, and cornstarch in a heavy saucepan; stir with a wire whisk until well blended. Cook over medium heat, stirring constantly, until thickened and smooth. Stir in liqueur. Chill thoroughly. Stir in coconut. Yield: about 2¾ cups.

Snow Peak Frosting:

1¼ cups light corn syrup
2 egg whites
Dash of salt
1 teaspoon vanilla extract

Bring corn syrup to a boil.

Combine egg whites (at room temperature) and salt in a large mixing bowl. Beat egg whites at high speed of an electric mixer until soft peaks form; continue to beat, slowly adding corn syrup. Add vanilla; beat until stiff peaks form and frosting is thick enough to spread. Yield: enough for one 9-inch layer cake.

PUMPKIN-PECAN PIE

½ cup pecan halves
4 pounds fresh pumpkin
1 (14-ounce) can sweetened condensed
   milk
2 eggs
1 teaspoon ground cinnamon
½ teaspoon ground nutmeg
½ teaspoon ground ginger
½ teaspoon salt
Pastry for 1 (9-inch) pie
3 tablespoons dark brown sugar
3 tablespoons whipping cream

Position knife blade in food processor bowl. Add pecans; top with cover, and pulse 6 times or until coarsely chopped. Remove pecans, and set aside.

Cut pumpkin in half crosswise. Place halves, cut side down, on a 15- x 10- x 1-inch jellyroll pan. Bake at 325° for 45 minutes or until tender; cool. Peel pumpkin, and discard seeds. Cut pumpkin into chunks; place in processor bowl. Process until pureed. Measure 3¾ cups pumpkin; reserve remaining pumpkin for use in other recipes.

Combine 3¾ cups pumpkin, milk, eggs, and seasonings in processor bowl. Pulse just until blended.

Fit pastry into pieplate; pour pumpkin mixture into pastry shell. Bake at 375° for 50 to 55 minutes or until knife inserted halfway between center and edge of pie comes out clean. Cool slightly. Sprinkle chopped pecans around outer edge of pie.

Combine sugar and whipping cream in a small saucepan; cook over medium heat, stirring constantly, until sugar dissolves. Reduce heat, and simmer 5 minutes; let cool 5 minutes. Spoon over pecans. Yield: one 9-inch pie.

Note: Two (16-ounce) cans pumpkin may be substituted for 3¾ cups fresh.

Tip: To prevent a soggy crust in custard pies or quiche, brush slightly beaten egg white on the uncooked pastry shell; bake at 425° for 5 to 10 minutes. Add filling, and bake according to the recipe directions.

Napkins To Help Set The Holiday Mood

Preparing all that delicious food for your holiday guests takes time. But save a few minutes for that final touch. Starched white linen napkins can add elegance. Try one of our two napkin folds to create a special setting.

— Our first example of a simple fold (right) shows off trimmed napkins.

To begin, fold the napkin in a square, and turn the point of each of the two trimmed edges down. Next, fold the top point down to desired length.

Bring the two sides together, creating a cone effect; then turn the napkin over. Flip up the top two trimmed layers, and fold in place.

For a brighter look, use a colored napkin inside the white one, or use two different colored napkins.

— Plain napkins become showy with this eye-catching standing fold (right). Using this folding technique adds height dimension to your table setting.

Fold the napkin in half diagonally, with the point at bottom, and bring the two ends together to the bottom. Fold in half again by placing bottom point underneath top point.

Next, bring right point under left point. Stand the napkin up, and place in the center of the dinner plate.

Beautiful lace trim peeks out from under these napkin folds in this elegant setting. The napkin opens easily for use.

A smartly tailored look is suggested by the careful fold of this napkin. The height also adds dimension to a table setting.

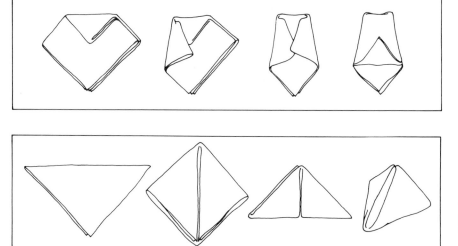

Flowers Add A Thoughtful Touch

What could be more special for your holiday table than individual flower arrangements? They tell your guests that you have taken a little extra care to make the occasion memorable.

These small-scale designs are done in the same manner as larger arrangements, and finding the containers for them is part of the fun. If you look around your home, you'll probably be amazed at the possibilities—tiny boxes, candlesticks, small pitchers, even kitchen utensils.

We've featured arrangements for formal as well as informal settings. A simple dinner served on a tray becomes more interesting when flowers are added. And for a formal dinner party, arrangements at each place setting or at each end of the table are elegant. You may even want to include placecards, coordinating them with the style of your arrangements.

Once you've decided on the type of place setting, consider the colors of the china and accessories. With these in mind, choose the flowers. Small flowers, such as hardy glads, are available from the florist year-round, as are Pinocchio chrysanthemums, miniature roses, and carnations. Depending on the season,

Arranged in a butter warmer, crabapples and leucothoe seedpods add visual interest while carrying out an apple theme in this casual setting.

you might use cones, seedpods, or fruit for filler material.

The designer of these arrangements, Naomi Thomason of Birmingham, Alabama, is never at a loss for creative ideas. She heads for her garden, collecting various vines and twigs, or even clipping foliage from houseplants, such as maidenhair fern. And she's not hesitant about combining fresh blooms with silk flowers in the same arrangement.

For these small-scale designs, be sure to cut the flowers ahead of time and put the stems in water at least one hour or longer before arranging. Misting the flowers the night before a party keeps them looking fresh.

Highlight The Flavor Of Cheese

Chances are good that some of your favorite holiday dishes feature cheese. The flavors of this rich dairy product may range from subtle to sharp, but even the mildest cheese can add unmistakable punch to a festive menu.

When cooking with cheese, always use low heat. If overcooked, it turns into a tough, stringy mass. To avoid this, sprinkle cheese over a dish or casserole during the last few minutes of cooking.

BRANDIED BLUE CHEESE BALL

2 cups (8 ounces) shredded sharp Cheddar cheese
1 (8-ounce) package cream cheese, softened
6 ounces blue cheese, crumbled
1 tablespoon instant minced onion
1 tablespoon chopped pecans
3 tablespoons brandy
1 teaspoon Pickapeppa Sauce
½ cup chopped pecans
2 tablespoons parsley flakes

Combine all ingredients except ½ cup pecans and parsley flakes; mix well.

Shape mixture into a ball. Roll in ½ cup chopped pecans and parsley. Chill 8 hours. Serve with crackers. Yield: one 6-inch cheese ball. *Gloria P. Different, Harvey, Louisiana.*

CHEESE-HERB BREAD

5½ to 6 cups all-purpose flour, divided
2 tablespoons sugar
2 teaspoons salt
1 package dry yeast
¾ teaspoon dried whole oregano
¾ teaspoon dried whole basil
1 cup milk
¼ cup butter or margarine
1 cup mashed cooked potatoes
2 eggs
2 cups (8 ounces) shredded Cheddar cheese
Melted butter or margarine

Combine 2 cups flour, sugar, salt, yeast, oregano, and basil. Heat milk and ¼ cup butter in a small saucepan to 120° to 130°. Gradually add hot mixture to flour mixture, beating 2 minutes at medium speed of electric mixer, scraping sides of bowl occasionally. Add 1 cup flour, potatoes, eggs, and cheese. Beat an additional 2 minutes at low speed. Gradually stir in enough of the remaining flour to make a soft dough.

Turn dough out onto a lightly floured surface, and knead 8 to 10 minutes until smooth and elastic. Shape into a ball, and place in a greased bowl, turning to grease top. Cover and let rise in a warm place (85°), free from drafts, 1 hour or until doubled in bulk.

Punch dough down, and divide in half; divide each half into thirds. Roll each third into a 10½-inch rope. Place 3 ropes, side by side, on a greased baking sheet. Tuck ends under to seal. Repeat with remaining 3 ropes. Place 3 inches apart on a lightly greased baking sheet. Brush with melted butter. Let rise in a warm place (85°), free from drafts, 45 minutes or until almost doubled in bulk.

Bake at 375° for 25 to 30 minutes. Cool on wire racks. Brush with melted butter. Yield: 2 loaves.

Sue-Sue Hartstern, Louisville, Kentucky.

SEASIDE CHEESE DIP

1 (6½-ounce) can minced clams, undrained
2 (5-ounce) jars sharp process cheese spread, softened
1 (8-ounce) package cream cheese, softened
½ cup chopped green pepper
2 green onions with tops, chopped
1 tablespoon Worcestershire sauce

Drain clams, reserving ¼ cup juice. Combine cheese in top of a double boiler; bring water to a boil. Reduce heat to low; cook until cheese melts. Stir in clams and remaining ingredients. Cook over medium heat, stirring occasionally until dip is smooth and bubbly. Serve warm with corn chips or fresh vegetables. Yield: 3 cups.

Carol Powell,
Charlottesville, Virginia.

APPLE-CHEESE PIE

¾ cup sugar
¼ cup all-purpose flour
¾ teaspoon ground cinnamon
⅛ teaspoon salt
5 cups peeled, sliced apples
Cheese Pastry Shell
¾ cup all-purpose flour
¼ cup sugar
⅛ teaspoon salt
⅓ cup butter or margarine
1 cup (4 ounces) shredded Cheddar cheese

Combine ¾ cup sugar, ¼ cup flour, cinnamon, and ⅛ teaspoon salt in a medium bowl. Add apples, tossing well. Spoon into Cheese Pastry Shell.

Combine ¾ cup flour, ¼ cup sugar, and ⅛ teaspoon salt in a small bowl; cut in butter with pastry blender until mixture is crumbly. Stir in cheese. Sprinkle over apples. Bake at 425° for 15 minutes; reduce heat to 350°, and bake an additional 30 minutes. Yield: one 9-inch pie.

Cheese Pastry Shell:

1 cup all-purpose flour
¼ teaspoon salt
⅓ cup shortening
⅓ cup shredded Cheddar cheese
2 to 3 tablespoons milk

Combine flour and salt; cut in shortening with pastry blender until mixture resembles coarse meal. Stir in shredded Cheddar cheese. Sprinkle milk, 1 tablespoon at a time, evenly over surface; stir mixture with fork until dry ingredients are moistened. Shape into a ball. Chill 30 minutes.

Roll out pastry to ⅛-inch thickness on a lightly floured surface. Place in a 9-inch pieplate; trim off excess pastry along edges. Fold edge under, and flute. Yield: one 9-inch pastry shell.

Janet Moer,
Windthorst, Texas.

HOT SOUFFLÉ CUPS

2 eggs
½ cup whipping cream
1 teaspoon prepared mustard
1 cup (4 ounces) shredded Cheddar cheese
Dash of red pepper

Lightly grease bottom of four 6-ounce custard cups or soufflé dishes; set aside.

Combine eggs, whipping cream, and mustard in a medium mixing bowl. Beat with an electric mixer until mixture is well blended. Stir in shredded cheese and red pepper. Spoon into prepared custard cups. Bake at 400° for 20 minutes or until tops are golden brown. Serve immediately. Yield: 4 servings.

Maggie Cates,
Orlando, Florida.

Ornaments To Make Ahead

Satisfy your handcrafting urge by making fragrant Cinnamon Ornaments. They're not edible, but all of the ingredients, except the wire loops and ribbon, come from the pantry. Hang them on the Christmas tree, tie them on packages, or give them as gifts.

CINNAMON ORNAMENTS

¾ cup ground cinnamon
1 tablespoon ground allspice
2 tablespoons ground cloves
1 tablespoon ground nutmeg
1 cup applesauce
Copper wire
⅛-inch or ¼-inch satin ribbon

Combine spices, blending well. Stir in applesauce; mix well. (Mixture will be stiff.) Roll out to ¼-inch thickness on an ungreased cookie sheet.

Using small or medium-size cookie cutters, cut dough into desired shapes. Peel away excess dough, and reroll as necessary.

Cut wire into 2-inch lengths as needed. Bend lengths of wire into horseshoe shapes, and insert ends into tops, leaving half-circles of wire exposed. Let ornaments dry uncovered for 4 to 5 days.

To hang, cut ribbon into 10-inch lengths as needed. Fold ribbon in half, knot ends together, and pull tight. Push loop of ribbon under wire, and pull knotted ends of ribbon through loop. Use additional ribbon to tie bow at top of wire, if desired. After ornaments have dried, store in sealed plastic bags until ready to use. Yield: 25 small ornaments or 18 medium-size ornaments.

Cinnamon Ornaments are shaped with cookie cutters and left to dry naturally.

Give Pasta
A New Look

At first glance, these recipes for a pie shell, pizza crust, and antipasto might seem like any other. But look again, and the shapes will tell a different story. They're all made from pasta.

Spinach-Pasta Pie bakes vermicelli into a piecrust that contains a vegetable filling. Butter, eggs, and Parmesan cheese bind the noodles and help hold the shape as it bakes. The noodle crust is so basic that you can use it with other fillings of a similar consistency. Be sure to keep it covered for most of the baking time to keep the noodles moist.

Line cooked jumbo macaroni shells with lettuce, and spoon in a salad mixture to make Salmon Salad Shells. It's an easy, make-ahead lunch idea that you might use during the hectic holiday season. Or fry some crisp Wonton Nibbles for parties. For this recipe, cut the wontons into little rectangles, pinch them into bows, and fry.

Instead of being boiled, the noodles in Chow Mein Over Crispy Noodles are fried into a patty as the base for the topping. You can find thin Chinese egg noodles for this recipe in most Oriental food stores. Thinner than vermicelli, they are usually marketed as clusters instead of traditional long strands.

To make the noodle patty, first rehydrate the noodles in boiling water until they're soft but not done. They cook very quickly, so watch them carefully.

Then rinse away the surface starch, and drain the noodles. Pick through the strands to separate them, and fry in hot oil until crisp. If rinsed and separated properly, the fried patty should break into crispy little noodles. (Use gentle pressure.) Check your patty before adding the topping, and if it doesn't break easily, loosen it by inserting and twisting a fork in several places. If you can't locate this type of noodle in your area, serve the tasty chow mein mixture over rice or crunchy commercial chow mein noodles that you find in the Oriental food section of most supermarkets.

Lasagna Pizza substitutes the traditional crust in favor of layered lasagna noodles. As it bakes, the cheese between the layers of noodles melts and binds the pasta into a "pizza crust" that's a snap to make—no more waiting for the yeast dough to rise.

Other recipes include Beef and Vegetables in a Noodle Ring and Fruit-Filled Wontons. The wontons are similar to the little fried pies your grandmother used to make.

Be sure to pick up a few extra packages of pasta on your next trip to the supermarket. We think you will enjoy using it in these recipes.

BEEF AND VEGETABLES
IN A NOODLE RING

2 pounds boneless sirloin, cut into ½-inch cubes
2 tablespoons vegetable oil
½ cup chopped onion
1 clove garlic, minced
½ cup Chablis or other dry white wine, divided
1 (8-ounce) can tomato sauce
½ teaspoon dried whole oregano
¼ teaspoon dried whole rosemary, crushed
¼ teaspoon salt
¼ teaspoon pepper
1 (10-ounce) package frozen mixed vegetables
⅓ cup water
½ pound fresh mushrooms, sliced
2 tablespoons butter or margarine, melted
2 teaspoons all-purpose flour
1 tablespoon water
Noodle Ring
Chopped fresh parsley (optional)

Brown meat in hot oil in a Dutch oven; remove meat with a slotted spoon. Add onion and garlic to pan drippings; sauté until tender. Add meat, ¼ cup wine, tomato sauce, and seasonings to onion mixture; bring to a boil. Cover, reduce heat, and simmer 30 minutes or until meat is almost tender. Add mixed vegetables and ⅓ cup water; cook over medium heat an additional 15 minutes or until meat is tender and vegetables are done.

Sauté mushrooms in butter until tender. Dissolve flour in 1 tablespoon water; add to mushrooms, and cook 1 minute, stirring constantly. Stir mushrooms into meat mixture. Add remaining ¼ cup wine, stirring well. Cover and cook over medium heat about 10 minutes, stirring occasionally. Spoon mixture in center of Noodle Ring; sprinkle with parsley. Yield: 6 servings.

Noodle Ring:

5 cups water
¾ teaspoon salt
1 (5-ounce) package medium egg noodles
2 eggs, beaten
1½ cups milk
2 tablespoons butter or margarine, melted
½ teaspoon salt

Combine water and ¾ teaspoon salt in a Dutch oven; bring to a boil. Add noodles; cook 4 to 5 minutes or until tender but slightly firm. Drain well.

Place noodles in a lightly greased 5-cup, ovenproof ring mold. Combine remaining ingredients, mixing well; pour over noodles. Lightly grease a piece of aluminum foil, and cover mold, greased side down. Bake at 325° for 30 minutes. Uncover and bake an additional 15 to 20 minutes or until set. Let stand 10 minutes before inverting. Yield: one 5-cup noodle ring.

LASAGNA PIZZA

16 lasagna noodles
4 cups (1 pound) shredded mozzarella cheese
Pizza sauce (recipe follows)
1 (3½-ounce) package sliced pepperoni
1 (8-ounce) can sliced mushrooms, drained
1 small green pepper, cut into strips
1 small onion, sliced and separated into rings
½ cup grated Parmesan cheese

Cook noodles according to package directions; drain. Rinse with cold water, and drain again.

Cover a buttered 15- x 10- x 1-inch jellyroll pan with half of noodles, arranging noodles lengthwise in pan, and overlapping sides slightly. (It may be necessary to cut one noodle into smaller pieces to cover pan.) Sprinkle noodles with half of mozzarella; top with remaining noodles. Spread pizza sauce evenly over noodles. Bake, uncovered, at 375° for 12 minutes. Arrange pepperoni, mushrooms, green pepper, and onion over pizza. Sprinkle with remaining mozzarella and Parmesan cheese. Bake an additional 15 minutes. Yield: 4 to 6 servings.

Pizza Sauce:

1 (8-ounce) can tomato sauce
1 (10¾-ounce) can tomato puree
1 clove garlic, minced
2 teaspoons dried whole oregano
1 teaspoon dried whole basil
1 teaspoon dried fennel seeds
¼ teaspoon pepper
⅛ teaspoon salt

Combine all ingredients, mixing well. Yield: about 2 cups.

PASTA ANTIPASTO

1 cup uncooked corkscrew macaroni
2 (6½-ounce) jars marinated artichoke
    hearts, undrained
¾ cup commercial Italian salad dressing
¼ teaspoon freshly ground pepper
1 pint cherry tomatoes
½ cup pimiento-stuffed olives
½ cup ripe olives
2 medium carrots, scraped and cut into
    julienne strips
½ pound fresh mushrooms
1 medium-size green pepper, cut into
    strips
3 to 4 ounces sliced pepperoni
3 to 4 ounces sliced salami

Cook macaroni according to package directions, omitting salt. Drain and rinse with cold water; set aside.

Drain artichoke hearts, reserving ½ cup artichoke liquid. Add Italian salad dressing and pepper to artichoke liquid to make marinade, stirring well.

Combine artichoke hearts, tomatoes, olives, carrots, mushrooms, and green pepper. Add about three-fourths of marinade to vegetable mixture, tossing gently. Cover and chill overnight. Add remaining marinade to pasta, tossing gently. Cover and chill overnight.

To serve, arrange pepperoni and salami around outer edges of a serving platter. Spoon pasta in a ring within meat, using a slotted spoon. Spoon vegetable mixture in center of platter, using a slotted spoon. Yield: 8 to 10 servings.

SALMON SALAD SHELLS

14 jumbo macaroni shells
1 (15-ounce) can salmon, drained and
    flaked
½ cup mayonnaise
⅓ cup chopped green pepper
¼ cup chopped onion
¼ cup sweet pickle relish
2 teaspoons lemon juice
¼ teaspoon salt
¼ teaspoon pepper
⅛ teaspoon hot sauce
Leaf lettuce

Cook pasta according to package directions; drain. Rinse with cold water; cover and chill.

Combine remaining ingredients except lettuce, mixing until blended; cover and chill.

To serve, tear lettuce into small pieces. Line each macaroni shell with lettuce; spoon salmon mixture into shells. Yield: 4 to 6 servings.

PASTA FRITTATA

3 ounces vermicelli
4 eggs
3 tablespoons milk
1 tablespoon chopped fresh basil or 1
    teaspoon dried whole basil
¼ teaspoon salt
¼ teaspoon freshly ground pepper
1 small onion, finely chopped
¼ cup chopped fresh parsley
1 clove garlic, crushed
¼ cup butter or margarine, melted
1 cup (4 ounces) shredded Swiss or
    Cheddar cheese
2 tablespoons chopped fresh parsley
    (optional)

Cook vermicelli according to package directions, omitting salt. Drain and set aside. Combine eggs, milk, basil, salt, and pepper; beat well. Stir in vermicelli, and set aside.

Sauté onion, ¼ cup parsley, and garlic in butter in a 10-inch nonstick skillet; remove from heat. Stir in vermicelli mixture; sprinkle with cheese and 2 tablespoons parsley, if desired. Cover and cook over low heat 5 to 7 minutes or until cheese melts and egg mixture is set. Let stand 5 minutes before serving. Cut into wedges. Yield: 4 servings.

SPINACH-PASTA PIE

1 (10-ounce) package frozen chopped
    spinach, thawed
½ (12-ounce) package vermicelli
2 tablespoons butter or margarine,
    softened
⅓ cup grated Parmesan cheese
2 eggs, well beaten
3 eggs, well beaten
1 cup (4 ounces) shredded mozzarella
    cheese
⅓ cup milk
½ teaspoon salt
¼ teaspoon freshly ground pepper
¼ teaspoon onion powder
⅛ teaspoon ground nutmeg
6 (3-inch) strips pimiento

Place spinach on paper towels, and squeeze until barely moist.

Cook vermicelli according to package directions; drain. Stir butter and Parmesan cheese into hot vermicelli. Add 2 eggs, stirring well. Spoon mixture into a lightly greased 9-inch pieplate. Use a spoon to shape vermicelli into a pie shell. Cover with aluminum foil, and bake at 350° for 10 minutes. Set aside.

Combine spinach, 3 eggs, mozzarella cheese, milk, and seasonings, stirring

until blended. Spoon spinach mixture into pasta shell.

Cover pie with aluminum foil. Bake at 350° for 35 minutes; uncover and bake an additional 5 minutes. Arrange pimiento strips around pie, radiating from center. Let stand 10 minutes before slicing. Yield: 6 servings.

CHOW MEIN
OVER CRISPY NOODLES

1 pound boneless sirloin steak
1 tablespoon cornstarch
½ cup water
¼ cup plus 2 tablespoons soy sauce
¼ pound thin Chinese egg noodles
6 cups boiling water
1 cup vegetable oil
2 teaspoons grated fresh ginger
1 large onion, thinly sliced and separated
    into rings
2 stalks celery, diagonally sliced
½ cup sliced fresh mushrooms
1 (8-ounce) can sliced water chestnuts,
    drained
1 (6-ounce) package frozen Chinese pea
    pods, thawed

Partially freeze steak; slice diagonally across grain into 2- x ¼-inch strips. Set aside. Dissolve cornstarch in water and soy sauce; set aside.

Place noodles in boiling water; cover and let stand 1 to 2 minutes or until softened but not done. Separate strands as they soften, using a fork. (The noodles cook quickly, so watch them carefully.) Drain noodles. Rinse thoroughly with cold water, and drain well. Sort through noodles to separate strands that mass together.

Heat oil in a 10-inch nonstick skillet with sloping sides. Carefully place noodles evenly into skillet, quickly shaping them into a patty using a fork. Fry about 3 to 4 minutes or until crisp on bottom and patty holds together when lifted. Gently turn patty over, using large spatulas; fry 2 to 3 minutes or until crisp on other side. Drain noodle patty well on paper towels. Place in warm oven while preparing beef.

Pour off all but about 3 tablespoons oil remaining in skillet. Sauté ginger in oil briefly; add steak, and stir-fry 3 minutes. Remove steak from skillet. Stir-fry onion, celery, mushrooms, and water chestnuts in skillet 2 to 3 minutes, adding additional oil if necessary. Add pea pods and meat. Stir in soy sauce mixture; cook over medium-high heat until mixture is thickened and bubbly, stirring constantly.

Place noodle patty on serving plate. Gently loosen noodle patty, if necessary, by inserting and twisting a fork in several places, keeping patty intact. Spoon beef mixture over noodles, and serve immediately. Yield: 4 servings.

WONTON NIBBLES

1 dozen frozen wonton skins, thawed
Peanut or vegetable oil
Sifted powdered sugar

Work with 1 wonton skin at a time, and keep others covered when not in use. They dry out quickly and are difficult to shape when dry.

Cut each wonton skin into 2 lengthwise strips. Cut each strip into 3 crosswise strips. Moisten fingers, and pinch each strip in center to make bow shape. Pinch center of bow again from another angle to make shape adhere. Set aside to dry.

Heat 1 inch oil to 375° in a large skillet. Fry bows, a few at a time, in hot oil a few seconds or until crisp and golden brown, turning once; drain well. Dust bows with powdered sugar while still warm. Let cool, and store in an airtight container. Yield: 6 dozen.

FRUIT-FILLED WONTONS

1 (8-ounce) package dried peaches
1 cup water
3 tablespoons sugar
⅛ teaspoon ground cinnamon
½ cup sugar
½ teaspoon ground cinnamon
About 18 frozen wonton skins, thawed
Peanut or vegetable oil

Combine peaches and water in a saucepan; bring to a boil. Cover, reduce heat, and simmer 30 minutes or until tender; mash. Add 3 tablespoons sugar and ⅛ teaspoon cinnamon. Cool.

Combine ½ cup sugar and ½ teaspoon cinnamon in a large plastic bag, mixing well; set aside.

Spoon about 2 teaspoons peach mixture in center of each wonton skin; brush edges of wonton lightly with water. Fold in half diagonally, and press the edges together to seal.

Heat 1 inch oil to 375° in a large skillet. Place 2 or 3 wontons in hot oil, and fry 30 seconds on each side or until golden brown; drain on paper towels. Repeat with remaining wontons.

While warm, place a few wontons at a time in sugar mixture in bag; shake gently to coat. Yield: about 1½ dozen.

COOKING LIGHT®

Don't Skip The Appetizer

The holiday weeks can be a frantic time for the weight-conscious individual whose palate and patience are tempted beyond good reasoning and discipline. Your first thought may be to decline an appetizer and save the calories. In fact, the concept of an appetizer as a food or beverage that stimulates the appetite is enough to frighten most people. Fortunately, appetizers don't have to be a threat to your diet if you keep a few tips in mind when selecting and enjoying the delicacies.

An appetizer can actually help you eat less. Warm soups and beverages start the digestive juices flowing and can help fill you up before you have the entrée. The key is to eat slowly. Once you start eating, it takes about 20 minutes for the stomach to signal the brain that it is getting satisfied. So the longer you take to eat, the less food you should need to make you feel full. Instead of rushing through the appetizer, slow your pace.

Reduce the temptation to overindulge with pick-up appetizers. Decide what type and amount of food you will allow yourself beforehand; then prepare your plate. Try leaving some food on your plate to discourage others from offering you more.

When appetizers are served after guests are seated, you can still take charge of the situation and stick to your regular diet routine. Sample the food, or eat only a portion of it.

If you're the one planning the appetizer for a gala occasion, remember that simple, unadorned fare is easier on the taste buds and takes less preparation. Do yourself and your dieting friends a favor. Leave off the deep-fried batters and fancy morsels laden with sweeteners and heavy cream. Use the extra time you'll save to enjoy guests more. Here are some ideas to help you get started.

Fresh snow peas are a low-calorie alternative to crackers for the tasty crabmeat filling in our Crab-Stuffed Snow Peas. Reduced-calorie mayonnaise, parsley, Parmesan cheese, lemon juice, and garlic lend flavor to the tasty mixture, and the snow peas add crunch.

Stuffed mushrooms are a favorite of almost everyone. And our Flavor-Stuffed Mushrooms are no exception, even though they are low in calories. Green onion, pimiento, Creole mustard, and basil add zest to the stuffing mixture, while dry breadcrumbs and part-skim mozzarella cheese help bind the ingredients together.

Mock Cream of Broccoli Soup has far fewer calories than it would appear. The secret is in the preparation. Broccoli and carrots are pureed to give the soup its thick consistency and rich color. At only 57 calories per serving, you can proudly boast that this "creamy" soup doesn't contain a drop of high-fat, high-calorie cream. Instead, skim milk and chicken broth are used.

TOMATO-CRAB ASPIC

3 cups tomato juice
2 envelopes unflavored gelatin
2 slices onion
½ cup beef broth
2 bay leaves
¼ teaspoon celery salt
½ cup beef broth
2 tablespoons lemon juice
1 cup chopped celery
1 (6½-ounce) can crabmeat, drained
½ cup chopped green pepper
Lettuce leaves (optional)

Combine tomato juice, gelatin, onion, ½ cup beef broth, bay leaves, and celery salt in a heavy saucepan; bring to a boil. Stir in ½ cup beef broth and lemon juice. Chill mixture until consistency of unbeaten egg white. Stir in celery, crabmeat, and green pepper. Remove bay leaves.

Spoon mixture into 8 lightly oiled ½-cup molds; chill until firm. Unmold on lettuce leaves, if desired. Yield: 8 servings (about 40 calories per serving).
Danella Neely,
Freeport, Florida.

November   287

CRAB-STUFFED SNOW PEAS

1 (6½-ounce) can crabmeat, drained
⅓ cup reduced-calorie mayonnaise
2 tablespoons grated Parmesan cheese
2 tablespoons chopped fresh parsley
1 tablespoon lemon juice
¼ teaspoon garlic powder
30 fresh large snow peas

Combine all ingredients except snow peas, mixing well. Chill.

Trim ends from snow peas. Using a sharp knife, carefully slit one side of each pea pod. Spoon crab mixture into a decorating bag fitted with a tip with a large opening. Pipe crab mixture into each snow pea. Cover and chill. Yield: 2½ dozen (about 16 calories per stuffed pod).
Traci Myers,
Boca Raton, Florida.

FLAVOR-STUFFED MUSHROOMS

16 large fresh mushrooms
Vegetable cooking spray
1 tablespoon thinly sliced green onion
1 tablespoon dry breadcrumbs
1 tablespoon diced pimiento
1 teaspoon Creole mustard
¼ teaspoon dried whole basil
3 tablespoons shredded mozzarella cheese
Green onion shreds (optional)

Clean mushrooms with a damp paper towel. Remove mushroom stems; finely chop stems, and set aside. Sauté mushroom caps in cooking spray in a skillet until almost tender; set aside.

Sauté mushroom stems and 1 tablespoon green onion in cooking spray in a skillet until tender. Remove from heat; add remaining ingredients except green onion shreds, stirring well. Spoon mushroom mixture into mushroom caps. Place mushroom caps in a shallow baking pan coated with cooking spray. Cover, and bake at 350° for 10 minutes or until tender. Drain on paper towels. Garnish stuffed mushrooms with green onion shreds, if desired. Yield: 16 stuffed mushrooms (about 12 calories per stuffed mushroom).

TARRAGON-VEGETABLE SALAD

¼ cup red wine vinegar
3 tablespoons vegetable oil
1 tablespoon Worcestershire sauce
½ teaspoon dried whole tarragon
¼ teaspoon salt
⅛ teaspoon pepper
1 cup sliced fresh mushrooms
1 cup thinly sliced carrots
½ medium-size green pepper, cut into
   strips
8 cherry tomatoes, halved
Lettuce leaves (optional)

Combine vinegar, oil, Worcestershire sauce, and seasonings in a jar. Cover tightly, and shake vigorously. Combine vegetables in a medium bowl. Pour dressing over vegetables; toss gently to coat. Cover and marinate in refrigerator about 4 hours.

Drain vegetables, and arrange on lettuce leaves, if desired. Yield: 4 servings (about 57 calories per serving).
Ginny Whitt,
Mount Washington, Kentucky.

MOCK CREAM
OF BROCCOLI SOUP

2 cups water
1 (14½-ounce) can chicken broth
6 cups (about 1¼ pounds) coarsely
   chopped broccoli
1 cup sliced carrots
1 medium onion, quartered
½ cup skim milk
½ teaspoon salt
⅛ teaspoon white pepper
Carrot curls (optional)

Combine water, broth, broccoli, carrots, and onion in a Dutch oven; bring to a boil. Cover, reduce heat, and simmer 15 minutes or until tender.

Place half of vegetable mixture in container of an electric blender; process until smooth. Repeat with remaining mixture. Return to Dutch oven; add milk, salt, and white pepper. Cook mixture until heated. Garnish soup with carrot curls, if desired. Yield: 6 cups (about 57 calories per 1-cup serving).
Kathryn Schubert,
Springfield, Virginia.

BROILED ORANGE HALVES

3 large oranges
3 tablespoons crème de cacao
1½ teaspoons reduced-calorie margarine
Ground cinnamon

Cut oranges in half crosswise; remove seeds, and loosen sections. Place cut side up in a broiler pan. Drizzle each half with 1½ teaspoons crème de cacao; dot with ¼ teaspoon reduced-calorie margarine, and sprinkle with cinnamon. Broil oranges 4 inches from heat 3 to 5 minutes or until thoroughly heated. Yield: 6 servings (about 71 calories per serving).

Serve Winter Vegetables At Their Freshest

If you like fresh vegetables, you don't have to give them up just because the season changes. While you may not be able to find some of your spring and summer favorites, a lot of other vegetables are available this time of the year. Look for turnips, cabbage, broccoli, brussels sprouts, spinach, and cauliflower, just to name a few. Then try our readers' recipes; these folks know how to make the most of what the season has to offer. They've added new seasonings or toppings to old favorites.

LEMON SPROUTS

1 pound fresh brussels sprouts
1 cup water
½ teaspoon salt
2 tablespoons butter or margarine
2 tablespoons all-purpose flour
½ cup milk
1 tablespoon lemon juice
½ teaspoon caraway seeds

Wash brussels sprouts thoroughly, and remove discolored leaves. Cut off stem ends, and slash bottom of each sprout with a shallow X. Place sprouts in a large saucepan; add water and salt, and bring to a boil. Cover, reduce heat, and simmer 5 minutes or until tender. (Do not drain.)

Melt butter in a heavy saucepan over low heat; add flour, stirring until smooth. Cook mixture 1 minute, stirring constantly.

Gradually add milk; cook over medium heat, stirring constantly, until mixture is thickened and bubbly. Add to sprouts. Stir in lemon juice and caraway seeds. Yield: 4 servings.
Eleanor Homer,
Round Rock, Texas.

BROCCOLI-AND-EGGS AU GRATIN

1 (1½-pound) bunch fresh broccoli
4 hard-cooked eggs, coarsely chopped
3 ounces Cheddar cheese, sliced
¼ cup butter or margarine
¼ cup all-purpose flour
2 cups milk
½ teaspoon Worcestershire sauce
¼ teaspoon salt
2 tablespoons butter or margarine
¼ cup fine, dry breadcrumbs

Trim off large leaves and tough ends of lower stalks of broccoli. Wash broccoli thoroughly, and separate into spears. Cook in a small amount of boiling water 10 minutes or until tender. Arrange broccoli spears in a greased 2-quart baking dish. Top with chopped eggs and cheese.

Melt ¼ cup butter in a heavy saucepan over low heat; add flour, stirring until smooth. Cook 1 minute, stirring constantly. Gradually add milk; cook over medium heat, stirring constantly, until mixture is thickened and bubbly. Stir in Worcestershire sauce and salt. Pour sauce over broccoli mixture.

Melt 2 tablespoons butter in a heavy saucepan; stir in breadcrumbs. Brown lightly, and sprinkle over sauce. Bake at 350° for 25 to 30 minutes. Yield: 6 to 8 servings.
Sherry Baynes,
North Wilkesboro, North Carolina.

CARAWAY CABBAGE

3 slices bacon
1 medium onion, cut into strips
1 medium cabbage, cut into strips
1 cup beef broth
¼ cup white wine
½ teaspoon salt
¼ teaspoon pepper
1 teaspoon caraway seeds
1 large apple, peeled and chopped
Additional cooked and crumbled bacon for
    garnish (optional)

Cook bacon in a large Dutch oven until crisp; remove bacon, reserving drippings in Dutch oven. Crumble bacon, and set aside.

Sauté onion in bacon drippings. Add cabbage, broth, wine, salt, pepper, and carraway seeds; cover and simmer 15 minutes, stirring occasionally. Gently stir in reserved bacon and apple; cook 5 minutes. Garnish with additional crumbled bacon, if desired. Yield: 6 servings.
Suzy Carter,
South Houston, Texas.

CAULIFLOWER TOSS

1 large head cauliflower, broken into
    flowerets
2 tablespoons chopped onion
1 clove garlic, crushed
¼ cup plus 2 tablespoons butter or
    margarine, melted
2 tablespoons soft breadcrumbs
1 tablespoon chopped fresh parsley
1 hard-cooked egg, finely chopped

Place cauliflower in a small amount of boiling water; return to a boil. Cover, reduce heat, and simmer 8 minutes or until tender. Drain.

Sauté onion and garlic in butter in a large saucepan until tender. Stir in remaining ingredients; pour over cauliflower, and toss gently. Yield: 4 to 6 servings.
Susan McLemore,
Knoxville, Tennessee.

CREAMY SPINACH

2¼ pounds fresh spinach
¼ cup chopped onion
3 tablespoons butter or margarine, melted
½ to ¾ cup commercial sour cream
1 teaspoon vinegar
Dash of salt

Remove stems from spinach; wash leaves thoroughly. Cook spinach, covered, in a large Dutch oven 3 to 5 minutes. (Do not add water.) Drain spinach well; chop.

Sauté onion in butter in a skillet until tender. Add spinach and remaining ingredients; heat thoroughly. (Do not boil.) Yield: 4 servings.
Mrs. Bill Cotton,
Edcouch, Texas.

GOLDEN TURNIP SOUFFLÉ

¼ cup butter or margarine
¼ cup all-purpose flour
⅓ cup whipping cream
1¼ cups mashed cooked turnips (about 1
    pound)
1 tablespoon grated onion
½ teaspoon salt
⅛ teaspoon pepper
4 eggs, separated

Melt butter in a heavy saucepan over low heat; add flour, stirring until smooth. Cook 1 minute, stirring constantly. Gradually stir in whipping cream; cook over medium heat, stirring constantly, until thickened and bubbly. Add turnips, onion, salt, and pepper.

Beat egg yolks, and stir about one-fourth of hot turnip mixture into yolks, mixing well. Add yolk mixture to turnip mixture, stirring constantly.

Beat egg whites (at room temperature) until stiff; fold into turnip mixture. Pour into a greased 1½-quart casserole. Bake at 350° for 30 minutes. Serve immediately. Yield: 6 servings.
Claire Bastable,
Reston, Virginia.

SAUCY TURNIPS

6 cups peeled, sliced turnips
1¼ cups water
3 small green onions, sliced
1 tablespoon butter or margarine
1 teaspoon garlic powder
1 teaspoon seasoning salt
1 tablespoon cornstarch
¼ cup water
1 cup (4 ounces) shredded Cheddar cheese

Place turnips in a large saucepan; add 1¼ cups water, and bring to a boil. Cover and cook 12 minutes. Add green onions, butter, garlic powder, and salt; cook an additional 5 minutes.

Dissolve cornstarch in ¼ cup water; add to turnips, stirring until combined. Add cheese; cook until cheese melts. Yield: 6 servings.
Erma Jackson,
Huntsville, Alabama.

Open A Can Of Vegetables

Fall and winter months are ideal for using canned vegetables, especially when some fresh produce isn't available. Because the canned versions are already cooked, you save time as well.

ORANGE-GLAZED BEETS

¼ cup butter or margarine
½ cup orange marmalade
¼ cup orange juice
1 (16-ounce) can sliced beets, drained

Melt butter in a medium saucepan; add marmalade and orange juice, mixing well. Gently stir in beets; cook 5 minutes or until thoroughly heated. Yield: about 4 servings.
Mrs. R. H. Manderscheid,
Houston, Texas.

BAKED SCALLOPED CORN

1 (17-ounce) can whole kernel corn,
  drained
1 (17-ounce) can cream-style corn
¼ cup milk
¼ cup crushed round buttery crackers
¼ cup chopped onion
2 eggs, beaten
1 (2-ounce) jar chopped pimiento, drained
¼ teaspoon salt
¼ teaspoon pepper
2 tablespoons grated Parmesan cheese
1 tablespoon butter or margarine

Combine all ingredients except cheese
and butter, mixing well. Pour into a
greased 1½-quart casserole. Sprinkle
top with cheese, and dot with butter.
Bake, uncovered, at 350° for 40 to 45
minutes or until center is almost set.
Let stand 5 minutes before serving.
Yield: 6 servings. *Gayle Wallace,*
Porter, Texas.

SWEET-AND-SOUR
BLACK-EYED PEAS

3 (17-ounce) cans black-eyed peas, drained
¼ cup molasses
¼ cup vinegar
1 teaspoon dry mustard
1 teaspoon garlic powder
1 tablespoon brown sugar
1 (8-ounce) can sliced pineapple, drained

Combine all ingredients except pineapple; pour into a lightly greased shallow 2-quart baking dish. Top with
pineapple slices. Bake, uncovered, at
375° for 40 minutes. Yield: 6 to 8
servings. *Ella Stanley,*
Coeburn, Virginia.

These Sweets Are
For Breakfast

If you're tired of the usual bacon and
eggs every morning, why not break the
routine and have a sweet roll or a slice
of coffee cake instead? Either makes a
nice change from the ordinary. We've
found just the recipes to inspire you.
You may want to make them ahead or
make them some morning when you've
got a little extra time.
The Cinnamon Crumb Cake recipe
makes two coffee cakes with a delectable, streusel-type topping. You can

freeze one for later use. If you thaw it
overnight and warm it in the oven, it
tastes as if it were just made.
Easy Cinnamon Rolls take less time
than you'd expect. There's no yeast in
the dough, so you don't have to allow
time for rising.
Jam Kolaches take a little longer, but
they're well worth the wait. These
tender rolls are lightly flavored with
lemon and mace and have a dollop of
jam in the center. We liked them with
blackberry and strawberry jam, but you
can experiment with your favorite.

JAM KOLACHES

1 package dry yeast
¼ cup warm milk (105° to 115°)
⅓ cup sugar, divided
About 2½ cups unbleached flour, divided
¼ cup plus 2 tablespoons butter or
  margarine, softened
2 eggs
¼ cup whipping cream
1 teaspoon salt
¼ teaspoon ground mace
1 teaspoon grated lemon rind
1 egg
1 tablespoon whipping cream
½ cup strawberry or blackberry jam

Dissolve yeast in warm milk; let stand
5 minutes. Stir in 2 tablespoons sugar
and 2 tablespoons flour. Cover and let
stand 10 minutes. Set aside.
Cream butter; gradually add remaining sugar, beating until light and fluffy.
Add 2 eggs, ¼ cup whipping cream,
salt, mace, lemon rind, and yeast mixture. Gradually stir in enough remaining
flour to make a soft dough. Place dough
in a greased bowl, turning to grease
top. Cover and let rise in a warm place
(85°), free from drafts, 1 to 1½ hours
or until doubled in bulk.
Punch dough down, and divide into
24 portions. Shape each portion into a
ball, and roll out into 2-inch rounds.
Place rounds 2 inches apart on greased
baking sheets.
Combine egg and 1 tablespoon whipping cream; mix well. Brush lightly over
each dough round. Dipping thumb in
flour, make an indentation in center of
each round; spoon about 1 teaspoon
jam into each indentation. Let rise in a
warm place (85°), free from drafts, 30
minutes or until doubled in bulk. Bake
at 375° for 8 to 10 minutes. Yield: 2
dozen. *Donna L. Ellett,*
Monroe, Louisiana.

CINNAMON CRUMB CAKE

3 cups all-purpose flour
2 cups sugar
¼ cup wheat germ
1 tablespoon baking powder
½ teaspoon salt
1 cup butter
2 teaspoons ground cinnamon
4 eggs, separated
1 cup milk
¼ cup butter, melted and divided

Combine flour, sugar, wheat germ,
baking powder, and salt; mix well. Cut
in 1 cup butter with a pastry blender
until mixture resembles coarse meal.
Remove 1 cup of mixture; combine with
cinnamon, and set aside.
Beat egg yolks at high speed of an
electric mixer 2 minutes or until thick
and lemon colored; gradually beat in
milk. Add the flour mixture, stirring
just until moistened.
Beat egg whites (at room temperature) at high speed of an electric mixer
until soft peaks form. Fold egg whites
into batter. Pour batter into two
greased and floured 9-inch round cakepans. Sprinkle tops with reserved flour
mixture. Bake at 400° for 30 minutes.
Drizzle each cake with 2 tablespoons
butter. Serve warm or at room temperature. Yield: two 9-inch coffee cakes.
Evelyn L. Griswold,
Spring City, Tennessee.

EASY CINNAMON ROLLS

¼ cup plus 1½ teaspoons shortening
3 cups self-rising flour
1 cup milk
½ cup butter or margarine, softened
½ cup sugar
½ cup firmly packed brown sugar
1 tablespoon ground cinnamon
¾ cup chopped pecans
½ cup raisins
1¼ cups sifted powdered sugar
3 tablespoons milk

Cut shortening into flour with pastry
blender until mixture resembles coarse
meal. Add 1 cup milk, stirring until dry
ingredients are moistened. Turn dough
out onto a floured surface; knead
lightly.

Roll dough into a 20- x 14-inch rectangle; spread butter on dough, leaving a ½-inch border. Combine sugar and cinnamon; mix well, and sprinkle over butter. Top with pecans and raisins. Beginning at long side, roll up jellyroll fashion; press edges and ends together securely. Cut into 1-inch slices; place cut side down in a greased 13- x 9- x 2-inch baking pan. Bake at 375° for 20 to 25 minutes.

Combine powdered sugar and 3 tablespoons milk; drizzle over warm rolls. Yield: 20 rolls.   *Kathryn Bibelhauser, Louisville, Kentucky.*

Wine Makes The Dish Elegant

If you appreciate the special quality that a glass of wine adds to a meal, chances are you've surmised that its distinctive taste can make an extraordinary difference in a recipe. This versatile liquid is becoming increasingly popular in preparing meats, fish, vegetables, and even desserts.

Our recipes are a good place to start if you would like to try your hand at cooking with wine, but you don't have to stop there. Use your imagination and experiment with leftover table wines and see what kinds of results you can achieve with different combinations of wine and food. Keep in mind, however, that just adding wine to a dish doesn't automatically enhance its flavor. Here are some guidelines that should help when you're planning to experiment.

First, never use wine for cooking that you wouldn't consider drinking for its own merit. It doesn't have to be expensive, but remember that although alcohol evaporates when wine is heated, the flavor remains the same. The quality of the wine will make a big difference in the overall taste of the dish.

White wines are generally used with foods that are light in color, such as chicken and fish, while red wines are usually reserved for darker meats and robust soups and stews. This is not a hard-and-fast rule because there are many exceptions, but it pays to keep this in mind for aesthetic reasons as well as taste. For example, red wine added to a white sauce turns the sauce gray.

Wine is a marvelous flavoring agent, but it should be used the same way you use herbs and spices—sparingly. Be careful not to overshadow the characteristic flavor of the food when you're adding wine to a recipe.

Overdoing it can also be a problem with wine-based marinades. Although they act as a tenderizer on meat, they can add an acidic flavor if the meat is allowed to marinate too long. (Choice cuts need less time than tougher cuts.)

Note: From a safety standpoint, there's concern on the part of some appliance manufacturers about the amount of wine and other types of liquor used in baked dishes. They feel that since alcohol is basically a fuel, there's danger of a fire or explosion if too much alcohol is heated in a small space, such as an oven. To be on the safe side, they recommend using only a small amount of liquor and not doubling the recipe if the dish is going to be baked. They also recommend that you not cover the dish with a lid or aluminum foil because the pressure created by the alcohol and heat could cause an explosion.

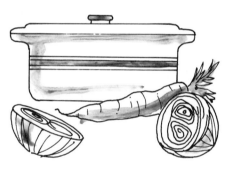

BEEF BURGUNDY ROAST

1½ cups Burgundy
1 bay leaf
½ teaspoon dried whole thyme
1 (4- to 5-pound) boneless rump roast
2 carrots, sliced
¾ cup chopped onion
¾ cup beef broth
½ teaspoon salt
⅛ teaspoon pepper
⅓ cup butter or margarine, melted
¼ to ⅓ cup all-purpose flour

Combine Burgundy, bay leaf, and thyme in a large bowl; add roast, turning to coat. Cover and marinate 8 hours in refrigerator.

Remove roast, reserving marinade. Wipe off surface with a paper towel. Brown roast in its own fat on all sides in a Dutch oven. Remove roast; add carrots and onion. Cook over low heat, stirring occasionally, 15 minutes or until tender. Add reserved marinade, broth, salt, and pepper; bring to a boil. Add roast; cover, reduce heat, and simmer 1 hour and 20 minutes or until meat reaches desired degree of doneness. Remove bay leaf.

Remove roast to serving platter, reserving cooking liquid in Dutch oven. Combine butter and flour; stir until smooth. Pour flour mixture into cooking liquid; cook, stirring constantly, until thickened and bubbly. Serve gravy with roast. Yield: 8 to 10 servings.

Donna L. Ellett, Monroe, Louisiana.

STUFFED CHICKEN BREASTS

8 chicken breast halves, skinned and boned
8 (1-ounce) slices boiled ham
8 (1-ounce) slices Swiss cheese
¼ cup all-purpose flour
1 egg, beaten
⅔ cup dry breadcrumbs
¼ cup butter or margarine
1 cup dry white wine
Cream Sauce
Chopped fresh parsley (optional)

Place each chicken breast on a sheet of waxed paper. Flatten chicken to ¼-inch thickness using a flat-sided meat mallet or rolling pin. Place a slice of ham and cheese in center of each piece of chicken. Roll up lengthwise, and secure with a wooden pick. Dredge each chicken roll in flour, dip in egg, and coat with breadcrumbs.

Melt butter in a large skillet. Add chicken, and brown on all sides. Pour wine over chicken; cover, reduce heat, and simmer 40 minutes.

Remove chicken from skillet; transfer to serving platter, and keep warm. Serve with Cream Sauce; sprinkle with parsley if desired. Yield: 8 servings.

Cream Sauce:

¼ cup finely chopped onion
¼ cup plus 2 tablespoons butter or margarine, melted
3 tablespoons all-purpose flour
1 cup milk
1 cup half-and-half
¼ teaspoon salt
Pinch of coarsely ground pepper

Sauté onion in butter in a heavy saucepan over low heat. Add flour, stirring until smooth. Cook 1 minute, stirring constantly. Gradually add milk and half-and-half; cook over medium heat, stirring constantly, until mixture is thickened and bubbly. Stir in salt and pepper. Yield: 1½ cups.

Kim Van Portfleet, Lake Park, Florida.

CREAMY BAKED GROUPER

3 pounds grouper fillets (6 fillets)
1 cup dry white wine
1 medium onion, chopped
1 clove garlic, minced
¼ cup plus 2 tablespoons butter or
  margarine, melted
½ pound mushrooms, sliced
2 tablespoons chopped fresh parsley
1 tablespoon dried whole dillweed
1½ tablespoons lime juice
1 cup commercial sour cream
1 cup mayonnaise
1 (1¼-ounce) package cheese sauce mix
¼ cup grated Parmesan cheese
½ teaspoon salt
½ teaspoon pepper
½ teaspoon paprika
½ cup chopped cashews
½ cup dry breadcrumbs

Place fish fillets in a greased 13- x 9- x 2-inch baking dish; pour wine over fillets. Refrigerate 30 minutes, turning once after 15 minutes.

Sauté onion and garlic in butter until onion is tender. Add mushrooms, and sauté an additional 3 minutes. Remove vegetables from heat; stir in parsley, dillweed, and lime juice. Let cool.

Combine sour cream, mayonnaise, cheese sauce mix, and Parmesan cheese. Add sour cream mixture to sautéed vegetables; mix well.

Combine salt, pepper, and paprika; sprinkle over fillets. Spoon mushroom-sour cream mixture evenly over top. Sprinkle with cashews and breadcrumbs. Bake, uncovered, at 400° for 30 minutes or until lightly browned. Yield: 6 servings. *Mrs. David Curry,*
Fort Lauderdale, Florida.

MUSHROOMS WITH WINE SAUCE

½ cup butter
1 pound medium mushrooms
¼ teaspoon seasoning blend
⅛ teaspoon garlic powder
⅓ cup dry white wine

Melt butter in a large skillet; add mushrooms, and stir gently. Sprinkle with seasonings. Cover and cook over low heat 5 minutes or until tender, stirring occasionally. Add wine; cover and continue cooking over low heat for 5 minutes. Yield: 4 to 6 servings.
Gene Eads,
Lubbock, Texas.

Tip: To keep mushrooms fresh longer, refrigerate in a brown paper bag.

BURGUNDY FRUITCAKE

6 cups chopped pecans
1 pound Brazil nuts, chopped
1 pound candied pineapple, chopped
1 (15-ounce) package raisins
1 (8-ounce) package chopped dates
2 cups all-purpose flour, divided
¾ cup sugar
1 teaspoon baking powder
½ teaspoon salt
½ teaspoon ground cinnamon
½ teaspoon ground nutmeg
4 eggs, beaten
½ cup Burgundy or other dry red wine

Combine pecans, Brazil nuts, pineapple, raisins, and dates in a large mixing bowl; add 1 cup flour, mixing well.

Combine remaining 1 cup flour, sugar, baking powder, salt, cinnamon, and nutmeg; mix well. Add eggs; beat with an electric mixer until well blended. Add batter to fruit mixture, stirring well.

Spoon batter into a greased and brown paper-lined 10-inch tube pan. Bake at 275° for 2½ hours or until a wooden pick inserted in center comes out clean. Cool cake completely in pan.

Remove from pan, and remove brown paper. Wrap cake in cheesecloth soaked in ½ cup wine; store in an airtight container at least 1 week before serving. Yield: one 10-inch cake.

Note: If cake is stored longer than a week, an additional ½ cup of Burgundy may need to be poured on top.
Sarah Walton,
Salisbury, North Carolina.

From Our Kitchen To Yours

Wines are gaining popularity in the South as the availability and selection broaden. This can make choosing the right wine a challenge. We would like to pass on some suggestions about selection as well as storage and serving.

Selection

The most important thing to remember is to choose a wine you'll enjoy. The strict rules on which wines go with certain foods are not observed as much as in the past, but there are some guidelines you should consider.

Generally, wines should complement the food, not overpower it. If you are planning to serve more than one type, it's best to serve lighter, drier wines before heavier and sweeter ones. Younger wines are usually served before older ones. Light dry wines, such as Sauvignon Blanc, Chardonnay, or any good white wine, go well with soups, salads, or appetizers.

When serving fish, choose a dry white wine or one with a little acidic character, such as Muscadet or Sauvignon Blanc. Chicken goes well with either a white or a light red wine. If a white sauce is served with the chicken, a white wine would be a good choice.

Choose a light red wine, such as a Beaujolais or a light Italian red, to accompany a roasted meat or one prepared Italian style. Red meat and game are best served with a full-bodied red wine, such as a Cabernet Sauvignon, Merlot, or Burgundy. Spicy or heavily seasoned meats require a robust, full-bodied red wine, such as Côtes du Rhône or Cabernet Sauvignon.

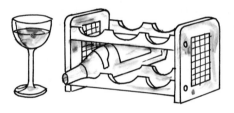

Storage

You don't need a wine cellar to store wine properly; a pantry, closet, or garage will do. Wherever you choose to store it, the area should be cool and away from direct sunlight. Temperatures between 55° and 65° F. (with little fluctuation) are most desirable. The area needs to be dark because long exposure to sunlight will warm up the wine and cause it to age improperly.

Wine bottles should be stored on their sides so that the wine is in contact with the cork. This storage keeps the cork from shrinking and the wine from aging too quickly.

Serving

To enjoy wine to the fullest, keep in mind that its serving temperature is important. White and light red wines are best served chilled to enhance flavor and fruitiness. White wine should be chilled for two to three hours in the refrigerator, while a light red wine needs only about one hour of chilling time. Most full-bodied red wines taste best when they are served between 65° F. and 70° F.

Champagne should be served at about 45° F. This temperature allows the bubbles to be released slowly over a longer period of time after being served.

Most young full-bodied red wines should be allowed to breathe for a period of 30 minutes to a few hours before serving to help them gain some maturity and softness. To let a wine breathe, uncork it and let it sit.

As for quantity, a standard wine bottle holds 25.5 ounces and serves about one glass for four to six people.

These Entrées Cook In A Skillet

You know the routine on a busy, hectic day: You rush home, head for the kitchen, and grab the skillet. Anyone who cooks on a regular basis probably has at least one skillet dish that can be counted on to carry the meal on days like these. Here are a few more suggestions for tasty yet easy recipes to add to your repertoire.

SMOTHERED BEEF AND ONIONS

4 to 6 cubed steaks (about 1 pound)
½ cup butter or margarine, melted
2 medium onions, sliced and separated into rings
3 tablespoons all-purpose flour
1 (10½-ounce) can beef consommé, undiluted
1 cup dry white wine
1½ tablespoons vinegar
½ teaspoon salt
¼ teaspoon pepper
Hot cooked rice (optional)
¼ cup chopped parsley

Brown steaks on both sides in butter in a large skillet; remove steaks, and set aside. Add onion, and cook until tender. Sprinkle flour over onion; stir well. Gradually add consommé and wine; cook until thickened, stirring constantly. Stir in vinegar, salt, and pepper. Place steaks in onion mixture; cover and simmer 20 minutes or until steaks are tender. Serve over rice, if desired, and sprinkle with parsley. Yield: 4 servings.
C. Jobe,
Tahlequah, Oklahoma.

TEXAS STRAW HAT

1 pound ground beef
1 cup chopped onion
⅔ cup chopped celery
⅔ cup chopped green pepper
2 (6-ounce) cans tomato paste
1 cup water
2 teaspoons chili powder
1 teaspoon Worcestershire sauce
½ teaspoon salt
¼ teaspoon dried whole thyme
⅛ teaspoon pepper
Dash of hot sauce
1 (6-ounce) package corn chips
2 cups (8 ounces) shredded Cheddar cheese

Combine ground beef and vegetables in a large skillet; cook until meat is browned, stirring to crumble. Drain off pan drippings. Stir in remaining ingredients except corn chips and cheese; bring to a boil. Cover, reduce heat, and simmer 20 minutes, stirring occasionally. Serve over corn chips, and top with cheese. Yield: 4 to 6 servings.
Linda E. Whitt,
Missouri City, Texas.

WALNUT-STUFFED CHICKEN BREASTS

½ cup (2 ounces) shredded Cheddar cheese
¼ cup soft breadcrumbs
¼ cup chopped walnuts
1 tablespoon minced onion
¼ teaspoon salt
Pinch of pepper
6 chicken breast halves, skinned and boned
¼ cup all-purpose flour
2 tablespoons butter or margarine, melted
½ cup chicken broth
¼ cup dry white wine
1 tablespoon chopped parsley

Combine cheese, breadcrumbs, walnuts, onion, salt, and pepper; mix well, and set aside.

Place each chicken breast half on a sheet of waxed paper. Flatten the chicken pieces to ¼-inch thickness, using a meat mallet or rolling pin.

Place a heaping tablespoon of cheese mixture in center of each chicken breast half, spreading to ½ inch from edge. Roll up each breast half jellyroll fashion; secure ends with a wooden pick. Roll chicken breasts in flour, and let stand 10 minutes.

Sauté chicken in butter in a skillet over medium heat, turning to lightly brown all sides. Add chicken broth and wine; cover, reduce heat to low, and simmer 10 minutes. Remove chicken to a warm platter; remove wooden picks. Bring broth mixture to a boil; cook, stirring occasionally, several minutes or until sauce thickens. Pour sauce over chicken; sprinkle with parsley. Yield: 6 servings.
Jean McKnight,
Abbeville, Alabama.

PORK CHOPS AND SPANISH RICE

1 cup uncooked regular rice
2 tablespoons vegetable oil
4 (1-inch-thick) pork chops
3 cups coarsely chopped tomatoes
1 green pepper, diced
1 small onion, chopped
1 teaspoon salt
¼ teaspoon pepper
¼ cup water

Sauté rice in a large skillet in oil over medium-high heat 3 to 5 minutes or until browned, stirring constantly. Remove rice, and set aside.

Add pork chops to skillet, and brown on both sides. Combine rice, tomatoes, green pepper, onion, salt, and pepper; spoon over pork chops. Add water; cover and simmer 50 to 55 minutes or until pork chops are tender. Yield: 4 servings.
Betty Czebotar,
Baltimore, Maryland.

SAUSAGE SKILLET SUPPER

1 pound bulk sausage
1 (16-ounce) can whole tomatoes, undrained and chopped
1 large green pepper, cut into 2- x ½-inch strips
1 large onion, chopped
1 teaspoon salt
¼ teaspoon pepper
½ teaspoon chili powder
3 cups cooked macaroni
1½ cups commercial sour cream

Cook sausage in a large skillet until browned, stirring to crumble; drain off pan drippings, and remove from heat. Stir in tomatoes, green pepper, onion, and seasonings; cover and cook over medium heat 10 minutes, stirring occasionally. Add the macaroni and sour cream; cook, stirring frequently, until mixture is thoroughly heated. Do not boil. Yield: 6 to 8 servings.
Carol S. Noble,
Burgaw, North Carolina.

Flavor The Dessert Chocolate

Most folks think of something rich and chocolate when it comes to special desserts. You can use the microwave oven to make some of these chocolate specialties and save time. Save cleanup, too, when you melt chocolate in the microwave instead of a conventional double boiler.

Semisweet chocolate morsels add the chocolate flavor to our Chocolate-Mint Brownies and Kahlúa Velvet Dessert. If you're using a recipe with no microwave directions, you can follow these general instructions to melt the morsels: Place ½ to 1 cup morsels in a microwave-safe measure or custard cup. Microwave at MEDIUM (50% power) for 2½ to 4 minutes or until the chocolate appears soft and shiny. Stir well. Use the same procedure to melt one square of unsweetened or semisweet chocolate, but be sure to stir after half the time.

The richest chocolate flavor comes from cocoa, as you'll see when you make our Chocolate-Praline Sauce. The pecan-studded chocolate sauce can be spooned over ice cream, pound cake, or angel food cake for a quick dessert. Keep some of the sauce refrigerated for drop-in company. Just reheat the sauce in the microwave before serving.

CHOCOLATE-AMARETTO CHEESECAKE

3 tablespoons butter or margarine
1 cup graham cracker crumbs
1½ tablespoons sugar
½ teaspoon ground cinnamon
1 (8-ounce) package cream cheese
⅔ cup sugar
2 eggs
¼ cup cocoa, sifted
3 tablespoons sugar
¼ cup amaretto
¾ cup commercial sour cream
1 teaspoon vanilla extract
¼ cup almonds, toasted
Sweetened whipped cream

Place butter in a 9-inch microwave-safe pieplate. Microwave at HIGH for 45 seconds or until melted. Stir in crumbs, 1½ tablespoons sugar, and cinnamon; mix well. Press into bottom and on sides of pieplate. Microwave at HIGH for 1½ minutes. Set aside.

Place cream cheese in a microwave-safe mixing bowl; microwave at MEDIUM LOW (30% power) for 1 minute or until softened. Beat with an electric mixer until light and fluffy. Gradually add ⅔ cup sugar, mixing well. Add eggs, one at a time, beating well after each addition.

Combine cocoa and 3 tablespoons sugar; stir into cream cheese mixture until well blended. Stir in amaretto, sour cream, and vanilla. Pour into prepared crust.

Microwave, uncovered, at MEDIUM LOW (30% power) for 17 to 19 minutes or until center is almost set, giving dish a half turn every 5 minutes. Remove from microwave, and let stand until cool. Cover and chill several hours or overnight. Garnish with almonds and whipped cream. Yield: one 9-inch cheesecake.

CHOCOLATE-MINT BROWNIES

½ cup butter or margarine
¾ cup sugar
2 eggs
1 cup all-purpose flour
1 (5.5-ounce) can chocolate-flavored syrup
1 teaspoon vanilla extract
2 tablespoons butter or margarine
1 cup sifted powdered sugar
2 tablespoons green crème de menthe
½ cup semisweet chocolate morsels
2 tablespoons butter or margarine

Place ½ cup butter in a microwave-safe mixing bowl; microwave at MEDIUM LOW (30% power) for 40 seconds or until softened. Cream butter; gradually add ¾ cup sugar, beating until light and fluffy. Add eggs, one at a time, beating well after each addition.

Add flour to creamed mixture alternately with chocolate syrup, beginning and ending with flour. Stir in vanilla. Pour batter into a greased and floured 8-inch square baking dish. Cover and microwave at HIGH for 5 to 6½ minutes or until surface is no longer doughy, turning dish twice. Cool.

Place 2 tablespoons butter in a microwave-safe mixing bowl. Microwave at MEDIUM LOW (30% power) 15 to 20 seconds or until softened. Cream butter; gradually add powdered sugar and crème de menthe, mixing well. Spread mixture evenly over chocolate layer; chill 1 hour.

Combine chocolate morsels and 2 tablespoons butter in a 2-cup measure. Microwave, uncovered, at HIGH for 45 seconds, stirring once. Stir mixture until smooth and glossy. Spread evenly over chilled filling. Chill brownies at least 1 hour or until set. Cut into squares. Yield: 1½ dozen.

Note: Store in refrigerator. Allow to stand at room temperature 10 minutes before cutting.

KAHLÚA VELVET DESSERT

1 (6-ounce) package semisweet chocolate morsels
2 eggs
2 tablespoons Kahlúa or other coffee-flavored liqueur, divided
½ teaspoon instant coffee granules
½ cup sugar
½ cup water
1 cup whipping cream, whipped
1 (3-ounce) package ladyfingers, split and halved crosswise
Sweetened whipped cream
1 (1⅛-ounce) English toffee candy bar, crushed

Place chocolate morsels in a 2-cup glass measure; microwave at HIGH for 1½ to 2 minutes, stirring once. Stir morsels until smooth and melted. Let chocolate cool several minutes.

Combine chocolate, eggs, 1 tablespoon Kahlúa, and coffee granules in a mixing bowl; set aside.

Combine sugar and water in a 2-cup glass measure. Microwave at HIGH for 2½ to 3 minutes, stirring once, until mixture boils and sugar dissolves.

Beat chocolate mixture at medium speed of an electric mixer, and gradually add hot sugar syrup in a thin stream. Continue beating mixture until well blended. Chill several hours or until mixture is thickened. Fold in whipped cream.

Divide ladyfinger halves evenly among eight 6-ounce dessert dishes. Lay halves against sides of dishes, cut side facing center of dish. Brush cut sides of ladyfingers with remaining 1 tablespoon Kahlúa. Spoon chocolate mixture into prepared dishes. Cover and chill at least 1 hour. Garnish with sweetened whipped cream and crushed candy before serving. Yield: 8 servings.

CHOCOLATE-PRALINE SAUCE

1½ cups chopped pecans
¼ cup butter or margarine
1½ cups firmly packed brown sugar
¼ cup cocoa
3 tablespoons all-purpose flour
¾ cup light corn syrup
1 (5-ounce) can evaporated milk

Spread pecans on a large glass pizza plate or pieplate. Microwave at HIGH for 5 to 6 minutes or until lightly toasted, stirring at 2-minute intervals. Set aside.

Place butter in a 1-quart glass bowl; microwave at HIGH for 50 seconds or until melted. Combine sugar, cocoa, and flour; add to butter, stirring well. Stir in corn syrup and milk.

Microwave at HIGH for 5 minutes or until mixture is very hot, stirring at 2-minute intervals. Stir in pecans. Serve over ice cream, pound cake, or angel food cake. Store in refrigerator. Yield: 3½ cups.

Have Fun Cooking A Meal For Two

Cooking for two may not always be a romantic candlelight event, but it certainly doesn't have to be an ordinary meal. With the entrées and desserts we offer here, you'll find it's a simple matter to make meals for two more exciting and interesting.

STEAKS BENEDICT FOR TWO

2 (6-ounce) cubed sirloin steaks, ½ inch thick
2 tablespoons butter or margarine, melted
2 poached eggs
Hollandaise sauce (recipe follows)

Sauté steaks in butter 2 minutes on each side or until lightly browned. Top each steak with a poached egg, and spoon hollandaise sauce over each. Serve immediately. Yield: 2 servings.

Hollandaise Sauce:

3 egg yolks
2 tablespoons lemon juice
½ cup butter or margarine, softened and divided
¼ teaspoon salt

Combine egg yolks and lemon juice in top of a double boiler; beat with a wire whisk until blended. Add one-third of butter. Bring water to a boil. (Water in bottom of double boiler should not touch top pan.) Reduce heat to low; cook, stirring constantly, until butter melts. Add second third of butter; stir constantly until butter begins to melt. Add remaining butter, stirring constantly until melted. Cook, stirring constantly, 2 to 3 minutes or until smooth and thickened. Remove from heat, and stir in salt. Yield: about ⅔ cup.

Zoe Newton,
Fort Smith, Arkansas.

VEAL SCALLOPINI MARSALA

¾ pound veal cutlets
½ teaspoon salt
⅛ teaspoon pepper
All-purpose flour
¼ cup butter or margarine, melted
⅓ cup Marsala wine
½ cup beef broth

Place cutlets on waxed paper, and flatten to ⅛-inch thickness with a meat mallet or rolling pin. Sprinkle with salt and pepper, and dredge in flour.

Sauté cutlets in butter 2 to 3 minutes on each side or until browned. Add wine; cook 1 minute over medium heat. Remove veal to a warm serving platter. Add broth to skillet; bring to a boil, stirring occasionally. Pour over veal. Yield: 2 servings. *Mrs. Rodger Giles,*
Augusta, Georgia.

VERMICELLI WITH CLAM SAUCE

1 (6½-ounce) can minced clams, undrained
½ cup finely chopped onion
1 clove garlic, minced
3 tablespoons vegetable oil
⅔ cup chicken broth
⅓ cup dry white wine
3 tablespoons butter or margarine
¼ teaspoon dried whole oregano
¼ pound vermicelli, cooked
⅓ cup grated Parmesan cheese
Fresh parsley (optional)
Lemon twists (optional)

Drain clams, reserving ¼ cup liquid; set aside.

Sauté onion and garlic in oil until tender; add chicken broth, wine, butter, and oregano. Simmer 20 minutes. Add clams and reserved liquid, and heat thoroughly. Serve over vermicelli; toss before serving. Sprinkle with cheese. Garnish with parsley and lemon twists, if desired. Yield: 2 servings.

Julie Earhart,
St. Louis, Missouri.

INDIVIDUAL PECAN PIES

⅓ cup dark corn syrup
¼ cup sugar
1 egg
2 tablespoons butter or margarine, melted
Dash of salt
¼ cup chopped pecans
2 (5-inch) unbaked pastry shells
8 pecan halves

Combine syrup, sugar, egg, butter, and salt; beat with an electric mixer until blended. Stir in chopped pecans. Pour mixture into pastry shells; arrange pecan halves on top. Bake at 350° for 30 to 35 minutes. Yield: 2 servings.

Alice Lewis,
Knoxville, Tennessee.

BAKED ALASKA

2 (2½-ounce) ice cream sandwiches
1 egg white
Dash of salt
2 tablespoons sugar

Cut ice cream sandwiches in half crosswise; stack each half on top of the other half. Place the two stacked sandwiches on a foil-lined cookie sheet, and place in freezer.

Beat egg white (at room temperature) and salt until foamy. Gradually add sugar, beating until stiff peaks form. Remove stacked sandwiches from freezer; quickly spread meringue over sandwiches, making sure edges are sealed to foil. Freeze at least 2 hours or overnight.

Bake at 500° for 2 minutes or until meringue begins to brown. Serve immediately. Yield: 2 servings.

Hazel Hurley,
Palm Springs, Florida.

Tip: When bits of shell fall into a broken egg, remove the bits by using half of the shell as a scoop. It works better than a spoon.

Tasty Ideas For A Potluck Meal

Whether it's an office party, a church supper, or a get-together with friends, when you pool the food to make a meal, not just any dish will do. These recipes should help you decide what to take, no matter the occasion.

If you're busy throughout the day and the event takes place in early evening, our chilled Marinated Bean Salad or Macaroni-Chicken Salad can be made the night before. Chilled salads are also ideal for office parties. But if you have no refrigeration there, bake our Coconut-Cream Cheese Pound Cake, and take it already sliced. Since it has no frosting or glaze, it can be eaten from a napkin, eliminating the need for plates and forks.

When you have a little more time just prior to the meal, you may want to prepare a hot main-dish casserole such as Chicken-Green Bean Casserole. It's an excellent way to make a whole chicken serve six to eight and offer a side dish in the same recipe.

For the best results with a cheese-topped casserole, such as our Mashed Potato Casserole, cook it according to directions, except for adding cheese. Later sprinkle on the cheese, cover, and bake the last five minutes after you reach your destination. This keeps the cheese from getting tough if it has to be reheated.

CHICKEN-GREEN BEAN CASSEROLE

1 (3-pound) broiler-fryer, cut up
¼ cup chopped celery
¼ cup chopped onion
2 cups herb-seasoned stuffing mix, divided
1 (16-ounce) can French-style green beans, drained
½ cup chopped fresh mushrooms
¼ cup chopped cashews
1 (10¾-ounce) can cream of mushroom soup, undiluted
½ cup milk
2 tablespoons butter or margarine, melted

Place chicken, celery, and onion in a Dutch oven, and cover with water. Bring to a boil; cover, reduce heat, and simmer 45 minutes or until tender. Remove chicken, and let cool, reserving ¾ cup broth. Bone chicken, and cut into ½-inch pieces; set aside.

Sprinkle 1 cup stuffing mix in a lightly greased 12- x 8- x 2-inch baking dish. Layer green beans, mushrooms, cashews, and chicken over stuffing mix. Combine soup, milk, and ½ cup reserved broth; mix well. Pour mixture over chicken.

Combine 1 cup stuffing mix, ¼ cup reserved broth, and butter, mixing well. Sprinkle on top of soup mixture. Bake, uncovered, at 350° for 25 to 30 minutes or until bubbly. Yield: 6 to 8 servings.

Tony Jones,
Atlanta, Georgia.

MACARONI-CHICKEN SALAD

1 (7¼-ounce) package macaroni-and-cheese dinner
1 cup diced cooked chicken
3 hard-cooked eggs, chopped
½ cup chopped green pepper
½ cup cooked green peas
¼ cup chopped celery
¼ cup sliced radishes
3 tablespoons chopped onion
⅓ cup salad dressing or mayonnaise

Cook macaroni-and-cheese dinner according to package directions. Combine mixture with remaining ingredients except salad dressing in a large bowl. Stir in salad dressing; toss gently. Chill. Yield: 6 to 8 servings.

Mrs. Clayton Turner,
De Funiak Springs, Florida.

MASHED POTATO CASSEROLE

6 large baking potatoes, peeled and cubed
1 (8-ounce) package cream cheese, softened
1 (8-ounce) carton commercial sour cream
1 cup small-curd cottage cheese
1 (2-ounce) package slivered almonds
⅛ teaspoon pepper
¼ cup (2 ounces) shredded Cheddar cheese
Paprika

Cook potatoes in boiling salted water until tender. Drain well, and mash.

Combine potatoes, cream cheese, sour cream, cottage cheese, almonds, and pepper, mixing well. Spoon the mixture into a lightly greased 12- x 8- x 2-inch baking dish; cover and bake at 325° for 35 minutes.

Sprinkle mixture with Cheddar cheese and paprika, and bake an additional 5 minutes. Yield: 10 servings.

Marie W. Harris,
Sevierville, Tennessee.

ZUCCHINI-JACK CASSEROLE

6 cups ¼-inch zucchini slices
4 eggs, beaten
½ cup milk
3 tablespoons all-purpose flour
2 teaspoons baking powder
½ teaspoon salt
2 cups (8 ounces) shredded Monterey Jack cheese
¼ cup plus 2 tablespoons finely chopped onion
¼ cup chopped parsley

Cook zucchini in a small amount of boiling water 5 minutes; drain well. Set zucchini aside.

Combine eggs, milk, flour, baking powder, and salt; mix well. Stir in zucchini and remaining ingredients. Pour into a lightly greased 2-quart casserole. Bake, uncovered, at 350° for 35 to 40 minutes. Let stand 10 minutes before serving. Yield: 6 to 8 servings.

Cheryl Keener,
Lenoir, North Carolina.

MARINATED BEAN SALAD

1 (17-ounce) can small English peas, drained
1 (16½-ounce) can whole kernel corn, drained
1 (16-ounce) can cut green beans, drained
1 (16-ounce) can cut golden wax beans, drained
1 (8¼-ounce) can sliced carrots, drained
1 (2-ounce) jar diced pimiento, drained
1 (2-ounce) can sliced mushrooms, drained
1 medium onion, chopped
1 cup sugar
¾ cup vinegar
½ cup vegetable oil
1 teaspoon pepper
½ teaspoon salt

Combine all vegetables in a large bowl, and set aside.

Combine sugar and vinegar in a small saucepan; bring to a boil. Stir in oil, pepper, and salt; bring to a boil. Remove from heat. Pour over vegetable mixture; cover and chill overnight. Yield: 10 to 12 servings. *Susie Butler,*
Goodman, Mississippi.

Tip: Use leftover liquid from canned or cooked fruit and vegetables in frozen desserts, gelatin molds, soups, stews, sauces, or casseroles.

CONFETTI MACARONI SALAD

1 (8-ounce) package elbow macaroni
2 hard-cooked eggs, grated
½ cup grated carrot
¼ cup finely chopped celery
1 (4-ounce) jar diced pimiento, drained
¼ cup chopped parsley
½ cup salad dressing or mayonnaise
1 tablespoon sugar
1 tablespoon milk
1 tablespoon vinegar
1 teaspoon prepared mustard
½ teaspoon salt
½ teaspoon celery salt
¼ teaspoon paprika
¼ teaspoon dry mustard

Cook macaroni according to package directions, omitting salt; drain. Rinse with cold water; drain well.

Combine macaroni, eggs, carrot, celery, pimiento, and parsley, tossing well. Combine remaining ingredients; toss with macaroni mixture. Cover and chill at least 30 minutes. Yield: 6 servings.

Mary Boden,
Stuart, Florida.

COCONUT-CREAM CHEESE POUND CAKE

½ cup butter or margarine, softened
½ cup shortening
1 (8-ounce) package cream cheese, softened
3 cups sugar
6 eggs
3 cups all-purpose flour
¼ teaspoon baking soda
¼ teaspoon salt
1 (6-ounce) package frozen coconut, thawed
1 teaspoon vanilla extract
1 teaspoon coconut flavoring

Cream butter, shortening, and cream cheese; gradually add sugar, beating at medium speed of an electric mixer until light and fluffy. Add eggs, one at a time, beating after each addition.

Combine flour, soda, and salt; add to creamed mixture, stirring just until blended. Stir in coconut and flavorings.

Spoon batter into a greased and floured 10-inch tube pan; bake at 350° for 1 hour and 15 minutes or until a wooden pick inserted in center comes out clean. Cool in pan 10 to 15 minutes; remove from pan, and cool completely. Yield: one 10-inch cake.   *Pat Belcher,*
Woodstock, Georgia.

Purees Stack Flavor

Here is an attractive way to present the true flavors and bright colors of pureed carrots and spinach. This dish has a middle creamy layer of Swiss cheese to set the two vegetable layers apart. Besides being colorful and flavorful, it's also versatile—it may be served either warm or chilled.

PUREED VEGETABLE-CHEESE LOAF

2 (10-ounce) packages frozen chopped spinach
¼ teaspoon salt
6 medium carrots, scraped and sliced
¼ cup water
2 tablespoons butter or margarine
¼ teaspoon curry powder
¼ teaspoon salt
6 eggs, slightly beaten
1 cup whipping cream
¾ cup (3 ounces) shredded Swiss cheese
¼ teaspoon salt
⅛ teaspoon ground nutmeg
Radish slices (optional)
Parsley sprigs (optional)

Grease an 8- x 4- x 3-inch loafpan; line the bottom with waxed paper. Grease waxed paper, and set pan aside.

Cook spinach according to package directions, using ¼ teaspoon salt. Drain; squeeze out excess water, and set aside.

Combine carrots, water, butter, curry, and ¼ teaspoon salt in a small saucepan; cover and bring to a boil. Reduce heat to low, and cook 15 minutes or until carrots are tender. Position knife blade in food processor bowl. Add carrots and cooking liquid; process until smooth, scraping sides as needed.

Combine eggs and whipping cream, stirring well. Add ¾ cup egg mixture to carrot puree, stirring to combine. Pour carrot mixture into prepared loafpan. Place loafpan in a 12- x 8- x 2-inch baking pan; pour hot water to depth of 1 inch into larger pan. Bake at 325° for 15 to 20 minutes or until carrot mixture is slightly firm on top. Remove loafpan to a wire rack.

Add ¾ cup egg mixture to cheese, stirring well. Spoon evenly over carrot layer; return to oven, and bake 25 to 30 minutes or until layer is slightly firm. Remove loafpan to a wire rack; let stand 10 minutes.

Position knife blade in food processor bowl. Add spinach, and process 30 seconds, scraping sides as needed. Add 2 tablespoons egg mixture to spinach; process until smooth. Stir in remaining egg mixture, ¼ teaspoon salt, and nutmeg, mixing well. Gently spoon spinach mixture over cheese layer; return to oven, and bake 25 minutes or until slightly firm. Remove loafpan to a wire rack; let cool 25 minutes. Unmold on a serving platter. Peel off waxed paper before slicing. Garnish with radish slices and parsley sprigs, if desired. Yield: 8 servings.

Note: Loaf may be chilled in pan several hours or overnight, if desired. Unmold on a serving platter, and serve chilled.   *Peggy S. Blackburn,*
Winston-Salem, North Carolina.

Candy Bar Desserts

If you think candy bars are strictly for snacking, take a look at these ingenious recipes from our readers. They all use candy bars as cooking ingredients. The same rich taste that tempts us between meals is a wonderful addition to cakes, pies, and other desserts.

You can use candy bars in other ways, too. Melted milk chocolate bars make a great frosting for brownies or snack cakes. A grated chocolate bar works well as a garnish for chocolate desserts. And crunchy candy bars can be crushed and used as a topping for ice cream and frozen desserts.

CHOCOLATE CHUNK-PEANUT BUTTER ICE CREAM

3 eggs
1½ cups sugar
2 tablespoons peanut butter
6 (2.16-ounce) chocolate-covered crispy peanut butter candy bars, crushed
3 (13-ounce) cans evaporated milk
3 cups milk

Beat eggs at high speed of an electric mixer; add sugar and peanut butter, and beat well. Stir in candy bars and evaporated milk, mixing until combined. Stir in milk.

Pour mixture into freezer can of a 5-quart hand-turned or electric freezer. Freeze according to manufacturer's instructions. Allow ice cream to ripen at least 1 hour. Yield: about 1 gallon.

Kim Wilkerson,
Birmingham, Alabama.

CREAMY CHOCOLATE PIE

6 (1.45-ounce) milk chocolate with
   almonds candy bars
2 tablespoons hot water
1 (8-ounce) carton frozen whipped
   topping, thawed
1 (9-inch) baked pastry shell

Place candy and water in top of a
double boiler; bring water to a boil.
Reduce heat to low; cook until candy
bars melt. Cool about 20 minutes.
Gradually fold in whipped topping.
Spoon into pastry shell. Chill 8 hours.
Yield: one 9-inch pie.   *Salli Ball,*
                          Atlanta, Georgia.

CANDY BAR CHEESECAKE

¾ cup graham cracker crumbs
⅔ cup finely chopped walnuts
2 tablespoons sugar
2 tablespoons butter or margarine, melted
1 (8-ounce) milk chocolate candy bar
4 (3-ounce) packages cream cheese,
   softened
¾ cup sugar
2 tablespoons cocoa
Dash of salt
2 eggs
½ cup commercial sour cream
½ teaspoon vanilla extract
Sour Cream Topping
Chopped walnuts

Combine crumbs, walnuts, 2 teaspoons sugar, and butter, and mix well;
firmly press mixture onto bottom and
sides of an 8-inch springform pan.
Break candy into several pieces, and
place in top of a double boiler; bring
water to a boil. Reduce heat to low;
cook until chocolate melts. Set aside.
Beat cream cheese with an electric
mixer until light and fluffy. Combine ¾
cup sugar, cocoa, and salt; gradually
add to cream cheese, mixing well. Add
eggs, one at a time, beating well after
each addition. Add melted chocolate;
beat until blended. Stir in sour cream
and vanilla, blending well.

Pour into prepared pan. Bake at 325°
for 40 minutes. Turn off oven, and let
cheesecake stand in closed oven 30 minutes. Let cool to room temperature;
then chill. Remove sides of springform
pan; spread with Sour Cream Topping,
and sprinkle on walnuts. Yield: one 8-
inch cheesecake.

Sour Cream Topping:

½ cup commercial sour cream
2 tablespoons sugar
½ teaspoon vanilla extract

Combine all ingredients; stir well.
Yield: ½ cup.   *W. N. Cottrell II,*
                  New Orleans, Louisiana.

A Cornbread Dressing Everyone Will Like

Cornbread dressing is often a regular
part of holiday meals. In fact, some of
us like to make dressing by the same
recipe year after year so it will always
taste the same. But if you are still
searching for that perfect recipe, we've
selected one for you to try. It's bound
to be a hit with family and guests alike.

TURKEY DRESSING

1½ cups white cornmeal
2 tablespoons all-purpose flour
1½ teaspoons sugar
1 teaspoon baking powder
¼ teaspoon baking soda
¼ teaspoon salt
1¼ cups buttermilk
2 eggs, beaten
1 tablespoon vegetable oil
1 tablespoon shortening or bacon
   drippings
2 stalks celery, diced
1½ medium onions, grated
3¼ to 3¾ cups turkey or chicken broth,
   divided
1¼ cups herb-flavored stuffing mix
1 to 1½ teaspoons rubbed sage
1 teaspoon white pepper
½ teaspoon garlic powder

Combine cornmeal, flour, sugar, baking powder, soda, and salt in a large
mixing bowl; add buttermilk, eggs, and
oil, mixing well.

Place 1 tablespoon shortening in a 10-
inch cast-iron skillet. Place skillet in a
450° oven for 3 to 4 minutes or until
hot. Tilt pan to evenly distribute shortening; pour batter into pan. Bake at
350° for 25 minutes. Cool; crumble the
cornbread into a large bowl.
Cook celery and onion in ¼ cup
broth in a skillet until tender. Add celery mixture, remaining broth (adjusting
for desired moistness), and remaining
ingredients to cornbread crumbs; mix
well. Spoon mixture into a lightly
greased 12- x 8- x 2-inch baking dish.
Bake dressing at 350° for 40 minutes.
Yield: 8 servings.
            Mary Emma Jefferson,
              Decatur, Alabama.

Sandwiches: The Heat Is On

Sandwiches don't have to be cold.
More than just a handful of great flavor, these hot sandwiches are so satisfying, they'll make the meal. We offer
one that's ideal for breakfast and others
that will liven up lunch or dinner.

APPLE-CINNAMON BREAKFAST SANDWICHES

1 tablespoon plus 1 teaspoon butter or
   margarine, divided
8 slices whole wheat bread
¾ cup applesauce, divided
½ teaspoon ground cinnamon, divided
1 egg, beaten
¼ cup milk
2 to 4 tablespoons vegetable oil
¼ cup sifted powdered sugar
⅛ teaspoon ground cinnamon

Butter each slice of bread on one side
with ½ teaspoon butter. Spread 3 tablespoons applesauce evenly on buttered
side of 4 slices of bread; sprinkle each
slice with ⅛ teaspoon cinnamon. Top
with remaining slices of bread, buttered
side down.
Combine egg and milk, beating well;
dip each sandwich in egg mixture, coating both sides.
Heat 2 tablespoons oil in a large skillet. Add 2 sandwiches, and cook over
medium heat 1 to 2 minutes or until
golden brown. Turn sandwiches, and

Fresh from the oven, our Grinder Sandwich is sliced into individual servings.

CRISPY REUBEN SANDWICHES

2 eggs, beaten
1 tablespoon milk
8 slices rye bread
1¼ cups corn chips, finely crushed
¼ cup commercial Thousand Island salad
    dressing or mayonnaise
4 (1-ounce) slices thinly sliced corned beef
4 (1-ounce) slices Swiss cheese
½ cup sauerkraut, drained

Combine eggs and milk, beating well.
Dip one side of each bread slice in egg mixture, and then in crushed corn chips. Place 4 slices of bread, chips side down, on baking sheet. Spread other side of bread with Thousand Island dressing. Top each bread slice with a slice of corned beef, cheese, and 2 tablespoons sauerkraut.

Top sandwiches with remaining bread, chips side up. Bake at 350° for 15 minutes or until cheese melts. Yield: 4 servings.
Mary Pappas,
Richmond, Virginia.

HOT TUNA SANDWICHES

1 (7-ounce) can white tuna, drained and
    flaked
½ cup mayonnaise, divided
2 teaspoons minced onion
1 teaspoon prepared mustard
¼ teaspoon Worcestershire sauce
6 slices bread
1 egg, beaten
¼ cup (1 ounce) shredded Cheddar cheese

Combine tuna, ¼ cup mayonnaise, onion, mustard, and Worcestershire sauce. Place bread on broiler pan, and toast lightly on one side. Spread the tuna mixture evenly over the toasted side of each bread slice.

Combine egg, cheese, and remaining ¼ cup mayonnaise; spread over tuna mixture. Return to lowest rack of oven, and broil 5 minutes or until lightly browned. Serve sandwiches immediately. Yield: 6 servings.
Mrs. Russell Spear,
Hilliard, Florida.

continue cooking until golden brown. Drain on paper towels. Repeat with remaining sandwiches, adding 2 tablespoons oil, if necessary.

Combine sifted powdered sugar and ⅛ teaspoon cinnamon. Sprinkle over sandwiches. Serve immediately. Yield: 4 servings.
Elma Bateman,
Asbury, Missouri.

Drizzle olive oil mixture over green pepper. Sprinkle with oregano; top with shredded mozzarella cheese. Cover with top of bread.

Wrap loaf in aluminum foil, and bake at 350° for 35 minutes or until cheese melts. Slice before serving. Yield: 6 servings.
Sally Pressley,
Birmingham, Alabama.

GRINDER SANDWICH

1 green pepper, cut into rings
1 clove garlic, minced
3 tablespoons olive oil
½ teaspoon onion salt
½ pound ham, thinly sliced
2 small tomatoes, thinly sliced
1 (14-ounce) loaf French bread, split
    lengthwise
½ teaspoon dried whole oregano
2 cups (8 ounces) shredded mozzarella
    cheese

Sauté green pepper and garlic in oil until pepper is crisp-tender. Sprinkle with onion salt. Remove green pepper, reserving olive oil mixture.

Layer ham, tomatoes, and green pepper on bottom half of French bread.

HOT HAM-AND-CHEESE SANDWICHES

1¼ cups diced ham
2 hard-cooked eggs, chopped
1 cup (4 ounces) shredded Cheddar cheese
½ cup chili sauce
⅓ cup sliced green onions with tops
¼ cup sliced pimiento-stuffed olives
1 tablespoon mayonnaise
8 hot dog buns

Combine all ingredients except buns; mix well. Spoon mixture into each hot dog bun. Wrap buns in aluminum foil, and bake at 350° for 20 minutes or until cheese melts. Yield: 8 servings.
Joan B. Piercy,
Memphis, Tennessee.

Tip: Disposable pans for heating vegetables, breads, or other foods on the grill are easily made from heavy-duty aluminum foil: Tear off a length of foil, and turn up edges to make 1½- to 2-inch sides; then pinch the corners of the foil to prevent leaking.

Make The Appetizers Special

If you want to get a party going in a hurry, serve an interesting appetizer—something new and different that has a little zip. We offer several suggestions.

Chunky Shrimp Spread, for example, is great paired with party rye or whole wheat bread. It's seasoned with curry powder, onion, and lemon juice. Coarse-chopped shrimp and minced onion give it texture.

Teriyaki Chicken Wings is another alternative. Start with chicken wings that are cut in half to make appetizer servings. The chicken is then marinated in a mixture of soy sauce, onion, and fresh gingerroot, and baked before serving.

If you like the distinctive taste of blue cheese, you'll love Blue Cheese Appetizer Tarts. They're like miniature quiches and have a topping of chopped walnuts. The tarts make a wonderful addition to a party tray or buffet.

CHUNKY SHRIMP SPREAD

3 cups water
1 pound unpeeled fresh shrimp
½ cup minced onion
1 tablespoon fresh lemon juice
½ teaspoon curry powder
¼ cup plus 2 tablespoons mayonnaise
¼ teaspoon salt
⅛ teaspoon white pepper
Parsley sprig (optional)

Bring water to a boil; add shrimp, and cook 3 to 5 minutes. Drain well; rinse with cold water. Chill.

Peel and devein shrimp; coarsely chop. Add remaining ingredients except parsley, mixing well; chill. Garnish with parsley, if desired. Serve spread with party-size rye or whole wheat bread. Yield: 2 cups.   *Elizabeth M. Watts, Panama City, Florida.*

TERIYAKI CHICKEN WINGS

2½ pounds chicken wings
¾ cup soy sauce
¼ cup water
⅔ cup chopped onion
1 teaspoon grated fresh gingerroot

Cut chicken wings in half at joint; cut off tips of wings, and discard. Combine chicken and remaining ingredients in a shallow container. Cover and refrigerate 8 hours, turning occasionally.

Remove chicken from marinade, discarding marinade; place in a single layer on a lightly greased 15- x 10- x 1-inch jellyroll pan. Bake, uncovered, at 350° for 30 minutes. Remove from oven; turn each piece, and continue baking 15 minutes or until done. Yield: about 12 appetizer servings.   *Betty Beske, Arlington, Virginia.*

BLUE CHEESE APPETIZER TARTS

1 cup (4 ounces) blue cheese, crumbled
1 tablespoon all-purpose flour
Tart shells (recipe follows)
1 egg, beaten
1 (5-ounce) can evaporated milk
Dash of salt
2 drops of hot sauce
¼ cup chopped walnuts

Combine blue cheese and flour; spoon evenly into tart shells.

Combine egg, milk, salt, and hot sauce; spoon evenly over blue cheese mixture in tart shells. Sprinkle with walnuts. Bake at 425° for 7 minutes. Reduce oven temperature to 300°, and bake an additional 17 minutes or until set. Yield: 2 dozen.

Tart Shells:

1 (3-ounce) package cream cheese, softened
½ cup butter or margarine, softened
1 cup all-purpose flour

Combine cream cheese and butter, mixing well. Stir in flour; chill. Shape dough into 24 (1-inch) balls. Place each ball into individual wells of ungreased 1¾-inch muffin pans, pressing dough onto bottom and sides of wells to form shells. Yield: 2 dozen.

Note: Tarts can be made ahead, baked, and frozen. When ready to serve, bake, frozen and uncovered, on a baking sheet at 350° for 20 minutes or until thoroughly heated.
    Gloria P. Different, Harvey, Louisiana.

BLACK-EYED PEA PINWHEELS

1 (15-ounce) can black-eyed peas, drained
¼ cup butter or margarine
¼ teaspoon seasoned salt
Two dashes of hot sauce
Dash of garlic powder
2 (3-ounce) packages cream cheese, softened
1 (10-ounce) package 6- x 4-inch ham slices
10 green onions, cut into 6-inch lengths

Combine peas, butter, seasoned salt, hot sauce, and garlic powder in a saucepan; bring to a boil. Reduce heat; simmer, uncovered, 15 minutes, stirring occasionally. Let cool.

Position knife blade in food processor bowl; add black-eyed pea mixture and cream cheese. Process 3 to 5 seconds. Stop processor, and scrape sides of bowl with a rubber spatula. Process an additional 5 seconds or until mixture is well blended. Spread about 3 tablespoons of pea mixture on each slice of ham; place a strip of green onion lengthwise in middle of ham slice. Roll up ham lengthwise; chill. To serve, cut each roll into ½-inch slices, and arrange cut side up on a serving platter. Yield: about 6½ dozen.   *Billy Archibald, Mexia, Texas.*

A Drink That Says "Welcome"

When friends drop in during the holidays, offer them cups of Creamy Eggnog. It's best if made a day ahead and stored in the refrigerator.

CREAMY EGGNOG

2 cups sugar
1 quart half-and-half
8 eggs, separated
1 cup bourbon
1 cup rum
½ cup brandy
1 quart whipping cream, whipped
Dash of salt
Freshly grated nutmeg

Combine sugar and half-and-half, stirring until sugar dissolves; set aside.

Beat egg yolks at medium speed of an electric mixer until thick and lemon colored. Gradually add bourbon, rum, and brandy, beating constantly at low speed of an electric mixer. Add half-and-half mixture gradually to yolk mixture, stirring well.

Beat egg whites (at room temperature) until stiff peaks form. Gently fold into yolk mixture. Fold in whipped cream and salt. Chill thoroughly. Stir before serving. Sprinkle with nutmeg. Yield: 1½ gallons.
    Mary Elizabeth Hughes, Memphis, Tennessee.

December

Memorable Entrées For Holiday Meals

Flickering candles, gleaming silver, and a beautifully appointed table create an elegant setting for holiday dining, but you need an exceptional entrée to make the meal truly distinctive. It might be something out of the ordinary that suggests it's an occasion—something like our Marinated Beef Tenderloin, a sumptuous main dish that makes the most of a fine piece of meat.

MARINATED BEEF TENDERLOIN

1 cup catsup
2 teaspoons prepared mustard
½ teaspoon Worcestershire sauce
1½ cups water
2 (0.7-ounce) envelopes Italian salad
    dressing mix
1 (4- to 6-pound) beef tenderloin, trimmed
Watercress (optional)
Red and green grapes (optional)

Combine catsup, mustard, Worcestershire sauce, water, and salad dressing mix; mix well. Spear meat in several places, and place in a zip-top, heavy-duty plastic bag. Pour marinade over meat, and seal bag tightly. Place bag in a shallow pan, and refrigerate 8 hours, turning occasionally.

Drain off and reserve marinade. Place tenderloin on a rack in a baking pan; insert meat thermometer. Bake at 425° for 30 to 45 minutes or until thermometer registers 140° (rare). Bake until thermometer registers 150° for medium-rare or 160° for medium. Baste occasionally with marinade while baking. Remove to serving platter, and garnish with watercress and grapes, if desired. Serve remaining marinade with meat. Yield: 12 to 15 servings.
Becky Rollins,
Birmingham, Alabama.

PRALINE HAM

1 (6- to 8-pound) fully cooked ham
1½ cups maple-flavored syrup
½ cup sugar
2 tablespoons butter or margarine
1 cup chopped pecans

Score outside of ham in a diamond design. Place ham in a shallow baking pan, fat side up. Insert meat thermometer, making sure it does not touch fat or bone. Bake, uncovered, at 325° for 2 hours or until meat thermometer registers 140°.

Combine maple syrup, sugar, and butter in a small saucepan; bring to a boil. Stir in pecans. Remove from heat. Spoon sauce over ham, and bake an additional 15 minutes. Serve remaining sauce with ham. Yield: 12 servings.
Ferrilyn Welsh,
Warner Robins, Georgia.

INDIAN TURKEY

1 (6-pound) turkey breast
½ teaspoon salt
¼ teaspoon pepper
1 (12-ounce) can frozen orange juice
    concentrate, thawed and undiluted
1 cup water
2 tablespoons brown sugar
1 teaspoon ground cinnamon
½ teaspoon ground cloves
½ teaspoon curry powder
1 (8-ounce) can pineapple chunks, drained
1 (2-ounce) package slivered almonds
¼ cup raisins
¼ cup currants
Cooked wild rice
3 tablespoons cornstarch
¼ cup water

Rub turkey breast with salt and pepper; brown in large Dutch oven.

Combine orange juice concentrate, 1 cup water, brown sugar, and spices, mixing well. Pour over turkey; add pineapple, almonds, raisins, and currants. Bring to a boil; cover, reduce heat, and simmer 2 hours. Remove turkey, and place on a bed of wild rice.

Combine cornstarch and ¼ cup water; gradually stir into juice mixture. Cook over medium heat, stirring constantly, until thickened and bubbly. Serve sauce with turkey and wild rice. Yield: 14 to 16 servings.
Mary C. Bohannon
Raleigh, North Carolina.

CHICKEN VÉRONIQUE

1 chicken-flavored bouillon cube
¼ cup hot water
¼ cup Chablis or other dry white wine
1 tablespoon chopped green onions with
    tops
4 chicken breast halves, skinned and
    boned
1 egg yolk
¼ cup whipping cream
¼ pound seedless green grapes, halved

Dissolve bouillon cube in hot water. Combine bouillon mixture, wine, and green onions in a large skillet. Add chicken; cover and cook 20 minutes over medium heat. Remove chicken, and set aside.

Combine egg yolk and whipping cream, stirring well. Gradually stir about one-fourth of hot mixture into yolk mixture; add to remaining hot mixture, stirring constantly. Add chicken and grapes; cook until thoroughly heated. (Do not boil.) Yield: 4 servings.
Lenah Miller Elliott,
Destin, Florida.

CHICKEN BREASTS WITH CRABMEAT STUFFING

12 chicken breast halves, skinned and
    boned
½ cup finely chopped onion
½ cup finely chopped celery
¼ cup finely chopped green pepper
¼ cup butter or margarine, melted
½ pound lump crabmeat
2 cups seasoned stuffing mix
1 egg, beaten
¼ teaspoon pepper
¼ teaspoon garlic salt
¼ teaspoon Creole seasoning
¾ cup butter or margarine, melted and
    divided
2 cups corn flake crumbs
1 (⅞-ounce) envelope béarnaise sauce mix
    (optional)

Place chicken breasts on a sheet of waxed paper. Flatten to ¼-inch thickness, using a meat mallet or rolling pin.

Sauté onion, celery, and green pepper in ¼ cup melted butter in a large skillet. Remove from heat. Add crabmeat, stuffing mix, egg, seasonings, and ¼ cup butter; mix well.

Spread about ¼ cup crabmeat mixture on each chicken breast; roll up jellyroll fashion, pressing edges to seal. Cover and refrigerate 30 minutes.

Dip each chicken roll in remaining ½ cup melted butter, and dredge in corn flake crumbs. Place seam side down in a greased 13- x 9- x 2-inch baking dish. Cover and bake at 350° for 45 minutes. Uncover and bake an additional 10 minutes or until golden brown. Prepare béarnaise sauce according to package directions, and serve over chicken rolls, if desired. Yield: 12 servings.
Chris Tortorici,
Pelham, Alabama.

COOKING LIGHT®

Shape Up With Citrus In Your Diet

If you are on a diet, there are probably an endless number of foods you've been told to avoid, but only a few you've actually been encouraged to include. An often overlooked food that should be on the list of foods for dieters to enjoy is citrus fruit. Full flavor, low-calorie content, and high nutritional value make this fruit a natural for dieters. And if you're also limiting sodium, you can depend on citrus to spruce up flavors in dishes that might otherwise taste bland without salt.

Citrus fruit is our best known source of ascorbic acid, or vitamin C, in the diet. This nutrient is important for maintaining collagen, the "cement" that binds body cells together. And because ascorbic acid can't be stored in the body, it's important to eat a rich source of the vitamin every day. Heat destroys ascorbic acid; for that reason, you can usually count on raw fruit and vegetables to provide more of the vitamin than cooked ones.

There's more good news about citrus. Many people who are limiting sodium intake to reduce high blood pressure take a medication known as a diuretic, or water pill. The drug helps flush excess water and sodium from the body, but, unfortunately, potassium is lost at the same time. This important mineral, which helps with normal muscle function and heartbeat, is found in generous amounts in citrus fruit.

From among our tasty calorie-trimmed recipes, Pink Grapefruit Ice makes a wonderful finale to any meal. Flavored with a bit of grenadine syrup, this delicious sweet-tart treat will make you think you're cheating on your diet. But at only 119 calories per serving, the treat is truly a dieter's delight.

Citrus Green Salad combines the best of fruit and vegetables. You'll find two kinds of lettuce, as well as grapefruit sections, orange sections, and avocado, in this flavorful dish.

You'll probably be pleased to know that a small amount of avocado can be included in your weight-reduction meal plan, especially when you choose those grown in Florida. These avocados have fewer calories, ounce for ounce, than the ones from California or Mexico because the varieties grown in Florida have a lower fat content.

CITRUS-HERB BAKED CHICKEN

1 (3-pound) broiler-fryer, cut up and skinned
Vegetable cooking spray
½ cup unsweetened orange juice
¼ cup lemon juice
½ teaspoon grated orange rind
½ teaspoon grated lemon rind
½ teaspoon dried whole thyme
¼ teaspoon dried whole tarragon
¾ teaspoon garlic powder
1 teaspoon paprika
¼ teaspoon pepper

Place chicken in a 13- x 9- x 2-inch baking dish coated with cooking spray. Combine remaining ingredients; mix well, and pour over chicken.

Cover and bake at 350° for 45 minutes, basting every 15 minutes. Uncover and bake an additional 15 minutes or until done. Serve with sauce. Yield: 6 servings (about 144 calories and 85 milligrams sodium per serving).
Jeanne R. Wood,
New Orleans, Louisiana.

ORANGE SCAMPI

3 cloves garlic
2 teaspoons vegetable oil
⅛ teaspoon salt
⅛ teaspoon white pepper
2 pounds medium fresh shrimp, peeled and deveined
⅔ cup unsweetened orange juice
2 tablespoons lemon juice
1 tablespoon plus 1 teaspoon chopped fresh chives
2 teaspoons cornstarch

Sauté garlic in oil in a large skillet until tender; stir in salt and pepper. Add shrimp; cook over medium heat 3 to 5 minutes, stirring occasionally. Drain off liquid, and discard.

Combine juice, chives, and cornstarch in a small saucepan, stirring well. Bring mixture to a boil; cook 1 minute, stirring constantly. Add orange sauce to shrimp, stirring well. Yield: 4 servings (about 280 calories and 427 milligrams sodium per serving).

CALICO CITRUS BRUSSELS SPROUTS

1 pound fresh brussels sprouts
1 cup chicken broth
1 medium carrot, scraped and coarsely grated
1½ teaspoons cornstarch
½ cup unsweetened orange juice
⅛ teaspoon orange rind
⅛ teaspoon ground nutmeg

Wash brussels sprouts thoroughly, and remove discolored leaves. Cut off stem ends, and slash bottom of each sprout with a shallow X. Combine brussels sprouts and broth in a medium saucepan; bring to a boil. Cover, reduce heat, and simmer 8 minutes. Add carrot, and cook an additional 2 to 3 minutes or until tender. Drain well, and place in a serving dish.

Combine cornstarch and orange juice in a small saucepan, stirring well. Bring mixture to a boil; cook 1 minute, stirring constantly. Stir in orange rind and nutmeg; pour over vegetables, and toss gently. Serve immediately. Yield: 4 servings (about 80 calories and 224 milligrams sodium per serving.)

GOLDEN CITRUS SALAD MOLD

1 (8-ounce) can unsweetened pineapple tidbits, undrained
1 envelope unflavored gelatin
1 cup unsweetened orange juice
¼ cup vinegar
½ cup orange sections, coarsely chopped
½ cup grated carrot
Vegetable cooking spray
Lettuce leaves
Orange sections (optional)

Drain pineapple, reserving juice. Set pineapple aside. Combine reserved juice and gelatin in a small saucepan. Cook over low heat 2 to 3 minutes, stirring until gelatin dissolves. Remove from heat, and stir in orange juice and vinegar; chill mixture until consistency of unbeaten egg white. Fold in pineapple, orange sections, and carrot.

Spoon mixture evenly into six 4-ounce molds coated with cooking spray. Chill until firm. Unmold on lettuce leaves, and garnish with additional orange sections, if desired. Yield: 6 servings (about 55 calories and 4 milligrams sodium per serving). *Ferrilyn Welsh,*
Warner Robins, Georgia.

Tip: Use slivered orange and lemon peel to season stews and other dishes.

PINK GRAPEFRUIT ICE

½ cup sugar
1 cup water
2½ cups fresh pink grapefruit juice, chilled
2 tablespoons grenadine syrup
Pink grapefruit wedges (optional)

Combine sugar and water in a small saucepan; bring to a boil, and boil 5 minutes. Remove from heat; let cool.

Combine sugar syrup, grapefruit juice, and grenadine syrup, stirring until well blended; freeze until firm. Remove from freezer.

Position knife blade in food processor bowl; add frozen mixture. Top with cover; process on high speed until smooth. Serve immediately or return to freezer. Garnish with pink grapefruit wedges, if desired. Yield: 6 servings (about 119 calories and a trace of sodium per ½-cup serving).

Mrs C. M. Conklin II,
Dallas, Texas.

Cool and refreshing Pink Grapefruit Ice adds contrast and interest to winter meals.

CITRUS GREEN SALAD

3 cups torn Boston lettuce
3 cups torn iceberg lettuce
2¼ cups grapefruit sections, drained
1½ cups orange sections, drained
1½ cups cubed avocado
2 teaspoons lemon juice
Orange-Yogurt Dressing

Combine lettuce, grapefruit sections, and orange sections in a salad bowl; set aside. Combine avocado and lemon juice in a small bowl; toss gently to coat avocado. Drain and add to lettuce mixture. Gently toss salad, and serve with Orange-Yogurt Dressing. Yield: 6 servings (about 95 calories and 6 milligrams sodium per serving plus 17 calories and 5 milligrams sodium per tablespoon dressing).

Orange-Yogurt Dressing:

1 medium banana, halved
1 tablespoon frozen orange juice concentrate, thawed and undiluted
2 teaspoons honey
⅛ teaspoon ground ginger
⅛ teaspoon ground cinnamon
1 (8-ounce) carton orange-flavored low-fat yogurt

Combine all ingredients except yogurt in container of an electric blender; process until smooth. Pour mixture into a bowl; gently stir in yogurt. Yield: about 1½ cups.

Eileen Wehling,
Austin, Texas.

LEMON FLUFF PUDDING

1 envelope unflavored gelatin
½ cup plus 1 tablespoon cold water, divided
1 cup boiling water
½ cup sugar
1¼ teaspoons grated lemon rind
¼ cup lemon juice
½ cup instant nonfat dry milk powder
½ cup ice water
4 or 5 drops yellow food coloring (optional)

Soften gelatin in 1 tablespoon cold water. Add 1 cup boiling water; stir until dissolved. Add ½ cup cold water, sugar, lemon rind, and lemon juice; mix well. Freeze until almost firm.

Chill a deep mixing bowl and beaters. Combine nonfat dry milk powder and ½ cup ice water in chilled bowl; beat until stiff peaks form. Chill.

Break up frozen lemon mixture with a fork; add whipped milk and food coloring, if desired. Beat at high speed of an electric mixer until smooth and fluffy. Serve immediately. Yield: 6 servings (about 103 calories and 54 milligrams sodium per serving).

Estelle Schwenke,
Waterloo, South Carolina.

Tip: For a great dessert, pour cream sherry over chilled grapefruit.

Holiday Desserts®

'Tis The Season For Glorious Desserts

For many Southerners, food preparation for the season begins early. There are pecans to crack, fruitcakes to soak, and sugar, candied fruit, and chocolate to stock up on. The most difficult part of all is deciding which desserts to prepare to celebrate the season.

Whether you're looking for confections to pack in gift boxes, spectacular desserts for entertaining, or sweet nibbles to share with guests, you'll find them here in one of our favorite special sections, *Holiday Desserts*.

On the pages that follow, you'll find many specialty desserts for dinner parties. If you really want to make an impression, turn the lights down low and serve one of our flaming desserts. As always, we've made sure that many of these desserts are easy to make when you have a busy schedule.

Cheese for Dessert?

To begin the special section, we're suggesting a new way to have a party—a dessert cheese party. Europeans have served cheese for dessert for years, and the custom is gaining popularity across the South as well, with a few regional preferences added.

European dessert trays traditionally team mild-flavored cheeses with savory crackers and breads. But instead of serving crackers, dessert cheese parties we've heard about lately offer slightly sweet bread bases, such as the Sweet Little Biscuits, Date-Nut Bread, Ginger Cookies, and Pound Cake in our menu. You might also set out a couple of types of commercial crackers or breadsticks. In addition to the store-bought cheeses, our party features a basic recipe from which you can make a variety of fruit-flavored, slightly sweet cream cheese spreads. You may have noticed the pretty pastel colors of similar cheese blends in supermarkets.

Our menu also features sweet jams and sauces to serve with the cheeses and sweetbreads. Recipes include Rosy Wine Jelly, but you can substitute commercial spreads, such as orange marmalade or apricot preserves.

When planning your menu, select commercial cheeses that are mild in flavor. We suggest Swiss, Gouda, mild Cheddar, Port Salut, and Brie. Serve lots of fresh fruit along with the cheeses. Apples, pears, and grapes go well with almost any cheese, and strawberries and kiwi look especially pretty in fruit-and-cheese arrangements. Serve chilled champagne or not-so-sweet punch as the beverage.

It's Easy To Do

Besides being a novel way to entertain, a dessert cheese party is quick and easy to plan. The fruit, champagne, and most of the cheeses can be purchased commercially. And if you're short of time, you can buy some of the sauces and breads as well. All of your cooking can be done ahead of time. The day of the party, just arrange the fruit and cheese on trays, and chill it until about 45 minutes before the guests arrive. Then set out the trays, so that the fruit and cheese can reach room temperature and offer their fullest flavor.

Slice and arrange the bread at the very last minute to keep it fresh. If you expect the bread to sit out very long at the party, start by slicing just a few pieces; set out the loaves and a knife so that guests can slice their own.

There are no real right or wrong choices when combining fruit, cheese, and bread for this type of party. The fun is in guests mixing and matching their own favorites. As you arrange the platters, group the items with an eye for color, flavor, and shape variation; let the guests take it from there.

SWEET LITTLE BISCUITS

3 cups all-purpose flour
⅓ cup sugar
1 tablespoon baking powder
½ teaspoon baking soda
½ teaspoon salt
¾ cup butter or margarine
1 cup buttermilk
Milk

Combine dry ingredients, mixing well; cut in butter with a pastry blender until mixture resembles coarse meal. Add buttermilk, stirring until dry ingredients are moistened. Shape dough into a ball, and knead lightly 4 or 5 times.

Roll dough to ½-inch thickness on a lightly floured surface; cut with a 1¾-inch biscuit cutter, and place on ungreased baking sheets. Brush lightly with milk. Bake at 400° for 12 to 15 minutes. Yield: 3 dozen.

Let guests mix and match cheeses, breads, and fruit as they prefer. No rules govern combinations of this type.

POUND CAKE LOAF

½ cup butter or margarine, softened
¼ cup shortening
1½ cups sugar
3 eggs
1½ cups sifted cake flour
¼ teaspoon baking powder
½ cup milk
¼ teaspoon almond extract
¼ teaspoon vanilla extract

Cream butter and shortening; gradually add sugar, beating well. Add eggs, one at a time, beating mixture after each addition.

Combine flour and baking powder; add to creamed mixture, mixing well. Add milk, and beat 5 minutes at medium speed of an electric mixer. Stir in flavorings.

Pour batter into a greased and floured 9- x 5- x 3-inch loafpan. Bake at 325° for 50 to 55 minutes or until a wooden pick inserted in center comes out clean.

Allow cake to cool in pan 10 minutes; remove from pan, and cool completely on wire rack. Yield: 1 loaf.

DATE-NUT BREAD

1½ cups all-purpose flour
½ cup sugar
2 teaspoons baking powder
¼ teaspoon salt
½ cup chopped walnuts
½ cup chopped dates
1 egg, beaten
⅔ cup milk
¼ cup butter or margarine, melted

Combine flour, sugar, baking powder, and salt; add walnuts and dates, stirring to lightly coat with flour mixture. Make a well in center of mixture.

Combine egg, milk, and butter. Add to dry ingredients; stir just until moistened. Spoon into 2 greased and floured 16-ounce vegetable cans. Bake at 350° for 40 to 45 minutes or until a wooden pick inserted in center comes out clean.

Allow bread to cool in cans 10 minutes, and remove to wire rack to cool completely. To serve, slice bread crosswise. Yield: 2 loaves.

GINGER COOKIES

¾ cup sugar
2 cups all-purpose flour
1 teaspoon baking soda
¼ teaspoon salt
½ teaspoon ground cinnamon
½ teaspoon ground ginger
¾ cup shortening
¼ cup molasses
1 egg, slightly beaten

Combine sugar, flour, soda, salt, and spices; stir lightly. Cut in shortening with a pastry blender until mixture resembles coarse meal. Stir in molasses and egg.

Shape dough into 1-inch balls. Place on ungreased cookie sheets; bake at 350° for 10 minutes. Let stand on cookie sheets 1 minute. Remove cookies to wire racks to cool completely. (Cookies will firm up as they cool.) Yield: about 3½ dozen.

ROSY WINE JELLY

2 cups rosé or Burgundy wine
3 cups sugar
1 (3-ounce) package liquid fruit pectin

Combine wine and sugar in top of a double boiler; bring water to a boil. Reduce heat to low; cook until sugar dissolves, stirring constantly. Remove from heat, and stir in pectin.

Quickly pour jelly into hot sterilized jars, leaving ¼ inch headspace; cover at once with metal lids, and screw on bands. Process in boiling-water bath 5 minutes. Yield: 4 half pints.

CHUNKY CREAM CHEESE

1 (8-ounce) package cream cheese, softened
¼ cup sifted powdered sugar
¼ teaspoon lemon extract
½ cup finely chopped pecans

Combine cream cheese, powdered sugar, and lemon extract; beat at medium speed of an electric mixer until smooth. Stir in pecans. Chill until ready to serve. Yield: about 1 cup.

FRUITED CREAM CHEESE

1 (8-ounce) package cream cheese, softened
Choice of prepared fruit (see below)
2 tablespoons powdered sugar

Combine cream cheese, prepared fruit, and powdered sugar; beat at medium speed of an electric mixer until smooth. Chill until ready to serve. Yield: about 1 cup.

Strawberry: Coarsely chop 6 medium strawberries. Gently press strawberries between paper towels to remove excess moisture.

Pineapple: Drain 1 (8-ounce) can crushed pineapple. Gently press pineapple between paper towels to remove excess moisture.

Orange: Gently press ¼ cup chopped orange sections between paper towels to remove excess moisture; stir in 1½ teaspoons Grand Marnier or other orange-flavored liqueur.

Peach: Coarsely chop 2 canned peach halves. Gently press peaches between paper towels to remove excess moisture; stir in ½ teaspoon almond extract.

Cherry: Coarsely chop ¼ cup drained maraschino cherries. Press chopped cherries between paper towels to remove excess moisture; stir in ¼ teaspoon almond extract.

Right: *Presented on a bed of watercress with jewel-like accents of red and green grapes, Marinated Beef Tenderloin (page 302) has a classic look that's well suited for a Christmas feast. A garland of watercress crowns the meat to complete the effect.*

Pages 308 and 309: *Arrange your trays with an eye for color, flavor, and shape variation. Aim for color variety in the fruit, and different shapes and sizes in the cheese; commercial breadsticks wedged between other foods give the tray extra visual interest. (Recipes begin on page 305.)*

Right: *Molded French Cream (page 311) looks elegant adorned with green grapes that have been dipped in egg whites and coated with sugar.*

Below right: *Dazzle your guests with Flaming Christmas Pudding (page 312). When the flames die down, slice and serve the pudding with Brandied Hard Sauce.*

Below: *Yule Log Spice Cake (page 314) is baked in coffee cans. The cake's heavier texture makes frosting and slicing easier.*

Favorite Sweets From Around The World

Holidays and sweets go hand in hand all around the world. As the Christmas and New Year season approaches, families enjoy preparing their favorite international dessert recipes.

MOLDED FRENCH CREAM

1 (8-ounce) carton commercial sour cream
1 cup whipping cream
¾ cup superfine sugar
1 envelope unflavored gelatin
¼ cup boiling water
1 (8-ounce) package cream cheese, softened
½ teaspoon vanilla extract
Additional whipped cream (optional)
Frosted green grapes (optional)

Combine sour cream and whipping cream in a medium saucepan; beat at medium speed of an electric mixer until blended. Gradually add sugar; beat well. Cook over low heat until warm.

Dissolve gelatin in boiling water. Add to cream mixture; remove from heat.

Beat cream cheese with an electric mixer until light and fluffy; add cream mixture and vanilla, beating until smooth. Pour into a lightly oiled 4-cup mold; chill until firm. Unmold on serving platter; garnish with additional whipped cream and frosted grapes, if desired. (To frost grapes, dip in unbeaten egg white and sugar. Let dry in a cool place, but do not refrigerate.) Yield: 8 servings.
Mrs. Herbert W. Rutherford,
Baltimore, Maryland.

DANISH PASTRY PUFFS

1 cup butter or margarine, divided
2 cups all-purpose flour, divided
2 tablespoons ice water
1 cup water
1 teaspoon almond extract
3 eggs
Frosting (recipe follows)
½ cup chopped pecans

Cut ½ cup butter into 1 cup flour with a pastry blender until mixture resembles coarse meal. Sprinkle 2 tablespoons ice water (1 tablespoon at a time) evenly over surface; stir with a fork until dry ingredients are moistened. Divide dough in half; pat each half into a 12- x 3-inch rectangle on a lightly greased baking sheet; set aside.

Place remaining ½ cup butter and 1 cup water in a saucepan; bring to a boil. Stir in almond extract. Reduce heat to low, and add remaining 1 cup flour, stirring vigorously until mixture leaves sides of pan and forms a smooth ball. Remove mixture from heat, and allow to cool slightly.

Add eggs, one at a time, beating with a wooden spoon after each addition; beat until batter is smooth. Spread evenly over pastry rectangles; bake at 350° for 55 to 60 minutes or until golden. Spread with frosting; sprinkle with pecans. Yield: 12 servings.

Frosting:

2¼ cups sifted powdered sugar
⅛ teaspoon salt
About 3 tablespoons milk
1½ tablespoons butter or margarine, melted
¾ teaspoon vanilla extract

Combine all ingredients in a small mixing bowl; beat until smooth. Yield: enough for 2 (12- x 3-inch) pastry puffs.
Sharon McClatchey,
Muskogee, Oklahoma.

SPANISH FLAN

½ cup sugar
⅔ cup sugar
6 eggs, beaten
3 cups milk
1 teaspoon vanilla extract
¼ teaspoon salt

Sprinkle ½ cup sugar evenly in a heavy skillet; place over low heat. Caramelize sugar by stirring often until it melts and is light golden. Quickly pour syrup into a 10-inch flan pan; tilt pan to evenly coat the bottom. Set aside.

Combine remaining ingredients in a mixing bowl; beat well. Pour over caramelized sugar in flan pan. Place pan in a large baking dish; pour hot water into baking dish to a depth of 1 inch.

Bake at 325° for 30 minutes or until a knife inserted near center comes out clean. Remove flan pan from water; cool. Chill thoroughly. Unmold onto serving platter. Yield: 8 to 10 servings.
Loy Witherspoon,
Charlotte, North Carolina.

ITALIAN SESAME COOKIES

1 cup butter or margarine, softened
1 cup sugar
3 egg yolks
1 teaspoon vanilla extract
2½ cups all-purpose flour
1 teaspoon baking powder
1 teaspoon ground cinnamon
⅛ teaspoon salt
Sesame seeds

Cream butter and sugar, beating until light and fluffy. Add egg yolks, one at a time, beating well after each addition. Stir in vanilla.

Combine flour, baking powder, cinnamon, and salt; add to creamed mixture, mixing well. Shape a heaping teaspoon of dough into a 2½-inch-long cookie; repeat with remaining dough. Lightly roll each cookie in sesame seeds; place about 2 inches apart on ungreased cookie sheets. Bake at 400° for 8 minutes or until cookies are lightly browned. Cool on wire racks. Yield: about 5 dozen. *Roxanna Alvarez,*
Casselberry, Florida.

SWEDISH ALMOND COOKIES

½ cup shortening
½ cup butter or margarine, softened
1 cup sifted powdered sugar
½ teaspoon salt
2 cups all-purpose flour
1 tablespoon water
1 tablespoon vanilla extract
1¼ cups finely chopped almonds
Additional sifted powdered sugar

Cream shortening and butter until light and fluffy. Add 1 cup powdered sugar and salt; mix well. Add flour, water, vanilla, and almonds, stirring well. Shape dough into 1-inch balls; place on ungreased cookie sheets. Slightly flatten each cookie; bake at 350° for 15 minutes. Remove from cookie sheets, and roll in additional powdered sugar. Yield: about 3 dozen.

Mrs. Wilson Brown,
Langdale, Alabama.

Try A Flaming Dessert

Whipped cream and chocolate curls make a pretty garnish, but if you really want to impress your guests, try a flamed dessert. Assemble everything ahead of time, and do the flaming right at the table for a dazzling show.

There are two ways to flame desserts; the most common way is to use *liquors.* To flame desserts in this manner, heat the alcohol quickly just until fumes are produced; then remove it from heat, ignite, and pour evenly over the dessert. Our Flaming Christmas Pudding and Cranberries Jubilee use this technique. When heating the alcohol, remember that it's the fumes that ignite, not the alcohol. Don't overheat the alcohol, or the fumes will evaporate and the alcohol won't ignite.

The higher the alcohol content, the better the fumes will flame. And sweet liqueurs, such as Triple Sec, which is used in our Flaming Flan, will produce a higher flame and burn slightly longer than liquor containing less sugar but the same amount of alcohol.

In this method, the alcohol vanishes completely as it burns, and only the flavor remains. Those who do not care for alcohol may still enjoy this type of flamed dessert.

You can also use selected *extracts* to flame desserts. The higher the alcohol content of the extract, the better it will flame. Orange or lemon extract with 80% alcohol produces a very good flame, and peppermint extract with 65% alcohol produces a smaller yet good flame; vanilla extract with 35% alcohol produces no flame at all. Extracts flame without being heated, in contrast to alcoholic beverages that must be heated.

Because the flavor is so concentrated in extracts, you won't want to use the larger amounts typically used when flaming with alcoholic beverages. When using extracts, it's best to soak just a small portion of the dessert, such as the garnish, in the extract; then set the soaked portion in place, and ignite it.

Dessert Orange Flambé uses the extract method for flaming. For this recipe, soak sugar cubes in orange extract for a couple of minutes; then tuck a sugar cube in a carved out maraschino cherry cup placed atop each individual orange dessert. Ignite the sugar cubes, and present dessert to each guest from a tray of individual flaming dishes.

It's not dangerous to flame desserts if you use common sense and caution. Do remember that if you are heating the spirit over an open flame (gas or table-top burner) prior to igniting, do not allow it to boil, as it can self-ignite. You only need to heat it long enough to begin producing fumes. And if you're nervous about igniting the dessert, you might be more comfortable using long-stemmed fireplace matches.

CRANBERRIES JUBILEE

1 cup sugar
1 cup water
⅛ teaspoon ground cinnamon
2 cups fresh cranberries
⅓ cup chopped pecans
3 tablespoons rum
Vanilla ice cream

Combine sugar, water, and cinnamon in a saucepan. Bring mixture to a boil, stirring occasionally; boil 5 minutes. Add cranberries, and return to a boil; cook 5 minutes, stirring occasionally. Stir in pecans. Remove from heat.

Heat rum in a saucepan just long enough to produce fumes (do not boil); remove mixture from heat, ignite, and pour over cranberries. When flames die down, spoon over ice cream. Yield: 4 to 6 servings.

FLAMING CHRISTMAS PUDDING

3 cups all-purpose flour
1 teaspoon baking soda
½ teaspoon salt
1½ teaspoons ground cinnamon
½ teaspoon ground nutmeg
½ teaspoon ground allspice
¼ teaspoon ground cloves
1½ cups cranberries
1½ cups raisins
1 cup peeled, chopped cooking apple
1 cup light molasses
1 cup cold water
1½ cups finely chopped suet
3 candied red cherry halves
3 orange rind strips tied into bows
⅓ cup brandy
Brandied Hard Sauce

Combine flour, soda, salt, and spices in a large bowl. Stir in cranberries, raisins, and apple.

Combine molasses, water, and suet; add to dry ingredients, stirring well. Spoon mixture into a well-buttered 10-cup steamed pudding mold; cover pudding with aluminum foil, and place lid securely in place.

Place mold on a shallow rack in a large, deep kettle with enough boiling water to come halfway up mold. Cover kettle. Steam pudding 3 hours in continuously boiling water. (Replace water as needed.)

Unmold pudding onto serving plate, and allow to cool slightly. Decorate pudding with candied cherries and orange rind bows, as desired.

Heat brandy in a small saucepan just long enough to produce fumes (do not boil); remove from heat, ignite, and pour over pudding. When flames die down, slice and serve with Brandied

Hard Sauce. (Pudding will flame whether warm or at room temperature.) Yield: 8 to 10 servings.

Brandied Hard Sauce:

½ cup butter or margarine, softened
1 cup sifted powdered sugar
2 to 3 tablespoons brandy

Combine softened butter, sugar, and brandy; beat until mixture is smooth and fluffy. Yield: ¾ cup.

DESSERT ORANGE FLAMBÉ

4 medium oranges
⅓ cup apricot jam
2 tablespoons orange juice
¼ cup flaked coconut, toasted
4 maraschino cherries
4 sugar cubes
1 to 2 tablespoons orange extract

Slice away rind from oranges. Cut a slice from bottom of each orange so it sits flat. Cut oranges crosswise into ½-inch slices; stack each in original shape, and secure with a wooden pick, if necessary. Hollow out a small area on top of each orange for cherry garnish. Place each orange in an individual serving compote. Combine jam, orange juice, and coconut; spoon over oranges.

Slice top from each cherry, and scoop out pulp, using a small paring knife. Place a cherry cup atop each orange, cut side up.

Using a paring knife, trim sides of sugar cubes, if necessary, to make cubes fit in cherries. Soak sugar cubes in orange extract about 2 minutes, tossing to coat well. Place a soaked sugar cube inside each cherry cup, and ignite. Serve flambé when flames die down. Yield: 4 servings.

ORANGE-POACHED PEARS FLAMBÉ

6 pears
½ cup firmly packed brown sugar
½ cup sugar
½ cup water
½ cup orange juice
⅛ teaspoon ground cinnamon
1 or 2 oranges
2 tablespoons orange extract

Peel each pear, and remove core from bottom end, leaving stem intact. Slice about ¼ inch from base of each pear so that it will sit flat.

Combine sugar, water, orange juice, and cinnamon in a Dutch oven; bring to a boil over medium heat, stirring until sugar dissolves. Add pears. Cover, reduce heat, and simmer 25 minutes or until pears are tender. Remove Dutch oven from heat, and allow pears to cool slightly. Spoon pears and syrup into individual dessert dishes.

Cut six 10-inch strips of orange rind from oranges, using a citrus zester. Soak strips of rind in orange extract at least 5 minutes, stirring occasionally to coat strips thoroughly.

Just before serving, quickly tie orange rind strips into bows, and attach to stems of pears. Ignite orange rind bows. Serve flambé when flames die down. Yield: 6 servings.

SHERRIED FRUIT FLAME

2 cups seedless green grapes, halved
2 large oranges, peeled and sectioned
1 (8-ounce) can pineapple chunks, undrained
1 teaspoon minced crystallized ginger
⅓ cup sliced almonds, toasted
¼ cup cream sherry

Combine fruit and ginger, tossing well. Cover and refrigerate at least 4 hours or until serving time for flavors to blend. Just before serving, cook fruit mixture over low heat until thoroughly heated. Spoon fruit mixture into heat-proof serving container, and sprinkle with almonds.

Heat sherry in a small saucepan just long enough to produce fumes (do not boil); remove from heat, ignite, and pour over fruit. When flames die down, spoon fruit into individual serving dishes. Yield: 4 to 6 servings.

FLAMING FLAN

½ cup sifted all-purpose flour
¼ cup sugar
½ teaspoon baking powder
⅛ teaspoon salt
2 tablespoons vegetable oil
2 eggs, separated
2 tablespoons water
½ teaspoon vanilla extract
¼ teaspoon cream of tartar
¼ cup sugar
1 (16-ounce) can sliced peaches, drained
8 maraschino cherries, halved
½ cup apricot jam
¼ cup Triple Sec or other orange-flavored liqueur, divided

Combine flour, ¼ cup sugar, baking powder, and salt in a medium-size mixing bowl. Make a well in center; add oil, egg yolks, water, and vanilla. Beat at high speed of an electric mixer about 5 minutes or until satiny smooth.

Combine egg whites (at room temperature) and cream of tartar in a large mixing bowl; beat at medium speed until soft peaks form. Add ¼ cup sugar, 1 tablespoon at a time, and beat about 4 minutes at medium speed or until stiff peaks form.

Pour egg yolk mixture in a thin, steady stream over entire surface of egg whites; then gently fold yolk mixture into whites.

Pour batter into an ungreased 10-inch flan pan, spreading evenly with a spatula. Bake at 325° for 20 minutes or until cake springs back when lightly touched. Remove from oven; invert pan on wire rack, and cool completely. Gently remove from pan, using a knife to loosen from sides, if necessary.

Just before serving, place flan on serving plate, and arrange peaches and cherries in center. Place jam in a small saucepan, and cook over low heat until melted. Press jam through a sieve to remove lumps. Return sieved jam to saucepan, and add 1 tablespoon Triple Sec. Cook over low heat just until warmed. Spoon jam mixture over fruit.

Heat remaining 3 tablespoons Triple Sec in a small saucepan just long enough to produce fumes (do not boil); remove from heat, ignite, and pour over fruit. When flames die down, slice into wedges to serve. Yield: 8 servings.

BLAZING BRANDY FLOAT

⅓ cup brandy
½ cup hot coffee
2 tablespoons honey
½ cup half-and-half
2 scoops vanilla ice cream

Heat brandy in a saucepan over low heat just long enough to produce fumes (do not boil). Rinse 2 mugs with hot water to warm mugs. Pour hot brandy into one mug. Combine coffee and honey in other mug, and stir until honey dissolves. Ignite brandy in mug. Carefully pour the brandy back and forth between mugs, pouring over a heatproof surface. When flames subside, divide brandy mixture evenly between mugs. Pour half-and-half evenly into each mug, and top each with a scoop of ice cream. Serve immediately. Yield: 2 servings.

Start Your Own Holiday Cake Tradition

Ask Southerners about their favorite holiday cake, and the answers may surprise you. Coconut cake and fruitcake are still popular, but to many of our readers a special holiday cake is one with a tradition behind it or simply a family favorite.

Mrs. Robert Humphrey of Palestine, Texas, serves a traditional Yule Log Spice Cake at holiday time. The cake is of English origin, and according to Mrs. Humphrey, it was customary to push two peas into one end of the baked cake and two beans into the other end. The end with peas was served only to ladies and the end with beans served only to gentlemen. Finding a pea or bean in a slice of cake was a sign of good luck for the coming year. Whether you follow the custom or not, the cake may become a family favorite.

ORANGE-CRANBERRY CAKE

2¼ cups all-purpose flour
1 cup sugar
1 teaspoon baking powder
1 teaspoon baking soda
¼ teaspoon salt
1 cup fresh cranberries
1 cup chopped pecans
1 cup chopped dates
2 tablespoons grated orange rind
2 eggs, beaten
1 cup buttermilk
¾ cup vegetable oil
Glaze (recipe follows)

Combine dry ingredients in a large mixing bowl. Add cranberries, pecans, dates, and orange rind; stir well.

Combine eggs, buttermilk, and oil; add to flour mixture, stirring until well blended.

Pour batter into a greased and floured 10-inch Bundt pan. Bake at 350° for 50 minutes or until a wooden pick inserted in center comes out clean. Cool in pan 10 minutes; remove from pan onto serving plate. Punch holes in top of warm cake with a wooden pick; spoon warm glaze over warm cake, and allow cake to cool completely. Yield: one 10-inch cake.

Glaze:

⅓ cup orange juice
⅓ cup sifted powdered sugar

Combine ingredients; mix well. Yield: about ½ cup.   *Stephanie J. Faskey, Washington, North Carolina.*

YULE LOG SPICE CAKE

½ cup butter, softened
¼ cup plus 2 tablespoons margarine, softened
1½ cups sugar
2 eggs
1⅔ cups all-purpose flour
½ teaspoon baking soda
1½ teaspoons ground cinnamon
¼ teaspoon ground nutmeg
½ cup buttermilk
1 cup raisins
½ cup currants
Creamy chocolate frosting (recipe follows)
Chocolate leaves (optional)

Cream butter and margarine; gradually add sugar, beating well. Add eggs, one at a time, beating well after each addition.

Combine flour, soda, cinnamon, and nutmeg. Add flour mixture to creamed mixture alternately with buttermilk, beginning and ending with flour mixture. Stir in raisins and currants.

Pour batter into 2 greased and floured 1-pound coffee cans, reserving 3 tablespoons batter. Bake at 300° for 1 hour and 10 minutes or until a wooden pick inserted in center comes out clean. Cool in cans 10 minutes. Remove from cans; cool completely on wire racks.

Place 1 tablespoon of reserved batter into each of 3 greased and floured miniature muffin pans. Bake at 300° for 20 minutes. Cool in pans 10 minutes; remove from pan, and cool completely on a wire rack.

Spread frosting on 1 end of each large cake; place frosted ends together, forming one log. Spread remaining frosting, reserving ½ cup, over cake. Place miniature cakes on cake log at intervals to represent knots; spread with reserved frosting. Score frosting with fork tines to resemble bark. Garnish with chocolate leaves, if desired. (See "Mold a Chocolate Garnish," page 16.) Yield: one 8-inch log cake.

Creamy Chocolate Frosting:

¼ cup butter or margarine
2 (1-ounce) squares unsweetened chocolate
2 cups sifted powdered sugar
⅓ cup evaporated milk
Pinch of salt
¼ teaspoon vanilla extract

Melt butter and chocolate in top of a double boiler. Add sugar, milk, and salt; beat until smooth. Stir in vanilla. Yield: about 1½ cups.
        Mrs. Robert L. Humphrey, Palestine, Texas.

Tip: Three tablespoons unsweetened cocoa powder plus 1 tablespoon shortening may be substituted for each 1-ounce square unsweetened chocolate called for in a recipe.

Holiday Desserts

BOURBON FRUITCAKE

2 cups candied mixed fruit
1½ cups raisins
1½ cups chopped pecans
3½ cups all-purpose flour, divided
1½ cups butter, softened
1¾ cups sugar
6 eggs
1½ teaspoons baking powder
¾ teaspoon ground nutmeg
⅓ cup milk
⅓ cup bourbon
½ cup bourbon

Combine candied fruit, raisins, and pecans; dredge in ½ cup flour, stirring to coat evenly. Set aside.

Cream butter in a large mixing bowl; gradually add sugar, beating at medium speed of an electric mixer until light and fluffy. Add eggs, one at a time, beating after each addition.

Combine remaining 3 cups flour, baking powder, and nutmeg. Add flour mixture to creamed mixture, alternately with milk and ⅓ cup bourbon, beginning and ending with flour mixture. Stir in fruit mixture.

Spoon batter into a greased and waxed paper-lined 10-inch tube pan. Bake at 300° for 1 hour and 30 minutes or until a wooden pick inserted in center comes out clean. Cool in pan 10 to 15 minutes; remove from pan, and cool completely on a wire rack.

Moisten several layers of cheesecloth with remaining ½ cup bourbon; cover cake completely with cheesecloth. Wrap with aluminum foil, and store in cool place at least one week, remoistening cheesecloth as needed. Yield: one 10-inch cake. *Peggy H. Amos, Martinsville, Virginia.*

Dried Fruit Desserts

Colorful raisins, apricots, dates, and other dried fruit gems add interest and nutrition to desserts. Dried fruit is abundant in grocery stores right now, but the price may be a shocker.

However, if you think about the amount of fresh fruit needed to produce

Show off Cinnamon Apples With Brandied Date Conserve by serving the tempting dessert in a footed compote or champagne glass.

a pound of dried fruit, the price doesn't seem so high. For example, to get just 1 pound of dried fruit, it takes 4 pounds of grapes (for raisins), 6 to 8 pounds of apricots, and 7 to 10 pounds of apples.

So go ahead and splurge this year; then after the holidays, stock up on dried fruit when certain kinds may be on sale. The fruit stores well on your cabinet shelf, and you'll have a headstart on next year's baking season.

CINNAMON APPLES WITH BRANDIED DATE CONSERVE

¾ cup sugar
2 cups water
⅓ cup red cinnamon candies
2 tablespoons lemon juice
2 to 3 drops red food coloring
10 to 12 medium-size cooking apples, peeled and cored
Brandied Date Conserve
Soft cream cheese

Combine sugar, water, and cinnamon candies in a large Dutch oven. Bring to

a boil; add lemon juice, food coloring, and apples. Return to a boil; cover, reduce heat, and simmer until apples are tender, turning occasionally. Remove apples. Bring cinnamon mixture to a boil, and continue to boil 10 minutes. Pour syrup over apples; chill.

To serve, fill each apple with Brandied Date Conserve, and top with a small dollop of cream cheese. Yield: 10 to 12 servings.

Brandied Date Conserve:

½ cup chopped dates
½ cup raisins
¼ cup sugar
¼ cup water
2 tablespoons brandy
1 tablespoon lemon juice
¼ cup coarsely chopped pecans

Combine dates, raisins, sugar, and water in a small saucepan. Bring to a boil; reduce heat and simmer, uncovered, 5 minutes. Stir in brandy, lemon juice, and pecans. Chill. Yield: 1 cup.
Doris T. Ramsey, Martinsville, Virginia.

APPLE-MINCEMEAT PIE

1 (9-ounce) package condensed mincemeat, crumbled
1 cup apple juice
2 large cooking apples, peeled and thinly sliced
1 unbaked 9-inch pastry shell
¼ cup all-purpose flour
¼ cup firmly packed brown sugar
⅓ cup chopped walnuts
1 teaspoon ground cinnamon
2 tablespoons butter or margarine, softened

Combine mincemeat and juice, and cook over medium heat, stirring constantly, until mixture thickens and comes to a boil; cook 1 minute, stirring occasionally. Remove from heat; cool.

Arrange apples in pastry shell; top with mincemeat mixture. Combine flour, sugar, walnuts, and cinnamon in mixing bowl; cut in butter with a pastry blender until mixture resembles coarse meal. Sprinkle over mincemeat. Bake at 425° for 25 minutes. Yield: one 9-inch pie.
Mrs. Thomas Lee Adams, Kingsport, Tennessee.

CRANBERRY-RAISIN PIE

Pastry for double-crust 9-inch pie
1½ cups cranberries, chopped
¾ cup raisins, chopped
1 cup sugar
1½ tablespoons all-purpose flour
½ cup water
1½ tablespoons butter or margarine
1½ teaspoons vanilla extract

Line a 9-inch pieplate with half of pastry; set aside. Chill remaining pastry.

Combine cranberries, raisins, sugar, flour, and water in a medium saucepan; cook over medium heat, stirring occasionally, until mixture thickens. Remove from heat; stir in butter and vanilla. Spoon into prepared pastry shell.

Roll out remaining pastry to ⅛-inch thickness; cut into ½-inch strips. Arrange pastry strips in lattice design over filling. Bake at 425° for 25 minutes. (Cover edges of pie with aluminum foil to prevent overbrowning, if necessary.) Yield: one 9-inch pie.
Holly Beatie, Lake Worth, Florida.

WHITE FRUITCAKE

¼ pound chopped candied citron
¼ pound chopped candied orange peel
¼ pound chopped candied lemon peel
¼ pound candied red cherries, chopped
⅝ pound chopped candied pineapple
½ cup chopped dates
½ cup chopped dried figs
½ cup chopped dried apricots
1½ cups golden raisins
2 cups all-purpose flour, divided
1 cup shortening
1 cup sugar
5 eggs
1½ teaspoons baking powder
½ teaspoon salt
¼ cup pineapple juice
2 cups flaked coconut
2 cups sliced almonds, toasted

Combine candied and dried fruit; dredge in ½ cup flour, stirring to coat evenly. Set aside.

Cream shortening; gradually add sugar, beating at medium speed of an electric mixer until light and fluffy. Add eggs, one at a time, beating well after each addition.

Combine remaining 1½ cups flour, baking powder, and salt; add to creamed mixture alternately with pineapple juice, beginning and ending with flour mixture. Mix well after each addition. Stir in fruit mixture, coconut, and almonds.

Spoon batter into 2 greased and waxed paper-lined 9- x 5- x 3-inch loafpans. Bake at 275° for 2 hours and 15 minutes or until a wooden pick inserted in center comes out clean. Cool in pans 10 minutes; remove loaves from pans, and let cool completely on wire racks. Yield: two 9- x 5- x 3-inch loaves.
Mrs. Gene O. Cross, Montgomery, Alabama.

Tip: Learn to judge food labels carefully and take advantage of products with nutrient information on the label. Nutrition labels indicate the number of calories and the amount of protein, carbohydrates, and fat in a serving of the product. They also give an indication of major vitamins and minerals present in the product.

COOKING LIGHT®

Envision A Luscious, Light Dessert

If the mere vision of sugarplums seems to add inches to your waistline, you've come to the right page. There's no need to gain back those pounds you've worked so hard to lose. But there's also no reason to deprive yourself of desserts.

Hostesses like Joan Banks of Brownsville, Tennessee, know that desserts for the holidays are usually too rich and high in calories for anyone on a reduced-calorie diet. Joan solves this dilemma with a delicious recipe called Raspberry-Topped Soufflé. Her creation certainly looks appetizing and, at only 152 calories per serving, it helps you keep off those unwanted pounds.

Like many of our calorie-trimmed desserts, Raspberry-Topped Soufflé calls for skim milk instead of whole milk (a calorie difference of about 90 per cup). Calories are kept low by adding only a small amount of sugar to the milk mixture. Stiffly beaten egg whites give the soufflé volume. The bright red raspberry topping is made by simply thickening raspberries (frozen in a light syrup) with cornstarch. No additional sugar is needed.

Marie Horbaly also uses skim milk to reduce calories in Chocolate Cream Roll. The cream filling of whipped topping mix and skim milk is about 70 calories lighter per serving than the sweetened whipped cream.

BANANA-PEACH FLAMBÉ

2 ripe bananas, sliced
1 tablespoon lemon juice
1 tablespoon brown sugar
2 teaspoons cornstarch
⅔ cup unsweetened orange juice
1 (16-ounce) can unsweetened sliced peaches, drained
Ground cinnamon
3 tablespoons light rum
3 cups vanilla ice milk

Toss sliced bananas with lemon juice; set aside.

Combine brown sugar and cornstarch in a saucepan; mix well. Stir in orange juice; cook over medium heat, stirring constantly, until smooth and thickened. Add bananas and peaches; stir gently, and cook 1 to 2 minutes or until thoroughly heated. Remove from heat; sprinkle with cinnamon.

Place rum in a small, long-handled saucepan; heat just until warm. (Do not boil.) Ignite rum with a long match, and pour over fruit mixture. Stir gently until flames die down. Serve immediately over ½-cup servings of ice milk. Yield: 6 servings (about 178 calories per serving). *Christine McQueen, Annville, Kentucky.*

CHOCOLATE CREAM ROLL

Vegetable cooking spray
½ cup sifted cake flour
3 tablespoons cocoa
¾ teaspoon baking powder
3 egg yolks
¼ cup sugar
2 tablespoons skim milk
4 egg whites
⅛ teaspoon salt
3 tablespoons sugar
1 (1.25-ounce) envelope whipped topping mix
½ cup skim milk
¾ teaspoon instant coffee powder
½ teaspoon vanilla extract
1 tablespoon powdered sugar
Fresh strawberries (optional)
Seedless green grapes (optional)

Coat a 15- x 10- x 1-inch jellyroll pan with cooking spray, and line with waxed paper. Coat waxed paper with cooking spray; set aside.

Sift together flour, cocoa, and baking powder; set aside.

Beat egg yolks at high speed of an electric mixer until thick. Gradually beat in ¼ cup sugar, 1 tablespoon at a time; add 2 tablespoons skim milk, beating well. Fold in flour mixture.

Beat egg whites (at room temperature) and salt until foamy; gradually add 3 tablespoons sugar, 1 tablespoon at a time, beating until peaks are stiff, but not dry. Fold egg whites into chocolate mixture. Spread batter evenly in prepared pan. Bake at 375° for 10 to 12 minutes.

Immediately loosen cake from sides of pan, and turn out onto a towel. Peel off waxed paper. Starting at short side, roll up cake and towel together. Place seam side down on a wire rack, and cool completely.

Combine whipped topping mix, ½ cup skim milk, coffee powder, and vanilla in a deep, narrow-bottom bowl. Whip at high speed of an electric mixer about 4 minutes or until topping is light and fluffy. Unroll cake, and remove towel. Spread cake with whipped topping mixture, and reroll. Place on serving plate, seam side down. Chill 3 to 4 hours. To serve, sift 1 tablespoon powdered sugar over top. Garnish with strawberries and grapes, if desired. Yield: 12 servings (about 95 calories per serving without garnish).
Marie T. Horbaly, Springfield, Virginia.

RICE CREAM WITH MANDARIN ORANGES

1 envelope unflavored gelatin
½ cup water
3 eggs, separated
¼ cup sugar
½ teaspoon salt
2 cups skim milk
1 cup cooked rice (no added salt or fat)
1½ teaspoons vanilla extract
⅓ cup sugar
1 (11-ounce) can unsweetened mandarin oranges, drained

Combine gelatin and water in a small bowl; set aside.

Combine egg yolks, ¼ cup sugar, and salt in top of a double boiler; gradually stir in milk. Bring water to a boil, and reduce heat to medium. Cook, stirring occasionally, until custard thickens and coats a metal spoon. Remove from heat; add gelatin mixture, stirring until dissolved. Stir in rice and vanilla. Chill mixture until the consistency of unbeaten egg white.

Beat egg whites (at room temperature) at high speed of an electric mixer until foamy. Gradually add sugar, 1 tablespoon at a time, until soft peaks form. Fold whites into rice mixture. Spoon into 8 (6-ounce) dessert dishes; chill until set. Top with mandarin oranges. Yield: 8 servings (about 150 calories per serving).
Phyllis Dupuy, Concord, Virginia.

RASPBERRY-TOPPED SOUFFLÉ

2 eggs, separated
2 tablespoons sugar
1½ teaspoons unflavored gelatin
1½ cups skim milk, scalded
½ teaspoon vanilla extract
¼ cup sugar
Raspberry Topping

Combine egg yolks, 2 tablespoons sugar, and gelatin in top of a double boiler. Gradually add scalded milk, stirring until smooth. Bring water to a boil. Reduce heat to medium low; cook custard, stirring frequently, 10 to 12 minutes or until custard thickens and coats a metal spoon. Remove from heat; stir in vanilla. Chill mixture until the consistency of unbeaten egg white.

Beat egg whites (at room temperature) until foamy. Gradually add ¼ cup sugar, 1 tablespoon at a time, beating until stiff peaks form. Fold into custard mixture; spoon into 6 (6-ounce) dessert dishes. Chill. Serve with Raspberry Topping. Yield: 6 servings (about 100 calories per serving plus 26 calories per tablespoon topping).

Raspberry Topping:

1 (10-ounce) package frozen raspberries in light syrup, thawed and undrained
2 teaspoons cornstarch

Drain raspberries, reserving juice. Combine juice and cornstarch in a small saucepan; cook over medium heat, stirring constantly, until mixture comes to a boil. Cook 1 minute, stirring constantly. Cool slightly, and add raspberries. Chill. Yield: ¾ cup. *Joan Banks, Brownsville, Tennessee.*

Combine gelatin mixture, cream cheese, lemon juice, salt, Worcestershire sauce, hot sauce, and onion in a mixing bowl; beat at medium speed of an electric mixer until smooth. Stir in crabmeat; pour into a lightly oiled 5½-cup mold, and chill until firm.

Unmold and garnish with olive slices and chopped parsley. Serve with crackers. Yield: 5½ cups.

ndies, and there's special pleasure in the Christmas Tree Peanut -and-Jelly Sandwiches and the erbread Men Cookies.

ood food is not the only reason this arty has become an important part of Collinwood's festivities. One of the most eagerly anticipated events occurs when the children gather in the Walkers' living room to share their last-minute wishes with Santa Claus. Seated next to the Christmas tree, Santa gives each child a turn in his lap and listens to requests that range from baby dolls to computers.

Before these neighbors know it, the Christmas party is over; it's time for parents to collect their children and head for home, the way lit by the flickering luminarias.

SHRIMP TREE

2 gallons water
2 (3-ounce) packages crab and shrimp boil
6 pounds fresh large or jumbo shrimp, unpeeled
Fresh parsley sprigs
Commercial seafood cocktail sauce

Bring water to a boil; add crab and shrimp boil. Boil 20 minutes. Add shrimp, and return to a boil. Reduce heat, and simmer, uncovered, 3 to 5 minutes. Drain well; chill shrimp. Peel and devein shrimp, leaving tails on, if desired.

Using florist picks, attach parsley sprigs to a 12-inch plastic foam cone. Place cone in center of serving tray.

Gently spear shrimp with wooden picks, and attach to cone tree. Arrange remaining shrimp on tray around base of tree. Serve with cocktail sauce. Yield: 24 appetizer servings.

Way
borhood Party

just before Christmas, the neighborhood in Opelika, glows from end to end with ias. Wreaths appear on front while mailboxes sport red and n bows. Carolers and a live nativity ne are assembled along the winding streets to entertain motorists.

The neighborhood works together to get the luminarias ready, and they all have a good time in the process, according to Martha Hill, chairman of the event. "Many of our children have grown up with the lights. They've become an annual tradition we all look forward to." (For instructions on making luminarias, see page 173.)

Another Collinwood neighborhood tradition is an open house party held in the home of Jane and Jacob Walker, Jr., following the lighting of the luminarias. "It's a time for all of us to get together, catch up on news, and welcome newcomers," Jane comments. "It's a special way for the neighbors to wish each other a Merry Christmas."

Getting enough food together to feed 50 families is no problem since the neighbors join efforts to plan and prepare the menu. "We've come up with a menu that's filling and varied enough to appeal to all ages," Jane explains. She tells us that they all start baking weeks in advance.

On party night, Jane has tables of food throughout her home. The dining room is set with a beautiful buffet for the adults. Favorite recipes requested every year include a molded crabmeat spread, a creamy spinach dip, and a large bowl of marinated vegetables.

The children's table, in another room, is the real center of excitement. Eyes widen at the assortment of cookies and

PARTY HAM ROLLS

1 (8-ounce) jar Dijon mustard
1 cup butter or margarine, softened
2 tablespoons poppy seeds
2 (7½-ounce) packages party rolls
About ¾ pound thinly sliced ham
About 8 ounces thinly sliced Swiss cheese

Combine mustard, butter, and poppy seeds; mix well.

Cut rolls in half; spread mustard mixture on each cut side. Place a small amount of ham and cheese on bottom of each roll. Cover with top half of rolls, and wrap in foil. Bake at 300° for 10 to 15 minutes or until cheese melts. Yield: about 3½ dozen.

Note: Rolls may be assembled ahead and frozen. To serve, thaw and bake rolls at 300° for 10 to 15 minutes or until cheese melts.

CRAB MOLD

2 envelopes unflavored gelatin
½ cup cold water
½ cup boiling water
3 (8-ounce) packages cream cheese, softened
¾ cup lemon juice
1 teaspoon salt
1 teaspoon Worcestershire sauce
½ teaspoon hot sauce
½ teaspoon grated onion
4 (6-ounce) cans lump crabmeat, drained
Pimiento-stuffed olive slices
Chopped fresh parsley

Sprinkle gelatin over cold water; let stand 5 minutes. Add boiling water; stir until gelatin dissolves.

MUSHROOM ROLLUPS

¼ pound fresh mushrooms, chopped
¼ cup butter or margarine, melted
1½ tablespoons all-purpose flour
½ cup half-and-half
1 teaspoon chopped fresh or freeze-dried chives
½ teaspoon lemon juice
¼ teaspoon salt
About 28 slices thin sandwich white bread
¼ cup butter or margarine, melted

Sauté mushrooms in ¼ cup butter in a skillet until tender. Add flour, stirring until smooth. Cook 1 minute, stirring constantly. Gradually add half-and-half; cook over medium heat, stirring constantly, until mixture is thickened and bubbly. Stir in chives, lemon juice, and salt. Remove from heat; set aside.

Trim crusts from bread; press each slice to ⅛- to ¼-inch thickness with a rolling pin. Spread each slice with a rounded teaspoonful of mushroom mixture; roll up tightly. Brush rolls with ¼ cup melted butter; cut each roll in half, and place on ungreased baking sheets. Bake at 400° for 10 minutes or until lightly browned. Serve warm. Yield: about 4½ dozen appetizers.

Note: If you're going to freeze rolls, do not brush with melted butter. Place unbaked rolls in an airtight container in freezer. To serve, remove rolls from freezer and thaw. Cut each roll in half, and brush with melted butter. Bake at 400° for 10 minutes or until rolls are lightly browned.

SPINACH MADELEINE IN CHAFING DISH

2 (10-ounce) packages frozen chopped spinach
2 tablespoons finely chopped onion
¼ cup butter or margarine, melted
2 tablespoons all-purpose flour
⅓ cup evaporated milk
1 (6-ounce) roll process cheese with jalapeño peppers, cubed
1 teaspoon Worcestershire sauce
¾ teaspoon celery salt
½ teaspoon pepper
⅛ teaspoon garlic powder
Red pepper to taste

Cook spinach according to package directions; drain well, reserving ½ cup liquid. Set spinach aside.

Sauté onion in butter in a heavy saucepan over low heat until tender. Add flour, stirring until smooth. Cook 1 minute, stirring constantly. Gradually add reserved spinach liquid and milk; cook over medium heat, stirring constantly, until mixture is thickened and bubbly. Add cheese, Worcestershire sauce, celery salt, pepper, garlic powder, and red pepper, stirring until cheese melts. Stir in spinach; transfer to a chafing dish. Serve with crackers. Yield: 2⅔ cups.

MARINATED VEGETABLE MEDLEY

¼ cup vinegar
¼ cup vegetable oil
½ cup mayonnaise
¼ cup chopped fresh or freeze-dried chives
1½ teaspoons prepared mustard
¼ teaspoon salt
¼ teaspoon garlic powder
2 cups broccoli flowerets
2 cups cauliflower flowerets
2 cups sliced carrots

Pour vinegar into a medium mixing bowl; slowly whisk in oil until combined. Whisk in mayonnaise, chives, mustard, and seasonings; mix well.

Combine vegetables; pour dressing, tossing well. Marinate in refrigerator several hours or overnight. Yield: 12 to 15 appetizer servings.

CHRISTMAS TREE PEANUT BUTTER-AND-JELLY SANDWICHES

Cut out Christmas tree shapes from slices of white bread with a cookie cutter. Spread each piece with peanut butter. Spoon strawberry or grape jelly into a pastry bag fitted with a small round tip. Pipe jelly in a thin line around borders of trees. Store in airtight containers until ready to serve.

CITRUS PUNCH

2 tablespoons citric acid
1 cup cold water
2 quarts cold water
1 (46-ounce) can unsweetened pineapple juice
1 (6-ounce) can frozen orange juice concentrate, thawed and undiluted
1¾ cups sugar
1 (33.8-ounce) bottle ginger ale, chilled

Combine citric acid and 1 cup cold water in a large bowl; cover and refrigerate 8 hours.

Combine citric mixture and remaining ingredients except ginger ale. Add ginger ale just before serving; serve over crushed ice. Yield: 5 quarts.

GINGERBREAD MEN COOKIES

⅓ cup water
½ cup shortening
¼ cup butter or margarine
4½ cups all-purpose flour
2 teaspoons baking soda
1½ teaspoons ground ginger
1 teaspoon ground cinnamon
Pinch of salt
1½ cups molasses
Raisins

Combine water, shortening, and butter in a small saucepan. Cook over medium heat, stirring constantly, until shortening melts.

Combine flour, soda, ginger, cinnamon, and salt in a mixing bowl; add

shortening mixture, stirring well. Stir in molasses; mix well. Chill overnight.

Divide dough in half; store one portion in refrigerator. Roll half of dough to ¼-inch thickness on a lightly floured surface. Cut with a 4-inch gingerbread man cutter, and place on lightly greased cookie sheets. Press raisins into dough for eyes, nose, and mouth.

Bake at 350° for 10 minutes. Cool cookies 2 minutes on cookie sheets; remove to wire racks, and allow to cool completely. Repeat the procedure with remaining dough. Yield: 3 dozen.

Note: Cookies will be soft. Store in an airtight container.

GRANDMOTHER'S COOKIES

1 cup butter or margarine, softened
1½ cups sugar
2 eggs
1½ teaspoons vanilla extract
3½ cups all-purpose flour
1 teaspoon baking powder
½ teaspoon salt
Red and green granulated sugar (optional)
Frosting (recipe follows)

Cream butter; gradually add 1½ cups sugar, beating until light and fluffy. Add eggs, one at a time, beating after each addition. Stir in vanilla. Combine flour, baking powder, and salt; add to creamed mixture, stirring well. Cover and refrigerate at least 8 hours.

Work with one-fourth of dough at a time; store remainder in refrigerator. Roll dough to ¼- to ⅛-inch thickness on a lightly floured surface. Cut with assorted Christmas cookie cutters, and place on ungreased cookie sheets. Bake at 375° for 8 to 9 minutes. Cool cookies slightly on cookie sheets. Sprinkle cookies with colored sugar, if desired. Or remove to wire racks, cool completely, and decorate with frosting. Repeat procedure with remaining dough. Yield: about 7 dozen 2½-inch cookies.

Frosting:

½ cup butter or margarine, softened
1 (16-ounce) package powdered sugar
3 tablespoons half-and-half
1 teaspoon vanilla extract
Red and green paste food coloring

Combine butter and powdered sugar, creaming until light and fluffy. Add half-and-half and vanilla; beat until of spreading consistency. Color one-third of frosting red and one-third green, leaving remaining frosting white. Yield: about 2½ cups.

CREAM PUFF CHRISTMAS TREE

1 cup water
½ cup butter or margarine, softened
1 cup all-purpose flour
4 eggs
Almond Cream Filling
Caramel Glaze

Combine water and butter in a large saucepan; bring to a boil. Add flour to butter mixture all at once, stirring vigorously over low heat until mixture leaves sides of pan and forms a smooth ball. Remove from heat, and cool 4 minutes. Add eggs, one at a time, beating thoroughly with a wooden spoon after each addition; then beat until batter is smooth.

Drop batter by heaping teaspoonfuls 2 inches apart onto lightly greased baking sheets. Bake at 400° for 20 to 25 minutes or until golden brown. Cool on wire racks away from drafts.

Cut a small slit in side of each cream puff. Fill a pastry bag with Almond Cream Filling. Pipe filling into each cream puff.

Dip top of each cream puff in Caramel Glaze, and stack in a pyramid shape on serving platter, beginning with a base of 16 cream puffs. Drizzle remaining glaze over pyramid. Yield: 35 cream puffs.

Almond Cream Filling:

1 (3½-ounce) package vanilla instant pudding mix
1¼ cups milk
1 cup whipping cream, whipped
1 teaspoon almond extract

Prepare pudding mix according to package directions using 1¼ cups milk. Fold in whipped cream and almond extract. Chill 2 hours. Yield: 3 cups.

Caramel Glaze:

1½ cups sugar
¾ cup boiling water

Place sugar in a heavy skillet; cook over medium-high heat. Stir constantly until sugar melts and forms a light-brown syrup. Reduce heat to low. Gradually add boiling water in a slow stream, stirring constantly with a wire whisk. (Do not add water rapidly; mixture may bubble up and overflow or form lumps.) Simmer 5 minutes or until mixture reaches (220°) on a candy thermometer. Remove from heat; cool to room temperature. Yield: about ¾ cup.

Tip: Use muffin pans to make extra large ice cubes for punch.

Their Tradition Is a Gift of Friendship

Everything about Winston-Salem, North Carolina, spells tradition. For over 200 years, the Moravians, a group of devout Germanic people who first settled there, have held an annual "love feast," where the close-knit people gather for worship and to share a simple meal of coffee and buns. And Christmas traditions are no exception for Joan and Murray Greason and family, who live in the area.

For 11 years, the Greasons have included invitations with their Christmas cards, asking relatives, neighbors, and friends to share a stand-up family supper and party on the Sunday night closest to Christmas. "When we were younger, there were always lots of parties at Christmastime, but the children were never invited. So we decided to have a party for families and include all the children," Joan explains. The Greasons' annual Christmas supper has mushroomed from a meager guest list of 40 the first year to 185 currently.

"I love Christmas and would have it all year-round if I could," says Joan. And the party guests echo her excitement. "The Greasons' Christmas supper is special because it is for families and because it is traditional and a gift of friendship," explains Linda Heckmann, a close friend who has attended the party every year since its beginning.

The menu for the party is always the same, and a familiar gingerbread house, made by Joan and the children, always serves as the table's centerpiece. There's always something for everyone in the family to enjoy. Adults look forward to sampling Pappa's Punch, an old family recipe, while the children gather in the playhouse out back to break a candy-filled piñata. And just in case one is not quick enough to scramble for the candy as it falls to the floor, there's always a little take-home treat. For the whole family, there's singing of Christmas carols and reminiscing with old friends.

"It's like a homecoming reunion," says college student Tripp, the oldest of the Greasons' three children. "You get to come back home and see all your buddies from childhood and high school that you haven't seen in a while."

According to Murray, what has changed most with the party over the years is the children. "We've always emphasized inviting families with children, and it's been a real joy to watch our friends' children and our children's friends grow up over the years."

■ One of the favorite recipes of Joan's Aunt Willette was Brunswick stew. It was the highlight of many church suppers, and no wonder—it's delicious.

AUNT WILLETTE'S BRUNSWICK STEW

1 (2½- to 3-pound) broiler-fryer
1½ pounds lean beef for stewing, cut into 1-inch cubes
1 pound pork tenderloin
3 (16-ounce) cans tomatoes, undrained and chopped
6 medium potatoes, peeled and cubed
4 cups frozen lima beans
1 (16-ounce) package frozen white shoepeg corn
4 cups chopped onion
2 cups sliced carrots
2 cups frozen sliced okra
1 cup frozen green peas
1 cup chopped cabbage
3 medium jalapeño peppers, seeded and chopped
1 (6-ounce) can tomato paste
3 tablespoons Worcestershire sauce
2 tablespoons lemon juice
1 tablespoon sugar
2 teaspoons salt
½ to 1 teaspoon pepper

Place broiler-fryer in a Dutch oven; cover with water. Bring to a boil. Cover, reduce heat, and simmer 1 hour. Remove chicken from broth, reserving broth; let chicken cool. Bone chicken, and coarsely chop meat; set aside.

Place beef and pork in a Dutch oven; cover with water. Bring to a boil. Cover, reduce heat, and simmer 2 hours. Remove meat from broth, reserving broth; let meat cool. Coarsely chop meat; set aside.

Combine chicken, beef, and pork broth; reserve 6 to 7 cups of broth mixture. Combine broth, chopped meat, all vegetables, jalapeño peppers, and tomato paste in a large Dutch oven. Bring to a boil. Cover, reduce heat, and simmer 2 hours.

Add Worcestershire sauce, lemon juice, sugar, salt, and pepper; mix well. Yield: 2 gallons.

Note: For a thicker stew, use only 5 cups of broth.

CURED HAM AND BISCUITS

1½ pounds thinly sliced cured ham
Buttermilk biscuits (recipe follows)

Place ham in a shallow baking pan. Bake at 350° for 10 to 15 minutes. Remove ham from pan, reserving pan drippings; set aside. Cut ham into bite-sized pieces.

Cut biscuits in half crosswise; dip cut side of biscuit in pan drippings. Place a small amount of ham on bottom half of biscuit; place top on biscuit. Repeat with remaining biscuits and ham. Yield: 3½ dozen.

Buttermilk Biscuits:

¼ cup plus 2 tablespoons shortening
2 cups self-rising flour
1¼ cups buttermilk

Cut shortening into flour with a pastry blender until mixture resembles coarse meal. Add buttermilk, stirring until dry ingredients are moistened. Turn dough out onto a floured surface; knead lightly 3 or 4 times.

Roll dough to ½-inch thickness; cut with a 2-inch biscuit cutter. Place biscuits on a greased baking sheet. Bake at 350° for 20 to 25 minutes or until lightly browned. Yield: 3½ dozen.

CRESCENTS

1 cup butter or margarine, softened
¼ cup plus 2 tablespoons sifted powdered sugar
2 cups all-purpose flour
2 teaspoons cold water
2 teaspoons vanilla extract
2 cups finely chopped pecans
Additional powdered sugar

Cream butter; gradually add ¼ cup plus 2 tablespoons powdered sugar, beating well. Gradually add flour, mixing well. Add water and vanilla; mix well. Stir in pecans. Chill 2 to 3 hours.

Break off dough by heaping teaspoonfuls, and shape into 2-inch crescents. Place on lightly greased cookie sheets. Bake at 325° for 17 to 18 minutes; do not brown. Cool on cookie sheets 1 minute; dust with additional powdered sugar. Remove cookies to wire racks, and cool completely. Yield: 4 dozen.

BUCKEYES

1½ (16-ounce) packages powdered sugar
1 (16-ounce) jar crunchy peanut butter
1 cup butter or margarine, softened
1 (12-ounce) package semisweet chocolate morsels
1 tablespoon shortening

Position knife blade in food processor bowl. Add half each of powdered sugar,

peanut butter, and butter; top with cover. Process until thoroughly mixed. Shape into 1-inch balls; chill. Repeat process.

Combine chocolate and shortening in top of a double boiler; bring water to a boil. Reduce heat to low; simmer until chocolate melts. Dip each ball in chocolate until partially coated; place on waxed paper until chocolate hardens. Store in an airtight container in refrigerator. Yield: about 7 dozen.

■ Joan remembers her mother making so much of this fruitcake that she had to mix the batter in a large stockpot.

MOM'S FRUITCAKE

1 pound pecans, chopped
½ pound red candied cherries, halved
½ pound green candied cherries, halved
½ pound candied mixed fruit
½ pound chopped dates
½ pound raisins
2 cups all-purpose flour, divided
½ teaspoon baking powder
½ teaspoon baking soda
½ teaspoon salt
½ teaspoon ground cinnamon
½ teaspoon ground cloves
½ teaspoon ground allspice
5 eggs
1 cup sugar
1 cup butter or margarine, melted
½ cup light corn syrup
½ teaspoon vanilla extract
½ cup brandy (optional)

Combine pecans and candied and dried fruit; dredge in 1 cup flour, stirring to coat evenly. Set aside.

Combine remaining 1 cup flour with baking powder, soda, salt, and spices; mix well, and set aside.

Beat eggs in a large mixing bowl; gradually add sugar, mixing well. Add butter, corn syrup, vanilla, and flour mixture, mixing well. Stir in fruit mixture, and blend well. Spoon batter into a greased, floured, and waxed paper-lined 10-inch tube pan. Bake at 250° for 2½ to 3 hours or until a wooden pick inserted in center comes out clean. Cool cake completely in pan. Remove from pan, and remove waxed paper.

Moisten several layers of cheesecloth with ½ cup brandy, if desired; cover cake completely with cheesecloth. Wrap with foil; store in a cool place at least one week, remoistening cheesecloth as needed. Yield: one 10-inch cake.

■ The custom in old Moravian homes was to keep a cloth-covered stick in a bucket of melted lard on top of the wood stove. It was used to grease the cookie sheets when Moravian sugar cookies were made.

MORAVIAN SUGAR COOKIES

½ cup butter, softened
1 cup sugar
1 egg
½ teaspoon vanilla extract
2¼ to 2½ cups all-purpose flour
½ teaspoon salt
½ teaspoon baking soda
¼ cup buttermilk
Superfine sugar

Cream butter and sugar, beating well. Add egg and vanilla; beat well. Combine 2¼ cups flour, salt, and soda; add to creamed mixture alternately with buttermilk, mixing well. Add extra flour if dough seems very sticky. Cover and chill 8 hours.

Work with one-fourth of dough at a time, and store remainder in refrigerator. Place stockinette cover on rolling pin; flour well. Roll dough to ⅛- to ¹⁄₁₆-inch thickness on a lightly floured pastry cloth. Cut with Christmas tree cookie cutters, and carefully place on lightly greased cookie sheets. Bake at 375° for 6 to 8 minutes or just until cookies begin to brown around edges. Cool slightly on cookie sheets, and sprinkle with superfine sugar. Remove cookies to wire racks, and cool completely. Store in airtight container. Yield: about 10 dozen 3¼-inch cookies.

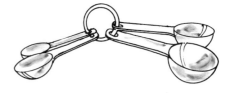

■ Pappa's Punch was the drink Murray's parents always served when they entertained.

PAPPA'S PUNCH

2 cups bourbon
2 cups water
1¼ cups sugar
1 cup fresh lemon juice
Rinds of 3 lemons

Combine all ingredients except lemon rinds; stir well until sugar dissolves. Add lemon rinds. Store overnight in an airtight container. (Do not refrigerate.) Remove lemon rinds. Serve over finely crushed ice. Yield: 5½ cups.

CHILDREN'S PUNCH

1 quart pineapple juice
1 quart orange juice
1 quart lemonade
1 (33.8-ounce) bottle ginger ale, chilled

Combine pineapple juice, orange juice, and lemonade. Gently stir in ginger ale just before serving. Serve over crushed ice. Yield: 1 gallon.

Cookies Make It Christmas

Like Christmas lights, shiny packages, and scents of evergreen, Christmas cookies hold their own special magic this time of year. We give and receive them as gifts, hang them on Christmas trees, and shape them into angels, reindeer, bells, and Santas. We don't mind taking the extra time to brighten them with colored frostings and decorations.

If you enjoy giving cookies as gifts, you'll find plenty of recipes here to add variety to your packages. Sturdy cookies that won't crumble easily are ideal. Just about all the recipes listed here are suitable. Soft cookies, such as our Melt-Away Peppermint Wreaths, are fragile and better for serving holiday guests in your home. Also, Butter Cookies decorated with soft, moist Buttercream Frosting are best served from a tray. To use Butter Cookies for gifts, you might skip the frosting and use colored sprinkles and candies to decorate instead.

Lemony Cutout Cookies are fun to eat or to turn into Christmas ornaments. Be sure to make a hole in the top of each cookie before baking so you can attach a ribbon for hanging. Then decorate with Royal Icing, which dries hard and lasts indefinitely.

We used the recipe for Lemony Cutout Cookies to make small and large gingerbread people for the Advent calendar sketched on page 325. Bake small cookies, and number each one with the 24 days before Christmas. Then tie a large cookie at the top of the calendar to be eaten on Christmas Day.

Making cookies takes time, but we found some Southerners who have discovered a way to serve lots of different cookies in their homes by baking several batches of only one recipe. They share cookies with friends at a cookie swap. The exchange provides a reason for a party. (See page 325.)

MAPLE SANDWICH COOKIES

1 cup butter or margarine, softened
⅔ cup sugar
2 egg yolks
½ teaspoon maple extract
2½ cups all-purpose flour
¼ teaspoon salt
Powdered sugar
Maple Frosting
Red and green sugar sprinkles
Red cinnamon candies (optional)
Buttercream frosting (optional)

Cream butter; gradually add sugar, beating until light and fluffy. Add egg yolks, one at a time, beating well after each addition. Stir in maple extract.

Combine flour and salt; add to creamed mixture, beating well. Shape dough into a ball; cover and chill at least 2 hours.

Work with half of dough at a time; store remainder in refrigerator. Sift powdered sugar lightly over working surface. Roll half of dough out to ¼-inch thickness; cut with 2½-inch round or rectangular cookie cutters. Repeat procedure with remaining dough. Cut centers from half of cookies with 1-inch canape cutters.

Place on lightly greased cookie sheets. Bake at 375° for 6 to 8 minutes or until cookies are lightly browned. Cool on wire racks.

The sketch below identifies all of the cookies pictured on the cover.

1. Chocolate-Cherry Cookies 2. Lemony Cutout Cookies 3. Swedish Ginger Cookies 4. Childhood Thumbprint Cookies 5. Maple Sandwich Cookies 6. Butter Cookies 7. Melt-Away Peppermint Wreaths 8. Snappin' Turtle Cookies 9. Santa's Whiskers

Spread bottom side of solid cookies with Maple Frosting, and top with cutout cookies. Fill cutout centers with red or green sugar sprinkles. If desired, decorate with cinnamon candies, and pipe designs with buttercream frosting. (See recipe for Butter Cookies, below, for buttercream frosting recipe.) Yield: about 2 dozen.

Maple Frosting:

¼ cup butter or margarine, softened
2 cups sifted powdered sugar, divided
2 tablespoons milk
¼ to ½ teaspoon maple extract

Cream butter; gradually add 1 cup sugar, beating well with an electric mixer. Add remaining sugar alternately with milk, beating until smooth enough to spread. Add maple extract, and mix well. Yield: 1 cup.

BUTTER COOKIES

1 cup butter or margarine, softened
¾ cup sugar
1 egg
½ teaspoon vanilla extract
2½ cups all-purpose flour
1 teaspoon baking powder
¼ teaspoon salt
Food coloring (optional)
Buttercream frosting (recipe follows)
Assorted candies and sprinkles

Cream butter; gradually add sugar, beating until light and fluffy. Add egg and vanilla; beat well. Combine flour, baking powder, and salt; add to creamed mixture, mixing well. Color dough with food coloring, if desired. Using a cookie press, press dough into desired shapes onto ungreased cookie sheets. Bake at 350° for 10 to 12 minutes. Cool on wire racks. Decorate with buttercream frosting, assorted candies, and decorator sprinkles. Yield: about 6 dozen (2-inch) cookies.

Buttercream Frosting:

3 tablespoons butter or margarine, softened
2⅓ cups sifted powdered sugar
Dash of salt
1½ to 2 tablespoons milk
½ teaspoon vanilla extract
Food coloring (optional)

Cream butter; gradually add powdered sugar, beating well. Add salt, milk, and vanilla; mix well. Color frosting with food coloring, if desired. Yield: about 1 cup.   *Ruth Griggs,
South Hill, Virginia.*

LEMONY CUTOUT COOKIES

1 cup butter or margarine, softened
2 cups sugar
3 eggs
2 tablespoons buttermilk
5 cups all-purpose flour
1 teaspoon baking soda
1 teaspoon grated lemon rind
1 teaspoon lemon extract
Royal icing (recipe follows)

Cream butter; gradually add sugar, beating well. Add eggs, one at a time, beating well after each addition. Add buttermilk, and beat well. Combine flour, soda, and lemon rind; gradually stir into creamed mixture. Stir in lemon extract. Chill dough several hours or overnight.

Roll dough to ⅛-inch thickness on a lightly floured surface; cut out with shaped cookie cutters. (Place unused dough in refrigerator.) Place cookies 1 inch apart on lightly greased cookie sheets. Bake at 400° for 6 to 7 minutes or until edges are lightly browned. Remove cookies, and cool completely on wire racks. Repeat procedure with remaining dough. Decorate as desired with royal icing. Yield: about 4 dozen (5-inch) cookies.

Royal Icing:

3 egg whites
½ teaspoon cream of tartar
1 (16-ounce) package powdered sugar, sifted
Red and green paste food coloring (optional)

Combine egg whites (at room temperature) and cream of tartar in a large mixing bowl. Beat at medium speed of an electric mixer until frothy. Gradually add powdered sugar, mixing well. Beat 5 to 7 minutes. Color portions of icing with paste food coloring, if desired. (Icing dries very quickly; keep covered at all times with plastic wrap.) Yield: about 2 cups.

Note: Royal icing dries very hard and is used for making decorations to last indefinitely. It is edible, but crunchy.

SANTA'S WHISKERS

1 cup butter or margarine, softened
1 cup sugar
2 tablespoons milk
1 teaspoon vanilla extract
2½ cups all-purpose flour
¾ cup chopped red and green candied cherries
½ cup chopped pecans
¾ cup flaked coconut

Cream butter; gradually add sugar, beating until light and fluffy. Add milk and vanilla; beating until smooth. Stir in remaining ingredients except coconut. Shape dough into two (8- x 2-inch) cylinders; roll each in coconut. Cover and chill 3 to 4 hours; cut into ¼-inch-thick slices. Place on ungreased cookie sheets; bake at 375° for 12 to 14 minutes. Cool on wire racks. Yield: about 4½ dozen.   *Sue W. Lankford, Memphis, Tennessee.*

SWEDISH GINGER COOKIES

1 cup butter or margarine, softened
1½ cups sugar
1 egg
2 tablespoons molasses
1 tablespoon water
3¼ cups all-purpose flour
2 teaspoons baking soda
2 teaspoons ground cinnamon
1 teaspoon ground ginger
½ teaspoon ground cloves
Red and green candied cherries
Almond slices

Cream butter; gradually add sugar, beating until light and fluffy. Add egg, molasses, and water; mix well. Combine flour, soda, and spices; add to creamed mixture, mixing until blended.

Roll dough to ⅛-inch thickness on a lightly floured surface. Cut dough with a 2-inch round cutter. Decorate with cherries and almond slices arranged in a flower design. Place on lightly greased cookie sheets; bake at 350° for 8 minutes. Cool on wire racks. Yield: about 9 dozen.   *Pearle E. Evans, Myrtle Beach, South Carolina.*

SNAPPIN' TURTLE COOKIES

½ cup butter or margarine, softened
½ cup firmly packed brown sugar
1 egg
1 egg, separated
¼ teaspoon vanilla extract
1½ cups all-purpose flour
¼ teaspoon baking soda
¼ teaspoon salt
12½ dozen pecan halves
Chocolate frosting (recipe follows)

Cream softened butter; gradually add brown sugar, beating until light and fluffy. Add 1 egg, 1 egg yolk, and vanilla, beating mixture well.

Combine flour, soda, and salt; add to creamed mixture, mixing well. Chill 1 to 2 hours. Arrange pecan halves in groups of 5 on ungreased cookie sheets, resembling head and legs of turtles. Shape dough into 1-inch balls and dip bottom edges into remaining egg white. Press gently onto pecans to resemble turtle bodies. Bake at 350° for 10 to 12 minutes; cool on wire racks. Spread chocolate frosting on tops of cookies. Yield: 2½ dozen.

Chocolate Frosting:

2 (1-ounce) squares unsweetened chocolate
¼ cup milk
1 tablespoon butter or margarine
About 1¾ cups sifted powdered sugar

Combine unsweetened chocolate squares, milk, and butter in a small saucepan; cook over low heat, stirring constantly, until chocolate melts. Remove from heat. Add powdered sugar; beat until smooth. Yield: about 1 cup.
   Donna DiRicco, Arlington, Virginia.

CHILDHOOD THUMBPRINT COOKIES

1 cup butter or margarine, softened
⅔ cup sugar
2 egg yolks
½ teaspoon vanilla extract
2¼ cups all-purpose flour
½ teaspoon salt
Chocolate frosting (recipe follows)

Cream butter; gradually add sugar, beating until light and fluffy. Add egg yolks, one at a time, beating well after each addition. Stir in vanilla.

Combine flour and salt; add to creamed mixture, mixing well. Chill.

Roll dough into 1-inch balls; place balls about 2 inches apart on ungreased cookie sheets. Press thumb in each ball of dough, leaving an indentation. Bake at 300° for 20 to 25 minutes; do not brown. Allow to cool on wire racks. Place about ½ teaspoon chocolate frosting in each cookie indentation. Yield: 3½ dozen.

Chocolate Frosting:

1 cup sugar
¼ cup cocoa
¼ cup milk
¼ cup butter or margarine
½ teaspoon vanilla extract

Combine sugar, cocoa, and milk in a heavy saucepan. Bring to a boil, and boil 1½ to 2 minutes, stirring constantly. Remove from heat; stir in butter and vanilla. Beat until mixture is of spreading consistency. Yield: 1 cup.
   Paula Stone, Hanceville, Alabama.

MELT-AWAY PEPPERMINT WREATHS

1¼ cups butter or margarine
¾ cup sifted powdered sugar
2½ cups all-purpose flour
¾ teaspoon peppermint extract
Red food coloring
Green food coloring

Cream butter; gradually add sugar, beating well. Add flour, and mix well. Stir in peppermint extract. Divide dough in half, and place in separate bowls. Tint half of dough with red food coloring and the other half with green food coloring.

Roll dough into balls using ½ teaspoon dough per ball. For each wreath-shaped cookie, place six balls in a circle on ungreased cookie sheets, alternating colors. Press together securely. Bake at 375° for 8 minutes. Let cool 10 minutes; remove to racks. Cool completely. Yield: 3 dozen.

CHOCOLATE-CHERRY COOKIES

1 cup butter or margarine, softened
1 cup sifted powdered sugar
1 egg
¼ teaspoon almond extract
2 (1-ounce) squares semisweet chocolate, melted and cooled
2½ cups all-purpose flour
¼ teaspoon cream of tartar
1 cup red candied cherries, coarsely chopped
½ cup finely chopped pecans

Cream butter; gradually add sugar, beating until light and fluffy. Add egg and beat well; stir in almond extract. Stir in melted chocolate, mixing well. Combine flour and cream of tartar; add to creamed mixture, and mix well. Stir in cherries and pecans.

Shape dough into two 10- x 2-inch blocks or cylinders. Wrap in plastic wrap; freeze several hours or overnight.

Cut dough into ¼-inch slices; place on ungreased cookie sheets. Bake at 375° for 10 to 12 minutes. Cool on wire racks. Yield: 5 dozen.

FROSTED NUTMEG LOGS

1 cup butter or margarine, softened
¾ cup sugar
1 egg
3 cups all-purpose flour
1 to 1¼ teaspoons ground nutmeg
2 teaspoons rum extract
2 teaspoons vanilla extract
Vanilla-Rum Frosting
Ground nutmeg

Cream butter; gradually add sugar, beating until light and fluffy. Add egg; mix well. Combine flour and 1 to 1¼ teaspoons nutmeg; add to creamed mixture, mixing until blended. Stir in the flavorings.

Shape dough into 3- x ½-inch logs. Place 2 inches apart on ungreased cookie sheets; bake at 350° for 12 minutes or until lightly browned. Cool on wire racks.

Spread Vanilla-Rum Frosting on cookies; run fork tines lengthwise in frosting on each cookie. Sprinkle with nutmeg. Yield: 4½ dozen.

Vanilla-Rum Frosting:

¼ cup butter or margarine, softened
3 cups sifted powdered sugar, divided
2 tablespoons half-and-half or milk
1 teaspoon vanilla extract
1 teaspoon rum extract

Cream butter; gradually add 1½ cups sugar, beating well. Add remaining ingredients and remaining 1½ cups sugar; beat until smooth. Yield: 1½ cups.

Jennie Callahan,
Louisville, Kentucky.

HEAVENLY DELIGHTS

½ cup butter or margarine, softened
½ cup shortening
⅔ cup sifted powdered sugar
1 teaspoon vanilla extract
1 teaspoon orange extract
2 cups all-purpose flour
½ cup chopped pecans
Sifted powdered sugar

Cream butter and shortening; gradually add ⅔ cup sugar and flavorings, beating until light and fluffy. Gradually add flour; beat well. Stir in pecans. Shape into 1-inch balls; place on ungreased cookie sheets. Bake at 350° for 20 minutes. Remove immediately from cookie sheets, and roll in powdered sugar. Cool and roll again in powdered sugar. Yield: about 3½ dozen.

Jean Voan,
Shepherd, Texas.

RAISIN GINGERSNAPS

¾ cup shortening
1 cup sugar
1 egg
¼ cup molasses
2¼ cups all-purpose flour
2 teaspoons baking soda
½ teaspoon salt
¾ to 1 teaspoon ground ginger
¼ teaspoon ground cinnamon
¼ teaspoon ground cloves
1½ cups seedless raisins, chopped
Sugar

Cream shortening; gradually add 1 cup sugar, beating until light and fluffy. Add egg and molasses; mix well. Combine flour, soda, salt, ginger, cinnamon, and cloves. Add to creamed mixture, mixing until blended. Stir in raisins. Chill dough.

Shape dough into 1-inch balls; roll in sugar. Place 2 inches apart on greased cookie sheets; bake at 375° for 10 minutes or until lightly browned. Allow to cool. Yield: 4 dozen.

Charlene Keebler,
Savannah, Georgia.

PECAN CRESCENT COOKIES

½ cup shortening
½ cup butter or margarine, softened
¼ cup plus 2 tablespoons sifted powdered sugar
1 tablespoon water
2 cups all-purpose flour
Pinch of salt
1 teaspoon vanilla extract
1 cup chopped pecans

Cream shortening and butter; gradually add sugar, beating until light and fluffy. Add water, beating well. Combine flour and salt; add to creamed mixture, stirring well. Stir in vanilla and pecans.

Shape dough into 1½-inch crescents. Place on lightly greased cookie sheets. Bake at 325° for 17 to 20 minutes. Yield: 3 dozen.

Mrs. Ray B. Sizemore,
Keysville, Virginia.

Tip: For perfectly shaped round cookies, pack homemade refrigerator cookie dough into clean 6-ounce juice cans (don't remove bottoms) and freeze dough. Thaw cookie dough about 15 minutes; then open bottom of can and push up, using the top edge as a cutting guide.

A Calendar Of Cookies

A fun way for children to count down the days until Christmas is with a cookie Advent calendar. A cookie for each of the first 24 days of December is attached to a long ribbon. The top of the ribbon holds an extra-special cookie to be eaten on Christmas Day. (See "Cookies Make It Christmas" on page 322 for suggested recipe.) Here's how to make a ribbon Advent calendar like the one sketched below.

Materials

You'll need 1½ yards of red grosgrain ribbon (at least 2 inches wide), 7 yards of red ⅛-inch satin ribbon, 3½ yards of green ⅛-inch satin ribbon, 3½ yards of white ⅛-inch satin ribbon, red thread, and a small holiday gift card. If you'd like, substitute different ribbon colors to match your holiday decor.

Construction

■ Fold the top of the grosgrain ribbon under ½ inch, and then 1 inch more.

Fold the bottom of ribbon under ½ inch, and then another ½ inch. Press and stitch both ends in place.
■ Cut a 23-inch length from each of the red and green satin ribbons. Run ribbons through hem at top of grosgrain ribbon. Tie in a bow, and use to hang calendar.
■ To make tie for large cookie, cut a 13-inch length from each of the red and white satin ribbons. Place ribbons together, and fold in half to find center. Hand sew to the center of grosgrain ribbon 3 inches from top of calendar.
■ For smaller cookie ties, cut remaining satin ribbon into 9-inch lengths. Use two ribbons of contrasting colors for each cookie tie. Measure 9 inches from top of calendar, and sew the center of the first small cookie tie ½ inch from the edge of the wide ribbon. Sew second cookie tie alongside first tie, ½ inch from the edge of opposite side of wide ribbon. Measure 3 inches below the first row of cookie ties, and sew on two more cookie ties, alternating ribbon colors. Repeat process until you have 12 rows with 2 cookie ties on each row.
■ Wrap 24 (2-inch) cookies and 1 (5-inch) cookie in plastic wrap, gathering the edges of plastic wrap at the top of each cookie. Tie the large cookie to the cookie tie at the top of the calendar. Tie small cookies onto the calendar using the ribbons sewed in place. If necessary, trim ribbons after tying bows. If cookies are numbered with icing, start with cookie marked "1" at the bottom of the calendar.
■ Sew the center of one ribbon to the top left corner of the calendar. Punch a hole in a holiday card, insert the ribbon, and tie to the top of the calendar. Use the card to write a holiday message or a Christmas poem. (This is an optional step.)

A Quick Alternative

You can use burlap and yarn instead of ribbons. Cut a strip of burlap 1½ yards long by 3½ inches wide. Pull threads on sides and bottom to leave ½-inch frayed edges. Fold top of burlap over 1 inch, and hand stitch to the back of calendar.

Cut a piece of yarn 23 inches long, and run through the hem at the top of the calendar. Tie in a bow, and use to hang calendar. Cut 25 (9-inch) lengths of yarn. Run both ends of each piece of yarn through burlap toward the front of the calendar, leaving three or four threads of burlap between each end of yarn. Use the same spacing as listed for cookie ties on ribbon calendar.

Host A Cookie-Swap Party

It's always fun to offer your family and holiday guests a choice of several kinds of cookies, but finding the time to prepare a variety of recipes isn't always possible. That's when a cookie swap party with your friends comes in handy—you each take home a delectable assortment.

■ Brenda Mitchell of Rockingham, North Carolina, has hosted a cookie exchange for the past four years. Planning is the key to a successful party, she says. Be sure everyone knows the procedure and what to bring. Knowing the type of cookie each guest will prepare helps also. "That way we don't wind up with half of them being chocolate chip," she explains.

Brenda invites 11 friends to her home every year, and each guest brings one dozen cookies packaged for each of the other participants—a total of 11 dozen cookies—and a copy of her recipe. If they wish, some guests prepare extra cookies for tasting at the party.

Guests have become creative with their packaging. The cookie bags often come tied with colorful yarn or plaid ribbons, or nestled in decorated baskets. Brenda suggests using plastic bags so that the cookies can be seen.

As for the party itself, Brenda provides an array of nibbles for the guests. She serves hot spiced tea, cheese straws, and other appetizers. When guests leave with their cookies, they are presented with a ribbon-tied booklet of cookie recipes from the previous year's cookie swap.

■ In Columbus, Georgia, Joanne Cavis participates in a church-wide cookie exchange each year. Over the past five years her group has experimented with several different ways to organize such a large party. "We have so many people, you can't possibly bake enough cookies for everyone to have one-half dozen," she remarks. To solve the problem, each person brings the number of cookies she would like to swap. "For example, if you bring 10 dozen cookies, you take home 10 dozen different cookies," explains Joanne.

It helps to decide ahead of time how many cookies to package for each person. "It's nice to have at least one-half dozen of each kind of cookie rather than two or three," says Joanne. "Also, it's good to plan to have some tasting ones for refreshments with coffee."

Joanne says that having the actual recipes to take home with the cookies was a highlight of the party for her group. She suggests having the recipes copied ahead of time so each person can leave with a copy of each recipe. "That's one of the things that makes a successful cookie swap," she says.

In addition to the fun of gathering with friends, sampling tasty cookies, and exchanging recipes, Joanne says that the cookie swap is a timesaver when it comes to holiday baking. "The beauty of a cookie swap is that for the time you've spent, you end up with a lot of different cookies," she says.

For some ideas for cookie recipes, turn to "Cookies Make It Christmas" on page 322.

■ Here are some additional tips for organizing a cookie swap:

—Send out invitations at least a month in advance so that everyone has time to bake cookies.

—On the invitations, be sure to explain the procedure of the party, and give detailed instructions for each guest. If you plan to present the recipes at the cookie swap, ask each person to give you a copy of her recipe before the cookie-swap party. Let the guests know that you may ask them to select another recipe if too many people plan to bring the same one.

—When compiling a booklet of recipes for guests to take home, be sure to list the contributor of each one. If the party is an annual event, don't forget to include the date.

—On each cookie package, use stick-on holiday labels noting the cook's name and the name of the recipe. For a fancier package, place plastic bags of cookies in small decorative gift boxes or baskets, line the bags with colorful tissue, or tie colorful ribbons or ornaments on each bag.

—Be sure to set up a table for displaying the cookies. For large parties, you may want to set up sampling trays in front of the packaged cookies. Cut the cookies in quarters if there is a large number to sample.

Bake A Sweet Quick Bread

Fresh from the oven, these quick breads flavored with fruit or nuts are great for morning meals or a midday snack. A loaf of Banana-Zucchini Bread or a warm fruit coffee cake is just perfect to share with a friend.

BANANA-ZUCCHINI BREAD

3 cups all-purpose flour
1 teaspoon baking soda
1 teaspoon salt
1 teaspoon ground cinnamon
½ teaspoon baking powder
1 cup vegetable oil
3 eggs
2 cups sugar
1 tablespoon vanilla extract
1 teaspoon imitation banana extract
2 cups mashed bananas
2 cups unpeeled shredded zucchini
1 cup chopped pecans or walnuts

Combine flour, soda, salt, cinnamon, and baking powder in a mixing bowl, and set aside.

Combine oil, eggs, sugar, and flavorings in a large bowl; beat well. Stir in bananas and zucchini. Add flour mixture, stirring just until moistened. Stir in pecans.

Pour batter into two greased and floured 8½- x 4½- x 3-inch loafpans. Bake at 350° for 1 hour or until a wooden pick inserted in center comes out clean. Cool in pans 10 minutes; remove from pans, and cool completely on wire racks. Yield: 2 loaves.

Gail Marshall,
Camden, Tennessee.

BLUEBERRY COFFEE CAKE

¼ cup butter or margarine, softened
¾ cup sugar
1 egg
2 cups all-purpose flour
2 teaspoons baking powder
½ teaspoon salt
½ cup milk
2 cups fresh blueberries
Streusel (recipe follows)

Cream butter in a large mixing bowl; gradually add sugar, beating well. Add egg, and beat well.

Combine flour, baking powder, and salt; add to creamed mixture alternately

with milk, beginning and ending with flour mixture. Mix well after each addition. Fold in blueberries.

Spoon batter into a greased and floured 9-inch springform pan. Sprinkle with streusel. Bake at 375° for 40 to 45 minutes or until lightly browned. Cool in pan 10 minutes; loosen edges of cake with a knife, and remove rim from springform pan. Serve warm. Yield: one 9-inch coffee cake.

Streusel:

½ cup firmly packed light brown sugar
3 tablespoons all-purpose flour
1 tablespoon ground cinnamon
3 tablespoons butter or margarine
½ cup finely chopped pecans

Combine sugar, flour, and cinnamon in bowl. Cut in butter with pastry blender until mixture resembles coarse meal. Stir in pecans. Yield: about 1⅓ cups.

Nancy Swinney,
Tallahassee, Florida.

MACADAMIA RING COFFEE CAKE

½ cup finely chopped macadamia nuts
2 cups all-purpose flour
1¼ cups sugar
1 teaspoon baking powder
1 teaspoon baking soda
1 teaspoon ground ginger
¼ teaspoon salt
½ teaspoon ground nutmeg
1 egg
1 cup buttermilk
⅔ cup butter or margarine, melted
1 teaspoon vanilla extract

Grease a 10-inch tube pan with butter and sprinkle macadamia nuts evenly in pan; set aside.

Combine dry ingredients in a large bowl. Combine egg, buttermilk, butter, and vanilla; stir into dry ingredients until smooth.

Pour batter into prepared pan. Bake at 350° for 35 to 40 minutes or until a wooden pick inserted in cake comes out clean. Cool in pan 10 to 15 minutes; invert onto a serving platter. Serve warm. Yield: one 10-inch coffee cake.

Note: Coffee cake will not rise to height of tube pan. Total height is about 2½ inches. *Liz Wade,*
Winston-Salem, North Carolina.

Tip: Bread is done if it sounds hollow when tapped. It will be pulled away from sides of the pan and golden brown in color.

Tree-Trimming Snack

More than likely, one of your family's favorite holiday activities is putting up the Christmas tree. This year before you take out the decorations, consider this suggestion: Make tree-trimming even more fun with some quick and easy snacks for the occasion.

Have Crunchy Rice Mix ready for nibbling when the festivities begin. Later in the evening, pop Little Pizza Turnovers into the oven for a hot, tasty treat. Easy to prepare, these snacks add an extra touch to a special evening.

LITTLE PIZZA TURNOVERS

1 cup ricotta cheese
½ cup (2 ounces) shredded mozzarella cheese
¼ cup grated Parmesan cheese
1 (10-ounce) package refrigerated flaky biscuits
20 thin pepperoni slices

Combine cheese; mix well, and set aside. Separate half the biscuits into 2 layers. Shape each biscuit layer into a 4- x 2-inch oval. Place one slice pepperoni and about 1 tablespoon cheese mixture on one side of each oval; moisten edges with water. Fold dough in half; press edges together, using a fork to seal. Transfer to a lightly greased baking sheet. Repeat with remaining biscuits.

Bake at 350° for 18 to 20 minutes or until golden. Serve pizzas warm. Yield: 20 appetizer servings.

Mary Kay Menees,
White Pine, Tennessee.

CRUNCHY RICE MIX

4 cups bite-size crispy rice square cereal
3 tablespoons butter or margarine, melted
2 teaspoons taco seasoning mix
2 teaspoons grated Parmesan cheese
1 (7-ounce) jar mixed salted nuts

Toss cereal with butter in a large mixing bowl; sprinkle with seasoning mix and cheese. Add nuts, and stir well. Spread mixture in a 15- x 10- x 1-inch jellyroll pan; bake at 325° for 10 minutes. Let cool, and store in an airtight container. Yield: 5 cups.

Catherine Bearden,
Bostwick, Georgia.

Combine leaf lettuce with alfalfa sprouts, celery, tomato, and avocado for Spanish Sprout Salad. Serve it with a sweet-and-tangy French dressing.

Give A New Twist To Salads

When you want the salad to be more than just tossed greens, these easy recipes will help you serve something different. They all start with basic salad greens and boast some unique combinations of fruit, vegetables, and flavors. Add the avocado to Spanish Sprout Salad just before serving.

SPANISH SPROUT SALAD

1 small head leaf lettuce, torn
1 large tomato, diced
1 cup alfalfa sprouts
½ cup sliced celery
2 small avocados, cut into bite-size pieces
2 tablespoons lemon juice
Dash of red pepper
Commercial French dressing (optional)

Combine vegetables and avocado pieces in a large salad bowl. Combine lemon juice and pepper; sprinkle over salad and toss gently. Serve with commercial French dressing, if desired. Yield: 6 servings.

Jan K. Sliwa,
Temple, Texas.

COMBINATION SPINACH SALAD

1 pound fresh spinach
5 small fresh mushrooms, sliced
3 green onions, sliced
1 (8-ounce) can pineapple chunks, drained
1 (14-ounce) can artichoke hearts, drained and quartered
1 (11-ounce) can mandarin oranges, drained
12 slices bacon, cooked and crumbled
Commercial ranch-style dressing

Remove stems from spinach; wash leaves, pat dry, and tear into bite-size pieces. Combine spinach, mushrooms, green onions, pineapple, artichoke hearts, and oranges in a large bowl. Sprinkle with bacon, and serve with dressing. Yield: 8 servings.

Arlene Margolis,
Little Rock, Arkansas.

DIFFERENT COTTAGE CHEESE SALAD

2 cups cream-style cottage cheese
½ cup mayonnaise
2 tablespoons prepared horseradish
1 medium head iceberg lettuce, torn
3 green onions, chopped
1 medium-size green pepper, chopped
Tomato wedges (optional)
Minced green pepper (optional)

Combine cottage cheese, mayonnaise, and horseradish; chill well.

Combine lettuce, green onions, and green pepper; toss lightly. Arrange lettuce mixture on individual plates; top with cottage cheese mixture. Garnish with tomato wedges and minced green pepper, if desired. Yield: 4 servings.

Cyndi Copenhaver,
Virginia Beach, Virginia.

HERBED GARDEN SALAD

1 head iceberg lettuce, torn
2 tomatoes, cut into wedges
½ cucumber, sliced
¼ green pepper, cut into strips
10 radishes, sliced
1 tablespoon chopped parsley
1 teaspoon salad herbs
½ teaspoon seasoned salt
⅛ teaspoon garlic powder
¼ teaspoon pepper
¼ cup vegetable oil
2 tablespoons cider vinegar
1 (3½-ounce) can French-fried onion rings

Combine lettuce, tomatoes, cucumber, green pepper, and radishes in a large salad bowl; sprinkle with parsley, salad herbs, seasoned salt, garlic powder, and pepper.

Combine oil and vinegar in a small jar; cover tightly, and shake vigorously until well blended. Pour over salad; toss gently. Sprinkle onion rings on top. Serve immediately. Yield: 8 servings.

Sue-Sue Hartstern,
Louisville, Kentucky.

Tip: To dry fresh herbs in the microwave oven, first remove stems from parsley, chives, basil, sage, and other herbs; rinse and pat dry. Spread ½ to 1 cup of the rinsed herbs between two sheets of paper towel, and microwave at HIGH for 2 to 2½ minutes. Store in airtight containers.

MICROWAVE COOKERY

A Quick Menu From The Microwave

Busy holiday schedules call for meals that are quick to fix. With this in mind, we turned to the microwave oven. In just minutes, you can put together a complete lunch or dinner that serves four. It includes salad, soup or sandwich, dessert, and beverage. For dinner, you may prefer serving the sandwich. The soup is ideal for a lighter lunch.

The key to making this meal quickly and fuss-free lies in the order the dishes are assembled and microwaved. Start by combining the ingredients for Shortcut French Onion Soup or Pocket Sloppy Joes. While this is microwaving, the Fast-and-Easy Salad ingredients can be collected and prepared.

After the salad is tossed, fill the microwave coffeemaker and get it started. Once this is done, if you're in a rush, you can start eating.

We suggest filling the peaches with the gingersnap crumb mixture ahead of time. This way, they are ready to pop in the microwave as soon as the coffeemaker is removed.

If you don't already have a microwave coffeemaker, you might want to know a little more about them. With most models, you can brew two to four cups of coffee in about 6 minutes. Models vary in the total amount of beverage they hold and in the placement of the water reservoir, but the proportions of coffee or tea to water are generally the same.

If your microwave oven is equipped with an automatic start, you can assemble the coffeemaker ahead, and fresh Mocha Coffee will be ready when you want it.

Fast-and-Easy Salad
Pocket Sloppy Joes or Shortcut French Onion Soup
Gingersnap Peaches
Mocha Coffee

FAST-AND-EASY SALAD

2 slices bacon
3 cups torn fresh spinach
1 cup torn iceberg lettuce
2 small green onions, sliced into ½-inch pieces
2 hard-cooked eggs, chopped
1 tablespoon sugar
2 tablespoons mayonnaise
1 tablespoon vinegar

Place bacon on a rack in a 12- x 8- x 2-inch baking dish; cover with paper towels, and microwave at HIGH for 2 to 3 minutes. Drain. Crumble bacon, and combine with spinach, lettuce, green onions, and eggs in a large bowl.

Combine sugar, mayonnaise, and vinegar in a small bowl; stir with a wire whisk. Microwave at HIGH for 30 seconds to 1 minute or just until mixture comes to a boil. Pour over salad; toss lightly, and serve immediately. Yield: 4 servings.

POCKET SLOPPY JOES

1 pound ground beef
1 small onion, chopped
⅓ cup chopped celery
1 (6-ounce) can tomato paste
¼ cup catsup
1 tablespoon vinegar
2 teaspoons Worcestershire sauce
½ teaspoon dry mustard
¼ teaspoon salt
⅛ teaspoon pepper
4 (6-inch) pocket bread rounds

Combine beef, onion, and celery in a large glass mixing bowl or baking dish, stirring to crumble beef. Cover tightly, and microwave at HIGH 5½ to 6½ minutes or until beef is browned, stirring at 2-minute intervals. Drain.

Stir in remaining ingredients except bread rounds. Cover and microwave at HIGH 3 to 4 minutes or until thoroughly heated.

Cut pocket bread rounds in half; fill each half with ⅓ cup meat sauce. Yield: 4 servings.

SHORTCUT FRENCH ONION SOUP

2 tablespoons butter or margarine
2 medium onions, sliced
2 (14½-ounce) cans beef broth, undiluted
1 teaspoon Worcestershire sauce
⅛ teaspoon ground thyme
4 (½-inch thick) slices French bread, toasted
¼ cup grated Parmesan cheese

Combine butter and onion in a 2-quart casserole. Cover and microwave at HIGH for 4 minutes, stirring after 2 minutes. Stir in broth, Worcestershire sauce, and thyme. Cover and microwave at HIGH for 8 to 12 minutes or until mixture comes to a boil.

Divide half of soup among 4 bowls. Top each bowl of soup with a slice of toasted French bread. Pour remaining soup over bread; sprinkle with cheese. Yield: 4 servings.

GINGERSNAP PEACHES

2 tablespoons butter or margarine
4 gingersnaps, crushed
1 teaspoon sugar
⅛ teaspoon ground cinnamon
4 canned peach halves
4 scoops vanilla ice cream

Microwave butter in a 1-cup glass measure on HIGH for 45 seconds or until melted; set aside. Combine gingersnap crumbs, sugar, and cinnamon.

Place peach halves in a 1½-quart casserole. Fill each peach cavity with crumb mixture; drizzle with butter. Cover and microwave at HIGH 3 to 4 minutes. Serve peaches in stemmed glasses; top each with a scoop of ice cream. Yield: 4 servings.

MOCHA COFFEE

2 cups water
¼ cup fresh ground coffee
¼ cup instant cocoa mix
Dash of ground cinnamon

Fill coffeemaker with water, and attach brewing unit securely. Place basket in brewing unit, and line with filter. Spoon coffee into filter. Replace top securely. (In some microwave coffeemakers, the water is placed in a reservoir above the brewing unit. Follow manufacturer's instructions for using your model.)

Place coffeemaker in center of microwave oven. Microwave at HIGH for 4 minutes. After all water has been drawn into brewing unit, stop the cooking process; allow to stand 2 minutes. Remove coffeemaker from oven. Carefully lift brewing unit just far enough to break seal. Let coffee drain into the bottom of the pot. Stir in instant cocoa mix and cinnamon. Yield: 2 cups.

From Our Kitchen To Yours

Some of the most important utensils in kitchens are pots and pans. With the variety of metals and styles now available, selecting and investing in new cookware can be a tough decision. Our test kitchens home economists would like to pass on suggestions for the selection and care of cookware.

—We encourage you to get the best cookware you can afford; it's wise to buy quality that will last.

—Choose pots and pans of heavy gauge or thickness and sturdy construction—those that will not warp, develop hot spots, or get dented. The gauge usually determines quality; the heavier the gauge, the better the product.

—To be energy efficient, cookware should have straight sides, tight-fitting lids, and flat bottoms for best contact with the heat source.

—The cookware material should be a good conductor of heat, such as aluminum or copper.

—The handle and knobs should be sturdy and attached securely to the pot or pan, and the handle should be strong enough to support the weight of the utensil when it's filled. Look for handles and knobs that are heat resistant and stay cool when being used.

Materials To Choose From

Aluminum is probably the most common material used for pots and pans. It's durable, and it's also a good heat conductor. It spreads heat evenly and responds quickly to temperature changes. Uncoated aluminum may react to highly acidic foods and wines, causing a slight metallic flavor. When cooking leafy green vegetables and eggs in aluminum, you may also have a change in food color or flavor, but these reactions are not a health hazard. You'll find some aluminum cookware is coated with a thin metal, stainless steel, nonstick, or porcelain finish; this type of coating helps prevent any reaction with foods during cooking.

Cast iron is the heaviest metal used in cooking. It heats slowly and retains heat well, but doesn't cook as evenly as aluminum or copper. Proper care of cast-iron cookware is very important; it will rust if it's not seasoned to protect the surface and dried thoroughly after each use. If cast iron is coated with porcelain enamel, it doesn't need to be seasoned; however, the enamel may have a tendency to chip and crack.

Stainless steel is strong, durable, lightweight, and easy to clean, but it's a poor heat conductor. Unless bonded with another metal—such as copper or aluminum—utensils may develop hot spots and warp. This material will keep its bright look and will not tarnish. But it needs to be dried carefully after each use to prevent water spots.

Copper is an excellent heat conductor that heats uniformly. Most copper utensils are lined with tin, stainless steel, or a nonstick coating; this keeps copper from reacting with food and causing a color change.

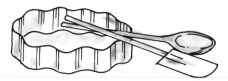

Care of Cookware

Whatever kind of cookware you choose, care will help it last a lifetime. Here are some general guidelines to keep in mind:

—Before using your new cookware, read all the instructions. It's best to wash cookware in soapy hot water before using. This will remove the manufacturing oils and any polishing compounds.

—Keep empty pots and pans away from high heat or sudden temperature changes. If you move a pan from the cooktop to cold water, it may warp.

—When cooking in porcelain-lined pans or cookware with a nonstick finish, use wooden or plastic spoons and spatulas to prevent scratching the finish.

—If undissolved salt is allowed to sit on aluminum or stainless steel, it may cause the inside of the utensils to pit or become marred.

—Cleaning pots and pans in the dishwasher will often cause the surfaces to become dull, discolored, and scratched.

—When cleaning cookware covered with a nonstick finish or copper, don't use an abrasive cleaner or pad.

—Avoid scrubbing cast-iron utensils with strong detergents; just gently clean with soapy hot water, rinse, and wipe dry immediately. Utensils can be quickly dried in a slightly warm oven.

—If cast iron has been washed with soap, it often needs to be reseasoned to prevent rusting. To do this, coat the surface of the utensil with unsalted vegetable oil or shortening, and put in a 350° oven for 2 hours. Remove it from the oven, and wipe away any excess oil. Store it in a dry place, uncovered. If covered, it may sweat and then rust.

Appendices

EQUIVALENT WEIGHTS AND MEASURES

Food	Weight or Count	Measure or Yield
Apples	1 pound (3 medium)	3 cups sliced
Bacon	8 slices cooked	½ cup crumbled
Bananas	1 pound (3 medium)	2½ cups sliced, or about 2 cups mashed
Bread	1 pound	12 to 16 slices
	About 1½ slices	1 cup soft crumbs
Butter or margarine	1 pound	2 cups
	¼-pound stick	½ cup
Cabbage	1 pound head	4½ cups shredded
Candied fruit or peels	½ pound	1¼ cups chopped
Carrots	1 pound	3 cups shredded
Cheese		
American or Cheddar	1 pound	About 4 cups shredded
cottage	1 pound	2 cups
cream	3-ounce package	6 tablespoons
Chocolate morsels	6-ounce package	1 cup
Cocoa	1 pound	4 cups
Coconut, flaked or shredded	1 pound	5 cups
Coffee	1 pound	80 tablespoons (40 cups perked)
Corn	2 medium ears	1 cup kernels
Cornmeal	1 pound	3 cups
Crab, in shell	1 pound	¾ to 1 cup flaked
Crackers		
chocolate wafers	19 wafers	1 cup crumbs
graham crackers	14 squares	1 cup fine crumbs
saltine crackers	28 crackers	1 cup finely crushed
vanilla wafers	22 wafers	1 cup finely crushed
Cream, whipping	1 cup (½ pint)	2 cups whipped
Dates, pitted	1 pound	3 cups chopped
	8-ounce package	1½ cups chopped
Eggs	5 large	1 cup
whites	8 to 11	1 cup
yolks	12 to 14	1 cup
Flour		
all-purpose	1 pound	3½ cups
cake	1 pound	4¾ to 5 cups sifted
whole wheat	1 pound	3½ cups unsifted
Green pepper	1 large	1 cup diced
Lemon	1 medium	2 to 3 tablespoons juice; 2 teaspoons grated rind
Lettuce	1 pound head	6¼ cups torn
Lime	1 medium	1½ to 2 tablespoons juice; 1½ teaspoons grated rind
Macaroni	4 ounces (1 cup)	2¼ cups cooked
Marshmallows	11 large	1 cup
	10 miniature	1 large marshmallow
Marshmallows, miniature	½ pound	4½ cups
Milk		
evaporated	5.33-ounce can	⅔ cup
evaporated	13-ounce can	1⅝ cups
sweetened condensed	14-ounce can	1¼ cups
Mushrooms	3 cups raw (8 ounces)	1 cup sliced cooked
Nuts		
almonds	1 pound	1 to 1¾ cups nutmeats
	1 pound shelled	3½ cups nutmeats
peanuts	1 pound	2¼ cups nutmeats
	1 pound shelled	3 cups

Food	Weight or Count	Measure or Yield
Nuts		
pecans	1 pound	2¼ cups nutmeats
	1 pound shelled	4 cups
walnuts	1 pound	1⅔ cups nutmeats
	1 pound shelled	4 cups
Oats, quick-cooking	1 cup	1¾ cups cooked
Onion	1 medium	½ cup chopped
Orange	1 medium	⅓ cup juice; 2 tablespoons grated rind
Peaches	2 medium	1 cup sliced
Pears	2 medium	1 cup sliced
Potatoes		
white	3 medium	2 cups cubed cooked or 1¾ cups mashed
sweet	3 medium	3 cups sliced
Raisins, seedless	1 pound	3 cups
Rice		
long-grain	1 cup	3 to 4 cups cooked
pre-cooked	1 cup	2 cups cooked
Shrimp, raw in shell	1½ pounds	2 cups (¾ pound) cleaned, cooked
Spaghetti	7 ounces	About 4 cups cooked
Strawberries	1 quart	4 cups sliced
Sugar		
brown	1 pound	2⅓ cups firmly packed
powdered	1 pound	3½ cups unsifted
granulated	1 pound	2 cups

HANDY SUBSTITUTIONS

Ingredient Called For	Substitution
1 cup self-rising flour	1 cup all-purpose flour plus 1 teaspoon baking powder and ½ teaspoon salt
1 cup cake flour	1 cup sifted all-purpose flour minus 2 tablespoons
1 cup all-purpose flour	1 cup cake flour plus 2 tablespoons
1 teaspoon baking powder	½ teaspoon cream of tartar plus ¼ teaspoon soda
1 tablespoon cornstarch or arrowroot	2 tablespoons all-purpose flour
1 tablespoon tapioca	1½ tablespoons all-purpose flour
2 large eggs	3 small eggs
1 egg	2 egg yolks (for custard)
1 egg	2 egg yolks plus 1 tablespoon water (for cookies)
1 (8-ounce) carton commercial sour cream	1 tablespoon lemon juice plus evaporated milk to equal 1 cup; or 3 tablespoons butter plus ⅞ cup sour milk
1 cup yogurt	1 cup buttermilk or sour milk
1 cup sour milk or buttermilk	1 tablespoon vinegar or lemon juice plus sweet milk to equal 1 cup
1 cup fresh milk	½ cup evaporated milk plus ½ cup water
1 cup fresh milk	3 to 5 tablespoons nonfat dry milk solids in 1 cup water
1 cup honey	1¼ cups sugar plus ¼ cup water
1 (1-ounce) square unsweetened chocolate	3 tablespoons cocoa plus 1 tablespoon butter or margarine
1 tablespoon fresh herbs	1 teaspoon dried herbs or ¼ teaspoon powdered herbs
¼ cup chopped fresh parsley	1 tablespoon dried parsley flakes
1 teaspoon dry mustard	1 tablespoon prepared mustard
1 pound fresh mushrooms	6 ounces canned mushrooms

METRIC MEASURE/CONVERSION CHART

Approximate Conversion to Metric Measures

When You Know . . .	Multiply by . . .	To Find . . .	Symbol
	Mass (weight)		
ounces	28	grams	g
pounds	0.45	kilograms	kg
	Volume		
teaspoons	5	milliliters	ml
tablespoons	15	milliliters	ml
fluid ounces	30	milliliters	ml
cups	0.24	liters	l
pints	0.47	liters	l
quarts	0.95	liters	l
gallons	3.8	liters	l

APPROXIMATE TEMPERATURE CONVERSIONS—FAHRENHEIT TO CELSIUS

	Fahrenheit (°F)	Celsius (°C)
Freezer		
coldest area	-10°	-23°
overall	0°	-17°
Water		
freezes	32°	0°
simmers	115°	46°
scalds	180°	55°
boils (sea level)	212°	100°
Soft Ball	234° to 240°	112° to 115°
Firm Ball	242° to 248°	116° to 120°
Hard Ball	250° to 268°	121° to 131°
Slow Oven	275° to 300°	135° to 148°

Fahrenheit to Celsius: Subtract 32 • Multiply by 5 • Divide by 9
Celsius to Fahrenheit: Multiply by 9 • Divide by 5 • Add 32

COOKING MEASURE EQUIVALENTS

Metric Cup	Volume (Liquid)	Liquid Solids (Butter)	Fine Powder (Flour)	Granular (Sugar)	Grain (Rice)
1	250 ml	200 g	140 g	190 g	150 g
¾	188 ml	150 g	105 g	143 g	113 g
⅔	167 ml	133 g	93 g	127 g	100 g
½	125 ml	100 g	70 g	95 g	75 g
⅓	83 ml	67 g	47 g	63 g	50 g
¼	63 ml	50 g	35 g	48 g	38 g
⅛	31 ml	25 g	18 g	24 g	19 g

TIMETABLE FOR ROASTING FRESH PORK

Cut	Approximate Weight	Internal Temperature	Approximate Cooking Times at 325°F.
	pounds		minutes per pound
Loin			
Center..............................	3 to 5	170°F.	30 to 35
Half..............................	5 to 7	170°F.	35 to 40
End..............................	3 to 4	170°F.	40 to 45
Roll..............................	3 to 5	170°F.	35 to 40
Boneless top..............................	2 to 4	170°F.	30 to 35
Crown..............................	4 to 6	170°F.	35 to 40
Picnic shoulder			
Bone-in..............................	5 to 8	170°F.	30 to 35
Rolled..............................	3 to 5	170°F.	35 to 40
Boston shoulder..............................	4 to 6	170°F.	40 to 45
Leg (fresh ham)			
Whole (bone-in)..............................	12 to 16	170°F.	22 to 26
Whole (boneless)..............................	10 to 14	170°F.	24 to 28
Half (bone-in)..............................	5 to 8	170°F.	35 to 40
Tenderloin..............................	½ to 1	170°F.	45 to 60
Back ribs..............................		cooked well done	1½ to 2½ hours
Country-style ribs..............................		cooked well done	1½ to 2½ hours
Spareribs..............................		cooked well done	1½ to 2½ hours
Pork Loaf..............................		cooked well done	1¾ hours

TIMETABLE FOR ROASTING SMOKED PORK

Cut	Approximate Weight	Internal Temperature	Approximate Cooking Times at 325°F.
	pounds		minutes per pound
Ham (cook before eating)			
Whole..............................	10 to 14	160°F.	18 to 20
Half..............................	5 to 7	160°F.	22 to 25
Shank portion..............................	3 to 4	160°F.	35 to 40
Butt portion..............................	3 to 4	160°F.	35 to 40
Ham (fully cooked)			
Whole..............................	10 to 12	140°F.	15 to 18
Half..............................	5 to 7	140°F.	18 to 24
Loin..............................	3 to 5	160°F.	25 to 30
Picnic shoulder (cook before eating)..............	5 to 8	170°F.	30 to 35
Picnic shoulder (fully cooked)..............................	5 to 8	140°F.	25 to 30
Shoulder roll (butt)..............................	2 to 4	170°F.	35 to 40
Canadian-style bacon..............................	2 to 4	160°F.	35 to 40

TIMETABLE FOR ROASTING BEEF AND LAMB

Kind and Cut	Approximate Weight	Internal Temperature	Approximate Total Cooking Times at 325°F.
	pounds		hours
Beef			
Standing ribs* (10-inch ribs)............................	4	140°F. (rare)	1¾
		160°F. (medium)	2
		170°F. (well done)	2½
	6	140°F. (rare)	2
		160°F. (medium)	2½
		170°F. (well done)	3½
	8	140°F. (rare)	2½
		160°F. (medium)	3
		170°F. (well done)	4½
Rolled ribs...	4	140°F. (rare)	2
		160°F. (medium)	2½
		170°F. (well done)	3
	6	140°F. (rare)	3
		160°F. (medium)	3¼
		170°F. (well done)	4
Rolled rump...	5	140°F. (rare)	2¼
		160°F. (medium)	3
		170°F. (well done)	3¼
Sirloin tip...	3	140°F. (rare)	1½
		160°F. (medium)	2
		170°F. (well done)	2¼
Lamb (bone in)			
Leg..	6 to 7	160°F. (medium)	2½ to 3¾
Leg (half).......................................	3 to 4	160°F. (medium)	2 to 2¾
Shoulder (boneless).............................	4 to 6	160°F. (medium)	2½ to 3¾
Rib roast†.......................................	1½ to 2½	160°F. (medium)	1 to 1⅔
Crown roast (unstuffed)†	2 to 3	160°F. (medium)	1 to 1½

*Standing ribs (8-inch ribs) allow 30 minutes longer.
†Oven set at 375°F. and not preheated.

TIMETABLE FOR ROASTING POULTRY

Kind of Poultry	Ready-to-Cook Weight	Oven Temperature	Internal Temperature	Approximate Total Roasting Time
	pounds			hours
Chicken (unstuffed)*	1½ to 2	400°F.	185°F.	1
	2 to 2½	375°F.	185°F.	1 to 1¼
	2½ to 3	375°F.	185°F.	1¼ to 1½
	3 to 4	375°F.	185°F.	1½ to 2
	4 to 5	375°F.	185°F.	2 to 2½
Capon (unstuffed)	4 to 7	325°F.	185°F.	2½ to 3
Cornish Hen (stuffed)	1 to 1½	375°F.	185°F.	1 to 1¼
Duckling (unstuffed)	3½ to 5½	325°F.	190°F.	2 to 3
Goose (unstuffed)	7 to 9	350°F.	190°F.	2½ to 3
	9 to 11	350°F.	190°F.	3 to 3½
	11 to 13	350°F.	190°F.	3½ to 4
Turkey (stuffed)†	4 to 8	325°F.	185°F.	3 to 3¾
	8 to 12	325°F.	185°F.	3¾ to 4½
	12 to 16	325°F.	185°F.	4½ to 5½
	16 to 20	325°F.	185°F.	5½ to 6½
	20 to 24	325°F.	185°F.	6½ to 7½

*Stuffed chickens require about 5 additional minutes per pound.
†Unstuffed turkeys require about 5 minutes less per pound.

TIMETABLE FOR COOKING FISH AND SHELLFISH

Method of Cooking	Product	Market Form	Approximate Weight or Thickness	Cooking Temperature	Approximate Total Cooking Times
Baking	Fish	Dressed	3 to 4 lbs.	350°F.	40 to 60 min.
		Pan-dressed	½ to 1 lb.	350°F.	25 to 30 min.
		Steaks	½ to 1 in.	350°F.	25 to 35 min.
		Fillets	1 in.	350°F.	9 to 10 min. per inch
	Clams	Live		450°F.	15 min.
	Lobster	Live	¾ to 1 lb.	400°F.	15 to 20 min.
			1 to 1½ lbs.	400°F.	20 to 25 min.
	Oysters	Live		450°F.	15 min.
		Shucked		400°F.	10 min.
	Scallops	Shucked		350°F.	25 to 30 min.
	Shrimp	Headless		350°F.	20 to 25 min.
	Spiny lobster tails	Headless	4 oz.	450°F.	20 to 25 min.
			8 oz.	450°F.	25 to 30 min.
Broiling	Fish	Pan-dressed	½ to 1 lb.		10 to 15 min.
		Steaks	½ to 1 in.		10 to 15 min.
		Fillets	1 in.		9 to 10 min. per inch
	Clams	Live			5 to 8 min.
	Lobster	Live	¾ to 1 lb.		10 to 12 min.
			1 to 1½ lbs.		12 to 15 min.
	Oysters	Live			5 min.
		Shucked			5 min.
	Scallops	Shucked			8 to 10 min.
	Shrimp	Headless			8 to 10 min.
	Spiny lobster tails	Headless	4 oz.		8 to 10 min.
			8 oz.		10 to 12 min.
Cooking in water	Fish	Pan-dressed	½ to 1 lb.	Simmer	10 min.
		Steaks	½ to 1 in.	Simmer	10 min.
		Fillets	1 in.	Simmer	9 min. per inch
	Crabs	Live		Simmer	15 min.
	Lobster	Live	¾ to 1 lb.	Simmer	10 to 15 min.
			1 to 1½ lbs.	Simmer	15 to 20 min.
	Scallops	Shucked		Simmer	4 to 5 min.
	Shrimp	Headless		Simmer	5 min.
	Spiny lobster tails	Headless	4 oz.	Simmer	10 min.
			8 oz.	Simmer	15 min.
Deep-fat frying	Fish	Pan-dressed	½ to 1 lb.	375°F.	2 to 4 min.
		Steaks	½ to 1 in.	375°F.	2 to 4 min.
		Fillets	½ to 1 in.	375°F.	1 to 5 min.
	Clams	Shucked		375°F.	2 to 3 min.
	Crabs	Soft-shell	¼ lb.	375°F.	3 to 4 min.
	Lobster	Live	¾ to 1 lb.	350°F.	3 to 4 min.
			1 to 1½ lbs.	350°F.	4 to 5 min.
	Oysters	Shucked		375°F.	2 min.
	Scallops	Shucked		350°F.	3 to 4 min.
	Shrimp	Headless		350°F.	2 to 3 min.
	Spiny lobster tails	Headless	4 oz.	350°F.	3 to 4 min.
			8 oz.	350°F.	4 to 5 min.

GLOSSARY

à la King—Food prepared in a creamy white sauce containing mushrooms and red and/or green peppers

à la Mode—Food served with ice cream

al Dente—The point in the cooking of pasta at which it is still fairly firm to the tooth; that is, very slightly undercooked

Aspic—A jellied meat juice or a liquid held together with gelatin

au Gratin—Food served crusted with breadcrumbs and/or shredded cheese

au Jus—Meat served in its own juice

Bake—To cook food in an oven by dry heat

Barbecue—To roast meat slowly over coals on a spit or framework, or in an oven, basting intermittently with a special sauce

Baste—To spoon pan liquid over meats while they are roasting to prevent surface from drying

Beat—To mix vigorously with a brisk motion with spoon, fork, egg beater, or electric mixer

Béchamel—A white sauce of butter, flour, cream (not milk), and seasonings

Bisque—A thick, creamy soup usually of shellfish, but sometimes made of pureed vegetables

Blanch—To dip briefly into boiling water

Blend—To stir 2 or more ingredients together until well mixed

Blintz—A cooked crêpe stuffed with cheese or other filling

Boil—To cook food in boiling water or liquid that is mostly water (at 212°F. at sea level) in which bubbles constantly rise to the surface and burst

Boiling-water-bath canning method—Used for processing acid foods, such as fruit, tomatoes, pickled vegetables, and sauerkraut. These acid foods are canned safely at boiling temperatures in a water-bath canner

Borscht—Soup containing beets and other vegetables, usually with a meat stock base

Bouillabaisse—A highly seasoned fish soup or chowder containing two or more kinds of fish

Bouillon—Clear soup made by boiling meat in water

Bouquet Garni—Herbs tied in cheese-cloth which are cooked in a mixture and removed before serving

Bourguignon—Name applied to dishes containing Burgundy and often braised onions and mushrooms

Braise—To cook slowly with liquid or steam in a covered utensil. Less-tender cuts of meat may be browned slowly on all sides in a small amount of shortening, seasoned, and water added

Bread, to—To coat with crumbs, usually in combination with egg or other binder

Broil—To cook by direct heat, either under the heat of a broiler, over hot coals, or between two hot surfaces

Broth—A thin soup, or a liquid in which meat, fish, or vegetables have been cooked

Capers—Buds from a Mediterranean plant, usually packed in brine and used as a condiment in dressings or sauces

Caramelize—To cook white sugar in a skillet over medium heat, stirring constantly, until sugar forms a golden-brown syrup

Casserole—An ovenproof baking dish, usually with a cover; also the food cooked inside it

Charlotte—A molded dessert containing gelatin, usually formed in a glass dish or a pan that is lined with ladyfingers or pieces of cake

Chop—A cut of meat usually attached to a rib

Chop, to—To cut into pieces, with a sharp knife or kitchen shears

Clarified butter—Butter that has been melted and chilled. The solid is then lifted away from the liquid and discarded. Clarification heightens the smoke point of butter. Clarified butter will stay fresh in the refrigerator for at least 2 months

Coat—To cover completely, as in "coat with flour"

Cocktail—An appetizer; either a beverage or a light, highly seasoned food served before a meal

Compote—Mixed fruit, raw or cooked, usually served in "compote" dishes

Condiments—Seasonings that enhance the flavor of foods with which they are served

Consommé—Clear broth made from meat

Cool—To let food stand at room temperature until not warm to the touch

Court Bouillon—A highly seasoned broth made with water and meat, fish or vegetables, and seasonings

Cream, to—To blend together, as sugar and butter, until mixture takes on a smooth, cream-like texture

Cream, whipped—Cream that has been whipped until it is stiff

Crème de Cacao—A chocolate-flavored liqueur

Crème de Café—A coffee-flavored liqueur

Crêpes—Very thin pancakes

Croquette—Minced food, shaped like a ball, patty, cone, or log, bound with a heavy sauce, breaded, and fried

Croutons—Cubes of bread, toasted or fried, served with soups or salads

Cruller—A doughnut of twisted shape, very light in texture

Cube, to—To cut into cube-shaped pieces

Curaçao—Orange-flavored liqueur

Cut in, to—To incorporate by cutting or chopping motions, as in cutting shortening into flour for pastry

Demitasse—A small cup of coffee served after dinner

Devil, to—To prepare with spicy seasoning or sauce

Dice—To cut into small cubes

Dissolve—To mix a dry substance with liquid until the dry substance becomes a part of the solution

Dot—To scatter small bits of butter over top of a food

Dredge—To coat with something, usually flour or sugar

Filé—Powder made of sassafras leaves used to season and thicken foods

Fillet—Boneless piece of meat or fish

Flambé—To flame, as in Crêpes Suzette or in some meat cookery, using alcohol as the burning agent; flame causes caramelization, enhancing flavor

Flan—In France, a filled pastry; in Spain, a custard

Florentine—A food containing or placed upon spinach

Flour, to—To coat with flour

Fold—To add a whipped ingredient, such as cream or egg white, to another ingredient by gentle over-and-under movement

Frappé—A drink whipped with ice to make a thick, frosty consistency

Fricassee—A stew, usually of poultry or veal

Fritter—Vegetable or fruit dipped into, or combined with, batter and fried

Fry—To cook in hot shortening

Garnish—A decoration for a food or drink

Glaze (To make a shiny surface)—In meat preparation, a jelled broth applied to meat surface; in breads and pastries, a wash of egg or syrup; for doughnuts and cakes, a sugar preparation for coating

Grate—To obtain small particles of food by rubbing on a grater or shredder

Grill—To broil under or over a source of direct heat

Grits—Coarsely ground dried corn, served boiled, or boiled and then fried

Gumbo—Soup or stew made with okra

Herb—Aromatic plant used for seasoning and garnishing foods

Hollandaise—A sauce made of butter, egg, and lemon juice or vinegar

Hominy—Whole corn grains from which hull and germ are removed

Jardiniere—Vegetables in a savory sauce or soup

Julienne—Vegetables cut into strips or a soup containing such vegetables

Kahlúa—A coffee-flavored liqueur

Kirsch—A cherry-flavored liqueur

Knead—To work a food (usually dough) by hand, using a folding-back and pressing-forward motion

Marinade—A seasoned liquid in which food is soaked

Marinate, to—To soak food in a seasoned liquid

Meringue—A whole family of egg white-sugar preparations including pie topping, poached meringue used to top custard, crisp meringue dessert shells, and divinity candy

Mince—To chop into very fine pieces

Mornay—White sauce with egg, cream, and cheese added

Mousse—A molded dish based on meat or sweet whipped cream stiffened with egg white and/or gelatin (if mousse contains ice cream, it is called bombe)

Panbroil—To cook over direct heat in an uncovered skillet containing little or no shortening

Panfry—To cook in an uncovered skillet in small amount of shortening

Parboil—To partially cook in boiling water before final cooking

Pasta—A large family of flour paste products, such as spaghetti, macaroni, and noodles

Pâté (French for paste)—A paste made of liver or meat

Petit Four—A small cake, which has been frosted and decorated

Pilau or pilaf—A dish of the Middle East consisting of rice and meat or vegetables in a seasoned stock

Poach—To cook in liquid held below the boiling point

Pot liquor—The liquid in which vegetables have been boiled

Preheat—To turn on oven so that desired temperature will be reached before food is inserted for baking

Puree—A thick sauce or paste made by forcing cooked food through a sieve

Reduce—To boil down, evaporating liquid from a cooked dish

Remoulade—A rich mayonnaise-based sauce containing anchovy paste, capers, herbs, and mustard

Render—To melt fat away from surrounding meat

Rind—Outer shell or peel of melon or fruit

Roast, to—To cook in oven by dry heat (usually applied to meats)

Roux—A mixture of butter and flour used to thicken gravies and sauces; it may be white or brown, if mixture is browned before liquid is added

Sauté—To fry food lightly over fairly high heat in a small amount of fat in a shallow, open pan

Scald—(1) To heat milk just below the boiling point (2) To dip certain foods into boiling water before freezing them (also called blanching)

Scallop—A bivalve mollusk of which only the muscle hinge is eaten; also to bake food in a sauce topped with crumbs

Score—To cut shallow gashes on surface of food, as in scoring fat on ham before glazing

Sear—To brown surface of meat over high heat to seal in juices

Set—Term used to describe the consistency of gelatin when it has jelled enough to unmold

Shred—Break into thread-like or stringy pieces, usually by rubbing over the surface of a vegetable shredder

Simmer—To cook gently at a temperature below boiling point

Skewer—To fasten with wooden or metal pins or skewers

Soak—To immerse in water for a period of time

Soufflé—A spongy hot dish, made from a sweet or savory mixture (often milk or cheese), lightened by stiffly beaten egg whites or whipped cream

Steam—To cook food with steam either in a pressure cooker, on a platform in a covered pan, or in a special steamer

Steam-pressure canning method—Used for processing low-acid foods, such as meats, fish, poultry, and most vegetables. A temperature higher than boiling is required to can these foods safely. The food is processed in a steam-pressure canner at 10 pounds' pressure (240°) to ensure that all of the spoilage micro-organisms are destroyed

Steep—To let food stand in not quite boiling water until the flavor is extracted

Stew—A mixture of meat or fish and vegetables cooked by simmering in its own juices and liquid, such as water and/or wine

Stir-fry—To cook quickly in oil over high heat, using light tossing and stirring motions to preserve shape of food

Stock—The broth in which meat, poultry, fish, or vegetables has been cooked

Syrupy—Thickened to about the consistency of egg white

Toast, to—To brown by direct heat, as in a toaster or under broiler

Torte—A round cake, sometimes made with breadcrumbs instead of flour

Tortilla—A Mexican flat bread made of corn or wheat flour

Toss—To mix together with light tossing motions, in order not to bruise delicate food, such as salad greens

Triple Sec—An orange-flavored liqueur

Truss, to—To tie or secure with string or skewers the legs and wings of poultry or game in order to make the bird easier to manage during cooking

Veal—Flesh of milk-fed calf up to 14 weeks of age

Velouté—White sauce made of flour, butter, and a chicken or veal stock, instead of milk

Vinaigrette—A cold sauce of oil and vinegar flavored with parsley, finely chopped onions, and other seasonings; served with cold meats or vegetables

Whip—To beat rapidly to increase air and increase volume

Wok—A round bowl-shaped metal cooking utensil of Chinese origin used for stir-frying and steaming (with rack inserted) of foods

GARNISHES

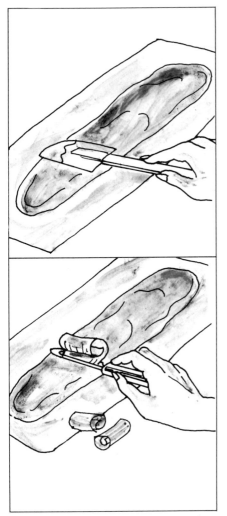

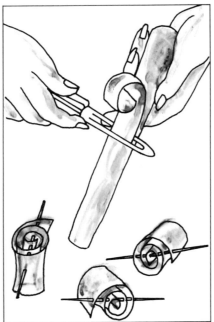

CARROT CURLS

Scrape carrot. Cut off ½ inch from each end; discard. Using a vegetable peeler, cut thin lengthwise strips from carrot. Roll strips jellyroll fashion; secure with wooden picks. Drop in ice water, and refrigerate at least 1 hour for curls to set. Remove picks before serving.

TOMATO ROSE

Cut a thin slice from bottom of a tomato, using a sharp paring knife; discard. Beginning at top, peel a continuous paper-thin strip (about ¾-inch wide for regular tomato, and about ¼-inch wide for cherry tomato) from entire tomato.

Beginning with first portion cut, shape the strip like a rose. With flesh side inward, coil the strip tightly at first to form the center of the rose, gradually letting it become looser to form the outer petals.

LEMON OR ORANGE ROSE: Follow the same directions to make a lemon or orange rose, cutting strip about ½- to ¾-inch wide.

CHOCOLATE CURLS

Place squares or morsels of semisweet chocolate in top of a double boiler; bring water to a boil. Reduce heat to low; cook until chocolate melts. Let cool slightly.

Pour chocolate out in a stream onto a waxed paper-lined baking sheet. Spread chocolate with a spatula into a 2- or 3-inch wide strip. (The width of strip determines the length of curls.) Smooth top of strip with spatula.

Let stand at room temperature until chocolate cools and feels slightly tacky, but is not firm. (If chocolate is too hard, curls will break; if too soft, chocolate will not curl.)

Gently pull a vegetable peeler across length of chocolate until curl forms, letting chocolate curl up on top of peeler. Insert wooden pick in curl to transfer. Chill until ready to use.

CARROT FLOWERS

Scrape carrot. Using a sharp knife, cut 4 or 5 grooves, evenly spaced, down the length of carrot; then slice the carrot to produce flowers.

FLUTED MUSHROOMS

Select firm white mushrooms. Cut several slits at even intervals around each mushroom cap, cutting from the center of the cap to the edge, using a curving motion with the knife. Make another set of slits parallel to the first slits, allowing about 1/16 inch between them. Remove and discard the thin strips of mushroom between the slits.

CELERY FANS

Slice celery stalks into 3- or 4-inch lengths, and place on a cutting board. Using a sharp knife, cut several slits at one or both ends of each piece of celery, cutting almost to, but not through, the center. Place in ice water, and refrigerate at least 1 hour for fans to curl.

GREEN ONION FANS: Follow same directions to make green onion fans, slicing off root and most of onion's top portion before beginning.

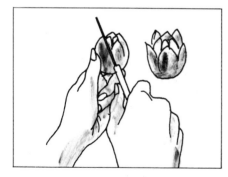

RADISH ROSE

Slice stem end and root tip from radish. Hold radish with root tip up, and slice 4 or 5 petals around the radish by slicing from top to, but not through, bottom. Leave a little red between each petal. Drop radish in ice water, and refrigerate at least 1 hour for rose to open.

ONION MUM

Select a firm white or red onion; peel onion. Set onion on cutting board, root end down. Cut onion almost into quarters, slicing to within ¼ inch of bottom. Continue slicing onion into smaller divisions, slicing to, but not through, bottom. Hold onion under warm running water, and gently separate sections. Place onion in ice water, and refrigerate at least 1 hour for onion to open. Drain well.

CITRUS CUPS

Cut a thin slice from each end of the fruit so that the cups will sit level. Insert the blade of a small knife at a downward angle into the middle of the fruit; remove the blade. Insert knife again at an upward angle to make a zigzag pattern. Continue cutting in this fashion completely around fruit.

Separate the halves by twisting slightly and carefully pulling them apart. Scoop out the pulp if the cups will be used as a container.

TOMATO OR GREEN PEPPER CUPS: Follow same directions to make tomato or green pepper cups.

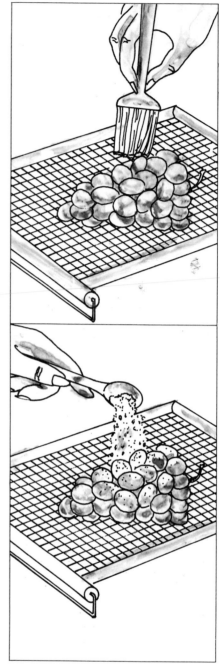

FROSTED GRAPES

Place purple, blue, or green grapes on a wire rack (individually or in bunches). Beat an egg white just until frothy. Paint grapes with egg white, using a soft pastry brush. While grapes are still wet, sprinkle with granulated sugar to create a frosted look, and allow to dry in a cool place. Don't refrigerate the frosted grapes because the moisture in the refrigerator will melt the sugar.

FROSTED CRANBERRIES: Follow the same directions to make frosted cranberries.

Recipe Title Index

An alphabetical listing of every recipe by exact title
All microwave recipe page numbers are preceded by an "M"

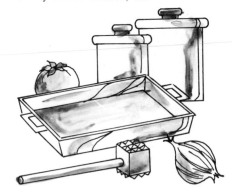

Month-by-Month Index

An alphabetical listing within the month of every food article and accompanying recipes
All microwave recipe page numbers are preceded by an "M"

General Recipe Index

A listing of every recipe by food category and/or major ingredient
All microwave recipe page numbers are preceded by an "M"

Sauces and Gravies. *See also* Dessert
Sauces.
Apricot-Sauced Pork Chops, 22
Barbecue Sauce, Bourbon, 90
Bean Sauce, Pork-and-Onions with, 76
Béarnaise Sauce, 37

General Recipe Index   369

Favorite Recipes

Record your favorite recipes below for quick and handy reference

Appetizers	Source/Page	Remarks

Beverages	Source/Page	Remarks

Breads   Source/Page   Remarks

Desserts   Source/Page   Remarks

Eggs and Cheese	Source/Page	Remarks

Main Dishes	Source/Page	Remarks

Salads   Source/Page   Remarks

Soups and Stews   Source/Page   Remarks

Vegetables and Side Dishes   Source/Page   Remarks